MICROWAVE GOURMET

Barbara Kafka is a well-known American food and
wine writer who contributes monthly columns on
food opinion, entertaining and microwave cooking to
The New York Times, *Vogue*, and *Family Circle*.
Microwave Gourmet has been a major critical and
popular success on both sides of the Atlantic. Her
follow-up book, *Microwave Gourmet Healthstyle
Cookbook*, is published in hardback by Barrie &
Jenkins.

Also by Barbara Kafka

Microwave Gourmet Healthstyle Cookbook

Microwave Gourmet

Barbara Kafka

HEADLINE

First published in Great Britain in 1989
by Barrie & Jenkins Ltd

First published in paperback in 1990
by HEADLINE BOOK PUBLISHING PLC

10 9 8 7 6 5 4 3 2 1

Cover photograph by Clive Streeter

ISBN 0 7472 3380 2

Printed and bound in Great Britain by
Collins, Glasgow

HEADLINE BOOK PUBLISHING PLC
Headline House
79 Great Titchfield Street
London W1P 7FN

CONTENTS

For My Father, James Beard, Robert Bak, and Steven Spector
Men who lived with style and a love of good food
In remembrance

ACKNOWLEDGEMENTS

·◆·◆·

A s a writer and cook, I have been extremely fortunate in the support I have received from professional friends, assistants and editors. It is probably impossible to distinguish between categories, but thanks are more than due. They are offered with my warm memories and chuckles of shared laughter and with recognition that without these people not only would my tasks have become chores, but they probably would have never got done. Affectionate thank you's to ...

Ann Bramson, who has shepherded me through three books, worrying about my tardiness and defending me and my books at every turn, who thought I was only mildly crazy to write a microwave cookery book, who loyally learned to use a microwave and now wants a second one, and who has elicited from me better books than I might otherwise have written.

Lois Bloom, who has worked with me for fifteen years without getting exasperated, but instead has offered warm support and much style.

Rebecca Marshall, who has worked with me on this and other projects for the last two years with enthusiasm, food knowledge, good hands, patience with both computer systems and boss, and a fine palate (her French isn't half bad, either).

Christopher Styler, who has worked with me for ten years off and on and helped with part of the testing for this book.

Rebecca Atwater, who sewed the pieces together and kept me in order when I seemed to be coming apart at the seams.

Joy Rosenberg, a recent recruit, who has transcribed recipes and tested valiantly.

Amy Schwartzman, Kathi Long and Prudence Hillburn, who helped keep the financial books and the research books in order.

Elsa Tobar, who kept the house.

Leo Lerman, who made me write about food in the first place.

Alex Liberman, who brought me back to *Vogue*.

Edouard Cournand and Jacques Guerin, who first made me equate France and culture.

And Paula Wolfert, Joseph Baum, Amy Gross, Marion Asnes, Corby Kummer, Warren Picower, Carl Jerome, Margot Slade—all great supporters.

NOTES ON MEASUREMENTS

—————— • ◆ • ——————

Both Metric and Imperial measurements are given in this book. Because exact equivalents in the two systems of measurement would be difficult for the cook to use, slight adjustments have been made, while still keeping the ingredients in the same proportions. So follow only one system of measuring when preparing a recipe.

Standard metric spoon measures have been used, and all spoon measures are level.
1 tablespoon = 15 ml
1 teaspoon = 5 ml

Australian readers please note that their tablespoon is equivalent to 20 ml; therefore, they should use 3 teaspoons (3 5-ml spoons) where tablespoon measures are given.

Coarsely ground sea salt is used in all recipes.

INTRODUCTION

O ne of the most exciting things to happen in my culinary life in recent years has been my discovery of microwave cooking. The exquisite flesh of perfectly cooked fish, vegetables of intense colour and full of vitamins without being soggy, Chicken in Red Wine ready just 20 minutes after I get home, perfect risottos without stirring and classic sauces are an easy part of my life. Efficiency and rapidity are only part of the story; better cooking and better eating are the true tale.

For many years, I was wrong about the microwave oven. I saw it abused in bad restaurants, and I thought that was the best it could do. I ate potatoes 'baked' in it and rebelled at the lack of quality. I read the manuals that came with microwaves and was repelled by the recipes I saw. I rejected the ovens along with their misuse. I was a microwave snob, as most of my chef and food-writing friends still are. When I finally announced, rather sheepishly, that I was writing a microwave cookery book, I felt I would have had a better reception had I announced my intention of going down to Times Square in New York City at 3 P.M. to take my clothes off.

I am a recent convert. I used to be wary of the microwave oven. I don't know if I was more frightened by what I (wrongly) thought was the danger of radiation or by having to learn a new technology. It took me a while to figure out how similar microwave cooking was to what I had always done, and just what the significant differences were.

I am still somewhat in awe of scientists and experts; therefore, as I learned, I was frequently astonished by the inaccuracies of the available information. I have had to puzzle out the truth for myself and combine it with what I already know of cooking to create a body of information and recipes on which I can rely. I am not willing to accept food that is one bit less good from the microwave oven than I would serve at any time. The testing procedure was lengthy as I juggled ingredients, times and techniques to create equally valid recipes for different quantities of food and different powers of ovens.

I started out an aborigine scared of fire and ended up a computer-age person. I am not about to give up my copper pans, my cast-iron wood-burning stove or my barbecue; but I have a new friend in my kitchen, the microwave oven, and I use it more and more every day.

I hope you will come to enjoy it as I do. If you are a free-wheeling cook, you may feel cramped at the beginning. You must follow recipes exactly until you find out how the oven works. My best advice is to use it a great deal. The more you use recipes that work, where the food tastes good and suits the way you live, the more comfortable you will be with microwave cooking. It will no longer just be a way to reheat your coffee, defrost frozen dinners and make bacon. It can be an important aid in the way you cook every day. It can encourage you to try foods you thought were too hard or too time-consuming to make, or restore foods to your repertoire that you thought you no longer had time to cook: pâtés made in 11 minutes, stocks that take 20 minutes, comforting soups that can be made in less time than it takes to set a table, stews and ragoûts ready in under half an hour, sauces that even good restaurants don't take the time to make any more done in 10 minutes—all these are liberations from limitation and invitations to creativity. The microwave oven makes it possible for all of us to cook and eat good homemade food again. We can return to entertaining without sacrificing our lives to it. If the microwave oven cooks something badly, I will be the first to tell you; but you will find that it cooks some things better than any other kind of cooking.

ABOUT THE RECIPES

These recipes are finicky about weights, measures, size of dishes and kinds of coverings. These elements influence microwave cooking fairly dramatically. Try to approximate them as closely as possible. You cannot simply multiply and divide microwave-cooking recipes; neither times nor ingredients work that way. To ease this problem, I have given several variations on very basic or much-used recipes. Use these prototype recipes as models for similar recipes that you are trying to develop, or turn to the Dictionary of Foods and Techniques in the back of the book for cooking times for different quantities.

All recipes were tested in large, full-power (650- to 700-watt) ovens. Where possible, I have supplied timings for different sizes and powers of ovens, both in the recipes and in the Dictionary. See page 17 for adapting recipes to different powers of ovens.

Compensating is something we have learned to do automatically when cooking in our regular ovens and on top of our regular hobs. We all know that our own cookers are just a little different from everybody else's. Our pans may be different, too. We adjust to these differences with hardly a thought. We will learn to do the same thing with microwave cooking. It just takes a little time.

CREATING OR ADAPTING YOUR OWN RECIPES

When you are comfortable with your microwave oven and these recipes, you may want to change them, or adapt other recipes that you know and love. Check similar recipes in the book to see what is done with the proportion of liquid to solids and to cooking times. Then try your own.

More aid is available from the Dictionary, which lists every food I worked with in the microwave oven and tells how it cooks, how long different quantities take to microwave-cook, and how to adjust spices, herbs and wine in your recipes. The Dictionary describes basic cooking techniques, as well as a few less common ones, to give you an idea of what does and does not work in the microwave oven. You will find, for instance, timings for defrosting or for reducing a certain amount of liquid or sauce.

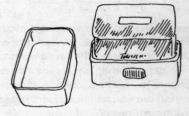

Scales are essential; food weight almost always determines cooking time.

USES OF THE MICROWAVE OVEN

Gradually, you will learn when and for what to use it. Rarely will you use it to make all the dishes in a meal unless some are make-ahead—desserts, pickles, relishes, sauces, a first course to be eaten cold. I seldom prepare foods and freeze them because it takes no longer to cook fresh than to defrost, and fresh is better.

Main courses, including meat and vegetables, casseroles, stews, plated meals, and the like, are good choices for microwave cooking. Once you have tried microwave-cooking fish, you may never cook it any other way unless you barbecue it outdoors. Most vegetables and fruits do well in the microwave oven, sometimes to cook fully, sometimes just for the first stage of their cooking before they are added to a pasta, soup or dessert. Many prepared components used in baking are made quickly and well in the microwave oven: caramel, custards, blanched or toasted nuts. The hotter the summer day, the greater its use. It doesn't heat up the kitchen—especially nice for preserving.

Polenta and risotto can now be everyday foods since you no longer have to stand stirring over a hot stove to the exclusion of all other activity. In fact, my prowess with risotto has converted more of my guests to microwave cooking than any promise of speed. Try the recipe on page 109; it will convert you, too.

On the other hand, there are things it cooks disastrously. I have followed every lead offered by overeager manufacturers and tried every solution suggested by overzealous writers. The microwave oven will not roast. It cannot make soufflés. Bread is beyond its limits. The suggestion of one blinkered writer that Hollandaise be made by opening the oven every 15 seconds in order to whisk vigorously would seem to be an advance backward. Do those things in the microwave that it does well—precooking duck, for example. Finish it under the grill while you cook the vegetable in the microwave oven. One modestly sized piece of equipment cannot be asked to do the work of a whole kitchen.

While testing ten microwave ovens of different manufacturers, sizes, control systems and powers, I kept in mind the reality that most of us are working with only one proud oven that efficiently cooks only one dish at a time. The day may come when we all lust for two microwave ovens—but not until we have learned that they are tools for cooking, not just for reheating and defrosting.

LEARNING PLEASANT TRUTHS AND A NEW COOKING STYLE

The only real problem you may discover is that cooking in a microwave oven upsets your time sense, in the same way that a food processor or a computer does. You get used to the speed—in fact addicted to it. It is difficult to stop and allow time to bring large pans of water to the boil—in cooking pasta, for instance. You will be spoiled by the ease of washing-up. There are no baked-on, boiled-on messes; frequently, there are no cooking dishes at all since many (or all) foods can be cooked right in their serving dishes or on individual plates.

Microwave cooking takes place in an enclosure, the oven, and cooking in that enclosed space takes a little getting used to. We all welcome the lack of heat, but we may miss the usual puttering—poking at the food, smelling it, reseasoning it. (Bakers are used to this, having few adjustments to make while the food cooks.) The virtues of microwave cooking—rapidity, simplicity and perfect results—will reconcile you to these changes. You will still enjoy delicious cooking odours; they just won't be as strong. You will create exceptional tastes. Most you will recognize; a few will be new, special and terrific.

I don't think I've ever had more fun working on a project. Do come along with me on the journey. I promise you'll taste some good food on the way.

THE OVEN

—————•◆•—————

W hen I first read about microwaves and how they cooked, it all seemed complicated and mysterious. Water molecules in food, it was explained, were set in motion by microwaves, causing friction that in turn caused heat. This made it all seem rather alien to me, unlike anything else I know, until a more logical friend pointed out that this was the way most cooking procedures worked. (Just think of boiling water.) Then, when I discovered that the available information was distorted and that other matter (sugars and fats, for example) also danced around in the presence of microwaves, everything began to seem more orderly. I learned that a large piece of food was not cooked entirely by microwaves, but as in other kinds of cooking by internal conduction of heat.

'Microwave' means tiny (micro) waves. Other kinds of energy also travel in waves, but they are waves of longer lengths. Because microwaves are so short, they travel quickly, making most microwave cooking a rapid process. They slip quickly past the outer layer of a structure, so that the food rarely browns. In most cases, this isn't an overwhelming problem. Food cooks so quickly that it doesn't lose its juices and doesn't need the protection of a brown layer or crust. If you miss the browned look or flavour, simply sauté the food on top of the stove before cooking it in the oven, just as you do when making a pot roast. A lick of grill heat at the last minute will gild rice puddings, cream-baked potatoes and cheese toppings.

The little rays quickly run out of energy, so food to be microwave-cooked is optimally cut into 7.5 cm/3 inch pieces. Since the waves don't get trapped on the food's surface, within the sphere of their power they cook extremely evenly—no fish with hard crusts and undercooked insides. The only problem occurs if the food being cooked is so small or so thin that it forces the waves to overlap in the middle of the food, burning it.

Because the microwaves really get the molecules jumping, food will stay very hot longer than if conventionally cooked, even though the surface may seem no hotter than usual. Remember that all foods, no matter how they are cooked, continue to cook after they are removed from heat—just think of scrambled eggs and roasts.

Fat seems to attract microwaves like a magnet, so there are advantages to cooking fatty foods in the microwave oven. Defatting ducks and spare ribs is easy. Cooking bone marrow for classic sauces is a snap. Rendering chicken fat ceases to be a major event. The attraction of microwaves to sugar means easy, controllable caramelizing. Tight covering keeps steam washing down the walls of the containers, neatly avoiding untoward crystals.

All those jumping molecules mean *steam*. Some of it comes from the water content of the food itself: the juices of meat, the water in vegetables. Some of it may come from added stock, water, wine or other liquids; you don't need much to work up a head of steam. When it is held tightly in the container rather than allowed to escape, it helps cook the food quickly and evenly and keeps it moist. This also means you need to add less liquid. When liquid is heated in an uncovered container, rapid evaporation takes place, which is highly desirable for reducing sauces.

Because microwave cooking creates steam—pressure—within foods, a particular food with a relatively nongiving enclosure (a chestnut, for example) will explode from the steam pressure created as it cooks, like a soccer ball pumped too full of air. That is why it is suggested that you prick the skin of potatoes and sausages and the membrane encasing egg yolks.

Other advantages of the microwave oven are that it will not heat up the kitchen (bliss in hot weather), and it uses relatively little energy.

THE FEATURES

If you are planning to buy a microwave oven, get one bigger than you think you need. You will soon discover how wonderfully useful it is. Tiny ovens are adequate if you mean never to do anything but reheat your coffee (ugh), defrost a lonely dinner, cook bacon, or cook very simply for only one or two. (Where it makes sense, I have given timings for these smaller quantities.)

Do not buy the space-age-control, multiuse (convection and grilling) oven to which you may be drawn. This suggestion comes from experience with washers and dryers: the simpler the appliance, the fewer repairs. In addition, there is an unsolved problem with multiuse ovens, which are metal-lined without any protective easy-to-clean plastic covering. Despite the introduction of fans, these ovens retain outrageous amounts of humidity, loosening the seal of plastic wrapping and distorting cooking results and times in other ways. Remember, most of these ovens do not cook two ways at once; you will be doing the procedures sequentially. The uncoated metal liners and shelves get so hot that you can easily burn yourself. Ordinary microwave ovens do not present this problem, and their plastic-lined interiors and glass liner at the bottom are also far easier to clean.

Since the walls of such ovens are exposed metal, they radiate heat back at the food. This will not change most of your cooking times, but small amounts of high-fat foods such as butter and chocolate may require a 30-second reduction in cooking times if they are not to scorch.

I don't like automatic cooking programmes, defrosting programmes, sensors and probes. They are too inaccurate to be reliable. In an orgy of proprietary paranoia, the oven manufacturers don't explain how their programmes work, so you cannot adjust them or use standard recipes in them. The basic information to look for is how many watts the oven uses and what the settings such as 'low' and 'medium' mean as a percentage of full power. There are as yet no industry standards for such things.

In this book, most recipes call for 100% power—'high' or '10' on some ovens—which is always the highest setting. Some recipes, notably those for custards and large joints of beef, sometimes use 50% power, variously designated as 'medium' or '5'. A few recipes and defrosting instructions use a power of 30%; that can be called 'low defrost', 'medium low', '3' or 'simmer' on ovens of different makes, which is frustrating. The power levels can also be erratic in some ovens. A little experimentation will probably straighten things out. You can try writing or calling the manufacturers; unfortunately, I have found that very unproductive. For most purposes, there is no reason to cook at anything less than 100%.

Most ovens have clocks; on some, the cooking timers can also function as general timers for your kitchen. Reconcile yourself to the irritating electronic beep the oven makes when it has accomplished its task. (With three or four beepers going off at any given time when I was testing this book, my kitchen began to sound like a zoo.)

There are two kinds of optional controls that are helpful. As with a clock, digital controls are more accurate than dials. Some ovens have a button you can touch for 'minute plus', which permits you to add a minute without turning the oven off and losing power if your food looks like it needs just a little more time.

Many of us are wary of microwaves, but anybody who can use a push-button telephone or set a digital clock should have no trouble using these machines— which are infinitely safer, in terms of radiation, than television sets. Different models have different opening devices, but they all are absolute controls: if the door is open, the power shuts off. Ovens that have a lever for opening instead of a handle are easier to use when your hands are full. All have doors that open from the right, so choose a place where you can open your oven fully without having to dance around the door.

ADJUSTING RECIPES FOR DIFFERENT OVENS

There is some variation between microwave ovens, but the differences are no more extreme than those between one make of cooker and another. There are three main categories. Most full-power-ovens use between 650 and 700 watts of power (the standard of power for this book); cooking times in these ovens will be almost identical. Some smaller ovens use only 400 watts, while most medium-power ovens use 500 to 600 watts. There is no simple arithmetical way of calculating relative cooking times for ovens of different power. Cooking times in lower-wattage ovens will be longer, but the increase in time is mainly in the first part of the cooking. A low-wattage oven is like a car without much power; it will take longer to get up to 70 miles an hour, but once it is there, it will cruise at speed as well as a more powerful car. On foods that cook extremely quickly, such as wafer-thin biscuits like Florentines, allow another 30 seconds of cooking time in less powerful ovens; for longer-cooking recipes, allow about one and a half times the full-power oven times: 15 minutes in a low-wattage oven versus 10 in a full-power oven. If there is 250ml/8fl oz or more of liquid in the recipe, allow an extra 3 minutes of cooking time.

Many small-scale recipes, usually variations for one or two people, offer times for smaller ovens. Use the Dictionary as a guide to small quantities when working out your own recipes in small ovens. Only some of the baking recipes have been worked out for lower-power ovens. They don't work well for baking large quantities.

Oven size is determined by the square footage of its internal capacity. The largest is about one-and-one-half cubic feet. The largest oven that will fit in your kitchen offers the greatest flexibility in cooking. The smallest ovens will accommodate no more than dinner for two. As these small ovens are usually of low wattage, they will also require timing adjustments. Ovens with little height usually meant to fit over existing wall ovens or attach to the undersides of cupboards also will allow less flexibility since they will not hold the larger cooking vessels such as 5 litre/8 pint casseroles.

EVENNESS OF COOKING

Microwaves are erratic; not even the oven manufacturers can tell you exactly the pattern the waves will make in any particular oven. This means hot spots and uneven cooking. Some models have fans or other mechanical means of rotating the microwaves or the microwave-producing element.

Some ovens come with a turntable in the bottom that rotates the food as it cooks. If yours does not have one, you can purchase an inexpensive one that

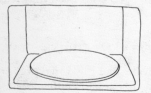

You can cook directly on oven's glass liner. In ovens with turntables, it is round (left); dishes must fit on the turntable. If oven has no turntable, buy a windup one (right).

works like a windup toy, or you can remember to *rotate foods that take a longer time to cook 45 degrees (a quarter turn) after half the cooking time has elapsed*. The turntable does slightly restrict the size of the dish that will fit in the oven—35 cm/14 inches with rounded corners is the maximum. I don't find that I need more than that, but you may. However, I find that much less rotating is necessary than commonly thought. Tight covering provides a mini-environment that evens out the cooking, and in recipes that call for stirring, the food is rotated without having to move the dish.

THE CONTROLS

Each make of oven, indeed each model, has controls that vary slightly. What you really need to discover is how to set a cooking time at 100% power, or 'high', for a given time since almost all your cooking will be done in that mode. It is not hard.

Time on most ovens is set as it is on a digital clock: you press the number for the minutes, and then for the seconds. If you are setting for an even number of minutes, you must remember to press in two zeros for the seconds. To set a time of 3½ minutes, press in 3, then 3, then 0, for 3 minutes 30 seconds.

THE EQUIPMENT

CONTAINERS. One of the saddest parts of cooking in the microwave oven is that your glorious copper pans will go unused. (Happily, you will not have to clean them.) This copper taboo extends to all metal pans. Don't get confused by Le Creuset and other enamelled wares; they have a heart of metal. Do not use any ceramics decorated with gold or other metals. Be careful with all-over blue or orange-red glazes, as they may be metal-based. A little bit of these glazes in a decoration will not matter.

The problem with metal is that it absolutely blocks microwaves so your food can't cook. A lot of metal may also create an arc, or flash of light, in the oven; this won't kill your oven, but it is unpleasantly dramatic. A little bit of gold, silver or platinum in decoration may melt or discolour, not nice for the dishes.

 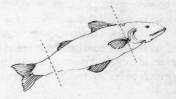

Shield banana (left) during ripening. Shield whole fish from either end to points indicated. If head and tail are removed, shield 2.5 cm/1 inch of cut ends.

Metal is sometimes used in special-purpose microwave dishes, such as browning dishes. Here it is perfectly fine, as is the limited use of aluminium foil to *shield* part of your food, like the thin tail part of a fish, and keep it from overcooking. It is called shielding because microwaves cannot pass through metal. Sometimes foil will be wrapped around dishes to keep the edges of the food from overcooking. Usually, the foil is removed at some time during the cooking to permit the shielded part to catch up.

The containers and dishes you can use in the microwave oven may be quite different from what you usually think of as cookware (except for glass and ceramic soufflé dishes and those wonderful earthenware casseroles you bought but don't use because they seem to break in your oven). Large gratin dishes, loaf dishes, flan dishes, lasagne dishes, ramekins made from glass or ceramic, and the occasional all-glass cooking pans are all usable. One special pleasure of cooking with these or indeed irregular plates in the microwave oven is the ease of washing-up; no burned-on food— simple washing, no scrubbing, will do the trick.

Your cupboards will yield all kinds of surprising containers hitherto unused for cooking. You can use ceramic and glass bowls, pudding basins, coffee cups, teacups, glass measuring jugs of all sizes (oversized with extra headroom is particularly useful), most of your plates and platters (including the best antique porcelains, as long as they don't have metal decoration, cracks or repairs), plastic storage containers marked 'microwave-safe', vases, mugs, crocks, tureens, pitchers, undecorated paper towels and paper plates, and microwave-safe polythene bags and wrap. Despite the attractions of frugality and ecology, do not use recycled paper; it may, strangely enough, contain small metal particles, causing it to catch fire. If you must, go ahead and use special pans designed for the microwave oven in hideous plastic or conventional-looking glass and ceramic. I have found that Japanese lacquer bowls do very well. I was apprehensive about using them, but now it is a favourite way to heat a calming cup of soup without having the bowl get hot.

There is one dish specially made for the microwave oven that I highly recommend. It is $27.5 \times 35 \times 5$ cm/$11 \times 14 \times 2$ inches and has rounded corners so that it can fit on a turntable and still turn. It has the greatest capacity that is reasonable in a microwave oven, and I use it very often for everything from risotto to stew to duck joints.

It would be nice if those very useful roasting bags suitable for microwave use came in more sizes. You cannot get an absolute seal (see page 26) although nylon ties sold with some roasting bags are microwave-safe, but turning the end of the bag under or loosely knotting it will do quite well. (The largest bags may swell up too much to rotate freely on a turntable unless you shorten them slightly by knotting.)

If the food is attractive, by all means cook it in glass; it shows it off, and, more important, you can see what is happening to it as it cooks. This is particularly

Twist polythene bag containing food. Knot to seal and shorten.

helpful when you are reducing a sauce. A glass measuring jug will let you see the reduction and measure it at the same time. When measuring jugs are used to cook in, I always use glass.

Microwave-safe plastic and polypropylene have one important asset. They are invisible to microwaves. Using them instead of glass will shorten cooking times by 10 or more seconds, depending on the size of the dish—something to remember when cooking very sensitive foods. However, plastic tends to craze if tranparent, and discolour with cooking over time. Worst of all, it is unattractive. Looks are more important in microwave-cooking containers than in other kitchen utensils, so try to save the plastic and polypropylene for storage and defrosting. Remember, much of the time the cooking dish, plate or platter will also be what you serve in or eat out of.

Use containers that approximate the shape and size suggested in the recipe. The size of the container (dish) and the way it lets you arrange the food influences the way food cooks and the timing. When divising your own recipes, use containers just large enough around to hold the food. Try to pick dishes deep enough to allow a little headroom so that sauces do not boil over, making a mess and loosening the covering. If you are using large dishes or platters, make sure they fit in the oven, and if you are using a turntable, make sure they have enough room to turn.

Casseroles or other dishes with tightly fitting lids are to be preferred. When covering with cling film (see page 26), it is preferable that the dishes have high enough sides so that the film does not touch the food and so that the steam from the cooking food has enough room.

The size and shape of a cooking dish is an important variable when cooking in the microwave oven. When you reach for a dish described in a recipe, do not panic if you do not have one with precisely the same dimensions. Try to approximate it as closely as possible. The primary considerations in choosing a dish are volume, surface area and depth (particularly if you are preparing a dish with a lot of liquid); the outline or form is really a secondary matter. As you can see from the illustrations below, 2 litre/3½ pint dishes can vary tremendously in shape.

Coffee cup   *Ramekin*   *Demitasse cup*

7.5 × 4 cm/3 × 1½ inch   9.4 × 4 cm/3½ × 1½ inch   9.5 × 5 cm/3¾ × 2 inch

These may all be used interchangeably.

10 × 6 × 4.5 cm/4 × 2½ × 1¾ inch   12.5 × 9 × 2.5 cm/5 × 3½ × 1 inch

16 × 11 × 2.5 cm/6½ × 4½ × 1 inch

Small ovals are good for baking eggs, larger ones for single portions of Macaroni Cheese.

15 × 6 cm/6 × 2½ inch   17.5 × 7.5 cm/7 × 3 inch   1.5 litre/2½ pint

Soufflé dishes come in all volumes. Glass are best.

5 litre/8 pint
to use as a stockpot

2 litre/3½ pint   2 litre/3½ pint

Use rimmed and rimless 2 litre/3½ pint dishes interchangeably; use rimless dish for cakes.

Glass measuring jugs in 1 litre/2 pint and 500 ml/1 pint sizes (plus other glass jugs)

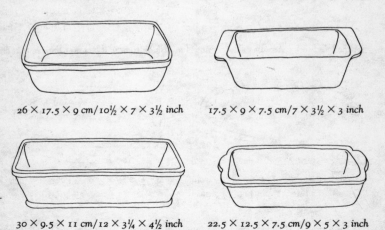

26 × 17.5 × 9 cm/10½ × 7 × 3½ inch   17.5 × 9 × 7.5 cm/7 × 3½ × 3 inch

30 × 9.5 × 11 cm/12 × 3¼ × 4½ inch   22.5 × 12.5 × 7.5 cm/9 × 5 × 3 inch

Use loaf dish specified in recipe; different shapes change cooking times even if the volumes are the same.

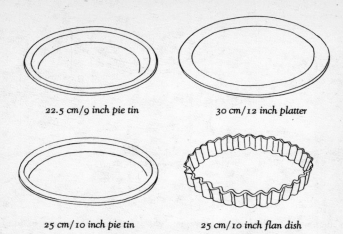

22.5 cm/9 inch pie tin 30 cm/12 inch platter

25 cm/10 inch pie tin 25 cm/10 inch flan dish

Use only where flat dishes are called for; they do not hold stews.

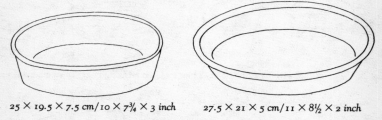

25 × 19.5 × 7.5 cm/10 × 7¾ × 3 inch 27.5 × 21 × 5 cm/11 × 8½ × 2 inch

Although dishes have same volume, liquid in dish on right will be lower than in that on left.

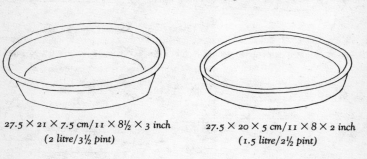

27.5 × 21 × 7.5 cm/11 × 8½ × 3 inch 27.5 × 20 × 5 cm/11 × 8 × 2 inch
(2 litre/3½ pint) (1.5 litre/2½ pint)

The flattened oval, though similar in dimension, cannot be substituted due to small volume.

Deep ovals can be used as same-volume soufflés. Use shallow ovals to replace similar-dimension rectangles. Measure volumes of all ovals.

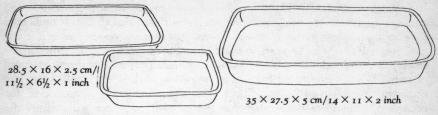

28.5 × 16 × 2.5 cm/
11½ × 6½ × 1 inch

35 × 27.5 × 5 cm/14 × 11 × 2 inch

18 × 12.5 × 2.5 cm/7¼ × 5 × 1 inch

Three good and useful rectangles; if it fits in your oven, buy the largest. If substituting ovals, go by length and width, not volume.

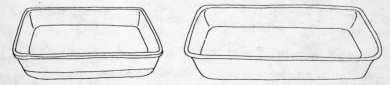

20 cm/8 inch square (left); 27 × 17.5 × 6 cm/10¾ × 7 × 2½ inch (right; can be used instead of 28.5 cm/11½ inch rectangle or 27.5 cm/11 inch oval)

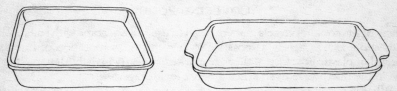

22.5 cm/9 inch square (left); 32.5 × 24 × 5 cm/13 × 9½ × 2 inch (right; can be used instead of 35 cm/14 inch rectangle)

TRIVETS. These are helpful when you want to cook more than one dish of plated food at a time. They are ugly, but at least their legs fold so they don't take too much room to store. Be very sure when you open the legs that you snap them into place so that the trivet does not collapse. If you are cooking two portions by cooking two platefuls at once, up the timing for two portions by 1 minute 30 seconds and exchange the position of the dishes halfway through the cooking time. Some ovens come equipped with trivets.

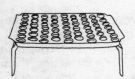 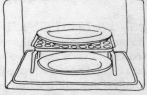

Trivet with folding legs (left) fits in all ovens; two dishes cook at once (right).

25

BROWNING DISHES. These are dishes with metal surfaces or metalicized patterns applied to the bottom. These special surfaces absorb heat if preheated for about 4 minutes in the microwave oven. Just as when you brown in a frying pan, you will need fat. You can, in this fashion, brown sandwiches, croûtons or small pieces of food like scallops or chicken joints. They are not the most useful of pans. When not heated for use as browning dishes, they will work like ordinary microwave dishes. Check the manufacturer's instructions for preheating your dish. Remember that flat metal-lined dishes will require the same cleaning as conventional saucepans.

22.5 cm/9 inch round metal-lined browning dish; it gets as hot as any pan.

20 cm/8 inch square browning dish with thin metal decal on bottom.

COVERING FOOD

Many of the cooking vessels that you wish to use will not come with suitable lids. Lids should fit as tightly as possible to prevent the evaporation of liquid. Be careful of plastic lids. Often, they are marked in nearly invisible letters, 'not for use in the microwave oven'; they are just for storage.

What you will use is paper towels for loose covering and to avoid spatters, aluminium foil to shield parts of foods that you want to cook or defrost more slowly, and microwave-safe cling film.

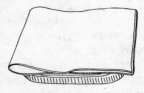

Loosely cover dish with doubled paper towel.

MAKING A TIGHT SEAL. Previous microwave recipes have frequently called for covering with cling film and leaving what is called a vent, a small flap of turned-back film at one edge or corner of the container. If covering in this way, be very careful not to remove the film from the loose, vent section; there will be the greatest amount of steam at this point. You may find that vented film sags down on to the food—undesirable.

I, rather differently, heartily recommend tight sealing with cling film as long as certain precautions are observed. All microwave-safe cling films are usable. However, there are differences in formulation that will require slightly different techniques. Polyvinyl-chloride (PVC) cling film stretches when subjected to steam pressure: it blows up like bubble gum. Don't be alarmed; this is correct. Watching the plastic bubble swell when you have a good seal is a childlike pleasure. This kind of film can be stretched smoothly over the rims of containers and patted against the sides.

Bubble forms during cooking if dish is tightly sealed.

Other cling films with more rigid formulations should have a little slack over the top of the container; it's like making a gusset in dressmaking. The edges of the cling film should still be tightly affixed to the rim and sides of the cooking container.

Again, when possible in selecting a container for microwave cooking, try to choose one with high enough sides or a deep enough well so that the film does not touch the food.

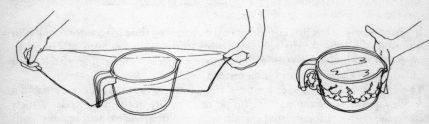

Place square of microwave cling film diagonally over jug.

Carefully seal under pouring lip and around and under handle.

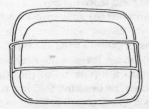

Overlap second piece of film by 5 cm/2 inches if necessary to assure good coverage and tight seal.

This kind of covering is very good since your foods will cook more evenly. It is like the environment in a terrarium where heat and humidity are evened out. It makes light of oven hot spots and provides what cooks have sought since time immemorial by baking in salt or clay, using a *bain-marie*, making *papillotes*, sealing the rims of casseroles with strips of dough, and more recently tightly covering with aluminium foil.

Be careful when removing film from hot food. Before removing cooked food from the oven, pierce the film with the tip of a knife to release any steam, and peel off carefully. To uncover a measuring jug or baking dish, hold on to one corner of the film and pull it away from the container, lifting at the same time. It is no more dangerous than uncovering a steaming pan.

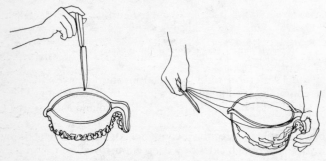

Prick small hole with point of sharp knife to release steam.
Pull film up and away from container to release.

If your container has just come out of the freezer or the refrigerator, cling film will not cling tightly. As the container heats in the oven, the film will begin to cling. It adheres less well to some plastics than to glass or china. If an airtight seal is called for, cook in glass or china instead.

The advantages of a tight covering of cling film are more rapid cooking and a lack of evaporation of the cooking liquid or moisture in the food itself. Which leads to the correct thought that certain recipes or ingredients will benefit from cooking, *uncovered*, so that evaporation can take place.

If you need to remove film during cooking in order to stir or turn food over, you should not remove the food from the oven. You can take all the film off and replace it. Or you can simply slit the film with a knife while your dish is still in the oven, then stir with a wooden spoon. Just patch the hold with a fresh piece of film, or re-cover the dish right over the slit film.

If you don't prick the film, a strange thing may happen. As the steam cools, the cling film gets drawn down tightly on to the surface of the food; it looks shrink-wrapped. Don't worry. By pricking the cling film before the cooking dish is withdrawn from the oven, the seal will release, and the film will not collapse and touch the food.

MICROWAVE BASICS

PLANNING YOUR MEAL

Before you start to cook, take your ingredients out of the refrigerator or freezer. Defrost what may need defrosting, following the information in the Dictionary under DEFROSTING. In this book timings are based on the assumption that ingredients are at room temperature unless instructions are given for defrosting, or, as in the case of butter, melting. Depending on the amount of cold food that is added to a recipe, the cooking time can increase anywhere from 15 seconds to a few minutes.

While you are getting used to the microwave oven, microwave-cook only one dish per meal, unless you can make the others ahead. The best way to time the main course is to figure out when your guests will get to it. Then count back for a starting time by the number of minutes the dish takes to cook. Often this means not putting food in the microwave until the guests are seated at the table, or have finished the previous course. Food cooked in the microwave oven will keep hot longer than foods cooked conventionally. Don't forget that if you are cooking an accompanying starch, you will need to start the water long before the main course goes in the oven.

BEFORE YOU BEGIN TO COOK

OVEN GLOVES. These are a must when cooking in the microwave oven. Tins and dishes *do* get hot, no matter what you have heard to the contrary. They won't get so hot that you will burn yourself, just hot enough so that you might drop them.

STIRRING. Because the walls of plastic-lined ovens do not get hot, it is easy to stir things without removing them from the oven. By doing so, you conserve heat and shorten cooking times. Slit the cling film, insert a spoon in the slit and stir rapidly. Re-cover the dish or simply patch the film with an overlapping sheet. The object is to move quickly so as to release as little retained heat from the oven and the food as possible. Be careful when cooking in a metal-lined microwave oven—its innards do get hot. Be very careful when you go back to regular cooking or you may burn yourself.

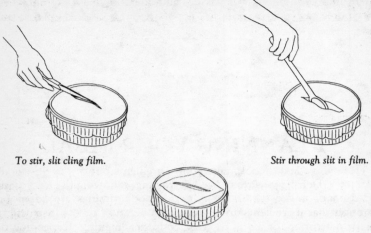

To stir, slit cling film.   Stir through slit in film.

Patch cling film with fresh square to make tight seal.

SETTING THE TIMER. When you are going to stir or turn something in the oven, set the timer for the full cooking time and then remember when it is time to stir. (As you open the door, you automatically interrupt the cooking. To resume cooking, close the door and press the Start button.) Alternatively, set the timer for only the time until stirring, shaking or turning. To resume cooking, close the oven door and reset the controls for the remaining time.

Timings in this book are based on this rapid, in-oven manipulation. If you are more comfortable working a little more slowly and removing the cooking dish from the oven, add 30 seconds (1 minute in less powerful ovens) to the cooking time in order to allow the heat to catch up with itself.

MICROWAVE OVENS 'PREHEAT'. You don't need to preheat ovens on purpose, but realize that the air in the oven, with its natural humidity, gets warm. This is important in two ways. First, successive batches of rapid-cooking foods—wafer biscuits, for example—will cook more quickly (by about 15 seconds) than the first batch. Second, because this heat helps cook food, it is better not to remove the food from the oven in order to stir.

OVERALL PREPARATION AND COOKING TIMES have been given in the introduction to some of the recipes to give you an idea of how long you will actually be in the kitchen. (Compare microwave cooking times to longer, standard times!) Unfortunately, the microwave oven does not eliminate the need for peeling, cutting and chopping. If you do those things in a more leisurely fashion, allow a little extra time. Since you do not have to watch the pot, some preparation can be done while the food cooks. A food processor is often called for to speed up the cutting. If you do not have one, allow a little more time.

Blenders are wonderful for some soups and sauces. Use a food mill when you want to purée and remove seeds and skins, or put the cooked mixture through a sieve.

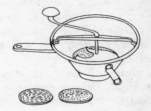

Food mill discs with different-size holes.

MULTIPLYING TIMES AND QUANTITIES. Microwave cooking is a funny business. You can't just multiply, divide or apply some other arithmetic formula to the business of increasing or decreasing recipes. Different multiples are involved for different basic ingredients. That is why there are so many variant recipes in this book: they ensure your success and give you models to follow for your own multiplication and division. Seasonings have to be changed when recipes are increased or decreased, since this change in size heralds a different cooking time. For example, the recipe for a briefly cooked food—say a fish fillet that is cooked for only 1 minute 30 seconds—pepped up with a smidgen of garlic and some dried herbs, will need ten times as much garlic but only four times as many herbs when the recipe is expanded for eight fillets that cook in 7 minutes. This, as you will see later in this chapter, has to do with the way garlic and dried herbs behave with longer microwave cooking.

Look ingredients up in the Dictionary to find out what special quirks they may have in microwave cooking, as well as additional cooking times.

Since microwave cooking frequently depends on a combination of steam cooking and the activity of different kinds of food molecules under the influence (sounds like Svengali) of microwaves, cooking times depend on the amount of liquid in the ingredients as well as the amounts of fat, sugar and protein.

When multiplying recipes, especially those that are cooked tightly covered, don't increase the amount of liquid arithmetically. Use as little liquid as is reasonable to achieve flavour. Liquid actually slows cooking. You can always add more at the end, or heat it separately and add it. With tight covering, almost no evaporation takes place. Indeed, liquid seems to appear from nowhere; it is drawn from the ingredients themselves. You may find that much less liquid is plenty.

Some examples of reduced liquid and reduced cooking time: Beef in Red Wine (page 211) microwave-cooks in 15 minutes with 350 ml/12 fl oz of liquid, as compared to conventional cooking, which takes 4 hours, with 750 ml/1¼ pints of liquid for the same amount of beef; 500 g/1 lb of acorn squash cooks to moist perfection without any added liquid in 7 minutes in the microwave oven, versus 45 to 50 minutes if conventionally cooked with liquid added.

Liquid can be water, wine, stock, cream, juice, milk, liquid vegetables like tomatoes, or anything else that you add to moisten food. This liquid, as well as the liquid in the foods themselves—meat juices, the water content of vegetables—comes to the boil in the microwave oven and turns to steam, which either evaporates out of the dish if the food is uncovered, or helps to cook the food when the food is tightly covered.

When dividing recipes, it does not always follow that the liquid can be proportionally reduced. You may not leave enough to get up a good head of steam, and your food may take longer to cook. Adding a little water that will boil quickly and make steam is like priming the pump.

SIZE OF FOOD AND COOKING TIME

When possible, it is better to avoid large hunks of food and big, empty hollows like the space inside a whole chicken. You will be spending time heating that space. Since birds cannot be roasted successfully in any case, it is much better to joint them before microwave-cooking them. Fairly large fish can be cooked whole; see FISH in the Dictionary. To get indications for the largest single piece of a given meat that can be cooked at one time—beef, for example—check the relevant recipe. If the largest quantity given is for 1.5 kg/3 lb, it is safe to assume that results with larger pieces of this meat have been unsatisfactory. See the section on cooking protein (page 33) for an explanation.

Relatively modest-size vegetables in the microwave oven will cook in roughly the same time whether cut up or whole (group cut-up pieces in cups).

You can slightly accelerate the cooking times of certain foods by cutting them into equal, optimal shapes and sizes and separating them in the dish to cook individually—fish medallions or meat loaves, for example. When you divide a recipe into individual containers for cooking, you may not be speeding the cooking process because each container will need to heat up. It is also the reason to increase the dish size, rather than use several dishes at once.

As in Chinese cooking, pieces of the major ingredient(s) should be about the same size. Pieces about 7.5 cm/3 inches cubed or discs 7.5 cm/3 inches in diameter and 5 cm/2 inches thick are optimal for rapid cooking. Food is best arranged so that large pieces do not touch; the microwaves can get at them better.

If a large piece of food is kept to a height dimension of around 7.5 cm/3 inches and is not allowed to get much fatter (wider) than that—for example, a whole fish, a pâté or a slim piece of veal—its length will be less important.

The sizes into which secondary ingredients are cut does not matter much, unless they are disproportionately large (the vegetables should be smaller than the meat in a stew) or unless they are the major ingredient at some point in the cooking process (onions cooked first in butter before other ingredients are added). When a dish, a soup for instance, is composed of many different but equally important ingredients, they should be pretty much the same size.

ARRANGING FOOD

There is more to arranging food than separating roughly evenly shaped major ingredients. When cooking food on top of the stove, the centre of the pan is the hottest. In a microwave oven, the food towards the outside of the dish cooks the most quickly. Arrange foods for microwave cooking either in a ring towards the outer perimeter of the cooking dish, with the quicker-cooking elements (such as vegetables) towards the centre, or arrange food like the spokes of a wheel, with the thickest parts of the food towards the rim.

Because food cooks differently depending on where it is placed in the cooking dish, vegetables that normally need different cooking times can all be cooked at the same time. Place the long-cooking vegetables towards the outside of the dish and quick-cooking vegetables in the centre. See VEGETABLES in the Dictionary for a list of long- and quick-cooking vegetables. Often, you can cook all the vegetables in the same time it would take to bring to the boil the water to cook just one vegetable. This permits you to cook a variety of vegetables even for one or two people.

The technique of arranging foods of different cooking times applies to more than vegetables. Follow the arrangement descriptions in the recipes, and refer to the illustrations that follow on page 34.

HOW DIFFERENT KINDS OF FOODS COOK

COOKING PROTEIN. You have only to cook an egg white—practically pure protein—to understand how rapidly proteins respond to microwaves. A few seconds too many and you achieve rubber. This rapid response is a fabulous benefit when cooking fish and chicken, foods that are not normally cooked in large quantities or for a long time. It is also a tremendous help in the cooking of stocks, where extraction of bone gelatine, proteins and meat flavours occurs incredibly quickly. Using a protein-rich stock as a cooking liquid rather than water will actually shorten cooking times.

A small joint of veal—a cut that toughens if really roasted—cooks sublimely well in the microwave oven. The rapidity makes it a joy to cook Ossobuco, Chicken in Red Wine or duck for one. Perhaps I should be content with these triumphs, but there are times when I crave a real stew or chilli. There are problems with these dishes, as you will see; but I think, within limits, I have licked them. At least I can now eat these foods without having to spend half the

Petal arrangement, skinned and boned chicken breasts.

Sections of foods (stuffed peppers) arranged in dish and covered.

Long-cooking ingredients not touching, around quick-cooking ones.

Pork chops with bones towards edge of dish.

Arrange meat loaf or figs to hold shape or position.

Fish fillets folded, thicker (fold part) towards the edge of dish.

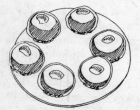

Singly wrapped foods, here apples, arranged for even cooking.

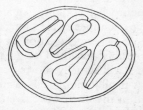

Pears or foods with thin ends (quick-cooking) towards centre.

day in the kitchen. See Lamb Stew (page 229), Chunky Beef Chilli (page 208), and Sliced Beef Casserole (page 211).

Cooking large joints of meat, or large quantities of meat that normally need to be stewed to be tender, is an iffy proposition. If the timing isn't correct, the meat will toughen up on you just when you think it is getting delightfully tender. Some microwave cooks solve the problem by cooking the meat at reduced power after it has been thoroughly heated at 100%. This seems logical; but I am not convinced. For one thing, the cooking time is sufficiently prolonged that it becomes a toss-up whether the meat might as well be cooked in the regular oven or on top of the cooker. For another, I find the results unreliable.

When preparing meat dishes, do not try to increase quantities; the resulting increased cooking times will be disastrous. Only a limited group of beef stews improves with waiting, a process I call *mellowing* (see page 206). Otherwise, eat meats as soon as they are cooked. Reheating and defrosting can be problematic. You do not want to overcook. In addition, some foods take as long to defrost and reheat as to cook from scratch. See REHEATING and DEFROSTING in the Dictionary for guidelines.

COOKING SUGAR. Sugar by itself or with a little butter or water caramelizes well in the microwave oven. See entries for BROWNING, SUGAR and CARAMEL in the Dictionary. This feature is a bonanza for bakers and the makers of sweets, who no longer have to worry about burned pans or sugar crystals ruining their sweets. Microwave techniques are fabulous for the making of syrups, jams and jellies: the sugar mixture gets dense (jells) before the fruit flavour dies. Onions will caramelize nicely, too, as they do on top of the stove when cooked long enough. This is good news for onion soup enthusiasts who don't want to stand over the cooker stirring for an hour.

Meat will not caramelize or crust in the microwave oven. Coloured glazes act only as concealments; they neither caramelize themselves nor affect the way meat cooks. Meat cannot be roasted or sautéed until brown in the microwave oven. On the other hand, I do not think it needs to be for stews—heresy!

COOKING WITH LIQUID. Use much less than normal; water takes a significant amount of time to come to the boil. Tight sealing will keep the food bathed in moisture. Most vegetables and fruits will cook wonderfully if tightly wrapped in microwave cling film or in a microwave-safe roasting bag—no liquid at all, no salt needed to keep the colours bright.

Vitamins are much less affected by rapid microwave cooking with very little liquid than they are by any other kind of cooking—a nice benefit for all of us.

FAT IN THE MICROWAVE OVEN. Fat is one of the things that cooks quickest in the microwave oven. It attracts the microwaves. This differential rapidity is useful when you want to render fat, particularly to separate it from another substance (like the flesh and skin of a duck) or from bone (to liberate marrow).

You have to add little fat when cooking with microwaves. Use it mainly for flavour or to coat something like rice (see Basic Risotto, page 109) to keep the pieces separate. You don't need it to keep food from sticking; it won't stick. You don't need it for sautéing; you cannot really sauté in the microwave oven anyhow. A little fat can accelerate the cooking process.

STARCH. Whether in flour, potatoes or rice, starch can behave oddly or beautifully in the microwave oven. If the starch, such as *wheat flour*, is part gluten (the protein part, which stretches and lets baked goods rise), it will absorb great quantities of liquid and become gluey; cooked without liquid, it gets hard. The microwave successes you can have with wheat flour are extremely limited. Refer to BAKING in the Dictionary and page 356 for a fuller discussion. One nice sideline of flour's odd cooking properties is that you can make Brown Roux (page 292), so essential to New Orleans Cajun and Creole cooking, without danger of scorching.

Other starches also behave differently in the microwave oven. *Rice starch* absorbs great quantities of liquid slowly, hence the perfect risotto. On one hand, this tells us that rice as a side dish is just as quickly cooked on the hob. On the other hand, in the case of a dish like paella or pilaf, where you do not want the rice to overcook before the other ingredients are ready, the special properties of rice in microwave cooking are quite an asset.

Cornflour behaves at its best in the microwave oven. It thickens sauces without lumps when added as a slurry, mixed until smooth with water or cooking liquid. It does not impart a raw taste; you do not need much of it; and it does not lose its binding power. It is also useful as a replacement for flour when baking cakes, as is potato starch.

Arrowroot behaves oddly. Since it is expensive, I have not worried about it much.

Vegetable starches absorb liquid, but less than they might in other kinds of cooking—a mixed bag of results. Potatoes cook, but they do not get mealy. This means you need to add more liquid when making mashed potatoes. It also means that potatoes cooked in stews and vegetable soups retain their shape, which is nice. Vegetables such as parsnips, orange-fleshed sweet potatoes and even carrots, which tend to get watery when cooked conventionally, do fabulously in the microwave oven. Vegetable cooking times are given in the Dictionary.

FLAVOURING AND SEASONING FOOD. Remember that microwave cooking tends to emphasize the inherent tastes of foods. If you want to gentle the flavour, as some people do with spinach and rhubarb, use more liquid, cook uncovered and lengthen the cooking time. In most cases, the added punch of natural flavour is a blessing. If you are in the habit of seasoning to compensate for bland ingredients, you may need to do less of this with microwave-cooked foods. If you have been seasoning to balance flavours, you may want to slightly increase seasoning amounts, but check the general indications for seasoning and entries for individual seasonings in the Dictionary.

Be careful with *salt*. Generally, you can use less than usual as foods tend to absorb it and you will be using less liquid than is customary. Also, the better flavour of microwave-cooked vegetables requires almost no salt. Since food is hot when it comes from the oven, it can be salted then and still absorb the salt. The flavour of salt does not change in microwave cooking. However, if you are cooking foods uncovered, the liquid will reduce substantially and make the dish seem very salty. If you are cooking vegetables on their own with little or no liquid, do not add salt. It will draw liquid from the vegetable, leaving it with a wrinkled look.

Where stock made from a cube can be substituted for homemade stock when you are in a hurry, the recipes say so. Never use the substitute in a dish where the liquid is going to be substantially reduced—foods that are cooked uncovered. When using stock cubes, it is necessary to adjust the recipe by being sure to use, or increase, water or another liquid to compensate for the liquid of the stock. Omit salt until the final tasting. Since the salt levels in stock cubes are so high, they are not suitable for making risotto, all glazes and many sauces. Fortunately, making stock is a speedy proposition in a microwave oven and it freezes well.

There are many ingredients that are often used canned. Always remember that salt is present in canned tomatoes, juices and tomato paste. Adjust recipes to suit your taste. If you are salt-sensitive, prepare your own ingredients to replace those in cans. You can do it quickly with the microwave oven.

Black or white pepper should be used in tiny quantities. It develops a terrific wallop in microwave cooking (though it does not get bitter as it does with prolonged cooking on the hob). If you are hesitant about controlling the punch of pepper, do not add it until the end of the cooking time, or until the food comes out of the oven.

Garlic, unless very briefly cooked or added at the end of the cooking time, should be used in quantities greater than you would imagine. It cooks to a soft sweetness in about 7 minutes.

When making a stew, increase the proportion of wine or *alcohol* to stock. The flavours dissipate rapidly, as do those of vanilla, almond, lemon and orange when added as an essence, since it is alcohol-based.

Increase the warm *spices* such as cumin, coriander, cardamom, anise, caraway and allspice; they tend to become quite gentle. Be careful with the pungent spices such as cinnamon, nutmeg, dried ginger and five-spice powder; they will become more dominant. The hot spices—ground pepper, Szechuan peppercorns, dried chillies and mustard powder—must be sharply decreased or they will knock the socks off all but those with palates of asbestos. Decrease dry *herb* quantities, as all of their flavour will be reconstituted; increase fresh herb quantities or stir them in late in the game (their essential oils tend to volatilize). *Aromatics*, such as parsley, celery and carrots, can be increased slightly when used as flavourings rather than as major ingredients. Spring onions and fresh ginger can be left at normal quantities, but should not be added too soon; they fade easily.

IMPORTANT NOTES

1. Unless specified otherwise, all ingredients are used at room temperature.
2. Whenever adding cool liquids to hot ones, pour slowly, as the mixture may initially boil up. Never set a hot container on a wet surface.
3. Do not use cracked, chipped or repaired bowls or plates in the oven.
4. Butter is the only ingredient that is always used directly from the refrigerator or freezer—*cold*. Butter quickly changes texture and flavour at room temperature. Cooking and melting times are based on this temperature.

FIRST COURSES

I dearly love first courses, and with the microwave oven I cook them up so speedily I sometimes have to stop myself, or there is just too much food. It is particularly rewarding to make pâtés. It is a matter of minutes to prepare one, instead of hours; and they can be ready and waiting when needed.

Besides the recipes for first courses in this chapter, there are many first courses that can be scooped out of cans and jars or be picked up at delicatessens. More gala are little homemade composed salads with bits of leftovers tossed in, or cracklings, or freshly cooked mushrooms, or a few chicken livers still warm and sprinkled with vinegar.

Other ideas for first courses can be found in the vegetable and grains chapters. Garlic Creams (page 264), Asparagus Creams (page 263), Parsnip Creams (page 263), and many others make perfect first courses. Small portions of risotto and polenta are also good for starters, as are small portions of vegetable stew. Soups, hot or cold, are always welcome as an introduction to a meal where the main course is not too saucy. Some fish and seafood dishes can be served in half portions as first courses at a more formal meal.

Herewith, a group of recipes for foods really meant to be first courses. They also function splendidly as part of a buffet. From time to time I have tried to give an indication of how long the dish takes to make working at an efficient rate. Sometimes I even tell how long it used to take to make it pre-microwave.

COLD FIRST COURSES

One of the nice things about most cold, or cool, first courses is that they can be made ahead. They should be interesting enough to awaken the appetite, but not so aggressive as to satisfy or kill it.

STUFFED VINE LEAVES

• ◆ •

Along the shores of the Mediterranean in Greece and Turkey they stuff young vine leaves and marinate them in olive oil and lemon juice. These make a super first course or hors d'oeuvre. Serve alone, or with some chunks of feta cheese, olives, and perhaps a few cold mussels as a first course. The stuffed leaves keep well for up to a week in the refrigerator. *Makes 2 dozen*

½ jar vine leaves (grape leaves in brine), or fresh vine leaves (see note)
200 ml/7 fl oz fruity olive oil
45 g/1½ oz chopped onion
2 cloves garlic, smashed, peeled and finely chopped

175 g/6 oz long-grain rice
60 g/2 oz fresh dill, chopped
30 g/1 oz fresh mint leaves, chopped
1 teaspoon sea salt
¼ teaspoon freshly ground black pepper
2 tablespoons fresh lemon juice

1 Place vine leaves in a large bowl and rinse well with running water. Drain and set aside.

2 Heat 175 ml/6 fl oz olive oil in a 27.5 × 22.5 cm/11 × 9 inch dish, uncovered, at 100% for 3 minutes. Add onions, garlic, rice, dill and mint. Stir to coat. Cover tightly with microwave cling film. Cook at 100% for 5 minutes.

3 Pierce film with the tip of a sharp knife, then remove dish from oven. Uncover and let stand until cool. Add salt and pepper.

4 To stuff the vine leaves, place a leaf on a work surface with the rough side up and stalk end closest to you. Place a teaspoonful of rice mixture at the stalk end. Roll away from you, folding in both sides of the leaf as you go. Arrange stuffed leaves in two rows in a 27.5 × 22.5 cm/11 × 9 inch dish (they should just touch each other). Pour 350 ml/12 fl oz water over leaves. Cover tightly with microwave cling film. Cook at 100% for 12 minutes.

5 Pierce film with the tip of a sharp knife, then remove dish from oven. Uncover and let stand until cool. Pour lemon juice and remaining 2 tablespoons olive oil over leaves. Cover tightly with microwave cling film. Refregerate for at least 6 hours, or up to a week. Serve at room temperature.

Note. If you have unsprayed fresh vine leaves, make a strong saltwater brine by boiling 350 g/12 oz sea salt in 1 litre/ 1¾ pints water in a 2.5 litre/4 pint soufflé dish, uncovered, for 10 minutes at 100%. Put in 12 vine leaves. Cook uncovered for 2 minutes at 100%. Lift out leaves with a fish slice or skimmer and place in iced water. Repeat with more leaves, if desired.

VARIATION

STUFFED VINE LEAVES WITH TOMATOES, RAISINS, OR NUTS To rice mixture, add one of the following ingredients, or any combination: 200 g/7 oz canned tomatoes, drained and crushed; 75 g/2½ oz raisins; 45g/1½ oz pine nuts.

Spread the vine leaf flat and place a teaspoon of rice mixture in centre. Fold in the edges of the leaf to enclose rice. Roll leaf away from you to make a neat package.

CLASSIC AUBERGINE APPETIZER

The flesh of aubergine cooked in a microwave oven retains a beautiful green colour, rather than taking on the dull brown of roasted aubergine. That gives these dips a fresh, appealing look and flavour that is delicious with raw vegetables or with warm pita bread. They are terrific for cocktail parties.

This wonderfully garlicky dish demands 1½ hours of baking in a conventional oven, but only 12 mintues in the microwave oven. *Makes 500 ml/16 fl oz*

1 large aubergine (about 500 g/1 lb), pricked several times with a fork
1 small onion, peeled and chopped
4 tablespoons chopped parsley
1 clove garlic, smashed, peeled and finely chopped

1 teaspoon sea salt
¼ teaspoon freshly ground black pepper
2 tablespoons olive oil
2 teaspoons fresh lemon juice

1 Place aubergine on a double thickness of paper towel and cook, uncovered, at 100% for 12 minutes. Remove from oven. Let cool.

2 When aubergine is cool enough to handle, cut it in half lengthways and scoop out flesh. Place in the container of a food processor. Add onion, parsley, garlic, salt and pepper and process just until mixture is coarsely chopped.

3 Transfer to a serving bowl. Stir in oil and lemon juice. Serve at room temperature.

VARIATIONS

RUSSIAN AUBERGINE ORIENTALE While waiting for aubergine to cool, core and seed 1 green pepper, then chop finely. Place in a 300 ml/½ pint glass jug with 1 tablespoon olive oil. Cover tightly with microwave cling film. Cook at 100% for 3 minutes. Pierce film, then remove from oven. Prepare aubergine mixture, stir in the pepper along with 125 ml/4 fl oz Lightly Cooked Crushed Tomatoes (page 293) or chopped tomatoes, 3 tablespoons tomato paste, 2 tablespoons fresh lemon juice, and a pinch of cayenne pepper. Serve with lemon wedges.

AUBERGINE WITH ORIENTAL SEASONINGS Cook aubergine for Classic Aubergine Appetizer. Omit all seasonings except lemon juice and garlic. Add 2 chopped spring onions, 4 tablespoons chopped fresh coriander, 1 tablespoon finely chopped fresh root ginger, 2 teaspoons soya sauce, and 2 teaspoons sesame oil. Proceed as for Classic Aubergine Appetizer.

CALAMARI SALAD

• ◆ •

It would be hard to think of a fresher-tasting or more quickly prepared salad.
Serves 4

350 g/12 oz medium squid, cleaned and sliced into rings (page 493)

3 centre celery sticks with leaves, sticks stringed and thinly sliced diagonally and leaves left whole

60 g/2 oz onion, peeled and thinly sliced

60 g/2 oz red pepper, cored, seeded and thinly sliced

2 tablespoons olive oil

2 tablespoons fresh lemon juice

1 teaspoon sea salt

¼ teaspoon freshly ground black pepper

12 oil-cured black olives, stoned and coarsely chopped

1 Toss together squid, sliced celery, onion and red pepper in a 1 litre/2 pint soufflé dish. Cover tightly with microwave cling film. Cook at 100% for 2 minutes 30 seconds, shaking the dish once.

2 Pierce film with the tip of a sharp knife, then remove dish from oven. Uncover and let cool slightly. When cool enough to handle, pour off liquid collected in bottom of dish. Add remaining ingredients and stir to coat. Serve at room temperature.

VARIATION

CALAMARI AND SEAFOOD SALAD Add 8 raw medium prawns, peeled and cut in half, and 8 cleaned mussels to the ingredients for Calamari Salad; increase squid to 500 g/1 lb, red pepper to 90 g/3 oz. Arrange prawns and mussels towards outside of a 2.5 litre/4 pint soufflé dish; place vegetables and squid in centre of dish. Cover tightly and cook for 5 minutes. Remove mussels from shells if desired. Proceed as for Calamari Salad, increasing lemon juice to 3 tablespoons. Taste to check seasonings. *Serves* 8.

GEFILTE FISH

• • •

This traditional Jewish dish for Passover makes a wonderful cold first course for anybody. It could also be served as a main course. Usually served with red and white horseradish, it could have a spicy rémoulade sauce or herb-rich mayonnaise instead. Always serve a little of the jellied stock and a few of the carrots with the fish. This must be made a day ahead. *Serves 12 as a first course, 6 as a light dish*

FISH STOCK
1.5 kg/3 lb fish heads, skin and bones (from the fish you are using and other similar fish), well rinsed and gills removed
1 medium carrot, trimmed, peeled and quartered
1 medium onion (about 250 g/8 oz), peeled and quartered
½ celery stick, stringed and quartered
1 bay leaf
1 litre/1¾ pints water
1½ tablespoons sea salt
3 medium carrots, trimmed, peeled and sliced crossways 3 mm/⅛ inch thick

FISH MIXTURE
250 g/8 oz fillets of freshwater white fish such as trout, skinned
250 g/8 oz carp fillets, skinned
250 g/8 oz pike fillets, skinned
2 medium onions, peeled and quartered
3 eggs
85 g/scant 3 oz matzo meal
175 ml/6 fl oz soda water, chilled (for Passover substitute cold water)
1 teaspoon sea salt
Large pinch freshly ground black pepper
1 teaspoon powdered gelatine, if necessary
Red and white horseradish (optional)

1 To prepare the stock, place fish heads, skin and bones, quartered carrot, onion, celery, bay leaf, water and salt in a 2 litre/3½ pint glass jug or bowl. Cover tightly with microwave cling film. Cook at 100% for 30 minutes.

2 Pierce film with the tip of a sharp knife, then remove jug from oven. Uncover and strain.

3 Add sliced carrots. Cover tightly with microwave cling film. Cook at 100% for 10 minutes. Pierce film, remove from oven and set aside.

4 To prepare the fish mixture, place the fillets and onions in the container of a food processor. Process until smooth. Add remaining ingredients except gelatine and horseradish and process just until combined. With damp hands, shape mixture into 12 ovals, 8.5 × 5 cm/3½ × 2 inches.

5 Arrange fish in a spoke around the edge of a 35 × 27.5 cm/14 × 11 inch oval dish. Spoon carrot slices into centre of dish and pour stock over all. Cover tightly with microwave cling film, leaving a small vent in one corner. Cook at 100% for 12 minutes.

6 Place a small plate in the freezer (to test setting of finished stock).

7 Remove fish from oven. Uncover and turn each piece over. Let fish cool in the stock for 30 minutes.

8 Test the jelly by pouring a spoonful of stock on to the cold plate. Place the plate in the freezer for 1 minute. Stock should be firm. If it is not, place cooled stock in a bowl and sprinkle gelatine on top. Leave to soak for 2 minutes. Stir well and repeat test with chilled plate. If stock is still not firm, add another teaspoon of gelatine.

9 Place gefilte fish in the smallest deep container that can hold it in one layer. Cover with stock. Refrigerate overnight.

10 Serve gefilte fish chilled, with some of the jellied stock and carrots. Serve horseradish in a separate bowl, if desired.

Gefilte fish arranged, not touching, around carrots.

VEGETABLES À LA GRECQUE

The French have many delightful ways of preparing vegetables to be served cool. One is based on a Greek way of preparing artichokes, which are often then served with little onions and potatoes. The Greek version is usually flavoured with dill or fresh or dried mint. The French version often has dried coriander seed, cardamom seed, and even mustard seed. The vegetables can be served singly, in an assortment, as part of a mixed hors d'oeuvre, or as an accompaniment to a pâté. The cooking liquid can be refrigerated for up to a month and reused for different vegetables. One nice thing about cooking artichokes this way is that much more of them, sometimes all, becomes edible with a knife and fork.

GLOBE ARTICHOKES AND ONIONS À LA GRECQUE

Large globe artichokes are more frequently cooked in Greece than the tiny ones described in the following recipe. If you plan to serve Spring Onions à la Grecque too, prepare the spring onions first, and then add the additional ingredients to the stock and reuse for the artichokes. *Serves 4 to 6 by itself, 8 to 16 as part of a mixed hors d'oeuvre*

4 globe artichokes (350 g/12 oz each), leaf tips trimmed, quartered through stem and choke removed (see note)
8 small (2.5–4 cm/1–1½ inch diameter) onions, peeled
Juice of 2 lemons, lemon shells reserved
500 ml/16 fl oz Chicken Stock (page 286) or stock from a cube

125 ml/4 fl oz olive oil
1 tablespoon sea salt (less if using stock cube)
4 fresh dill sprigs
4 tablespoons chopped fresh mint or dill

1 Arrange artichokes, cut side down, in a 30 × 18.5 × 5 cm/12 × 7½ × 2 inch dish, with the fat stalk ends towards the outside of the dish. Tuck onions and lemon shells among artichokes. Add stock, oil, salt and dill sprigs. Cover tightly with microwave cling film. Cook at 100% for 12 minutes.

2 Pierce film with the tip of a sharp knife, then remove dish from oven. Uncover and turn artichokes over. Re-cover tightly and cook for 8 minutes more.

3 Pierce film, then remove from oven. Let stand, covered, until cool. Just before serving, stir in 4 tablespoons of the lemon juice, salt to taste, and sprinkle with mint or dill.

Note. Artichokes weighing 350–500 g/¾-1 lb should be quartered lengthways; 250 g/8 oz artichokes should be cut in half lengthways. If using 250 g/8 oz artichokes, use five and plan on serving at least one half artichoke per person.

VARIATIONS

LATE AUTUMN ARTICHOKES À LA GRECQUE Add ½ teaspoon cardamom pods, crushed, and a pinch of dried oregano to the stock before cooking.

SPRING ONIONS À LA GRECQUE These spring onions are more truly braised; they could be served hot as a side dish with Poached Chicken Breasts in Sauce Suprême or with a simple fish dish. Substitute 18 medium spring onions (about 3 bunches), trimmed and cut into 12.5 cm/5 inch lengths, for artichokes and onions. Reduce lemon juice to 1 tablespoon and reduce stock and oil by half. Omit lemon shells, dill and mint. Proceed as for Globe Artichokes and Onions, cooking spring onions in a 15 × 5 cm/6 × 2 inch round dish for 6 minutes.

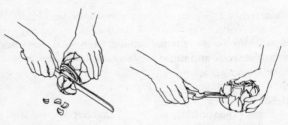

To trim artichokes, first cut off 2.5 cm/1 inch from the top of the artichoke. Then, with scissors, clip the remaining leaf tips around artichoke bottom.

MINIATURE ARTICHOKES À LA GRECQUE

When very tiny artichokes are available, they can be cooked whole, and every bit is edible and delicious. *Serves 6*

500 g/1 lb baby artichokes (about 16), round bottom leaves and any really hard outer leaves removed and leaf tips trimmed by 1 cm/½ inch
500 ml/16 fl oz Chicken Stock (page 286) or stock from a cube

175 ml/6 fl oz olive oil
3 cloves garlic, smashed and peeled
2 tablespoons fresh lemon juice
1 tablespoon sea salt (less if using stock cube)
4 tablespoons finely chopped fresh dill

1 Place artichokes, stock, oil and garlic in a 1.5 litre/2½ pint soufflé dish. Cover tightly with microwave cling film. Cook at 100% for 8 minutes.

2 Pierce film with the point of a sharp knife, then remove dish from oven. Uncover and turn artichokes over. Re-cover tightly and cook at 100% for 4 minutes more.

3 Pierce film, then remove from oven. Uncover and pour off all but 250 ml/8 fl oz cooking liquid. Stir in lemon juice and salt. Sprinkle with dill just before serving.

BABY ARTICHOKES À LA GRECQUE

This recipe is for those spring days when you find small artichokes in the greengrocer. Ideally, they should be the pointy artichokes the French call *violets*, not globe artichokes. *Violets* are the ones the Italians flatten out to look like the flowers they are and then deep-fry. *Serves 4*

8 baby artichokes (about 60 g/2 oz each), round bottom leaves removed and leaf tips trimmed, then cut in half lengthways
4 tablespoons fresh lemon juice
150 ml/¼ pint Chicken Stock (page 286) or stock from a cube

5½ tablespoons olive oil
2 cloves garlic, smashed and peeled
½ teaspoon coriander seed
½ teaspoon crushed cardamom pods
¼ teaspoon mustard seed
Sea salt

1 Rub artichokes with lemon juice. Remove any inner leaves that have a reddish tinge at the edge.

2 Combine artichokes, any remaining lemon juice, stock, oil, garlic, spices and salt in a 2.5 litre/4 pint soufflé dish. Cover tightly with microwave cling film. Cook at 100% for 10 minutes.

3 Pierce film with the point of a sharp knife, then remove dish from oven. Uncover and turn artichokes over. Re-cover and cook at 100% for 3 minutes more.

4 Pierce film, then remove from oven. Let stand, covered, until cool.

ONIONS À LA MONÉGASQUE

·•·•·

This is one of those dishes that is nice to have in the refrigerator to serve as part of a mixed hors d'oeuvre. Allow onions to come to room temperature before using. They are also delicious with grilled fish or chicken, or nestled up to a pâté. Another nice side dish of onions is Onions in Barbecue Sauce (page 262). *Serves 6 in a mixed hors d'oeuvre, 8 to 10 with pâté*

250 g/8 oz button onions, peeled (page 472)	Pinch dried oregano
2 tablespoons red wine vinegar	75 g/2½ oz raisins
2 tablespoons white wine	2 tablespoons water
2 tablespoons olive oil	¼ teaspoon sea salt
3 tablespoons tomato paste	Pinch freshly ground black pepper
½ bay leaf	2 drops Tabasco sauce
	1 teaspoon sugar (optional)

1 Stir together onions, vinegar, wine, oil, tomato paste, bay leaf, oregano and raisins in a 1 litre/2 pint soufflé dish. Cover tightly with microwave cling film. Cook at 100% for 10 minutes.

2 Pierce film with the tip of a sharp knife, then remove dish from oven. Uncover and stir in water, salt, pepper, Tabasco sauce and sugar, if used. Serve warm or cool. If you like it a little looser, add another tablespoon of water.

To double the recipe. Double all ingredients and cook for 15 minutes, stirring once after 8 minutes.

VARIATION

SAFFRON ONIONS Omit tomato paste, bay leaf, oregano and Tabasco sauce. Substitute white wine vinegar for red wine vinegar and 2 tablespoon sultanas for raisins. Increase sugar to 1 tablespoon. Add ¼ teaspoon ground cumin, a large pinch of powdered saffron or a small pinch of thread saffron, mixed with the white wine, and a knife-point each of ground coriander and cardamom. Proceed as for Onions à la Monégasque, cooking for 8 minutes. Remove from oven and stir in 1 tablespoon water, ⅛ teaspoon salt, a pinch of black pepper, and an additional ½ teaspoon vinegar.

PEPPER SALAD

— ◆ ◆ ◆ —

This is a very pretty cooked salad, light and easy to prepare. It is delightful when you want something before dinner that is not too filling. It is served at room temperature. *Serves 2*

1 yellow pepper, cored, seeded and
  julienned
1 green pepper, cored, seeded and
  julienned
1 red pepper, cored, seeded and
  julienned

1 tablespoon vegetable oil
½ teaspoon sea salt
1 teaspoon fennel seed
½ teaspoon dried oregano
Large pinch freshly ground black pepper
1 tablespoon water

1 Arrange peppers in a 1 litre/2 pint soufflé dish with yellow peppers on the bottom, green in the middle, and red on top.

2 Stir together remaining ingredients and pour over peppers. Cover tightly with microwave cling film. Cook at 100% for 6 minutes.

3 Pierce film with the tip of a sharp knife, then remove dish from oven. Uncover and serve warm or chilled.

CANNELLINI BEANS

— ◆ ◆ ◆ —

These Italian favourites are available in cans. The canned beans are mushier than the freshly cooked beans, but they will do (see variation). *Makes 600 ml/ 1 pint*

175 g/6 oz dried cannellini beans
8 large cloves garlic, smashed and peeled
3 parsley sprigs
4 tablespoons olive oil
2 tablespoons chopped fresh basil

1 teaspoon sea salt
Pinch freshly ground black pepper
1 can (200 g/7 oz) water-packed tuna
  fish, drained (optional)
8 thin slices peeled red onion (optional)

1 Place cannellini in a 2.5 litre/4 pint soufflé dish with 500 ml/16 fl oz water. Cover tightly with microwave cling film. Cook at 100% for 15 minutes.

2 Pierce film with the tip of a sharp knife, then remove dish from oven. Let stand for 5 minutes. Uncover and add 500 ml/16 fl oz very hot tap water. Recover with a fresh piece of microwave cling film. Let stand for 1 hour.

3 Uncover, drain and rinse. Return to soufflé dish and add garlic, parsley and 1 litre/1¾ pints water. Cook, tightly covered, at 100% for 35 minutes.

4 Pierce film, then remove from oven. Let stand, covered, for 20 minutes.

5 Uncover, drain and remove parsley. Let cool. Add oil, basil, salt and pepper; stir well. Serve cold.

6 If desired, top with chunks of tuna and sliced red onions.

VARIATION

SALAD WITH CANNED CANNELLINI BEANS Drain and rinse 2 cans of cooked cannellini. Place in a 1 litre/2 pint glass measuring jug with 4 tablespoons water, garlic and parsley. Cover tightly. Cook at 100% for 5 minutes. Continue as in step 5.

BRANDADE DE MORUE

Before the food processor and microwave oven, this took days of work. First the cod had to be soaked to soften and get rid of the excess salt. Then it had to be pounded into a purée, with or without potato, then sauced and seasoned. Now, it goes quickly and makes a good dip for vegetables or filling for salty pastry as an hors d'oeuvre. As a first course, serve in little ramekins with fried bread. You can also use it under Baked Eggs (page 66) instead of vegetable purée.
Makes 500 ml/16 fl oz

1 small (125 g/4 oz) potato, pricked
  twice with a fork
250 g/8 oz salt cod fillet, washed in
  cold running water for 2 minutes

175 ml/6 fl oz Garlic Cream (page 302)
2 tablespoons fruity olive oil

1 Place potato on paper towel in the oven. Cook at 100% for 6 minutes. When cool enough to handle, peel and pass through medium disc of a food mill. Set aside.

2 Place the fish in a 25 × 7.5 cm/10 × 3 inch round dish and pour 750 ml/1¼ pints cold water over it. Cover tightly with microwave cling film. Cook at 100% for 5 minutes.

3 Pierce film with the tip of a sharp knife, then remove dish from oven. Uncover and drain. Rinse fish with cold water and repeat the soaking process 2 more times.

4 Place fish in the container of a food processor. Add Garlic Cream and process for 2 minutes. Add potato and oil. Process for 2 minutes longer, or until smooth and creamy.

SWORDFISH QUENELLES

· ·

This classic recipe, usually made with pike, is an excellent way to use trimmings from swordfish medallions (page 154). Serve with Watercress Sauce (page 320), Beurre Blanc (page 314), or Sauce Américaine (page 322). Other fish trimmings such as salmon can be substituted, or try prawns or scallops. *Serves 2 to 3*

250 g/8 oz skinned and boned
   swordfish, cut into 5 cm/2 inch
   chunks
1 egg white

1 teaspoon sea salt
Pinch freshly ground black pepper
Pinch freshly grated nutmeg
125 ml/4 fl oz double cream, very cold

1 Place fish in the container of a food processor. Process for 30 seconds. Add egg white and process for 30 seconds. Scrape down the sides of the container. Add salt, pepper and nutmeg, and process until mixture forms a ball (as for a dough). With machine running, add cream to mixture in a thin stream.

2 Remove container from food processor and refrigerate for 15 minutes.

3 Put 2 tablespoons of water in a 27.5 × 21 × 5 cm/11 × 8½ × 2 inch rectangular or oval dish. To form the quenelles, use two tablespoons to shape mixture into elongated ovals, or pipe mixture into 2.5 × 5 cm/1 × 2 inch strips using a piping bag fitted with a 1 cm/½ inch tube. Place each quenelle as it is formed in the dish, arranging the quenelles around inside rim. Do not allow them to touch. Cover tightly with microwave cling film. Cook at 100% for 2 minutes.

4 Pierce film with the point of a sharp knife, then remove dish from oven. Uncover and serve hot with sauce.

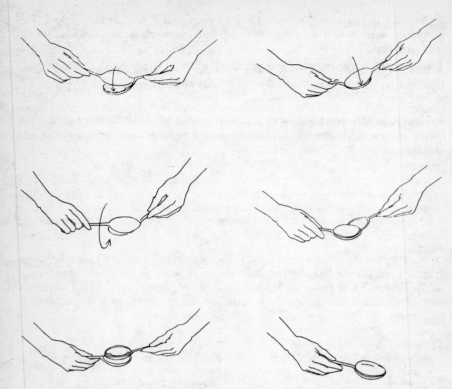

Scoop up a tablespoonful of quenelle mixture and shape, using two tablespoons. Scrape the mixture from spoon to spoon, working from the outside edge of the spoon towards the inside.

PÂTÉS

Cooking pâtés used to be an all-day affair with messy *bain-maries*. The microwave oven has virtually turned them into fast food. Make them the night before you want to use them, or several days before for the meat and liver pâtés.

With this ease of preparation, a totally pâté cocktail party or buffet with salad and cheese is easily in reach. Either prepare each pâté while the previous one is cooking or cook one a night for three or four nights, starting with the heavier pâtés and ending with the fish or chicken. As pâtés keep well for up to two weeks, you can have them on hand in case you want to invite people at the last minute.

After being removed from the oven and cooled, many pâtés need to be weighted in order to firm up their texture. To do so, cool the pâté to skin temperature (not cold). Cut a piece of card to fit just inside the pâté mould or loaf dish. Wrap it in two layers of aluminium foil. Place it on top of the pâté and weight with a brick or two heavy tins. Place in refrigerator. If the mould is very full, set it on a plate before weighting to catch any spills.

Almost all the recipes on the pages that follow can be cooked in a standard glass loaf dish.

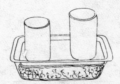

Place a piece of foil-covered card on top of cooked, cooled pâté and weight with tins.

CHICKEN PÂTÉ

◆ ◆ ◆

This is a beautiful pâté to look at, almost white and flecked with green. Full slices can be served on sprigs of parsley or on a pool of Red Pepper Purée (page 296). Little quarter-slices can be put on small, brown cocktail pumpernickel rounds as canapés for a party.

The pâté cooks for just 6 minutes and can be served warm (let it cool for 10 minutes after it comes out of the oven) or cold (it will need to be weighted in the refrigerator overnight). Serve it warm as a first course; it will be lighter as it is not weighted. Serve it chilled for a canapé; it will have a firmer texture. *Serves 8 to 10 as a first course, 20 for cocktails*

350 g/12 oz boneless, skinless chicken breast, cut into 5 cm/2 inch chunks
550 ml/18 fl oz double cream
90 g/3 oz watercress leaves, or 60 g/ 2 oz flat-leaf parsley and 2 tablespoons fresh tarragon, finely chopped

2 shallots, peeled and finely chopped
1½ teaspoons sea salt
⅛ teaspoon cayenne pepper
⅛ teaspoon freshly ground black pepper

1 Place chicken in the container of a food processor and process until very finely chopped. With motor running, pour in 300 ml/½ pint of the cream in a thin stream. Process until smooth.

2 Pass mixture through a sieve into a bowl. Stir in rest of cream and remaining ingredients. Pour into a 17.5 × 8.5 cm/7 × 3½ inch loaf dish. Cover tightly with microwave cling film. Cook at 100% for 6 minutes.

3 Pierce film with the tip of a sharp knife, then remove dish from oven. To serve warm, uncover and let cool slightly before slicing in dish. To serve cold, uncover and let come to room temperature. Wrap tightly, weight and refrigerate for 8 to 12 hours.

SMOOTH COUNTRY TERRINE

⋅ ◆ ⋅

This pâté, while also smooth, is much more robust in flavour than the Scandinavian Liver Pâté (page 58). It would be very good before Chicken in Red Wine (page 191), with bread and gherkins or Onions à la Monégasque (page 48). *Serves 12 as a first course, up to 40 as part of a mixed hors d'oeuvre*

500 g/1lb sausagemeat
500 g/1 lb chicken livers, rinsed, and connective tissue removed
250 g/8 oz cold unsalted butter, cut into 1 cm/½ inch cubes
175 ml/6 fl oz white wine
1 tablespoon sea salt

½ teaspoon freshly ground black pepper
1 teaspoon Quatre-Épices (page 478)
2 tablespoons Cognac or brandy
1 bay leaf
350 ml/12 fl oz Aspic (page 287) (optional)

1 Place sausagemeat, livers and butter in the container of a food processor. Process until well combined. Stir in remaining ingredients, except bay leaf and Aspic, if using. Pass through a fine sieve and discard all gristle.

2 Pour mixture into a 1.5 litre/2½ pint soufflé dish. Place bay leaf in centre. Cover tightly with microwave cling film. Cook at 100% for 18 minutes.

3 Pierce film with the tip of a sharp knife, then remove dish from oven. Uncover and chill. Cover with Aspic if desired.

CHICKEN LIVER MOUSSE

◆ ◆

While this seems very similar to other smooth pâtés, it is made differently. The chicken livers are gently cooked, then puréed. It cannot be sliced; it must be spooned. Serve it with toasted white bread or sliced toasted brioche. *Makes 6 individual first course ramekins, or 1 large mousse to serve 18 with other hors d'oeuvres*

350 g/12 oz unsalted butter, cut into small pieces
90 g/3 oz onion, peeled and finely chopped
4 bruised juniper berries
2 cloves garlic, smashed and peeled
500 g/1 lb chicken livers, rinsed, and connective tissue removed

4 tablespoons dry vermouth
Large pinch freshly ground black pepper
2 teaspoons sea salt
250 ml/8 fl oz Aspic (page 287) (optional)

1 Place butter, onions, juniper berries and garlic in a 27.5 × 21 × 5 cm/11 × 8½ × 2 inch dish. Cook, uncovered, at 100% for 4 minutes.

2 Remove from oven. Add livers in a single layer. Cover tightly with microwave cling film. Cook at 100% for 3 minutes, stirring once after 1 minute 30 seconds.

3 Pierce film with the tip of a sharp knife, then remove dish from oven. Uncover and stir in remaining ingredients, except Aspic, if used. Pour into the container of a food processor. Process until smooth. Pour mixture into six 10 cm/4 inch ramekins, or a 1 litre/2 pint soufflé dish. Chill for at least 1 hour. When chilled, cover each mousse with 3 tablespoons of Aspic, if desired.

VARIATION

DUCK LIVER MOUSSE Substitute equal weight duck livers, cleaned.

PRAWN PÂTÉ

A simple and delicious first course. It is beautiful when its pale pink colour is contrasted with the clear orangy-yellow of Papaya Cumin Sauce (page 331) or the bright green of Watercress Sauce (page 320). Make a pool of the sauce on a serving plate, top with a slice of pâté, and sprinkle with glossy, black-brown papaya seeds or a sprig of watercress.

Shelling the prawns takes about 15 minutes; if you are pressed for time, scallops are a good alternative. The entire pâté can be assembled and baked in just 8 minutes. Allow for an additional 20 minutes of standing time. Serve the pâté warm or cold. *Serves 8*

350 g/12 oz raw prawns, shelled and deveined
350 ml/12 fl oz double cream
1 tablespoon fresh lemon juice

¾ teaspoon sea salt
⅛ teaspoon cayenne pepper
⅛ teaspoon freshly ground black pepper

1 Place the prawns in the container of a food processor. Process until coarsely puréed. Stop processor three or four times to scrape down sides of the container.

2 Combine cream with remaining ingredients. With the processor motor running, add to prawn purée in a thin stream. Stop the processor, scrape down sides, and continue processing until the cream is incorporated and the mixture is very smooth, about 1 minute. Do not overprocess or the cream will curdle.

3 Pour mixture into a 17.5×8.5 cm/$7 \times 3\frac{1}{2}$ inch loaf dish. Cover tightly with microwave cling film. Cook at 100% for 4 minutes.

4 Pierce film with the tip of a sharp knife, then remove dish from oven. Uncover the pâté, wrap in a tea towel, and let stand for 20 minutes. Unmould on to a serving plate and serve warm or cool.

VARIATION

SCALLOP MOUSSE Substitute 350 g/12 oz scallops for prawns and 1 tablespoon white wine for lemon juice. Omit cayenne and add 2 tablespoons finely sliced fresh chives. Proceed as for Prawn Pâté. Serve warm or cool.

SUMMER PÂTÉ WITH VEAL, SWEETBREADS AND SPINACH

• • •

This is a bit fancier and more work than some of the other pâtés, but it still can be put together and cooked in about 30 minutes. In 10 minutes, you can clean and trim your sweetbreads and vegetables (the vegetables can all go into the food processor). While the sweetbreads cook (16 minutes), you can make the pâté mixture. The assembled pâté cooks for only 10 minutes. If you want it simpler yet, eliminate the sweetbreads; mince all pâté ingredients together and cook in about 15 minutes for a pretty, pale green pâté. Make these pâtés a day before they are served, as they need to cool and be weighted.

This is really three recipes in one. It is the best way to cook sweetbreads that I know, and you get a wonderful dividend in the braised vegetables. Purée them in the blender for a sauce or thin the purée with 250 ml/8 fl oz Chicken Stock to make a wonderful soup for two. *Serves 10 to 12*

SWEETBREADS
1 teaspoon mild vegetable oil
45 g/1½ oz unsalted butter
2 carrots, trimmed, peeled and coarsely chopped
2 sticks celery, stringed, trimmed and coarsely chopped
½ small onion, peeled and coarsely chopped
600 g/1¼ lb sweetbreads, cleaned and trimmed (see note)
250 ml/8 fl oz Chicken Stock (page 286) or stock from a cube

FORCEMEAT
4 large shallots, peeled
1 kg/2 lb pie veal without fat, cubed
300 g/10 oz unsalted butter, cut into tablespoon-size chunks
½ teaspoon fresh rosemary
2 teaspoons freshly ground fennel seed
¼ teaspoon ground allspice
2 teaspoons sea salt
¼ teaspoon freshly ground black pepper
500 g/1 lb spinach, stalks removed, well rinsed and dried

1 Brush the interior of a 30 × 10 cm/12 × 4 inch loaf dish with the vegetable oil. Set aside.

2 To prepare the sweetbreads, heat butter in a 2.5 litre/4 pint soufflé dish, uncovered, at 100% for 3 minutes. Add carrots, celery and onions and stir to coat. Cook, uncovered, at 100% for 3 minutes.

3 Remove from oven. Arrange sweetbreads on top of vegetables and pour stock over all. Cover tightly with microwave cling film. Cook at 100% for 5 minutes. Pierce film with tip of a sharp knife, then remove dish from oven. Uncover and turn sweetbreads over. Re-cover and cook for 5 minutes more.

4 Pierce film, then remove from oven. Uncover and set aside.

5 To prepare the forcemeat, place shallots and veal in the container of a food processor. Process until veal is coarsely minced. Add remaining ingredients except spinach and process until combined.

6 Remove 600 g/1¼ lb of veal mixture and set aside. Add spinach to remaining veal mixture in container. Process until smooth.

7 To assemble the pâté, spread half the veal mixture without spinach in the bottom of prepared loaf dish. Spread one third of spinach mixture on top. Arrange a strip of sweetbreads (if necessary cut sweetbreads in half lengthways) down the length of the dish, leaving a 1 cm/½ inch border on all sides. Cover sweetbreads with remaining spinach mixture. Spread remaining veal mixture on top. Cover tightly with microwave cling film. Cook at 100% for 10 minutes.

8 Pierce film, then remove dish from oven. Uncover. Let cool to room temperature. Weight and refrigerate for 12 to 24 hours. Slice and serve.

Note. I have called for 600 g/1¼ lb of sweetbreads since a pair usually weighs that much. If you can buy them by weight, you will need only 350 g/12 oz. If you have leftover sweetbreads, or if you want to serve sweetbreads as a separate dish, remove them from the microwave oven after cooking; set aside on another plate and cover loosely while you purée the vegetables in a blender for a light and delicious sauce. Serve the sweetbreads sliced with the sauce to four people. The leftover 250 g/8 oz quantity will feed two as a first course.

SCANDINAVIAN LIVER PÂTÉ

This creamy, mild-tasting liver pâté is a Scandinavian standard called Leverpostej. Ordinarily it requires an hour and a half of cooking time in a messy *bain-marie*. With my microwave method, it takes 25 minutes to prepare and exactly 12 minutes to cook. Like all pâtés, it does need to be made the night before you want to serve it. Unmoulded and wrapped in foil and then in polythene, it will keep refrigerated for a week. Though it can be frozen, it hardly seems worthwhile when it is so quickly made. Sliced and served with bread and mustard, it makes an easy cold main course for a summer luncheon, and it is perfect for a cocktail party or when people stop by. *Serves 12 as a first course, 6 as lunch, and up to 40 for cocktails*

500 g/1 lb chicken or calf's liver, rinsed, and connective tissue removed	3 eggs
350 g/12 oz fresh pork fat, trimmed of any meat	2 teaspoons sea salt
1 small onion (about 125 g/4 oz), peeled and quartered	¾ teaspoon freshly ground white pepper
1½ tablespoons anchovy paste	½ teaspoon ground allspice
750 ml/1¼ pints double cream	¼ teaspoon ground cloves
	350 g/12 oz fresh (unsalted) pork back fat, thinly sliced

1 Place liver, pork fat, onion and anchovy paste in the container of a food processor. Process until liquid. Add remaining ingredients except back fat. Process thoroughly. Pass mixture through a fine sieve.

2 Line a 22.5 × 12.5 × 7.5 cm/9 × 5 × 3 inch loaf dish with the back fat, making sure it does not overlap inside dish. Leave a 5 cm/2 inch overhang around top of dish. Pour liver mixture into prepared dish and fold overhanging fat over top of pâté. Cover loosely with paper towel. Cook at 100% for 12 minutes.

3 Remove from oven. Uncover and let stand until cool. Cover tightly, weight top of pâté, and refrigerate for 8 to 12 hours.

To make a smaller pâté. Halve all ingredients and cook in a 17.5 × 10 × 10 cm/ 7 × 4 × 4 inch loaf dish for 8 minutes.

VARIATION

CHUNKY PÂTÉ Process liver coarsely and set aside. Process pork fat coarsely and combine with liver. Do not pass through sieve. Proceed as for Scandinavian Liver Pâté.

PÂTÉ WITH CHINESE BLACK BEANS

This is a classic pâté jazzed up with a few Chinese seasonings. Everybody seems to like it. If you are serving it as a first course, you can put a dollop of plum sauce in one corner of the plate, some Chinese mustard in another corner, and a short piece of spring onion across the middle of each slice of pâté.

The French Pâté and Pâté with Walnuts variations go back to basics. Serve them with Dijon mustard, gherkins or sliced pickled cucumbers, and good French bread. *Serves 10 to 12 as a first course, 20 for cocktails*

350 g/12 oz chicken livers, rinsed, and connective tissue removed

1 small onion (about 125 g/4 oz), peeled and quartered

3 cloves garlic, smashed and peeled

4 tablespoons Chinese salted black beans, soaked for 5 minutes and drained

750 g/1½ lb boned pork shoulder, coarsely minced (by the butcher, if possible)

45 g/1½ oz cooked, smoked ham, cut into 5 mm/¼ inch dice

400 g/14 oz unsalted (fresh) pork back fat, 6 tablespoons cut into 5 mm/¼ inch dice and the rest thinly sliced

¾ teaspoon dried oregano

1½ teaspoons dried thyme

2 tablespoons plus ¼ teaspoon mirin

1½ teaspoons Worcestershire sauce

1½ tablespoons tamari soya sauce

1 teaspoon sea salt

½ teaspoon freshly ground black pepper

1 Place livers, onion and garlic in the container of a food processor. Process until coarsely chopped. Remove to a mixing bowl. Stir in remaining ingredients except back fat slices.

2 Test pâté for flavour: bring some water to the boil, make a small ball of pâté mixture and cook for 2 minutes. Taste and adjust seasoning if necessary, and add more salt and pepper and garlic or herbs if desired.

3 Line a 22.5 × 12.5 × 7.5 cm/9 × 5 × 3 inch loaf dish with fat, making sure it does not overlap inside dish. Leave a 5 cm/2 inch overhang around top of dish. Pour liver mixture into prepared dish and fold fat over top of pâté.

4 Cover loosely with paper towel. Cook at 100% for 15 minutes.

5 Remove from oven. Uncover and let stand until cool. Cover tightly, weight top of pâté, and refrigerate for 8 to 12 hours. Slice and serve.

VARIATIONS

FRENCH PÂTÉ Omit Chinese black beans, mirin and soya sauce. Increase salt to 2 teaspoons, oregano to 1½ teaspoons, thyme to 1 tablespoon, and add 2 teaspoons Quatre-Épices (page 478) made from equal quantities of nutmeg, ginger, cinnamon and cloves. Add 2 tablespoons brandy. Proceed as for Pâte with Chinese Black Beans.

PÂTÉ WITH WALNUTS Add 125 g/4 oz broken walnuts to liver and pork when chopping. Omit ham. Season as for French Pâté, using 3 tablespoons port instead of brandy. Garnish plate with walnut halves.

VEAL AND HAM PÂTÉ

◆ ◆

This is most elegant looking, with rosy flecks of ham and darker mushroom flecks in a creamy-coloured pâté. It has a robust flavour and is a good choice for almost any kind of meal. *Serves 10 as a first course, 20 to 40 as an hors d'oeuvre*

1 teaspoon mild vegetable oil
500 g/1 lb cooked ham, cut into 5 cm/ 2 inch chunks
500 g/1 lb boned pork shoulder, cut into chunks
250 g/8 oz pie veal
250 g/8 oz fresh (unsalted) pork back fat, cut into chunks
75 g/2½ oz mushrooms, quartered

½ bunch parsley, stalks removed (flat-leaf if available)
1 tablespoon sea salt
1 teaspoon freshly ground black pepper
1½ teaspoons crushed juniper berries
5 shallots (about 75 g/2½ oz), peeled and quartered
4 tablespoons dry vermouth

1 Brush the interior of a 22.5 × 12.5 cm/9 × 5 inch loaf dish with the vegetable oil. Set aside.

2 Place 250 g/8 oz of the ham and all of the pork, veal and fat in the container of a food processor. Pulse on and off until coarsely minced and well combined. Remove mixture to a large bowl.

3 Place mushrooms, parsley, shallots and remaining ham in processor. Pulse on and off until finely minced.

4 Combine with meat mixture and add vermouth, salt, pepper and juniper berries, mixing well. Pack into prepared dish. Cover tightly with microwave cling film. Cook at 100% for 20 minutes.

5 Pierce film with the tip of a sharp knife, then remove dish from oven. Let cool to room temperature. Weight and refrigerate for 8 to 12 hours or overnight.

HOT FIRST COURSES

Many of the more substantial or elegant first courses—some hearty enough to be used as a main course—are served hot. That used to be a logistical problem that sometimes left me feeling like a general instead of a cook. Microwave cooking makes it easy to assemble or partly cook everything ahead and do the last-minute cooking while guests have a glass of wine. Clams Casino and Oysters Florentine can be finished while your guests are already sitting at the table.

PRAWN BOIL

In Texas they have little hard-shelled shrimp that they cook in buckets of beer and shell with their fingers, washing them down with more cold beer. It's an ideal informal meal (or a start to one for solid eaters). Away from the Gulf of Mexico, we have to make do with whatever prawns or shrimp are available. Either way, this dish is still a hands-on proposition best shared with good friends. It's not necessary, but a bowl of fresh Mayonnaise (page 332), for dipping, couldn't hurt anything except your outline. *Serves 4 to 6 as a first course, 1 or 2 as a main course*

500 g/1 lb raw medium prawns (24 to 26 prawns)

2 tablespoons Crab Boil (page 300)
½ lemon, cut into quarters

Place prawns in a 2.5 litre/4 pint soufflé dish. Add Crab Boil and stir to coat. Add lemon. Cover tightly with microwave cling film. Cook at 100% for 1 minute 30 seconds. Shake dish to redistribute prawns. Cook for 1 minute 30 seconds longer. Pierce film with the tip of a sharp knife before removing dish from oven.

To serve 12–15 as a first course. Use 3 kg/6 lb raw medium prawns, unpeeled, and 2 recipes Crab Boil (page 300). Toss together prawns and crab boil in a 5 litre/8 pint casserole with a tight-fitting lid. Cover with lid and cook at 100% for 20 minutes, stirring 3 times.

CLAMS CASINO

This is one of those really good dishes that can still be found in old-fashioned Italian restaurants. It is quick to make using the microwave oven to open the clams and blanch the bacon. You can prepare this recipe without the salt; it just keeps the clams from tilting. The dish can be made entirely ahead and then tucked under the grill after your guests sit down. Serve the clams on warm plates with little oyster forks or salad forks and plenty of French bread. Cold white wine, beer or a not-too-refined red wine would all be good. *Serves 4 to 6*

24 small clams (1.5 kg/3 lb total weight), well scrubbed
90 g/3 oz Snail Butter (page 310)

Coarse salt, for grilling clams
2 rashers bacon, cut into 4 cm/1½ inch pieces

1 Arrange clams, hinge end down, in a 5 cm/2 inch deep dish just large enough to hold them. Cover tightly with microwave cling film. Cook at 100% for 7 minutes (any clams that do not open may be cooked for 1 additional minute; then discard any that remain closed).

2 Pierce film with the tip of a sharp knife, then remove dish from oven. Uncover and remove clams from shells. Reserve clams and the deeper side of each shell. (Save clam liquor for use in another recipe. It can be frozen.)

3 Heat a conventional grill.

4 Melt Snail Butter in a 500 ml/1 pint glass measuring jug, uncovered, at 100% for 3 minutes.

5 Pour salt into a 25 cm/10 inch round ovenproof dish to a depth of 1 cm/½ inch. Arrange clam shells on salt. Divide melted Snail Butter evenly among shells. Place a clam in each and place a piece of bacon on top. Grill 12.5 cm/5 inches from heat source for 2 minutes, until bacon is crisp.

To make 48 clams. Double all ingredients, cooking clams for 11 minutes to open. Proceed as for Clams Casino, but use a large baking tray and double the amount of salt for grilling.

Clams arranged, hinge end down, in a dish just large enough to hold them.

DIJON SNAILS

— • • • —

Far from the vineyard, snails come in cans, cooked and ready to be seasoned and reheated. Usually they are tucked into snail shells or covered with Snail Butter and grilled. It seems like a lot of useless labour to stuff them back into shells. Try this gentler version, served in individual soufflé dishes or small gratin dishes, or use the sauced snails as a topping for modest amounts of fine egg noodles. If you do not use noodles, serve with a spoon and bread for mopping up the sauce. *Serves* 6

250 ml/8 fl oz double cream
1½ tablespoons Dijon mustard
15 g/½ oz Snail Butter (page 310)
15 g/½ oz unsalted butter, cut into 4
  pieces

4 tablespoons white wine
36 large snails (two 210 g/7½ oz cans),
  drained and rinsed

1 Combine cream and mustard in a 1 litre/2 pint glass measuring jug. Cook, uncovered, at 100% for 5 minutes.

2 Remove from oven. Stir in Snail Butter and unsalted butter and keep warm.

3 Place wine and snails in a 1.5 litre/2½ pint soufflé dish. Cover tightly with microwave cling film. Cook at 100% for 1 minute 30 seconds.

4 Pierce film with the tip of a sharp knife, then remove dish from oven. Uncover and drain. Stir snails into warm sauce.

VARIATIONS

SNAILS WITH DUXELLES Substitute 2 tablespoons Duxelles (page 294) for both Snail Butter and unsalted butter. Proceed as for Dijon Snails.

SNAILS IN SNAIL BUTTER Heat 90 g/3 oz Snail Butter in a 1 litre/2 pint glass measuring jug, uncovered, at 100% for 2 minutes 30 seconds. Stir in snails and proceed as for Dijon Snails.

OYSTERS FLORENTINE

— • • • —

This Parisian dish is not too far removed from Clams Casino (page 62). Another member of the family is Oysters Rockefeller, of New Orleans origin, which I think is somewhat overrated. To make this recipe more like Oysters

Rockefeller, add some mint and tarragon to the spinach when you are puréeing it. All these recipes can be made ahead, and grilled at the last minute. *Makes 12 oysters*

12 oysters (about 1 kg/2 lb), well
   scrubbed
250 g/8 oz spinach, cooked, rinsed, and
   squeezed
5½ tablespoons Thick Béchamel (page
   317), nutmeg omitted

¼ teaspoon sea salt
Freshly ground black pepper
Coarse salt, for grilling oysters
125 ml/4 fl oz Mornay (page 317)

1 Place oysters, hinge end down, in a 5 cm/2 inch deep dish just large enough to hold them. Cover tightly with microwave cling flim. Cook at 100% for 4 minutes. (Oysters will be just barely open. Any oysters that do not open may be cooked for 1 additional minute; then discard any that remain closed.)

2 Pierce film with the tip of a sharp knife, then remove dish from oven. Uncover and pry oysters open with a blunt knife. Free oysters from shell. Set aside oysters and the deeper half of each shell. (Save and freeze liquor for use in another recipe.)

3 Place spinach, Béchamel, salt and pepper in the container of a food processor. Process until well combined; set aside.

4 Heat a conventional grill.

5 Pour salt into a 25 cm/10 inch ovenproof dish to a depth of 1 cm/½ inch. Arrange oyster shells on salt. Place a tablespoon of spinach mixture in each shell and place an oyster on top. Cover each with 2 teaspoons Mornay. Grill 12.5 cm/5 inches from heat source for 2 to 3 minutes, until browned and bubbly. Serve hot.

To make 24 oysters. Double all ingredients and cook oysters for 9 minutes to open. Grill on a large baking tray or in two batches.

STUFFED CALAMARI

· · ·

The looks of some foods seem to dictate their destiny. The conical bodies of medium-size squid seem designed for stuffing. In this recipe, cooked stuffed squid are sliced into white-rimmed green circles and set on a sea of red. *Serves 4 as a first course, 2 as a main course*

500 g/1 lb fresh spinach with stalks, well rinsed and drained

2 tablespoons olive oil

750 g/1½ lb squid, bodies 12.5–15 cm/ 5–6 inches long, cleaned, with tentacles chopped (page 493)

45 g/1½ oz chopped onion

30 g/1 oz chopped celery

1 clove garlic, smashed and peeled

45 g/1½ oz Breadcrumbs (page 306), coarsely ground

2 teaspoons sea salt

2 teaspoons fresh lemon juice

100 g/3½ drained canned Italian plum tomatoes, diced

2 tablespoons white wine

¼ teaspoon freshly ground black pepper

1 Place spinach in a 35 × 27.5 × 5 cm/14 × 11 × 2 inch dish and cook, uncovered, at 100% for 4 minutes.

2 Remove from oven. Squeeze spinach well to remove excess water. Roughly chop spinach and set aside.

3 Heat oil in a 1 litre/2 pint glass measuring jug, uncovered, at 100% for 2 minutes. Add chopped squid tentacles, onions, celery and garlic. Cook, uncovered, for 2 minutes, stirring once.

4 Remove from oven and place in the container of a food processor. Add spinach, Breadcrumbs, 1 teaspoon of the salt and 1 teaspoon of the lemon juice. Process until finely chopped.

5 Divide the stuffing evenly among the squid bodies (use about 2 tablespoons, loosely packed, per squid).

6 Place tomatoes, wine, pepper, remaining 1 teaspoon salt and 1 teaspoon lemon juice in a shallow 30 cm/12 inch round dish. Arrange squid on top of sauce spoke-fashion with tails towards the centre. Cook, uncovered, at 100% for 5 minutes.

7 Remove from oven and remove squid from dish. Cook sauce, uncovered, for 2 minutes longer.

8 Remove from oven. Spoon sauce on to serving plates. Slice squid, crossways, into 1 cm/½ inch slices and arrange, overlapping, on sauce.

BAKED EGGS

Now that eggs no longer are a daily breakfast occurrence, because of concern about cholesterol, maybe we can bring back some of the festive versions developed by the French. Eggs do not do uniformly well in the microwave oven; but what are variously called baked eggs or *oeufs en cocotte* do very well indeed if, once you break them into their cooking dishes, you take a knife with a very sharp tip and gently prick the yolk twice, breaking the membrane. This will keep the egg from exploding; strangely enough, the yolk will not run all over. I was scared to death the first time I tried this, but it works like a charm. *Serves 1*

4 tablespoons vegetable purée, such as
    Lightly Cooked Crushed Tomatoes
    (page 293), Duxelles (page 294) or
    Broccoli (page 254)
Pinch dried oregano (optional)

Sea salt
1 egg
½ teaspoon unsalted butter, cut into
    bits
Freshly ground black pepper

1 Spread purée in bottom of an 8.5 × 5 cm/3½ × 2 inch round ramekin. Stir in oregano, if used, and a pinch of salt. Carefully break egg on top of purée and prick yolk twice with knife tip.

2 Scatter butter over egg and season lightly with pepper and salt.

3 Cover loosely with paper towel. Cook at 100% for 1 minute. (In a small oven, cook for 1 minute 45 seconds.)

To multiply recipe. Place each egg in a separate ramekin and use 4 tablespoons purée for each. Place ramekins 10 cm/4 inches apart and cover loosely with paper towel. For 2 eggs, cook for 1 minute 45 seconds. For 4 eggs, cook for 3 minutes. For 6 eggs, cook for 5 minutes. (In a small oven, cook 2 eggs for 3 minutes 30 seconds, using a turntable.)

To bake 2 eggs in one gratin dish. Place 125 ml/4 fl oz purée in a 10 × 5 cm/4 × 2 inch glass or ceramic ramekin. Top with 2 eggs. Pierce yolks with knife tip. Top with 2 teaspoons butter cut in 5 mm/¼ inch dice, sprinkle with salt and freshly ground black pepper. Cook at 100% for 1 minute 30 seconds. (In a small oven, cook for 3 minutes.)

VARIATIONS

HERB-BAKED EGGS WITH CREAM Place egg or eggs on the purée of your choice. Prick yolks. Top each egg with 1 teaspoon finely chopped fresh herbs—parsley, chervil, tarragon, chives and summer savory are all good, alone or in combination. Top each egg with 2 tablespoons double cream. Omit butter. Cook as for Baked Eggs.

EGGS WITH CREAMED SPINACH AND PERNOD Mix ½ teaspoon Pernod into each 4 tablespoons Creamed Spinach (page 260). Top each egg with 3 tablespoons Mornay (page 317) gently seasoned with Tabasco sauce, or with Fiery Pepper Sauce (page 297). Cook as for Baked Eggs.

EGGS WITH REFRIED BEANS, CHILLIES AND CHEESE With the rim of the ramekin as a guide, cut 1 round slice of Cheddar cheese for each egg. Use 4 tablespoons Refried Beans (page 128) per egg, breaking egg on top of beans; sprinkle with a little chopped fresh chilli, and cover with circle of cheese. Cook as for Baked Eggs.

BAKED HAM AND EGGS WITH MORNAY Cut rounds of 3 mm/⅛ inch thick cooked ham slices. Place a ham slice in the bottom of each ramekin; top with an egg. Top each egg with 3 tablespoons Mornay (page 317). Cook as for Baked Eggs.

BAKED EGGS WITH MUSHROOMS For each egg, thinly slice ½ medium mushroom. Toss with 2 teaspoons melted butter, salt and ½ teaspoon chopped dill or other fresh herb. Place 4 tablespoons Duxelles (page 294) in bottom of each ramekin; top with an egg. Spoon sliced mushrooms, butter and seasonings over egg. Cook as for Baked Eggs.

POACHED EGGS IN SOUP Boil 750 ml/1¼ pints Chicken Stock (page 286), stock from a cube, or any of the seasoned chicken stocks (pages 79–80) in a wide 2 litre/3½ pint glass jug or bowl. Cook, uncovered, at 100% for 1 minute 30 seconds. (In a small oven, cook for 3 minutes.) Serves 2 as a soup.

EGGS IN RED WINE

• ◆ •

This unlikely-sounding dish is a French classic and very good. It is usually served with triangular pieces of toast stuck around it. *Serves 4*

125 g/4 oz bacon, cut into lardons (page 415)	½ bay leaf
	2 parsley sprigs
1 tablespoon chopped shallots	4 eggs
1 clove garlic, smashed, peeled and finely chopped	2 teaspoons cornflour dissolved in 2 tablespoons water
125 ml/4 fl oz red wine	1 teaspoon sea salt
125 ml/4 fl oz water	Freshly ground black pepper

1 Place lardons in a 25 × 5 cm/10 × 2 inch round flan dish. Cook, uncovered, at 100% for 2 minutes. Stir in shallots and garlic and cook, uncovered, for 2 minutes more. Add wine, water, bay leaf and parsley. Cook, uncovered, at 100% for 8 minutes.

2 Remove from oven. Carefully break eggs into liquid and prick each yolk twice with the tip of a sharp knife. Cook, uncovered, at 100% for 1 minute 30 seconds.

3 Remove from oven. Remove eggs to a heated serving platter with a slotted spoon. Stir cornflour mixture into wine mixture. Cook, uncovered, at 100% for 2 minutes 30 seconds.

4 Remove from oven. Remove bay leaf and parsley sprigs. Stir in salt and pepper and pour over eggs. Serve hot.

STROGANOFF MEATBALLS

I nto every life a cocktail party must from time to time fall, and this easy, rapidly made dish can be left in an old-fashioned chafing dish to solace the souls and dilute the liquor of the guests. It is an inexpensive version of an expensive Forties favourite, Boeuf Stroganoff. *Makes 65–70 meatballs*

MEATBALLS
150 g/5 oz mushrooms, stalks trimmed
  and quartered
150 g/5 oz onion, peeled and cut into
  5 cm/2 inch chunks
750 g/1½ lb minced beef
1½ teaspoons Hungarian paprika
1 tablespoon Worcestershire sauce
½ teaspoon dry mustard
2 teaspoons sea salt
Freshly ground black pepper, to taste

SAUCE
250 ml/8 fl oz soured cream
250 ml/8 fl oz Chicken Stock (page
  286) or stock from a cube
1 tablespoon cornflour dissolved in
  2 tablespoons cold water
4 tablespoons chopped fresh dill
Sea salt, to taste
Freshly ground black pepper, to taste

1 Place mushrooms and onions in the container of a food processor. Process until coarsely chopped. Scrape into a mixing bowl and stir in minced beef and seasonings. Shape mixture into teaspoon-sized meatballs.

2 Arrange half the meatballs in a 27.5 × 20 × 5 cm/11 × 8 × 2 inch oval or rectangular dish, leaving a 1 cm/½ inch space between each meatball. Cover with a tightly fitting lid or microwave cling film. Cook at 100% for 2 minutes 30 seconds. If using cling film, pierce to release steam.

3 Remove from oven and uncover. Remove cooked meatballs to serving plate to keep warm, and reserve any cooking juices. Repeat with remaining meatballs.

4 To prepare sauce, stir together soured cream, stock, cornflour and reserved liquid from meatballs in a 1 litre/2 pint glass measuring jug. Cook, uncovered, at 100% for 4 minutes 30 seconds, stirring twice.

5 Remove from oven and stir in dill. Add salt and pepper to taste. Pour sauce over meatballs and serve with wooden cocktail sticks.

STUFFED VEGETABLES

In many countries, vegetables are stuffed at home and then taken to the baker to be slowly cooked after the day's breads have been taken out and the wood-fired heat has abated. In Turkey, one can still see children returning home just before mealtime, carrying pans filled with a tempting assortment of peppers, aubergines and tomatoes. Oddly, the slow cooking of the dying oven produces results very similar to the magical speed of the microwave oven. The major difference is that the vegetables have better colour and shape when cooked in the microwave oven.

For a lovely buffet or barely warm summer dinner, prepare an assortment of vegetables with a variety of stuffings—an inexpensive feast.

STUFFED PEPPERS

• • •

Mix red and green peppers for more visual interest. This recipe may be doubled; just extend the cooking time to 30 minutes. *Serves 4 as a first course or side dish, 2 as a main course*

4 medium-to-large green or red peppers (about 1 kg/2 lb)
Greek or Moroccan Stuffing (see following recipes)

125 ml/4 fl oz water
2 tablespoons Basic Tomato Paste (page 294) or canned tomato paste
½ teaspoon sea salt

1 Slice 1 cm/½ inch 'lids' off tops of peppers and set aside. Remove seeds from peppers and lids.

2 Divide stuffing evenly among peppers and replace their lids. Fit peppers, right side up, in a 25 × 20 cm/10 × 8 inch oval dish.

3 To make cooking liquid, whisk together water, tomato paste and salt until smooth. Pour mixture around peppers. Cover tightly with microwave cling film. Cook at 100% for 20 minutes, until couscous or rice in stuffing is tender. Halfway through cooking, poke a small hole in film with the tip of a sharp knife.

4 Remove from oven. Uncover and let stand 5 minutes before serving.

Note. Peppers may be stuffed, then frozen uncooked. To cook, place frozen peppers in a 25 × 20 cm/10 × 8 inch oval dish. Cover tightly with microwave cling film. Cook with prepared cooking liquid at 100% for 30 minutes.

GREEK STUFFING

There was a time when this would have been made with lamb in Greece. Sadly, lamb is in short supply today, and imported beef is used instead. The flavours are fairly straightforward, much like those in Italian cooking.

4 tablespoons olive oil
1 large onion, peeled and finely
    chopped
175 g/6 oz minced beef or lamb
1 can (400 g/14 oz) Italian plum
    tomatoes, drained, coarsely chopped
    and liquid reserved

60 g/2 oz long-grain rice
2 teaspoons sea salt
1 teaspoon dried thyme
1 teaspoon dried oregano
¼ teaspoon freshly ground black pepper

1 Heat oil in a 2.5 litre/4 pint soufflé dish, uncovered, at 100% for 2 minutes. Stir in onions and beef. Continue cooking, uncovered, for 5 mintues, stirring once.

2 Remove from oven. Pour off all but 4 tablespoons drippings from pan. Place mixture in the container of a food processor. Add tomatoes and process just until meat is finely chopped. Stir in remaining ingredients.

Note. Add 1 tablespoon fresh lemon juice to the cooking liquid for Stuffed Peppers when using Greek Stuffing.

MOROCCAN STUFFING

This is less an authentic Moroccan dish than an evocation of characteristic Moroccan ingredients and flavours.

4 tablespoons olive oil
1 large onion, peeled and finely
    chopped
175 g/6 oz minced lamb
2 cloves garlic, smashed and peeled
90 g/3 oz couscous or slightly
    undercooked rice

4 tablespoons raisins
2 tablespoons dried mint
2 tablespoons fresh lemon juice
1 teaspoon sea salt
1 teaspoon ground cumin
¼ teaspoon freshly ground black pepper

1 Heat oil in a 2.5 litre/4 pint soufflé dish, uncovered, at 100% for 2 minutes. Add onions, lamb and garlic. Cook, uncovered, at 100% for 5 minutes, stirring once.

2 Remove from oven. Pour off all but 4 tablespoons drippings from dish. Place mixture in the container of a food processor. Process until meat is finely chopped. Stir in remaining ingredients.

STUFFED AUBERGINE

• • •

Aubergines are perfect candidates for stuffing; but large ones provide altogether too much food for an attractive portion and have a nasty tendency to be bitter. Make this when smallish aubergines are available, or use the long, thin Chinese or Middle Eastern aubergines in any shade from purple to almost white. The flesh gets combined with the stuffing to luscious effect. *Serves 6 as a first course or side dish, 12 as part of a mixed stuffed vegetable dish*

6 small aubergines (about 10 cm/4 inches long), stalks removed and cut in half lengthways
Sea salt
⅓ recipe quantity Duxelles (page 294)
1 small onion (about 125 g/4 oz), peeled and quartered
3 tablespoons freshly grated Parmesan cheese
½ teaspoon ground cumin
Freshly ground black pepper

3 tablespoons fresh lemon juice
1 tablespoon Chicken Stock (page 286), stock from a cube or water

CRUMB MIXTURE
70 g/2¼ oz Breadcrumbs (page 306)
4 tablespoons coarsely chopped flat-leaf parsley
3 tablespoons freshly grated Parmesan cheese
2 to 3 tablespoons virgin olive oil

1 Scoop flesh out of each aubergine half, leaving a shell about 3 mm/⅛ inch thick. Generously salt inside of shells and reserved flesh.

2 Place a sheet of paper towel in a 22.5 cm/9 inch flan dish. Arrange shells on paper towel, cut side down, spoke-fashion with narrow ends towards centre of dish. Place flesh in centre of dish. Cover tightly with microwave cling film. Cook at 100% for 3 minutes.

3 Pierce film with the tip of a sharp knife, then remove dish from oven. Uncover and rinse both shells and flesh well. Pat dry with paper towel, pressing on flesh to remove excess moisture. Set shells aside.

4 Place flesh and remaining ingredients in the container of a food processor. Process until thoroughly combined and flesh is finely chopped.

5 Spoon mixture loosely into shells and arrange in the same dish spoke-fashion, this time with narrow ends towards the outside of the dish. Cover with a sheet of paper towel and then cover tightly with microwave cling film. Cook at 100% for 4 minutes.

6 Pierce film, then remove dish from oven. Remove film, but leave paper towel in place. Let stand for 3 minutes.

7 Heat a conventional grill. Toss together ingredients for crumb mixture. Sprinkle 1 to 2 teaspoons of mixture over each aubergine half and grill until lightly browned. Serve immediately.

VARIATIONS

AUBERGINE STUFFED WITH GREEK OR MOROCCAN STUFFING
Prepare aubergine shells and flesh as for Stuffed Aubergine through step 3. Do not make crumb mixture. Coarsely chop aubergine flesh and combine with a half recipe of either Greek or Moroccan stuffing (page 71). Cook for 10 minutes, tightly covered, at 100%. Stuff aubergine shells. Continue as for Stuffed Aubergine, but without paper towel.

COURGETTES STUFFED WITH GREEK OR MOROCCAN STUFFING Use young, 15 cm/6 inch long courgettes. Prepare and stuff as in first variation.

STUFFED ARTICHOKES

— • • —

Stuffed artichokes are prepared somewhat differently from other stuffed vegetables, but they are equally delicious. Cooking artichokes this way permits you to easily obtain perfectly cooked artichoke bottoms for the many classic French recipes that use them. See the illustration for how to clean the bottom once the artichoke is cooked. *Serves 4 as a first course or side dish*

4 globe artichokes (about 250 g/8 oz each), stalks removed, 2.5 cm/1 inch trimmed from top and leaf tips trimmed
1 lemon, cut in half

Salt Pork and Sage Stuffing, or Garlic and Parsley Stuffing (see following recipes)
2 tablespoons Chicken Stock (page 286) or stock from a cube
1 tablespoon olive oil

1 Rub artichokes with lemon halves to keep them from discolouring. Place artichokes in a 2.5 litre/4 pint soufflé dish or casserole with tightly fitting lid. If using casserole, add 2 tablespoons water. If using a soufflé dish, cover tightly with microwave cling film. Cook at 100% for 10 minutes or until the bottoms feel tender to your thumb nail. If using cling film, pierce with tip of a sharp knife to release steam.

2 Remove from oven. Lightly cover artichokes with a doubled tea towel and let stand for 5 minutes.

3 Uncover and remove purple-tipped leaves and chokes from the centre of each. The artichokes may be prepared ahead up to this point. Keep them tightly wrapped and refrigerated for up to 1 day.

4 About 10 minutes before serving, divide the stuffing evenly among the artichokes, placing most of it in the cavity and sprinkling about 1 tablespoon between the leaves. Arrange artichokes in a 25 × 20 cm/10 × 8 inch oval dish.

5 Stir together stock and oil and pour over artichokes. Cover with tightly fitting lid or microwave cling film. Cook at 100% for 5 minutes.

6 Pierce film, remove dish from oven, uncover, and serve hot.

SALT PORK AND SAGE STUFFING

175 g/6 oz salt pork, cut into 1 cm/
½ inch cubes
1 small onion (about 125 g/4 oz),
peeled and quartered
125 g/4 oz celery, trimmed, stringed
and cut into 5 cm/2 inch lengths
½ teaspoon dried sage

45 g/1½ oz fine dry Breadcrumbs (page
306) or unflavoured store-bought
breadcrumbs
3 tablespoons Chicken Stock (page
286) or stock from a cube
¼ teaspoon freshly ground black pepper
1 tablespoon olive oil

1 Place salt pork in a 25 cm/10 inch flan dish and cook, uncovered, at 100% for 4 minutes. Remove from oven and set aside.

2 Place onion and celery in the container of a food processor. Process until coarsely chopped.

3 Combine vegetables and salt pork and stir to coat. Cook, uncovered, at 100% for 2 minutes.

4 Remove from oven. Stir in remaining ingredients. Cook, uncovered, at 100% for 2 minutes.

5 Remove from oven and use to stuff artichokes.

GARLIC AND PARSLEY STUFFING

4 tablespoons olive oil
30 g/1 oz flat-leaf parsley, finely
chopped
2 cloves garlic, smashed, peeled and
finely chopped
70 g/2¼ oz fine dry Breadcrumbs (page
306) or unflavoured store-bought
breadcrumbs

1 tablespoon fresh lemon juice
1 teaspoon sea salt
¼ teaspoon freshly ground black pepper

1 Heat oil in a 500 ml/1 pint glass measuring jug, uncovered, at 100% for 2 minutes. Add parsley and garlic. Cook, uncovered, at 100% for 4 minutes.

2 Remove from oven. Stir in remaining ingredients.

Spread leaves apart to expose choke and pale, inner, small leaves.

Remove small leaves by picking up and pinching.

Scrape out remaining choke with a metal spoon.

Trim artichoke—all leaves removed—for artichoke bottom.

TOMATOES STUFFED WITH TABBOULEH

S ince tomatoes retain their vivid colour and do not burst when cooked in the microwave oven, it is ideal for cooking stuffed tomatoes. This dish, which is good hot or cold, has an intense tomato flavour. It is good as a vegetarian first course or as part of a stuffed vegetable main course (see Stuffed Kohlrabi, page 76, Stuffed Aubergine, page 72, and Grilled Stuffed Mushroom Caps, page 294) or as an accompaniment to grilled fish or roast lamb or chicken. The juice from the cooked tomatoes can become a vegetarian base for soup or, mixed with lemon juice and a minimum of olive oil, a light salad dressing. *Serves 6 to 8 as a first course or side dish*

8 small (6–7.5 cm/2½–3 inch) or 6 medium (10 cm/4 inch) tomatoes
Sea salt
90 g/3 oz burghul
500 ml/16 fl oz tomato juice, fresh or canned
7 tablespoons olive oil

4 tablespoons chopped fresh mint leaves
1 tablespoon finely chopped garlic
½ teaspoon dried hot chilli flakes
60 g/2 oz spring onions (green and white parts), chopped
freshly ground black pepper
2 tablespoons fresh lemon juice

1 Cut a small slice from the top of each tomato. Scoop out inside of tomatoes, preferably with a silver spoon, leaving a shell 3 mm/⅛ inch thick. Chop flesh and set aside together with seeds and juice.

2 Sprinkle salt inside each tomato. Prick the skin of each two or three times and rub with oil. Place tomatoes cut side down on paper towels to drain.

3 Combine burghul, tomato juice, oil, mint, garlic, chilli flakes and spring onions. Let stand 15 minutes.

4 Pour burghul mixture into a sieve set over a bowl. Drain 20 minutes, stirring several times; reserve liquid. Pour mixture into a clean bowl and stir in pepper, lemon juice, salt to taste, and reserved tomato flesh, seeds and juice.

5 Arrange tomato shells cut side up around the inside edge of a 22.5 cm/9 inch dish. Fill shells with burghul mixture, mounding it slightly. Pour reserved drained liquid around tomatoes. Cover tightly with microwave cling film. Cook at 100% for 7 to 9 minutes, until tender when pricked with a sharp knife.

6 Pierce film with the tip of a sharp knife, then remove dish from oven. Uncover and transfer tomatoes with a slotted spoon to serving plate.

STUFFED KOHLRABI

Briefly cooked in the microwave oven, kohlrabi is revealed to be a wholly new vegetable, elegant and pale jade green. Pre-microwave, kohlrabi had to be cooked so long that it became white, watery and fibrous. *Serves 4 to 8*

8 small kohlrabi, trimmed and peeled   75 g/2½ oz cooked rice
2 tablespoons anchovy paste   Freshly ground black pepper
1 tablespoon olive oil

1 Using a melon baller, remove the centre of each kohlrabi and set aside. Place cored kohlrabi in a ring around the inside edge of a deep pie dish or flan dish.

2 Finely chop reserved centres. Combine with remaining ingredients.

3 Divide stuffing between kohlrabi, mounding slightly.

4 Pour 1 tablespoon water into centre of dish. Cover dish tightly with microwave cling film. Cook at 100% for 7 minutes. Pierce film with the tip of a sharp knife, remove dish from oven and serve.

To double the recipe. Double all ingredients. Use a 35 × 27.5 cm/14 × 11 inch dish and lengthen cooking time to 10 minutes.

To make 2 kohlrabi. Use 2 small kohlrabi, trimmed and peeled, 1½ teaspoons anchovy paste, ¾ teaspoon olive oil, 2 tablespoons cooked rice, and freshly ground black pepper. Proceed as for 8 kohlrabi, using a 10 cm/4 inch soufflé dish. Add 1 teaspoon water. Cover tightly with microwave cling film. Cook at 100% for 3 to 4 minutes. Pierce cling film before removing from oven.

STUFFED CHRISTOPHENE

It is time for the northerners among us to become familiar with this southern and Caribbean speciality, variously called chayote, chow-chow and christophene. It cooks fabulously in the microwave oven. Just grill it at the very end. This is rich. *Serves 4 as a first course or side dish*

2 christophenes, each pricked 4 times with the tip of a sharp knife
60 g/2 oz plus extra knob unsalted butter
1 small onion, peeled and thinly sliced
1 clove garlic, smashed, peeled and finely chopped
1 tablespoon finely chopped parsley
½ teaspoon dried thyme

250 ml/8 fl oz milk
½ teaspoon sea salt
Freshly ground black pepper
Pinch cayenne pepper
125 g/4 oz Gruyère cheese, grated
45 g/1½ oz fine dry Breadcrumbs (page 306) or store-bought unflavoured breadcrumbs

1 Place christophenes in the microwave oven and cook, uncovered, at 100% for 7 minutes. Remove from oven. When cool enough to handle, scoop out flesh and reserve flesh and shells.

2 Melt 60 g/2 oz butter in a 25 cm/10 inch flan dish, uncovered, at 100% for 2 minutes. Add onion and garlic and stir to coat. Cook, uncovered, at 100% for 4 minutes. Add parsley, thyme and reserved christophene flesh. Cook, uncovered, at 100% for 5 minutes, stirring twice.

3 Remove from oven. Add milk, stirring constantly until it is absorbed. Stir in salt, pepper and cayenne. Cook, uncovered, at 100% for 2 minutes.

4 Preheat conventional grill with rack in highest postion.

5 Divide half the christophene mixture between the reserved shells. Using half the Gruyère, cover each layer of filling with a layer of cheese. Spread remaining christophene mixture over cheese and top with remaining cheese. (This dish may be prepared to this point up to one day in advance.)

6 Place stuffed christophenes on grill pan. Sprinkle each with Breadcrumbs and dot with remaining butter. Grill until brown and bubbly.

SOUPS

—— ❖ ——

S oup restores me and gives me comfort. I like it hot or cold, thick or thin, as the preamble to a meal or as the meal itself. I find there are soups to entertain with and soups for personal pleasure. One of my greatest delights in microwave cooking is the possibility of making good soup every night if I wish.

Most soups are made with a meat stock base, but many are made without stock at all and others are made with a vegetarian base. Look through the recipes on pages 286-291 for stocks that can be made rapidly in the microwave oven and used as soups or the basis for soup. If your time is very limited, use a good stock cube or canned consommé as the starting point. In that case, add salt carefully; stock cubes and canned consommé are salted.

Soups can be clear or they can be thickened—with a purée, with cornflour, with eggs, with a cooked potato, with cream or with soured cream or yogurt.

Besides the soups in this chapter, there are others among the beans, grains, pulses and vegetable purées; you can find them in the Index. Of course, you can create your own. Look in the Dictionary at the end of the book to see how to cook vegetables, grains and purées that can be put together with stock in endless combinations to make new soups.

If you have any soup left over, reheat 250 ml/8 fl oz in a 500 ml/1 pint glass measuring jug, uncovered, at 100% for 2 minutes; 500 ml/16 fl oz in a 1 litre/ 2 pint jug, uncovered, at 100% for 3 minutes; 1 litre/ 2 pints in a 2 litre/3½–4 pint jug or bowl, uncovered, at 100% for 4 minutes.

CHICKEN STOCK & ...

—— ◆ ◆ ——

These variations on Chicken Stock are richly flavoured and sustaining. The garlic becomes sweet and adds body, making it a soup version of Chicken and Rice (page 189). *Makes 500 ml/16 fl oz*

500 ml/16 fl oz Chicken Stock (page 286) or stock from a cube
6 cloves garlic, smashed and peeled

2 tablespoons fresh lemon juice
Sea salt
Freshly ground black pepper

1 Place stock and garlic in a 1 litre/2 pint glass measuring jug.

2 Cover tightly with microwave cling film and cook at 100% for 8 minutes.

3 Pierce film to release steam, then remove jug from oven. Uncover and stir in lemon juice. Correct seasonings.

To make 1 litre/1¾ pints. Double all quantities in recipe or any variation and cook at 100% for 10 minutes.

VARIATIONS

EGG DROP SOUP Omit garlic. Make Chicken Stock & .... Whisk 1 or 2 eggs. Remove cling film, leaving soup in oven. Whisk in eggs. Cook, uncovered, at 100% for 2 minutes. Do not use lemon juice. Serve with grated Parmesan cheese, if desired.

HEALTH SOUP Reduce garlic to 2 cloves. In the container of a food processor, chop leaves from 4 parsley sprigs with 5 spinach leaves and some watercress sprigs. Cook with Chicken Stock & .... Omit lemon juice. Correct seasonings.

BATAVIA SOUP Reduce garlic to 3 cloves. Cut 5 leaves of batavia (ideally leftovers from salad fixings) into thin strips across the veins. Put in jug with Chicken Stock & .... Add 45 g/1½ oz cooked or canned chickpeas, if available. Cook. Omit lemon juice. Correct seasonings.

HOT AND SPICY CHICKEN SOUP

This soup, inspired by a Thai soup, is one I like to make for myself, especially if I have a cold—it clears the nose. *Makes 500 ml/16 fl oz*

500 ml/16 fl oz Chicken Stock (page 286) or stock from a cube
6 slices peeled fresh root ginger, about 5 mm/¼ inch thick
3 cloves garlic, smashed, peeled and sliced
⅛ teaspoon dried hot chilli flakes

1 teaspoon Worcestershire sauce
1 tablespoon fresh coriander leaves, cut into ribbons across the vein
2 tablespoons thinly sliced spring onion greens
3 teaspoons light soya sauce

1 In a 2 litre/3½ pint glass jug or bowl, combine stock, ginger, garlic, chilli flakes and Worcestershire sauce. Cook, uncovered, at 100% for 8 minutes.

2 Remove from oven and stir in remaining ingredients. Serve hot.

NEW ENGLAND CLAM CHOWDER

This is the classic American cream-based clam chowder. *Serves 4 to 5*

8 large clams (1.5–2 kg/3–4 lb total weight), well scrubbed
75 g/2½ oz bacon (about 3 rashers, 5 mm/¼ inch thick), cut into lardons
1 large onion, peeled and finely chopped

3 medium potatoes, diced
1 tablespoon plain flour
250 ml/8 fl oz milk
250 ml/8 fl oz double cream
Sea salt
Freshly ground black pepper

1 Arrange clams, standing them on their hinge ends, in a 5 cm/2 inch deep dish. Cover tightly with microwave cling film. Cook at 100% for 7 minutes.

2 Pierce film with the tip of a sharp knife, remove dish from oven and uncover. Remove clams from shells, reserving meat and any liquor. Strain liquor through a sieve lined with paper towels and reserve (you will have about 250 ml/8 fl oz). Chop clams coarsely and reserve with any juices they give off.

3 Put bacon in a 2.5 litre/4 pint soufflé dish. Cover loosely with paper towels. Cook at 100% for 4 minutes.

4 Remove from oven. Stir in onions, potatoes, flour and reserved liquor. Cover tightly with microwave cling film. Cook at 100% for 10 minutes. Pierce film, remove from oven and set aside.

5 Combine milk and cream in a 1 litre/2 pint glass measuring jug. Heat, uncovered, at 100% for 4 minutes 30 seconds.

6 Remove from oven and stir into reserved vegetable mixture. Add clams and their juices. Stir well, add salt and pepper to taste, and serve hot.

To serve 12. Double all ingredients except bacon and onion. Increase bacon to 125 g/4 oz, and use 1½ onions. Cook clams as above for 20 minutes. Cook bacon as above for 8 minutes. Add onions, potatoes, flour and reserved liquor and cook, covered, for 20 minutes. Heat milk and cream in a 2 litre/3½ pint glass jug or bowl for 7 minutes. Combine all as above and heat, uncovered, for 3 minutes.

Arrange clams in a dish just large enough to hold them.

SALT COD CHOWDER

One of the microwave oven's star turns is the rapidity and efficiency with which it freshens salt cod. If you are unlucky enough to have an exceptionally salty or dried out piece of fish, add one more round of blanching and rinsing.

Chowders, or *chaudières*, have been made from clams, potatoes and sweet-corn. In America, they have been either cream- or tomato-based. In this recipe you can see the influence of people from warm lands—Italian or Portugese—living in a cold climate. *Serves 10 or more*

500 g/1 lb salt cod, washed in cold running water for 2 minutes
60 g/2 oz piece streaky bacon, cut into 5 × 1 × 1 cm/2 × ½ × ½ inch lardons
3 medium carrots, trimmed, peeled and cut into 7.5 cm/3 inch lengths
2 celery sticks, trimmed, stringed and cut into 7.5 cm/3 inch lengths
2 small onions (about 350 g/12 oz), peeled and quartered
4 cloves garlic, smashed and peeled

1.25 kg/2½ lb potatoes, peeled and diced
2 cans (400 g/14 oz each) chopped tomatoes with juice
¼ teaspoon dried thyme
¼ teaspoon dried oregano
½ bay leaf
1 litre/1¾ pints Fish Stock (page 289), Clam Liquor (page 435) or chicken stock from a cube
Freshly ground black pepper
Tabasco sauce

1 Place salt cod in a 2.5 litre/4 pint soufflé dish or casserole. Cover with 1 litre/1¾ pints of cold water. Cover with a tightly fitting lid or with microwave cling film. Cook at 100% for 5 minutes. If using cling film, pierce to release steam.

2 Remove from oven and uncover. Drain fish and rinse with cold water. Repeat the soaking process 2 more times. Drain fish, cut into 2.5 cm/1 inch chunks and reserve.

3 Place bacon, carrots, celery, onions and garlic in the container of a food processor. Process until coarsely chopped.

4 Place mixture in a 2.5 litre/4 pint soufflé dish or casserole. Cook, uncovered, at 100% for 10 minutes, stirring twice. Add potatoes, tomatoes and their juice, thyme, oregano and bay leaf. Cover tightly with a lid or microwave cling film. Cook at 100% for 30 minutes. If using cling film, pierce to release steam.

5 Remove from oven and uncover. Discard bay leaf and stir in reserved salt cod and remaining ingredients. Cook, uncovered, for 4 minutes or until hot. Serve immediately.

To serve 4 to 5. Halve all ingredients except carrots, potatoes and tomatoes. Use 1 carrot, 400 g/14 oz potatoes and 250 g/8 oz tomatoes. Cook salt cod as above, using 750 ml/1¼ pints water. Cook chopped bacon, carrots, celery, onions and garlic, uncovered, for 6 minutes. Add potatoes, tomatoes and their juice, thyme, oregano and bay leaf. Cook, covered, for 20 minutes. Add reserved salt cod and remaining ingredients. Cook, uncovered, for 3 minutes or until hot.

MUSSEL SOUP

M ussel soups are easy to make because cooked mussels give off a rich-tasting liquor as they cook. The only real work is in cleaning the mussels. Discard any that feel strangely heavy; they may have gunk inside. The liquor needs to be strained to remove any dirty bits and sand. Depending on how elegant you want dinner to be and how clean the hands of the eaters, you can serve the mussels in the shell or shelled. The cold variations are wonderful summer fare, but are always better with shelled mussels. *Serves 4 as a light dish, 6 as a first course*

6 dozen mussels, scrubbed and beards removed
600 ml/1 pint white wine
12 whole peppercorns
8 cloves garlic, smashed and peeled
2 medium fennel bulbs (about 500 g/1 lb), cored, quartered and sliced, or

125 g/4 oz celery, trimmed, stringed and sliced
200 g/7 oz onions, peeled and sliced
3 cans (250 g/8 oz each) chopped tomatoes with juice
2 tablespoons sea salt

1 Arrange mussels, hinge side down, in a single layer in a deep 35 × 12.5 × 5 cm/14 × 11 × 2 inch dish. Add 350 ml/12 fl oz of the wine, the peppercorns and the garlic. Cover tightly with microwave cling film. Cook at 100% for 8 minutes.

2 Pierce film with the tip of a sharp knife, then remove dish from oven and uncover. Holding mussels over dish to catch their liquor, remove meat from shells and set aside. Leave any unopened mussels in dish. Re-cover tightly with microwave cling film. Cook at 100% for 3 to 4 minutes, until they open. Pierce film.

3 Remove remaining mussels from shells, discarding any unopened mussels. Strain cooking liquid through a sieve lined with a double thickness of muslin. Reserve cooking liquid with mussels.

4 Combine fennel, onions, tomatoes and remaining wine in a 2.5 litre/4 pint soufflé dish. Cover tightly with microwave cling film. Cook at 100% for 13 minutes.

5 Pierce film, remove dish from oven and uncover. Add reserved mussels with their cooking liquid, and salt. Stir well and serve hot.

VARIATIONS

BILLI BI Prepare as for Mussel Soup through step 4. In a 2 litre/3½ pint glass jug or bowl, whisk 250 ml/8 fl oz each cream and Mussel Liquor (page 465) or Chicken Stock (page 286) and 4 egg yolks. Cover tightly with microwave cling film and cook for 6 minutes at 100%. Pierce film, remove from oven and uncover. Whisk into reserved mussel cooking liquid; add salt and pepper to taste. Refrigerate. When cold, stir in reserved mussels. Serves 6.

COLD CURRIED MUSSEL SOUP Cook as for Billi Bi, adding ½ teaspoon curry powder or Spice Powder I (page 299) to cream-liquor mixture before cooking.

PRAWN AND SWEETCORN CHOWDER

—— • • ——

A ll chowders are not made with clams. Here is one festive enough for any party.
Serves 6

1 red pepper, cored, seeded and finely
    chopped
1 green pepper, cored, seeded and finely
    chopped
500 ml/16 fl oz Prawn Cream (page
    305) or double cream
500 ml/16 fl oz Fish Stock (page 289),
    Clam Liquor (page 435) or fish stock
    from a cube
1 baking potato, peeled and diced
165 g/5½ oz sweetcorn kernels, fresh or
    canned

125 g/4 oz raw prawns, peeled,
    deveined and cut into small pieces
4 tablespoons chopped celery leaves,
    taken from the centre of the celery
    bunch, or ½ teaspoon celery seed
½ teaspoon dried thyme
2 teaspoons fresh lemon juice
1 teaspoon sea salt (less if using a stock
    cube)
¼ teaspoon freshly ground black pepper

1 Combine peppers, Prawn Cream, stock and potato in a 2.5 litre/4 pint soufflé
dish. Cover with microwave cling film. Cook at 100% for 12 minutes.

2 Pierce film with the tip of a sharp knife, remove dish from oven and uncover.
Add remaining ingredients and stir well. Cook, uncovered, at 100% for 2
minutes. Serve hot.

TOMATO SOUP & ...

—— • • ——

T hese are some of my favourite, virtually instant soups. I always make and eat
two cups. Then I feel happy. Sometimes I double the recipe to serve guests, and
they seem to feel happy, too. *Makes 500 ml/16 fl oz*

250 ml/8 fl oz Chicken Stock (page
    286) or stock from a cube
4 cloves garlic, smashed and peeled
1 can (250 g/8 oz) plum tomatoes

4 leaves fresh basil (optional)
15 g/½ oz unsalted butter (optional)
Sea salt
Freshly ground black pepper

1 Put stock with garlic in a 1 litre/2 pint glass measuring jug.

2 Open can of tomatoes and cut through tomatoes in can until coarsely cut up.
Add tomatoes and liquid to stock. Stir in basil, if desired.

3 Cover tightly with microwave cling film. Cook at 100% for 7 minutes.

4 Pierce film with the tip of a sharp knife, then remove jug from oven. Uncover and stir in butter, if desired. Taste and add salt and pepper, if needed. Serve hot.

To make 1 litre/1¾ pints. Double all ingredients. Cook for 10 minutes.

VARIATIONS

TOMATO SOUP WITH COUSCOUS Substitute 4 tablespoons couscous for the garlic. Omit basil.

TOMATO MINESTRONE Precook 40 g/1¼ oz macaroni or small pasta shells in salted boiling water on top of the stove. Measure out 45 g/1½ oz canned white cannellini beans and set aside. Add 1 pinch of dried oregano, 1 pinch of dried thyme, 1 tablespoon peeled and thinly sliced carrots, 1 tablespoon chopped onions, 1 tablespoon stringed and thinly sliced celery, and 1 small mushroom, sliced, to the stock, tomatoes, garlic and basil. Cover tightly; cook at 100% for 10 minutes. Pierce film, remove from oven and uncover. Stir in drained macaroni and beans. Add more stock if you want a thinner soup. Add salt and pepper to taste. Serves 4.

CREAM OF TOMATO SOUP

◆·◆

There was a time when I could be satisfied with tomato soup out of a can—no more. I don't know if I have changed or the soup has. This makes me as happy as the canned soup used to. It is one good reason to make Chunky Tomato Sauce and keep it on hand, fresh or frozen. (Defrost frozen sauce before making soup.)
Makes 1.25 litres/2 pints, serves 4 to 6

250 ml/8 fl oz Chunky Tomato Sauce (page 324)
500 ml/16 fl oz Chicken Stock (page 286) or stock from a cube
1 teaspoon sugar
¼ teaspoon freshly ground black pepper
125 ml/4 fl oz double cream
1 tablespoon thinly shredded fresh basil leaves or chopped fresh dill (both optional)

1 Place all ingredients except basil or dill in a 2 litre/3½ pint glass jug or bowl. Cook, uncovered, at 100% for 6 minutes.

2 Remove from oven and stir well. Serve hot, sprinkled with basil leaves or dill, if desired.

SIMPLE SEAFOOD STEW

• • •

This stew needs only a green salad and a bit of cheese afterwards to make a meal of it. Put an extra bowl on the table for the empty shells. *Serves 4 as a main course, 6 as a substantial first course if extra mussels and clams are added*

2 small whole fish such as mackerel (about 750 g/1½ lb each), gills and fins removed, head and tail discarded, cut across into 4 cm/1½ inch slices
1 small onion, peeled and sliced
2½ tablespoons good-quality olive oil
6 mussels, well scrubbed and beards removed
6 clams, well scrubbed
6 to 7 raw prawns (about 125 g/4 oz), shelled and deveined
10 scallops, muscle removed, cut in half horizontally if very large
4 to 6 cloves garlic, smashed, peeled and thinly sliced
2 large ripe tomatoes, cored and cut into chunks, or 4 whole canned tomatoes, squeezed to remove juice

Large pinch saffron threads
1 tablespoon sea salt
Freshly ground black pepper
350 ml/12 fl oz Lightly Cooked Crushed Tomatoes (page 293) or whole canned tomatoes, drained, squeezed and coarsely chopped
2 tablespoons Pernod
175 ml/6 fl oz Fish Stock (page 289) or Clam Liquor (page 435)
175 ml/6 fl oz white wine
Fiery Pepper Sauce (page 297) or bottled Tabasco sauce (optional)
Aïoli (page 332) (optional)

1 Arrange fish in a 2.5 litre/4 pint soufflé dish with skin of fish against sides of dish. Place onions in centre and drizzle with oil. Arrange mussels and clams around sides of dish on top of fish.

2 Arrange prawns in a single layer on top of onions. Arrange scallops over prawns. Scatter garlic and tomato chunks over top. Sprinkle with saffron, salt and pepper. Pour crushed tomatoes, Pernod, stock and wine over all. Cover tightly with microwave cling film. Cook at 100% for 15 to 17 minutes, just until clams open.

3 Pierce film to release steam, then remove dish from oven. Uncover, add pepper sauce, if desired, and stir. Serve with boiled potatoes, croûtons or rice, and pass Aïoli, if desired, in a separate dish.

ANISE SEAFOOD STEW

—— • ❖ • ——

Anise is a liquorice-tasting spice that goes very well with seafood and fish. It adds a little special oomph to this brightly coloured stew. Serve some Aïoli (page 332) on the side, if you like. *Serves 3 to 4 as a main course, 6 as an ample first course*

Pinch saffron
125 ml/4 fl oz white wine
6 large clams, well scrubbed
1 can (400 g/14 oz) tomatoes, cut into chunks
6 cloves garlic, smashed and peeled
½ teaspoon freshly ground aniseed

Freshly ground black pepper
Pinch dried hot chilli flakes
250 g/8 oz cod fillet, cut into chunks
6 large raw prawns (about 250 g/8 oz)
8 mussels, well scrubbed and beards removed

1 Stir saffron into white wine and let stand.

2 Arrange clams, hinge side down, in a 2.5 litre/4 pint soufflé dish. Cover tightly with microwave cling film. Cook at 100% for 3 minutes.

3 Pierce film with the tip of a sharp knife, then remove from oven. Uncover and remove clams from their shells, reserving meat and any liquor.

4 Stir together tomatoes, garlic, aniseed, pepper and chilli flakes in the soufflé dish. Place cod in centre of dish. Arrange prawns and mussels around cod. Cover tightly with microwave cling film. Cook at 100% for 9 minutes 30 seconds, until mussels open.

5 Pierce film, then remove dish from oven. Gently stir in reserved saffron-wine mixture and clams with their liquor. Reheat, if necessary, tightly covered, at 100% for 3 minutes.

FRENCH ONION SOUP

—— • ❖ • ——

This is one of the most cheering of soups. Here it is made *blonde*, without browning (caramelizing) the onions. To make it *brune*, with the onions thoroughly caramelized, see Traditional French Onion Soup. The browned-onion version takes longer. You may want to serve the soup with a melted cheese crust on top (gratinéed). *Makes 1.25 litres/2 pints, to serve 5, or 6 if croûtons and cheese are added*

125 g/4 oz unsalted butter
1 kg/2 lb onions, peeled and sliced
500 ml/16 fl oz white wine or
   Champagne, not acid or sour

500 ml/16 fl oz Chicken or Veal Stock
   (page 286) or stock from a cube
Sea salt
Freshly ground black pepper

1 Heat butter in a 35 × 27.5 × 5 cm/14 × 11 × 2 inch dish, uncovered, at 100% for 4 minutes. Stir in onions. Cook, uncovered, at 100% for 15 minutes, until onions are soft.

2 Add wine and stock. Continue cooking for 15 minutes longer.

3 Remove from oven. Season to taste with salt and pepper. Serve hot.

Note. If you are using stock made from a cube, you will probably not need salt.

To make 600 ml/1 pint. Halve all ingredients. Heat butter in a 1 litre/2 pint soufflé dish, uncovered, at 100% for 2 minutes. Add onions and cook for 10 minutes. Stir in wine and stock and cook for 10 minutes longer.

VARIATIONS

HEARTY ONION SOUP Prick 2 baking potatoes twice each with a fork. Place on a sheet of paper towel and cook, uncovered, at 100% for 11 minutes. Remove from oven. When cool enough to handle, scoop out flesh and place in container of a food processor. Add French Onion Soup and process until smooth. For half this quantity, cook 1 potato for 7 minutes and use only 600 ml/1 pint soup.

TRADITIONAL FRENCH ONION SOUP Cook onions for 40 to 50 minutes, stirring 3 times, until golden brown. They will not have a uniform colour. Continue as for French Onion Soup, preferably using Veal Stock. If desired, you may substitute 4 tablespoons port for that amount of wine. For a thinner soup, stir in 250 ml/8 fl oz additional hot stock at the end of the cooking. Serves 6 to 8. To serve 3 to 4, halve ingredients; cook butter for 2 minutes; cook onions for 30 minutes; cook with stock and wine for 10 mintues.

GRATINÉED FRENCH ONION SOUP To gratiné, heat the grill when you add the stock for French Onion Soup. Put a croûton (page 308) in the bottom of each of 6 ovenproof bowls. Divide soup among bowls. Sprinkle top of soup in each bowl with 1½ tablespoons (9 in all) grated Gruyère cheese. Place bowls on a baking sheet. Place under grill for 3 minutes, or until cheese melts.

FISH SOUP

◆ ◆

In one of the most unlikely parts of Rome, Trastevere, there is a wonderfully elegant restaurant that serves only fish and is owned by Alberto Ciarla, a man consumed with a passion for food and the history of Italian food. Once, he served me the most extraordinary fish soup based, he said, on an antique recipe. He used borlotti beans, lobster bisque and pasta to make a symphony of complex flavours based on a fish stock and made joyous with the tiniest of seafoods. I have taken liberties to change this into a recipe that I can make in a reasonable time at home. It is still wonderful and, surprisingly, the well-cooked paprika does much to make up for the missing lobster.

The microwave oven does wonders with the stock, and keeps the seafood unusually tender. *Serves 4*

500 g/1 lb fish bones, broken into
    5 cm/2 inch pieces
500 ml/16 fl oz water
125 g/4 oz piece streaky bacon, cut into
    5 × 5 × 10 mm/¼ × ¼ × ½ inch
    lardons
1 tablespoon olive oil
1 tablespoon medium-hot paprika
½ large onion, peeled and chopped
3 cloves garlic, smashed and peeled
125 ml/4 fl oz white wine
3 sheets dry lasagne noodles, broken
    across into 2.5 cm/1 inch pieces
    (about 60 g/2 oz)

8 small clams (about 500 g/1 lb),
    scrubbed
125 ml/4 fl oz Lightly Cooked Crushed
    Tomatoes (page 293)
4 mussels, scrubbed and debearded
400 g/14 oz canned borlotti beans,
    drained and rinsed
250 g/8 oz squid, cleaned, bodies sliced
    into rings and tentacles quartered,
    OR 250 g/8 oz queen scallops
Pinch dried sage
Pinch dried thyme
Pinch freshly ground black pepper

1 Combine fish bones and water in a 2.5 litre/4 pint soufflé dish or casserole. Cover with a tightly fitting lid or with microwave cling film. Cook at 100% for 15 minutes. If using cling film, pierce to release steam.

2 Remove from oven and uncover. Strain stock through a fine sieve and reserve. If using a lidded dish, measure. If you do not have 500 ml/16 fl oz stock, top up with water.

3 Place bacon in a 5 litre/8 pint casserole. Cover loosely with paper towel. Cook at 100% for 7 minutes.

4 Remove from oven and uncover. Remove lardons with a slotted spoon and drain on additional paper towels. Reserve lardons. Pour off most of the fat, leaving about 1 tablespoon in the casserole. Add oil and paprika and stir to combine. Mound in the centre of the dish. Cook, uncovered, at 100% for 2 minutes.

5 Remove from oven. Add onion and garlic and toss to coat. Cook, uncovered, for 2 minutes 30 seconds. Stir in wine, 350 ml/12 fl oz of the fish stock and the lasagne. Cover with lid and cook at 100% for 5 minutes.

6 Remove from oven and uncover carefully. Arrange clams, hinge-end down, around the inside edge of the dish. Re-cover and cook for 5 minutes or until clams open.

7 Remove from oven and uncover carefully. Stir in crushed tomatoes. Arrange mussels, hinge-end down, in the centre of the dish. Cover and cook for 5 minutes or until mussels open.

8 Remove from oven and uncover carefully. Add remaining ingredients and stir to combine. Cover and cook for 4 minutes or until squid is opaque. Remove from oven, stir in reserved lardons and serve.

RUSSIAN STURGEON SOUP

The Russians have a kind of soup—really a meal—called solianka, which is at its best made with sturgeon. (Monkfish is a good substitute.) The broth turns a beautiful golden colour and the fish does not dissolve, as so often happens in fish soups. The surprise is in the seasonings. Don't be afraid; the gherkins, olives and capers give emphatic flavour without spiciness. It is fresh-tasting, thinning, and very good. *Serves 4 as a main course, 8 as a first course*

1 kg/2 lb sturgeon or monkfish bones and head, cleaned of all blood
1 litre/1¾ pints water
30 g/1 oz unsalted butter
125 g/4 oz onion, peeled and finely chopped
125 g/4 oz mushrooms, cut into 5 mm/ ¼ inch slices
1 kg/2 lb sturgeon or monkfish fillet, cut into 15 × 7.5 cm/6 × 3 inch pieces
5 shallots, peeled
1 carrot, trimmed, peeled and sliced in food processor

1 celery stick, trimmed, stringed and sliced across in food processor
1 leek, trimmed, well rinsed and sliced across in food processor
1 parsnip, peeled and sliced across in food processor
2 teaspoons Basic Tomato Paste (page 294) or canned tomato paste
2 teaspoons capers
1 tablespoon stoned and chopped Kalamata olives
3 sour gherkins, chopped
Large pinch freshly ground black pepper
1 tablespoon sea salt

1 Place fish bones, head and water in a 2.5 litre/4 pint soufflé dish. Cover tightly with microwave cling film. Cook at 100% for 25 minutes. Pierce film with the tip of a sharp knife, then remove dish from oven. Strain stock and set aside.

2 Heat butter in a 35 × 27.5 × 5 cm/14 × 11 × 2 inch dish, uncovered, at 100% for 2 minutes. Stir in onion and mushrooms. Cook, uncovered, for 4 minutes longer.

3 Remove from oven. Arrange sturgeon on top of onion mixture in a single layer. Scatter shallots and sliced vegetables over fish. Pour reserved stock over all. Cover tightly with microwave cling film. Cook at 100% for 18 minutes.

4 Pierce film, then remove from oven. Uncover and stir in remaining ingredients. Serve hot.

TRADITIONAL HOT BORSCHT

When winter comes on as it does very heavily in Russia, they make hot borscht that is thick with meat and vegetables. Wine-coloured by beetroot and tomatoes, it is made sweet and sour by the vegetables, sugar and vinegar. It often makes a meal; but it could go before a light fish or chicken main course. The flavour of this soup improves with mellowing (see page 206). *Serves 10 to 12 as a first course, 8 as a main course*

1 litre/1¾ pints Light Beef or Veal Stock (page 287) or stock from a cube
750 g/1½ lb beetroot, scrubbed, 2.5 cm/1 inch of stem left on
1 carrot, trimmed and peeled
6 cloves garlic, smashed and peeled
250 g/8 oz green cabbage, shredded as for fine coleslaw
500 g/1 lb fresh tomatoes, cored and coarsely chopped
500 g/1 lb beef chuck, cut into 1 cm/½ inch cubes

6 tablespoons Basic Tomato Paste (page 294) or canned tomato paste
½ bay leaf
4 tablespoons red wine vinegar
2 tablespoons sugar
2 teaspoons sea salt
Freshly ground black pepper
2 baking potatoes, cooked just prior to serving (page 475), peeled and quartered (optional)
30 g/1 oz fresh dill, chopped, for serving
Soured cream, for serving

1 Combine stock and beetroot in a 1.5 litre/2½ pint soufflé dish. Cover tightly with microwave cling film. Cook at 100% for 10 to 12 minutes (it will take less time if beetroot are small).

2 Pierce film with the tip of a sharp knife, then remove from oven and uncover. Remove beetroot and reserve stock.

3 When beetroot are cool enough to handle, cut off stems and root ends and slip off their skins, holding them over the container of a food processor to catch any liquid. Put medium grating disc in food processor. Grate beetroot and carrot.

4 Scrape grated vegetables into reserved stock. Stir in remaining ingredients except for potatoes, dill and soured cream. Cover tightly with microwave cling film. Cook at 100% for 8 minutes. Leaving dish in oven, uncover and stir well. Re-cover and cook for 8 minutes more.

5 Pierce film, then remove from oven. Soup may be mellowed at this point (page 206). Place a piece of potato in each soup bowl. Stir dill into soup just before serving. Ladle hot soup over potato. Top each serving with soured cream.

Hot Beetroot and Red Cabbage Borscht

This version of borscht is easily made from leftover Sweet and Sour Red Cabbage (page 270). If you don't have leftovers, make the Traditional Hot Borscht (page 91) instead. *Serves 4*

150 g/5 oz Sweet and Sour Red Cabbage (page 270)
1 beetroot (125 g/4 oz) cooked (page 419), then grated
600 ml/1 pint Chicken Stock (page 286) or stock from a cube

2 teaspoons fresh lemon juice
1 teaspoon sea salt (less if using a stock cube)
2 tablespoons plus 2 teaspoons chopped fresh dill
1 tablespoon soured cream, for serving

1 Combine cabbage, grated beetroot and stock in a 1 litre/2 pint glass measuring jug. Stir in lemon juice, salt and 2 tablespoons of the dill. Cover tightly with microwave cling film. Cook at 100% for 4 minutes.

2 Pierce film with the tip of a sharp knife, remove from oven and uncover carefully. Serve each portion with a dollop of soured cream and ½ teaspoon of the remaining dill.

TOMATO AND CABBAGE SOUP

Make this soup in autumn or winter when the whole world seems grey.
Serves 4

1 can (400 g/14 oz) whole tomatoes,
   with juice
45 g/1½ oz spring onion greens,
   coarsely chopped
30 g/1 oz flat-leaf parsley, chopped
2 tablespoons chopped fresh dill
175 g/6 oz white cabbage, shredded

1 small courgette, trimmed and cut
   across into 5 mm/¼ inch slices
⅛ teaspoon dried oregano
⅛ teaspoon dried thyme
1 tablespoon sea salt
Freshly ground black pepper

1 Combine tomatoes, spring onion greens, parsley and dill in a 1 litre/2 pint glass measuring jug. Cover tightly with microwave cling film. Cook at 100% for 5 minutes.

2 Pierce film with the tip of a sharp knife, remove from oven, uncover, and place in the container of a food processor. Purée until smooth. Remove from food processor, leaving about 125 ml/4 fl oz in container. Set aside the rest.

3 Place cabbage and courgette in a 1 litre/2 pint glass measuring jug. Cover tightly with microwave cling film. Cook at 100% for 5 minutes.

4 Pierce film, remove from oven, uncover, and place in container of food processor. Purée until smooth.

5 Combine cabbage and reserved tomato mixture in 1 litre/2 pint glass measuring jug. Stir in oregano, thyme, salt and pepper. Cover tightly with microwave cling film. Cook at 100% for 5 minutes. Serve hot, or allow to come to room temperature and refrigerate for Cold Yogurt-Vegetable Soup.

VARIATIONS

COLD YOGURT-VEGETABLE SOUP For an extremely refreshing hot-weather soup, combine 500 ml/16 fl oz chilled Tomato and Cabbage Soup with 350 ml/12 fl oz low fat plain yogurt and 2 tablespoons water in a food processor or blender; blend well. Just before serving, stir ½ teaspoon chopped fresh dill into each portion. This will serve 4; repeat with remaining soup to serve 8.

STRAINED TOMATO VEGETABLE SOUP Place tomatoes in the container of a food processor and purée. Scrape into a 2 litre/3½ pint glass jug or bowl. Add remaining vegetables and 250 ml/8 fl oz water. Cook, covered, at 100% for 15 minutes. Add oregano, thyme, salt and pepper to taste.

CREAMY CABBAGE SOUP

◆ ◆ ◆

An unusual and surprisingly elegant soup. *Serves 4*

1 large or 2 small baking potatoes (about 500 g/1 lb), washed, dried and pricked several times
1 small onion, peeled and thinly sliced
15 g/½ oz unsalted butter, cut into bits
175 g/6 oz green cabbage, shredded

250 ml/8 fl oz Chicken Stock (page 286) or stock from a cube
125 ml/4 fl oz double cream
Sea salt
Freshly ground black pepper
Finely chopped parsley (optional)

1 Cook potato, uncovered, at 100% for 7 minutes. If cooking 2 potatoes, cook for 9 to 10 minutes. Remove from oven and set aside.

2 Place onions and butter in a 1 litre/2 pint glass measuring jug. Cover tightly with microwave cling film. Cook at 100% for 3 minutes.

3 Pierce film with the tip of a sharp knife, then remove from oven. Uncover and stir in cabbage. Re-cover and cook at 100% for 4 minutes.

4 Peel potato and cut into chunks. Place in the container of a food processor. Add cabbage and stock to potato. Process until well combined but not completely smooth. Remove mixture to a bowl.

5 Stir in cream. Add salt and pepper to taste. Sprinkle individual servings with parsley, if desired.

WINTER VEGETABLE SOUP

◆ ◆ ◆

A slightly unusual group of vegetables gives this a special taste. Quadratini are little squares of pasta. If you can't find them, substitute other tiny pasta shapes. *Makes 1 litre/1¾ pints*

3 carrots, trimmed, peeled and cut in half lengthways
2 heads chicory, trimmed
1½ medium turnips, trimmed, peeled and quartered
2 medium leeks (white part only), thinly sliced
6 celery sticks, stringed and diced
1 litre/1¾ pints Chicken Stock (page 286) or stock from a cube

½ clove garlic, smashed and peeled
75 g/2½ oz quadratini
3 fresh basil leaves, ¼ teaspoon dried thyme, or 1 tablespoon chopped fresh dill
30 g/1 oz unsalted butter, cut into bits
Sea salt
Freshly ground black pepper

1 Put 500 ml/16 fl oz of water on the stove to boil for the pasta.

2 Using a food processor fitted with the slicing disc, thinly slice carrots, chicory and turnips.

3 Place vegetables, stock and garlic in a 2.5 litre/4 pint soufflé dish. Cover tightly with microwave cling film. Cook at 100% for 15 to 17 minutes, until carrots are tender.

4 Meanwhile, cook pasta for 5 minutes and drain.

5 Pierce film with the tip of a sharp knife, remove soup from oven and uncover. Add herbs, butter, salt and pepper. Stir in pasta and serve hot.

GREEN LENTIL SOUP

Lentils make a wonderful, substantial soup. You can substitute other colour lentils if they are easier to find. *Serves 6 to 8*

200 g/7 oz dried green lentils
2 sticks celery, trimmed, stringed and cut into 5 cm/2 inch pieces
1 leek, white part only, cut into 5 cm/2 inch pieces
3 cloves garlic, smashed and peeled
2 medium carrots, trimmed, peeled and cut into 5 cm/2 inch pieces

3 parsley sprigs
3 tablespoons olive oil
1 litre/1¾ pints Chicken Stock (page 286), Lamb Stock (page 287) or stock from a cube
1 tablespoon sea salt (less if using a stock cube)
Pinch freshly ground black pepper

1 Put lentils in a 2.5 litre/4 pint soufflé dish with 1 litre/1¾ pints water. Cover tightly with microwave cling film. Cook at 100% for 35 minutes.

2 Pierce film with the tip of a sharp knife, then remove from oven. Let stand, covered, for 20 minutes. Uncover and drain lentils. Set aside.

3 Place celery, leeks, garlic, carrots and parsley in the container of a food processor. Process until finely chopped.

4 Add vegetables to reserved lentils. Stir in oil, stock, salt and pepper. Cover tightly with microwave cling film. Cook at 100% for 15 minutes.

5 Pierce film, remove from oven and uncover. Purée about half the soup in the food processor. Stir purée into remaining soup and serve.

Split Pea Soup

• • •

This is usually family soup, but my version is so creamy and lovely I think you will be tempted to serve it for elegant winter dinners. With sausages, it can be an informal main course. I would add salad, cheese, and a spicy red wine like a Californian zinfandel. *Serves 4*

200 g/7 oz green or yellow split peas   ⅛ teaspoon ground or rubbed sage
350 ml/12 fl oz Chicken Stock (page 286) or stock from a cube

1 Place peas and 500 ml/16 fl oz water in a 2.5 litre/4 pint soufflé dish. Cover tightly with microwave cling film. Cook at 100% for 15 minutes.

2 Pierce film with the tip of a sharp knife, then remove from oven. Let stand for 5 minutes. Uncover and add 500 ml/16 fl oz very hot tap water. Re-cover and let stand for 1 hour.

3 Uncover, drain, and rinse peas. Return to soufflé dish. Add 1 litre/1¾ pints warm water. Cover tightly. Cook at 100% for 35 mintues.

4 Pierce film, then remove from oven. Let stand, covered, for 20 minutes. Uncover and place in the container of a food processor. Process until smooth. Add stock and sage.

5 Return to soufflé dish. Heat, uncovered, at 100% for 4 minutes, stirring once.

6 Remove from oven. Serve hot.

VARIATION

YELLOW SPLIT PEA SOUP WITH KIELBASA Cook a smoked gammon hock (knuckle) (page 292). Reserve cooking liquid and discard hock, or save for another use. Proceed as for Split Pea Soup, adding reserved gammon cooking liquid with enough water to measure 1 litre/1¾ pints. Add 165 g/5½ oz kielbasa, cut into slices and each slice quartered, to soup before reheating. You could also use your choice of cooked sausage.

BLACK BEAN SOUP

———— • • • ————

This is a wonderful, heartwarming soup. You can stir 1 tablespoon of sherry into the finished soup and place a thin slice of hard-boiled egg on each portion instead of the soured cream and coriander. *Serves 6*

175 g/6 oz dried black beans
1 litre/1¾ pints Chicken Stock (page 286) or stock from a cube
1 tablespoon vegetable oil
1 medium onion, peeled and finely chopped
2 cloves garlic, smashed and peeled
1 leek, white part only, washed and chopped
½ celery stick with leaves, stringed and chopped

1 bay leaf
1 whole clove
2 teaspoons sea salt (less if using a stock cube)
Pinch freshly ground black pepper
Hot and Sweet Red Pepper Sauce (page 297) or Fiery Pepper Sauce (page 297) to taste
4 tablespoons soured cream, for serving
2 tablespoons chopped fresh coriander, for serving

1 Place beans in a 2.5 litre/4 pint soufflé dish. Add 500 ml/16 fl oz water. Cover tightly with microwave cling film. Cook at 100% for 15 minutes.

2 Pierce film with the tip of a sharp knife, then remove from oven. Let stand for 5 minutes. Uncover and add 500 ml/16 fl oz very hot tap water. Re-cover tightly and let stand for 1 hour.

3 Uncover, drain, and rinse beans. Return to soufflé dish and add remaining ingredients except soured cream and coriander. Stir well. Cover tightly with 2 sheets of microwave cling film. Cook at 100% for 35 minutes.

4 Pierce film, then remove from oven. Let stand, covered, for 20 minutes. Uncover and place in the container of a food processor. Process until smooth. Stir in salt, pepper and pepper sauce to taste. Serve with a dollop of soured cream and a sprinkle of coriander.

VARIATIONS

BLACK BEANS Make beans through step 3. Let stand as for Black Bean Soup. Do not process, simply drain and serve. Omit pepper sauce, soured cream and coriander.

BLACK BEAN PURÉE Make beans as for Black Bean Soup. Drain, process until smooth, and serve. Omit pepper sauce, soured cream and coriander.

CREAM OF CAULIFLOWER SOUP

— • ◆ • —

This is a rich cream soup, a good choice to begin a light meal of filleted fish or roast chicken. Make the main course colourful. Any vegetable purée (pages 251–261) could be substituted for the cauliflower. *Makes 1.25 litres/2 pints; serves 6*

600 ml/1 pint Cauliflower Purée (page 256)
250 ml/8 fl oz Basic Béchamel (page 316)
30 g/1 oz unsalted butter

500 ml/16 fl oz Chicken Stock (page 286) or stock from a cube
Sea salt
Freshly ground black pepper
Fresh chives (optional)

1 In a 2 litre/3½ pint glass jug or bowl, whisk together Cauliflower Purée, Béchamel, butter and stock. Cover loosely with paper towel. Cook at 100% for 5 minutes.

2 Remove from oven. Stir well and season with salt and pepper. To serve, snip some fresh chives over each portion, if desired.

CARROT SOUP

— • ◆ • —

This cream soup, a delightful orange-salmon in colour, can be served hot or chilled. *Serves 2*

350 g/12 oz carrots, trimmed, peeled and sliced in 5 mm/¼ inch rounds
250 ml/8 fl oz Chicken Stock (page 286) or stock from a cube
30 g/1 oz unsalted butter

½ teaspoon paprika
½ teaspoon sea salt
4 tablespoons double cream
Freshly grated nutmeg (for cold soup)

1 Arrange carrots in 2 or 3 layers in a dish just large enough to hold them. Cover tightly with microwave cling film. Cook at 100% for 7 minutes.

2 Pierce film with the tip of a sharp knife, then remove from oven. Uncover and place in the container of a food processor. Add stock, butter, paprika and salt and process to a smooth purée. Pour into a 1 litre/2 pint glass measuring jug and stir in cream.

3 Cover tightly with microwave cling film. Cook for 3 minutes.

4 Pierce film, then remove from oven. Serve hot, or allow to cool to room temperature and refrigerate. To serve chilled, dust each bowl of soup with grated nutmeg.

To serve 4. Double all ingredients. Cook carrots for 10 minutes. Purée in two batches, then stir in cream. Pour into a 2 litre/3½ pint glass jug or bowl and cover tightly with microwave cling film. Cook at 100% for 5 minutes.

VARIATION

LIGHT CARROT SOUP Increase the stock to 300 ml/½ pint and add 2 teaspoons cornflour to carrots in food processor. Omit the cream. Increase final cooking time to 5 minutes.

LEEK AND POTATO SOUP

This is the French mother's equivalent of chicken soup. If you are cold and tired, try it. You'll feel a lot better soon. *Serves 4*

2 small potatoes (350 g/12 oz), peeled and diced, or sliced with the chip cutter on food processor
2 medium leeks (white part and 2.5 cm/1 inch of the green), diced

500 ml/16 fl oz Chicken Stock (page 286) or stock from a cube
250 ml/8 fl oz double cream
30 g/1 oz unsalted butter
Sea salt
Freshly ground black pepper

1 Place potatoes, leeks and 250 ml/8 fl oz of the stock in 2 litre/3½ pint glass jug or bowl. Cover tightly with microwave cling film. Cook at 100% for 12 minutes.

2 Pierce film with the tip of a sharp knife, then remove from oven. Uncover and pass through a food mill fitted with a medium disc . Stir in cream, butter and remaining stock. Season with salt and pepper. Heat in a 2 litre/3½ pint soufflé dish, covered tightly, for 5 minutes. Serve piping hot.

VARIATION

VICHYSSOISE Increase cream by 125 ml/4 fl oz and stir in 2 teaspoons snipped fresh chives with cream, stock and butter. Chill well and serve with additional chives sprinkled on top, if desired.

MUSHROOM SOUP

A few wild mushrooms added to the cultivated ones will jazz up this soup no end. Russians who love mushroom soup, would probably add a dollop of soured cream to each bowl when serving. It makes a robust vegetarian soup if you use Vegetable Stock. *Serves 4*

30 g/1 oz unsalted butter
500 g/1 lb mushrooms, stalks trimmed, wiped clean and thinly sliced
1 celery stick, trimmed, stringed and finely chopped
1 small onion, peeled and finely chopped
500 ml/16 fl oz Chicken Stock (page 286), Vegetable Stock (page 290) or stock from a cube

4 teaspoons cornflour
125 ml/4 fl oz double cream
2 teaspoons fresh lemon juice
2 tablespoons chopped fresh dill
1 teaspoon sea salt (less if using a stock cube)
¼ teaspoon freshly ground black pepper

1 Heat butter in a 2.5 litre/4 pint soufflé dish, uncovered, at 100% for 2 minutes. Stir in mushrooms, celery and onions. Cover tightly with microwave cling film. Cook at 100% for 6 minutes.

2 Pierce film with the tip of a sharp knife, remove from oven and uncover. Stir in 125 ml/4 fl oz of the stock and let cool for 5 minutes.

3 Stir cornflour into cream. Add to mushroom mixture and stir well. Add lemon juice, dill, salt, pepper, and remaining stock; stir. Cover tightly with microwave cling film. Cook at 100% for 6 minutes. Serve hot.

To serve 8. Double all ingredients except butter. Cook mushroom mixture for 4 minutes. Cook an additional 8 minutes in step 3 after adding final ingredients.

DUXELLES SOUP

Duxelles is a kind of mushroom hash, finely chopped mushrooms sautéed in butter, that can be frozen or refrigerated for weeks. If you have some on hand, you can make a cup of mushroom soup in 5 minutes. *Serves 1*

250 ml/8 fl oz Chicken Stock (page 286) or stock from a cube
1 teaspoon cornflour
4 tablespoons Duxelles (page 294), fresh or defrosted (page 439)

1 tablespoon double cream or soured cream
2 drops Tabasco sauce
Large pinch freshly ground black pepper
Chopped fresh dill (optional)

1 Combine stock, cornflour, Duxelles and cream in a 500 ml/1 pint glass measuring jug. Cover tightly with microwave cling film. Cook at 100% for 5 minutes.

2 Pierce film with tip of a sharp knife, then remove from oven. Uncover and stir in Tabasco sauce and pepper. Sprinkle with fresh dill, if used.

To serve 2. Double all ingredients. Place in a 1 litre/2 pint glass measuring jug and cook for 7 minutes.

To serve 4. Use 4 times the amount for all ingredients. Place in a 2 litre/3½–4 pint glass measuring jug or bowl and cook for 10 minutes.

VARIATION

HEARTY MUSHROOM SOUP Make Duxelles Soup and place a quarter of a cooked baking potato, peeled, in each bowl.

VEGETABLE SOUP

— • • • —

This is a good, home-style vegetable soup. Add 30 g/1 oz cooked pasta if you want to make it heartier. *Makes 1 litre/1¾ pints*

30 g/1 oz unsalted butter or chicken fat
125 g/4 oz onion, peeled and chopped
2 medium or 3 small carrots, trimmed, peeled and chopped
2 celery sticks, trimmed, stringed and chopped

Pinch dried thyme
300 ml/½ pint tomato juice
500 ml/16 fl oz Chicken Stock (page 286) or stock from a cube
Sea salt
Freshly ground black pepper

1 Heat butter in a 2 litre/3½ pint glass jug or bowl, uncovered, at 100% for 2 minutes. Add onions and cook for 3 minutes longer.

2 Add carrots and celery. Add thyme and 4 tablespoons of the tomato juice and cook, uncovered, at 100% for 10 minutes.

3 Remove from oven. Pour into the container of a food processor and purée.

4 Return purée to the glass jug or bowl. Add as much of the remaining tomato juice as needed to make 500 ml/16 fl oz.

5 Add stock, and salt and pepper to taste. Cook, uncovered, at 100% for 2 minutes.

BEEF-BARLEY SOUP

◆ ◆ ◆

There is no winter day so cold that you won't warm up with this homestyle classic. Miraculously, the microwave oven cooks the beef perfectly in this tiny bit of time. Do remember to allow the time for the cooking of the barley. I sometimes make soup the day after I have made barley as a starch with dinner. The ideal leftover. *Serves 4*

600 ml/1 pint Creamy Barley (page 120)
900 ml/1½ pints Chicken or Lamb Stock (page 286) or stock from a cube
15 g/½ oz Italian dried mushrooms (*funghi porcini*) or ceps
2 medium carrots, trimmed, peeled and sliced in thin rounds

2 cloves garlic, smashed and peeled
¼ bay leaf
125 g/4 oz beef chuck, in 5 mm/¼ inch cubes
5 tablespoons chopped fresh dill
Sea salt
Freshly ground black pepper

1 Combine barley, 500 ml/16 fl oz of the stock, mushrooms, carrots, garlic, bay leaf and beef in a 2 litre/3½ pint glass jug or bowl. Cover tightly with microwave cling film. Cook at 100% for 14 minutes.

2 Pierce film with the tip of a sharp knife, then remove from oven. Uncover and discard bay leaf. Add dill and remaining stock. Season with salt and pepper and serve hot.

ACORN SQUASH SOUP

◆ ◆ ◆

Before the microwave oven, I would never have made this soup, because it took so long to cook acorn squash. Today, I make it frequently. The taste and golden colour are sensational. It is elegant enough for even the most sophisticated dinner party. *Serves 4*

1 medium acorn squash (about 500 g/ 1 lb), cut in half and seeded
3 cloves garlic, smashed and peeled
600 ml/1 pint Chicken Stock (page 286) or stock from a cube

1 tablespoon sea salt (less if using a stock cube)
Pinch freshly ground black pepper
Scant ⅛ teaspoon ground cardamom
30 g/1 oz unsalted butter, cut into small pieces (optional)

1 Arrange squash halves, cut sides down, in a suitable-size dish and cover tightly with microwave cling film. Cook at 100% for 7 minutes. Pierce film with the tip of a sharp knife, remove from oven and unwrap carefully. Scoop out flesh and purée with garlic in a food processor.

2 Combine the purée, stock and seasonings in a 1 litre/2 pint glass measuring jug and stir well. Cover tightly with microwave cling film. Cook at 100% for 10 minutes.

3 Pierce film, then remove from oven. Uncover and stir in butter, if desired.

To serve 8. Double all ingredients. Cook squash for 15 minutes. Use a 2 litre/3½ pint glass jug or bowl for step 2. Cook soup for 12 minutes.

ASPARAGUS SOUP

When asparagus have been in season for a while and all the hot and cold preparations, with vinaigrette, butter or Hollandaise, have begun to pall, then I make asparagus soup. I use only the trimmings, saving the tips for another dish. Asparagus soup made in the microwave oven is a delight, as it has a much clearer green colour than soup made on the stove. It may be served hot or chilled. *Serves 2*

Stalks and peelings from 500 g/1 lb asparagus, about 165 g/5½ oz trimmings (cleaned tips saved for another use)
350 ml/12 fl oz Chicken Stock (page 286) or stock from a cube

1 small onion, peeled and thinly sliced
2 teaspoons cornflour
1 teaspoon fresh lemon juice
½ teaspoon sea salt (less if using a stock cube)
⅛ teaspoon freshly ground black pepper

1 Place asparagus, stock and onions in a 1.5 litre/2½ pint soufflé dish. Cover tightly with microwave cling film. Cook at 100% for 15 minutes.

2 Pierce film with the tip of a sharp knife, then remove from oven. Uncover and pass through a food mill fitted with a fine disc.

3 Measure out 4 tablespoons of mixture; stir in cornflour and blend well. Stir this back into remaining mixture. Add lemon juice, salt and pepper. Cook, uncovered, at 100% for 6 minutes, until boiling and thickened. Serve hot or let cool to room temperature and refrigerate to serve chilled.

To serve 6. Multiply all ingredient quantities by 3 except lemon juice (double it). Cook asparagus with stock and onions in a 2 litre/3½ pint soufflé dish for 20 minutes. Increase final cooking time to 10 minutes.

SORREL SOUP

• ◆ •

Served cold, this is among the best of summer soups, lightly acid, refreshing, and smooth. In summer, I often keep a glass jar of it in the refrigerator. It can be thickened either with egg yolks or cornflour. If substituting cornflour use 2 tablespoons cornflour and follow technique in 250 ml/8 fl oz version. These basic ways of thickening are good to keep in mind for a host of cold summer soups. *Makes 1.5 litres/2½ pints; serves 6*

60 g/2 oz unsalted butter
250 g/8 oz chiffonade of sorrel (see note)
1 tablespoon sea salt (less if using a stock cube)
Freshly ground black pepper

125 ml/4 fl oz double cream
1 litre/1¾ pints Chicken Stock (page 286) or stock from a cube
6 egg yolks or 2 tablespoons cornflour, to thicken

1 Combine butter, sorrel, salt and pepper in a 2.5 litre/4 pint soufflé dish. Cook, uncovered, at 100% for 3 minutes.

2 Remove from oven. Stir in cream and stock. Cook, uncovered, at 100% for 7 minutes.

3 Remove from oven. Whisk 250 ml/8 fl oz of hot liquid into yolks and stir into remaining liquid. Cook, uncovered, at 100% for 2 minutes. Chill well before serving.

Note. To make a chiffonade, stack the sorrel leaves and cut into thin strips, 3 mm/⅛ inch wide, across the central vein. This keeps the soup from getting stringy.

To make 250 ml/8 fl oz. Combine 15 g/½ oz butter, 60 g/2 oz sorrel, ¾ teaspoon salt, and pepper in a 1 litre/2 pint glass measuring jug. Cook, uncovered, at 100% for 2 minutes. Add 2 tablespoons cream, 175 ml/6 fl oz stock and 1 teaspoon cornflour dissolved in 2 teaspoons cold water. Cook, uncovered, at 100% for 1 minute 30 seconds. Chill before serving.

VARIATION

HEARTY SORREL SOUP Before making the basic version of this soup, cook 2 baking potatoes for 11 minutes at 100%. While soup cooks for 7 minutes, peel potatoes and cut into 1 cm/½ inch dice. Add to soup when adding egg yolks; extend final cooking time to 4 minutes. *Serves 8.*

COLD BEETROOT BORSCHT

◆ ◆

Borscht is one of the world's most beautiful and best-tasting soups. Frankly, it has always been a little bit of a hassle to make. Now that I know how to cook beetroots in the microwave oven, I cook them ahead, keep them on hand, and make this soup for family or friends whenever it seems appropriate.

There are varying views of how to serve it. I eat it plain, but if I am giving a party, I set out little bowls of spring onions (both the green and white parts), chopped dill, soured cream, cooked peeled potato chunks (cold), and lemon wedges. *Serves 4*

500 ml/16 fl oz water
2 tablespoons white vinegar
100 g/3½ oz sugar
175 g/6 oz cooked beetroot, peeled and grated (page 419)
2 tablespoons fresh lemon juice or more, to taste

2 teaspoons sea salt
125 ml/4 fl oz double cream
175 ml/6 fl oz soured cream
4 teaspoons chopped fresh dill, for serving

1 Combine water, vinegar and sugar in a 1 litre/2 pint glass measuring jug. Cover tightly with microwave cling film. Cook at 100% for 5 minutes.

2 Pierce film with the tip of a sharp knife, then remove from oven. Uncover and stir in beetroot. Let cool.

3 When cool, add lemon juice, salt, cream and 125 ml/4 fl oz of the soured cream. Stir to combine. Add more lemon juice, if desired, and chill. Garnish each serving with a tablespoon of remaining soured cream and a teaspoon of dill.

To serve 8. Double ingredients. Cook water mixture 10 minutes in a 2 litre/3½ pint glass jug or bowl. Continue as for Cold Beetroot Borscht.

COLD CURRIED TOMATO SOUP WITH YOGURT

◆ ◆

Curried soups are somehow more cooling than other iced soups, as the British discovered in India more than a century ago. Make this ahead. *Serves 4*

2 tablespoons vegetable oil
1 clove garlic, smashed and peeled
1 small onion, peeled and sliced
1 tablespoon curry powder
250 ml/8 fl oz Lightly Cooked Crushed Tomatoes (page 293)

750 ml/1¼ pints Chicken Stock (page 286) or stock from a cube
150 g/5 oz frozen peas, defrosted in a sieve under warm running water
250 ml/8 fl oz plain yogurt
2 teaspoons fresh lemon juice

1 Heat oil in 2.5 litre/4 pint soufflé dish, uncovered, at 100% for 2 minutes. Stir in garlic, onion and curry powder. Cook, uncovered, at 100% for 8 minutes, stirring once.

2 Remove from oven. Add tomatoes, stock and peas. Cover tightly with microwave cling film. Cook at 100% for 5 minutes.

3 Pierce film with the tip of a sharp knife, then remove from oven and let stand, covered, until tepid.

4 Uncover. Stir in yogurt and lemon juice, and chill before serving.

GOOD GRAINS, PASTA & ...

———— ❖ ————

S ome of my favourite foods are starches. Now that the experts have told us all that we would be healthier if more of our daily diet came from such foods, I can feel virtuous as I indulge myself. While I sometimes eat these Italian style, as a first course, I like risottos, pastas, polentas and other grains enough to make them the whole meal. Sometimes that meal is breakfast—porridge and the like.

Vegetarians, of course, do make starches the heart of the meal a lot of the time. While some vegetarians do not eat milk or eggs, it is a good idea to combine milk products and eggs in a restricted diet to be sure of getting a full array of proteins. Cheese is often combined with rice, pasta and polenta in many lovely dishes. Cheese dishes are used as first courses when they are not being served as lunch or dinner.

RICE

I love rice. I love risotto. I think pilafs are spiffy, rice pudding delish. I have been known to crave paella, lap up arroz con pollo, giggle over Cajun dirty rice. There, it's out: I make a fool of myself over rice.

If I am just making boiled or steamed rice to go with dinner or to put in soup, I probably won't make it in the microwave oven. It takes about the same time as it does on top of the stove: of course, on top of the stove I have to allow time for the water to come to the boil. When it comes to the really good rice dishes, though, I turn to the microwave oven.

To identify different kinds of rice, learn more about them, and find out what substitutions you can make, see the entry on RICE in the Dictionary.

RISOTTO

If anything could convince the true cook, or even the ardent eater, that the microwave oven is a tool worth having, it would be that it makes risotto divinely, effortlessly, and relatively rapidly while the cook talks to the guests. From being a once-a-year treat, it can go to being an everyday delight.

Risotto is one of the great dishes that the Italians have given the world. It is rich and creamy in texture, much moister than ordinary rice without having the rice get overcooked. Partly this is achieved by using a special kind of rice, arborio, grown in the Po Valley, and partly by a special cooking method that flourishes from Milan to Venice. Traditionally, the rice is cooked in a hot fat until it turns white and then slow-cooked and continuously stirred as hot stock is added, spoonful by spoonful, as the rice absorbs the liquid in the pan.

With the microwave oven, all that stirring is a thing of the past. The very idiosyncrasy of cooking that makes the microwave oven generally unacceptable for the cooking of floury dishes makes risotto work well. Starch absorbs liquid slowly in the microwave oven, and it also absorbs too much. That is exactly what you want the rice to do in a risotto.

The reason there are so many recipes in this section is not only to give a panoply of wonderful flavours, but to deal with the fact that these are recipes that cannot be simply multipled or divided either by time or quantity. All the recipes are based on room temperature stock. Cold or hot will change the cooking time. The cooking dish may seem large for the quantities; but that is essential to allow for sufficient evaporation. Risotto is never covered as it cooks. Since you will get so much evaporation, be careful with salt if you are using stock from a cube. You may even want to dilute it with a further one-quarter water. Arborio is the rice of choice in most of these recipes; but you can also use another Italian rice called ambra if you want a slightly less glutinous texture, as I did in the Prawn and Spring Vegetable Risotto. You can cook long-grain rice the same way; it will taste wonderful but the texture will be entirely different.

Vegetarians should feel free to substitute Vegetable Stock or Oriental Vegetable Stock (page 290). Those who eat fish and seafood, but not meat, can use one of the fish stocks or *fumets* (page 289). Liquid left from soaking dried wild mushrooms, vegetable juices (see Tomato Risotto), cooked vegetables, purées, herbs, spices and leftover cooked meats can all be included in risottos and in the pilafs that follow. One of my favourites is made with leftover cooked duck and Duck Stock (page 286), made with the carcasses.

For a creamier risotto, additional stock may be added at the outset of standing time. For 200 g/7 oz arborio rice, add 4 tablespoons stock; for 100 g/3½ oz rice, add 2 tablespoons stock; for 50 g/1¾ oz rice, add 1 tablespoon stock. The Venetians would add even more stock and eat their risotto with a spoon. In most cases—aside from seafood risottos—they would also sprinkle it liberally with freshly grated Parmesan cheese.

Risotto is one of the great dishes subject to many variations once the technique is mastered. Unfortunately, it has always been time-consuming and last-minute. Except for Saffron Risotto, which is served in Milan as a side dish with Ossobuco, risotto is always a first course in Italy. I like risotto best as a side dish with grilled foods; it is too creamy to be used with most sauced dishes. Some risottos, like Prawn and Spring Vegetable Risotto, make light meals.

Risotto can be made ahead and reheated in the microwave oven. Make the risotto, but withhold one sixth of the liquid and stop cooking 2 minutes before the full time. Cover the partly cooked risotto loosely with paper towels. When your guests sit down, stir in the remaining liquid and cook at 100% for 3 minutes 30 seconds.

BASIC RISOTTO

There are numerous kinds of risotto. This is the classic, the one to return to. It doesn't get much better than this. I have a friend who makes the whole recipe as a meal for one—admittedly, exceptional. *Serves 3 as a first course, 6 as a side dish*

30 g/1 oz unsalted butter
2 tablespoons olive oil
125 g/4 oz onion, peeled and finely chopped
200 g/7 oz arborio rice
750 ml/1¼ pints Chicken Stock (page 286), stock from a cube or any other stock (see pages 286–291)

2 teaspoons sea salt (less if using a stock cube)
Freshly ground black pepper
Freshly grated Parmesan cheese (optional)

1 Heat butter and oil in a 25 cm/10 inch flan or deep pie dish, or 27.5 × 21 × 5 cm/11 × 8½ × 2 inch dish, uncovered, at 100% for 2 minutes. Add onions and stir to coat. Cook, uncovered, at 100% for 4 minutes. Add rice and stir to coat. Cook, uncovered, for 4 minutes more. (If using a small oven, cook onions for 7 minutes; add rice and cook for 7 minutes more.)

2 Stir in stock. Cook, uncovered, at 100% for 9 minutes. Stir well and cook for 9 minutes. (If using a small oven, cook for 12 minutes, stir and cook for 12 minutes more.)

3 Remove from oven. Let stand, uncovered, for 5 minutes to let rice absorb remaining liquid, stirring several times. Stir in salt, pepper and Parmesan cheese, if desired.

To serve 6 as a first course, 10 to 12 as a side dish. Double all ingredients. Cook butter, oil and onions as in step 1, using a 35 × 27.5 × 5 cm/14 × 11 × 2 inch dish. Add rice and cook for 4 minutes. Add stock and cook, uncovered, for 12 minutes. Stir and cook for 12 minutes more. Finish as for Basic Risotto.

To serve 2 as a first course, 4 as a side dish. Halve all ingredients and use a 22.5 cm/ 9 inch flan dish or 20 cm/8 inch square dish. Cook onions for 2 minutes and rice for 2 minutes more. Finish as for Basic Risotto.

To serve 1 as a first course, 2 as a side dish. Reduce butter and oil to 2 teaspoons each, onions to 1 tablespoon, rice to 50 g/1¾ oz, and stock to 300 ml/½ pint. Heat butter and oil in a large soup plate or flan dish. Add onions and rice and cook for 2 minutes. Finish as for Basic Risotto, cooking for 12 minutes total. Let stand for 3 minutes.

RISOTTO WITH RADICCHIO AND RED VERMOUTH

In this country, we are becoming used to seeing the leaves of round, red radicchio in salad. In Italy, radicchio comes in many shapes and is eaten more often cooked than raw. It loses most of its beautiful red colour, but it acquires a wonderful, slightly bitter taste. The flavour reminds me of aged red vermouth, so I have combined them. *Serves 4 as a first course or side dish*

30 g/1 oz unsalted butter
2 tablespoons olive oil
5½ tablespoons finely chopped onion
200 g/7 oz arborio rice
750 ml/1¼ pints Veal or Chicken Stock (page 286) or stock from a cube
4 tablespoon finely chopped parsley

125 g/4 oz radicchio, any kind, cored and shredded
2 tablespoons aged red Italian vermouth or other bitter vermouth
1½ teaspoons sea salt (less if using a stock cube)
Freshly gound black pepper
4 tablespoons freshly grated Parmesan cheese

1 Heat butter and oil in a 25 cm/10 inch flan dish or 27.5 × 21 × 5 cm/11 × 8½ × 2 inch dish, uncovered, at 100% for 2 minutes. Add onions and stir to coat. Cook, uncovered, at 100% for 2 minutes. Add rice and stir to coat. Cook for 2 minutes more.

2 Stir in stock and cook, uncovered, at 100% for 9 minutes. Stir in parsley and radicchio. Cook, uncovered, for 9 minutes more.

3 Remove from oven. Stir in vermouth, salt and pepper. Let stand for 6 minutes. Stir in cheese and serve.

SAFFRON RISOTTO

———— ◆ ◆ ————

This is the famous Milanese risotto that goes with Italian-Style Veal Knuckle (page 226). Its Buddhist-monk's-robe colour makes a great background for vegetable curries, casseroles and stews. *Serves 1 as a first course, 2 as a side dish*

1 teaspoon unsalted butter
1 teaspoon olive oil
2 tablespoons finely chopped onion
1 clove garlic, smashed, peeled and
  finely chopped (optional)
50 g/1¾ oz arborio rice

250 ml/8 fl oz Chicken Stock (page
  286) or stock from a cube
4 tablespoons white wine
9 threads saffron
Sea salt
Freshly ground black pepper

1 Heat butter and oil in a large soup plate or flan dish, uncovered, at 100% for 2 minutes.

2 Add onions, garlic and rice; stir to coat. Cook, uncovered, at 100% for 2 minutes.

3 Add stock, wine and saffron. Cook, uncovered, for 6 minutes. Stir well and cook for 6 minutes more.

4 Remove from oven. Stir in salt and pepper and serve hot.

To serve 2 as a first course, 4 as a side dish. Increase saffron to 12 threads and double all other ingredients. Heat butter in a 22.5 cm/9 inch flan dish or 20 cm/ 8 inch square dish. Continue as for single serving. Remove from oven and stir in salt and pepper.

To serve 3 as a first course, 6 as a side dish. Increase saffron to 16 threads and multiply all other ingredients by 4. Heat butter in a 27.5 × 21 × 5 cm/11 × 8½ × 2 inch dish or a 25 cm/10 inch flan dish. Cook onions for 4 minutes. Add rice and cook for 4 minutes more. Add stock and cook for 9 minutes. Stir and cook for 9 minutes more. Remove from oven and stir in salt and pepper.

TOMATO RISOTTO

———— ◆ ◆ ————

This dish is one you can play with: add a few dried mushrooms when you add the stock, or stir in some chopped fresh herbs as soon as you take the risotto out of the microwave oven. Because of the thickness of the tomato mixture, you get somewhat crunchy rice at the indicated cooking time. If you like your rice a little creamier—more traditional—cook it 5 minutes longer. Add salt with discretion, as both stock cubes and canned tomatoes can be salty. *Serves 3 as a first course, 6 as a side dish*

30 g/1 oz unsalted butter
2 tablespoons olive oil
125 g/4 oz onion, peeled and finely chopped
1 tablespoon finely chopped garlic (about 4 cloves)
200 g/7 oz arborio rice

400 g/14 oz can Italian tomatoes, puréed with juice
300 ml/½ pint Chicken Stock (page 286) or stock from a cube
Freshly ground black pepper
5½ tablespoons freshly grated Parmesan cheese
Sea salt (optional)

1 Heat butter and oil in a 25 cm/10 inch flan dish or 27.5 × 21 × 5 cm/11 × 8½ × 2 inch dish, uncovered, at 100% for 2 minutes.

2 Stir in onions and garlic. Cook, uncovered, at 100% for 4 minutes. Add rice and stir to coat. Cook for 4 minutes more.

3 Add tomatoes and stock. Cook, uncovered, at 100% for 9 minutes. Stir well and cook for 9 minutes more, 14 minutes for a thoroughly creamy risotto.

4 Remove from oven. Stir in pepper and cheese, add salt to taste, if desired, and serve hot.

To serve 6 as a first course, 10 as a side dish. Increase stock to 650 ml/22 fl oz and double all other ingredients. Heat butter in a 35 × 27.5 × 5 cm/14 × 11 × 2 dish for 2 minutes. Add onions and garlic and cook for 3 minutes. Add rice and cook for 4 minutes more. Stir in tomatoes and stock and cook for 18 minutes. Stir and cook for 18 minutes more. Remove from oven. Stir in pepper, cheese and salt to taste.

OLIVADA RISOTTO

◆ ◆ ◆

This is an absolutely untraditional recipe. It is delicious and decorative, with a rich olive flavour and a lightly black colour. It makes use of the jars of Italian olivada that can be bought in delicatessens. Don't add salt; the olivada is salty.
Serves 2 as a first course, 4 as a side dish

15 g/½ oz unsalted butter
1 tablespoon olive oil
2½ teaspoons finely chopped garlic (about 3 cloves)
100 g/3½ oz arborio rice
175 ml/6 fl oz canned chopped tomatoes with juice
250 ml/8 fl oz Chicken Stock (page 286) or stock from a cube

2 tablespoons olivada, Kalamata olive purée or tapenade
2 tablespoon freshly grated Parmesan cheese
2 tablespoons (packed) shredded fresh basil leaves
Freshly ground black pepper

1 Place butter, oil and 1½ teaspoons of the garlic in a 22.5 cm/9 inch flan dish or 20 cm/8 inch square dish. Heat, uncovered, at 100% for 2 minutes. Add rice and stir to coat. Cook, uncovered, at 100% for 2 minutes.

2 Stir in tomatoes and stock. Cook, uncovered, at 100% for 8 minutes. Stir well and cook for 8 minutes more.

3 Stir in remaining 1 teaspoon garlic, the olivada and the cheese. Cook, uncovered, at 100% for 2 minutes.

4 Remove from oven. Stir in basil and pepper. Serve hot.

To serve 4 as a first course, 8 as a side dish. Double all ingredients. Heat butter, oil and 4 teaspoons finely chopped garlic in a 27.5 × 21 × 5 cm/11 × 8½ × 2 inch dish. Add rice and cook for 4 minutes. Add tomatoes and stock and cook for 18 minutes, stirring after 9 minutes. Finish as for Olivada Risotto.

CABBAGE RISOTTO

◆ ◆ ◆

This unusual risotto is good on its own, but its combination with cabbage makes it a great vegetable dish. I never make small quantities of this because it hardly seems worth shredding the cabbage for a small amount. This riotto takes a little less than the usual amount of liquid because of the juice from the cabbage.
Serves 3 as a first course, 6 as a side dish

30 g/1 oz unsalted butter
2 tablespoons olive oil
5½ tablespoons finely chopped onion
200 g/7 oz arborio rice
650 ml/22 fl oz Chicken Stock (page 286) or stock from a cube
90 g/3 oz cabbage, shredded

4 tablespoons chopped parsley
2 teaspoons sea salt (less if using a stock cube)
Freshly ground black pepper
4 tablespoons freshly grated Parmesan cheese

1 Heat butter and oil in a 35 × 27.5 × 5 cm/14 × 11 × 2 inch dish, uncovered, at 100% for 2 minutes. Add onions and stir to coat. Cook, uncovered, at 100% for 2 minutes. Add rice and stir to coat. Cook, uncovered, for 2 minutes more.

2 Stir in stock. Cook, uncovered, at 100% for 9 minutes. Add cabbage and parsley and stir well. Cook, uncovered, for 9 minutes longer.

3 Remove from oven. Stir in salt, pepper and cheese. Serve hot.

To serve 6 as a first course, 12 as a side dish. Increase stock to 900 ml/1½ pints and double all other ingredients. Cook onions for 3 minutes. Add rice and cook for 4 minutes more. Add stock and cook for 12 minutes. Stir and cook for 12 minutes more. Remove from oven and stir in salt, pepper and cheese.

PRAWN AND SPRING VEGETABLE RISOTTO

❖ ❖ ❖

This dish is so beautiful that when *The New York Times* asked me to provide a microwave recipe that would be photographed for their entertaining issue, this is the one I chose. Italians use ambra rice rather than arborio in this recipe, both for its pale golden colour and for its lighter, less glutinous consistency, but arborio can be substituted. *Serves 6 as a main course, 10 as a first course*

45 g/1½ oz unsalted butter
3 tablespoons fruity olive oil
60 g/2 oz spring onions (white part only), trimmed and chopped
2 celery sticks, stringed and chopped
30 g/1 oz flat-leaf parsley, chopped
400 g/14 oz ambra rice
1 litre/1¾ pints Fish Stock (page 289), Clam Liquor (page 435), Chicken Stock (page 286) or fish stock from a cube
350 g/12 oz asparagus, trimmed, peeled and cut into 5 cm/2 inch lengths

500 g/1 lb raw medium prawns, peeled, deveined and cut in half crossways
125 g/4 oz shelled fresh peas or frozen petits pois, defrosted in a sieve under warm running water
1 to 2 teaspoons sea salt (less if using stock cubes)
½ teaspoon freshly ground black pepper
4 tablespoons chopped spring onion (green part only)
60 g/2 oz Parmesan cheese, freshly grated

1 Heat butter and oil in a 35 × 27.5 × 5 cm/14 × 11 × 2 inch dish, uncovered, at 100% for 3 minutes. Add spring onion whites, celery, parsley and rice and stir to coat. Cook, uncovered, at 100% for 4 minutes.

2 Stir in stock and cook, uncovered, at 100% for 12 minutes. Add asparagus, prawns and peas and stir well. Cook, uncovered, for 12 minutes more.

3 Remove from oven. Stir in salt and pepper. Cover loosely with paper towel and let stand for 8 to 10 minutes. Uncover, sprinkle with spring onion greens and cheese, and serve.

WILD RICE

••••

Wild rice is expensive. It is normally a nuisance to prepare because it requires a succession of soakings in fresh water. I find this microwave method infallible and rapid. Try it in a very festive meal. *Serves 4 as a side dish*

160 g/scant 5½ oz wild rice   Sea salt
500 ml/16 fl oz cold water   Freshly ground black pepper

1 Combine wild rice and water in a 2 litre/3½ pint glass jug or bowl. Cover tightly with microwave cling film. Cook at 100% for 12 minutes. (If using a small oven, cook for 20 minutes.)

2 Pierce film with the tip of the sharp knife, remove from oven and cover with a plate. Allow rice to stand for 15 minutes. Uncover. (If using a small oven, return to oven and cook, uncovered, at 100% for 10 minutes.) Drain. Add salt and pepper to taste and serve hot.

To serve 2. Combine 80 g/2¾ oz rice and 250 ml/8 fl oz water in a 1 litre/2 pint glass measuring jug. Cook for 7 minutes. Finish as for Wild Rice.

To serve 8. Combine 250 g/8 oz rice with 750 ml/1¼ pints water in a 27.5 × 20 × 7.5 cm/11 × 8 × 3 inch oval dish. Cook for 18 minutes. Pierce film, remove from oven and cover with a baking sheet. Let stand for 15 minutes. Uncover and cook for 10 minutes more. Finish as for Wild Rice.

MUSHROOMS AND LIVERS WITH WILD RICE

This is a delicious dish with roasted birds. Use it, without the rice, in omelets.
Serves 8

90 g/3 oz unsalted butter

125 g/4 oz onion, peeled, cut in half and sliced 3 mm/⅛ inch thick

90 g/3 oz mushrooms, rinsed and cut into 5 mm/¼ inch slices

4 cloves garlic, smashed and peeled

1 celery stick, stringed and cut on the diagonal into 5 mm/¼ inch slices

1 green apple (125 g/4 oz), peeled, cored and cut into 2.5 cm/1 inch chunks

175 g/6 oz livers from whatever bird you are using (chicken, duck, turkey, etc.), cleaned and cut into 4 cm/1½ inch chunks

1 teaspoon sea salt

¼ teaspoon freshly ground black pepper

240 g/8 oz cooked Wild Rice to serve 8 (see preceding recipe)

1 Heat butter in a 32.5 × 22.5 cm/13 × 9 inch dish, uncovered, at 100% for 3 minutes. Add onions, mushrooms, garlic, celery and apples and stir to coat. Cook, uncovered, at 100% for 4 minutes, stirring twice.

2 Remove from oven. Stir in remaining ingredients except rice. Cook, uncovered, at 100% for 2 minutes.

3 Remove from oven. Stir in Wild Rice and serve hot.

PILAF

The Indians, the Turks, the Persians and numerous peoples of Europe share a secret, the secret of pilaf. It's a good secret and, with the microwave oven, an easy one to unlock.

At first, a pilaf seems very much like risotto. The rice is cooked in fat with seasonings. Liquid is added for the final cooking. The difference is in the kind of rice used and in the covering of the rice for the final cooking with liquid. Less liquid is used, and the grains of rice remain separate and fairly dry. The long, thin grains of basmati rice are particularly suitable for pilaf, but you can use ordinary long-grain rice, or, even better, parboiled (not instant) rice (see RICE in the Dictionary).

Pilaf is more often used as an accompanying starch than risotto. Since it is less creamy, pilaf is better at absorbing sauces. Yet it has enough texture to serve as a contrast to simple fish dishes. When deciding what kind of pilaf to make, pick one whose seasonings and colour set off the main dish. Instead of Curried Pilaf with Curried Prawns, for example, serve Tomato Pilaf or Coriander Pilaf. Use the Curried Pilaf as a surprising contrast to Veal Fricassee (page 224), or to go with Chicken Breasts Normande (page 184). With Irish Stew (page 230), try Basic Pilaf or Green Pilaf.

If you are making the main course in the microwave oven, you will probably make the pilaf first. If so, uncover the pilaf when removing from the oven. After the main course is cooked, sprinkle 1 tablespoons water per portion over the pilaf. Cover tightly and heat for 2 minutes at 100% for four portions, 5 minutes for eight portions. That way, all parts of the meal will be hot.

Some pilafs serve as the main dish of a meal. These tend to be family meals rather than special dinners. In main course pilafs, the kind with meat, seafood or vegetables added to them, the same amount of rice serves fewer people than in side dish pilafs. This is true because people eat more pilaf when it is a main course. This means that if 175 g/6 oz of raw rice serves four people when cooked as a side dish, it will serve three when cooked in a main course combination.

BASIC PILAF

•‌•‌•

This can be made with any of the basic stocks in the Savoury Basics chapter, including the vegetarian stocks. There is virtually no limit to the variations you can ring on this theme. *Serves 4 as a side dish*

45 g/1½ oz unsalted butter
175 g/6 oz basmati rice, parboiled, or
  Carolina rice

350 ml/12 fl oz stock of choice
Sea salt
Freshly ground black pepper

1 Heat butter in a 2.5 litre/4 pint soufflé dish at 100% for 4 minutes. Stir in rice. Cook, uncovered, at 100% for 4 minutes. (In a small oven, cook 7 minutes.)

2 Add stock. Stir. Cover tightly with microwave cling film. Cook at 100% for 13 minutes. (If using a small oven, cook for 19 minutes.) Pierce film with the tip of a sharp knife, remove from oven and uncover; season to taste with salt and pepper.

To serve 8. Heat 60 g/2 oz butter in a 35 × 27.5 × 5 cm/14 × 11 × 2 inch dish for 5 minutes. Add 350 g/12 oz rice and cook as a for Basic Pilaf for 5 minutes. Add 750 ml/1¼ pints and cook for 16 minutes more. Finish as for Basic Pilaf.

VARIATIONS

CORIANDER PILAF FOR 4 Proceed as for Basic Pilaf. Add 4 cloves smashed and peeled garlic to melted butter. Cook, uncovered, for 3 minutes. Add rice and cook. Add stock and cook. One minute before end of cooking time, remove film; stir in 5½ tablespoons chopped fresh coriander and 45 g/1½ oz peeled, seeded and chopped cucumber. Re-cover with microwave cling film and cook for 2 minutes 30 seconds. Season to taste with salt and pepper. Serve topped with yogurt.

CORIANDER PILAF FOR 8 Double quantities of rice and stock. Increase butter to 60 g/2 oz. Use 10 cloves garlic, 30 g/1 oz coriander, and 100 g/3½ oz cucumber. Proceed as for Basic Pilaf.

GREEN PILAF FOR 4 Proceed as for Basic Pilaf. At end, stir in 45 g/1½ oz spinach washed, stemmed and chopped, and 5 tablespoons chopped parsley. Cook, uncovered, 1 minute 30 seconds.

GREEN PILAF FOR 8 Proceed as for Basic Pilaf, stirring in 45 g/1½ oz chopped parsley and 90 g/3 oz spinach washed, stemmed and chopped, at end. Increase final cooking time by 2 minutes.

TOMATO PILAF

— • • —

This pilaf may seem to use more liquid than some others, but that is because puréed tomatoes are thicker, part solid, so you have to use more. The mustard seeds add a surprising little crunch. *Serves 8 as a side dish*

60 g/2 oz unsalted butter
1 tablespoon mustard seed
350 g/12 oz basmati rice or Carolina rice

300 ml/½ pint Chicken Stock (page 286) or stock from a cube
400 g/14 oz can tomatoes with juice
Sea salt
Freshly ground black pepper

1 Heat butter in a 35 × 27.5 × 5cm/14 × 11 × 2 inch dish, uncovered, at 100% for 3 minutes. Stir in mustard seed and cook, uncovered, at 100% for 5 minutes. Add rice and stir to coat. Cook, uncovered, for 5 minutes longer.

2 Remove from oven. Stir in stock and tomatoes. Cover tightly with microwave cling film. Cook at 100% for 16 minutes.

3 Pierce film with the tip of a sharp knife, then remove from oven. Uncover and stir in salt and pepper to taste. Serve hot.

CURRIED PILAF

— • • —

If this weren't so special, it could be Basic Pilaf. It isn't dinner; but I am willing to think up excuses for using it. *Serves 4 as a side dish*

45 g/1½ oz unsalted butter
1 tablespoon Spice Powder III (page 299) or curry powder
125 g/4 oz onion, peeled and chopped
2 tablespoons raisins or flaked almonds
3 cloves garlic, smashed, peeled and sliced

175/6 oz basmati rice or Carolina rice
350 ml/12 fl oz Chicken Stock (page 286) or stock from a cube
75 g/2½ oz frozen peas, defrosted in a sieve under warm running water, or any cooked vegetable
Sea salt
Freshly ground black pepper

1 Heat butter in a 2.5 litre/4 pint soufflé dish, uncovered, at 100% for 2 minutes. Stir in spice powder, onions, raisins and garlic. Cook, uncovered, at 100% for 4 minutes. Add rice and stir to coat. Cook, uncovered, for 4 minutes more.

2 Pour stock over all. Stir. Cover tightly with microwave cling film. Cook at 100% for 13 minutes.

3 Pierce film with the tip of a sharp knife, then remove from oven. Uncover and stir in peas; add salt and pepper to taste. Serve hot.

To serve 8. Heat 60 g/2 oz butter in a 35 × 27.5 × 5 cm/14 × 11 × 2 inch dish for 5 minutes. Add 2 tablespoons spice powder, 60 g/2 oz onions, 30 g/1 oz raisins, and 5 cloves garlic; cook as for Curried Pilaf for 5 minutes. Add 350 g/ 12 oz rice and cook for 5 minutes more. Stir in 750 ml/1¼ pints stock and cook, covered, for 16 minutes. Double remaining ingredients; finish as Curried Pilaf.

VARIATIONS

VEGETARIAN CURRIED PILAF FOR 4 OR 8 For chicken stock, substitute half Coconut Milk (page 305) and half water. Proceed as for Curried Pilaf. For every 4 portions, stir in 30 g/1 oz desiccated coconut with peas, salt and pepper.

CURRIED PILAF WITH CHICKEN FOR 4 OR 8 Cook 6 chicken breasts to serve 4, cook 12 breasts for 8 (see page 430); cut into 2.5 cm/1 inch cubes. Prepare Curried Pilaf. Stir in chicken with peas, salt and pepper. Cover tightly with microwave cling film. Cook at 100% for 2 minutes for smaller amount, 4 minutes for larger amount.

CURRIED PILAF WITH LAMB FOR 4 OR 8 Substitute Lamb Stock (page 287) for chicken stock. Make Curried Pilaf, adding 250 g/8 oz lamb for 4 servings, 500 g/1 lb lamb for 8 servings, cut into 5 mm/¼ inch cubes, to rice. Add stock and cook, covered, for 15 minutes for smaller amount, 18 minutes for larger amount. Finish as for Curried Pilaf.

PILAF WITH HERBS AND LAMB FOR 4 OR 8 Eliminate spice powder. Cook as for Curried Pilaf with lamb. At end, stir in 15 g/½ oz chopped fresh dill or mint for 4 servings, 30 g/1 oz for 8 servings.

CREAMY BARLEY

◆·◆

We tend to overlook barley as a side dish. I use it more conventionally as part of a soup, as in Beef Barley Soup (page 102). But barley can be cooked like rice for risotto; it is creamy and delicious, a wonderful side dish for roast meat. *Serves 6 as a side dish*

30 g/1 oz unsalted butter
2 tablespoons olive oil
125 g/4oz onion, peeled and finely chopped
200 g/7 oz medium pearl barley

750 ml/1¼ pints Meat Stock (page 287) or stock from a cube
2 teaspoons sea salt (less if using a stock cube)
Freshly ground black pepper

1 Heat butter and oil in a 37.5 × 21 × 5 cm/11 × 8½ × 2 inch dish, uncovered, at 100% for 2 minutes. Add onions and stir to coat, Cook, uncovered, at 100% for 4 minutes. (If using a small oven, cook for 7 minutes.) Add barley and stir to coat. Cook for 2 minutes more. (In a small oven, cook for 5 minutes.)

2 Remove from oven. Stir in stock. Cook, uncovered, at 100% for 10 minutes. Stir well and cook for 15 minutes more. (If using a small oven, cook for 15 minutes, stir well, and cook for 23 minutes more.)

3 Remove from oven. Add salt and pepper and serve hot.

To serve 1 Heat 2 teaspoons each butter and oil in a 20 × 15 cm/8 × 6 inch dish. Stir in 1 tablespoon finely chopped onion and 50 g/1¾ oz barley and cook at 100% for 2 minutes. Add 300 ml/½ pint stock and finish as for Creamy Barley, cooking for 14 minutes total.

COUNTRY MACARONI WITH POTATOES AND PESTO

This delicious dish made with a sort-of-pesto is an ample dinner for vegans or vegetarians as well as people who don't have such an idea in their head. It is ideally made at the end of autumn when there is aplethora of basil. You can make the sauce in the time of abundance (through Step 3) and freeze it for a winter meal. The absence of nuts and cheese improves the keeping quality. You can, of course, sprinkle the whole thing with freshly grated Parmesan and even include pine nuts, but I don't think it's necessary. It will only make the dish more expensive and caloric. *Serves 7 as a side dish, 5 as a main course*

500 g/1 lb small, elbow macaroni
5½ tablespoons olive oil
125 g/4 oz onion, peeled and coarsely chopped
20 cloves garlic, smashed and peeled
500 g/1 lb spinach, stalks removed, washed and well dried

60 g/2 oz fresh basil leaves, washed
1½ teaspoons sea salt
Freshly ground black pepper, to taste
500 g/1 lb new potatoes, washed and cut into 5 mm/¼ inch dice

1 Bring a large pan of salted water to the boil on top of the stove. Continue with recipe while water comes to the boil. Cook macaroni and drain in a colander. Reserve.

2 Combine oil and onion in a 2.5 litre/4 pint soufflé dish. Cook, uncovered, at 100% for 3 minutes. Stir in garlic and cook, uncovered, for 3 minutes more. (If using a small oven, cook oil and onion for 6 minutes, add garlic and cook for 6 minutes more.)

3 Add spinach and basil and stir to combine. Cook, uncovered, at 100% for 7 minutes, stirring twice. (If using a small oven, cook for 12 minutes.) Remove from oven and transfer mixture to the container of a food processor or a blender. Process until very smooth. Add salt and pepper to taste. You will have 350 ml/12 fl oz sauce. Set aside.

4 Place potatoes around the inside edge of a 25 cm/10 inch flan dish. Sprinkle with 2 tablespoons of water. Cover tightly with microwave cling film. Cook at 100% for 10 minutes, or until potatoes are tender. (If using a small oven, cook for 15 minutes.) Prick film to release steam.

5 Remove from oven and uncover. Toss potatoes with 250 ml/8 fl oz of the reserved sauce and the cooked macaroni. Adjust seasoning and serve warm or cold. Remaining sauce can be frozen and used to sauce pasta or stir into soups.

SOFT POLENTA

• • •

The Italians are the most convincing thieves in the culinary business. They took tomatoes from the New World and made us think they were as Italian as pasta. Then they took American cornmeal mush and convinced us they knew more about it. Both Italian coarse-ground polenta and the finer cornmeal (also called maize meal) can be used to make this dish, which is a wonderful accompaniment to all sorts of foods. You can serve it (with or without Gorgonzola cheese) drizzled with the pan juices of roasted meats or birds, with grilled fish or with rich stews.

I think polenta has been less popular than potatoes because, cooked on top of the stove, it demands long and constant stirring, and even then there are likely to be lumps. Also, it has always worked best in quantity: no polenta for one or two. With the microwave oven, the polenta is stirred only once during the entire cooking time; it is guaranteed lumpless, and it can be made for one or for a crowd. If you can cook this in a serving dish, choose one with a cover; it will prevent the polenta from forming a skin and will, at the same time, keep it hot. *Serves 8 as a side dish*

1 litre/1¾ pints water
90 g/3 oz cornmeal
2 teaspoons sea salt
45 g/1½ oz unsalted butter

⅛ teaspoon freshly ground black pepper
60 g/2 oz softened Gorgonzola cheese
or 60 g/2 oz additional butter

1 Combine water, cornmeal and salt in a 2.5 litre/4 pint soufflé dish. Cook, uncovered, at 100% for 6 minutes. Stir well, cover loosely with paper towel, and cook for 6 minutes more. (If using a small oven, cook uncovered for 9 minutes; cover loosely and cook for 9 minutes.)

2 Remove from oven. Uncover and stir in butter, pepper and cheese (or additional butter). Let stand for 3 minutes. Serve hot.

To serve 1 or 2. Quarter all ingredients (use 3 tablespoons cornmeal). Proceed as for Soft Polenta, cooking in a soup bowl for 1 minute 30 seconds, uncovered, and then for another 1 minute 30 seconds, covered.

To serve 3 or 4. Combine 600 ml/1 pint water, 60 g/2 oz cornmeal, and 1 teaspoon salt in a 2 litre/3½ pint glass jug or bowl. Cook as for Soft Polenta for 5 minutes. Stir and continue cooking for 5 minutes longer. Finish as for Soft Polenta, stirring in 30 g/1 oz butter and a pinch of pepper.

VARIATION

SPICY POLENTA Use Cheddar or fresh goat cheese instead of Gorgonzola and add 1 fresh green chilli, stemmed, seeded and chopped.

FIRM POLENTA

This is a firmer polenta. Usually it is chilled, sliced and fried or grilled. Serve fried or grilled slices plain as a side dish or top with Chicken Livers (page 432) or Mushrooms and Livers with Wild Rice (page 116); or top each slice with a slice of Fontina or mozzarella cheese and grill until melted and bubbly. Fried or grilled polenta is also delicious with Bitter Broccoli Sauce (page 135). *Serves 8 as part of a first course or as a side dish*

1 litre/1¾ pints water
150 g/5 oz cornmeal
2 teaspoons sea salt

60 g/2 oz unsalted butter
⅛ teaspoon freshly ground black pepper

1 Combine water, cornmeal and salt in a 2.5 litre/4 pint soufflé dish. Cook, uncovered, at 100% for 12 minutes, stirring once.

2 Remove from oven, stir in 45 g/1½ oz of the butter, and add the pepper. Let stand for 3 minutes.

3 Lightly grease a 17.5 × 10 × 5 cm/7 × 4 × 2 inch loaf dish with half the remaining butter. Pour polenta into dish and brush lightly with the last of the butter. Let stand until cool.

4 Cover and refrigerate until chilled. To serve, slice the polenta about 1 cm/½ inch thick and fry or grill.

VARIATIONS

'FRIED' POLENTA Slice polenta 1 cm/½ inch thick and set the slices on a wire rack to dry for about 20 minutes. Heat 30 g/1 oz butter in a 25 cm/10 inch square browning dish at 100% for 3 minutes. Preheat conventional oven to lowest setting. Arrange half the polenta slices in a single layer in the dish. Cook, uncovered, at 100% for 6 minutes, turning once, until golden brown and firm. Remove from oven. Place slices on a baking sheet and place in conventional oven to keep warm. Repeat with remaining slices, using 15 g/½ oz butter or more, if needed. Serve immediately.

GRILLED POLENTA Preheat grill. Slice polenta 1 cm/½ inch thick and let dry as for Fried Polenta. Brush with olive oil and grill until crusty, about 2 minutes on each side.

MILLET

◆ ◆ ◆

Millet is a grain, small, round and yellowish. It is unfamiliar to many of us, but before sweetcorn (maize) came to Italy, it was widely used, ground, for polenta. I like to cook it whole as I do risotto. It is quick, and it is an unusual side dish. Of course, a vegetarian stock can be used. *Makes 2 litres/3½ pints*

125 g/4 oz unsalted butter
400 g/14 oz millet
1 litre/1¾ pints Chicken Stock (page 286), stock from a cube or Vegetable Stock (page 290)

1½ teaspoons sea salt (less if using a stock cube)
Freshly ground black pepper

1 Heat butter in a 35 × 27.5 × 5 cm/14 × 11 × 2 inch dish, uncovered, at 100% for 2 minutes.

2 Add millet and stir to coat. Pour stock over all. Cook, uncovered, at 100% for 10 minutes.

3 Remove from oven. Stir in salt and pepper and serve hot.

COUSCOUS

—— ◆ ◆ ◆ ——

Couscous is a pasta, although we seldom think of it that way. The traditional way to cook it calls for several steamings and rubbings. I like this as much, and it is much easier. *Serves 10 to 12 as a side dish*

1 medium onion, peeled and quartered
10 cloves garlic, smashed and peeled
125 g/4 oz unsalted butter
3 tablespoons ground cumin, preferably freshly ground
1 tablespoon curry powder
350 g/12 oz couscous

1 litre/1¾ pints Chicken Stock (page 286), stock from a cube, Vegetable Stock (page 290), tomato juice or water
1½ teaspoons sea salt (less if using a stock cube)
Freshly ground black pepper

1 Place onion, garlic and butter in the container of a food processor. Process until finely chopped. Scrape mixture into a 35 × 27.5 × 5 cm/14 × 11 × 2 inch dish. Cook, uncovered, at 100% for 2 minutes.

2 Stir in cumin and curry powder. Cook, uncovered, at 100% for 3 minutes.

3 Add couscous and stir to coat. Pour stock over all. Cook, uncovered, at 100% for 10 minutes.

4 Remove from oven. Stir in salt and pepper and serve.

To serve 5 or 6 as a side dish. Halve all ingredients. Cook onion mixture in a 2.5 litre/4 pint soufflé dish for 2 minutes. Add cumin and curry powder and cook for 2 minutes more. Add couscous, stir to coat, and pour stock on top. Cook, uncovered, at 100% for 6 minutes. Stir in salt and pepper and serve.

To serve 3 as a side dish. Divide all ingredient quantities by 4. Cook onion mixture in a 17.5 × 12.5 cm/7 × 5 inch oval or rectangular dish for 2 minutes. Add cumin and curry powder and cook for 2 minutes more. Add couscous, stir to coat, and add stock. Cook at 100% for 4 minutes. Season to taste with salt and pepper.

OLD-FASHIONED PORRIDGE

—— ◆ ◆ ◆ ——

When I was a child, every morning I was given cod liver oil, which I hated, hot cereal, which I loved, with butter melting on top, and a pitcher of double cream. That was good mothering. Maybe hot cereal will make a comeback because, with a microwave oven, it doesn't take too long at all. Cook porridge in a large container because it tends to boil over. Then sprinkle it with demerara sugar or spoon honey on top. Maybe we can bring back family breakfasts, especially on weekends. *Serves* 1

30 g/1 oz rolled oats (not 'quick-
   cooking')

Pinch sea salt
75 ml/6 fl oz water

1 Combine all ingredients in a 500 ml/1 pint glass measuring jug. Cover tightly with microwave cling film. Cook at 100% for 1 minute. Pierce film to release steam, then uncover and cook for 1 minute 30 seconds more. (If using a small oven, cook for 2 minutes, uncover and cook for 2 minutes more.)

2 Remove from oven. Let stand for 1 minute. Serve hot.

Serve 2 or 3. Double all ingredients. Combine in a 1 litre/2 pint glass measuring jug. Cover and cook at 100% for 2 minutes 30 seconds. Uncover and cook for 1 minute more. Remove from oven and let stand for 1 minute.

IRISH PORRIDGE

◆ ◆

These coarse-cut cereals once permitted poor people to thrive. Today, they are the luxury version of porridge. *Serves* 1

250 ml/8 fl oz water
15 g/½ oz coarse oatmeal

Pinch salt

1 Combine water and oatmeal in a 2 litre/3½ pint glass jug or bowl. Cover tightly with microwave cling film. Cook at 100% for 4 minutes and 30 seconds. Pierce film to release steam, then uncover and cook for 5 to 6 minutes more.

2 Remove from oven. Stir in salt and serve hot.

To serve 2 or 3. Combine 500 ml/16 fl oz water with 30 g/1 oz oatmeal in a 2 litre/3½ pint glass jug or bowl. Cover tightly with microwave cling film. Cook at 100% for 5 minutes. Uncover and cook for 5 minutes more. Stir and cook for 3 to 4 minutes more. Remove from oven, stir in salt to taste and serve hot.

SEMOLINA

— ❖ ❖ —

A nursery breakfast food made easy, to enjoy with butter and cream and sweetners if you want. I find cream is enough. It makes me feel like a happy child again. *Serves 4*

750 ml/1¼ pints water	1 teaspoon sea salt
90 g/3 oz fine wheat semolina	

1 Heat water in a 2 litre/3½ pint glass jug or bowl, uncovered, at 100% for 6 minutes. Add semolina and salt and stir well. Cook, uncovered, at 100% for 3 minutes.

2 Remove from oven. Serve hot.

To serve 2. Halve all ingredients. Heat water in a 1 litre/2 pint glass measuring jug for 3 minutes 30 seconds. Add remaining ingredients and cook for 2 minutes.

To serve 1. Heat 175 ml/6 fl oz water in a 600 ml/1 pint glass measuring jug for 2 minutes. Add 2 tablespoons semolina and ¼ teaspoon salt and cook for 1 minute.

CHILLIED BEANS

— ❖ ❖ —

My Chilli (page 208) doesn't have beans in it, but I often serve beans on the side, as I do with many Mexican and Texan dishes, either straight up or as Refried Beans (see variation that follows). These I think, are very tasty. *Serves 4*

175 g/6 oz dried pink, red or black beans	Pinch freshly ground black pepper
1 medium onion, peeled and quartered	1 teaspoon chilli powder
4 cloves garlic, smashed and peeled	1 teaspoon ground cumin
	1 bay leaf

1 Put beans in a 2.5 litre/4 pint soufflé dish and cover with 500 ml/16 fl oz water. Cover tightly with microwave cling film. Cook at 100% for 15 minutes.

2 Pierce film with the tip of a sharp knife, then remove from oven. Let stand for 5 minutes. Uncover and add 500 ml/16 fl oz very hot tap water. Re-cover tightly and let stand for 1 hour.

3 Uncover beans, drain, and rinse. Return them to soufflé dish and add remaining ingredients. Stir to combine. Add 1 litre/1¾ pints warm water. Cover tightly with two sheets of microwave cling film. Cook at 100% for 35 minutes.

4 Pierce film, then remove from oven. Let stand, covered, for 20 minutes. Uncover, stir, and serve.

VARIATION

REFRIED BEANS Make Chillied Beans and pass through a food mill fitted with a medium disc. Reserve. Combine 30 g/1 oz lard or 2 tablespoons vegetable oil and 2 tablespoons finely chopped onions in a 25 cm/10 inch flan dish. Cook, uncovered, at 100% for 2 minutes. Remove from oven. Stir in Chillied Beans and 1 teaspoon sea salt and spread mixture evenly in dish. Cook, uncovered, at 100%, for 4 minutes. Leaving dish in oven, stir and smooth mixture again. Cook for 3 minutes more.

BLACK-EYE BEANS

Black-eye beans are much loved in the Southern United States and, in the guise of Hoppin' John (see below), are traditional on New Year's Day. They are so filling that no extra meat is needed. *Makes 750 ml/1¼ pints*

1 smoked gammon hock (knuckle), about 250 g/8 oz, split and washed	150 g/5 oz black-eye beans

1 Place hock in a 1 litre/2 pint glass measuring jug with 500 ml/16 fl oz water. Cover tightly with 2 sheets of microwave cling film. Cook at 100% for 35 minutes.

2 Pierce film, then remove from oven. Uncover and drain; reserve liquid and gammon hock.

3 Place beans and 500 ml/16 fl oz water in a 2.5 litre/4 pint soufflé dish. Cover tightly with microwave cling film. Cook at 100% for 15 minutes.

4 Pierce film with the tip of a sharp knife, then remove from oven. Let stand for 5 minutes. Uncover and add 500 ml/16 fl oz very hot tap water. Re-cover with a fresh piece of microwave cling film. Let stand for 1 hour.

5 Uncover, drain, and rinse beans. Return to soufflé dish and add reserved gammon hock. Place reserved cooking liquid in a 1 litre/2 pint glass measuring jug and add enough water to fill. Pour over beans and ham. Cook, tightly covered, at 100% for 35 minutes.

6 Pierce film, then remove from oven. Let stand, covered, for 20 minutes. Uncover and drain cooking liquid back into 1 litre/2 pint jug. Cook, uncovered, at 100% for 16 minutes, until reduced to 175 ml/6 fl oz. Remove meat from gammon hock and discard bone and skin. Place meat with beans.

7 Remove liquid from oven. Add to meat and beans; stir. Serve hot.

VARIATION

HOPPIN'JOHN Omit gammon hock and prepare beans through step 4. Drain and rinse beans. Use all water instead of part gammon hock cooking liquid. Cook 4 thick rashers bacon in a 27.5 × 20 × 5 cm/11 × 8 × 2 inch dish, uncovered, at 100% for 3 minutes. Add 90 g/3 oz chopped onions and 175 g/ 6 oz long-grain rice. Cook, uncovered, at 100% for 4 minutes. Add 2 teaspoons salt, 500 ml/16 fl oz water and beans. Cover tightly with microwave cling film. Cook at 100% for 20 minutes. Finish as for Black-Eye Beans.

POTATOES

Here are a few very special recipes for potato dishes that fare exceptionally well in the microwave oven. Consult the Index and the Dictionary for more ways to cook potatoes.

GARLIC POTATOES

This is a microwave version of my favourite potato recipe. I find you can never have too many of these potatoes. They are good cold and they can be reheated. Serve them with roast meat, grilled chicken, or as good company to stewed vegetables. *Serves 4 as a side dish*

500 g/1 lb small new potatoes (about 10 potatoes), scrubbed and patted dry
6 large cloves garlic, smashed and peeled

3 tablespoons good-quality olive oil
½ teaspoon sea salt
Freshly ground black pepper

1 Place potatoes in a 1.5 litre/2½ pint soufflé dish. Add remaining ingredients and stir to coat potatoes. Cover tightly with microwave cling film. Cook at 100% for 10 to 15 minutes (depending on size of potatoes), shaking dish once to redistribute potatoes. Potatoes are done when the tip of a small knife easily pierces the flesh to the centre.

2 Pierce film with the tip of a sharp knife, then remove from oven. Uncover and serve hot.

To serve 8 to 10. Combine 2 kg/4 lb potatoes, 15 cloves garlic, 175 ml/6 fl oz oil, 2 teaspoons salt, and pepper to taste in a 35 × 27.5 × 5 cm/14 × 11 × 2 inch dish. Cook at 100% for 20 minutes, shaking dish once to redistribute potatoes.

POTATO GALETTE

This is a thin little cake of crisply cooked potatoes such as you would find in any major French restaurant. Serve it with lightly sauced foods. The reason you have to arrange the potatoes beforehand is to be able to transfer them quickly to the preheated browning dish before it cools. *Serves 1*

20 g/⅔ oz unsalted butter
1 waxy potato (250 g/8 oz), peeled and very thinly sliced

Sea salt
Freshly ground black pepper

1 Heat half of the butter in a ramekin, uncovered, at 100% for 1 minute. Reserve.

2 Arrange potato slices to overlap in a circle on a dinner plate.

3 Heat remaining butter in a 20 cm/8 inch square browning dish, uncovered, at 100% for 2 minutes.

4 Remove from oven. With a wide metal spatula transfer potatoes to browning dish, being careful to keep them in a circle. Brush with reserved melted butter. Cook, uncovered, at 100% for 3 minutes. Carefully turn potatoes over and cook for 1 minute 30 seconds more.

5 Remove from oven. Season with salt and pepper and serve hot.

To serve 4. Increase butter to 45 g/1½ oz and use 4 potatoes (about 1 kg/2 lb). Proceed as for single serving, using a 25 cm/10 inch square browning dish; arrange potato slices in four rows (1 potato per row). Heat second half of butter in the dish for 3 minutes and cook potatoes for 5 minutes. Turn and cook for 3 minutes more. Season and serve hot.

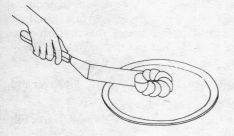

Arrange thinly sliced potatoes in a circle—for 1—transfer with spatula.

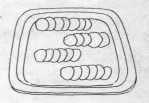

Arrange potatoes in lines—for 4—and transfer to browning dish.

SWEET POTATO PURÉE

This is a smooth creamy purée in the French style. Try it for a change instead of mashed potatoes. *Serves 4 as a side dish*

1 kg/2 lb orange-fleshed sweet potatoes (about 2 large potatoes), each pricked 3 or 4 times with a fork
275 ml/9 fl oz double cream

125 g/4 oz unsalted butter
2 teaspoons sea salt
Freshly ground black pepper

1 Cook potatoes, uncovered, at 100% for 13 to 15 minutes, until tender. Remove from oven and peel.

2 Pass potatoes through the medium disc of a food mill. Add remaining ingredients and mix well. Serve hot.

To serve 8. Double all ingredients. Cook potatoes at 100% for 25 minutes.

Note. Mixture may be made in advance and kept, tightly covered and refrigerated, for up to 3 days. Then heat purée, uncovered, at 100% for 5 minutes before serving.

PASTA

I use the Italian word because it is the best known. Most parts of the world have at least one kind of noodle made with various kinds of grains and with or without eggs.

The nice thing about pasta is it permits you to invent endlessly and make something to eat when there is nothing in the house. You can chop up 250 g/8 oz or so of any vegetable mix that appeals to you—generally including some onion and garlic—and cook. Put 45 g/1½ oz of butter or 3 tablespoons olive oil in a 22.5 × 32.5 cm/9 × 13 inch dish; cook for 3 minutes, uncovered, at 100%. Stir in vegetables and 2 tablespoons of fresh chopped herbs, if you want. Cover tightly with microwave cling film and cook for 5 minutes at 100%. Pierce film, then uncover. Add 5–6 tablespoons double cream or Lightly Cooked Crushed Tomatoes (page 293). Cook, uncovered, for 3 minutes. Use to top 500 g/1 lb linguine, cooked.

See Savoury Sauces (pages 312–333) for some pasta sauces. Fish and Seafood (pages 143–179) has some nice recipes for saucy clams and mussels. They are very good served over pasta.

The only thing to remember is that the water for the pasta must be started well before the sauce.

PASTA PRIMAVERA
• • •

While I tend to think that the flavour obtained by cooking the vegetables with sauce is best, in recent years many versions of Pasta Primavera, a dish made famous by Le Cirque restaurant in New York, have become popular. The problem has been that each vegetable needed to be cooked separately in its own pan of boiling salted water. The preparation was endless. Thanks to the way the microwave oven cooks differentially from the outside to the inside of a dish, all the vegetables can be cooked together quickly and come out as if each were lovingly and separately tended. You can bring the array of vegetables to the table in their cooking dish and toss them into the pasta that has previously been mixed with the two sauces—spectacular. *Serves 8 to 10 as a first course, 6 to 8 as a main course*

60 g/2 oz unsalted butter
2 tablespoons Chicken Stock (page 286) or stock from a cube
125 ml/4 fl oz double cream
500 ml/16 fl oz Lightly Cooked Crushed Tomatoes (page 293)
3 tablespoons olive oil
2 cloves garlic, smashed, peeled and finely chopped
1 tablespoon finely chopped fresh hot red or green chillies, or ½ teaspoon dried chilli flakes
4 tablespoons finely chopped parsley
175 g/6 oz broccoli florets
350 g/12 oz green beans, trimmed and cut into 2.5 cm/1 inch lengths

250 g/8 oz courgettes, trimmed and cut into 5 × 1 × 1 cm/2 × ½ × ½ inch strips
90 g/3 oz mange-touts, trimmed
4 asparagus spears, trimmed, peeled and cut into 5 cm/2 inch lengths
75 g/2½ oz peas, fresh or frozen
250 g/8 oz mushrooms, thinly sliced
30 g/1 oz pine nuts
1 tablespoon vegetable oil
500 g/1 lb spaghetti or spaghettini
60 g/2 oz Parmesan cheese, freshly grated
2 tablespoons sea salt
6 fresh basil leaves

1 Combine butter, stock and cream in a 500 ml/1 pint glass measuring jug. Cook, uncovered, at 100% for 5 minutes. Reserve.

2 Combine tomatoes, olive oil, garlic, chillies and parsley in a 1 litre/2 pint glass measuring jug. Cook, uncovered, at 100% for 5 minutes. Reserve.

3 Place a large pan of water on the stove to boil for the spaghetti.

4 In a 35 × 27.5 × 5 cm/14 × 11 × 2 inch dish, arrange the vegetables in concentric rings, with broccoli inside rim, then green beans, courgettes, mange-touts and asparagus. Mound peas in centre.

5 Toss mushroom slices and pine nuts in oil and sprinkle over vegetables. Cover tightly with microwave cling film. Cook at 100% for 7 minutes.

6 Cook pasta in boiling water and drain.

7 Pierce film with tip of a sharp knife, then remove dish from oven.

Arrange vegetables in concentric rings with the slowest-cooking around the inside rim of dish and the quick-cooking vegetables in the centre.

8 Reheat reserved sauces at the same time, in their separate measures, uncovered, at 100% for 4 minutes.

9 Place drained pasta in a large ceramic dish that will fit into the microwave oven. While pasta is hot, toss with vegetables, cream sauce and half of the tomato sauce.

10 Reheat pasta, uncovered, at 100% for 4 minutes.

11 Remove from oven and toss with Parmesan cheese, salt and basil. To serve, spoon some of remaining tomato sauce over each portion.

PASTA WITH BITTER BROCCOLI SAUCE

This is a simple, classic Italian pasta dish made with what is called broccoli di rape (see BROCCOLI DI RAPE in the Dictionary). It's a shame bitter broccoli isn't better known in this country. I often eat it without the pasta as a first course or with poached fish. Without pasta, but combined with the seasonings, it will serve four. *Serves 8 as a first course, 4 as a light dish*

500 g/1 lb spaghetti
175 ml/6 fl oz olive oil
14 cloves garlic, smashed and peeled
½ teaspoon dried chilli flakes

750 g/1½ lb broccoli di rape (2 bunches), cleaned and trimmed
2 teaspoons sea salt
Freshly grated Parmesan cheese

1 Bring a large pan of salted water to the boil for the pasta. When the water is boiling, add pasta and cook until al dente. Drain well.

2 Combine oil, garlic and chilli flakes in a 35 × 27.5 × 5 cm/14 × 11 × 2 inch dish. Heat, uncovered, at 100% for 4 minutes. Add broccoli and stir to coat. Cover tightly with microwave cling film. Cook at 100% for 10 minutes.

3 Pierce film with the tip of a sharp knife, then remove from oven. Uncover and stir well. Add drained pasta and salt and toss to combine. Serve hot with cheese on the side.

To serve 4 as a first course, 2 as a light dish. Cook and drain 250 g/8 oz pasta. Heat 5 tablespoons oil, 6 cloves garlic and a pinch of dried chilli flakes in a 27.5 × 21 × 5 cm/11 × 8½ × 2 inch dish, uncovered, for 3 minutes. Add 350 g/ 12 oz broccoli, cover, and cook for 7 minutes.

LASAGNE

• • •

Is there anybody who doesn't like lasagne? I don't think so. This one is made with meat sauce, but vegetarian versions can be made by substituting Duxelles (page 294) or Creamed Spinach (page 260) with some chopped basil for 500 ml/16 fl oz of the Bolognese Sauce and using 250 ml/8 fl oz of Chunky Tomato Sauce (page 324). Just make more layers. *Serves 8 as a main course*

5 sheets (about 250 g/8 oz) store-bought fresh lasagne noodles, 20 × 25 cm/8 × 10 inches (see note)
1 litre/1¾ pints Salsa Bolognese (page 326)

750 ml/1¼ pints Basic Béchamel (page 316)
350 g/12 oz Parmesan cheese, freshly grated

1 Bring a large pan of salted water to the boil.

2 Slip the pasta sheets, one at a time, into the boiling water. When the water returns to the boil, remove from heat. Drain immediately and refresh pasta under cold running water. Leave the pasta in cool water while you assemble the lasagne.

3 Cover the bottom of a 25 × 20 × 10 cm/10 × 8 × 4 inch dish with a thin layer of Bolognese Sauce. Lay a sheet of pasta on top. Pour about 250 ml/8 fl oz of the sauce over the pasta, then spoon over it 125 ml/4 fl oz of Béchamel. Sprinkle with 75 g/2½ oz of the cheese. Repeat these layers 3 times, ending with pasta. Spoon remaining Béchamel on top an sprinkle with remaining cheese. Cook, uncovered, at 100% for 15 minutes.

4 Remove from oven. Let stand for 5 to 10 minutes before serving.

Note. If fresh lasagne noodles are not available, use dried noodles, cooking them for 5 minutes.

MACARONI CHEESE

• • •

Do you know people so sophisticated they won't admit to loving macaroni cheese? I do. They are missing something very good. This is quicker than what you get in a packet and a lot better. To make a more authentic brown and bubbly macaroni cheese, run the dish under the grill after cooking. *Serves 1 as a main course, 2 as a side dish*

175 ml/6 fl oz milk
1 tablespoon cornflour
45 g/1½ oz Cheddar cheese, grated

½ teaspoon sea salt
1 teaspoon unsalted butter
Freshly ground black pepper
60 g/2 oz macaroni, cooked

1 Combine milk and cornflour in a 1 litre/2 pint glass measuring jug. Heat, uncovered, at 100% for 3 minutes.

2 Whisk in cheese, salt, butter and pepper. Fold in cooked macaroni and pour mixture into a large soup bowl or serving dish. Cook, uncovered, at 100% for 3 minutes.

3 Remove from oven. Serve hot.

To serve 2 as a main course. Combine 250 ml/8 fl oz milk and 2 tablespoons cornflour in a 1 litre/2 pint soufflé dish and cook for 3 minutes. Add 75 g/2½ oz cheese, 1½ teaspoons salt, 1 teaspoon butter, pepper and 150 g/5 oz macaroni, cooked. Cook, uncovered, at 100% for 4 minutes.

To serve 4 as a main course. Combine 500 ml/16 fl oz milk and 3 tablespoons cornflour in a 25 × 20 cm/10 × 8 inch dish and cook for 4 minutes. Add 135 g/4½ oz cheese, 2½ teaspoons salt, pepper and 30 g/1 oz butter. Fold in 300 g/10 oz macaroni, cooked. Cook, uncovered, at 100: for 4 minutes 30 seconds.

Note. This dish may be frozen. Turn out cooked and cooled food on to a large sheet of aluminium foil. Close tightly, retaining shape of cooked food. Freeze. To defrost, unwrap, return food to original cooking dish and cover tightly with microwave cling film. Heat at 100% for 3 minutes. Prick film, then remove from oven and uncover. Grill until bubbly.

CHEESE

Not every day needs meat, and cheese is a natural replacement. A nice thing about most cheese dishes, as you can see from Macaroni Cheese (page 136) and Lasagne (page 136), is that they are equally appropriate as first and main courses.

QUICHE LORRAINE

When done right, this much-abused dish is simple and delicious. Here is a light, crustless version. If you want a pastry case, blind-bake it in standard fashion. Pour in quiche mixture after step 3 and continue with recipe. *Serves 6 as a first course, 4 as a light dish*

175 g/6 oz cooked ham, cut into 1 cm/ ½ inch cubes
1 small onion, diced
22 g/¾ oz unsalted butter
4 eggs
175 ml/6 fl oz milk

125 ml/4 fl oz double cream
175 g/6 oz Gruyère cheese, grated
½ teaspoon sea salt
Pinch freshly ground black pepper
Pinch freshly grated nutmeg

1 Preheat conventional grill.

2 Combine ham, onions and butter in a 25 cm/10 inch flan dish. Cook, uncovered, at 100% for 3 minutes.

3 Stir together remaining ingredients. Pour over ham mixture and stir to combine. Cook, uncovered, at 50% for 3 minutes. Stir well and cook, uncovered, at 50% for 3 minutes more. Cover with a very tightly fitting lid or microwave cling film. Cook at 50% for 3 minutes.

4 If using cling film, pierce to release steam, then remove from oven and uncover. Cover with a tea towel and let stand for 8 to 10 minutes. Just before serving, carefully brown top under the grill.

CHEDDAR TOASTS

—— • ◆ • ——

When friends drop by for a glass of wine, or you need a simple savoury for a rare, Port occasion, these quickly prepared toasts do the trick. You could put some anchovy paste on the toasted bread slices before adding the cheese to vary the taste. *Makes 10 toasts*

60 g/2 oz Cheddar cheese, grated
1 tablespoon Dijon mustard
Pinch cayenne pepper

10 slices French bread, cut on the
   diagonal into 1 cm/½ inch thick
   slices

1 Combine cheese, mustard and cayenne in a small bowl. Reserve.

2 Place bread slices around the inside rim of a 25 cm/10 inch ceramic platter or flan dish. Cook at 100% for 2 minutes.

3 Remove dish from oven. Turn slices over. Divide cheese mixture evenly among slices, pressing it into the bread. Cook, uncovered, for 1 minute, or until cheese is melted.

4 Remove from oven. Let cool for several minutes and serve.

GILDED CHEESE

—— • ◆ • ——

A toasted cheese sandwich is probably the best use of browning dishes. A thin slice of ham may be added to each sandwich without changing the cooking time. Varying the cheese or adding a light coating of mustard will give you changes of pace. Consider removing the crusts from the bread and slicing each sandwich into 3 strips to make a hot hors d'oeuvre. Be careful: the cheese in these gets very hot. *Serves 1*

2 slices white bread
2 slices Cheddar cheese

15 g/½ oz unsalted butter, softened

1 Preheat a 25 cm/10 inch round browning dish (preferably one with a metal cooking surface) at 100% for 5 minutes.

2 Put together the sandwich. Butter each side of the sandwich. Place in the browning dish and cook, uncovered, at 100% for 1 minute. Flip the sandwich over and cook for 1 minute more.

3 Remove from oven. Serve hot.

To serve 2. Double all ingredients and proceed as for single serving.

FONDUTA

— • • —

Fondue is Swiss. Just to Switzerland's south, over a mountain peak, Italy starts. Italians make a dish with melted cheese that I prefer to fondue called fonduta. In its most luxurious version, it is served without bread but with freshly shaved, beastly expensive white truffles and freshly ground black pepper on top.

Fontina cheese melts evenly and has a mildly nutty flavour. *Makes 1 litre/1¾ pints, to serve 8 to 10 as a first course*

500 ml/16 fl oz milk
250 g/8 oz Italian Fontina cheese, grated
60 g/2 oz unsalted butter
2 egg yolks
Sea salt

Freshly ground black pepper
1 loaf country-style French bread (optional)
Italian white truffles, thinly shaved (optional)

1 Heat milk in a 2 litre/3½ pint glass jug or bowl, uncovered, for 4 minutes at 100%.

2 Place cheese, butter and egg yolks in the container of a food processor. Quickly pour in hot milk. Process for 2 minutes.

3 Scrape mixture back into the jug. Cook, uncovered, for 3 minutes at 100%. Whisk. Cook for 3 minutes longer.

4 Return hot mixture to food procesor. Process for 30 seconds. Season to taste with salt and pepper.

5 Serve in individual bowls or ramekins. Fonduta can be served with grilled pieces of country-style bread. The ultimate luxury is to top the creamy cheese mixture with thin shavings of white truffle.

FONDUE

— • • —

There was a time when fondue parties were all the thing, and every bride received a fondue set with a small burner to keep the fondue warm and long-handled forks to stick the chunks of bread on as they were stirred in the cheese. Ah, we are fickle: the fondue sets got stashed in the cupboard, partly, I think, because the fondue had a nasty trick of coming apart just when you needed to serve it and there was no way of reheating it. Well, I think fondue is still good, and the microwave oven makes it fail-safe; it can even be reheated. So dust off the fondue set, but use a soufflé dish instead of the little pot. If you like, pass a bowl of toasted caraway seeds separately. Dip cheese-covered bread into seeds. Don't be tempted to experiment with the cheese: the natural Swiss cheeses work, while others often don't. *Makes 250 ml/8 fl oz, to serve 4 as a light meal or first course*

250 ml/8 fl oz dry white wine
2 cloves garlic, smashed and peeled
250 g/8 oz Swiss Gruyère or
  Emmentaler cheese
2 teaspoons kirsch

1 loaf country-style French bread, cut in
  4 cm/1½ inch cubes, each with some
  crust
Toasted caraway seeds (optional)

1 Put white wine and garlic in a 1 litre/2 pint soufflé dish. Cook, uncovered, at 100% for 5 minutes.

2 Place cheese in the container of a food processor. Pour in hot wine. Process for 2 minutes.

3 Return mixture to soufflé dish. Cook, uncovered, at 100% for 2 minutes; stir; cook for 2 minutes longer.

4 Put soufflé dish on heat source at the table. Stir in kirsch. Serve with bread chunks.

To reheat fondue. Fondue can be made ahead without risk, even a day ahead. The cooled fondue will congeal into a piece of rubber covered with liquid. Fear not; the microwave is here. Let fondue come to room temperature in the soufflé dish. Cook, uncovered, at 100% for 4 minutes. Remove from oven and whisk vigorously. Serve.

CHEDDAR CHEESE SAUCE

Just because we have learned to be fancy doesn't mean that we should ignore the homely pleasures of Cheddar Cheese Sauce. It can make a meal poured over toast and briefly grilled in the guise of Welsh Rarebit. Topped with a fried egg, it is a Golden Buck. Mixed with fresh chillies and spread on tortilla chips and lightly grilled, it becomes nachos. Mixed with the same chillies but with the chips on the side, it is a dip. Use it as a topping for hamburgers, Old-Fashioned Meat Loaf (page 214) or broccoli.

One thing to beware of: if you want to add Tabasco sauce, Worcestershire sauce, bitters or prepared mustard to spice up your cheese sauce or rarebits, follow the directions in the Welsh Rarebit variation or you will find yourself with a grainy mess.

This sauce stores, refrigerated, virtually forever. It can easily be reheated by placing it in the microwave oven for 2 minutes 30 seconds, uncovered, at 100%. Stir before serving. *Makes 300 ml/½ pint*

125 ml/4 fl oz milk
250 g/8 oz Cheddar cheese, grated

Sea salt
Freshly ground black pepper

1 Heat milk in a 500 ml/1 pint glass measuring jug, uncovered, at 100% for 1 minute.

2 Remove from oven. Add cheese and stir to moisten. Scrape mixture into a blender or food processor and purée until smooth.

3 Return to jug. Heat, uncovered, at 100% for 30 seconds. Remove from oven and stir.

VARIATIONS

NACHO SAUCE Before heating cheese sauce for final 30 seconds, add 1 thinly sliced fresh green chilli or 1 teaspoon Fiery Pepper Sauce (page 297).

WELSH RAREBIT Prepare cheese sauce. Place in blender or food processor, add 1 teaspoon Tabasco sauce, Worcestershire sauce, or bitters, or a combination of the three, and purée for 30 seconds. Add 15 g/½ oz cold unsalted butter and purée for another 30 seconds.

FISH AND SEAFOOD

O ne of the microwave oven's star turns is cooking seafood. It has become my preferred way to cook fish since the fish stays moist and cooks through absolutely evenly. It is no longer necessary to eat fish that verges on raw in the centre in order to have fish that isn't dry and overcooked on the outside.

While all the seafood first courses and main courses can be cooked in the microwave oven, it is the answer to a prayer when you are in a hurry to make dinner for one or two people. Simply plop the fish into one or two dinner plates with deep rims, flat soup plates, or 25 cm/10 inch flan dishes with seasonings and a vegetable, if you wish; cover it tightly with microwave cling film and cook. If you are cooking shellfish, use a soup bowl so as to catch all the delicious juices. For timings, see the recipes in this chapter and on pages 447–450.

Not all recipes can be adapted to a small oven. For those seafood recipes that are reasonable in a small oven, particularly recipes for one or two people, times are given. You can adapt the fish dishes yourself by consulting FISH in the Dictionary for timings. If you are cooking a recipe for two portions and wish to cook it in two dishes, up the timing for the two portions by 1½ minutes and switch the dishes halfway through the cooking: put the dish on the microwave trivet on the bottom of the oven and the dish on the bottom of the oven on the trivet. Or you can cook each dish separately; the first will stay warm while the second cooks.

If you like fish and shellfish combinations, remember to time the cooking of the dish by the shellfish, which takes longer to cook. Always place the shellfish towards the edge of the dish. See Cod and Clams Livornese (page 172) as an example. For soups and stews using combinations of fish and shellfish, see Soups, pages 78–106.

I often serve fish in small portions as a first course. Aside from portion size, I don't know too many other distinctions between a first course seafood dish and a main course one. If I am serving fish as a main course, I serve a soup or a vegetable dish first. Pâté would also be good.

Make sure that the flavours or sauce of one course don't interfere with the next. See Savoury Sauces (pages 312–333) for wonderful embellishments for seafood.

Once you've got the hang of preparing fish in the microwave oven, I think you will do it often.

CLAMS POSILLIPO

◆ ◆ ◆

This can be made even more quickly and easily by substituting bottled spaghetti sauce for the Lightly Cooked Crushed Tomatoes. Decrease the salt and seasonings if you use bottled sauce. Be sure to serve the clams with a large spoon and French bread to mop up every last trace of sauce. Have an empty bowl ready for the shells. This dish is also good on top of pasta; 250 g/8 oz very thin ribbon noodles or spaghetti, cooked, will serve four.

If you want to use more than 24 clams, don't try to increase the recipe. Instead, once everyone has sat down, put a second batch in the oven. Cook the parsley and garlic ahead. That way, the last clams served are as hot as the first ones. *Serves 1 to 2 as a main course, 2 to 3 as a first course*

3 tablespoons olive oil
15 g/½ oz parsley leaves, preferably flat-leaf parsley
3 large cloves garlic, smashed, peeled and sliced
2 tablespoons white wine
125 ml/4 fl oz Lightly Cooked Crushed Tomatoes (page 293), canned chopped tomatoes, drained, or bottled spaghetti sauce

¾ teaspoon sea salt
⅛ teaspoon dried oregano
⅛ teaspoon freshly ground black pepper
18 small clams (about 1 kg/2¼ lb), well scrubbed and drained

1 Heat oil in a 2.5 litre/4 pint soufflé dish, uncovered, at 100% for 3 minutes. Add parsley and garlic and cook, uncovered, for 3 minutes longer.

2 Remove from oven. Stir in wine, tomatoes or tomato sauce, salt, oregano and pepper. Arrange clams on top, hinge ends down. Cover tightly with microwave cling film. Cook at 100% for 7 minutes, until clams open.

3 Remove from oven. Uncover and serve hot.

To serve 2 to 3 as a main course. Use 25 g/¾ oz parsley, increase garlic to 5 cloves and tomatoes or tomato sauce to 150 ml/¼ pint, and use 24 clams. Cook clams, covered, in a 35 × 27.5 × 5 cm/14 × 11 × 2 inch dish at 100% for 9 minutes.

VARIATION

MUSSELS POSILLIPO Substitute 1 kg/2 lb mussels for 24 clams and proceed as for Clams Posillipo for 2 to 3. *Serves 2 to 3 as a main course, 6 as a first course.*

MOULES MARINIÈRES

— • • —

This is an addictive French classic. Fortunately, it is also easy to make. Never judge mussels by their size: little shells often have better-tasting mussels. There will be more per 500 g/1 lb, but the timing will be the same.

Serve with bread and spoons and put a bowl for shells on the table. If you want to serve more than 2 kg/4 lb, cook in two batches as for Clams Posillipo (page 144). *Serves 2 as a main course, 3 to 4 as a first course*

2 kg/4 lb mussels (about 18 per 500 g/ 1 lb), well scrubbed and beards removed	Freshly ground black pepper
	4 tablespoons chopped parsley
125 ml/4 fl oz white wine	5 tablespoons double cream
4 cloves garlic, smashed, peeled and cut in half	Sea salt

1 Combine mussels, wine, garlic and pepper in a 2.5 litre/4 pint soufflé dish. Cover tightly with microwave cling film. Cook at 100% for 8 minutes.

2 Pierce film with the tip of a sharp knife, then remove from oven. Uncover and remove mussels to a serving bowl. Strain liquid. Add parsley, cream and salt. Cook, uncovered, at 100% for 1 minute.

3 Remove from oven. Pour liquid over mussels and serve hot.

To serve 4 as a main course. Double all ingredients. Divide ingredients equally between two 27.5 × 21 cm/11 × 8½ inch dishes. Cook simultaneously, using a trivet (page 25), for 14 minutes. Prepare sauce as for 2 servings and serve hot.

To serve 1 as a main course. Use 500 g/1 lb mussels. Halve remaining ingredients. Cook in a very large soup bowl or in a 1.5 litre/2½ pint soufflé dish, tightly covered, for 3 minutes. Prepare sauce as for 2 servings and serve hot. (If using a small oven, cook for 6 minutes.)

VARIATIONS

MUSSELS WITH FENNEL Strew 250 g/8 oz thinly sliced fennel bulb over each 1 kg/2 lb of mussels; substitute 1 tablespoon finely chopped fennel tops for the parsley. Add a knife-point of powdered saffron to the white wine. Add 1 tablespoon Pernod, if you like. Cook as for Moules Marinières. Serve as is for a thinning version, or add the cream, or substitute 1 tablespoon olive oil for the cream.

MUSSELS WITH DILL Line the bottom of a 2.5 litre/4 pint soufflé dish with 1 carrot, trimmed, peeled and sliced. Proceed as for Moules Marinières, covering 1 kg/2 lb of mussels and 8 large dill sprigs. Substitute 1 tablespoon fresh lemon juice for cream at end.

FINE NOODLES WITH MUSSELS, PESTO AND PEPPER RELISH

◆ ◆ ◆

Seafood can be a fabulous topping for pasta, especially mussels, which exude lots of rich-tasting liquid when cooked. In this beautiful dish, which can now be made in winter as well as summer, the black of the mussel shells, the brilliant colours of the pepper relish, and the green of the sauce combine for a delightful dish. *Serves 4 as a main course, 8 as a first course*

500 g/1 lb fine ribbon noodles (linguine) or spaghetti
4 tablespoons white wine
4 cloves garlic, smashed, peeled and sliced
Pepper Relish (page 148) made with flat-leaf parsley

750 g/1½ lb mussels (about 18 mussels per 500 g/1 lb), well scrubbed and beards removed
125 ml/4 fl oz Pesto (page 333)
Sea salt
Freshly ground black pepper

1 Put a large pan of salted water on to boil for the pasta. When it is boiling, add pasta and cook until al dente.

2 While the pasta cooks, combine wine and garlic in a 2.5 litre/4 pint soufflé dish. Mound relish in the centre of the dish. Arrange mussels around relish. Cover tightly with microwave cling film. Cook at 100% for 6 minutes, until mussels open.

3 Drain pasta well.

4 Remove mussels from oven. Uncover and transfer mussels to a bowl. Stir Pesto, salt and pepper into relish mixture. Add drained pasta and stir to coat. Scatter mussels over all and serve warm.

SAUTÉ OF SCALLOPS

◆ ◆ ◆

A browning dish really comes into its own here. If you have gloriously good scallops, this is the simplest way to cook them. Serve them accompanied by nothing but a wedge of lemon. If small queen scallops are unavailable, cut ordinary scallops in quarters. Scallops have a small, hard, shiny muscle running up the outside of the main muscle in a small strip. Remove these external muscles; they pull off easily. They may be saved to include in fish stock. *Serves 2 as a main course, 4 as a first course*

15 g/½ oz unsalted butter, cut into bits	350 g/12 oz queen scallops, external muscle removed, rinsed and patted dry

1 Heat a 22.5 cm/9 inch round or 20 cm/8 inch square browning dish at 100% for 4 minutes. Add butter and quickly swirl it around the dish. When butter is nearly melted, add scallops. Stir to coat with the butter and arrange in a single layer. Cook, uncovered, at 100% for 1 minute 30 seconds.

2 Remove from oven. Serve hot.

To serve 1. Cook 250 g/8 oz queen scallops with 15 g/½ oz butter in a small oven as for Sauté of Scallops for 2 minutes.

VARIATIONS

HERBED SCALLOPS Add 2 tablespoons finely chopped parsley, 1 finely chopped shallot, and 1 tablespoon finely chopped fresh herb—tarragon, basil, thyme, mint, or dill—to listed ingredients. Toss scallops with herbs and shallots before cooking. *Serves 2 as a main course, 4 as a first course.*

CURRIED SCALLOPS Heat a 25 cm/10 inch square browning dish for 4 minutes. Add 30 g/1 oz butter and heat, uncovered, for 3 minutes. Add 600 g/ 1¼ lb scallops and 1 tablespoon curry powder and stir well. Cook for 2 minutes. Remove scallops to a serving dish. Add 1 tablespoon fresh lemon juice and ¼ teaspoon salt to liquid and pour over scallops. *Serves 4 as a main course, 8 as a first course.*

SCALLOPS WITH PEPPER RELISH

— ◆ ◆ —

The fresh-tasting relish is used in Fine Noodles with Mussels (page 146), but it would be good under any simple fish fillet. Timings would be as for fillets.
Serves 2

250 g/8 oz scallops, external muscle
  removed (see preceding recipe),
  rinsed and patted dry
1 teaspoon fresh lemon juice
1 teaspoon sea salt
⅛ teaspoon freshly ground black pepper

PEPPER RELISH
45 g/1½ oz red pepper, cored, seeded
  and diced
45 g/1½ oz green pepper, cored, seeded
  and diced

60 g/2 oz canned sweetcorn kernels in
  water, drained
60 g/2 oz canned tomatoes with liquid,
  diced
1 spring onion, trimmed and thinly
  sliced (green and white parts)
1 tablespoon coarsely chopped fresh
  coriander or flat-leaf parsley
½ teaspoon Fiery Pepper Sauce (page
  297) or 1½ teaspoons roasted chilli,
  finely chopped

1 Stir together scallops, lemon juice, ½ teaspoon of the salt and the pepper. Set aside.

2 Combine relish ingredients. Spread in an even layer in a 25 cm/10 inch flan dish. Arrange scallops in a single layer on top of relish. Cover tightly with microwave cling film. Cook at 100% for 3 minutes.

3 Pierce film with the tip of a sharp knife, then remove from oven. Let stand, covered with a tea towel, for 2 minutes. Uncover, add remaining salt and serve immediately.

To serve 4. Increase peppers to 60 g/2 oz each, sweetcorn and tomatoes to 75 g/2½ oz each and double remaining ingredients. Proceed as for 2 servings, cooking in a 2.5 litre/4 pint soufflé dish for 7 minutes.

To serve 8. Increase peppers to 100 g/3½ oz each, sweetcorn and tomatoes to 150 g/5 oz each and double remaining ingredients. Proceed as for 2 servings, cooking in a 35 × 27.5 × 5 cm/14 × 11 × 2 inch dish for 11 minutes.

PRAWNS WITH COURGETTES

— ◆ ◆ —

This is a pretty pink and green dish to have when you want to be nice to yourself or a cherished friend. If you are not having a first course, add some cooked rice or a large salad. If you cannot find large prawns, substitute the same weight of medium prawns. *Serves* 1

1 small courgette, grated with skin	½ teaspoon fresh lemon juice
1 teaspoon sea salt	⅛ teaspoon finely chopped fresh
¼ teaspoon plus a pinch freshly ground	tarragon
black pepper	6 large raw prawns (about 165 g/5½
3 tablespoons Prawn Cream (page 305)	oz), peeled and deveined

1 Stir together courgette, salt and ¼ teaspoon pepper.

2 Combine Prawn Cream, lemon juice, remaining pepper and tarragon. Spread mixture in a 25 cm/10 inch flan dish. Mound courgette in centre of dish and arrange prawns in a circle around courgette. Cover tightly with microwave cling film. Cook at 100% for 1 minute 15 seconds. (If using a small oven, cook for 2 minutes 30 seconds.)

3 Pierce film with the tip of a sharp knife, then remove from oven. Uncover and serve hot.

To serve 2. Double all ingredients. Proceed as for 1 serving, cooking prawns and courgettes in a 25 cm/10 inch flan dish for 2 minutes 30 seconds, until prawns are pink.

To serve 6. Multiply all ingredient quantities by 6. Proceed as for 1 serving, cooking prawns and courgettes in a 35 × 27.5 × 5 cm/14 × 11 × 2 inch dish for 4 minutes. Slit film, stir and re-cover. Cook for 3 minutes longer, until prawns are pink.

SZECHUAN PRAWNS WITH CHILLI PASTE

This is a simply prepared version of one of the hot and spicy dishes so popular today. *Serves* 1 *as a main course,* 3 *as a first course*

250 g/8 oz medium raw prawns, (20 to	2 teaspoons Super Hot Chilli Paste
24 per 500 g/1 lb), peeled and	(page 298) or bottled paste
deveined	2 teaspoons soya sauce
1 spring onion, thinly sliced	1 teaspoon freshly grated root ginger
1 clove garlic, smashed and peeled	1 teaspoon mirin or dry sherry

1 Toss together all ingredients until prawns are evenly coated. Let stand for 5 minutes.

2 Arrange prawns spoke-fashion, with tails in the centre in a 25 cm/10 inch flan dish. Cover tightly with microwave cling film. Cook at 100% for 2 minutes. (If using a small oven, cook for 3 minutes.)

3 Pierce film with the tip of a sharp knife, then remove from oven. Uncover and serve hot.

To serve 3 as a main course. Double all ingredients. Proceed as for 1 serving, arranging prawns in a 25 cm/10 inch flan dish and cooking for 3 minutes.

To serve 6 as a main course. Multiply all ingredient quantities by 4. Arrange prawns in a 35 × 27.5 × 5 cm/14 × 11 × 2 inch dish. Cover and cook at 100% for 4 minutes. Slit film, stir and re-cover. Cook for 3 minutes longer, until prawns are pink.

PRAWNS CREOLE

—— • ◆ • ——

Prawns turned into a pretty, rich and fragrant concoction with vegetables, Tabasco and Louisiana's characteristic Brown Roux is a great American classic. The microwave oven turns the usually patience-trying Brown Roux into an easy success. The Prawn Butter is a French touch worth trying. If you don't have time, substitute 30 g/1 oz unsalted butter. *Serves 6 as a main course with rice*

60 g/2 oz Prawn Butter (page 304)
500 g/1 lb onions, peeled and chopped
5 cloves garlic, smashed and peeled
250 g/8 oz red peppers, cored, seeded and cubed
250 g/8 oz green peppers, cored, seeded and cubed
600 g/1¼ lb medium raw prawns (20 to 24 per 500 g/1 lb), peeled and deveined (shells saved for Prawn Butter)

250 g/8 oz fresh Italian plum tomatoes, cored and quartered
1 teaspoon Tabasco sauce
Freshly ground black pepper
2 teaspoons sea salt
4 tablespoons Brown Roux (page 292)
750 g/1½ lb cooked white rice, hot

1 Heat Prawn Butter in a 2.5 litre/4 pint soufflé dish, uncovered, at 100% for 1 minute. Add onions and garlic and stir to coat. Cook, uncovered, at 100% for 2 minutes. Stir in peppers. Cook, uncovered, for 3 minutes longer.

2 Remove dish from oven. Mound vegetables in centre and arrange prawns around vegetables. Scatter tomatoes over all. Cover tightly with microwave cling film. Cook at 100% for 2 minutes. Uncover and stir well. Re-cover and cook for 2 minutes longer.

3 Remove from oven. Uncover and add Tabasco sauce, pepper salt and roux; combine well. Cover tightly and cook at 100% for 3 minutes. Serve over rice.

CURRIED PRAWNS

This is another recipe where prawns lend their rich taste and light texture to a vibrantly flavoured dish. Serve with Tomato Pilaf (page 119), made ahead and left covered, or steamed rice—white, brown or saffron.

It's nice to know that you can feed so many people with 1 kg/2 lb of prawns, considering what they cost. This is a great dish for a buffet. *Serves 8 to 10*

60 g/2 oz unsalted butter
10 cloves garlic, smashed and peeled
175 g/6 oz onion, peeled and chopped
15 g/½ oz fresh coriander leaves, coarsely chopped
1½ teaspoons Spice Powder III (page 299)
2 red peppers, cored, seeded and cut into 5 cm/2 inch chunks
500 g/1 lb green apples, peeled and cut into 5 cm/2 inch chunks
500 g/1 lb cauliflower florets

1 kg/2 lb medium raw prawns (20 to 24 per 500 g/1 lb), peeled and deveined
125 ml/4 fl oz Coconut Cream (page 306) or canned unsweetened coconut cream
125 ml/4 fl oz Chicken Stock (page 286) or stock from a cube
¼ teaspoon Fiery Pepper Sauce (page 297)
2 tablespoons fresh lime juice
Sea salt
Freshly ground black pepper

1 Heat butter in a 35 × 27.5 × 5 cm/14 × 11 × 2 inch dish, uncovered, at 100% for 3 minutes. Stir in garlic, onions, coriander and spice powder. Cook, uncovered, at 100% for 4 minutes.

2 Remove from oven. Add peppers, apples and cauliflower and stir to coat. Cook, uncovered, at 100% for 5 minutes.

3 Remove from oven. Mound vegetables in centre of dish. Arrange prawns around inside rim of dish. Pour Coconut Cream and stock over all. Cover tightly with microwave cling film. Cook at 100% for 4 minutes.

4 Pierce film with the tip of a sharp knife, then uncover and stir well. Add pepper sauce. Cover tightly and cook at 100% for 4 minutes.

5 Pierce film, remove from oven and uncover. Season with lime juice, salt and pepper. Serve with rice.

CRAB NEWBURG

——— • • ———

This very rich dish—originally made with cooked lobster meat—was created at New York's Delmonico restaurant around the turn of the century. Supposedly, it was invented to honour a Mr. Wenberg. Unfortunately, he fell out with the chef and the two syllables of the name were inverted to avoid mentioning him. This is usually served in vol-au-vents or with buttered rice. You will need much less than you think because of the cream and voluptuous flavours which makes it a good way to stretch a small amount of an ingredient as expensive as crab meat. *Serves 4 as a main course, 6 as a first course*

275/9 oz white crab meat, defrosted if frozen, and picked over to remove any shell or cartilage
250 ml/8 fl oz double cream
4 tablespoons Madeira or dry sherry
⅛ teaspoon cayenne pepper
3 egg yolks, beaten
1 teaspoon fresh lemon juice
½ teaspoon sea salt

1 Combine crab meat, cream, Madeira and cayenne in a 2.5 litre/4 pint soufflé dish. Cover tightly with microwave cling film. Cook at 100% for 3 minutes 30 seconds. (If using a small oven, cook for 5 minutes.) Prick film to release steam.

2 Remove from oven and uncover. Remove 4 tablespoons of the cream to a small bowl. Whisk in the egg yolks and whisk mixture back into cooking dish. Cover tightly with microwave cling film. Cook at 100% for 2 minutes 30 seconds, stirring three times through slit cut in film and re-covering again each time. (If using a small oven, cook for 4 minutes, 30 seconds, stirring four times.) Prick film to release steam.

3 Remove from oven and uncover. Stir in lemon juice and salt. Serve over rice or triangular croûtes or in vol-au-vents, if desired.

FISH KEBABS

◆ ◆ ◆

In to each life a cocktail party falls from time to time. These little kebabs are quick to make and perfect. Larger kebabs make an easy dinner and use up odds and ends of fish from making Harlequin of Fish Medallions (page 154). *Makes 24 cocktail kebabs*

6 slices fresh root ginger, peeled and
    sliced 3 mm/⅛ inch thick
125 ml/4 fl oz canned pineapple juice
3 tablespoons tamari soya sauce
3 cloves garlic, smashed and peeled
¼ teaspoon Tabasco sauce

½ red pepper, cored, seeded and cut
    into 1 cm/½ inch pieces
2 spring onions, cut into 1 cm/½ inch
    pieces
175 g/6 oz fish fillet (any fish is fine),
    cut into 24 cubes, 1 cm/½ inch each

1 Combine ginger, pineapple juice, soya sauce, garlic and Tabasco sauce in a 30 cm/12 inch flan dish. Cook, uncovered, at 100% for 5 minutes.

2 Skewer pepper, spring onion and fish pieces on wooden cocktail sticks, alternating 2 pieces of fish with pepper and spring onion on each. Roll each in prepared sauce. Arrange spoke-fashion around the inside rim of a 25 cm/10 inch flan dish. Cover tightly with microwave cling film. Cook at 100% for 1 minute to 1 minute 30 seconds.

3 Pierce film with the tip of a sharp knife, then remove from oven. Uncover and serve hot with sauce on the side.

To serve 2 as a main course. Prepare sauce; increase fish or chicken to 250 g/8 oz. Use 1 whole pepper and 4 spring onions. Cut fillet and vegetables into 5 cm/2 inch chunks and arrange on 20 cm/8 inch wooden skewers. Proceed as for Fish Kebabs, cooking for 2 minutes 30 seconds. Serve over rice, if desired.

VARIATION

CHICKEN KEBABS Substitute 175 g/6 oz boneless chicken breast for the fish fillet. Proceed as for Fish Kebabs.

Arrange skewers spoke-fashion.

HARLEQUIN OF FISH MEDALLIONS

$\bullet \bullet$

This is one of the prettiest and best dishes I made while working on this book. The evenly shaped medallions cook perfectly and look attractive. They do, however, leave lots of fish trimmings. These can be used in Swordfish Quenelles (page 51) or in fish farce to stuff Paupiettes (page 156). The fish can be cut into 5 cm/2 inch cubes; it will be a less striking dish, but there will be almost no odds and ends. Swordfish medallions are prettier with all three kinds of peppers; for salmon, use only the red and yellow. Tuna can be substituted, but it is less decorative than the others because of its colour when cooked. *Serves 6 as a main course, 12 as a first course*

350 ml/12 fl oz Red Pepper Purée (page 296)
1.25 kg/2½ lb swordfish or salmon steaks (about 4 cm/1½ inches thick), skinned, boned and cut into 12 medallions, 5 cm/2 inches each (page 448)
Sea salt
Freshly ground black pepper

60 g/2 oz red pepper, cored, seeded and cut into julienne strips 5 mm/¼ inch wide
60 g/2 oz yellow pepper, cored, seeded and cut into julienne strips 5 mm/¼ inch wide
60 g/2 oz green pepper, cored, seeded and cut into julienne strips 5 mm/¼ inch wide

1 Pour purée over the bottom of a 35 × 27.5 × 5 cm/14 × 11 × 2 inch dish to a depth of 5 mm/¼ inch. Arrange medallions on top of purée, 2.5 cm/1 inch apart, in a ring around inside edge of dish. Sprinkle with salt and pepper. Scatter pepper strips over fish and in centre of dish. Cover tightly with microwave cling film. Cook at 100% for 6 minutes.

2 Pierce film with the tip of a sharp knife, then remove from oven. Uncover and serve hot.

To serve 1 as a main course. Pool 3 tablespoons purée in a large dinner plate with a deep rim or in a soup plate. Arrange 2 medallions (cut from 250 g/8 oz fish) on purée; scatter juliennes from ¼ pepper of each colour on top. Cover and cook at 100% for 1 minutes 30 seconds.

To serve 2 as a main course. Pool 5½ tablespoons purée on a 22.5 cm/9 inch flan dish. Arrange 4 medallions (cut from 500 g/1 lb fish) on purée; scatter juliennes from ½ pepper of each colour on top. Cover and cook at 100% for 2 minutes 30 seconds to 3 minutes.

To serve 3 as a main course. Pool 175 ml/6 fl oz purée in a 27.5 × 21 × 5 cm/11 × 8½ × 2 inch dish. Arrange 6 medallions (cut from 750 g/1½ lb fish) on purée; scatter juliennes from ¾ pepper of each colour on top. Cover and cook at 100% for 4 minutes.

VARIATION

HARLEQUIN OF FISH MEDALLIONS WITH WATERCRESS SAUCE

Substitute an equal amount of Watercress Sauce (page 320) for Red Pepper Purée.

Use a biscuit cutter to cut fish steaks into medallions.
Save scraps for another use.

SALMON MEDALLIONS

⎯ • ◆ • ⎯

This is quick, simple and good. Cod would be very good in this recipe in place of salmon. If you want a second vegetable, add spinach. For a slightly spicy dish, add 1 tablespoon Dijon mustard to marinade. (See Harlequin of Fish Medallions, page 154.) *Serves 3*

1 tablespoon olive oil
1½ teaspoons fresh lemon juice
1 teaspoon sea salt
Large pinch freshly ground black pepper
750 g/1½ lb filleted salmon or cod (4 cm/1½ inches thick), cut into 6 medallions, 5 cm/2 inches each (page 448)

3 medium mushrooms (about 125 g/4 oz), cut into 5 mm/¼ inch slices
1 small onion, peeled and cut into 3 mm/⅛ inch slices
750 g/1½ lb spinach, stalks removed, washed and dried (optional)

1 Combine oil, lemon juice, salt and pepper in a 27.5 × 21 × 5 cm/11 × 8½ × 2 inch oval dish. Dip both sides of medallions in marinade to coat; let stand in marinade for 15 minutes.

2 Arrange 3 medallions along each short side of dish. Toss together mushrooms and onions and place in centre of dish. Cover tightly with microwave cling film. Cook at 100% for 4 minutes.

3 Pierce film with the tip of a sharp knife, then remove from oven. Uncover and remove fish to a serving platter.

4 Return vegetables to oven. If spinach is used, make a circle of it around vegetables. Cook, uncovered, at 100% for 2 minutes longer.

5 Remove from oven. Pour remaining vegetables and cooking juices over fish and serve immediately.

To serve 1. Combine 2 medallions (cut from 250 g/8 oz of fish), 1 teaspoon oil, ½ teaspoon lemon juice, ¼ teaspoon salt, and pepper. Proceed as for 3 servings, using 1 mushroom and ⅓ small onion. Cook in a large dinner plate with a deep rim or a soup plate, reducing time to 1 minute 30 seconds.

To serve 2. Combine 4 medallions (cut from 500 g/1 lb of fish), 2 teaspoons oil, 1 teaspoon lemon juice, ½ teaspoon salt, and pepper. Proceed as for 3 servings, using 2 mushrooms and ⅔ small onion. Cook in a 22.5 cm/9 inch flan dish for 2 minutes 30 seconds to 3 minutes.

To serve 6. Double all ingredients. Proceed as for 3 servings, cooking medallions in a 35 × 27.5 × 5 cm/14 × 11 × 2 inch dish for 6 minutes.

Arrange medallions around the inside rim of dish and place vegetables in centre.

PAUPIETTES OF SOLE STUFFED WITH SALMON

This is the kind of food that people usually ate only in restaurants. With the advent of the microwave oven, paupiettes can be made easily at home. Yours will be better than the restaurant's because the stuffing will cook through without the fish getting overcooked. Paupiettes are usually served with a sauce, but it is no longer absolutely necessary since microwave-cooked fish stays moist. Use a Fish Velouté (page 318), Curry Velouté (page 318), Watercress Sauce (page 320), Prawn Cream (page 305), or Beurre Blanc (page 314), if you like. Allow 3 tablespoons of sauce under each first course serving of a single paupiette, 5–6 tablespoons under each main course portion. One butterflied prawn for each paupiette is an elegant addition. Add 5 seconds to the cooking time for each prawn added. *Serves 2 as a main course, 4 as a first course*

2 sole fillets (about 150 g/5 oz each),
  each cut in half lengthways

STUFFING
125 g/4 oz skinless, boneless salmon

2 tablespoons double cream
½ teaspoon sea salt
Large pinch freshly ground black pepper
½ teaspoon fresh lemon juice

1 Place stuffing ingredients in the container of a food processor. Process until smooth.

2 Place 2 tablespoons of the mixture on one end of fillet. Starting from that end, roll fillet lengthways around mixture. Secure ends together. Repeat until all are done. You should have 4 white circles with pink centres. Arrange paupiettes in a circle around inside rim of a 22.5 × 1 cm/9 × ½ inch round dish. Do not let them touch. Cover tightly with microwave cling film. Cook at 100% for 3 minutes.

3 Pierce film with the tip of a sharp knife, then remove from oven. Uncover carefully and serve hot with or without sauce.

To serve 4 as a main course, 8 as a first course. Double all ingredients. Proceed as for 2 servings, arranging paupiettes inside the rim of a 35 × 27.5 × 5 cm/14 × 11 × 2 inch dish and cooking for 5 minutes.

VARIATIONS

PAUPIETTES STUFFED WITH DUXELLES Stuff fillets with about ⅓ recipe quantity Duxelles (page 294) and cook as for Paupiettes of Sole Stuffed with Salmon.

PAUPIETTES WITH PROVENÇALE FISH FARCE Make a fish purée by mincing 175 g/6 oz skinned and boned fatty fish in food processor. Add 4 tablespoons finely chopped red pepper, 1½ tablespoons stoned and chopped Niçoise olives, 1½ teaspoons chopped spring onion, and freshly ground black pepper. Stir to combine. Stuff fillets with mixture and proceed as for Paupiettes of Sole Stuffed with Salmon.

SWORDFISH WITH TOMATO AND BASIL

◆ ◆ ◆

This tastes as fresh as summer, and it is diet food as well. This makes a good deal of light fresh sauce, perfect with rice, couscous or millet if the diet isn't too strict. Monkfish, tuna and mahi-mahi (dolphin fish) may all be substituted for swordfish. *Serves 2 as a main course*

3 large slices ripe tomato
4 large fresh basil leaves
350 g/12 oz swordfish steak (2.5 cm/1 inch thick)

½ teaspoon olive oil
½ teaspoon fresh lemon juice
Sea salt
Freshly ground black pepper

1 Arrange tomato slices in a single layer in a 25 cm/10 inch flan or deep pie dish. Top with 2 basil leaves. Centre fish on top of tomatoes. If using 2 pieces of monkfish make sure that thin, tail end of one piece abuts the thick end of the other piece. Add oil, lemon juice, salt and pepper. Top fish with remaining basil leaves. Cover with tightly fitting lid or microwave cling film. Cook at 100% for 4 minutes. If using film, pierce it with the tip of a sharp knife.

2 Remove from oven and uncover. Cover with a doubled tea towel and let stand for 2 minutes. Serve hot.

To serve 3 to 4. Double all ingredients. Cook fish in a 27.5 × 21 × 5 cm/11 × 8½ × 2 inch dish for 5 minutes 30 seconds.

To serve 6 to 8. Multiply all ingredient quantities by 4. Cook fish in a 35 × 27.5 × 5 cm/14 × 11 × 2 inch dish for 9 minutes.

SALAD COUNTER DIET DELIGHT

For people in a hurry and cooking for themselves or a small number of people, there is a new and convenient way to shop abroad in the land. It is the salad counter, where you can find an assortment of vegetables, washed, cut up, and ready to use. For this recipe, there is no single group of vegetables that you have to use. Make up an assortment that has colour and contrast. Put the slower-cooking vegetables around the fish, the quicker-cooking vegetables on top. If you are using cherry tomatoes, prick the skin once with the tip of a knife. Do not use all the vegetables mentioned below, just an attractive selection. For those not on a diet, serve with a bowl of Watercress Sauce (page 320). *Serves 1*

1 swordfish, tuna, monkfish or mahi-mahi (dolphin fish) steak, 2 cm/¼ inch thick (about 250 g/8 oz)
175 g/6 oz assorted vegetables: some *slow-cooking*, such as peeled and sliced carrots, green beans, red cabbage, broccoli florets, cauliflower florets, peas, mange-touts, cherry tomatoes;

some *quick-cooking*, such as asparagus, sliced red onion or spring onion, sliced mushrooms, sliced green or yellow courgettes, sliced red and green peppers
Sea salt
Freshly ground black pepper

1 Centre fish in a dinner plate with a deep rim or a 25 cm/10 inch flan dish. Arrange slower-cooking vegetables around fish. Scatter remaining, quicker-cooking vegetables over all. Cover tightly with microwave cling film. Cook at 100% for 4 minutes. (If using a small oven, cook for 5 or 6 minutes.)

2 Pierce film with the tip of a sharp knife, then remove from oven. Uncover and sprinkle with salt and pepper to taste. Serve hot.

To serve 2. Double all ingredients. Divide ingredients equally between 2 dishes. Cook simultaneously, using a trivet (page 25), for 8 minutes-10 minutes in a small oven.

JUST FOR THE HALIBUT

This is another simple, quickly prepared fish dish. To butterfly a prawn firmly hold it flat on a kitchen surface. Cut it in half from head to tail, leaving the tail intact. *Serves 1*

1 teaspoon olive oil
250 g/8 oz halibut fillet (about 1 cm/½ inch thick)
4 medium raw prawns in shell, butterflied

4 sprigs fresh chervil, fresh tarragon or flat-leaf parsley
2 thin slices lemon, with peel
1 tablespoon white wine
Sea salt
Freshly ground black pepper

1 Brush a large dinner plate with a deep rim, or a 25 cm/10 inch flan dish, with oil. Place fish in centre and arrange 2 prawns on either side. Sprinkle with herbs. Place lemon slices on top. Add wine, salt and pepper. Cover tightly with microwave cling film. Cook at 100% for 3 minutes. (If using a small oven, cook for 4 minutes 30 seconds.)

2 Pierce film with the tip of a sharp knife, then remove from oven. Let stand, covered, for 3 minutes. Uncover and serve hot.

To serve 2. Double all ingredients. Proceed as for single serving, cooking in a 25 cm/10 inch flan dish for 4 minutes 30 seconds.

To serve 4. Multiply all ingredient quantities by 4. Proceed as for single serving, cooking in a 33.5 × 23.5 × 5 cm/13½ × 9½ × 2 inch dish for 6 minutes.

To serve 6. Multiply all ingredient quantities, except prawns, by 6. Use 12 prawns. Proceed as for single serving, cooking in a 35 × 27.5 × 5 cm/14 × 11 × 2 inch dish for 8 minutes.

FISH WITH CURRIED CABBAGE

I invented this dish one day when I had salmon left from making the Harlequin of Fish Medallions on page 154. I liked it so much that I now make it on purpose with a wide variety of fish. Cod, swordfish, scallops, plaice, whiting, tuna and monkfish all work as well as salmon. If using monkfish, increase cooking time to 10 minutes. *Serves 3 to 4 as a main course*

30 g/1 oz unsalted butter
2 teaspoons curry powder
90 g/3 oz onion, peeled and thinly
  sliced
275 g/9 oz green cabbage, finely
  shredded

350 g/12 oz salmon fillet, skinned and
  cut into 5 cm/2 inch chunks
2 teaspoons sea salt
Freshly ground black pepper
1 teaspoon fresh lemon juice

1 Heat butter in a 2.5 litre/4 pint soufflé dish, uncovered, at 100% for 2 minutes. Add curry powder, onions and cabbage and stir to coat.

2 Cover tightly with microwave cling film and cook at 100% for 4 minutes. Pierce film with the tip of a sharp knife, then remove from oven and stir.

3 Mound cabbage mixture in centre of dish and arrange salmon around cabbage. Sprinkle salt, pepper and lemon juice over all. Cover tightly with microwave cling film and cook at 100% for 8 minutes.

4 Pierce film, then remove from oven. Uncover and stir. Re-cover dish and let stand for 3 minutes before serving.

SALMON FILLETS WITH MUSTARD AND DILL

This extremely quick sauce is akin to the sauce served with gravlax. It lets the flavour of the salmon shine through. If you are using frozen salmon—those who fish often have a surplus—increase cooking time to 3 minutes 30 seconds. *Serves 1*

2 teaspoons Dijon mustard
2 teaspoons chopped fresh dill
3/4 teaspoon fresh lemon juice
1/2 teaspoon vegetable oil
1/4 teaspoon sea salt
1/4 teaspoon sugar

1/4 teaspoon freshly ground black pepper
1 piece salmon fillet with skin (about
  250 g/8 oz)
4 thin slices tomato
4 thin slices courgette, cut on the
  diagonal

1 Combine mustard, dill, lemon juice, oil, salt, sugar and pepper and stir until smooth. Set aside one quarter of mustard mixture. Rub remaining mixture into fish on both sides.

2 Arrange fish on half of a large dinner plate with a deep rim or a 25 cm/10 inch flan dish. Cover the other half of the plate with alternating, overlapping slices of tomato and courgette. Spread remaining mustard mixture over vegetables. Cover tightly with microwave cling film. Cook at 100% for 2 minutes. (If using a small oven, cook for 3 minutes 30 seconds.)

3 Pierce film with the tip of a sharp knife, then remove from oven. Uncover and serve hot.

To serve 2. Double all ingredients. Divide ingredients equally between 2 dishes and arrange each as for single serving. Cook simultaneously, tightly covered, using a trivet (page 25), for 4 minutes.

To serve 4. Multiply all ingredient quantities by 4. Proceed as for single serving, arranging fillets around the inside rim of a 27.5 × 21 × 5 cm/11 × 8½ × 2 inch dish and placing vegetables in the centre. Cook, tightly covered, for 5 minutes.

MACKEREL WITH FENNEL

Mackerel, which is quite oily, pairs well with ingredients with a vigorous taste. Fennel is just about perfect and provides a little crunch as well. *Serves 2*

1 tablespoon olive oil
½ large fennel bulb, split, cored and cut into 5 cm/¼ inch slices; also use leaves

2 mackerel fillets (350 g/12 oz)
½ teaspoon sea salt
Large pinch freshly ground black pepper
1 tablespoon Pernod

1 Place oil and fennel in a 20 cm/8 inch square dish. Cook, uncovered, at 100% for 1 minute.

2 Remove from oven. Arrange fillets on top of fennel, head to tail. If the fillets are too long for the dish, tuck excess under the tail end. Sprinkle with salt and pepper; drizzle Pernod over all. Cover tightly with microwave cling film. Cook at 100% for 3 minutes 30 seconds.

3 Pierce film with the tip of a sharp knife, then remove from oven. Uncover and serve hot.

To serve 4. Double all ingredients. Cook fennel and oil in a 27.5 × 21 × 5 cm/ 11 × 8½ × 2 inch dish for 2 minutes. Add fillets, sprinkle with salt, pepper and Pernod, cover, and cook at 100% for 5 minutes.

COD FILLETS WITH PASTA AND PESTO

• • •

Sole or plaice can also be used. *Serves 1*

60 g/2 oz fine ribbon noodles (linguine) or spaghetti	4 tablespoons Pesto (page 333) 1 cod fillet (about 175 g/6 oz)

1 Cook pasta until al dente. Drain well.

2 Toss three quarters of the Pesto with pasta while still warm. Arrange in a layer on a large dinner plate with a deep rim, or a 25 cm/10 inch flan dish. Place fish on top of pasta. Drizzle remaining Pesto over all. Cover tightly with microwave cling film. Cook at 100% for 4 minutes. (If using a small oven, cook for 6 to 7 minutes.)

3 Pierce film with the tip of a sharp knife, then remove from oven. Uncover and serve hot.

To serve 2. Increase Pesto to 6 tablespoons and double amounts of pasta and fish. Follow recipe for single serving, cooking in a 25 cm/10 inch flan dish for 6 minutes. You can also use 2 large dinner plates with deep rims: double all ingredients, divide them between the plates, and cook simultaneously, using a trivet (page 25) and switching plates from top to bottom after 4 minutes, for a total of 7 to 8 minutes.

To serve 4. Increase Pesto to 150 ml/¼ pint and multiply quantities of pasta and fish by 4. Proceed as for single serving, cooking in a 27.5 × 21 × 5 cm/11 × 8½ × 2 inch dish for 8 minutes.

SLICED FRESH TUNA WITH BROCCOLI FLORETS

• • •

This recipe and the next one both use fish and broccoli. The results are very different due to variations in the seasoning, the fish, and the cooking method. In this recipe, the broccoli and tomato can be replaced with mange-touts and sliced mushrooms, cauliflower and courgettes, or green beans and 1 teaspoon sesame oil. *Serves 1*

1 tuna steak (125 g/4 oz), cut across the grain into 1 cm/½ inch thick slices 45 g/1½ oz broccoli florets 2 tablespoons finely diced fresh tomato 1 spring onion, trimmed and thinly sliced into rings	2 teaspoons soya sauce 1 teaspoon rice wine vinegar ½ teaspoon grated fresh root ginger 1 small clove garlic, smashed and peeled ¼ teaspoon sugar

1 Arrange tuna in a single layer to cover about half a large dinner plate with a deep rim, or a 25 cm/10 inch flan dish. Toss together broccoli and tomato and place on uncovered part of plate.

2 Combine remaining ingredients. Drizzle over tuna and broccoli. Cover tightly with microwave cling film. Cook at 100% for 1 minutes 30 seconds. (If using a small oven, cook for 3 minutes.)

3 Pierce film with the tip of a sharp knife, then remove from oven. Uncover and serve hot.

To serve 2. Double all ingredients. Divide ingredients equally between 2 large dinner plates with deep rims and arrange each as for single serving. Cook simultaneously, tightly covered, using a trivet (page 25), for 3 minutes, changing position of the plates after 1 minute 30 seconds.

To serve 4. Multiply all ingredient quantities by 4. Arrange tuna slices around the inside rim of a 27.5 × 21 × 5 cm/11 × 8½ × 2 inch dish and place vegetables in the centre. Cover and cook at 100% for 4 minutes.

PLAICE FILLETS WITH BROCCOLI FLORETS

This is a contemporary, 5-minute fish version of one of my old favourite, chicken divan. It is pretty and festive. The cheese makes the sauce, but it could be a herbed goat cheese or one of those readily available cheeses that come in foil-wrapped packages. Any simple white fillet of fish can be used instead of plaice. *Serves* 1

1 skinned plaice fillet (about 150 g/5 oz)
Sea salt
Freshly ground black pepper
3 broccoli stalks with florets, stems no longer than 5 cm/2 inches
2 tablespoons double cream

1 tablespoon soft garlic and herb cheese, at room temperature
1 tablespoon Fish Stock (page 289), Chicken Stock (page 286) or stock from a cube
2 teaspoons finely chopped shallots
¼ teaspoon cornflour

1 Sprinkle the skin side of fillet with salt and pepper. Fold fillet in half lengthways, skin side in, and centre on a large dinner plate with a deep rim, or a 25 cm/10 inch flan dish.

2 Arrange the broccoli stalks in spoke-fashion around the fish, tucking the ends under the fillet, if necessary.

3 Stir together cream, cheese, stock, shallots and cornflour until blended. Pour mixture over fish and broccoli. Cover tightly with microwave cling film. Cook at 100% for 2 minutes 30 seconds. If using a small oven, cook for 4 minutes.

4 Pierce film with the tip of a sharp knife, then remove from oven. Uncover and serve hot.

To serve 2. Double all ingredients. Proceed as for single serving, cooking fillets in a 27.5 × 21 × 5 cm/11 × 8½ × 2 inch dish for 3 minutes 30 seconds to 4 minutes.

To serve 4. Multiply ingredient quantities by 4. Proceed as for single serving, cooking fillets in a 33.5 × 23.5 × 5 cm/13½ × 9½ × 2 inch dish for 5 minutes.

Fillet of fish with thin end doubled over for even cooking.

FILLET OF SOLE WITH ALMONDS

• ◆ •

The French discovered long ago that amonds are perfect with sole. *Serves* 1

30 g/1 oz unsalted butter
2 tablespoons blanched, flaked almonds
1 tablespoon chopped parsley,
   preferably flat-leaf parsley

1 tablespoon white wine
2 tablespoons Chicken Stock (page
   286) or stock from a cube
1 sole fillet (about 175 g/6 oz)

1 Heat half of the butter in a 20 cm/8 inch square browning dish, uncovered, at 100% for 1 minute 30 seconds. Stir in almonds and parsley. Cook for 1 minute longer, stirring once.

2 Remove from oven. Add wine and stock. Fold the fillet in half lengthways and place in centre of dish. Cover tightly with microwave cling film. Cook at 100% for 2 minutes. (If using a small oven, cook for 3 minutes 30 seconds.)

3 Pierce film with the tip of a sharp knife, then remove from oven. Uncover and remove fillet to a serving plate. Whisk the remaining butter into the sauce and spoon over fillet. Serve hot.

To serve 2. Use the same amount of butter and double remaining ingredients. Heat half the butter for 2 minutes and cook for 2 minutes with almonds and parsley. Proceed as for single serving, cooking fish for 2 minutes 30 seconds.

To serve 4. Increase butter 60 g/2 oz and stock to 125 ml/4 fl oz. Multiply other ingredient quantities by 4. Heat half the butter in a 25 cm/10 inch square browning dish for 4 minutes and cook for 2 minutes with almonds and parsley. Proceed as for single serving, cooking fish for 4 to 5 minutes.

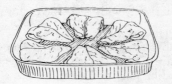

MONKFISH IN GREEN SAUCE

This recipe is a variation of a Basque way of cooking fish. Serve it with baking potatoes that have been cooked in the microwave oven, then peeled and cut in chunks, or with steamed rice.

Monkfish takes longer to cook than most fish. If you wish to substitute hake or whiting, reduce cooking time for fish to 3 minutes for two pieces.

Sometimes this cooking liquid is thickened with a sort of scrambled egg-white mixture instead of cornflour, as in the recipe to serve 6. *Serves 2*

5½ tablespoons white wine
5½ tablespoons Chicken Stock (page 286) or stock from a cube
5½ tablespoons Mussel Liquor (page 465), Fish Stock (page 289) or fish stock from a cube
½ small Spanish onion, peeled and cut in half
15 g/½ oz parsley leaves, preferably flat-leaf parsley
1 large clove garlic, smashed and peeled

3 tablespoons good-quality olive oil
2 pieces monkfish fillet (about 150 g/5 oz each), trimmed of outer membrane
Sea salt
Freshly ground black pepper
1 teaspoon cornflour
1 tablespoon water
75 g/2½ oz frozen peas, defrosted in a sieve under warm running water
1 tablespoon fresh lemon juice

1 Combine wine, Chicken Stock and Mussel Liquor in a 22.5 cm/9 inch flan dish. Cook, uncovered, at 100% for 9 minutes.

2 Place onion, parsley and garlic in the container of a food processor. Process until finely chopped. Scrape into stock mixture. Add 1 tablespoon of the olive oil and stir to combine.

3 Rub fillets with remaining 2 tablespoons olive oil and sprinkle with salt and pepper. Place fillets petal-fashion on top of onion mixture with the wide ends towards the outside of the dish and the narrow ends towards the centre. Cover tightly with microwave cling film. Cook at 100% for 5 minutes.

4 Pierce film with the tip of a sharp knife, then remove from oven. Uncover and remove fish to a serving platter; keep warm.

5 Mix cornflour and water. Stir into onion mixture. Sprinkle peas around inside edge of dish. Cover tightly with microwave cling film. Cook at 100% for 2 minutes.

6 Pierce film, then remove from oven. Uncover and add salt and pepper to taste. Spoon mixture on to 2 dinner plates and place a fillet on top of each. Drizzle each fillet with lemon juice and serve.

To serve 6. Combine 125 ml/4 fl oz *each* wine, Chicken Stock and Mussel Liquor in 27.5 × 20 cm/11 × 8 inch oval dish. Chop 250 g/8 oz Spanish onion, 45 g/1½ oz parsley leaves, and 4 cloves garlic in the food procesor. Add to wine and stock with 125 ml/4 fl oz oil. Cook, uncovered, at 100% for 10 minutes. Prepare 6 pieces monkfish fillets and arrange in sauce as in step 3. Cover and cook at 100% for 8 minutes. Remove fish to a serving platter. Beat together 4 egg whites with 2 tablespoons lemon juice; whisk into sauce, and add peas. Cover and cook at 100% for 4 minutes, stirring once with a fork after 3 minutes. Remove from oven and stir again. Pour over fish. This larger quantity can also be thickened with cornflour instead of egg whites. In that case, reduce oil to 3 tablespoons and use 2 tablespoons cornflour mixed with 4 tablespoons water to thicken.

TURBOT WITH BRUSSELS SPROUTS

No more soggy, yellow-green Brussels sprouts, or alternatively hard, green sprouts. In the microwave oven, they cook to a perfectly tender, green crispness right along with turbot fillets. If there is no turbot or it is just too expensive, equivalent plaice fillets may be substituted. *Serves* 1

30 g/1 oz unsalted butter
¼ teaspoon sea salt
¼ teaspoon dried savory
Freshly ground black pepper
½ turbot fillet, taken lengthways (150 g/5 oz)

5 Brussels sprouts (about 150 g/5 oz), stalks trimmed, any brown leaves removed and halved through the base
1 teaspoon fresh lemon juice

1 Place butter, salt, savory and pepper to taste in a 250 ml/8 fl oz glass jug or bowl. Cook, uncovered, at 100% for 1 minute.

2 Place the half fillet, both ends doubled under to achieve a double thickness, in the centre of a 25 cm/10 inch flan dish. Arrange Brussels sprouts around fillet with root ends against the edge of the dish. Pour over butter mixture. Cover tightly with microwave cling film.

3 Cook at 100% for 3 minutes. Pierce film to release steam. Remove from oven and uncover. Sprinkle over lemon juice and serve.

To serve 2. Double all ingredients. Melt butter with seasonings for 1 minute 30 seconds. Divide fish and Brussels sprouts between 2 flan dishes. Cook simultaneously, using a trivet, for 4 minutes, switching dishes after 2 minutes. Finish as above.

To serve 4. Multiply ingredient quantities except butter by 4. Proceed as for single serving, melting 90 g/3 oz of butter with seasonings in a 250 ml/8 fl oz glass jug or bowl for 2 minutes. Arrange fish and Brussels sprouts in a 35 × 27.5 × 5 cm/ 14 × 11 × 2 inch rectangular dish. Fold under ends of fillets and place in the centre of dish. Place Brussels sprouts around the inside edge. Pour over butter. Cover and cook for 5 minutes 30 seconds.

FILLET OF SOLE OVER CELERY

In this recipe, the sole is cut into strips that curl up alluringly when cooked. The dish looks like spring, all white and pale green, and has a light but especially good flavour. *Serves 1*

2 centre sticks celery with leaves, stringed and sliced across, leaves left whole
1 tablespoon Fish Stock (page 289), Chicken Stock (page 286) or stock from a cube
10 g/⅓ oz unsalted butter

1 teaspoon green peppercorns in brine, drained
¼ teaspoon sea salt
1 sole fillet (about 175 g/6 oz), cut across width into 4 strips
½ teaspoon fresh lemon juice
¼ teaspoon celery seed

1 Place sliced celery, stock, butter, peppercorns and salt on a large dinner plate with a deep rim or a 25 cm/10 inch flan dish. Cover with microwave cling film. Cook at 100% for 2 minutes.

2 Pierce film with the tip of a sharp knife, then remove from oven. Uncover and scatter celery leaves over mixture. Place fish, evenly spaced, on top of celery. Sprinkle with lemon juice and celery seeds. Cover tightly with microwave cling film. Cook at 100% for 1 minute. (If using a small oven, cook for 2 minutes.)

3 Pierce film, then remove from oven. Uncover and serve hot.

To serve 2. Double all ingredients. Divide ingredients equally between 2 large dinner plates with deep rims, or flan dishes. Proceed as for single serving, heating stock mixture simultaneously using a trivet (see page 25), for 4 minutes. Cook fish as in step 2 for 2 minutes.

SALMON STEAKS OVER CURRIED RICE

This is a good party dish. To serve eight, double the quantity of rice. Prepare two separate portions for four, first cooking one and then the other. Serve at the same time. *Serves 4*

250 g/8 oz long-grain rice
15 g/½ oz unsalted butter
1 tablespoon vegetable oil
1 small onion, peeled and finely chopped
1 small carrot, trimmed, peeled and finely chopped
2 teaspoons curry powder
650 ml/22 fl oz Chicken Stock (page 286) or stock from a cube

2 spring onions (white and green parts), thinly sliced into rings
2 tablespoons plain yogurt
1 teaspoon fresh lemon juice
4 salmon steaks (about 275 g/9 oz each), 2 cm/¾ inch thick
2 tablespoons Fresh Mango Chutney (page 407) or store-bought chutney
1 tablespoon water

1 Cook rice conventionally on the stove: heat butter and oil in a small heavy saucepan over medium heat; add onions, carrots and curry powder and sauté until the onion is wilted, about 5 minutes. Add rice and stir until well coated. Pour in the stock and heat to boiling. Reduce the heat to a simmer, cover the pan and cook just until rice is tender but firm, about 15 minutes.

2 Stir together spring onions, yogurt and lemon juice. Add the rice and stir to coat.

3 Spread rice in a single layer in a 27.5 × 21 × 5 cm/11 × 8½ × 2 inch oval dish. Arrange the steaks on top of the rice spoke-fashion, with tails towards the centre of the dish.

4 Combine chutney and water and brush over the steaks. Cover tightly with microwave cling film. Cook at 100% for 9 minutes.

5 Pierce film with the tip of a sharp knife, then remove from oven. Uncover and serve hot.

COD MEXICAN

◆ ◆

This is spicy, pretty and quick, especially when you have Hot Pepper Sauce in the refrigerator. If you are planning to make this dish for a party, make the sauce the day before. Slip the fish into the oven just as everybody sits down. *Serves 2*

4 tablespoons Hot Pepper Sauce (page 297)
500 g/1 lb skinned cod fillet, cut into four 5 × 5 × 4 cm/2 × 2 × 1½ inch chunks

8 fresh coriander leaves
1 teaspoon fresh lime juice

1 Place sauce in a 2.5 litre/4 pint soufflé dish. Arrange fish chunks, skin side down, spoke-fashion inside the rim of dish, with the wide ends towards the centre.

2 Place 2 coriander leaves on each chunk and sprinkle juice over all. Cover tightly with microwave cling film. Cook at 100% for 2 minutes 30 seconds. (In a small oven, cook for 5 minutes.)

3 Remove from oven. Uncover and serve hot.

To serve 4. Double all ingredients. Pour sauce into a 27.5 × 21 × 5 cm/11 × 8½ × 2 inch oval dish and add fish chunks. Cook as for 2 servings for 4 minutes 30 seconds.

To serve 6. Pour 250 ml/8 fl oz sauce into a 35 × 27.5 × 5 cm/14 × 11 × 2 inch dish. Add 12 fish chunks (cut from 1.25 kg/2½ lb), 1 tablespoon lime juice and 24 coriander leaves. Cook as for 2 servings for 6 minutes.

PLAICE WITH LEEKS

◆ ◆

Since this dish is so light, it is a good introduction to a meal. *Serves 4 as a first course, 2 as a main course*

1 plaice (750 g–1 kg/1½–2 lb), skinned and filleted, each fillet cut in half along the centre, head and bones cleaned and set aside
½ bay leaf
250 ml/8 fl oz water
125 ml/4 fl oz white wine
2 small onions, peeled and quartered

2 pieces lemon zest, 5 cm/2 inches each
Large pinch freshly ground black pepper
2 medium leeks, rinsed well, trimmed and cut into 3 mm/⅛ inch slices
15 g/½ oz unsalted butter, cut into small bits
2 teaspoons sea salt

1 Place head, bones and tail of fish, bay leaf, water, wine, onions, lemon zest and pepper in a 1 litre/2 pint glass measuring jug. Cover tightly with microwave cling film. Cook at 100% for 20 minutes.

2 Pierce film with the tip of a sharp knife, then remove from oven. Uncover and strain. Reserve.

3 Arrange fillets around inside rim of a 25 × 4 cm/10 × 1½ inch round dish. Place leeks in centre and dot with butter. Pour reserved stock over fish and sprinkle salt over all. Cover tightly with microwave cling film. Cook at 100% for 6 minutes.

4 Pierce film, then remove from oven. Uncover and remove fillets to a serving dish. Stir together leeks and liquid and let stand for 1 minute. Spoon over fish. Serve hot.

TOMATO-CURRIED HALIBUT

This is a quick and easy, mildly spicy way to cook a rather inexpensive fish. If you want a more dominant curry flavour, up the curry powder to 1 tablespoon. There is just enough sauce here to sauce the fish. If you want to have enough sauce for rice, double the sauce mixture. Cook the butter and seasonings for the same 2 minutes. Cook for 4 minutes after adding the tomatoes. Remove half of the sauce and reserve for the rice. Continue with the recipe. *Serves 4*

1 small onion (125 g/4 oz), peeled and
  chopped
2 cloves garlic, smashed and peeled
2 teaspoons curry powder
30 g/1 oz unsalted butter
175 ml/6 fl oz drained canned plum
  tomatoes, seeded and chopped

2 tablespoons chopped fresh coriander
½ teaspoon black mustard seed
800 g/1¾ lb halibut fillets, cut into 4
  equal pieces
½ teaspoon sea salt
1 tablespoon fresh lime juice

1 Place onion, garlic, curry powder and butter in a 32.5 × 22.5 × 5 cm/13 × 9 × 3 inch oval dish, Cook, uncovered, at 100% for 2 minutes. Leaving dish in oven, stir well and cook, uncovered, for 1 minute more.

2 Stir in tomatoes, coriander and mustard seed. Cook, uncovered, at 100% for 2 minutes. Remove from oven.

3 Arrange fish in a single layer over tomato mixture. Cover tightly with microwave cling film. Cook at 100% for 6 minutes or until fish is opaque. Prick film to release steam.

4 Remove from oven and uncover. Stir in salt and lime juice, and serve.

SOFT ROES

— • • • —

Soft roes, with their creamy texture, are cooked perfectly in the microwave oven. *Serves 1 as a main course, 2 as a first course*

175 ml/6 fl oz water
1 tablespoon white vinegar

1 pair large herring or other soft roes (200–250 g/7–8 oz), pricked 5 times on each side with the tip of a sharp knife

1 Heat water and vinegar in a 22.5 × 12.5 × 7.5 cm/9 × 5 × 3 inch oval dish at 100% for 2 minutes 30 seconds. (If using a small oven, heat for 4 minutes.)

2 Add roes to liquid. Cover tightly with microwave cling film. Cook at 100% for 2 minutes 45 seconds. (If using a small oven, cook for 5 minutes.)

3 Pierce film with the tip of a sharp knife, then remove from oven. Uncover and serve hot.

To serve 2 as a main course, 4 as a first course. Double all ingredients in recipe or variations. Cook roes for 7 minutes.

To serve 4 as a main course, 8 as a first course. Multiply all ingredient quantities in recipe or variations by 4. Heat liquid in a 35 × 27.5 × 5 cm/14 × 11 × 2 inch dish for 5 minutes. Cook roes for 10 minutes.

VARIATIONS

SOFT ROES IN BUTTER Heat 175/6 oz unsalted butter for 3 minutes. Add roes, cover with paper towels and cook at 100% for 2 minutes 45 seconds. Serve with fresh lemon juice and some of the butter spooned on top.

SOFT ROES WITH SORREL SAUCE For each pair of roes, stir together 60 g/2 oz fine sorrel chiffonade (page 433), 15 g/½ oz butter, and 2 finely chopped shallots in the appropriate size dish. Cook, uncovered, for 2 minutes. Add roes, 3 tablespoons double cream, and ½ teaspoon salt. Cover tightly with microwave cling film and cook at 100% for 2 minutes 45 seconds for 1 pair, 7 minutes for 2 pairs, and 10 minutes for 4 pairs.

COD WITH CLAMS LIVORNESE

— • • • —

I just love this dish. It is hard to get right in a conventional oven; the fish tends to overcook by the time the shellfish opens. In the microwave oven, it is fail-safe. When you prepare this recipe for more than a couple of people, use a whole fish—it will be much more attractive. *Serves 1*

250 g/8 oz cod fillet, 2.5 cm/1 inch thick fillet
6 small clams, well scrubbed
1 tablespoon olive oil
2 teaspoons white wine

Sea salt
Freshly ground black pepper
1 clove garlic, smashed, peeled and cut in three

1 Place fillet in the centre of a large dinner plate with a deep rim, or a 25 cm/ 10 inch flan dish. Arrange clams, hinge side down, in sets of two around fillet.

2 Sprinkle oil, wine, salt and pepper on fillet. Place garlic between clams. Cover tightly with microwave cling film. Cook at 100% for 3 minutes 30 seconds.

3 Pierce film with the tip of a sharp knife, then remove from oven. Uncover and serve hot.

To serve 2. Use 2 cod fillets (about 500 g/1 lb) and 10 clams; double the remaining ingredients. Cook in a 30 × 27 × 7.5 cm/12 × 10¾ × 3 inch oval dish for 6 minutes. Let stand, covered, for 1 minute and serve hot.

VARIATIONS

COD WITH MUSSELS Substitute mussels, scrubbed and beards removed, for clams. Proceed as for Cod with Clams Livornese, cooking single portion for 3 minutes, double portion for 5 minutes.

RED SNAPPER LIVORNESE This will generously serve 4 as a main course, 6 as a first course. Any other white fleshed, firm fish can be substituted for snapper. Arrange a 1.25 kg/2½ lb fish, head and tail on, diagonally in a 35 × 27.5 × 5 cm/14 × 11 × 2 inch dish. Sprinkle with 4 tablespoons white wine, 3 tablespoons olive oil, 1 teaspoon salt, and 2 grinds of black pepper. Cover tightly. Cook at 100% for 6 minutes. Add 20 clams, hinge side down, and 6 cloves smashed and peeled garlic in empty space around fish. Re-cover; cook for 10 minutes at 100%.

STEAMED WHOLE FISH

There are many times when I want to steam a whole fish to serve hot or cold. If you are serving it cold, be sure to remove the skin as soon as you can handle the fish; otherwise it tends to stick. The only limit to the amount of whole fish you can cook in the microwave oven is the length of the fish. That is why I have removed the head or both the head and the tail of larger fish. The fish steams in its own juice, when can be used to make a sauce such as Fish Velouté, Curry Velouté, Pesto, Chunky Tomato Sauce, Mayonnaise, Aïoli, Watercress Sauce, Béarnaise sauce or Parsley Sauce. *Each 250–350 g/8–12 oz of cooked fish feeds one person*

1 whole fish, 750 g/1½ lb with head
    and tail on

Place fish in a 35 × 20 cm/14 × 8 inch oval dish. Cover tightly with microwave cling film. Cook at 100% for 8 minutes.

To steam a 1.25 kg/2½ lb fish, head and tail on. Arrange in a 35 × 20 cm/14 × 8 inch oval dish. Cover tightly with microwave cling film. Cook at 100% for 11 minutes. (To cook in a small oven, use a 27.5 × 20 cm/11 × 8 inch dish, making sure to wrap tail-piece that juts out over edge. Cook for 14 minutes.)

To steam a 1.25 kg/2½ lb fish, head and tail on. Arrange diagonally in a 35 × 27.5 × 2 cm/11 × 14 × 2 inch dish. Cover tightly with microwave cling film. Cook 14 minutes at 100%.

To steam a 1.5 kg/3 lb fish, head and tail on. Arrange in a 35 × 27.5 × 5 cm/14 × 11 × 2 inch dish, curling tail if necessary. Cover tightly with microwave cling film. Cook at 100% for 16 minutes.

To steam a 3 kg/6 lb fish, head removed, cooking weight 2.25 kg/4½ lb. Arrange diagonally in a 35 × 27.5 × 5 cm/14 × 11 × 2 inch dish. Cover tightly with microwave cling film. Cook for 18 minutes at 100%.

To steam a 4 kg/8 lb fish, head and tail removed, cooking weight 3 kg/6 lb. This can be done only in a full-size microwave oven without a turntable. Place fish in a 42.5 cm/17 inch oval dish. Cover tightly with microwave cling film. Place dish diagonally in oven. Cook for 22 minutes at 100%.

VARIATIONS

CHINESE STEAMED FISH Sprinkle each 500 g/1 lb of fish with 1 piece of fresh root ginger the size of a 5p coin, peeled and slivered, 1 clove garlic, smashed and peeled, 1 coriander sprig, 2 teaspoons salted Chinese black beans, 2 teaspoons sesame oil, 2 teaspoons rice wine vinegar, and 2 tablespoons tamari soya sauce or hoisin sauce. A spring onion, both green and white parts, cut in 2.5 cm/1 inch lengths, may also be included. Cook as for plain Steamed Whole Fish.

VEGETABLE STEAMED FISH Sprinkle each 500 g/1 lb of fish with 1 tablespoon peeled and chopped carrot, 1 tablespoon chopped onion, 1 tablespoon chopped celery, 1 tablespoon chopped parsley, ¼ teaspoon salt and 2 tablespoons white wine. Cook as for Steamed Whole Fish. To serve, the vegetables can be poured over fish or they can be puréed in a blender with a little butter or cream to make a sauce.

HERB STEAMED FISH For each 500 g/1 lb of fish, add 1 tablespoon of a chopped fresh herb or of a combination of herbs. Tarragon, lovage or dill are good alone. Thyme goes well with savory and a tiny bit of oregano. If using rosemary, use only ½ tablespoon per 500 g/1 lb. Place half the herbs in cavity of fish. Cook as for Steamed Whole Fish; sprinkle with remaining herbs. Season with salt and pepper to taste when cooking is finished.

MARINATED SARDINES

The wily Venetians discovered a way (in saor) to preserve sardines in hot weather. The sardines are cooked, then left to steep in a marinade for several days. This dish needs to be made and refrigerated at least two days before serving; it will keep for five days. Bring it to room temperature before serving.

Two to three sardines make a main course with a salad. One sardine is enough for a first course, especially if accompanied by other hors d'oeuvres. *Makes 8 sardines*

5½ tablespoons olive oil
1 small onion, peeled and finely
   chopped
1 celery stick, stringed and sliced
2 carrots, peeled and cut into 5 mm/
   ¼ inch slices
150 ml/¼ pint white wine
150 ml/¼ pint white wine vinegar

3 fresh sage leaves or ½ teaspoon dried
   sage
2 bay leaves
1 teaspoon sea salt
Freshly ground black pepper
3 tablespoons raisins
3 tablespoons pine nuts
8 fresh sardines (about 250 g/8 oz)

1 Place oil and onions in a 27.5 × 18.5 × 6 cm/11 × 7½ × 2½ inch dish and cook, uncovered, at 100% for 2 minutes. Add celery, carrots, wine, vinegar, sage, bay leaves, salt and pepper. Cook, uncovered, at 100% for 8 minutes.

2 Stir in raisins and pine nuts. Cook, uncovered, at 100% for 2 minutes. Add sardines and cook, uncovered, at 100% for 1 minute 30 seconds.

3 Remove from oven. Remove fish to a storage container. Let liquid stand until cool. Pour over fish and refrigerate, tightly covered, for at least 2 days before serving.

To make 16 sardines. Use same amount of ingredients for marinade. Proceed as for 8 sardines. When first 8 sardines are cooked, remove from liquid. Reheat liquid, uncovered, at 100% for 2 minutes. Add remaining sardines and cook, uncovered, for 1 minute 30 seconds. Store all sardines covered with liquid in a single container.

TURBOT WITH NEW POTATOES

Nothing is better than simply cooked turbot and new potatoes. You can either spoil yourself or up to four worthy eaters. A good Chablis, a green salad and a piece of cheese make this a feast. *Serves 1*

30 g/1 oz unsalted butter
½ teaspoon chopped fresh tarragon
¼ teaspoon sea salt
1 turbot steak (175–250 g/6–8 oz),
   bone in and skin left on, about 2.5
   cm/1 inch thick

125 g/4 oz new potatoes (2 potatoes),
   cut into 5 mm/¼ inch slices
1 teaspoon fresh lemon juice

1 Place butter, tarragon and salt in a 250 ml/8 fl oz glass jug or bowl. Cook, uncovered, at 100% for 1 minute. (If using a small oven, cook for 1 minute 30 seconds.) Remove from oven.

2 Place fish in the centre of a 25 cm/10 inch flan dish. Arrange potato slices around fish and pour butter mixture over all. Cover tightly with microwave cling film. Cook at 100% for 5 minutes. (If using a small oven, cook for 8 minutes.) Pierce film to release steam.

3 Remove from oven and uncover. Sprinkle on lemon juice and serve.

To serve 2. Double all ingredients. Melt butter with seasonings in a 250 ml/8 fl oz jug or bowl for 1 minute 30 seconds. Arrange fish and potatoes in two 25 cm/ 10 inch flan dishes as above. Cover and cook, using a trivet, for 7 minutes, switching dishes halfway through cooking. Finish as above.

To serve 4. Use 90 g/3 oz unsalted butter and multiply all other ingredients by 4. Melt butter with seasonings in a 250 ml/8 fl oz jug or bowl for 2 minutes. Arrange fish in the centre of a 35 × 27.5 × 5 cm/14 × 11 × 2 inch dish and arrange potatoes around fish. Cover and cook for 10 minutes. Finish as above.

WHOLE TROUT WITH LEMON BUTTER

I find a whole trout a luxurious dinner for myself alone or with a good friend. There are too many bones for a dinner party.

Most of the trout we get to eat are farm-raised. They are often frozen but can sometimes be bought fresh. When you find fresh trout, ask the fishmonger to butterfly a few, taking the bones out but leaving the two fillets attached at the back and the head and tail on. You can stuff these with Duxelles (page 294), wrap each one in freezer film and freeze. Then they will be ready to cook when you want. Since trout freezes so well, this is an always at-hand luxury. All you need to do is to unwrap the fish and place in a 25 cm/10 inch flan dish. Cover tightly with microwave cling film. Defrost at 100% for 2 minutes 45 seconds. Prick film; remove from oven and let stand for 10 minutes while you assemble the rest of dinner and then cook as below. *Serves* 1

1 whole river, brown or rainbow trout, defrosted if frozen (page 442)
2 teaspoons fresh lemon juice
Sea salt

Freshly ground black pepper
30 g/1 oz unsalted butter, cut into 6 pieces

1 Place fish in an oval or rectangular cooking dish just large enough to hold it. Sprinkle the inside of fish with half the lemon juice, salt and pepper. Tuck half the butter inside. Scatter remaining lemon juice and butter on top. Cover dish tightly with microwave cling film. Cook at 100% for 1 minute. Slit film with a sharp knife and turn fish over. Re-cover and cook for 1 minute 30 seconds.

2 Pierce film, then remove from oven. Let stand, covered, for 1 minute. Uncover and serve hot.

To serve 2. Double all ingredients. Divide ingredients equally between the fish. Arrange, head to tail, in a 27.5 × 21 × 5 cm/11 × 8½ × 2 inch dish; cover tightly with microwave cling film; cook for 3 minutes 30 seconds, turning once. Remove from oven and let stand, covered, for 1 minute.

VARIATION

BUTTERFLIED TROUT WITH DUXELLES Substitute a whole butterflied trout for the whole trout. Halve butter and add 2 tablespoons Duxelles (page 294). Stuff fish with Duxelles and dot butter on top. Cook as for Whole Trout with Lemon Butter for 2 minutes 30 seconds.

TRUITE AU BLEU

◆ ◆ ◆

This is a classic preparation for trout. The skin turns blue in the acid cooking liquid. I was happy to find that this dish, which can usually be made only with impeccably fresh trout, can be prepared with frozen trout in the microwave oven. *Serves 1 as a main course, 2 as a first course*

125 ml/4 fl oz water
125 ml/4 fl oz tarragon vinegar
1 teaspoon sea salt
¼ teaspoon freshly ground black pepper

1 whole river, brown or rainbow trout (400–500 g/14–16 oz), defrosted if frozen (page 491)

1 Combine water, vinegar, salt and pepper in a 33.5 × 18.5 × 5 cm/13½ × 9½ × 2 inch dish. Cook, uncovered, at 100% for 8 minutes.

2 Remove from oven. Slip the trout into the hot liquid. Cover tightly with microwave cling film. Cook at 100% for 2 minutes. Pierce film with the tip of a sharp knife, then remove from oven, uncover and carefully turn the fish over. Re-cover and cook for 2 minutes longer.

3 Pierce film, then remove from oven. Uncover and transfer fish with a wide fish slice to a serving plate.

To serve 2. Increase water and vinegar to 175 ml/6 fl oz each and double remaining ingredients. Proceeding as for single serving, arrange fish head to tail in a 35 × 27.5 × 5 cm/14 × 11 × 2 inch dish and cook for 3 minutes. Turn both fish over, re-cover and cook for 3 minutes longer.

HERRING

Herring is the favourite fish of much of the world. Made this way, it can be served hot with a Beurre Blanc (page 314) or cold. Allow it to cool in its cooking liquid. *Serves 1 as a main course, 2 as a first course*

1 whole fresh herring (about 250 g/8 oz), scaled and gutted
125 g/4 oz onion, peeled and sliced
30 g/1 oz young carrot, trimmed, peeled and thinly sliced
175 ml/6 fl oz white wine

½ teaspoon sea salt
6 whole juniper berries
2 whole cloves
4 whole allspice berries
½ bay leaf

1 Place herring in a 27.5 × 12.5 cm/11 × 5 inch dish. Add remaining ingredients. Cover tightly with microwave cling film. Cook at 100% for 4 minutes.

2 Pierce film with the tip of a sharp knife, then remove from oven. Let stand, covered, for 1 minute. Uncover; fillet and serve.

To serve 4 as a main course, 8 as a first course. Use 4 herrings, 2 teaspoons salt, a large pinch freshly ground black pepper and 6 cloves. Double remaining ingredients. Proceed as for 1 fish, cooking in a 35 × 27.5 × 5 cm/14 × 11 × 2 inch dish for 10 minutes. Let stand, covered, for 2 minutes.

WHITING WITH PARSLEY SAUCE

Whiting *en colère* ('in a rage'), a fish arranged in a circle as if it were angrily biting its own tail, is a very good French standard served with a light parsley sauce. *Serves 4*

1 whiting (1.25 kg/2½ lb)
1 tablespoon plus 1 teaspoon cornflour
150 ml/¼ pint milk
5½ tablespoons double cream

30 g/1 oz parsley, finely chopped
2 tablespoons thinly sliced chives
1 teaspoon salt

1 Arrange fish in a 2.5 litre/4 pint soufflé dish, spine up, with its head and tail touching.

2 Stir together cornflour, milk and cream and mix well. Stir in parsley, chives and salt. Pour mixture over fish. Cover tightly with microwave cling film. Cook at 100% for 7 minutes.

3 Pierce film with the tip of a sharp knife, then remove from oven. Uncover and serve hot.

Place whiting in soufflé dish with the head and tail touching.

FAIR IS FOWL

I know that puns are inexcusable, but this really expresses the way I feel about cooking birds in the microwave oven: good. Once you know how to cook skinned and boned chicken breasts alone, or with a sauce, or with a vegetable, there are countless variations you can try, including having the breasts on hand, individually wrapped and frozen, to cook directly with their accompaniments for yourself, or yourself and one other person. If you look at the Chicken Breasts with Sofrito recipe and its variations, you will know how to time the frozen chicken breasts. Then you can try them with any sauce or with any of the vegetable purées in this book. If you have questions about any cooking times or quantities, look up CHICKEN in the Dictionary.

Once you have tried a few of the stews that follow, have fun. Change the vegetables, change the cooking liquid, or change the seasonings. Almost anything goes as long as you keep the proportion of solid to liquid consistent. If you want to cut down on calories, remove the skin from chicken for stews, fricassees and the like. Don't remove the bones or you will lose flavour and gelatine. Don't try to cook a whole bird that isn't jointed. It doesn't work well. Don't think of any version of this as roasting. It isn't.

Duck is divine in the microwave oven. It is easy, and you really get rid of that fat. Turkey is more limited. A whole turkey really needs to go into a conventional oven; see page 308 for one of my stuffings. Little birds—a half, a whole, or several to an eater—do well in the microwave oven.

Remember, for most of these dishes you will want an accompanying starch (pages 107–142), or make plain rice or noodles. For some you will want a vegetable (see pages 238–284). Of course, a few contain their own rice or vegetables. Don't overdo it.

POACHED CHICKEN BREASTS

◆•◆

With this simple recipe, you can create an endless series of dinners by adding different sauces or vegetables. This is also the way to cook breast meat for chicken salads or to substitute in Turkey à la King (page 198).

Poached chicken breasts are very good and elegant with Braised Lettuce (page 249) and Sauce Suprême (page 319). Plain rice and Velouté (page 318) work well. Think about snipping some fresh herbs into the sauce. Allow 4 tablespoons sauce for each breast and 1 teaspoon finely chopped herbs for each 4 tablespoons sauce. If you are putting tarragon on the chicken, add tarragon to the sauce. The lavish can top each breast with thin slices of black truffle and add some chopped truffle to the sauce. Another possibility is to stir ½ teaspoon tomato paste or 1 teaspoon Chunky Tomato Sauce (page 324) into each 4 tablespoons of Velouté for a gently pink dish that can be sharpened with a few drops of fresh lemon juice and Tabasco sauce. Parsley Sauce (page 320) and Watercress Sauce (page 320) provide nice colour contrasts.

How many breasts to prepare depends on individual appetites and what else you are serving. If there is going to be a first course, count on 1½ breasts per person, 2 breasts per person if there is no first course. *Serves 4 to 8*

8 chicken breasts, skinned and boned
125 ml/4 fl oz Chicken Stock (page 286) or stock from a cube

3 sprigs fresh tarragon (optional)
Sauce Suprême (page 319), for serving

1 Arrange chicken petal-fashion in a 30 × 4 cm/12 × 1½ inch round dish, with thin ends towards the centre. Pour stock over chicken and scatter tarragon on top.

2 Cover tightly with microwave cling film. Cook at 100% for 8 minutes.

3 Pierce film with the tip of a sharp knife, then remove from oven. Uncover and serve with sauce; you may stir a tablespoon or two of the cooking liquid into the sauce, if you like.

To make 1 breast. Place breast in a small flan dish with 4 tablespoons stock and a sprig of tarragon, if desired. Cover and cook at 100% for 3 minutes.

To make 2 breasts. Place breasts, thin edges towards each other, in a small flan dish with 4 tablespoons stock and a sprig of tarragon, if desired. Cover and cook at 100% for 4 minutes.

To make 4 breasts. Arrange breasts spoke-fashion in a 22.5 cm/9 inch dish with the thick ends towards the outside of the dish. Add 4 tablespoons stock and 2 sprigs of tarragon, if desired. Cover and cook at 100% for 6 minutes.

To make 6 breasts. **Arrange breasts spoke-fashion in a large round serving dish about 7.5 cm/3 inches deep, with the thick ends towards the outside of the dish. Add 4 tablespoons stock and 3 sprigs of tarragon, if desired. Cover and cook at 100% for 7 minutes.**

A whole, skinned, boneless breast of a chicken cut in half, thick sides facing.

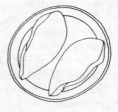

Chicken breasts cooked with the thick sides towards the edge of dish.

CHICKEN BREAST WITH DUXELLES

This simple dish makes a whole meal, super-easy if you have Duxelles in the freezer. Chicken, mushrooms and spinach go together perfectly. The mushrooms add a richness here that really makes a breast per person enough. If you want a sauce, add 1 tablespoon of Duxelles to 4 tablespoons Velouté (page 318) per person. Heat briefly, uncovered, in the microwave oven. *Serves* 1

1 chicken breast, skinned and boned
2 tablespoons Duxelles (page 294)
125 g/4 oz spinach leaves, stalks
   removed, washed thoroughly and
   dried

Sea salt
Freshly ground black pepper

1 Using your fingers, gently open up the pocket along the underside of the breast, being careful not to break the breast in two. Fill pocket loosely with Duxelles.

2 Arrange spinach in a layer in a large dinner plate with a deep rim or in a 25 cm/10 inch flan dish and centre chicken on top. Cover tightly with microwave cling film. Cook at 100% for 3 minutes.

3 Pierce film with the tip of a sharp knife, then remove from oven. Let stand for 1 minute. Uncover. If there is too much liquid on the plate, carefully pour off; a little is fine. Season to taste with salt and pepper.

To serve 2. Double all ingredients. Proceed as for single serving, arranging in a 25 cm/10 inch flan dish. Cover and cook at 100% for 4 minutes.

To serve 4. Multiply all ingredient quantities by 4. Proceed as for single serving, arranging chicken spoke-fashion in a 25 cm/10 inch flan dish. Cover and cook at 100% for 6 minutes.

CHICKEN CURRY

Everybody likes this. It can be made more of an event by serving it with little dishes of freshly grated coconut, raisins, chopped coriander, bananas sliced and dipped in lemon juice, toasted unsalted peanuts, and Fresh Mango Chutney (page 407). Add plain boiled rice or Tomato Pilaf (page 119). *Serves 4*

45 g/1½ oz unsalted butter
2 large onions, peeled and cut into 4 cm/1½ inch square chunks
1 slightly underripe papaya, peeled and cut into 4 cm/1½ inch square chunks
2 tablespoons Spice Powder III (page 299) or curry powder
500 g/1 lb chicken breasts (about 4 breasts), skinned, boned and cut into 5 cm/2 inch chunks

1 tablespoon Coconut Milk (page 306) or 1 tablespoon milk
2 tablespoons Chicken Stock (page 286) or stock from a cube
3½ teaspoons sea salt
2 teaspoons fresh lemon juice
4 tablespoons freshly grated coconut (see page 305 to open) or store-bought desiccated coconut (optional)

1 Heat butter in a 2.5 litre/4 pint soufflé dish, uncovered, at 100% for 3 minutes.

2 Remove from oven. Add onions, papaya and Spice Powder III. Stir to coat well. Cook, uncovered, at 100% for 6 minutes.

3 Add chicken, Coconut Milk and stock. Stir. Cover tightly with microwave cling film. Cook at 100% for 6 minutes, shaking dish after 3 minutes to distribute mixture.

4 Pierce film with the tip of a sharp knife, then remove from oven. Uncover carefully. Stir in salt and lemon juice; sprinkle with coconut, if desired.

FROZEN CHICKEN BREASTS

When you come home tired and need a quick dinner for yourself or for friends and family, think of those tidy, individually wrapped, skinned and boned chicken breasts in the freezer. Here they are cooked on a bed of braised chopped vegetables, but you could use anything else you have around—maybe some Hispanic Sofrito or leftover vegetable purée or Chunky Tomato Sauce (page 324), just awaiting defrosting. Substitute your gleanings for Sofrito in the recipe. Refer to Poached Chicken Breasts (page 181) for additional ideas. *Serves 2*

½ recipe quantity Sofrito (page 301)
2 frozen chicken breasts, skinned and
  boned

125 ml/4 fl oz Chicken Stock (page
  286) or stock from a cube
Sea salt
Freshly ground black pepper

1 Put Sofrito in a 2.5 litre/4 pint soufflé dish. Place chicken on top and add stock. Cover tightly with microwave cling film. Cook at 100% for 5 minutes.

2 Pierce film with the tip of a sharp knife, then remove from oven. Uncover and turn chicken over. Re-cover with fresh microwave cling film. Cook at 100% for 5 minutes more.

3 Pierce film, uncover and continue cooking for 2 minutes.

4 Remove from oven. Add salt and pepper to taste.

CHICKEN BREASTS NORMANDE

Normandy is too far north for grapes, but it is an ideal climate for apples. In autumn, they make cider and from it a kind of brandy called Calvados. Normandy is rich in butter and cream, and its dishes are rich also—elegant for a party. This dish is very white. If you are serving a vegetable, try for colour. Cut the peels of the apples into thin strips and scatter them on top, or sprinkle with finely chopped parsley. Noodles and rice are good to sop up the sauce. *Serves 8*

45 g/1½ unsalted butter
1 kg/2 lb Granny Smith apples, peeled,
  cored and cut into 5 cm/2 inch
  chunks
2½ tablespoons cornflour
5½ tablespoons apple juice
250 ml/8 fl oz Chicken Stock (page
  286) or stock from a cube

125 ml/4 fl oz double cream
2 tablespoons Calvados
2 teaspoons sea salt
Fresh ground black pepper
Pinch cayenne pepper
8 chicken breasts, skinned and boned

1 Heat butter in a 35 × 27.5 × 5 cm/14 × 11 × 2 inch dish, uncovered, at 100% for 1 minute.

2 Remove from oven. Add apples and stir to coat with butter. Cook, uncovered, at 100% for 5 minutes.

3 Stir cornflour into apple juice. Remove apples from oven. Stir in cornflour mixture and remaining ingredients except chicken. Cook, uncovered, at 100% for 8 minutes.

4 Remove from oven. Slip chicken into sauce, arranging with thick ends towards outside of dish. Cover tightly with microwave cling film. Cook at 100% for 8 minutes.

5 Pierce film with the tip of a sharp knife, then remove from oven. Uncover carefully and serve immediately.

CHICKEN DINNER IN TWENTY MINUTES

Serve this chicken dish over rice and with broccoli on the side. Boil water for the rice before doing anything else. Cook the rice (on top of the stove) and the chicken (in the microwave oven) at the same time. Cook the broccoli while you season the rice. Set out crusty French bread and chilled white wine, and you have a chicken dinner on the table in twenty minutes. *Serves 2 to 4*

4 chicken breasts, skinned and boned
1 small ripe tomato, cored and sliced 5 mm/¼ inch thick
1 medium courgette, trimmed and sliced 5 mm/¼ inch thick
1 leek, trimmed and sliced 5 mm/¼ inch thick (including 2.5 cm/1 inch of the green)
½ bunch flat-leaf parsley, coarsely chopped
3 tablespoons Chicken Stock (page 286) or stock from a cube
1 tablespoon olive oil
1 teaspoon sea salt
6 grinds fresh black pepper
1½ tablespoons fresh lemon juice

1 Arrange chicken pieces in half of a 30 cm/12 inch flan dish so that the pieces are fanned out but do not touch. Fan tomato slices opposite chicken and place courgette in centre. Scatter leeks and parsley over all.

2 Stir together remaining ingredients and drizzle over chicken and vegetables. Cover tightly with microwave cling film. Cook at 100% for 9 minutes.

3 Pierce film with the tip of a sharp knife, then remove from oven. Uncover and serve. Spoon the ample cooking juices over the rice and broccoli or whatever you are serving with the chicken.

CHICKEN WITH YELLOW PEPPERS AND TOMATOES

◆ ◆

This is a ravishingly fresh-tasting, late-summer dish when peppers and tomatoes are sweet and juicy. It produces its own sauce. Serve it with Rich, French Potato Purée (page 253) or just lots of crusty bread and a cold, dry white wine. At a party, I serve Chunky Pâté (page 59) first. *Serves 4*

4 tablespoons fruity olive oil
1 large onion, peeled and sliced
2 yellow peppers, cored, seeded and cut
 into 4 cm/1½ inch wide strips

5 ripe plum tomatoes, cored and cut
 across into 4 slices each
1 teaspoon sea salt
2 pinches freshly ground black pepper
4 chicken breasts, skinned and boned

1 Heat oil in a 35 × 27.5 × 5 cm/14 × 11 × 2 inch dish, uncovered, at 100% for 2 minutes. Add onions and stir to coat. Cook, uncovered, at 100% for 2 minutes.

2 Remove from oven. Add peppers, tomatoes, salt and pepper. Stir to coat with oil. Mound vegetables in centre of dish. Arrange chicken around vegetables, thinner sides facing the centre. Cover tightly with microwave cling film. Cook at 100% for 8 minutes.

3 Pierce film with the tip of a sharp knife, then remove from oven. Uncover carefully and serve hot.

To *serve* 2. Halve all ingredients. Cook onions for 1 minute 30 seconds and chicken for 5 minutes.

CHICKEN SALAD

◆ ◆

Make the chicken first and let it cool while the vegetables cook. Then assemble the salad. For cooking times for chicken, see Poached Chicken Breasts (page 181) or refer to the entry on CHICKEN in the Dictionary. *Serves 4*

1 medium fennel bulb, chopped
1 large onion, peeled and chopped
90–125 g/3–4 oz asparagus, trimmed
 and cut into 2.5 cm/1 inch lengths

500 g/1 lb cooked chicken, cut into
 1 cm/½ inch chunks
30 g/1 oz spring onion greens, thinly
 sliced
175 ml/6 fl oz Mayonnaise (page 332)

1 Put fennel in a 500 ml/1 pint glass measuring jug with 1 tablespoon water. Cover tightly with microwave cling film. Cook at 100% for 1 minute.

2 Pierce film with the tip of a sharp knife, then remove from oven. Drain and put into a mixing bowl. Cook onions and asparagus, separately, as for fennel in step 1.

3 Add chicken to vegetables and toss with remaining ingredients. Serve at room temperature.

CHICKEN LEGS WITH GARLIC CREAM

The lightly browned chicken combines wonderfully with the creamy richness of the sauce. Serve with rice or noodles. Peas with Mint and Spring Onions (page 241) would be pretty and good with this. You may substitute any combination of thighs and drumsticks or thighs alone in this recipe. *Serves 2*

10 g/⅔ oz unsalted butter
2 whole chicken legs, cut into thighs and drumsticks, each drumstick cut to the bone all the way around the thin end
Sea salt

Freshly ground black pepper
5½ tablespoons Garlic Cream (page 302)
2 tablespoons dry white wine
1 teaspoon fresh lemon juice

1 Place butter in a 22.5 cm/9 inch square browning dish. Heat, uncovered, at 100% for 3 minutes.

2 Sprinkle chicken with salt and pepper. Place, skin side down, in the butter. Cook, uncovered, at 100% for 6 minutes, turning chicken over after 3 minutes.

3 Remove from oven. Pour off fat. Add Garlic Cream, wine and lemon juice. Cook, uncovered, at 100% for 1 minute.

4 Remove from oven. Transfer chicken to a serving plate and keep warm. Stir the sauce well, scraping up the browned bits from the bottom of the dish. Adjust seasoning if necessary, and pour the sauce over the chicken.

Slit the skin and tendon on the drumsticks so the skin does not burst.

To serve 4. Double all ingredients. Heat butter for 5 minutes in a 25 cm/10 inch square or 25 cm/10 inch round browning dish. Cook chicken for 10 minutes 30 seconds.

To serve 8. Multiply all ingredient quantities by 4. Cook the legs in 2 batches, 4 at a time, as for 4 servings.

CHICKEN WITH BARBECUE SAUCE

No, this is not cooked on a barbecue. If you want a charred outside, shorten cooking time by 1 minute and place the chicken under a preheated grill or on the barbecue just until browned.

You can substitute thighs or any combination of thighs and drumsticks for drumsticks. Arrange the chicken with the meatiest parts towards the outside of the dish.

Made with drumsticks, this is a good snack before an outdoor meal. Made with thighs or drumsticks and thighs, it is dinner. I like Mashed Potatoes (page 252) with it. Made with wings, it is an irresistible hors d'oeuvre; be sure to have plenty of paper napkins. *Serves 6 to 8 for hors d'oeuvres, 3 to 4 as a main course*

8 chicken drumsticks (about 850 g/1¾ lb), each cut to the bone all the way around the thin end

1 recipe Mustard Barbecue Sauce (page 327) or ½ recipe Red Barbecue Sauce (page 327)

1 Arrange legs spoke-fashion in a 32.5 cm/13 inch round dish, with the thick ends towards the outside of the dish and the leg ends stacked one on top of another. Spoon enough sauce over chicken to coat well. Cover tightly with microwave cling film. Cook at 100% for 12 minutes.

2 Pierce film with the tip of a sharp knife, then remove from oven. Uncover and remove chicken to a serving plate.

3 Stir cooking juices into remaining sauce. Cover sauce tightly with microwave cling film and cook at 100% for 5 minutes. Pass separately as a dipping sauce.

To make 2 drumsticks. Place drumsticks in a 15 cm/6 inch round dish, cooking for 5 minutes.

To make 4 drumsticks. Place drumsticks in a 27.5 × 15 × 5 cm/11 × 6 × 2 inch rectangular dish, cooking for 7 minutes 30 seconds.

To make 6 chicken wings. Baste 6 wings, about 500 g/1 lb (split, tips removed and reserved for stock), with 5–6 tablespoons sauce. Arrange in a single layer in a 22.5 cm/9 inch flan dish. Cover and cook for 6 minutes. Proceed as for Chicken with Barbecue Sauce.

To make 12 chicken wings. Use 350 ml/12 fl oz sauce. Prepare and baste 12 wings, about 1 kg/2 lb, as for 6 wings, using about 125 ml/4 fl oz sauce. Arrange in a 25 × 20 cm/10 × 8 inch rectangular dish and cook for 10 minutes. Proceed as for Chicken with Barbecue Sauce.

To make 24 chicken wings. Use 350 ml/12 fl oz sauce. Prepare and baste 24 wings, about 2 kg/4 lb, as for 6 wings, using about 150 ml/¼ pint sauce. Arrange in a 35 × 27.5 × 5 cm/14 × 11 × 2 inch dish and cool for 14 minutes. Proceed as for Chicken with Barbecue Sauce.

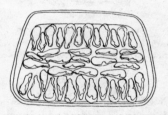

Arrange wings in a single layer in dish. Alternate different sections, meatier side to edge of dish.

CHICKEN AND RICE

This dish, or any of its variations (with lemon and eggs, with mint, with tomatoes), is just about as good as simplicity gets. It's the simplicity of a good black dress, right for any occasion. *Serves 4 to 6*

1 chicken (2.25 kg/4½ lb), jointed into serving pieces
2½ medium heads garlic, cloves smashed and peeled
600 ml/1 pint Chicken Stock (page 286) or stock from a cube
Freshly ground black pepper

175 g/6 oz long-grain rice
300 g/10 oz frozen petits pois, defrosted in a sieve under warm running water
2 teaspoons sea salt (less if using a stock cube)

1 Arrange chicken, skin side down, in a 2.5 litre/4 pint soufflé dish: place breasts in centre of dish, with legs, thighs, wings and backs around them. Scatter garlic over and pour 350 ml/12 fl oz of the stock over all. Add 6 grinds pepper. Cover tightly with microwave cling film. Cook at 100% for 20 minutes.

2 Pierce film with the tip of a sharp knife, then remove from oven and uncover. Remove chicken and keep warm. Strain cooking liquid into a 500 ml/1 pint glass measuring jug and add stock to make 500 ml/16 fl oz.

3 Bring cooking liquid and stock to the boil in a saucepan on top of the stove. Add rice and cook. When done, add peas, chicken and salt, heat through and serve.

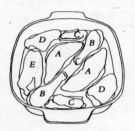

A: *Breasts*
B: *Drumsticks*
C: *Wings*
D: *Second joints*
E: *Back*

Arrange chicken pieces with the breasts in the centre, and legs and thighs around them. Drumsticks should have bone end pointing to centre.

VARIATIONS

AVGOLEMONO CHICKEN Cook chicken as for Chicken and Rice. Measure out 350 ml/12 fl oz cooking liquid, adding additional stock if necessary. Pour into a 1 litre/2 pint glass measuring jug and whisk in 4 tablespoons fresh lemon juice and 3 egg yolks. Cook, uncovered, at 100% for 2 minutes; whisk and cook for 2 minutes longer. Cook rice in addition stock. Add lemon sauce with peas and chicken.

CHICKEN WITH RICE AND MINT Add 1 teaspoon dried mint when cooking chicken, or add 2 tablespoons chopped fresh mint to rice after cooking.

CHICKEN WITH TOMATO AND BASIL Substitute 500 ml/16 fl oz Lightly Cooked Crushed Tomatoes (page 293) for stock and increase salt to 1 tablespoon. Omit garlic, rice and peas. Arrange a 1.25 kg/2½ lb chicken in dish as for Chicken and Rice and season with salt and pepper. Scatter 45 g/1½ oz fresh basil leaves over chicken and pour crushed tomatoes over all. Cook at 100% for 14 minutes. Pierce film, remove from oven, uncover and stir in 2 tablespoons cornflour dissolved in 4 tablespoons cold water. Cook, uncovered, for 4 minutes, until sauce thickens. Stir. Cook rice separately with stock. Serves 3 to 4 as a main course.

CHICKEN WITH TOMATO, BASIL AND GARLIC Arrange a 1.25 kg/2½ lb chicken in dish as for Chicken and Rice. Substitute Lightly Cooked Crushed Tomatoes (page 293) for stock, increase salt, and omit rice and peas; reduce garlic to 8 cloves. Drizzle chicken with 2 tablespoons olive oil; cook and thicken sauce as in Chicken with Tomato and Basil.

CHICKEN IN RED WINE

E arly on in my love affair with the microwave oven, a gust of emotion overcame me when I realized that it was possible to come home tired and slightly lonely and 15 minutes later have made myself a deep-tasting dark-sauced, authentic single portion of Chicken in Red Wine. Moreover, it would only take about 22 minutes to make the same thing for a group of friends, including the preparation time.

This is an absolutely splendid version of coq au vin. The chicken is perfectly tender when done, without being dried out, and the aromatic elements in the sauce retain their flavour. If you want to cut down on calories, skin the chicken, but leave the bones in for flavour and gelatine.

Before you start preparing your chicken, put salted water on to boil for rice, noodles or new potatoes. When the chicken goes into the microwave oven, put the starch in to cook (wait a few minutes for noodles). Every thing will be done at the same time. Choose a gutsy wine like Californian zinfandel or Cahors for both cooking and drinking. Serve a green salad and a simple dessert, like Light Poached Pears (page 335), that can be made ahead or while you are eating.

While it would occur to few to prepare coq au vin for one, you can do that quickly and well in the microwave oven, and you can choose your favourite part of the chicken. *Serves 4*

125 g/4 oz piece streaky bacon, cut into 5 × 5 × 10 mm/¼ × ¼ × ½ inch lardons
125 g/4 oz mushrooms, cleaned and sliced with stalks attached
125 g/4 oz button onions, peeled
1 chicken (1.25 kg/2½ lb), jointed into serving pieces
2 tablespoons brandy
2 tablespoons Meat Glaze (page 291), preferably Chicken Glaze
1 tablespoon red wine vinegar

2 tablespoons Basic Tomato Paste (page 294) or canned tomato paste
¼ teaspoon dried thyme
1 bay leaf
1 tablespoon sea salt
8 large cloves garlic, smashed and peeled
125 ml/4 fl oz Chicken Stock (page 286) or stock from a cube
250 ml/8 fl oz good red wine
2 tablespoons cornflour
Freshly ground black pepper

1 Put lardons in a 2.5 litre/4 pint soufflé dish. Cover loosely with paper towel. Cook at 100% for 7 minutes.

2 Remove from oven. With a slotted spoon, remove lardons and drain on paper towel.

3 Add mushrooms to bacon fat and toss. Mound in the centre of the dish. Place onions around inside edge of dish. Fit chicken breasts, skin side down, in centre of dish on top of mushrooms. Put legs, thighs, wings and the 2 meatiest pieces of the back around breasts, skin side down.

4 Pour brandy, Meat Glaze, vinegar and tomato paste over chicken. Add thyme, bay leaf and salt. Tuck garlic between chicken pieces. Pour stock and wine over chicken. Cover tightly with microwave cling film. Cook at 100% for 15 minutes.

5 Pierce film with the tip of a sharp knife, then remove from oven. Uncover carefully. Skim fat.

6 Stir cornflour into 4 tablespoons of the cooking liquid. Stir into sauce, making sure to stir up liquid from bottom of dish. Add pepper to taste and scatter lardons on top. Cook, uncovered, at 100% for 2 minutes.

7 Remove from oven. Stir well and serve.

To serve 1. Cut 1 thick rasher streaky bacon into 1 × 2.5 cm/½ × 1 inch lardons. Put lardons in a 1 litre/2 pint soufflé dish. Cook as for 4 servings for 4 minutes; skim out. Stir into fat 4 small mushrooms, quartered; 2 cloves garlic, smashed, peeled and cut in half lengthways; and 6 peeled button onions or 2 small white onions, peeled and quartered; stir to coat. Add 1 chicken leg and thigh or a breast with bone in, skin side down. Add 4 tablespoons stock, 4 tablespoons wine, 1 teaspoon brandy, 1 tablespoon Meat Glaze, ¼ teaspoon vinegar, 1½ teaspoons tomato paste, ¼ bay leaf, a pinch of thyme, ½ teaspoon salt, and pepper to taste. Cover and cook for 8 minutes. Dissolve 1 tablespoon cornflour in 2 tablespoons cooking liquid; stir into sauce. Cook for 4 minutes. Remove from oven, turn chicken skin side up, and stir sauce thoroughly. Scatter lardons on top and serve.

To serve 2. Use 2 rashers bacon; cut and cook in a 2.5 litre/4 pint soufflé dish as for single serving. Increase mushrooms to 8, button onions to 12, garlic to 6 cloves, red wine to 125 ml/4 fl oz, brandy to 2 teaspoons, vinegar to ½ teaspoon, tomato paste to 1 tablespoon, and salt to 1 teaspoon; use ½ bay leaf, 1 chicken breast and 1 leg and thigh. Use same amount of stock, Meat Glaze, thyme and cornflour. Increase first cooking time of chicken to 10 minutes. Proceed as for single serving.

CHICKEN GUMBO

———— • ◆ • ————

Although *gumbo* comes from an African word for okra, not all gumbos contain okra, nor do they have to have tomatoes and peppers. This gumbo is wonderful without any of them. Serve it with rice. It isn't wildly spicy; it *is* extra good. Since there are no tomatoes in the gumbo, you could add some to your salad. *Serves 4 to 6*

4 tablespoons Brown Roux (page 292)
1 large onion (about 350 g/12 oz), peeled and cut into 1 cm/½ inch wedges (leaving part of the core)
175 g/6 oz celery, stringed and cut 5 mm/¼ inch thick on the diagonal
30 g/1 oz celery leaves, coarsely chopped
8 cloves garlic, smashed and peeled
2 teaspoons filé powder, or 250 g/8 oz whole okra, trimmed (page 268)

500 ml/16 fl oz Chicken Stock (page 286) or stock from a cube
1 chicken (1.5 kg/3 lb), skinned and jointed into serving pieces, wings split and breasts cut into 3 pieces each
1 tablespoon fresh lemon juice
2 teaspoons sea salt (less if using a stock cube)
½ teaspoon freshly ground black pepper
½ teaspoon Fiery Pepper Sauce (page 297) or 1 teaspoon Tabasco sauce

1 Stir together roux, onions, celery, celery leaves and garlic in a 27.5 × 20 × 7.5 cm/11 × 8 × 3 inch dish. Cook, uncovered, at 100% for 5 minutes.

2 Remove from oven. Stir in filé powder, if used, and stock. Arrange chicken with the meatiest pieces towards the outside of the dish. Cover tightly with microwave cling flim. Cook at 100% for 8 minutes.

3 Pierce film with the tip of a sharp knife, then remove from oven. Uncover carefully and stir well. Cook, uncovered, at 100% for 7 minutes.

4 Remove from oven. Stir in lemon juice, salt, pepper and pepper sauce.

CHICKEN PAPRIKÁS

• • •

This is a Hungarian classic. Serve it with boiled noodles or half a microwave-cooked baking potato, peeled, per person. It is worth searching out Hungarian paprika paste— it comes in tubes and jars— or making Hot and Sweet Red Pepper Sauce (page 297) in order to experience this dish at its best. *Serves 4*

30 g/1 oz unsalted butter
2 large onions, peeled and chopped
2 cloves garlic, smashed and peeled
100 g/3½ oz peeled, seeded and finely chopped tomatoes or crushed and drained canned tomatoes
1 tablespoon plus 2 teaspoons paprika powder
1 chicken (1.5 kg/3 lb), jointed into serving pieces

250 ml/8 fl oz Chicken Stock (page 286) or stock from a cube
2 tablespoons cornflour
350 ml/12 fl oz soured cream
1 tablespoon sea salt
2 tablespoons fresh lemon juice
2 tablespoons Hot and Sweet Red Pepper Sauce (page 297) or Hungarian paprika paste

1 Heat butter in a 2.5 litre/4 pint soufflé dish, uncovered, at 100% for 2 minutes. Add onions and garlic and stir to coat with butter. Cook, uncovered, at 100% for 1 minute.

2 Remove from oven. Stir in tomatoes and paprika powder. Add chicken, skin side down. Place breasts in centre of dish and arrange remaining pieces around them, with the meatiest portions towards the outside of the dish. Pour stock over chicken. Cover tightly with microwave cling film. Cook at 100% for 15 minutes.

3 Pierce film with the tip of a sharp knife, then remove from oven. Uncover. Remove chicken to a serving platter and keep warm. Dissolve cornflour in 4 tablespoons cooking liquid. Stir thoroughly into remaining cooking liquid; stir in soured cream. Cook, uncovered, at 100% for 5 to 7 minutes, until thickened.

4 Remove from oven. Adjust seasoning with salt and lemon juice. Whisk in pepper sauce. Return chicken to the sauce and cook, uncovered, at 100% for 3 minutes, until heated through.

CHICKEN FRICASSEE

• • •

This is as good a Sunday dinner as any you can imagine. It has vegetables in it, but you can throw in a handful of peas along with the carrots if you like. Serve

the fricassee with rice. Put spoons on the table; the sauce is that good.
Serves 4 to 6

30 g/1 oz unsalted butter
1 medium onion (about 250 g/8 oz), peeled and sliced
1 carrot, trimmed, peeled and cut into 4 cm/1½ inch lengths
250 g/8 oz mushrooms, cleaned, trimmed and quartered
1 tablespoon lovage or celery leaves
1 bay leaf
1 chicken (2 kg/4 lb), trimmed of excess fat and jointed into serving pieces, breasts cut in half across the bone

350 ml/12 fl oz Chicken Stock (page 286) or stock from a cube
Sea salt
Freshly ground black pepper
2 tablespoons cornflour
125 ml/4 fl oz double cream
3 egg yolks
2 tablespoons fresh lemon juice
3 tablespoons chopped parsley

1 Heat butter, uncovered, in a 2.5 litre/4 pint soufflé dish at 100% for 2 minutes. Add onions, carrots, mushrooms and lovage; stir to coat with butter. Add bay leaf. Arrange chicken, skin side down, on vegetables. Place breast pieces in centre of dish and arrange remaining pieces around them, with the meatiest portions towards the outside of the dish. Add stock, salt and pepper. Cover tightly with microwave cling film. Cook at 100% for 18 minutes.

2 Pierce film with the tip of a sharp knife, then remove from oven. Let stand for 6 minutes. Uncover and skim fat. Stir cornflour into 4 tablespoons of the cream. Stir in remaining cream and egg yolks, then add 4 tablespoons cooking liquid. Stir cream mixture thoroughly into stew. Cover tightly with microwave cling film. Cook at 100% for 4 minutes.

3 Pierce film, then remove from oven. Uncover and stir in lemon juice and parsley. Taste and correct seasoning.

VARIATION

CHICKEN FRICASSEE WITH ANISE Substitute 1½ tablespoons aniseed or 1 teaspoon crushed anise for lovage or celery leaves.

CHICKEN LIVERS WITH MUSTARD AND CREAM

• • •

Microwave-cooked chicken livers are creamy and delicious, never tough and hard. You can serve them as a first course or as a main course with rice or an unsauced vegetable. Chicken livers are not expensive. Be sure to clean them well and remove all the connective tissue. When you buy a chicken, it sometimes comes with livers tucked inside. They are a dividend. (To freeze and defrost, see page 432.) *Serves 1 as a main course, 2 as a first course*

250 g/8 oz chicken livers, trimmed of connective tissue and cut in half
1 tablespoon finely chopped shallots
½ teaspoon sea salt
Large pinch freshly ground black pepper
2 tablespoons double cream

2 tablespoons Chicken Stock (page 286) or stock from a cube
1 tablespoon dry white wine
1 tablespoon Dijon mustard
15 g/½ oz unsalted butter

1 Toss livers with shallots, salt and pepper. Whisk together cream, stock, wine and mustard until well blended. Reserve.

2 Heat butter in a 22.5 cm/9 inch square browning dish, uncovered, at 100% for 2 minutes 30 seconds. Shake dish once or twice, if necessary, to ensure that butter browns evenly. Add livers. Cook, uncovered, at 100% for 2 minutes, turning livers over once.

3 Remove from oven. Remove livers to a serving plate and keep warm. Pour cream mixture into browning dish and stir well. Cook, uncovered, at 100% for 2 minutes. The sauce should be slightly reduced and thickened.

4 Remove from oven. Return livers to the dish and toss to coat with sauce. Serve at once.

To serve 2 as a main course, 4 as a first course. Double all ingredients. Heat butter in a 25 cm/10 inch square or round browning dish for 3 minutes. Cook livers for 3 minutes and reduce sauce for 3 minutes 30 seconds.

SPRING CHICKEN WITH GRAPES

This makes a gala party meal. I find that people really don't want more than half a spring chicken. It also is much easier to cut the birds. Rice, noodles or Mashed Potatoes (page 252) go with this. A few asparagus spears never hurt anybody. *Serves 2*

175 g/6 oz seedless green grapes
4 tablespoons Chicken Stock (page 286) or stock from a cube

Large pinch sea salt
1 spring chicken (850 g/1¾ lb), split, backbone removed

1 Place grapes and stock in a 25 × 17.5 × 10 cm/10 × 7 × 4 inch oval dish. Sprinkle with salt. Place split chicken, skin side up, over grapes. Cover tightly with microwave cling film. Cook at 100% for 8 minutes.

2 Pierce film with the tip of a sharp knife, then remove from oven. Serve piping hot.

To serve 4. Double all ingredients. Use a 2.5 litre/4 pint soufflé dish, arranging chicken with legs towards outside of dish and breasts towards the centre. Cook for 12 minutes.

To serve 6. Multiply all ingredient quantities by 3. Arrange chicken as for 4 servings in a 30 × 25 × 5 cm/12 × 10 × 2 inch dish and cook for 15 minutes.

VARIATION

SPRING CHICKEN WITH GRAPES IN CREAM SAUCE Cook chicken as for Spring Chicken with Grapes. Remove to a serving plate. Add 1 teaspoon sea salt, 2 tablespoons double cream, a squeeze of fresh lemon juice and a large pinch of cayenne pepper to grapes; stir well. Stir 1 teaspoon cornflour into 2 tablespoons cooking liquid; add to sauce and stir to incorporate thoroughly. Cook, uncovered, at 100% for 1 minute. Remove from oven. Spoon hot sauce and grapes over chicken.

COCOTTE OF SPRING CHICKENS

❖❖

This simple dish is rich with herbs and vegetables. It is good with either Garlic Potatoes (page 130) or boiled new potatoes. *Serves 4*

2 spring chickens (850 g/1¾ lb each), fresh or defrosted, split and backbones removed
3 teaspoons sea salt
¾ teaspoon freshly ground black pepper
300 g/10 oz frozen peas, defrosted in a sieve under warm running water
12 spring onions, trimmed, leaving 5 cm/2 inches of the green

2 medium carrots, trimmed, peeled and cut into 5 cm × 5 mm/2 × ¼ inch lengths
2 teaspoons dried oregano
1 teaspoon dried thyme
30 g/1 oz unsalted butter (optional)

1 Sprinkle chickens lightly on both sides with salt and pepper. Toss together remaining ingredients except butter in a large bowl.

2 Put half of vegetable mixture in a 2.5 litre/4 pint soufflé dish. Place the birds over the vegetables, with legs towards the outside of the dish and breasts towards the centre. Cover with remaining vegetables. Cover dish tightly with microwave cling film. Cook at 100% for 20 minutes; halfway through cooking time, uncover and turn chickens over; re-cover.

3 Pierce film with the tip of a sharp knife, then remove from oven. Uncover and remove birds to a serving platter. Stir butter into vegetables, if desired, and pour them over birds.

TURKEY À LA KING

❖❖

This is a wonderful dish for leftover turkey or chicken. Since poultry is so quick to cook in the microwave oven, it is now easy to make it from scratch when there are no leftovers. Serve Turkey à la King with rice, mashed potatoes or vol-au-vents so that you can enjoy all of the lovely gravy. This is one dish that is really not at its best made with stock from a cube. *Serves 4*

60 g/2 oz unsalted butter
2 tablespoons plain flour
60 g/2 oz celery, stringed and chopped
90 g/3 oz onion, peeled and chopped
250 ml/8 fl oz Chicken Stock (page 286)
125 ml/4 fl oz double cream
75 g/2½ oz frozen petits pois, defrosted

in a sieve under warm running water
1 teaspoon sea salt
8 drops Tabasco sauce
300 g/10 oz cooked turkey or chicken (page 181 and page 429), cut into large chunks and kept warm, if possible

1 Heat half of the butter in a 2 litre/3½ pint glass jug, uncovered, at 100% for 2 minutes. Remove from oven and whisk in flour.

2 Add celery and onions and cook, uncovered, at 100% for 3 minutes.

3 Remove from oven. Add half of the stock and whisk until smooth. Whisk in remaining stock and cream. Stir in peas. Cook, uncovered, at 100% for 8 minutes.

4 Remove from oven. Add salt, Tabasco sauce and remaining butter, stirring until butter melts. Add turkey, stir and serve.

Note. To make Turkey à la King from leftovers, use cold or room-temperature turkey and proceed as above. Stir an additional 4 tablespoons stock into final mixture. Cook, uncovered, at 100% for 2 minutes.

PIGEON WITH SEASONED BUTTER UNDER THE SKIN

• • •

This recipe is really intended for the richer-tasting pigeons, but it can be made with poussins instead.

This is a beautiful way to cook pigeon. The skin browns lightly, the flesh stays moist, and the flavours all blend together. Serve it on a bed of watercress. The butter and juices will wilt the cress a bit, and it will all taste delicious. Half of this bird satisfied me; but I suppose many will want the whole thing. *Serves* 1

30 g/1 oz Seasoned Butter (see
    following recipes)

1 squab pigeon (about 500 g/1 lb)

1 Prepare the seasoned butter of your choice.

2 Carefully work your fingers between the skin and meat of the breast and legs of the pigeon. Place all but 10 g/⅓ oz of the butter under the skin. Smear remaining butter over the skin.

3 Place the bird on a serving plate. Cook, uncovered, at 100% for 4 minutes.

To serve 2. Double all ingredients, cooking birds for 6 minutes.

To serve 4. Multiply all ingredient quantities by 4. Cook for 11 minutes in a 30 × 20 cm/12 × 8 inch dish.

SEASONED BUTTERS

◆ ◆

Makes 60 g/2 oz, enough for 2 pigeons

To make either of these compound butters, simply blend all ingredients well.
Use at room temperature. Either recipe may be doubled.

SEASONED BUTTER 1
45 g/1½ oz unsalted butter
10 g/⅓ oz flat-leaf parsley leaves
1 teaspoon fresh lemon juice

½ teaspoon ground cumin
½ teaspoon sea salt
⅛ teaspoon freshly ground pepper

SEASONED BUTTER 2
60 g/2 oz unsalted butter
1 teaspoon Spice Powder I (page 299)

1 teaspoon fresh lemon juice
1 teaspoon soya sauce

CRISPIEST DUCK

◆ ◆

This is the best and easiest way I have ever found for cooking duck. This recipe
should turn duck from a rarely cooked special dish into an easy, frequent one.
You can even make it just for one or two people without any problem.

Because fat cooks more quickly than protein in the microwave oven, the
excess fat under the duck skin is rendered, leaving the meat tender, not dried
out. The stock also helps protect the meat and keep it moist. Duck's rich taste
welcomes spicy flavours and rich, slightly acid sauces. Any of the following
sauces would be a treat: Blackberry Sauce (page 330), Cranberry Sauce for Duck
or Goose (page 329), or Cherry Sauce for Roast Birds (page 329). Allow 4
tablespoons of sauce for each portion of duck. *Serves 4 to 6*

1 duck, jointed into serving pieces, legs,
thighs, and breasts cut in half across
the bone, wing tips removed and
reserved for stock

250–300 ml/8–10 fl oz Duck Stock
(page 286), Chicken Stock (page
286) or stock from a cube

1 Remove any loose fat from duck. Prick the skin of each piece of duck several
times with a fork.

2 Heat the grill of a conventional oven. Move rack to position closest to heat
source.

3 Put duck, skin side up, in a 30 × 20 × 5 cm/12 × 8 × 2 inch dish. Add enough
stock to cover meat and bone; leave skin and fat above the liquid. Cover loosely
with paper towel. Cook in the microwave oven at 100% for 17 minutes.

4 Remove from oven. Remove duck from dish and place on grill pan. Slash fat and skin crosshatch-fashion. Grill for 6 to 8 minutes, until browned and crisp.

To serve 1. Cut a duck breast in half across the bone; each piece will be approximately 7.5 to 10 cm/3 to 4 inches square. Prick skin several times with a fork. Fit duck, skin side up, into a deep dish just large enough to hold the pieces. Add stock, 4–8 tablespoons, as for Crispiest Duck. Cook for 6 minutes, slash, and grill as for Crispiest Duck for 5 to 7 minutes.

To serve 2. Use about 750 g/1½ lb of duck, cut in half across the bone, and about 125 ml/4 fl oz stock. Prick skin several times with a fork. Cook as for Crispiest Duck in a 27.5 × 21 × 7.5 cm/11 × 8½ × 3 inch dish for 9 minutes. Grill for 5 to 7 minutes.

VARIATIONS

SPICE-RUBBED DUCK To make spice mixture, combine 1½ tablespoons freshly ground cumin, 2 teaspoons sea salt, ¼ teaspoon freshly ground black pepper, and 2 tablespoons fresh lemon juice. Rub microwave-cooked duck pieces all over with spice mixture. Grill as for Cripsiest Duck.

ORIENTAL GLAZED DUCK Joint 2 ducks into serving pieces; cut each breast, leg and thigh into 2 or 3 pieces across the bone; remove wing tips (reserve for stock) and split wings.

Put wing tips, necks, giblets and hearts in a 2 litre/3½ pint glass jug or bowl. Add 500 ml/16 fl oz Chicken Stock (page 286) or stock from a cube, 4 smashed, unpeeled cloves garlic, and ½ teaspoon ground cumin. Cover tightly with microwave cling film. Cook at 100% for 20 minutes. Strain and skim; reserve.

Prick skin of each piece of duck several times with a fork. Arrange duck in a 35 × 27.5 × 5 cm/14 × 11 × 2 inch dish and proceed as for Crispiest Duck, using reserved duck stock. Remove from oven. Place duck on grill pan and brush with Oriental Glaze (page 304). Heat grill. When duck has marinated for 10 minutes, brush again with glaze and grill close to heat source for 8 minutes. Remove duck to a serving platter and keep warm. Deglaze grill pan with a little of the reserved stock; serve as gravy with duck. Use reserved stock for soups. *Serves 8*

DUCK GUMBO
—— •◆• ——

This wonderful party fare is best partly cooked ahead, refrigerated overnight, skimmed, reheated with the vegetables and tasted for seasonings. If you are in a screaming hurry, you can serve this dish the day you make it. Skim very well after first cooking time; add vegetables. Reduce final cooking time to 10 minutes.

Serve the gumbo with a pilaf, such as Basic Pilaf (page 117), but substitute duck fat for butter and use chicken or duck stock for the liquid. This can be done while you are skimming the gumbo, before you start reheating. *Serves 10 to 12*

2 ducks, jointed into serving pieces, breasts, thighs and legs cut across the bone into 2 or 3 pieces, wing tips removed (reserve for stock) and wings split
1 large onion (about 500 g/1 lb), peeled and cut into 5 cm/2 inch chunks
12 cloves garlic, smashed and peeled
2 teaspoons Fiery Pepper Sauce (page 297)
3 cans (400 g/14 oz each) tomatoes in juice, drained and crushed
1 tablespoon filé powder (optional)
250 ml/8 fl oz Chicken Stock (page 286) or stock from a cube
200 g/7 oz okra pods, trimmed (page 268) or 300 g/10 oz frozen sliced okra, run under hot water until block of okra can be broken into 4 pieces

250 g/8 oz carrots, trimmed, peeled and julienned
150 g/5 oz frozen peas
500 g/1 lb asparagus, trimmed and stalks peeled and cut into 4 cm/1½ inch lengths
90 g/3 oz spring onions, cut on the diagonal into 2.5 cm/1 inch lengths (both white and green parts)
2 tablespoons fresh lemon juice
Sea salt
Freshly ground black pepper
Fiery Pepper Sauce or Searing Pepper Sauce (page 297) (optional)

1 Combine duck, onions, garlic, pepper sauce, tomatoes, filé if used, and stock in a 35 × 27.5 × 5 cm/14 × 11 × 2 inch dish. Stir to combine well. Cover tightly with microwave cling film. Cook at 100% for 20 minutes.

2 Pierce film with the tip of a sharp knife, then remove from oven. Let come to room temperature, covered. Refrigerate overnight.

3 Uncover; skim and reserve fat. Add remaining ingredients except for lemon juice, salt, pepper and pepper sauce. Stir well. If using frozen okra, put each quarter of frozen block in a corner of the dish. Cook, uncovered, at 100% for 15 minutes, or until heated through, stirring once during cooking time. Break up frozen okra when stirring.

4 Remove from oven. Skim off any remaining surface fat. Add lemon juice, salt, pepper and additional pepper sauce if desired. Serve with rice.

DUCK CONFIT

— • • —

This is one of the few lengthy recipes in this book. It needs to be made at least two weeks before you want to use it; but then you have a store of duck in the refrigerator available as needed. Remove as much duck as you want from the fat. Scrape off excess fat and put it back in the storage container.

Use duck in any recipe calling for confit or grill it briefly and serve it with a vegetable purée (pages 251–261). Another possibility is to rub the duck with the spice mixture in Spice-Rubbed Duck (page 201) and grill. The duck is good sliced on top of a salad with curly endive, duck cracklings (see entry on RENDERING in the Dictionary), and an onion vinaigrette.

When making confit, I start from Paula Wolfert's ideas in *The Cooking of Southwest France. Makes 2 ducks.*

6 large shallots, peeled
½ bunch parsley, preferably flat-leaf parsley
2 cloves garlic, smashed and peeled
6 tablespoons plus 2 teaspoons sea salt
2 teaspoons black peppercorns, coarsely ground
1 bay leaf, crumbled

Pinch dried thyme
2 ducks (about 2 kg/4 lb each), jointed into serving pieces, wing tips removed and saved for stock, extra skin and fat trimmed and reserved for rendered fat
800 g–1.2 kg/1¾–2½ lb rendered duck and pork fat (see note)

1 Place shallots, parsley and garlic in the container of a food processor and process until chopped. Stir in 6 tablespoons salt, ground peppercorns, bay leaf and thyme. Rub mixture on to each piece of duck. Arrange seasoned duck pieces on a large tray in a single layer. Cover loosely with a tea towel or polythene. Refrigerate for 24 hours.

2 Heat rendered fat in a 2.5 litre/4 pint soufflé dish, loosely covered with paper towel, at 100% for 10 minutes, until melted.

3 While melting fat, rinse duck pieces under cold running water. Dry. Fit legs and thighs into a 27.5 × 20 × 5 cm/11 × 8 × 2 inch dish in a single layer. Remove fat from oven and carefully ladle over duck until pieces are completely covered. Reserve remaining fat. Cover duck loosly with paper towel. Cook at 100% for 15 to 18 minutes, until thigh meat is easily pierced with a skewer.

4 Remove from oven. Allow duck to cool in fat for 30 minutes.

5 Choose a deep, narrow 2 litre/3½ pint ceramic or glass container to store confit, or 2 smaller, similarly shaped containers. Put a teaspoon of salt in bottom of container to absorb meat juices. Place legs and thighs in one container. Tent it with aluminium foil while preparing breasts and wings. Add fat from cooked leg pieces to reserved melted fat.

6 Fit breast pieces and wings into 27.5 × 20 × 5 cm/11 × 8 × 2 inch dish. Ladle reserved fat to cover as before. Cover loosely with paper towel. Cook at 100% for 10 to 12 minutes, until breast meat is easily pierced with a skewer. Proceed as in steps 4 and 5, placing breasts and wings on top of leg pieces if container is large or into their own storage container if not, with 1 teaspoon salt sprinkled over the bottom.

7 Ladle fat through a fine sieve over duck. Let cool to room temperature. Cover tightly with polythene and refrigerate overnight.

8 When duck has been refrigerated overnight, melt 250 g/8 oz rendered duck or pork fat in a 2.5 litre/4 pint soufflé dish, lightly covered with paper towel at 100% for 2 minutes 30 seconds. Pour a 1 cm/½ inch layer on top of the congealed fat that covers the duck. Cover with a double layer of polythene. Tie it down to seal well. Cover with doubled aluminium foil. Tie again. Store, refrigerated, for at least 2 weeks, and up to 4 months.

Note. For rendered fat, see entry on RENDERING in the Dictionary. Use reserved skin and fat from the ducks plus duck fat saved from cooking other ducks, such as Crispiest Duck or Duck Gumbo. Each piece of duck should have a covering of skin, but there are usually extra flaps between the leg and backbone and around the neck area. Render pork fat, allowing about 500 g/1 lb for every 300 g/10 oz needed.

MINI-CHARTREUSE WITH SAUSAGE AND QUAIL

This is another ornate dish. Perfect for impressing a significant other or someone you hope will become a significant other. The French make this into an even fancier, moulded dish, but I like it just like this with the flavours flowing together. It makes two portions from two quail—thrifty. *Serves 2*

½ teaspoon dried thyme
1 celery stick, trimmed and cut in half lengthways
½ bay leaf
10 sprigs flat-leaf parsley
500 g/1 lb white cabbage, shredded
1 carrot, trimmed, peeled and cut into 6 pieces

1 small onion, peeled and quartered
250 g/8 oz garlic sausage (kielbasa or any good smoked sausage)
500 ml/16 fl oz Chicken Stock (page 286) or stock from a cube
2 quail, cut in half
125 g/4 oz smoked ham, sliced thick

1 Make a bouquet garni: sprinkle thyme over one piece of celery, then arrange bay leaf and parsley over thyme and cover with the other piece of celery. Tie the bundle securely with kitchen string.

2 In a 2.5 litre/4 pint soufflé dish, toss together cabbage, carrots, onions and bouquet garni. Tuck sausage into the vegetables and add stock. Cover tightly with microwave cling film. Cook at 100% for 10 minutes.

3 Pierce film with the tip of a sharp knife, then remove from oven. Uncover and tuck quail around the sides of the dish under the vegetables; place ham on top of vegetables. Re-cover tightly with fresh microwave cling film. Cook at 100% for 3 minutes.

4 Pierce film, remove from oven, uncover, and divide between 2 serving dishes.

PHEASANT WITH REDCURRANT CREAM

This is absolutely fabulous. It cannot be made very often since it uses fresh redcurrants and pheasant. That makes it all the more special. This is the time for a big Burgundy wine. *Serves 2*

½ teaspoon dried oregano
½ bay leaf
1 pheasant (1.1–1.25 kg/2¼–2½ lb),
  fresh or defrosted, rinsed inside and
  out and patted dry

10 g/⅓ oz unsalted butter, softened
Sea salt
Freshly ground black pepper
250 g/8 oz redcurrants with stems
2 tablespoons double cream

1 Put oregano and bay leaf in a pheasant cavity. Rub the skin with butter and sprinkle with salt and pepper. Place in the centre of a shallow 30 cm/12 inch oval dish. Arrange redcurrants around the bird. Cook, uncovered, at 100% for 15 minutes.

2 Remove from oven. Let stand while you prepare the sauce. Drain cooking juices into a bowl and skim. Strain through a fine sieve into a clean bowl, and force redcurrants through sieve into juices. Stir in the cream, and salt and pepper to taste.

3 Cut off the legs and place one on each of 2 serving plates. Slice the breasts, arrange on the plates, and spoon some of the sauce around the meat. Pass the remaining sauce separately.

MAINLY MEAT

The microwave oven stews, braises, poaches and steams meat to perfection
It cooks it in sauce splendidly. It does not roast or shallow-fry or sauté, so
after much soul-searching and many failed attempts, I have decided to eliminate
all such recipes. Those that are left are first-rate.

MELLOWING

If you have a little extra time, mellow your stews by cooking them ahead, and
letting them cool to room temperature. Then either reheat immediately or
refrigerate and reheat the next day. The stew will not overcook, not even the
vegetables. (When you mellow, your meat will not overcook because it cools
before simply being brought back to the appropriate temperature.)

Not all meats benefit from such treatment. For those that do, instructions
appear at the end of the recipe. Food enough for eight will take 15 minutes to
reheat at 100% and should be stirred once during the cooking time. It does not
need to be covered. If it has not be refrigerated, reheat for 5 to 6 minutes.

Smaller quantities, leftovers for instance, will take less time to reheat for
mellowing—let's say 3 minutes for a portion for one from refrigerated, 5 to 6
minutes for two, and 10 minutes four. I would cover the portion for one; there
is a greater chance of its getting too dry. If the food has not been refrigerated, it
will take only 1 minute for a portion for one, 3 minutes for two, 5 minutes for
four, and 8 minutes for six.

STIRRING

In several of these recipes, you need to stir once or twice during the cooking
time. You don't need to remove the dish from the oven; indeed, it is better not
to. You can either carefully raise the film by pulling it away from the dish with
a knife—releasing the seal, but keeping your hand away from the steam—or cut
a slit in the film with a knife and stir through that. If you have cut a slit, patch
it with an overlapping square of fresh microwave cling film. If you have lifted the
cling film, you can reseal it, or put on fresh microwave cling film. You do not
have to remove the old film.

To stir, slit cling film.   *Stir through slit in film.*   *Patch cling film with fresh square to make tight seal.*

You can remove the cooking dish from the oven each time you need to stir—but I wouldn't do it any more than I would take a roasting pan out of a conventional oven each time I needed to baste a joint. You lose moisture, steam and heat.

Thanks to the microwave oven's ability to cook in serving dishes and attractive ceramic casseroles, you may want to cook many of the saucy dishes in a container that can come to the table. Keep it roughly the same size as the dish called for in the recipe, making sure that it has high enough sides so that, if you are using microwave cling film, it will not touch the food. Alternatively, choose a presentation dish that can accept a tightly fitting cover.

Unless potatoes or another starch are called for in the recipe, you probably are going to want to make potatoes, rice, noodles or another starch to go with these saucy dishes and sop up the good gravy. If you are cooking the starch in the microwave oven, make it before the meat and reheat it while the meat is mellowing or while you complete the seasoning. If you are making the starch on top of the stove, check your meat recipe and make sure you start the water for the starch early enough so it will be done at the same time as the main course. Of course, a crusty loaf of bread needs no cooking and will do the job just as well. For many of these homely, welcoming dishes, I give my guests a spoon. If they are a little timid at first, they quickly get into the spirit and use it to get up every last bit.

BEEF

For these saucy dishes, stews and pot roasts, the meat cooks better if marbled and aged. Use the cuts indicated. Do not use better cuts; you are likely to get dry meat.

HEART OF THE HOME BEEF STEW

———— • ————

This is basic eats, good solid food. Stir in some cooked potatoes, peeled and cubed, or serve with Mashed Potatoes (page 252) or Garlic Potatoes (page 130). *Serves 6 to 8*

1 tablespoon vegetable oil
250 g/8 oz small white onions (about
    4 cm/1½ inches in diameter), peeled
    and quartered
6 cloves garlic, smashed and peeled
3 small carrots, trimmed, peeled and
    sliced 3 mm/⅛ inch thick
6 mushrooms, trimmed and quartered
30 g/1 oz parsley, chopped
3 tablespoons Basic Tomato Paste (page
    294) or canned tomato paste
1 kg/2 lb stewing beef, cut into 2.5 cm/
    1 inch cubes

½ bay leaf
2 teaspoons dried marjoram
1 teaspoon dried oregano
1 teaspoon dried thyme
250 ml/8 fl oz Veal Stock (page 287)
    or stock from a cube
1 tablespoon cornflour dissolved in
    2 tablespoons cold water
1½ tablespoons sea salt (less if using a
    stock cube)
Freshly ground black pepper

1 Combine oil, onions, garlic, carrots, mushrooms, parsley and tomato paste in a 2.5 litre/4 pint soufflé dish. Cook, uncovered, at 100% for 4 minutes.

2 Stir in remaining ingredients. Cover tightly with microwave cling film. Cook at 100% for 10 minutes.

3 Stir well; re-cover. Cook at 100% for 5 minutes.

4 Stir again and re-cover. Cook for 3 minutes more.

5 Pierce film with the tip of a sharp knife, then remove from oven. Mellow (page 206), if you wish. Serve hot.

CHUNKY BEEF CHILLI

———— • ————

Fights have broken out, marriages broken up, and restaurants broken down over the proper recipe for chilli. Serious chilli people call for the beef or other meat to be cut into little cubes and say there should be no beans in the chilli. Beans are served, if at all, on the side. The truly austere don't even include tomatoes. They say the red colour should come only from the chilli and other spices. I don't go that far. You can substitute other meat or game for beef—pork, lamb or venison, alone or in a combination. This chilli can also be prepared with minced beef. If you like, serve Chillied Beans (page 127) on the side along with rice, soured cream, grated Cheddar cheese, chopped onions or spring onions, and even shredded lettuce. *Serves 6 as a main course without beans or rice, 8 to 10 as a main course with beans and/or rice, or 8 to 10 as a first course on its own*

1 large onion (about 350 g/12 oz), peeled and quartered
2 cloves garlic, smashed and peeled
2 tablespoons whole dried red chillies (each 2.5 cm/1 inch long)
1.1 kg/36 oz canned Italian plum tomatoes
1½ teaspoons ground cumin
1½ teaspoons ground coriander
2 teaspoons chilli powder, or to taste
½ teaspoon dried oregano
½ teaspoon dried marjoram
¼ teaspoon cayenne pepper

1 piece (5 cm/2 inches) cinnamon stick
1 kg/2 lb beef chuck, cut into 5 mm/ ¼ inch cubes
30 g/1 oz/fresh coriander leaves, coarsely chopped
30 g/1 oz dark plain chocolate (*chocolat pâtissier*), chopped
2 tablespoon red wine vinegar
2½ teaspoons sea salt
Soured cream, for serving (optional)
Grated Cheddar cheese, for serving (optional)

1 Place onions, garlic and chillies in the container of a food processor. Process until coarsely chopped. Drain tomatoes (reserving juice) and add them to food processor. Process until coarsely chopped.

2 Put reserved juice and tomato mixture in a 35 × 27.5 × 5 cm/14 × 11 × 2 inch dish. Stir in cumin, coriander, chilli powder, oregano, marjoram, cayenne and cinnamon. Cook, uncovered, at 100% for 9 minutes.

3 Stir in beef. Cover tightly with microwave cling film. Cook at 100% for 15 minutes.

4 If mellowing or planning to reheat, do not add remaining ingredients until reheated. Otherwise, stir in coriander, chocolate, vinegar and salt. Serve chilli with soured cream and grated cheese, if desired.

VARIATION

CHILLI WITH MINCED BEEF Substitute 1 kg/2 lb lean minced beef for cubed beef. Cook for only 5 minutes in step 3. If minced beef clumps together, whirl in food processor for a few pulses to break up.

TRADITIONAL POT ROAST

———— • ◆ • ————

This takes 10 minutes to prepare and 1 hour to cook, longer than almost any other recipe in this book; but it is worth it, especially considering that top-of-the-stove cooking time is 3 to 4 hours. Serve with Mashed Potatoes (page 276) or noodles. *Serves 6 to 8*

1.25 kg/2¼ lb boned and rolled brisket of beef, trimmed
250 g/8 oz medium carrots, trimmed, peeled and cut into 6 cm/2½ inch lengths
1 medium onion (about 250 g/8 oz), peeled and quartered
½ bay leaf

4 cloves garlic, smashed and peeled
125 ml/4 fl oz Veal or Chicken Stock (page 286) or stock from a cube
2 teaspoons sea salt (less if using a stock cube)
250 ml/8 fl oz Lightly Cooked Crushed Tomatoes (page 293) or canned chopped tomatoes with juice.

1 Place brisket, fat side down, in a 2.5 litre/4 pint soufflé dish. Arrange carrots, onions, bay leaf and garlic around brisket. Pour stock over vegetables and sprinkle salt over all. Pour crushed tomatoes over brisket. Cover tightly with microwave fling film. Cook at 100% for 35 minutes.

2 Pierce film with the tip of a sharp knife, then uncover and turn brisket over. Re-cover tightly. Cook at 100% for 25 minutes.

3 Pierce film, then remove from oven. Mellow (page 206) if time allows. Slice thin across the grain. Serve hot.

BEEF IN RED WINE

———— • • ————

This dish, called boeuf bourguignon by the French, is like most traditional stews: it is better the day after it is made. Store, tightly covered, in the refrigerator overnight. To reheat, see Mellowing (page 206). *Serves 6*

60 g/2 oz piece streaky bacon, cut into 5 cm × 5 mm/2 × ¼ inch lardons
125 g/4 oz small mushrooms, trimmed, wiped clean and quartered through stalk
125 g/4 oz small white onions, peeled and quartered
1 kg/2 lb beef chuck, cut into 4 cm/1½ inch cubes
2 teaspoons sea salt
Freshly ground black pepper
125 ml/4 fl oz red wine
125 ml/4 fl oz Veal or Chicken Stock (page 286), or stock from a cube

125 ml/4 fl oz canned tomatoes, drained and crushed
3 tablespoons Basic Tomato Paste (page 294) or canned tomato paste
¼ teaspoon dried thyme
¼ teaspoon dried rosemary
¼ teaspoon dried tarragon
6 cloves garlic, smashed and peeled
1 tablespoon cornflour dissolved in 2 tablespoons cold water
2 tablespoons Meat Glaze (page 291) (optional)
2 tablespoons Cognac or brandy

1 Place lardons in a 2.5 litre/4 pint soufflé dish. Cook, uncovered, at 100% for 4 minutes.

2 Remove from oven. Remove lardons to paper towel to drain and reserve.

3 Stir mushrooms and onions into hot fat. Cook, uncovered, at 100% for 4 minutes.

4 Sprinkle beef with salt and pepper. Stir into onion mixture and add remaining ingredients except cornflour, glaze, Cognac and reserved lardons. Cover tightly with microwave cling film. Cook at 100% for 15 minutes.

5 Pierce film with the tip of a sharp knife, then uncover. Stir in cornflour, glaze, Cognac and reserved lardons, stirring well to combine. Cook, uncovered, at 100% for 4 minutes.

6 Remove from oven. Allow the stew to mellow (page 206). Reheat and serve hot.

SLICED BEEF CASSEROLE

———— • • ————

The French call this dish boeuf en daube. Elizabeth David, the post-World War II English guru of French cooking, devised a method of slicing the beef for daube to shorten the cooking time and allow it to become more thoroughly imbued with the flavours of the sauce. This works well in the microwave oven. You might consider it as a way of cooking other pot roasts. The traditional cooking time for boeuf en daube, even with sliced beef, is 4 to 6 bours. In the microwave oven, total cooking time is 15 minutes. *Serves 6 to 8*

15 g/½ oz unsalted butter
1 medium onion, peeled and cut into 1 cm/½ inch dice
4 medium carrots, trimmed, peeled and cut into 1 cm/½ inch dice
½ teaspoon dried tangerine zest or dried orange zest, or 3 strips (7.5 × 1 cm/ 3 × ½ inch) fresh orange zest
4 tablespoons finely chopped parsley
8 cloves garlic, smashed and peeled
1 bay leaf
1 teaspoon dried thyme

2 teaspoons sea salt
1.5 kg/3 lb boned beef top rib joint, sliced across the grain, 1 cm/½ inch thick
125 ml/4 fl oz Chicken Stock (page 286) or stock from a cube
175 ml/6 fl oz red wine
4 tablespoons brandy
1 tablespoon Meat Glaze (Page 291), preferably Veal Glaze (optional)
1 piece bacon rind (15 × 5 cm/6 × 2 inches)

1 In a 2.5 litre/4 pint soufflé dish, combine butter, onions, carrots, tangerine or orange zest, parsley and garlic. Cook, uncovered, at 100% for 4 minutes.

2 Remove from oven. Stir in bay leaf, thyme and salt. Arrange sliced beef overlapping in dish. Pour stock, wine, brandy and glaze, if used, on beef. Tuck bacon rind between meat slices. Cover tightly with microwave cling film. Cook at 100% for 10 minutes.

3 Pierce film with the tip of a sharp knife, then uncover and stir well, pushing meat from the top towards the bottom of the dish. Cook, uncovered, at 100% for 5 minutes.

4 Remove from oven. Mellow (page 206) daube, if desired. Serve hot.

LEONARD SCHWARTZ'S MEAT LOAF

A colleague at *Vogue* tasted this meat loaf at Leonard Schwartz's 72 Market Street restaurant in California. She loved it so much that we got, tested and printed the recipe to applause. Here is a microwave version, which can't shorten the ingredient list or the chopping time, although you can chop in the food processor. It does shorten the cooking time. It is definitely good enough to be a dinner party meat loaf. *Serves* 8

1 medium onion, peeled and cut into
  2.5 cm/1 inch chunks
125 g/4 oz spring onions, trimmed and
  cut into 2.5 cm/1 inch lengths (white
  and some of the green)
100 g/3½ oz celery, stringed and cut
  into 5 cm/2 inch pieces
125 g/4 oz carrot, peeled and cut into
  2.5 cm/1 inch pieces
90 g/3 oz red pepper, cored, seeded and
  cut into 2.5 cm/1 inch pieces
90 g/3 oz green pepper, cored, seeded
  and cut into 2.5 cm/1 inch pieces
2 large cloves garlic, smashed and peeled
45 g/1½ oz unsalted butter

1 teaspoon sea salt
¼ teaspoon cayenne pepper
1 teaspoon freshly ground black pepper
½ teaspoon freshly ground white pepper
½ teaspoon ground cumin
½ teaspoon freshly grated nutmeg
125 ml/4 fl oz half cream
125 ml/4 fl oz tomato ketchup
750 g/1½ lb lean minced beef
250 g/8 oz lean minced pork
3 eggs, beaten
70 g/2⅓ oz fine, dry Breadcrumbs (page
  306) or store-bought unflavoured
  breadcrumbs

1 Place vegetables and garlic in the container of a food processor. Process until very finely chopped. Reserve.

2 Heat butter in a 27.5 × 21 × 5 cm/11 × 8½ × 2 inch dish, uncovered, at 100% for 3 minutes. Add chopped vegetables and stir to coat. Cover loosely with paper towel. Cook at 100% for 8 minutes.

3 Remove from oven. Uncover and let stand for 2 minutes.

4 Combine remaining ingredients in a large bowl, mixing well to make sure seasonings are evenly distributed. Knead in cooled, cooked vegetables.

5 Divide the mixture into 8 balls. Shape each ball into a small, rounded, oval loaf, 12.5 × 8.5 × 2.5 cm/5 × 3½ × 1 inch. Arrange loaves inside the rim of a 30 cm/12 inch flan dish. Cover tightly with microwave cling film. Cook at 100% for 4 minutes. Uncover and cook for 4 minutes more.

6 Remove from oven. Remove meat loaves to a warm platter. Serve with cooking juices spooned over, if desired.

To serve 4. Halve all ingredients. Prepare mixture as for 8 servings. Pack prepared mixture into a 22.5 cm/9 inch glass ring mould (loaf should be about 6 cm/2½ inches thick). Cook, tightly covered with microwave cling film, at 100% for 5 minutes; uncover and cook for 4 minutes longer.

To serve 2. Use ½ small onion, 30 g/1 oz spring onions, 30 g/1 oz celery, 45 g/1½ oz carrots, 2 tablespoons *each* chopped red and green pepper, ½ clove garlic, 10 g/⅓ oz butter, ¼ teaspoon salt, a pinch of cayenne, ½ teaspoon black pepper, ⅛ teaspoon white pepper, ⅛ teaspoon cumin, ⅛ teaspoon nutmeg, 2 tablespoons *each* cream and ketchup, 175 g/6 oz minced beef, 60 g/2 oz minced pork, 1 small egg and 20 g/⅔ oz Breadcrumbs. Prepare mixture as for 8 servings. Shape into a rounded loaf. Cook in an oval dish, covered, at 100% for 4 minutes; uncover and cook for 3 minutes longer.

To serve 1. Prepare mixture as for 4 servings. Shape prepared mixture into 4 loaves (250 g/8 oz each). If you wish, wrap and freeze 3 loaves. Cook each loaf by itself, in an oval dish, tightly covered, at 100% for 3 minutes; uncover and continue cooking for 1 minute. To defrost a frozen loaf, place it in an oval dish and cover tightly with microwave cling film. Cook at 100% for 4 minutes 30 seconds; the meat loaf will be defrosted and ready to cook.

Cook meat loaf in a ring mould so that it cooks evenly.

OLD-FASHIONED MEAT LOAF

When I was a child, I loved—almost best of all—the meat loaf nights with slices of juicy meat loaf, swirls of Mashed Potatoes (page 252), and extra cooking juice from the meat loaf nestled into a back-of-the-spoon indent in the potatoes. Creamed Spinach (page 260) completed childhood bliss. It was the kind of food my parents told me not to play with; but the rivers of gravy that would flow out of my potato mountain were irresistible. This is a recipe that doesn't let memory down. I wish more people would serve me food like this when I come to dinner.

If I have extra, I pretend I'm a grown-up and serve it cold the next day as pâté. *Serves 6 to 8*

1 celery stick, trimmed, stringed and broken into 3 pieces
1 small onion, peeled
500 ml/16 fl oz Lightly Cooked Crushed Tomatoes (page 293), or canned tomato purée
60 g/2 oz fresh breadcrumbs

1 tablespoon coarse mustard
2 teaspoons Hot Pepper Sauce (page 297) or Tabasco sauce
1 tablespoon Worcestershire sauce
1½ teaspoons sea salt
Freshly ground black pepper
1 kg/2 lb minced beef

1 Put all ingredients except beef in the container of a food processor. Process until well mixed. Scrape mixture into a large bowl and, using your hands, combine with beef. Pack into a 22.5 × 12.5 × 7.5 cm/9 × 5 × 3 inch loaf dish. Cook, uncovered, at 100% for 12 minutes.

2 Remove from oven. Let stand for 10 minutes. Carefully drain off cooking juices. Serve hot or cold. Skim cooking juices. Use as a gravy over mashed potatoes, rice or noodles.

FILLET OF BEEF PROVENÇALE

There is no doubt that fillet of beef is an expensive cut. Its redeeming values are tenderness and no waste—you can get it by the piece. There is a common notion that microwave-cooked beef must be tough, but this recipe and the following one prove that fillet is at its best in this rapid, moist mode of cooking. The beef never gets stringy. The sauce has a robust Provençale flavour to compensate for any blandness in the meat. I like to serve it with mashed potatoes or steamed new potatoes so that every bit of sauce gets enjoyed. *Serves 4 to 6*

1 medium onion, peeled and cut into
  5 mm/¼ inch dice
125 ml/4 fl oz dry red wine
4 tablespoons Cognac
12 cloves garlic, smashed and peeled
1 tablespoon Basic Tomato Paste (page 294) or canned tomato paste
3 strips (7.5 × 1 cm/3 × ½ inch) orange zest
4 tablespoons fresh orange juice

1 tablespoon cornflour
90 g/3 oz Niçoise olives, stoned (optional)
4 tablespoons finely chopped parsley
750 g/1½ lb joint fillet of beef, cut into six 1 cm/½ inch thick slices
Sea salt
Freshly ground black pepper
1½ tablespoons fresh lemon juice

1 Combine onion, wine, Cognac, garlic, tomato paste and orange zest in a 2.5 litre/4 pint soufflé dish or casserole with a tight-fitting lid. Cook, uncovered, at 100% for 6 minutes, stirring every several minutes.

2 Remove from oven. Combine orange juice with cornflour and stir into sauce along with olives and parsley. Sprinkle beef with salt and pepper and make two layers of slices on top of sauce in dish. Cover tightly with microwave cling film or with lid. Cook at 100% for 6 minutes, stirring every 2 minutes and moving beef slices from top to bottom in the dish so that they cook evenly. If using cling film, pierce it with tip of sharp knife to release steam.

3 Remove from oven and uncover. Stir in lemon juice and taste for seasoning. Serve.

FILLET OF BEEF WITH MORELS

— • ◆ • —

This is a party dish, elegant and—unfortunately expensive enough—to make any evening gala. Start with a cold terrine. The sauce can be made ahead. Put the beef in to cook while your guests are having their first course and glass of wine. When you go into the kitchen, finish the sauce while you are cutting the beef into easy portions. Pour some of the sauce around the beef and put the rest in a sauce boat or bowl. Serve with sauce spoons or large soup spoons; your guests won't want to waste a drop. Crusty French bread for sauce mopping wouldn't go amiss either. *Serves 8*

60 g/2 oz dried morels
750 ml/1¼ pints Veal Stock (page 287)
  or chicken stock from a cube
175 g/6 oz button onions, peeled
¼ teaspoon dried thyme
1.25 kg/2½ lb joint fillet of beef, tied
  with string but not barded

Sea salt
Freshly ground black pepper
125 ml/4 fl oz double cream
2 teaspoons Dijon mustard
1½ tablespoons cornflour

1 Place mushrooms in a 2.5 litre/4 pint soufflé dish. Cover with 500 ml/16 fl oz of the stock. Cover tightly with microwave cling film. Cook at 100% for 4 minutes. Pierce film to release steam.

2 Remove from oven and let stand, covered, for 2 minutes. Uncover. Drain liquid through a sieve lined with a double thickness of dampened muslin and reserve. Rinse mushrooms well in cold water. If mushrooms are large, cut into halves or quarters and reserve.

3 Place remaining stock in a 27.5 × 17.5 × 5 cm/11 × 7 × 2 inch loaf dish. Add onions and thyme. Season the beef with salt and pepper and place in dish. Cover tightly with microwave cling film. Cook at 100% for 13 minutes for rare beef, turning beef over halfway through cooking. Add 2 minutes to the timing if you like your beef better done. Pierce film to release steam.

4 Remove from oven and uncover. Remove beef to a carving board. Remove strings.

5 Combine cream, mustard and cornflour in a small bowl. Whisk into cooking dish along with reserved mushroom liquid and mushrooms. Cover tightly with microwave cling film. Cook at 100% for 4 minutes. Remove from oven, stir well and serve with beef sliced about 2.5 cm/1 inch thick.

TOPSIDE STEAKS WITH TOMATO SAUCE

——— ◆ ◆ ———

Nothing could be quicker or easier. It is a nice way to cook a less expensive cut of beef so that it stays tender. Don't lengthen the cooking time or you will toughen the beef. If you don't have time to make one of my tomato sauces (pages 323–325), use your favourite brand of bottled tomato or spaghetti sauce. Either way, the tomato sauce and the meat juices will combine to enliven the pasta—spaghettini or fine noodles—that you will have cooked ahead allowing 60 g/2 oz per person. *Serves 4*

4 slices beef topside, each weighing 125 g/4 oz, and cut 8 mm/⅓ inch thick

250 ml/8 fl oz homemade tomato sauce, or bottled spaghetti sauce

1 Place slices of beef in one layer in a 32.5 × 22.5 × 5 cm/13 × 9 × 2 inch oval dish. Cover each slice with 4 tablespoons of sauce. Cover tightly with microwave cling film. Cook at 50% for 7 minutes 30 seconds. Pierce film to release steam.

2 Remove from oven and uncover. Serve surrounded by cooked pasta, if desired.

To serve 1. Divide ingredients by four. Arrange as above in a 25 cm/10 inch flan dish and cook, covered, at 50% for 2 minutes. (Same time at 100% in a small oven.)

To serve 2. Halve all ingredients. Arrange as above in a 25 cm/10 inch flan dish and cook, covered, at 50% for 5 minutes. (Same time at 100% in a small oven.)

PORK

Pork has been one of the great revelations of working on this book. I have always liked pork; but it rises to a new level of succulence with microwave cooking. It cooks through before it dries out. Even with the reduced fat content of today's pork, it bastes itself to perfection. Clearly, it doesn't brown. I think that is an improvement; the pork doesn't develop those nasty stringy bits. The only place where the browning seems important is in the Smothered Pork Roast (page 220). There, you grill the roast briefly after it is cooked, to crisp and brown the surface fat.

When cooking pork, it is important to make sure the meat is cooked through. The best way to tell is to use a small, instant-reading meat thermometer. Insert the thermometer halfway into the fleshiest part of the meat, not too close to the bone. Watch for a temperature of 60° to 63°C/140° to 145°F. The meat will keep cooking for a while after it comes out of the oven. All these recipes work for the time and temperature that are given, but your piece of meat may have a slightly different weight or shape. It is not critical; but it makes it worth using the thermometer.

PORK CHOP WITH SAUERKRAUT

•◦•

The Hungarians know a thing or two about food. One of the things they know is an extraordinary stew of pork and sauerkraut called Szekely Gulyas. This meatier version is made with pork chops.

I defy anybody to eat two of these pork chops and the savoury sauerkraut that goes with them—too much. These are big chops. Steam some potatoes or butter some noodles. Drink icy beer or a white riesling wine. *Serves 4*

30 g/1 oz unsalted butter
1 large onion (about 350 g/12 oz), peeled, thinly sliced and separated into rings
4 loin pork chops (2.5–4 cm/1–1½ inches thick), 1–1.25 kg/1–2½ lb
1.5 kg/3 lb sauerkraut, drained and rinsed

1 tablespoon caraway seeds
6 cloves garlic, smashed and peeled
500 ml/16 fl oz soured cream
2 to 3 tablespoons Hot and Sweet Red Pepper Sauce (page 297) or Hungarian paprika paste

1 Heat butter in a 35 × 27.5 × 5 cm/14 × 11 × 2 inch dish, uncovered, at 100% for 2 minutes. Stir in onions. Cook, uncovered, for 2 minutes more.

2 Remove from oven. Arrange pork chops on top of onions; place one in each corner of the dish with the bone against the side of the dish. Spread sauerkraut over chops and stir in caraway. Press garlic into sauerkraut. Cover tightly with microwave cling film. Cook at 100% for 16 minutes.

3 Insert an instant-reading thermmeter right through the film into the thickest part of a chop, without letting it touch the bone. If it reads 63°C/145°F, the chops are done. If it reads less than that, patch the hole in the film with a small piece of film and cook at 100% for 1 to 2 minutes more.

4 Pierce film with the tip of a sharp knife, then uncover. Stir in soured cream and pepper sauce. Cover tightly with microwave cling film. Cook at 100% for 2 minutes.

5 Pierce film, then remove from oven. Uncover and serve hot.

6 This reheats and mellows (page 206) well. Add 125 ml/4 fl oz water or stock when reheating.

PORK CHOPS IN TOMATO SAUCE
—— • ◆ • ——

If there is a meal easier than this, I don't know it. No one will know that you make it using bought spaghetti sauce. The only important thing is that it tastes good. This dish is meant to be served with spaghetti or noodles, with the sauce from the chops poured over the pasta. Since the chops are thin, they sop up a maximum of flavour. One chop and a portion of spaghetti and sauce feeds me; but I have known a small, if admittedly athletic, person to inhale 3 chops. You will have to be the judge. When you have figured it out, allow about 60 g/2 oz of dry pasta per person. That makes 125 g/4 oz if each person eats 3 chops, and 350 g/12 oz if there are 6 eaters like me. I usually make about 250 g/8 oz of pasta and figure it will work out. Toss pasta with 1 tablespoon of olive oil before adding sauce. *Serves 6, 1 chop each*

6 thin pork chops (1–2 cm/½–¾ inch thick), about 1 kg/2 lb
250 ml/8 fl oz bottled or canned spaghetti sauce
1 tablespoon olive oil

3 large cloves garlic, smashed and peeled
2 tablespoons chopped parsley
Large pinch dried thyme
Sea salt
Freshly ground black pepper

1 Arrange chops in a 30 cm/12 inch square dish with their bony sides against the sides of the dish.

Pork chops with bones towards edge of dish.

2 Stir together spaghetti sauce, olive oil, garlic, parsley and thyme and spoon over chops. Cover tightly with microwave cling film. Cook at 100% for 8 minutes.

3 Insert an instant-reading thermometer right through the film into the thickest part of a chop, without touching the bone. If it reads 63°C/145°F, the chops are done. If it reads less than that, patch film with a small piece of film and return to oven for 1 to 2 minutes more.

4 Pierce film with the tip of a sharp knife, then remove from oven and uncover. Stir in salt and pepper to taste and serve.

To serve 1. Use 1 pork chop, 4 tablespoons sauce, 1 teaspoon oil, 1 small clove garlic, 2 teaspoons parsley, a small pinch of thyme, salt and pepper. Centre chop in a 15 cm/6 inch round dish. Cover tightly with microwave cling film. Cook as for Pork Chops in Tomato Sauce for 4 minutes.

To serve 12. Double all ingredients. Cook in 2 batches: spoon half the sauce over 6 chops and cook as for Pork Chops in Tomato sauce. Serve the first 6 to keep them warm while preparing the rest.

SMOTHERED PORK ROAST
◆ ◆ ◆

This is a cross between a pot roast and a real roast, and it is the best pork joint I have ever had, with the plus of a great vegetable. If you want to add something, it should be a simple, colourful vegetable like Glazed Carrots (page 242) or leaf spinach. Leftover meat is good cold in sandwiches or sliced and reheated with some of the vegetale purée. *Serves 6 to 8 as a main course*

3 baking potatoes, each pierced twice with a fork
45 g/1½ oz unsalted butter
500 g/1 lb onions, peeled and sliced
250 g/8 oz celery, stringed and sliced
4 tablespoons finely chopped parsley

1 boneless pork loin joint (1.75 kg/ 3½ lb, 10 cm/4 inches in diameter)
2 teaspoons sea salt
Freshly ground black pepper
½ teaspoon caraway seeds

1 Cook potatoes (page 476). Remove from oven. Cover with an inverted pan or two tea towels to keep warm.

2 Heat butter in a 27.5 × 20 × 5 cm/11 × 8 × 2 inch dish, uncovered, at 100% for 2 minutes. Stir in onions. Cook, uncovered, at 100% for 5 minutes. Stir in celery and parsley.

3 Sprinkle joint with salt, pepper and caraway. Place in onion mixture, fat side down. Cover tightly with microwave cling film. Cook at 100% for 10 minutes.

4 Pierce film with the tip of a sharp knife, uncover and turn joint over. Re-cover; cook for 10 minutes more.

5 Preheat conventional grill.

6 Uncover joint and turn over again. Cook, uncovered, for 15 minutes.

7 Put joint in a pan that can go under the grill. Grill until brown, if desired.

8 Scrape vegetables into a food processor. Peel and dice potatoes. Add to vegetables; purée until smooth. Serve with the roast.

SAUSAGE AND PEPPERS

• ◆ •

This is super easy and very good. The spiciness of the dish will depend on the spiciness of the sausage you can find or want to use. If you cannot find fresh basil, substitute ½ teaspoon dried basil. *Serves 3 to 4*

1 kg/2 lb fresh spicy pork sausages, cut into 5 cm/2 inch lengths
250 g/8 oz onion, peeled and cut into 1 cm/½ inch cubes
1 green pepper, cored, seeded and cut into 5 cm/2 inch chunks

1 red pepper, cored, seeded and cut into 5 cm/2 inch chunks
15 g/½ oz fresh basil leaves
4 tablespoons store-bought spaghetti or tomato sauce
Sea salt

1 Place sausage in a 27.5 × 20 × 5 cm/11 × 8 × 2 inch oval dish and cover loosely with paper towels. Cook at 100% for 10 minutes, stirring twice.

2 Remove from oven. Uncover, drain well and discard fat.

3 Add remaining ingredients except salt. Stir to coat. Cover tightly with microwave cling film. Cook at 100% for 7 minutes.

4 Remove from oven. Uncover and sprinkle with salt. Serve with mashed potatoes or pasta, or on French bread.

VARIATION

SAUSAGE AND FENNEL Substitute 100 g/3½ oz bulb fennel cut into 5 cm/2 inch chunks for green pepper and 1 teaspoon fennel seeds for basil. *Serves 3 to 4*

BARBECUED SPARERIBS

Finish these out of doors on a barbecue or under your grill. Eat hot or cold, as picnic food. Lamb breast riblets are particularly good for a cocktail party. The recipe gives you, as a dividend, 250 ml/8 fl oz of cooking juices, which are delicious spooned over Mashed Potatoes (page 252). *Serves 3 to 4*

1.75 kg/3½ lb pork spareribs   1 recipe Red Barbecue Sauce (page 327), made with finely chopped garlic

1 Arrange ribs in a single layer in a 35 × 27.5 × 5 cm/14 × 11 × 2 inch dish. Brush on one side with half of sauce. Cover tightly with microwave cling film. Cook at 100% for 10 minutes.

2 If using grill, preheat.

3 Pierce film with the tip of a sharp knife, remove meat from oven and uncover. Turn ribs over and brush with remaining sauce. Re-cover tightly with fresh microwave cling film. Cook at 100% for 10 minutes.

4 Barbecue for 4 minutes, turning once, or grill, in grill pan, 15 cm/6 inches from heat source for 5 minutes, turning once. Serve hot.

VARIATIONS

ORIENTAL SPARERIBS Replace barbecue sauce with a sauce made by combining 4 tablespoons Chicken Stock (page 286) or stock from a cube, 125 ml/4 fl oz tamari soya sauce, 5½ tablespoons sugar, ½ crushed star-anise pod or ½ teaspoon five-spice powder, 6 cloves smashed and peeled garlic, and 6 crushed dried chillies in a 1 litre/2 pint glass measuring jug. Cover tightly with microwave cling film. Cook at 100% for 3 minutes. Proceed as for Barbecued Spareribs.

BARBECUED LAMB RIBLETS Substitute an equal weight of lamb breast riblets for spareribs. Cook as for Barbecued Spareribs. Grill without turning.
Serves 14 with drinks

VEAL

Veal has become incredibly expensive. I don't like the quality of most of what is available and it's hard to get butchers to pay proper attention to it—separating it into individual muscles and so forth. Consequently, most of these recipes are for less expensive and less fussy cuts of veal. These are exactly the recipes that usually take a long time to cook, but not with a microwave oven.

Don't overcook veal: since it contains little fat, it dries out. Veal is pale in colour. Pick colourful accompaniments—purées like Carrot and Potato (page 254) or Creamed Spinach (page 260)—or Wild Rice (page 115) to brighten the plate. Simply cooked veal can be accompanied by Stuffed Vegetables (pages 70–77), and it does well with a Mushroom Sauce (page 318), or Sauce Espagnole (page 321), or Sauce Poulette (page 319) made with veal stock.

VEAL FRICASSEE

• • •

This ivory-coloured stew, the French blanquette de veau, is enlivened with a few nontraditional carrots. It is almost always served with plain rice. You could use Green Pilaf (page 118) instead, for a nice colour contrast. Make the fricassee first. Let it mellow (page 206) before adding the egg-yolk mixture, while you cook the pilaf. Then reheat for 30 seconds more than the time given. *Serves 4 to 6*

15 g/½ oz unsalted butter
250 g/8 oz mushrooms, trimmed and
   quartered
250 g/8 oz button onions, peeled
2 carrots, trimmed, peeled and cut into
   5 cm/2 inch lengths
1 kg/2 lb boneless veal shoulder or leg,
   trimmed and cut into 5 cm/2 inch
   cubes
500 ml/16 fl oz Veal or Chicken Stock
   (page 286) or chicken stock from a
   cube

1 teaspoon dried thyme
½ bay leaf
1 clove garlic, smashed and peeled
2 tablespoons cornflour
175 ml/6 fl oz double cream
3 egg yolks
Pinch freshly grated nutmeg
Sea salt
Freshly ground black pepper
2 tablespoons fresh lemon juice

1 Heat butter in 2.5 litre/4 pint soufflé dish, uncovered, at 100% for 30 seconds.

2 Toss mushrooms and onions in butter and mound in centre of dish. Arrange carrots and veal in a circle around the onions.

3 Cover with stock. Add thyme, bay leaf and garlic. Cover tightly with microwave cling film. Cook at 100% for 15 minutes.

4 Pierce film with the tip of a sharp knife, then remove from oven. Remove film. Let stew stand for 10 minutes, to cool slightly so the eggs do not curdle when added.

5 Stir cornflour into about 4 tablespoons of cream. Stir in remaining cream, egg yolks and nutmeg and blend thoroughly. Add to stew and stir well. Cover tightly with microwave cling film. Cook at 100% for 4 minutes.

6 Pierce film, then remove from oven. Uncover and stir. Taste and correct seasoning with salt, pepper and lemon juice.

VARIATION

VEAL FRICASSEE WITH ANISE Add 1½ tablespoons aniseed or 1 teaspoon crushed anise when you add garlic.

LOIN OF VEAL

Admitted that veal is expensive, this is the way to get the maximum of what you pay for in the least possible amount of time with a minimum of fuss. The cooking takes all of 6 minutes. The meat doesn't shrink and stays white and tender. You can also serve it cold, thinly sliced, as a first course Italian-fashion (vitello tonnato), to an unexpectedly large group, or as a main course on a hot day, with a lettuce and tomato salad, cold white wine and bread sticks. See page 333 for Tomato Sauce. *Serves 4*

1 boneless joint loin of veal
  (750 g/1½ lb)

125 ml/4 fl oz Veal or Chicken Stock
  (page 286) or chicken stock from a
  cube

1 Put veal in a 22.5 × 12.5 × 7.5 cm/9 × 5 × 3 inch dish. Add stock and cover tightly with microwave cling film. Cook at 100% for 6 minutes.

2 Insert an instant-reading thermometer right through the film into the centre of the joint. At 63° C/145° F, the veal is done; it will be pale pink in the centre. (For a loin cooked through, not at all pink, cook for 8 minutes.) If it is not done to your liking, patch film with a small piece of film and cook for 1 to 2 minutes longer.

VEAL STEW

• • •

This is an utterly delicious stew with an elegant sauce. Sauces today are seldom thickened with breadcrumbs the way this one is. It used to be commonplace and was called thickening with panade, a French word derived from *pain* (bread). The stew is rich, the sauce ample. Serve it with rice and it will serve more people than you might imagine. *Serves 6 to 8*

1 kg/2 lb boneless veal shoulder or leg, trimmed and cut into 5 cm/2 inch cubes
4 teaspoons sea salt
Freshly ground black pepper
500 ml/16 fl oz Veal Stock (page 287)
1 celery stick, trimmed, stringed and cut into 3 pieces
1 carrot, trimmed, peeled and cut into 3 pieces
1 small onion (about 125 g/4 oz), peeled and quartered
15 g/½ oz parsley, preferably flat-leaf parsley
30 g/1 oz unsalted butter
Pinch dried thyme
125 g/4 oz fresh breadcrumbs
2 egg whites

1 Season veal with 2 teaspoons of the salt and the pepper. Put in a 2.5 litre/4 pint soufflé dish and add 350 ml/12 fl oz of the stock. Cover tightly with microwave cling film. Cook at 100% for 10 minutes.

2 Put celery, carrots, onions and parsley in the container of a food processor. Process until coarsely chopped. Scrape into a 2 litre/3½ pint glass jug or bowl. Add butter, thyme, remaining salt, and pepper to taste and stir to combine.

3 Remove veal from oven and set aside. Cook chopped vegetables, uncovered, at 100% for 4 minutes.

4 Remove from oven. Whisk in breadcrumbs and egg whites. Add remaining stock and stir. Cover tightly with microwave cling film. Cook at 100% for 5 minutes.

5 Pierce film with the tip of a sharp knife, then remove from oven. Uncover veal and remove with a slotted spoon to a small container. Pour cooking liquid from veal into a blender. Add vegetable mixture and blend for 20 seconds. Return veal to soufflé dish and pour sauce over it.

ITALIAN-STYLE VEAL KNUCKLE

• • •

Veal knuckle makes a wonderful Italian winter dish called ossobuco. It is usually served with Saffron Risotto (page 116) and sprinkled on top with an attractive and sharp aromatic mix called gremolata. It used to take so long to make that it was only worth doing for a party. Now that it can be quickly made in the microwave oven, it is still good party fare, but is wonderfully heartwarming. Made in 12 minutes, it is a comfort to the soul. Some veal knuckles make very large and meaty slices and will feed two. Give your guests coffee spoons to scoop out the marrow from the centre of the bone. It is a succulent, if not terribly healthy, prize. *Serves 4*

VEAL KNUCKLES
1 small onion, peeled and cut in half
125 g/4 oz celery sticks, trimmed, stringed and broken into 3 pieces each
125 g/4 oz carrots, trimmed, peeled and cut into 5 cm/2 inch lengths
4 pieces veal knuckle (about 350 g/12 oz each), cut across the bone 6 cm/ 2½ inches thick
2 tablespoons olive oil
3 cloves garlic, smashed and peeled
1 piece orange zest (7.5 × 1 cm/3 × ½ inch)
1 piece lemon zest (7.5 × 1 cm/3 × ½ inch)
1 teaspoon sea salt
⅛ teaspoon freshly ground black pepper
¼ teaspoon dried thyme
½ bay leaf

3 parsley sprigs
Pinch cayenne pepper
60 g/2 oz canned tomatoes, drained and crushed
3 tablespoons Basic Tomato Paste (page 323) or canned tomato paste
4 tablespoons white wine
4 tablespoons Chicken Stock (page 314) or stock from a cube
2 tablespoons Veal or Chicken Glaze (page 320)

GREMOLATA
5 cloves garlic, smashed and peeled
1 bunch parsley
5 pieces orange zest (7.5 × 1 cm/3 × ½ inch)
1 piece lemon zest (7.5 × 1 cm/3 × ½ inch)

1 Place onions, celery and carrots in the container of a food processor. Process until coarsely chopped.

2 On top of the stove, brown veal on all sides in oil; this will take about 10 minutes.

3 Put veal in a 27.5 × 20 × 5 cm/11 × 8 × 2 inch oval or rectangular dish. Scatter chopped vegetables over veal pieces. Tuck garlic and zests between pieces. Combine remaining ingredients for veal and pour over. Cover tightly with microwave cling film. Cook at 100% for 16 minutes.

4 Place ingredients for gremolata in food processor and process until finely chopped. Reserve.

5 Pierce film with the tip of a sharp knife, then remove veal from oven. Let sit for 15 minutes before serving or mellow (page 225) for a longer time. Just before serving, top each piece of veal with gremolata.

To serve 2. Halve all ingredients. Cook as for 4 servings in a 23.5 × 17.5 × 4.5 cm/9½ × 7 × 1¾ inch oval dish for 12 minutes.

To serve 6. Use 6 pieces veal knuckle as above, 3 tablespoons oil, 1 medium onion, 175 g/6 oz each celery and carrots, 4 to 5 cloves garlic, 1½ pieces *each* orange and lemon zest, 1½ teaspoons salt, a scant ¼ teaspoon pepper, ½ teaspoon thyme, ¾ bay leaf, 5 parsley sprigs, large pinch cayenne, 90 g/3 oz crushed tomatoes, 4½ tablespoons tomato paste, 6 tablespoons *each* wine and stock, and 3 tablespoons glaze. Prepare gremolata and proceed as for cooking veal in a 35 × 27.5 × 5 cm/14 × 11 × 2 inch dish for 22 minutes.

LAMB

Lamb has wonderful flavour, it goes with a wide variety of seasonings, and it is relatively inexpensive. Lamb makes one of the best roast joints, is terrific in curry, loves spinach, and goes with beans—fresh French beans or dried flageolets (pages 417 and 418), in particular.

When making lamb stew for close friends or family, buy lamb with the bone in. It will be more succulent. Middle neck, scrag and shoulder are good, inexpensive stew cuts. Sometimes lamb or gigot steaks, cut from the top of the leg, are available at a good price; they can be cut up for stew, as can regular lamb chops, if they are cheaply bought on special offer. For guests, use stew meat that has been taken off the bone.

Lamb likes the stronger-tasting purées. Swede Purée (page 257) or Winter Vegetable Purée (page 255) would both be good with stew. Szechuan Green Beans (page 268) and Chinese Stewed Tomatoes (page 269) are unusual partners for roast lamb.

LAMB STEW

— • ◆ • —

Lamb stew is rich and full of flavour, even richer when made with bones. It can be a spring dish made with peas and green herbs or that midwinter classic, Irish Stew. The latter may sound plain, but I guarantee that it tastes terrific—ideal family fare. *Serves 4 to 6*

1 kg/2 lb lamb on the bone, cut into chunks no larger than 6 cm/2½ inches square
750 ml/1¼ pints Lamb Stock (page 287), Chicken Stock (page 286) or chicken stock from a cube
3 medium carrots, trimmed, peeled and cut into sticks 5 cm × 5 mm/2 × ¼ inch
250 g/8 oz onions, peeled and quartered

30 g/1 oz celery, stringed and sliced
5 cloves garlic, smashed and peeled
1 tablespoon plus 2 teaspoons cornflour
150 g/5 oz peas
30 g/1 oz parsley, finely chopped
1½ tablespoons fresh mint leaves
2 tablespoons fresh lemon juice
Sea salt
Freshly ground black pepper

1 Place lamb, stock, carrots, onions, celery and garlic in a 2.5 litre/4 pint soufflé dish. Cover tightly with microwave cling film. Cook at 100% for 20 minutes.

2 Pierce film with the tip of a sharp knife, then uncover. Dissolve cornflour in about 4 tablespoons cooking liquid. Add to lamb mixture and stir thoroughly. Add peas, parsley and mint. Re-cover tightly with fresh microwave cling film. Cook at 100% for 4 minutes, until sauce has thickened.

3 Pierce film, then remove from oven. Uncover and season to taste with lemon juice, salt and pepper.

VARIATION

IRISH STEW Use 1 kg/2 lb lamb as for Lamb Stew; 250 g/8 oz peeled small white onions (not button); 500 g/1 lb peeled small white potatoes, cut in 5 cm/ 2 inch chunks; 250 g/8 oz small turnips, about 5 cm/2 inches in diameter, peeled and cut into 1 cm/½ inch wedges; 1½ tablespoons sea salt; freshly ground black pepper; and 350 ml/12 fl oz water. Omit other ingredients. Arrange lamb around inside edge of a 2.5 litre/4 pint soufflé dish. Put vegetables in centre. Dissolve salt in water and add with pepper to taste. Cover tightly with microwave cling film and cook at 100% for 25 minutes. *Serves 4 to 6*

GREEN LAMB CURRY

—◆◆—

Not all curries are yellow; a few of my favourites are green with herbs, like this one, which is a good dish for family or guests. Don't be discouraged by the long list of ingredients. Most of them are spices.

The curry goes well with Tomato Pilaf (page 119). If you have a little time, or have it on hand, try Peach Chutney (page 407) or Fresh Mango Chutney (page 407). All the usual curry accompaniments (page 183) can be served. *Serves 4*

2 teaspoons vegetable oil
1½ teaspoons sesame seed
½ teaspoon fennel seed
1½ teaspoons cumin seed
1½ teaspoons mustard seed
8 to 10 cloves garlic, smashed and peeled
45 g/1½ oz parsley leaves
2 medium onions, peeled and quartered
750 g/1½ lb boneless lamb, cut into 1 cm/1½ inch cubes
300 g/10 oz frozen broad beans, defrosted in a sieve under warm running water

5½ tablespoons Lamb or Chicken Stock (page 286) or chicken stock from a cube plus any accumulated juices from lamb
500 g/1 lb spinach, thoroughly washed, stalks removed and dried
45 g/1½ oz dill sprigs
1 fresh green Indian chilli, stemmed, seeded, deribbed and cut into 1 cm/ ½ inch pieces
1 tablespoon grated fresh root ginger
⅛ teaspoon grated nutmeg
½ teaspoon dried thyme
1 bay leaf, broken in half
Sea salt

1 Heat oil in a 2.5 litre/4 pint soufflé dish, uncovered, at 100% for 2 minutes.

2 Add sesame, fennel, cumin and mustard seeds. Cover loosely with a sheet of paper towel, Cook at 100% for 4 minutes.

3 Put garlic and parsley in the container of a food processor and process until finely chopped. Add onions and process until coarsely chopped.

4 Scrape mixture into soufflé dish, add lamb and toss to combine. Stir in broad beans and stock. Cover tightly with microwave cling film. Cook at 100% for 4 minutes. Pierce film with the tip of a sharp knife to release steam.

5 Put spinach, dill, chilli, ginger, nutmeg and thyme in food processor. Process until finely chopped. Add this mixture and bay leaf to lamb and stir well. Re-cover tightly with microwave cling film. Cook at 100% for 2 minutes.

6 Pierce film, remove from oven and uncover. Stir in salt to taste and serve hot.

LEG OF LAMB

This is not a true microwave recipe, but it is a useful trick for which you can use the microwave oven. Since we sometimes buy leg of lamb already frozen or freeze it for storage, it is nice to be able to defrost and cook it in the same time or less than it would ordinarily take just to cook it. This makes leg of lamb good emergency rations to keep on hand for last-minute guests.

The meat is actually cooked at a very high temperature in a conventional oven, but since it heats somewhat during defrosting, the roasting time is reduced. The result is very good. For convenience's sake, defrost the lamb in a dish that can also go in the regular oven. *Serves 6*

1 frozen 2 kg/4 lb leg of lamb
3 cloves garlic, smashed, peeled and slivered
1 teaspoon sea salt
¼ teaspoon freshly ground black pepper

½ teaspoon rosemary leaves, fresh or dried
250 ml/8 fl oz Lamb Stock (page 287), chicken stock from a cube, red wine or a mixture of half wine and half stock

1 Preheat conventional oven to 260° C/500° F, Gas Mark 9–10.

2 Place leg of lamb in a 33.5 × 23.5 × 5 cm/13½ × 9½ × 2 inch dish. Shield the knuckle bone with aluminium foil (page 19). Cover tightly with microwave cling film. Cook at 100% for 15 minutes. Without removing from oven, pierce film, uncover and remove foil shield. Re-cover and cook for 6 minutes more.

3 Pierce film, remove from oven and uncover. Move joint to roasting pan, if necessary. Prick all over with a small knife and insert slivers of garlic in meat. Sprinkle all surfaces with salt, pepper and rosemary.

4 Place in preheated oven. Cook for 20 minutes for rare, 25 to 27 minutes for medium rare.

5 Remove from oven. Put meat on a platter. Let stand for 15 minutes before carving. Pour fat out of cooking pan, leaving juices in pan.

6 If lamb was roasted in a microwavable dish, add stock or other liquids to dish. Place in microwave oven, uncovered, for 3 minutes at 100%. Remove and stir to dissolve all the meat juices in pan. Correct seasoning. Serve as gravy.

7 If meat was roasted in a metal pan, place on stove over high heat. Pour in stock or other liquids while scraping pan with a wooden spoon to dissolve all the meat juices. Cook for 3 minutes, stirring constantly. Season and serve.

LAMB STEAKS WITH MINT

Tender leg or gigot steaks, cut from the fillet end of a leg of lamb, are delicious served rare after quick cooking in a microwave oven. This simply prepared dish has middle-eastern overtones of mint although they would want their lamb well done. Try reinforcing the ethnic idea by serving couscous. Lamb chump chops may also be cooked this way. *Serves 8*

6 lamb steaks, about 350 g/12 oz each, cut 5 cm/2 inches thick
1 tablespoon sea salt

6 cloves garlic, smashed and peeled
4 tablespoons very finely chopped fresh mint

1 Place steaks in a single layer in a 35 × 27.5 × 5 cm/14 × 11 × 2 inch rectangular dish. Sprinkle with salt, garlic and half the mint. Cover tightly with microwave cling film. Cook at 100% for 20 minutes. Pierce film to release steam.

2 Remove from oven and uncover. Sprinkle with remaining mint and serve hot, or mellow (page 206) then reheat.

To serve 3–4. Place 2 steaks in a 32.5 × 22.5 × 5 cm/13 × 9 × 2 inch dish. Sprinkle with 1 teaspoon salt, 2 cloves garlic and ¾ tablespoon fresh mint. Cover as above and cook for 18 minutes. Uncover, sprinkle with an additional ¾ tablespoon mint and serve.

LAMB STEAKS WITH SPINACH

Unfortunately, this recipe cannot be made for a crowd as can Lamb Steaks with Mint. All that spinach just won't fit in the oven. It makes a delicious, healthy, complete family meal. As lamb steaks are rather large, you will have to look and see if you think you will get two or three servings. *Serves 2–3*

1 baking potato, peeled and cut into
  4 cm/1½ inch cubes
1 kg/2 lb spinach, stalks removed, well
  washed and squeezed of excess water,
  chopped in the food processor
2 lamb steaks, about 350 g/12 oz each,
  cut 5 cm/2 inches thick

6 cloves garlic, smashed and peeled
1 teaspoon dried oregano
½ teaspoon dried thyme
125 ml/4 fl oz plain yogurt
½ teaspoon sea salt
Freshly ground black pepper
½ teaspoon ground cumin

1 Bring 1 litre/1¾ pints lightly salted water to the boil on the stove. Add potatoes and cook until tender.

2 Spread half the spinach over the bottom of a 32.5 × 22.5 × 5 cm/13 × 9 × 2 inch dish. Arrange steaks over spinach. Sprinkle the meat with garlic, oregano and thyme. Cover with remaining spinach. Cover tightly with microwave cling film. Cook at 100% for 12 minutes. (If using a small oven, cook for 22 minutes.) Pierce film with the tip of a sharp knife to release steam.

3 Remove from oven and uncover. Put steaks on a platter or plates and keep warm. Return dish with spinach to oven. Cook, uncovered, at 100% for 5 minutes. (If using a small oven, cook for 10 minutes.) If mellowing (page 225) or making ahead, stop at this point. Then reheat.

4 Remove from oven. Stir in yogurt, salt, pepper to taste and cumin. Drain potato and stir into spinach mixture. Arrange around steaks and serve hot.

To serve 4. Use 1 large potato, 1.5 kg/3 lb spinach, 3 lamb steaks, 9 cloves garlic, 1½ teaspoons oregano, ¾ teaspoon thyme, 175 ml/6 fl oz yogurt, 1 teaspoon salt and ¾ teaspoon cumin. Cook potato as above. Arrange spinach, meat, garlic, oregano and thyme as above and cook for 18 minutes. (If using a small oven, cook for 35 minutes.) Remove lamb and cook for 8 minutes more. (If using a small oven, cook for 20 minutes.) Finish as above.

OTHER MEATS

When we think of meat, we usually think of beef, pork, lamb and veal. Here, I have recipes for rabbit, tongue and brains. They may not be everyday fare, but they are definitely worth trying in the microwave oven. To cook sweetbreads, see page 57.

RABBIT IN MUSTARD SAUCE

I t is a commonplace that every time someone does not know how to describe a meat, from rattlesnake to alligator to frogs' legs, they say that it tastes like chicken. Well, rabbit does taste a bit like chicken, but better. Now that rabbits are available, frozen, in many supermarkets, you should give them a try. They are usually already cut into serving pieces. Serve with noodles, rice or Potato Galette (page 130). *Serves 4 to 6*

1–1.25 kg/2–2½ lb frozen rabbit, jointed into serving pieces
500 ml/16 fl oz milk
250 ml/8 fl oz double cream

250 g/8 oz Dijon mustard
2 tablespoons fresh lemon juice
½ teaspoon sea salt
½ teaspoon freshly ground black pepper

1 Arrange rabbit, bonier side up, in a 27.5 × 20 × 5 cm/11 × 8 × 2 inch oval dish.

2 Whisk together remaining ingredients. Pour over rabbit. Cover tightly with microwave cling film. Cook at 30% (see page 17) for 15 minutes; halfway through cooking time, pierce film, uncover dish and turn rabbit over.

3 Re-cover and increase power to 100% and cook for 17 minutes. Preheat conventional grill.

4 Pierce film, then remove rabbit from oven. Uncover and remove rabbit to grill pan. Brush with some of the cooking liquid and grill 15 cm/6 inches from the heat source for 2 to 3 minutes, until lightly browned. Serve with the additional sauce.

TONGUE

I love tongue, both smoked and pickled and hot or cold for sandwiches on rye bread with mustard and with Bread and Butter Pickles (page 404) or as a family meal. The problem—pre-microwave—was that with blanching (par-cooking to remove salt) and cooking the pickled tongue or cooking the smoked tongue, the time required could be from 3 to 6 hours. In the microwave oven, smoked tongue cooks perfectly in 30 minutes, pickled tongue in just over an hour. If you do not want to serve either of them hot with cabbage, Creamed Spinach (page 260) is good. Beer is the thing to drink with this. *Serves 8 to 10 as a main course.*

1 pickled tongue (1.8 kg/4 lb), trimmed of root end, or 1 smoked tongue of the same weight 150 ml/¼ pint ale	330 ml/11 fl oz water 2 tablespoons brown sugar 2 cloves garlic, smashed and peeled 1 allspice berry

1 If using smoked tongue, go directly to Step 3. If using pickled tongue, place tongue in a 5 litre/8 pint casserole and cover with 2 litres/3½ pints of cold water. Cover tightly with microwave cling film or a tightly fitted lid. Cook at 100% for 20 minutes. Prick film to release steam. Remove from oven and uncover. Turn tongue over and repeat blanching process with an equal amount of cold water. Prick film to release steam.

2 Remove from oven and uncover. Drain tongue and remove from dish. Trim of all visible fat and any bones.

3 Shield 6 cm/2½ inches of tip of tongue with aluminium foil (page 19). Place in a 2.5 litre/4 pint soufflé dish. Combine remaining ingredients and pour over tongue. Cover tightly with microwave cling film. Cook at 100% for 15 minutes. Prick film to release steam.

4 Remove from oven and uncover. Turn tongue over and remove foil shield. Re-cover and cook for 15 minutes more. Prick film to release steam.

5 Remove from oven and uncover. Remove tongue from dish and allow to cool slightly. When tongue is cool enough to handle, peel and cut off base end. Slice tongue thinly. Store in cooking juices.

BRAINS

I once lost a boyfriend who saw me cleaning brains. I didn't find out what happened until years later. Clearly, we were not fated for each other. Nevertheless, if I had had this recipe and a microwave oven then he never would have had to see me doing that icky chore. The microwave oven miraculously eliminates the need for tedious preparation of brains. Brains are good hot with Browned Butter Sauce (page 313) or cold in a salad. *Serves 2 as a main course*

1 set brains, washed and medulla (connecting part in centre) removed (about 350 g/12 oz)
125 ml/4 fl oz water

2 tablespoons sherry vinegar
Browned Butter Sauce (page 313) for serving (optional)

1 Place brains, rounded side up, in a 2.5 litre/4 pint soufflé dish. Combine water and vinegar and pour over brains. Cover tightly wih microwave cling film. Cook at 100% for 4 minutes.

2 Without removing dish from oven, pierce film, then uncover and turn brains over. Re-cover and cook for 4 minutes more.

3 Pierce film, then remove from oven. Uncover, drain and serve hot with Browned Butter Sauce, if desired.

VARIATION

BRAIN SALAD Prepare brains, substituting malt vinegar or white vinegar for sherry vinegar. Drain and let stand until cool. Cut into 5 mm/¼ inch slices and arrange on a bed of batavia or other bitter salad leaves. Combine 1 tablespoon tarragon vinegar, 3 tablespoons good-quality olive oil, 1 tablespoon finely chopped fresh tarragon, ½ teaspoon salt, 1 hard-boiled egg (peeled, white finely chopped and yolk forced through a sieve), and 1 tablespoon finely chopped shallot. Pour over brains and serve with freshly ground black pepper. *Serves 4 as a main course, 2 as a first course*

BRAISED BRAINS WITH TURNIP SAUCE

This dish tastes so good I hope you will be tempted to try it. It is very elegant. *Serves 4 as a main course*

125 g/4 oz turnips, peeled and diced
125 g/4 oz onion, peeled and diced
1–2 celery sticks, stringed and diced
4 tablespoons very finely chopped plus 4 tablespoons finely chopped parsley
125 ml/4 fl oz Chicken Stock (page 286) or stock from a cube

2 sets brains (about 600 g/1¼ lb), washed and medulla (centre connecting part) removed
125 ml/4 fl oz double cream
75 g/2½ oz cooked smoked tongue or ham, julienned (optional)

1 Combine turnips, onions, celery, very finely chopped parsley and stock in a 2.5 litre/4 pint soufflé dish. Place brains on top, rounded side up. Cover tightly with microwave cling film. Cook at 100% for 6 minutes.

2 Leaving dish in oven, pierce film, uncover and turn brains over. Re-cover and cook for 6 minutes more.

3 Pierce film, then remove from oven. Uncover and remove brains to a warm dish. Place vegetables in the container of a food processor. Add cream and process until smooth. Spoon some sauce on to each of 4 serving plates and place 1 piece of brain on top of each. Sprinkle with julienned smoked tongue or ham, if desired. Sprinkle with chopped parsley.

VEGETABLES

C ooking vegetables in the microwave oven is a pleasure, and not just because it is quick. They are better. They have much better colour and flavour than vegetables cooked conventionally, and they retain more of their vitamins. They cook evenly, and their texture is better, no more water-logged or stringy vegetables. They keep their shape better whether stuffed and cooked, cooked whole or in pieces, either on their own or in soups and stews.

Now that we are getting very good vegetables from our farmers and from the southern Europe, the Caribbean, Israel, Central and South America, Australia, New Zealand and the Orient, where vegetables ripen in what seem to us strange seasons, we have harvest season year-round. As you need barely any fat in microwave cooking, what you add is a very small amount, mainly for flavour.

To prepare vegetables in the microwave oven, consult the Dictionary at the end of the book. Under the name of the vegetable you want to cook, you will find how to prepare it and cover it, and how long to cook it in large and small ovens. You will find how much you will get, raw and cooked, from the amount you buy or pick. You will also find some general information in the Dictionary about vegetables that may be new to you.

If you are using an oven with less than 650 to 700 watts, read page 17 to find out how to adapt the recipes. If you still have questions or need to defrost frozen vegetables, you should find the answers in the Dictionary.

Most of the recipes in this chapter are for fresh vegetables. With few exceptions, notably frozen petits pois, which are better than all but fresh local peas, fresh vegetables are far better and cheaper than frozen or canned vegetables (except for tomatoes out of season). The microwave oven makes cooking vegetables so rapid and easy it seems a pity to cheat. Where you can, I have noted the fact. Remember, though that vegetables that have been frozen have generally been blanched (lightly cooked). You have to shorten the cooking time or add them later in a recipe. Be careful. Since they often give off some of the water they were cooked in, you will need to drain them once they have been defrosted or to add less liquid when you cook them.

The recipes in this chapter go beyond basics. The chapter starts with the simplest recipes for the season's best and goes on to the kind that turn simple grilled fish or meat, poached fish, chicken or veal into party fare. It ends with a few recipes meant to be whole meals. There are other vegetable recipes in this book, notably among the First Courses (pages 39–77). Starchy vegetables like potatoes and dried beans, as well as pastas and risottos with vegetables, are in the chapter beginning on page 107.

If you want to find a recipe for a sauce to serve with hot or cold vegetables, look in Savoury Sauces (pages 312–333) or in the Index. Mornay (page 317), Cheddar Cheese Sauce (page 141), Parsley Sauce (page 320), Watercress Sauce (page 320), Chunky Tomato Sauce (page 324) and Mayonnaise (page 332) for cold vegetables are all good sauces to keep in mind. Several of the purées in this chapter can be thinned with cream or milk to make good and attractive sauces.

The number of people that I indicate a recipe will serve is based on one vegetable as a side dish. If you are preparing two vegetables, you can assume that each recipe will serve a third again as many people. If you are preparing three vegetables, double the number each recipe will serve.

When you are choosing a vegetable to go with a main course, the first rule of thumb is the saucier the main course, the simpler the vegetable. Vegetables should complement the main dish and each other in colour, texture and flavour, not repeat it or fight with it. A curried vegetable does not go with a curried main course, nor does Sweet and Sour Red Cabbage. The vegetable can give oomph to the main course when it is very simple, like poached fish or chicken, but it shouldn't overwhelm it. If you are serving more than one vegetable, do only one that is saucy. Combine it with a crisp vegetable or a puréed one.

If you are preparing the main course as well as the vegetables in the microwave oven, make the vegetables first and stick them back in for 1 or 2 minutes at 100% while you finish seasoning the main course. You can arrange the food on plates with deep rims, in wide-rimmed soup plates, or in 25 cm/10 inch flan dishes, and put them in two by two, using a trivet (see page 25) for 30 seconds to 1 minute to reheat.

I hope I will succeed in convincing you as you read this chapter to cook more vegetables and to make them a larger part of your diet, along with the grains and other starches I have given recipes for in other parts of the book. We all know it is a healthier way to eat. Let's make it a pleasure as well.

SIMPLE VEGETABLES

Even non-vegetarians sometimes get a craving for a summery meal of vegetables. In the microwave oven, it can be quick, fresh and easy. You can try a few of the recipes that follow; but, simpler yet, you could stop at a supermarket and pick up an assortment of already cleaned and cut-up vegetables (300 g/10 oz per person). Arrange them on a dinner plate, with the quicker-cooking vegetables in the centre and the slower-cooking ones around them. See the Dictionary (page 501) for a list of which is which. Sprinkle with 1 tablespoon of fresh herbs and/or other seasonings, not salt. Add salt only after removing the plate from oven. Cover tightly with another, upturned plate and cook at 100% for 3 minutes 30 seconds. Voilà, Instant Vegetable Dinner. If you want to add protein, top each portion with an egg after cooking 2 minutes. Prick the yolk twice with the tip of a very sharp knife and replace the dish, uncovered, in the oven for 2 minutes at 100%. Or serve the vegetables with Cheddar Cheese Sauce (page 141) or Mornay (page 317) or with an added starch. (Put any leftover cooked starch in the middle of the plate.) For more people, cook just the vegetables of Pasta Primavera (page 133) and serve with either of the cheese sauces or with Watercress Sauce (page 320).

Vegetables as in Pasta Primavera   Instant Vegetable Dinner

Arrange long-cooking vegetables towards the rim, quick-cooking vegetables in the centre.

BROCCOLI

I thought it might be interesting to take a vegetable like broccoli and follow it through this chapter, going from simple to complex recipes, especially to illustrate some of the basic ways to cook vegetables.

Broccoli is generally available all year-round. If you want to cook it so that it stays bright green, loses none of its vitamins and also has both stalk and flowers perfectly cooked, this is the way. Serve with Cheddar Cheese Sauce (page 141) or one of the other sauces. You could top the broccoli with a Poached Chicken

Breast (page 181); top that in turn with Mornay (page 317) and then pass the dish quickly under the grill for Chicken Divan. If you season the broccoli with lemon juice, serve it immediately, or it will discolour. This is true for all vegetables seasoned with lemon juice. *Serve 4 to 6 as a side dish*

1.25 kg/2½ lb broccoli, trimmed of leaves and cut into 10–12.5 cm/4–5 inch stalks with florets	4 tablespoons water Sea salt Fresh lemon juice

1 Arrange broccoli in a single layer, spoke-fashion with florets pointing towards the centre of a 30 cm/12 inch flan dish. Pour water over broccoli. Cover tightly with microwave cling film. Cook at 100% for 12 minutes.

2 Pierce film with the tip of a sharp knife, then remove from oven. Uncover and add salt and lemon juice.

To make 750 g/1½ lb broccoli. Trim the broccoli stalks. Peel stalks. Cut off florets. Cut stalks across into 5 mm/¼ inch thick coins. Place broccoli florets and stalks in a 27.5 × 20 × 5 cm/11 × 8 × 2 inch oval dish or a casserole with a tightly fitting lid. If using oval dish, cover tightly with microwave cling film. If using casserole, add 4 tablespoons water. Cook at 100% for 6 minutes. If using cling film, pierce it before removing from oven. Add salt and lemon juice to taste.

To make 250 g/8 oz broccoli. Trim broccoli. Peel stalks. Cut off florets. Slice stalks thin. Place florets and sliced stalks in a 1 litre/2 pint glass measuring jug. Cover tightly. Cook at 100% for 4 minutes. Add salt and lemon juice to taste.

PEAS WITH MINT AND SPRING ONIONS

This is a classic way to prepare peas. There is none better when the peas are good. If you can get fresh home-grown peas in summer, so much the better. If not, use frozen petits pois. They will be much more tender than old peas. *Serves 4 to 6*

60 g/2 oz unsalted butter 600 g/1¼ lb frozen petits pois, defrosted in a sieve under warm running water, or 750 g/1½ lb fresh peas, shelled	1 bunch spring onions, trimmed and cut into 4 cm/1½ inch lengths 10 g/⅓ oz fresh mint leaves, shredded, or 1 teaspoon dried mint Sea salt Freshly ground black pepper

1 Heat butter in a 1.5 litre/2½ pint soufflé dish, uncovered, at 100% for 2 minutes. Stir in peas, spring onions and mint. Cover tightly with microwave cling film. Cook at 100% for 3 minutes.

2 Pierce film with the tip of a sharp knife, then remove from oven. Uncover and stir in salt and pepper. Serve hot.

To serve 2. Place 100 g/3½ oz freshly shelled peas, 7 g/¼ oz butter, a pinch salt and a mint sprig in a 250 ml/8 fl oz glass jug or bowl. Cover tightly with microwave cling film. Cook for 3 minutes.

VARIATION

PEAS WITH MINT, SPRING ONIONS AND LETTUCE Stir in 90 g/3 oz shredded soft-leaved (round) lettuce before final seasoning. Cook, uncovered, at 100% for 1 minute. Salt and pepper to taste. *Serves* 4 to 6

GLAZED CARROTS

◆ ▪ ◆

This recipe was devised for whole young carrots in their prime. If you use larger carrots, peel them and cut them in quarters lengthways and then into 5 cm/2 inch lengths. If the carrots are very young, chop 1 tablespoon of the very tip leaves and sprinkle on top before cooking. *Serves* 2

6 small carrots, each about 15 cm/6 inches long (250 g/8 oz), peeled and left whole with 2.5 cm/1 inch of green stalk

15 g/½ oz unsalted butter, cut into bits
1 tablespoon sugar

1 Arrange carrots, alternating tip and root ends in a 21 × 16 × 5 cm/8½ × 6½ × 2 inch oval dish. Scatter butter and sugar on top of carrots. Cover tightly with microwave cling film. Cook at 100% for 8 minutes.

2 Pierce film with the tip of a sharp knife, then remove from oven and let stand for 1 to 2 minutes. Uncover, toss, and serve.

To serve 4. Double all ingredients. Cook in a 27.5 × 21 × 5 cm/11 × 8½ × 2 inch dish for 12 minutes. Finish as for 2 servings.

FENNEL

— • • —

Florence fennel, or bulb fennel, is a delicious vegetable that looks like round, white celery and tastes mildly like liquorice. It is good cooked and also raw, thinly sliced in salads with a lemon dressing. Except to Italians, fennel is less familiar than it should be, but it is becoming widely available. It makes a nice change. It goes well with fish, chicken and veal. If the fennel is brown or stringy on the outside, go over it lightly with a potato peeler. Cut off the stems and just enough of the root end to make it tidy, but not so much that it falls apart. *Serves 4*

2 large bulbs fennel (about 7.5 cm/3 inches across), cored, trimmed and cut into 6 wedges each
2 tablespoons finely chopped feathery tops of fennel (optional)

15 g/½ oz unsalted butter, cut into small pieces
Sea salt
Freshly ground black pepper

1 Place fennel in the centre of a 2.5 litre/4 pint soufflé dish. Top with fennel tops, if desired and available. Cover tightly with microwave cling film. Cook at 100% for 5 minutes.

2 Pierce film with the tip of a sharp knife, then remove from oven. Let stand, covered, for 2 minutes. Uncover and remove to a serving platter. Top or toss with remaining ingredients and serve hot.

To serve 1. Use 1 small or half a large bulb fennel and quarter the amount butter. Proceed as for 4 servings, cooking for 2 minutes 30 seconds. Let stand for 2 minutes.

To serve 2. Use 1 large bulb fennel and half the amount butter. Proceed as for 4 servings, cooking for 3 minutes 30 seconds. Let stand for 2 minutes.

VARIATIONS

FENNEL WITH LEMON BUTTER Proceed as for Fennel. Add 1 teaspoon fresh lemon juice with other seasonings.

FENNEL WITH OLIVE OIL AND LEMON Combine 1½ tablespoons olive oil, 1 tablespoon fresh lemon juice, ¾ teaspoon salt and ¼ teaspoon pepper. Proceed as for Fennel. Add oil mixture instead of butter to warm fennel. Let stand until cool and serve at room temperature.

CREAMED ONIONS

This is delicious. It is very white, however; if it is not being served with an assortment of colourful foods, top the dish with 3 tablespoons finely chopped parsley. *Serves 8 to 10*

60 g/2 oz unsalted butter
2 tablespoons plain flour
400 ml/14 fl oz milk
1½ teaspoons sea salt

1 kg/2 lb small white onions (about 24), peeled
Freshly ground black pepper

1 Heat half of the butter in a 25 cm/10 inch dish, uncovered, at 100% for 1 minute. Whisk in flour and cook, uncovered, at 100% for 2 minutes more.

2 Remove from oven. Whisk in milk and salt, making sure there are no lumps. Add onions and stir to coat. Cover tightly with microwave cling film. Cook at 100% for 10 minutes.

3 Pierce film with the tip of a sharp knife, then remove from oven. Uncover and stir in remaining butter and pepper. Serve hot.

CURRIED OKRA

Okra is one of those vegetables that take an astonishing leap up the scale of quality in the microwave oven. The okra stays bright green, and if you are careful when cutting off the stalk to not cut into the pod, it doesn't get slimey. Here, it combines with curry in a sort of quick Franco-African sauce that lets it go happily with any simple grilled or microwave-cooked fish, chicken or lamb. *Serves 4 as a side dish*

1 small onion (125 g/4 oz), peeled and sliced
4 cloves garlic, smashed and peeled
1 tablespoon curry powder
30 g/1 oz unsalted butter
1 tablespoon plain flour

250 ml/8 fl oz milk
500 g/1 lb okra, stalks removed without cutting into the okra
2 tablespoons fresh lime juice
1 teaspoon sea salt
3 tablespoons plain yogurt (optional)

1 Place onions, garlic, curry powder and butter in a 2.5 litre/4 pint soufflé dish or casserole. Cook, uncovered, at 100% for 3 minutes.

2 Add flour and stir well to combine. Cook, uncovered, for 2 minutes.

3 Remove from oven. Whisking constantly, slowly add milk. Cook, uncovered, for 3 minutes. Add okra and stir to coat with the sauce. Cover with a tightly fitting lid or with microwave cling film. Cook at 100% for 9 minutes. If using cling film, pierce to release steam.

4 Remove from oven and uncover. Stir in remaining ingredients and serve.

To serve 2. Halve all ingredients. Cook onion mixture in a 2.5 litre/4 pint soufflé dish, uncovered, for 2 minutes. Add flour and cook, uncovered, for 1 minute 30 seconds. Stir in milk and cook, uncovered, for 2 minutes. Add okra. Cover and cook for 6 minutes. Uncover, add remaining ingredients and serve.

HOT DILLED CUCUMBERS

◆ • ◆

Most of us think of cucumbers in salad and leave it at that. They make an interesting hot vegetable, whose smell freshens the air of the kitchen when they are being prepared and delights the dining room when they are served. These cooked cucumbers go very well with fish and chicken. *Serves 4*

1.25 kg/2½ lb medium cucumbers (5 to 6), trimmed, peeled, quartered lengthways and seeded, cut into 2.5–4 cm/1–1½ inch lengths

15 g/½ oz fresh dill, snipped into 5 mm/¼ inch pieces
2 teaspoons cornflour
30 g/1 oz unsalted butter
2 teaspoons sea salt

1 Combine cucumbers and dill in a 1 litre/2 pint glass measuring jug. Cover tightly with microwave cling film. Cook at 100% for 6 minutes.

2 Pierce film with the tip of a sharp knife, then remove from oven and uncover. Pour 4 tablespoons of the liquid into a small bowl. Stir in cornflour and mix well; pour back over cucumbers. Add butter and salt and stir until butter melts. Cook, uncovered, at 100% for 4 minutes.

3 Remove from oven. Stir well and serve hot.

To serve 2. Halve all ingredients. Cook cucumbers for 4 minutes. Add cornflour and cook for 4 minutes more.

ROASTED GARLIC

This is not an ordinary, everyday idea. You need to know your guests. They have to be adventurous eaters who are willing to use their hands since the way to eat the garlic is for them to pull off a clove with their fingers and, holding it by the root end, scrape the sweet and soft pulp out with their teeth. It is much like eating an artichoke. Everybody will be surprised. The garlic is not sharp— it is sweet and nutty. This can be a first course on its own, or can jazz up roast leg of lamb or roast chicken. *Serves 4 as a side dish*

4 heads garlic, tips cut as illustrated below

5½ tablespoons Chicken Stock (page 286) or stock from a cube
3 tablespoons olive oil

1 Place all ingredients in a 1 litre/2 pint glass measuring jug. Cover tightly with microwave cling film. Cook at 100% for 6 to 8 minutes, cooking longer if bulbs are large.

2 Pierce film with the tip of a sharp knife, then remove from oven. Let stand, covered, for 10 minutes.

To serve 2. Combine 2 heads garlic, 4 tablespoons stock and 2 tablespoons oil in the measuring jug. Cook, covered, for 5 minutes. Let stand for 5 to 10 minutes.

Cut tips off entire head of garlic revealing cut cloves.

BRAISED LEEKS

This is one of my favourites. I often substitute it for creamed onions at holidays. It takes a long time to cook on top of the stove or in the oven, but in the microwave oven, it is so easy I will even make it for myself. Then I eat two large leeks. The recipe allows one large leek per person as a vegetable side dish. As a first course, hot or cold, serve two. Cold leeks can be drained and served with a mustard vinaigrette. Warm, they are special when made with Veal or Meat

Stock and Glaze. It is easy to turn braised leeks into a main course with ham and Mornay Sauce. *Serves 8*

8 leeks, white and 2.5 cm/1 inch of
  green, trimmed and well rinsed
350 ml/12 fl oz Chicken Stock (page
  286), stock from a cube or Meat
  Stock with Vegetables (page 287)
45 g/1½ oz unsalted butter

60 g/2 oz Veal Glaze (page 291) or
  Sauce Espagnole (page 321)
  (optional)
Sea salt
Freshly ground black pepper

1 Arrange leeks alternating white and green ends in a 27.5 × 21 × 5 cm/11 × 8½ × 2 inch dish. Add stock, butter, glaze, if used, and salt. Cover tightly with microwave cling film and cook at 100% for 20 minutes.

2 Pierce film with the tip of a sharp knife, then remove from oven. Uncover and turn leeks over. Re-cover and cook at 100% for 20 minutes more.

3 Pierce film, then remove from oven. Uncover and add pepper. Serve hot.

To serve 4. Combine 4 leeks, 250 ml/8 fl oz stock, 30 g/1 oz butter and salt in a 22.5 × 20 × 5 cm/9 × 8 × 2 inch oval dish. Cook as for 8 servings for 15 minutes. Turn leeks and cook for 15 minutes more. Finish as for 8 servings.

To serve 2. Combine 2 leeks, 5½ tablespoons stock, 15 g/½ oz butter and salt in a soup bowl. Cook as for 8 servings for 10 minutes. Turn leeks over and cook for 8 to 10 minutes more. Finish as for 8 servings.

VARIATION

BRAISED LEEKS WITH HAM Preheat grill. After the leeks are cooked, remove in pairs to a lightly oiled grill pan. Cover each pair of leeks with 2 thin slices of cooked ham. Cover each leek and ham serving with 4 tablespoons Mornay Sauce (page 317). Place pan under grill until sauce is lightly gilded. Serve hot. *Serves 4 as a main course*

MELTED LEEKS

◆·◆

This is a lovely vegetable recipe. Melted Leeks make a welcome addition to any main course, or can be used as an ingredient. Two tablespoons of it can be tucked under each fillet of fish or chicken before cooking without changing the timing but adding flavour. It is also good stirred into Velouté (page 318) and spooned over poached or steamed fish or chicken. *Serves 6*

500 g/1 lb leeks, white and 2.5 cm/1
   inch of the green, trimmed, rinsed
   and sliced across 3 mm/⅛ inch thick
   (about 6 leeks)

30 g/1 oz unsalted butter
Sea salt

1 Place leeks and butter in a 30 × 18.5 × 7.5 cm/12 × 7½ × 3 inch dish. Cook, uncovered, at 100% for 6 minutes 15 seconds.

2 Remove from oven. Stir and add salt to taste; serve hot.

To serve 3. Halve all ingredients, cooking in a 22.5 × 20 × 5 cm/9 × 8 × 2 inch oval dish for 4 minutes.

BRAISED ONIONS

◆ ◆

This is a light and easy way to prepare onions. It would be good when you are serving Creamed Spinach (page 260). *Serves 4 to 6*

750 g/1½ lb onions, peeled and thinly
   sliced
1 tablespoon sugar
2 tablespoons Chicken Stock (page
   286) or stock from a cube

2 teaspoons sea salt
4 whole cloves

1 Combine all ingredients in a 35 × 27.5 × 5 cm/14 × 11 × 2 inch dish. Cover tightly with microwave cling film. Cook at 100% for 12 minutes.

2 Pierce film with the tip of a sharp knife, then remove from oven. Uncover and serve hot.

BRAISED CHICORY

◆ ◆

Braised chicory is not beautiful, but it looks better cooked in the microwave oven than it does any other way. People go on cooking chicory because it tastes so good. It has a faintly bittersweet quality that is terrific with roast veal, roast chicken or grilled fish. Chicory can be transformed into a main dish by treating it like the leeks in Braised Leeks with Ham (page 247). Braised Chicory Oriental, the variation, is not a classic, but I am rather proud of it. It goes well with poached or steamed fish, giving a little extra flavour. *Serves 8 as a side dish*

8 heads chicory, trimmed and well rinsed
150 ml/¼ pint Chicken Stock (page 286) or stock from a cube

60 g/2 oz unsalted butter, cut into 4 pieces
Sea salt
Freshly ground black pepper

1 Place chicory in a 30 × 18.5 × 7.5 cm/12 × 7½ × 3 inch dish. Pour in stock and dot with butter. Sprinkle with a pinch of salt. Cover tightly with microwave cling film. Cook at 100% for 8 minutes.

2 Pierce film with the tip of a sharp knife, then remove from oven. Uncover and turn chicory over. Cook, uncovered, for 8 minutes more.

3 Remove from oven. Add salt and pepper and serve hot.

To serve 2. Use 2 heads chicory and halve all other ingredients. Cook as for 8 servings in a 22.5 × 12.5 × 7.5 cm/9 × 5 × 3 inch loaf dish for 6 minutes. Uncover and cook for 2 minutes more. Season and serve hot.

VARIATION

BRAISED CHICORY ORIENTAL Increase stock to 250 ml/8 fl oz, omit butter and add 4 teaspoons mirin, 8 teaspoons rice wine vinegar, 4 teaspoons sesame oil and salt. Cook as for Braised Chicory for 8 minutes. Turn chicory over, re-cover and cook for 8 minutes more. *Serves 8.*

To serve 2. Quarter all ingredients in Braised Chicory Oriental for 8, cooking in a 22.5 × 12.5 × 7.5 cm/9 × 5 × 3 inch dish for 6 minutes. Turn chicory over, re-cover and cook for 2 minutes more.

BRAISED LETTUCE

This is another of those vegetables like cucumbers that we use mainly in salads. It is surprisingly good cooked, something the clever French have known for a long time. Here is a dish that looks and tastes so much better made in the microwave oven than conventionally and is so much quicker that I really cannot imagine doing it any other way ever again. *Serves 8*

60 g/2 oz unsalted butter
250 ml/8 fl oz Chicken or Veal stock (page 286) or stock from a cube
125 ml/4 fl oz Sauce Espagnole (page 321) or Meat Glaze (page 291)
1½ teaspoons sea salt

4 heads soft-leaved lettuce (250 g/8 oz each), large outer leaves removed, washed and heads cut in half lengthways
1 tablespoon cornflour dissolved in 2 tablespoons cold water

1 Heat butter and stock in a 35 × 27.5 × 5 cm/14 × 11 × 2 inch dish, uncovered, at 100% for 3 minutes. Stir in Sauce Espagnole and salt. Arange lettuce halves with core ends pointing towards the outside of the dish. Cover tightly with microwave cling film. Cook at 100% for 15 minutes.

2 Pierce film with the tip of a sharp knife, then remove from oven. Uncover and remove lettuce to a warmed serving platter, folding ragged leaf edges under. Stir cornflour into liquid in dish. Cook, uncovered, at 100% for 7 minutes.

3 Remove from oven. Spoon sauce over lettuce and serve immediately.

To serve 4. Halve all ingredients and omit cornflour. Proceed, cooking lettuce in a 27.5 × 21 × 5 cm/11 × 8½ × 2 inch dish for 8 minutes. Finish cooking sauce for 4 minutes.

To serve 2. Quarter all ingredients and omit cornflour. Proceed, cooking lettuce in a 23.5 × 17.5 × 3.5 cm/9½ × 7 × 1¾ inch oval dish for 5 minutes 30 seconds. Finish cooking sauce for 3 minutes.

THE PURÉES

There was a time after everyone got a food processor and figured out how to use it when I thought I never wanted to see another purée. That time has passed. Purées are really delicious on their own, or thinned as sauces, and they are endlessly useful in soups, custards and timbales. I never mind having leftover purées for that reason. However, purées are a good way to use up leftover vegetables that were cooked simply.

The simplest purées are made from the cooked vegetable on its own. If you want, season the purée with butter, cream, salt and spices, but you may find that microwave-cooked vegetables have such good flavour that a minimum of seasoning is needed. Microwave-cooked and peeled baking potatoes can be used to thicken purées of watery vegetables or to dilute the taste of strong vegetables. See the Dictionary for weights, preparation, cooking times and puréed yield for individual vegetables.

Purée vegetables in a food processor or blender (with a little extra liquid) or with a food mill (see page 31 for illustration). The blender will give a somewhat silkier, more liquid result. The result with a food mill depends on which of its three discs you are using; it can go from slightly chunky to quite smooth. The food mill will separate the skin and seeds from vegetables such as tomatoes.

TO MAKE SOUPS FROM PURÉES. There are some recipes for puréed vegetable soups in the chapter on soups and as variations in this chapter. Almost any vegetable purée can be made into a soup by adding 3 parts of liquid to 1 part of purée and heating it, covered. Do not overseason. The microwave-cooked vegetables have delightful flavours of their own. Even the most mundane vegetables like parsnips, carrots, swede and vegetable marrow make surprisingly elegant soups; they can be served hot or cold. For soups, as well as purées and custards, watery vegetables do better when puréed with a cooked potato.

The liquid for a soup could be Chicken Stock, homemade (page 286) or from a cube, Vegetable Stock (page 290), Velouté (page 318), Sauce Suprême (page 319), Thin Béchamel (page 317), cream, milk, or a combination of stock and cream or milk. When reheating soups with milk, cream or butter in them, use large containers and cook covered. They tend to boil over. It is better to use some cream, soured cream or plain yogurt—low fat is fine—in soups that will be cold. Whisk in the soured cream or yogurt after removing the soup from the oven and letting it cool somewhat; that way it is less likely to separate.

If additional thickening is called for after a hot soup is taken from the oven, you can swirl in a little butter or add some cornflour—1 teaspoon to each 250 ml/8 fl oz—mixed with cold water and cook, uncovered, at 100% for 3 to 4 minutes. You can also thicken soup with egg yolks as described on page 104. If you are using leftover butter-rich purées to make soup, reduce the amount of cream you add, and unless the purée contains potato, thicken the soup in one of the ways described.

TO MAKE VEGETABLE FLANS, CUSTARDS AND TIMBALES To the cooked purée from 250 g/8 oz of vegetables (about 125 ml/4 fl oz), add 4 whole eggs and 175 ml/ 6 fl oz double cream. Mix well. Taste for seasoning. Place 4 tablespoons of the mixture in each of 10 lightly greased 7.5 cm/3 inch soufflé dishes or ramekins. Those with a bowl shape will cook more evenly. (See page 22 for illustrations.) Cover each tightly with microwave cling film. Arrange in oven in a circle so they do not touch. Cook at 100% for 3 minutes 30 seconds. Pierce film. Unmould on to individual plates atop 3 tablespoons of sauce, for a first course. Unmould on to a dinner plate, to serve as a side dish.

TO MAKE GRATINS FROM PURÉES. Take 500 ml/16 fl oz of purée. If it is potato thickened but has no butter or cream, add 2 tablespoons cream and 2 lightly beaten whole eggs. Add 60 g/2 oz grated Parmesan or Gruyère cheese. If the purée is not already thickened and not made from a starchy vegetable, purée ½ of a microwave-cooked potato with the purée. Then follow rules for flans, custards and timbales. Preheat grill. Smooth gratin mixture into a 27.5 × 20 × 5 cm/11 × 8 × 2 inch dish that can go under the grill. Cook the gratin in microwave oven 2 minutes, then put under grill until lightly browned. If you like, sprinkle gratin with 90 g/3 oz grated cheese before placing under grill. If you don't care if the gratin browns, smooth purée about 1 cm/½ inch deep into the dish; grate 2 tablespoons per 4 tablespoons or purée of Gruyère, Fontina or Doux de Montagne cheese over purée. Cook, uncovered, for 4 minutes.

TO MAKE SAUCES FROM PURÉES. Purées without potatoes or starchy vegetables make better sauces than those with them. For cold sauces, thin with a little plain yogurt, stock and a bit of olive oil, or mix with Mayonnaise (page 332). Season. For hot sauces, proceed as for soups, but add only ½ to 1 part extra liquid to each part of purée. Choose a liquid that goes with but does not repeat the food you are saucing. For instance, if you are making a sauce for a custard, make one without butter, cream or eggs.

MASHED POTATOES

Mashed potatoes are really one kind of potato purée. They happen to be one of my favourite things in the world when I permit myself to indulge. I am capable of making dinner from a bowl of super mashed potatoes. Baking potatoes cooked in the microwave oven make superior baked potatoes for mashing or purées. They have more potato taste and no extra water. Potatoes cooked in water will give you a somewhat lighter, less fatty mashed potato. See the Dictionary for cooking times.

There are many different ways to make mashed potatoes: with cream, milk, butter, or any combination of the three. The potatoes can be mashed with a fork or potato masher or put through a food mill. They should not be put in a food processor or blender unless they are being combined with another vegetable for a mixed purée: they tend to turn to glue. *Serves 4*

2 baking potatoes (200–250 g/7–8 oz each)175 ml/6 fl oz milk

30 g/1 oz unsalted butter
½ teaspoon sea salt

1 Prick potatoes twice with a knife tip. Cook, uncovered, at 100% for 11 minutes. (In a small oven, cook for 18 minutes.)

2 Remove from oven with oven glove or towel. Holding it in same, carefully peel with a small knife. Cut in about 2.5 cm/1 inch cubes. Mash or put through food mill into a 1 litre/2 pint glass measuring jug.

3 With a whisk, beat in milk, butter and salt.

4 Place jug, uncovered, in oven for 1 minute 30 seconds. (In a small oven, cook for 3 minutes.)

5 Adjust seasoning as desired and serve hot.

VARIATION

LIGHT MASHED POTATOES Scrub and peel 2 potatoes (200–250 g/7–8 oz each). Cut in 2.5 cm/1 inch chunks. Arrange in a circle arround the rim of a 22.5 cm/9 inch flan dish. Add 125 ml/4 fl oz water. Cook, tightly covered, for 12 minutes. Drain, mash and stir in 175 ml/6 fl oz milk, 30 g/1 oz unsalted butter and salt. Cook, uncovered, for 1 minute 30 seconds. Adjust seasoning as desired and serve hot.

RICH, FRENCH POTATO PURÉE
• ◆ •

This is just a fancy version of mashed potatoes. It is the richest potato purée of all. It is much creamier than ordinary mashed potatoes, almost a sauce. For your ultimate self-indulgence I give the recipe. I love it; but can't be responsible to your arteries.

The French would probably add even more milk at the end; they like the purée to be very silky. This must be beaten by hand. *Serves 2*

1 small baking potato (about 200–250 g/7–8 oz)
45 g/1½ oz unsalted butter, at room temperature, cut into chunks
¼ teaspoon sea salt

4 tablespoons double cream
1 tablespoon or more milk (optional)
Sea salt
Freshly ground black pepper (optional)

1 Prick potato twice with a knife tip. Cook, uncovered, at 100% for 7 minutes.

2 Remove from oven with oven glove or towel. Holding it in same, carefully peel with a small knife. Cut in about 2.5 cm/1 inch cubes. Mash or put through food mill into a 500 ml/1 pint glass measuring jug.

3 With a fork or tiny whisk, beat in butter and salt. Potatoes will appear to shrink.

4 Place jug, uncovered, in oven for 30 seconds at 100%.

5 Beat in cream, 1 tablespoon at a time. The purée absorbs more as it goes. If desired, beat in milk to thin and add more salt and pepper to taste.

6 Reheat for 30 seconds, covered with paper towel.

VARIATION

CARROT AND POTATO PURÉE Cook 2 baking potatoes (200 g/7 oz each). To make carrot purée, cook 750 g/1½ lb carrots, cut into 3–5 mm/⅛–¼ inch slices, in a dish large enough to hold them in 2 to 3 layers. Cover tightly with microwave cling film and cook for 9 minutes 30 seconds. Remove from oven and purée in the container of a food processor with peeled, sliced potatoes, unsalted butter, and salt and pepper to taste. Serve hot. *Serves 6*

BROCCOLI PURÉE

H ere is our friend broccoli again. Use broccoli cooking instructions on page 240. *Makes about 600 ml/1 pint*

750 g/1½ lb broccoli, stalks and florets
90 g/3 oz unsalted butter

1 teaspoon sea salt

1 Cook broccoli.

2 Remove from oven. Put cooked broccoli in the container of a food processor. Process to a coarse purée. Add butter and salt and process briefly to combine.

To make 125 ml/4 fl oz. Wash and trim 250 g/8 oz broccoli. Cut into florets and thinly slice the stalks. Place in a 1 litre/2 pint glass measuring jug. Cover tightly with microwave cling film. Cook for 4 minutes at 100%. Purée in food processor. Use in Broccoli Timbale (page 262). For a rich purée to serve 2, add 45 g/1½ oz melted butter (2 minutes in microwave oven), 2 tablespoons double cream and ¼ teaspoon salt; purée in blender.

CELERIAC PURÉE

This knobby, ugly, midwinter root vegetable is good shredded raw to make a salad with a mustard mayonnaise. It makes a subtle purée that needs no fat, unless you decide you want something richer. Combine this purée with a potato purée for variety. *Makes 250 ml/8 fl oz*

750 g/1½ lb celeriac, peeled and cubed   ½ teaspoon celery seed (optional)
30 g/1 oz unsalted butter

1 Place celeriac in a 17.5 × 20 × 5 cm/11 × 8 × 2 inch oval dish. Cover tightly with microwave cling film. Cook at 100% for 9 minutes.

2 Pierce film with the tip of a sharp knife, then remove from oven. Uncover and place in the container of a food processor with butter. Process until smooth.

3 Serve sprinkled with celery seeds, if liked.

VARIATIONS

CELERIAC AND POTATO PURÉE Cook celeriac. Cook a 200 g/7 oz baking potato. Peel; purée with celeriac, 30 g/1 oz butter, and 4 tablespoons double cream. Add salt to taste. *Makes 500 ml/16 fl oz.*

WINTER VEGETABLE PURÉE Combine Celeriac Root and Potato Purée with 250 ml/8 fl oz Parsnip Purée (page 258). Season to taste. *Makes 750 ml/1¼ pints.*

THREE-VEGETABLE WINTER CREAM SOUP Combine Winter Vegetable Purée with 600 ml/1 pint Chicken Stock (page 286) or stock from a cube, 125 ml/4 fl oz double cream and 1 teaspoon sea salt. Heat in a 2 litre/3½ pint glass jug or bowl, tightly covered, for 5 minutes at 100%. *Serves 6*

CELERY PURÉE

—— • • ——

This is a pale, pale green purée that is aromatic. *Makes 350 ml/12 fl oz*

500 g/1 lb celery, stringed and cut
    across into 5 mm/¼ inch pieces
2 tablespoons chopped celery leaves, if
    available
1 baking potato (200 g/7 oz), cooked
    and mashed

125 ml/4 fl oz double cream
45 g/1 ½ oz unsalted butter
Sea salt
Freshly ground black pepper

1 Place celery in a 1 litre/2 pint glass measuring jug with 1 tablespoon water. Cover tightly with microwave cling film. Cook at 100% for 5 to 6 minutes, until tender.

2 Pierce film with the tip of a sharp knife, then remove from oven. Uncover and place in the container of a food processor. Process until smooth. Add remaining ingredients and process until well combined. Season to taste.

VARIATION

CELERY SOUP Add 750 ml/12 fl oz Chicken Stock (page 286) or stock from a cube to finished purée. Stir to combine and serve hot. *Serves 4*

CAULIFLOWER PURÉE

—— • • ——

Cauliflower makes one of the most elegant purées. The potato version has more body, but is not necessarily better. Cauliflower cooks more evenly divided into florets. *Makes 500 ml/16 fl oz (750 ml/1¼ pints with potato added)*

1 small cauliflower, cored, trimmed and
    florets removed
2 baking potatoes (200 g/7 oz each),
    cooked (optional)

125 ml/4 fl oz double cream
Sea salt
1 tablespoon packed, finely snipped or
    sliced chives (optional)

1 Place cauliflower florets in a rectangular dish just large enough to hold them in a single layer. Cover tightly with microwave cling film. Cook at 100% for 7 minutes.

2 Remove from oven. Uncover and place in the container of a food processor with peeled, sliced potato, if used. Process until smooth with cream and salt to taste.

3 Sprinkle chives on top, if used, or stir in.

ACORN SQUASH PURÉE

The winter squashes, which are becoming more and more available in Britain, make silky-smooth purées of great elegance in varying shades of gold and yellow. They are quick and delicious, and they are easily transformed into party soups to serve hot or cold. If serving soup cold, make it one day ahead. *Makes about 600 ml/1 pint*

2 acorn squash, cut in half and seeded
250 ml/8 fl oz double cream
125 g/4 oz unsalted butter

Pinch cayenne pepper
1½ teaspoons sea salt

1 Place squash halves side by side in a deep, rectangular dish just large enough to hold them. Cover tightly with microwave cling film or with a tightly fitting lid. Cook at 100% for 12 to 15 minutes or until flesh is easily pierced with a fork. If using cling film, pierce it with tip of a sharp knife.

2 Remove from oven. Uncover and scoop out flesh. Pass through the medium disc of a food mill. Stir in remaining ingredients and serve hot.

VARIATIONS

BUTTERNUT SQUASH PURÉE Substitute 1.25 kg/2½ lb butternut squash for acorn squash. Proceed as for Acorn Squash Purée.

WINTER SQUASH SOUP Combine any of the squash purées with 500 ml/16 fl oz of Velouté (page 318). Season to taste with sea salt, freshly ground white pepper and a tiny pinch of nutmeg. Heat in 2 litre/3½ pint glass jug or bowl for 5 minutes at 100%. Whisk and serve. *Serves 4 to 5*

SWEDE PURÉE

Swede is a strangly homely, strong tasting and old-fashioned vegetable generally overlooked in the search for the new. It makes a creamy, pale gold purée that would be useful with Heart of the Home Beef Stew (page 208) or Lamb Stew (page 229). *Makes 750 ml/1¼ pints*

750 ml/1½ lb swede, trimmed, peeled
   and cut into 1 cm/½ inch cubes
125 ml/4 fl oz water
250 ml/8 fl oz double cream

60 g/2 oz unsalted butter
2 teaspoons sea salt
Pinch cayenne pepper

1 Put swede and water in a 2 litre/3½ pint glass jug or bowl. Cover tightly with microwave cling film. Cook at 100% for 15 minutes.

2 Pierce film with the tip of a sharp knife, then remove from oven. Uncover and place in the container of a food processor. Process until smooth. Add remaining ingredients and process until well combined.

3 To reheat, if necessary, return to jug or bowl. Cook, uncovered, at 100% for 3 minutes. Stir well.

PARSNIP PURÉE

Parsnips are another old-fashioned winter vegetable. They have a sweet and spicy taste. *Makes 1 litre/1¾ pints*

500 g/1 lb parsnips, trimmed, peeled
   and cut into 4 cm/1½ inch chunks
250 ml/8 fl oz water
1 potato, baked, peeled and mashed
   (page 476)

60 g/2 oz unsalted butter
250–350 ml/8–12 fl oz double cream
2 teaspoons sea salt
½ teaspoon freshly ground black pepper

1 Combine parsnips and water in a 1 litre/2 pint glass measuring jug. Cover tightly with microwave cling film. Cook at 100% for 8 minutes.

2 Pierce film with the tip of a sharp knife, then remove from oven. Uncover and place in the container of a food processor. Process until smooth. Add remaining ingredients and process until well combined.

VARIATION

UNSEASONED PARSNIP PURÉE Combine 250 g/8 oz peeled and cubed parsnips in a 1 litre/2 pint glass measuring jug with 7.5 g/¼ oz butter and 125 ml/4 fl oz Chicken Stock (page 286) or stock from a cube. Cover tightly. Cook for 5 minutes. Purée. *Makes 250 ml/8 fl oz*

TURNIP PURÉE

— • • —

Turnips are always around. They can be added to dinner any night. When people are served this purée, they will think they are getting mashed potatoes. The slight bite of turnips will come as a pleasant surprise. Think of this with Smothered Pork Roast (page 220), or with something as unexpected as Green Lamb Curry (page 230). *Makes 300 ml/½ pint*

500 g/1 lb turnips (about 4 turnips)
   trimmed, peeled and diced
1 potato, baked, peeled and mashed
   (page 476)

30 g/1 oz unsalted butter
½ teaspoon sea salt

1 Place turnips in a 1 litre/2 pint glass measuring jug. Cover tightly with microwave cling film. Cook at 100% for 6 minutes.

2 Pierce film with the tip of a sharp knife, then remove from oven. Uncover and place in the container of a food processor. Add remaining ingredients and process until smooth.

3 Return mixture to jug and reheat, uncovered, at 100% for 3 minutes.

4 Remove from oven. Uncover and serve hot.

BEETROOT AND POTATO PURÉE

— • • —

This is a luscious shade of pink. It would add colour and interest to Poached Chicken Breasts (page 181) or steamed fish fillets. Without the potato, is makes an unusual sauce. *Makes 300 ml/½ pint*

250 g/8 oz beetroot, rinsed and stalks
   removed
1 small potato, baked, peeled and
   mashed (page 476)

90 g/3 oz unsalted butter
1 teaspoon cider vinegar
¼ teaspoon sea salt
Freshly ground black pepper

1 Place beetroots, so they are not touching, just inside the rim of a 2.5 litre/4 pint soufflé dish or a casserole with a tightly fitting lid. If using soufflé dish, cover tightly with microwave cling film. Cook at 100% for 8 minutes. If using cling film, pierce it with the tip of a sharp knife.

2 Remove from oven. Uncover and drain beetroot juices into a bowl. Remove skins and place beetroots and juice in the container of a food processor. Process until smooth.

3 Combine beetroots with remaining ingredients in a 1 litre/2 pint glass measuring jug. Heat, uncovered, at 100% for 4 minutes.

4 Remove from oven. Serve hot.

VARIATION

SWEET AND SOUR BEETROOT SAUCE Cook beetroots as for Beetroot and Potato Purée. Purée in blender with all ingredients except for potato purée. Taste and add a little sugar, if needed. Serve with other vegetables or with steamed fish.

CREAMED SPINACH

Most of us don't think of this as a purée, yet not only is it one of the best tasting, it is also one of the most versatile. It can be a base for spinach soufflé with the possible addition of grated cheese. It can be baked as a gratin. It also makes good soup that can be sharpened with the acid of sorrel in spring or the pepperiness of watercress in winter. *Makes 600 ml/1 pint*

1 kg/2 lb spinach, stalks removed and rinsed
500 ml/16 fl oz Thick Béchamel (page 317)

1½ teaspoons sea salt
Freshly ground black pepper
Freshly grated nutmeg

1 Place spinach in a 5 litre/8 pint casserole with a tightly fitting lid. Cook at 100% for 5 minutes 30 seconds. Remove from oven. Rinse spinach in cold water. Drain well and squeeze out excess water.

2 Place spinach and remaining ingredients in the container of a food processor. Process until well combined and smooth.

3 To reheat, place mixture in a 2.5 litre/4 pint soufflé dish and cook, uncovered, at 100% for 4 minutes, stirring twice.

4 Remove from oven and serve hot.

VARIATIONS

CREAM OF SPINACH SOUP To Creamed Spinach add 500 ml/16 fl oz Chicken Stock (page 286), stock from a cube, or Vegetable Stock (page 290). Season to taste and heat in a 2 litre/3½ pint glass jug or bowl, tightly covered, at 100% for 4 minutes. To serve cold, chill in refrigerator overnight. Then whisk in 125 ml/4 fl oz plain yogurt. *Serves 4 to 5*

GREEN CREAM SOUP Make Creamed Spinach, substituting 250 g/8 oz sorrel, cut in thin strips across the centre vein, or 250 g/8 oz watercress leaves, for 250 g/8 oz of the spinach. Cook with spinach. Proceed as for Cream of Spinach Soup.

Savoury Creams and Timbales

These are some of the most elegant of vegetable creations. Between the food processor and the microwave oven, they have become so easy I feel slightly guilty. A little leftover purée can show up in this disguise—125 ml/4 fl oz of purée will make 10 servings (see pages 251–261).

These dishes are equally good as first courses and side dishes. For a first course, you serve them with a garnish or sauce (see pages 312–333 and the Index for a choice of sauces). When planning the vegetables for a meal, don't serve a purée with savoury cream; the textures are too similar. Pick an elegant stewed vegetable like Mushroom Ragoût (page 274), or something simple like Glazed Carrots (page 242) or Peas with Mint and Spring Onions (page 241). Although these moulds are rich, you probably would not serve a starch as well, so they don't make the meal heavy.

Individual servings can be baked in custard cups or as 7.5 cm/3 inch soufflés; they do best in bowl-shaped ramekins (see page 22). You can use small teacups or demitasse cups instead. Point the handles to the centre of the oven.

Broccoli Timbale

• ◆ •

As a first course, this would look beautiful on Sweet and Sour Beetroot Sauce (page 260). Put a small, blanched broccoli floret on each plate. *Serves 10*

125 ml/4 fl oz Broccoli Purée (125 ml/
    4 fl oz variation, page 254)
4 eggs

175 ml/6 fl oz double cream
Sea salt to taste
Vegetable oil for greasing moulds

1 In a food processor or with a whisk, just combine all ingredients except oil.

2 Lightly oil 10 demitasse cups or small custard cups. Fill each with 4 tablespoons of broccoli mixture. Cover each tightly with microwave cling film.

3 Place in microwave oven in a large ring, not touching. Cook at 100% for 3 minutes 30 seconds.

4 Pierce film. Remove from oven. Uncover. Unmould on to dinner plate, platter or first course plates with about 3 tablespoons of sauce on each.

PARSNIP CREAMS

──────── ◆ ◆ ◆ ────────

This is one of the best of the savoury creams. As a first course it is sensational counterpointed by a thin slice of smoked salmon. *Serves 8*

Vegetable oil for greasing moulds
250 g/8 oz parsnips, trimmed, peeled
  and cut in chunks
1 shallot, peeled
7 g/¼ oz unsalted butter, cut into bits
125 ml/4 fl oz Chicken Stock (page
  286) or stock from a cube

4 tablespoons double cream
2 egg yolks
Sea salt
Freshly ground black pepper

1 Lightly grease 8 ramekins (125 ml/4 fl oz size) with oil. Set aside.

2 Place parsnips and shallot in a 2.5 litre/4 pint soufflé dish. Add butter and stock. Cover tightly with microwave cling film. Cook at 100% for 5 minutes.

3 Pierce film with the tip of a sharp knife, then remove from oven. Place in the container of a food processor. Process until smooth. Add cream and egg yolks. Process again until well combined. Stir in salt and pepper.

4 Pour 4 tablespoons of mixture into each prepared ramekin. Place ramekins in a 35 × 27.5 × 5 cm/14 × 11 × 2 inch dish and add water to a depth of 2.5 cm/ 1 inch. Cover tightly with microwave cling film. Cook at 100% for 8 minutes.

5 Pierce film, then remove ramekins from oven. Let stand for 3 minutes. Uncover and unmould on to a serving platter or individual dishes. Serve immediately.

ASPARAGUS CREAMS

──────── ◆ ◆ ◆ ────────

This is terrific tasting, and luxury on the cheap as a little bit of asparagus feeds a lot of people. This is fine with fish. As a first course, serve the creams with a few lightly cooked asparagus. *Serves 10*

Vegetable oil for greasing moulds
350 g/12 oz asparagus, ends snapped
  off, peeled and cut into 5 cm/2 inch
  lengths (250 g/8 oz trimmed)
2½ teaspoons sea salt

1 tablespoon water
250 ml/8 fl oz double cream
4 eggs
Freshly ground black pepper

1 Lightly grease 10 ramekins (6 cm/2½ inch size) with oil. Reserve.

2 Place asparagus pieces in a 25 cm/10 inch flan dish. Sprinkle with ½ teaspoon of the salt dissolved in the water. Cover tightly with microwave cling film. Cook at 100% for 2 minutes 30 seconds. Pierce film with the tip of a sharp knife, then remove from oven. Uncover and reserve.

3 Place cream in a 1 litre/2 pint glass measuring jug. Cook, uncovered, at 100% for 1 minute 30 seconds.

4 Place asparagus and eggs in the container of a food processor. Process until smooth. With machine running, add hot cream in a thin stream until incorporated. Stir in remaining salt and pepper.

5 Pour 4 tablespoons of mixture into each prepared ramekin. Cover each tightly with microwave cling film. Arrange ramekins around inside rim of a 30 cm/12 inch platter or on turntable. Cook at 100% for 3 minutes 30 seconds.

6 Pierce film with the tip of a sharp knife. Remove from oven. Uncover and unmould on to a serving platter. Serve immediately.

GARLIC CREAMS

These are fantastic. Your guests won't know what they are, only that they're good. The garlic is sweet and nutty, not sharp. The custard is smooth and creamy—just right with roast leg of lamb or roast chicken or grilled fish. They could be the centrepiece of a vegetable dinner with Curried Mushroom Caps with Peas (page 273), Szechuan Green Beans (page 268), and Chinese Stewed Tomatoes (page 269). As a first course, serve them on Red Pepper Purée (page 296), topped with a few strips of red pepper. *Serves* 8

Vegetable oil for greasing moulds	2 tablespoons olive oil
4 heads garlic, split into cloves and smashed	250 ml/8 fl oz double cream
	3 eggs
4 tablespoons Chicken Stock (page 286) or stock from a cube	1 teaspoon sea salt

1 Lightly grease 8 ramekins (6 cm/2½ inch size) with oil. Set aside.

2 Combine garlic, stock, olive oil and cream in a 1 litre/2 pint glass measuring jug. Cover tightly with microwave cling film. Cook at 100% for 10 minutes.

3 Pierce film with the tip of a sharp knife, then remove from oven. Uncover and pass through the medium disc of a food mill. Stir in eggs and salt.

4 Pour 4 tablespoons of mixture into each prepared ramekin. Cover each tightly with microwave cling film. Arrange around inside rim of a 30 cm/12 inch platter or on turntable. Cook at 100% for 3 minutes 30 seconds.

5 Pierce film with the tip of a sharp knife. Remove from oven. Uncover each and unmould on to a serving platter. Serve immediately.

RADICCHIO GRATIN

If we know radicchio at all, we know it as a salad ingredient, leaves peeled from a round, dark red vegetable that looks like a small cabbage. In its native Italy, radicchio is eaten as often cooked as raw, and there are many different varieties. It does lose most of its glorious colour when cooked, but its slightly bitter, mysterious taste compensates for the loss. Try this gratin with a simple fish dish, Loin of Veal (page 225), Smothered Pork Roast (page 220), or a roast chicken. *Serves 4 to 6*

500 g/1 lb radicchio, well rinsed	4 tablespoons double cream
1 teaspoon balsamic vinegar	Freshly ground black pepper
1 teaspoon sea salt	2 tablespoons freshly grated Parmesan
30 g/1 oz unsalted butter	cheese
3 egg yolks	

1 Place radicchio in microwave-safe roasting bag and close tight. Cook at 100% for 5 minutes.

2 Remove from oven. Unwrap, and remove and discard cores. Place the rest in the container of a food processor and process until smooth. Add remaining ingredients except cheese. Process until well combined.

3 Place mixture in a 20 cm/8 inch square dish. Sprinkle with cheese. Cook, uncovered, at 100% for 14 minutes.

4 Remove from oven. Cover with a plate and let stand for 15 minutes. Serve warm.

To serve 8. Double all ingredients. Cook radicchio for 8 minutes. Proceed, cooking custard in a 25 cm/10 inch square dish for 20 to 22 minutes, until firm. Let stand for 15 minutes.

SWEETCORN CREAM

This is a delight. It is light enough to serve with a simple main course, from fish to meat. It can stand on its own as an egg dish at a brunch or luncheon. You can spice it up, but try it this way at least once. *Serves 8 as a side dish or 4 to 6 as a brunch dish*

30 g/1 oz unsalted butter
½ small onion, peeled and chopped
30 g/1 oz spring onion greens, chopped
330 g/11 oz fresh sweetcorn kernels
4 eggs

300 ml/½ pint milk
175 ml/6 fl oz double cream
2 teaspoons sea salt
¼ teaspoon Fiery Pepper Sauce (page 297)

1 Preheat conventional grill.

2 Combine butter, onions, spring onion greens and sweetcorn in a 27.5 × 20 × 5 cm/11 × 8 × 2 inch dish. Cook, uncovered, at 100% for 3 minutes. Remove from oven and stir well.

3 Whisk together remaining ingredients. Pour over sweetcorn mixture. Cook, uncovered, at 100% for 3 minutes. Stir well and cook for 3 minutes more.

4 Without removing dish from oven, cover tightly with microwave cling film. Cook at 100% for 1 minute 30 seconds.

5 Pierce film with the tip of a sharp knife, then remove from oven. Uncover and place under grill 5 inches from heat source, until golden brown. Serve hot.

VARIATION

MEXICAN SWEETCORN CREAM Add 100 g/3 ½ oz peeled, seeded and diced tomato (5 mm/¼ inch pieces) and 45 g/1½ oz each green and red pepper, cored, seeded and diced, to the other vegetables in step 2. Increase cooking time to 4 minutes. Add 60 g/2 oz grated mature Cheddar cheese to the ingredients in step 3 and increase Fiery Pepper Sauce to 1 teaspoon. Cook as for Sweetcorn Cream.

EXCITING VEGETABLES

These are spectacular vegetable dishes, the kind that make a dinner memorable no matter how simple. I hope they become as much a part of your repertoire as they have mine. You can cook one or two of these while the roast is in the oven. They can also be cooked before the main course and briefly reheated. Almost all of them can be served at room temperature. An assortment adds wonders to a buffet. I can imagine a whole buffet of vegetable dishes with a grain like Couscous (page 125) or a pilaf and with a green salad and a few cheeses. That would be great summer entertaining with no last-minute work.

ONIONS IN BARBECUE SAUCE

These are best in the early spring, when you can sometimes buy cipolline, small, flat Italian onions; but the recipe can be made with small white onions (not button size) and it is still sensational. The onions go with anything, can be eaten on their own, are good as a first course and simply terrific for cocktail onions. The only thing they do not go with is a barbecue. To prepare them, you do need an assortment of vinegars and spices, but it is quickly done, especially if you start with bottled tomato sauce. *Serves 8 as a side dish*

750 g/1½ lb Italian flat onions (6–8 × 1 cm/2½–3¼ × ½ inch), skinned and roots trimmed, or small round white onions (about 4 cm/1½ inches in diameter)
125 ml/4 fl oz white wine vinegar
4 tablespoons balsamic vinegar
4 tablespoons white wine
175 ml/6 fl oz Chunky Tomato Sauce (page 324) or store-bought tomato or spaghetti sauce

2 tablespoons olive oil
¼ teaspoon ground cumin
¼ teaspoon ground cardomom
¼ teaspoon dry mustard
½ teaspoon ground ginger
¼ teaspoon Searing Pepper Sauce (page 297) or commercial Tabasco sauce
2 tablespoons sugar (optional)
Sea salt (optional)

1 Combine all ingredients except sugar and salt in a 35 × 27.5 × 5 cm/14 × 11 × 2 inch dish. Pat the onions into a single layer, pushing larger onions to the outside of the dish. Cover tightly with microwave cling film. Cook at 100% for 15 minutes. Pierce film with the tip of a sharp knife, then uncover and cook 10 minutes more.

2 Remove from oven and stir well. Add sugar and salt, if desired.

SZECHUAN GREEN BEANS

— ◆ ◆ ◆ —

This dish is a triumph. It takes only 1 tablespoon of oil for 500 g/1 lb of beans. The colour is good, the flavour delicious. Be careful if you make them ahead. They will disappear. People love to munch on them. I use them as a satisfying, low-calorie snack before dinner and as a picnic dish. *Serves 8 as a side dish*

6 cloves garlic, smashed and peeled
2 5p piece-size slices fresh root ginger, peeled
2 spring onion, trimmed and cut into 5 cm/2 inch lengths
1 tablespoon vegetable oil

1 teaspoon dried chilli pepper flakes
1 tablespoon tamari soya sauce
1 tablespoon rice wine vinegar
500 g/1 lb green beans, topped and tailed

1 Place garlic, ginger and spring onions in the container of a food processor. Process until finely chopped. Remove to a 35 × 27.5 × 5 cm/14 × 11 × 2 inch dish. Add oil and chilli flakes. Cook, uncovered, at 100% for 3 minutes.

2 Remove from oven. Stir in remaining ingredients. Cook, uncovered, at 100% for 15 minutes, stirring 4 to 5 times.

3 Remove from oven. Stir and serve hot or cold.

STEWED OKRA

— ◆ ◆ ◆ —

Even people who thought they didn't like okra will like this. It is just about perfect with fish or lamb or pork chops. Be sure to cut off the stalks of the okra carefully, without cutting into the okra itself. As long as the okra isn't cut, it won't get slimy. *Serves 6 as a side dish*

125 g/4 oz onion, peeled and sliced
4 cloves garlic, smashed and peeled
½ teaspoon dried chilli flakes
4 tablespoons olive oil
250 g/8 oz okra, stalks removed without cutting into the okra

400 g/14 oz can chopped tomatoes with juice
1 teaspoon sea salt
1 tablespoon fresh lemon juice
Freshly ground black pepper

1 Combine onions, garlic, chilli flakes and oil in a 20 cm/8 inch square dish. Heat, uncovered, at 100% for 3 minutes. Add okra and cook, uncovered, at 100% for 3 minutes.

2 Remove from oven. Stir in tomatoes. Cover tightly with microwave cling film. Cook at 100% for 6 minutes.

3 Pierce film with the tip of a sharp knife, then remove from oven. Uncover and stir in remaining ingredients. Serve hot.

VARIATION

CREOLE STEWED OKRA WITH PRAWNS Add ¼ teaspoon Tabasco sauce plus 1 teaspoon filé powder, if liked, to oil and onion mixture. Add 12 raw prawns, peeled and deveined, or 4 boneless chicken breasts, cut into 6 × 2.5 cm/ 2½ × 1 inch strips, with tomatoes. Cook for an additional 2 minutes. Finish as for Stewed Okra. *Serves 6 as a first course, 2 to 4 as a main course with rice*

CHINESE STEWED TOMATOES

Make all of this. You will never regret it. If there are leftovers, they are good in an omelet or with scrambled eggs. You can cook fish or chicken in them. Use this as a sauce for angel hair pasta. Serve some with a sandwich or sliced ham instead of coleslaw. Serve it as a vegetable with almost any main course that does not have tomatoes or sauce. Think of it as a pickle with a robust pâté. You may have gathered that I like it. If you want to start small, there are directions for making less at the end of the recipe. *Serves 8 to 10 as a side dish*

6 cloves garlic, smashed and peeled
2 spring onions, cut into 5 cm/2 inch lengths
30 g/1 oz fresh coriander leaves and 5 cm/2 inches of stalks
1 tablespoon vegetable oil

1.5 kg/3 lb tomatoes, cored and cut into 8 wedges each
4 tablespoons dried Chinese black beans
2 tablespoons tamari soya sauce
1 tablespoon rice wine vinegar
2 tablespoons cornflour

1 Place garlic, spring onions and coriander in the container of a food processor. Process until coarsely chopped. Scrape into a 35 × 27.5 × 5 cm/14 × 11 × 2 inch dish and add oil. Cook, uncovered, at 100% for 3 minutes.

2 Remove from oven. Add tomatoes and beans and stir to coat. Cover tightly with microwave cling film. Cook at 100% for 10 minutes.

3 Combine soya sauce, vinegar and cornflour in a small bowl.

4 Pierce film on tomato mixture with the tip of a sharp knife, then remove from oven. Uncover and stir in cornflour mixture. Cook, uncovered, at 100% for 3 minuted.

5 Remove from oven. Serve hot.

To serve 2. Chop 1 clove garlic, ½ spring onion (white only), and 2 tablespoons coriander leaves in the food processor. Scrape into a 20 cm/8 inch square dish with 1 teaspoon oil. Cook for 2 minutes. Add 2 tomatoes and 1 tablespoon beans. Cover and cook for 3 minutes. Combine 2 teaspoons tamari soya sauce, 1 teaspoon vinegar and 2 teaspoons cornflour and stir in. Cook, uncovered, at 100% for 2 minutes.

SWEET AND SOUR RED CABBAGE

◆ ◆ ◆

This has that warm, sweet and sour taste I like so much. It is good with boiled beef or Traditional Pot Roast (page 210). Leftovers can be made into Hot Beetroot and Red Cabbage Borscht (page 92). A dollop of soured cream and a sprinkling of finely chopped dill on each portion would not go amiss. *Serves 6*

1 medium onion, peeled and thinly
  sliced
35 g/1⅙ oz unsalted butter
1 medium red cabbage (about 1.25 kg/
  2½ lb) washed, cored and shredded
175 ml/6 fl oz red wine vinegar
4 teaspoons granulated sugar
2 tablespoons (packed) dark brown
  sugar

1 teaspoon sea salt
½ teaspoon freshly ground black pepper
6 cloves garlic, smashed and peeled
1 bay leaf
10 juniper berries
2 tablespoons fresh lemon juice
1 tablespoon treacle

1 Place onions and 2 tablespoons of the butter in a 30 × 25 × 75 cm/12 × 10 × 3 inch dish. Cook, uncovered, at 100% for 2 minutes.

2 Remove from oven and stir in cabbage. Cover tightly with microwave cling film. Cook at 100% for 8 minutes.

3 In a 1 litre/2 pint measure, combine vinegar, granulated and brown sugars, salt, pepper, garlic, bay leaf, and juniper berries. Without removing cabbage from oven, uncover and pour vinegar mixture over all. Re-cover tightly and cook for 10 minutes more.

4 Remove from oven. Let stand, covered.

5 Combine lemon juice, treacle, and remaining butter in a 500 ml/1 pint glass measure. Cook, uncovered, at 100% for 30 seconds.

6 Remove from oven. Uncover cabbage and stir in treacle mixture. Serve hot.

PAK CHOI

The leaves of large pak choi, or Chinese white cabbage, need to be cooked separately from the stalks. To separate them, hold the stalk between the outstretched thumb and fingers of one hand. With the other hand, sharply pull off the green leaves. This recipe can be mixed into the following one for Pak Choi Stalks if you are serving it warm, but I prefer to keep them separate, serving the leaves with fish or seafood another day. If you get really beautiful little pak choi heads, no longer than 15 cm/6 inches in all, cook them whole this way. You can cook up to six at a time, one per person. Increase cooking time by 2 minutes. Note that the widely available Chinese leaves (petai) is a different oriental vegetable. *Serves 2 to 3*

2 tablespoons sesame oil
1 tablespoon sesame seeds
Leaves from 2 heads pak choi (about
    200 g/7 oz), cut into 5 mm/¼ inch
    chiffonade

2 tablespoons mirin
1 tablespoon soya sauce
1 tablespoon Worcestershire sauce
2 teaspoons sugar

1 Combine oil and seeds in a 35 × 27.5 × 5 cm/14 × 11 × 2 inch dish. Cover tightly with microwave cling film. Cook at 100% for 3 minutes.

2 Pierce film with the tip of a sharp knife, then remove from oven. Uncover and add pak choi. Stir well. Cover tightly with microwave cling film. Cook at 100% for 3 minutes.

3 Pierce film, then remove from oven. Uncover and stir in remaining ingredients. Re-cover and cook for 2 minutes more.

4 Pierce film, then remove from oven. Uncover and serve.

PAK CHOI STALKS

— • ◆ • —

The pale, white-green stalks of pak choi are slightly crunchy and mildly spicy. They can be served hot as a vegetable. They will also keep up to a week in the refrigerator and can be used as pickle. See the recipe for Pak Choi for directions on how to separate the leaves from the stalks. *Serves 6*

Stalks from 2 heads pak choi, cut into
    5–7.5 cm/2–3 inch lengths
1 tablespoon water
2 tablespoons cornflour
5½ tablespoons vegetable oil

1 teaspoon small dried chillies
6 large cloves garlic, smashed and peeled
2 tablespoons sugar
1 tablespoon sea salt
4 tablespoons rice wine vinegar

1 Place pak choi in a 35 × 27.5 × 5 cm/14 × 11 × 2 inch dish. Sprinkle with water. Cover tightly with microwave cling film. Cook at 100% for 6 minutes.

2 Pierce film with the tip of a sharp knife, then remove from oven. Uncover, remove cooking juices to a small bowl and stir in cornflour. Remove pak choi to a warm plate. Reserve liquid and pak choi.

3 Combine oil, chillies and garlic in same dish. Cook, uncovered, at 100% for 4 minutes.

4 Remove from oven. Add reserved cornflour mixture and stir well. Stir in sugar, salt, vinegar and reserved pak choi. Cover tightly with microwave cling film. Cook at 100% for 5 minutes.

5 Pierce film, then remove from oven. Uncover and serve hot.

CURRIED MUSHROOM CAPS WITH PEAS

This is a mild curry meant to accompany non-curry main courses. If you want it hotter, double the amount of Spice Powder; if using curry powder, double the amount and add ¼ teaspoon Tabasco sauce. This is good with hamburgers, roasts or grilled chops of any kind. *Serves 6*

1 tablespoon plus 1 teaspoon vegetable oil

2 teaspoons black or yellow mustard seeds

1 teaspoon Spice Powder III (page 299) or curry powder

1 clove garlic, smashed and peeled

½ teaspoon sea salt

500 g/1 lb medium (4 cm/1½ inch size) mushrooms, wiped clean and stalks removed

4 tablespoons Chicken Stock (page 286) or stock from a cube

75 g/2½ oz frozen petit pois, defrosted in a sieve under warm running water

5½ tablespoons Coconut Milk (page 306) or canned unsweetened coconut milk

1 teaspoon fresh lime juice

1 Heat 1 teaspoon of the oil in a 1.5 litre/2½ pint soufflé dish, uncovered, at 100% for 2 minutes. Add the mustard seeds and cover loosely with paper towels. Cook at 100% for 4 minutes, shaking dish once.

2 Remove from oven. Add remaining oil, spice powder, garlic and salt. Add the mushroom caps and stock and stir to coat. Cover tightly with microwave cling film. Cook at 100% for 12 minutes.

3 Pierce film with the tip of a sharp knife, then remove from oven. Uncover and stir in remaining ingredients. Cook, uncovered, at 100% for 1 minute 30 seconds.

4 Remove from oven. Stir and serve hot or warm.

MUSHROOM CAPS WITH CUMIN AND SOURED CREAM

This is almost the best vegetable there is with steak and Mashed Potatoes (page 252). It can also be served cold as a first course on some lettuce. If you want to cut down on calories, use plain low fat yogurt instead of soured cream. *Serves 4*

2 tablespoons vegetable oil
1 teaspoon ground cumin
500 g/1 lb medium (4 cm/1½ inch size) mushrooms, wiped clean and stalks removed
½ teaspoon sea salt

4 tablespoons soured cream
1 tablespoon very finely chopped flat-leaf parsley
1 teaspoon fresh lemon juice
¼ teaspoon freshly ground black pepper

1 Heat oil and cumin in a 2.5 litre/4 pint soufflé dish, uncovered, at 100% for 2 minutes. Add mushrooms and salt and stir to coat. Cover tightly with microwave cling film. Cook at 100% for 12 minutes.

2 Pierce film with the tip of a sharp knife, then remove from oven. Uncover and stir in soured cream, parsley, lemon juice and pepper. Cook, uncovered, at 100% for 1 minute 30 seconds.

3 Remove from oven. Stir and serve hot.

MUSHROOM RAGOÛT

No doubt about it, this is special occasion food unless you feel like treating yourself to expensive dried mushrooms. If you have some wild mushrooms, freshly picked or store-bought, substitute cèps (boletus) or chanterelles, cut in strips, for some or all of the store-bought mushrooms. Canned Chinese straw mushrooms can also be added. Stir it into Velouté (page 318) for a fabulous veal or chicken sauce serving 10 to 12 people. Save the soaking liquid from the dried morels to add to stocks or sauces. It will do wonders for Vegetable Stock (page 290).

Serve the ragoût with steak, veal or chicken. You don't need much; it is rich. Add a green vegetable without sauce, like asparagus. Spoon the ragoût into Vol-au-Vents (page 384) as a first course. *Serves 6 as a side dish*

30 g/1 oz dried morels (8 to 12
  mushrooms)
500 g/1 lb cultivated mushrooms,
  sliced 5 mm/¼ inch thick
2 teaspoons fresh lemon juice
30 g/1 oz dried shiitake mushrooms
1 tablespoon very finely chopped
  shallot
2 tablespoons Meat Glaze (page 291) or
  Sauce Espagnole (page 321)

2 tablespoons red wine
1 tablespoon Cognac
2 tablespoons very finely chopped
  parsley
15 g/½ oz unsalted butter
Sea salt
Freshly ground black pepper
1 tablespoon (packed) finely chopped
  fresh dill (optional)
1 tablespoon Dijon mustard (optional)

1 Place morels in a 1 litre/2 pint glass measuring jug and cover with 250 ml/8 fl oz cold water. Cover tightly with microwave cling film. Cook at 100% for 3 minutes. Remove from oven and let stand, covered, for 3 minutes. Pierce film with the tip of a sharp knife, then uncover and strain. Keep soaking liquid for another use. Use small morels whole. Slice large morels across into 5 cm/2 inch pieces and reserve.

2 Combine sliced cultivated mushrooms and lemon juice in a 22.5 cm/9 inch flan dish. Crumble dried shiitake mushrooms over mixture, discarding stalks; stir. Cover tightly with microwave cling film. Cook at 100% for 3 minutes.

3 Pierce film, then remove from oven. Uncover and stir in reserved morels. Add remaining ingredients except salt and pepper, dill and mustard. Cook, uncovered, at 100% for 3 minutes.

4 Remove from oven. Stir in salt and pepper, dill and/or mustard, if used. Serve hot.

VARIATIONS

CREAMY MUSHROOM RAGOÛT Dissolve 2 teaspoons cornflour in 125 ml/4 fl oz double cream. Stir into mushrooms along with morels in step 3 and cook as for Mushroom Ragoût. Finish, adding 1 tablespoon of the morel-soaking liquid and dill and/or mustard, if you like.

MUSHROOM RAGOÛT WITH STRAW MUSHROOMS Add 175 ml/6 fl oz canned straw mushrooms, drained and rinsed, along with morels. Increase red wine and Meat Glaze *each* to 3 tablespoons. Cook for 4 minutes. If desired, finish as Creamy Mushroom Ragoût, using 1 tablespoon cornflour.

WILD MUSHROOM SAUCE Add cooked Mushroom Ragoût to 350 ml/12 fl oz Velouté (page 318). Season with salt, a little pepper and a pinch of cayenne. Reheat in a 2 litre/3½ pint glass jug or bowl, loosely covered with paper towel, at 100% for 4 minutes.

SUMMER VEGETABLES WITH BASIL

• • •

The quality of olive oil is particularly important in this dish. If you are not using one of the exceptionally fruity oils (which can also be exceptionally expensive), double the amount of oil and reduce cooking time by 1 minute. If small tomatoes (5 cm/2 inches in diameter) are not available, core and quarter large tomatoes.

This combination was devised at the height of summer, when I returned from Vermont with a bounty of perfect produce. There are alternatives for some of the ingredients, but one item that is indispensable is fresh basil. Best of all was a version using half bush basil and half large leaf basil.

At once refreshing and comforting, this is one of my favourite recipes for a ripened garden on a warm day. The oil from the peppers is absorbed into all the other vegetables—delightful. It is also good over pasta. *Serves 8 as a first course or side dish*

500 g/1 lb very small yellow or green courgettes (about 8 to 10 , with flowers intact, if possible) or larger courgettes cut into 2.5 × 2.5 × 7.5 cm/1 × 1 × 3 inch pieces
4 medium Hungarian peppers, or 3 red peppers, cored, seeded and cut into 7.5 cm/3 inch strips, and 1 teaspoon dried chilli flakes

500 g/1 lb small tomatoes, pricked 3 or 4 times each
15 g/½ oz fresh basil leaves
2 tablespoons water
2 tablespoons fruity olive oil
1 teaspoon sea salt

1 Arrange courgettes in a 2.5 litre/4 pint soufflé dish spoke-fashion with flowers pointing towards the centre. Place peppers in centre and arrange tomatoes on top of courgettes. Tuck basil between vegetables. Pour water, oil and salt over all. Cover dish tightly with microwave cling film. Cook at 100% for 12 minutes 30 seconds, until vegetables are tender.

2 Pierce film with the tip of a sharp knife, then remove from oven. Uncover and cut peppers in half. Serve hot or let cool to room temperature and serve with cold leftover meat or an omelet.

To serve 4. Use 3 Hungarian peppers or 2 red peppers plus ¾ teaspoon dried chilli flakes. Halve all other ingredients. Arrange in a 16 × 7.5 cm/6½ × 3 inch soufflé dish. Cover and cook for 9 minutes. Finish as for 8 servings.

To serve 2. Use 1 Hungarian pepper or ½ red pepper plus ⅛ teaspoon dried chilli flakes and 2 teaspoons oil. Divide all other ingredient quantities by 4. Arrange in a large soup bowl. Cover and cook for 8 minutes. Finish as for 8 servings.

MAIN COURSE VEGETABLES

It isn't just vegetarians who from time to time relish making a meal out of vegetables. Slimmers and delighters in the season's produce do so as well. The chapter on grains (page 107) has pasta and rice dishes that make good meatless main courses. Cook the vegetables for Pasta Primavera (page 133) and top with eggs as in Summer Vegetable Bonanza (page 283) or, even simpler, serve them with Watercress Sauce (page 320). You might want to pick three of your favourite vegetable recipes and serve them with a simple starch. Use one of the vegetable purées under Baked Eggs (page 66).

VEGETABLES FOR ONE

If you are cooking just for one, pick up already cleaned and sliced vegetables from a salad counter. There is no simpler way to satisfy a craving for a dish of crunchy, assorted fresh vegetables, with absolutely no work involved. *Serves 1*

250–300 g/8–10 oz assorted vegetables, trimmed, peeled and sliced (see note)

2 tablespoons finely chopped fresh herbs, such as basil, chives, dill, parsley or tarragon

Sea salt

Freshly ground black pepper

15 g/½ oz unsalted butter, cut into bits (optional)

1 Arrange vegetables in a 20 cm/8 inch flan dish or deep pie dish, with slower-cooking vegetables towards the outside. Sprinkle with herbs, salt, pepper and butter, if used. Cover tightly with microwave cling film. Cook at 100% for 5 minutes.

2 Pierce film with the tip of a sharp knife, then remove from oven. Uncover immediately.

Note. Slower-cooking vegetables include carrots, green beans, red cabbage, broccoli florets, cauliflower florets, peas, mange-touts, cherry tomatoes. Quick-cooking vegetables include asparagus, red onions or spring onions, mushrooms, courgettes, red and green peppers.

STUFFED CABBAGE LEAVES

• ◆ •

There are people who can eat a piece of stuffed cabbage and live to eat their main course; I find it too filling. This recipe makes 8 to 10 stuffed leaves. You really have to know your guests' appetites to figure out how much to serve. One may be enough with a dollop of soured cream on top; but I have known grown people and growing boys to eat three.

Drink beer, or a cold red wine like Beaujolais. I would have a salad and relax. *Serves 4 to 8*

60 g/2 oz long-grain rice
1 cabbage, broken outer leaves removed and cored, leaving head whole
1 medium onion, peeled and quartered (about 250 g/8 oz)
1 clove garlic, smashed and peeled
1 5p piece-size fresh root ginger, peeled
500 g/1 lb minced beef
1 tablespoon sea salt
⅛ teaspoon grated nutmeg

SAUCE
400 g/14 oz canned tomatoes, drained and crushed
4 tablespoons cider vinegar
75 g/2½ oz brown sugar
1 tablespoon Meat Glaze (page 291) (optional)
2 tablespoons paprika, 2 teaspoons paprika paste or 1 teaspoon Hot Pepper Sauce (page 297)
2 cloves garlic, smashed and peeled
75 g/2½ oz raisins
4 tablespoons sweet wine, like riesling or Tokay

1 Place rice in a 1 litre/2 pint glass measuring jug and cover with 250 ml/8 fl oz cold water. Cover with microwave cling film. Cook at 100% for 5 minutes. Pierce film with the tip of a sharp knife, then remove from oven. Drain, rinse and reserve.

2 Place whole cabbage in centre of oven and cook, uncovered, at 100% for 5 to 6 minutes. Remove from oven and let cool slightly. Peel back and remove 8 large or 10 small leaves.

3 Place onions, garlic and ginger in the container of a food processor. Process until finely chopped. Remove from processor and combine with minced beef, salt, nutmeg and reserved rice.

4 Position a cabbage leaf, outside down, on a work surface. Fill with 2 tablespoons of meat mixture and fold sides of leaf over on both sides to enclose filling. Then roll up. Repeat with all leaves. Place stuffed cabbage rolls, seam sides down, in a 27.5 × 22.5 × 10 cm/11 × 9 × 4 inch dish (see vine leaves, page 41).

5 Stir together sauce ingredients just to combine. Pour over prepared cabbage. Cover tightly with microwave cling film. Cook at 100% for 15 minutes.

6 Pierce film, then remove from oven. Uncover and remove cabbage to a warm serving dish. Return sauce to oven and cook, uncovered, at 100% for 5 minutes.

7 Remove from oven. Pour sauce over cabbage and serve.

GREEN VEGETABLE CURRY

Served with a pilaf like Tomato Pilaf (page 119), this is enough for two to three as a main course. *Serves 4 as a side dish*

2 tablespoons vegetable oil
1 medium onion (about 250 g/8 oz), peeled and thinly sliced
1 clove garlic, smashed, peeled and very finely chopped
1 teaspoon Spice Powder I (page 299)
Large pinch cayenne pepper
500 g/1 lb spinach, stalks removed, washed and dried
3 spring onions, trimmed and coarsely chopped

3 tablespoons chopped fresh dill
4 tablespoons Chicken Stock (page 286) or stock from a cube
1 teaspoon sea salt
4 medium courgettes (about 250 g/8 oz), preferably 2 green and 2 yellow, cut into 5 cm/2 inch rounds and each round cut into eights

1 Heat oil in a 2.5 litre/4 pint soufflé dish, uncovered, at 100% for 2 minutes. Add onions, garlic, spice powder and cayenne. Cook, uncovered, at 100% for 4 minutes.

2 Remove from oven. Add remaining ingredients except courgettes. Cover tightly with microwave cling film. Cook at 100% for 5 minutes. Pierce film with the tip of a sharp knife, then uncover and stir in courgettes. Re-cover and cook for 5 minutes more, stirring once.

3 Pierce film, then remove from oven. Uncover and let stand 3 minutes before serving.

VEGETABLE CURRY

＋·＋·＋

This makes a wonderful meal with plain rice or a pilaf, or as an accompaniment to grilled chicken, fish, lamb or beef. Here, making your own spice powder really pays off. If you like things spicy, double the amount of Spice Powder or curry powder.

This curry is very good cold. Reduce the final cooking period to 10 minutes; let stand, covered, until cool. Refrigerate until ready to serve. *Serves 8 as a main dish, 12 to 16 as a side dish*

1 large baking potato (about 300 g/10 oz), peeled and thinly sliced in a food processor
60 g/2 oz Clarified Butter (page 424) or unsalted butter
1 large onion, peeled, quartered and thinly sliced in a food processor
3 cloves garlic, smashed and peeled
1 tablespoon Spice Powder III (page 299) or curry powder
500 ml/16 fl oz Chicken Stock (page 286) or stock from a cube
250 ml/8 fl oz Lightly Cooked Crushed Tomatoes (page 293)

200 g/7 oz cauliflower florets
2 large carrots, trimmed, peeled and thinly sliced in a food processor
1 large red pepper, cored, seeded and cut in 2.5 cm/1 inch dice
90 g/3 oz broccoli florets
125 g/4 oz green beans, trimmed and cut in half
2 tablespoons fresh lime juice
2 tablespoons chopped fresh coriander
Sea salt
Freshly ground black pepper

1 Put a pan of salted water on to blanch potatoes and blanch for 5 minutes. Drain and reserve.

2 Heat butter in a 2.5 litre/4 pint soufflé dish, uncovered, at 100% for 3 minutes. Add the onions, garlic and spice or curry powder. Cook, uncovered, at 100% for 8 minutes, stirring once.

3 Add stock, crushed tomatoes, cauliflower, carrots and reserved potatoes. Cover tightly with microwave cling film. Cook at 100% for 12 minutes.

4 Pierce film with the tip of a sharp knife, then uncover and stir in peppers, broccoli and beans. Re-cover and cook at 100% for 12 minutes.

5 Pierce film, then remove from oven. Let stand, covered, for 2 minutes. Uncover and stir in lime juice and coriander; add salt and pepper to taste.

To serve 4. Blanch 1 small potato. Heat 45 g/1 ½ oz butter in a 1.5 litre/2½ pint soufflé dish. Add 1 large sliced onion, 2 cloves garlic and 2 teaspoons spice powder and cook for 6 minutes. Halve quantities of stock, crushed tomatoes, cauliflower and carrots and cook as for 8 servings for 10 minutes. Uncover and add 1 pepper, 45 g/1½ oz broccoli, and 90 g/3 oz beans. Cover and cook for 10 minutes more. Halve remaining ingredients and finish as for 8 servings, letting the curry stand for 2 minutes. To serve cold, reduce final cooking time to 8 minutes. Taste to see if it requires more lime juice or a little bit of vegetable oil.

To serve 2. Blanch 1 small potato. Heat 30 g/1 oz butter in a 1 litre/2 pint soufflé dish. To butter add 1 small sliced onion, 1 clove garlic and 1 teaspoon spice powder and cook for 6 minutes. Add 1 small pepper, 30 g/1 oz broccoli, and 45 g/1½ oz beans. Cook for 6 minutes more. Finish as for 8 servings, adding 2 teaspoons lime juice and 2 teaspoons coriander with the salt and pepper at end. To serve cold, reduce final cooking time to 5 minutes.

AUBERGINE, TOMATO AND FENNEL

This is a seansational first course, major vegetable course or vegetarian main dish that could not be made anywhere as well as in the microwave oven, which permits the vegetables to stay whole and still blend their juices. *Serves 4 as a first course, 2 as a main course*

4 small aubergines (about 8.5 cm/3½ inches long), each pricked 4 times with a fork, or 2 large aubergines, each cut into 7.5 × 4 cm/3 × 1½ inch rectangles
4 large plum tomatoes (about 300 g/ 10 oz), each pricked 4 times with a fork
½ bulb fennel, cored and quartered lengthways

4 large cloves garlic, smashed and peeled
3 sprigs fresh basil
¼ teaspoon fresh thyme
2 tablespoons olive oil
1 tablespoon water
1 teaspoon sea salt
Freshly ground black pepper

1 Arrange aubergines spoke-fashion, stalks towards the centre, around the inside rim of a 2.5 litre/4 pint soufflé dish. Place tomatoes in centre. Scatter fennel on top of aubergines. Tuck garlic, basil and thyme between vegetables. Pour oil, water, salt and pepper over all. Cover tightly with microwave cling film. Cook at 100% for 15 minutes.

2 Pierce film with the tip of a sharp knife, then remove from oven. Uncover and let stand for 3 minutes before serving.

SPICY VEGETABLE RAGOÛT

• ◆ •

This stew is meant to be ladled over a heap of Couscous (page 125) in a soup plate. It is not authentic couscous, but no one will mind, or miss the meat. It is a great dish for a party with a sliced roast and a salad. It makes a good buffet dish, kept warm in a chafing dish or on a hot plate. In that scenario it would serve a small army.

The flavours are spicy, but they don't shout. The surprise comes from the cinnamon, which gives a hint of sweetness that is typical of Moroccan cooking. It will take you about half an hour to prepare all the vegetables, but the ragoût cooks quickly, so you can entertain without fuss. Make the Couscous ahead and reheat it, covered, for 3 minutes at 100%. The vegetables will stay hot. With so many vegetables and the tomato-based sauce, it's a pretty dish. *Serves 6 to 8 as a main course*

COOKING LIQUID
1 litre/1¾ pints tomato juice
12 cloves garlic, mashed and peeled
2 teaspoons aniseed
1 tablespoon ground cumin
2 teaspoons ground coriander
2 teaspoons ground ginger
½ teaspoon ground allspice
¼ teaspoon freshly grated nutmeg
1 teaspoon dried chilli flakes
1 teaspoon ground cardamom
¾ teaspoon ground cinnamon
1 teaspoon Fiery Pepper Sauce (page 297) or 1 teaspoon *each* sambal olek and harissa
2 tablespoons olive oil

VEGETABLES
175 g/6 oz canned chick-peas, drained and rinsed

8 baby artichokes, trimmed and cut in half lengthways
2 medium carrots, trimmed, peeled and cut into 2.5 cm/1 inch rounds, or 4 small turnips, trimmed, peeled and cut into 4 cm/1½ inch chunks
12 okra pods or cauliflower florets
400 g/14 oz can baby sweetcorn, drained and rinsed
750 g/1½ lb tomatoes, cored and cut into 4 cm/1½ inch wedges
750 g/1½ lb aubergines, cut into 2.5 cm/1 inch cubes
500 g/1 lb asparagus spears, trimmed and cut in 5 cm/2 inch lengths

1 tablespoon sea salt
30 g/1 oz fresh coriander leaves and stalks, shredded
2 tablespoons fresh lemon juice
1 tablespoon fresh lime juice
Couscous (page 125)

1 Combine cooking liquid ingredients in a 35 × 27.5 × 5 cm/14 × 11 × 2 inch dish. Add all vegetables and salt. Stir to coat. Cover tightly with microwave cling film. Cook at 100% for 20 minutes.

2 Pierce film with the tip of a sharp knife, then remove from oven. Uncover and cook at 100% for 10 minutes.

3 Remove from oven and stir in coriander, lemon juice and lime juice. Serve over Couscous.

SUMMER VEGETABLE BONANZA

◆ ◆ ◆

This is terrific in early summer when the first of the vegetables start coming on. Serve it with Garlic Potatoes (page 130) or BURGHUL (see entry in the Dictionary). You can add eggs or stir in 350 g/12 oz feta cheese or tofu, rinsed and cut in 1 cm/½ inch cubes, at the last minute. Serve lots of chunky bread, please. *Serves 12 as a side dish or first course, 6 as a vegetarian main course*

1 kg/2 lb small aubergines (11–15 cm/ 4½–6 inches long), each pricked 4 times with a fork, or 1 kg/2 lb larger aubergines, cut into 5 × 5 × 7.5 cm/ 2 × 2 × 3 inch pieces
500 g/1 lb baby courgettes (7.5–10 cm/3–4 inches long), preferably 250 g/8 oz green and 250 g/8 oz yellow, trimmed, or larger courgettes cut into 2.5 × 2.5 × 7.5 cm/1 × 1 × 3 inch pieces

1 kg/ 2 lb plum tomatoes (about 12), cored, each pricked 4 times with a fork
12 cloves garlic, smashed and peeled
60 g/2 oz fresh basil leaves
1 tablespoon sea salt
1 teaspoon dried thyme
8 grinds fresh black pepper
6 tablespoons olive oil
Extra sprigs of basil, for serving (optional)

1 Arrange aubergines around the inside rim of a 35 × 27.5 × 5 cm/14 × 11 × 2 inch dish. Place courgettes in centre and arrange tomatoes in a ring on top. Tuck garlic and basil between the vegetables. Sprinkle salt, thyme, pepper and oil over all. Cover tightly with microwave cling film. Cook at 100% for 20 minutes.

2 Pierce film with the tip of a sharp knife, then remove from oven. Uncover and let stand for 3 minutes. Serve with extra basil sprigs scattered on top, if desired.

VARIATION

SUMMER VEGETABLE BONANZA WITH EGGS For a vegetarian meal for a hungry troop, break one egg per person on top of the cooked vegetables in a ring around the edge. Prick each yolk twice with the tip of a very sharp knife. Re-cover and cook at 100% for 2 minutes longer. Serve with burghul. *Serves 6*

Oriental Green Vegetable Casserole

— • ◆ • —

Who would believe these everyday vegetables would taste so special when brought together with rather simple seasonings? Tasting is believing. *Serves 2 as a main course with rice, 4 as a side dish*

1 small green pepper, cored, seeded and cut into 5 cm/2 inch strips
6 spring onions, trimmed, whites cut into 7.5 cm/3 inch lengths and greens cut into 5 mm/¼ inch rounds
125 g/4 oz courgettes, trimmed, cut in half lengthways, then cut into 2 inch pieces

125 g/4 oz mange-touts, stringed
15 g/½ oz fresh coriander leaves
2 tablespoons tamari soya sauce
1½ tablespoons rice wine vinegar
6 thin slices fresh root ginger, peeled
2 teaspoons vegetable oil

1 Toss together all ingredients in a 1 litre/2 pint casserole. Cover tightly with microwave cling film. Cook at 100% for 6 minutes.

2 Pierce with the tip of a sharp knife, then remove from oven. Uncover and stir well once or twice before serving.

SAVOURY BASICS

—◆◆—

Cooking, particularly microwave cooking, takes little time. It's usually the assembling of the ingredients, particularly the cooked ones, that takes so long. This is when the microwave oven is of incalculable aid. If you need some cooked vegetables for a soup, a sauce or a purée, if you need melted chocolate or butter, look in the Dictionary and you'll be able to whip them out in good order. If you need to blanch nuts or defrost meat, look in the Dictionary. You will find other basics in the sections on Savoury Sauces, Sweet Basics and Sweet Sauces. That still leaves you with lots of other things you will need to prepare as parts of a recipe. Perhaps the most frequently called for are stocks, which can be found in this chapter. The other recipes included here are good for unregenerate, top-of-the-stove cooks. They may even end up getting attached to their microwave ovens.

MEAT STOCKS

You will have better stocks if you chop the bones into small pieces (or, much better, get the butcher to do it for you). When buying meat, even if you are buying it boned, ask for the bones and freeze them until you have enough to make stock. Stock can be made with or without vegetables; it is a matter of taste and depends, too, on what sort of recipe you are going to use the stock in. I tend to use vegetables in making stock for fricassées and clear soups, and not to use them in stocks for vegetable soups. When making Chicken Stock, you may add hearts and gizzards to the bones, but do not add chicken livers. It is a good habit to ask for the bones when buying filleted chicken or fish. When removing wing tips to prepare chicken wings in Chicken with Barbecue Sauce (page 188), save those as well. When you roast a chicken, save the gizzards if you are not using them for Chicken Gravy (page 288). Pop your gleanings into a freezer container and make stock when you have enough bones and other good stuff.

If you want an absolutely clear stock, as for Aspic, clarify. See CLARIFYING in the Dictionary. *Makes 1 litre/1¾ pints*

1 kg/2 lb chicken, duck, veal, beef
marrow or lamb bones (see following
instructions)

1 litre/1¾ pints water

1 Place bones and water in a 2.5 litre/4 pint soufflé dish. Cover tightly with microwave cling film. Cook at 100% for 30 minutes, or 40 minutes for a stock that will jell.

2 Pierce film with the tip of a sharp knife, then remove from oven. Let stand, covered, until liquid stops bubbling. Uncover carefully and strain through a fine sieve. Cool. Store tightly covered, in the refrigerator or freezer. Remove fat.

To make 500 ml/16 fl oz stock. Use 500 g/1 lb bones and 500 ml/16 fl oz water. Cook for 20 minutes.

CHICKEN STOCK Use bones, necks, backs and even giblets (gizzards and hearts, not liver); cut into 5–7.5 cm/2–3 inch pieces.

DUCK STOCK Chip bones into 7.5–10 cm/3–4 inch pieces. You may substitute Chicken Stock or stock from a cube for the water. Do not use stock from a cube if you are planning to make Duck Glaze; it will be too salty.

To make 1.75 litres/3 pints: Make Duck Stock and transfer hot stock and bones to a 3 litre/5 pint soufflé dish. Add 750 ml/1¼ pint Chicken Stock or stock from a cube (not if planning to make a Glaze), and 350 g/12 oz raw duck bones, chopped. Cover and cook at 100% for 30 additional minutes.

VEAL STOCK Use veal knuckles sawed across the bone to expose the marrow and hacked into 5 cm/2 inch pieces.

To make 2 litres/3½ pints: Use 2.5 kg/5 lb raw veal knuckles and 2 litres/3½ pints water. Cook for 45 minutes.

LIGHT BEEF STOCK Use beef marrow bones. Add 1 small carrot, trimmed, peeled and quartered.

LAMB STOCK Hack 500 g/1 lb lamb bones into 2.5 cm/1 inch pieces. Substitute Chicken Stock or stock from a cube for the water. Cook for only 20 minutes.

To make 500 ml/16 fl oz: Halve ingredients and cook for only 15 minutes.

Aspic. Clarify (see CLARIFYING in the Dictionary) 1 litre/1¾ pints stock. If your stock will not jell, sprinkle 1 tablespoon powdered gelatine on top of warm, clarified stock; return to the oven and heat at 100% for 5 minutes.

MEAT STOCK WITH VEGETABLES

◆ ◆ ◆

1 kg/2 lb chicken bones and giblets, or veal bones or leg bones of beef, or a combination
250 g/8 oz onions, peeled and quartered
125 g/4 oz celery, cut into 7.5 cm/ 3 inch lengths

250 g/8 oz tomatoes, cored and halved
125 g/4 oz carrots, cut into 7.5 cm/ 3 inch lengths
3 parsley sprigs
1 litre/1¾ pints water

1 Preheat grill.

2 Chop bones as for Meat Stocks (page 286). Spread bones and vegetables in a single layer in a roasting pan. Grill 15 cm/6 inches from the heat source for 40 minutes, shaking the pan occasionally, until well browned.

3 Remove bones and vegetables to a 2 litre/3½ pint glass jug or bowl. Pour water over solids and cover tightly with microwave cling film. Cook at 100% for 30 minutes.

4 Pierce with the tip of a sharp knife, then remove from oven. Uncover and strain stock through a fine sieve. Cool. Store, tightly covered, in the refrigerator or freezer. Remove fat.

VARIATIONS

LIGHT VEGETABLE AND CHICKEN STOCK Use the same ingredients plus 1 clove garlic, smashed and peeled, and 3 fresh dill sprigs. Do not brown bones and vegetables first.

RICH AND MEATY STOCK This really goes beyond stock if you serve the sliced beef in the soup with vegetables. Add some cooked noodles and you have a lovely dinner for 6.

Make Meat Stock with Vegetables using veal knuckles. Strain and skim off fat. Place in a 2.5 litre/4 pint soufflé dish with 500 g/1 lb beef shin meat cut across the grain into 5 mm/¼ inch thick slices. Cover tightly and cook at 100% for 10 minutes. Remove from oven. Remove meat with a slotted spoon. If using stock for a thick soup, do not strain. If you want a clear stock, line a sieve with a wet cloth and pour the stock through. You will have 1 litre/1¾ pints of enriched stock, which can be used in any recipe after skimming off fat and, if desired, clarifying.

To use as a whole meal, do not strain stock. Reserve meat. Add to stock 1 small carrot, peeled and thinly sliced, ½ bay leaf, a pinch of thyme, 150 g/5 oz peas, 1 small turnip, peeled and thinly sliced. 1 tablespoon finely chopped parsley and, if desired, 1 small parsnip, peeled and thinly sliced. Cover tightly and cook for 4 minutes at 100% . Pierce film, then remove soup from oven; season to taste with salt and pepper. Add meat and cooked noodles or cooked cubed potatoes. Serve with horseradish sauce and mustard.

CHICKEN GRAVY Break chicken neck in half. Place in a 1 litre/2 pint glass measuring jug with all the giblets (not the liver), 3 cloves garlic, 2 parsley sprigs, ½ small peeled onion, ½ bay leaf and 1 small peeled carrot cut into 2.5 cm/1 inch lengths. Cover with 250–350 ml/8–12 fl oz Chicken Stock, a version of meat stock with vegetables, or stock from a cube. Cover tightly with microwave cling film. Cook for 20 minutes at 100%. Strain and skim stock. Cut giblets into small pieces. If you have the patience, pick the meat off the neck bones, discarding the bones. (If making gravy for a roast chicken, deglaze the roasting pan with the skimmed stock.) In any case, whisk 2 tablespoons Roux (page 320) into hot stock. Return sliced giblets and neck meat to thickened stock. Cook, uncovered, for 2 minutes at 100%. Season to taste with salt and pepper and chopped dill, parsley, lovage or tarragon, if desired.

You can quickly poach 6 skinned and boned chicken breasts in the Chicken Gravy for 7 minutes. The gravy won't need its last 2 minutes of cooking, because it will get that while the chicken cooks. Serve with noodles, rice, broccoli or spinach.

FISH STOCK

— • ♦ • —

Fish stock should not be made with the bones of flatfish—sole, plaice and the like—or the stock will be bitter. Blood will do the same thing. For basic fish stock, use the bones of white-fleshed fish. Salmon and sturgeon bones give a flavourful and beautifully coloured stock—pale gold for sturgeon, pale pink for salmon—but they are too definite in flavour to use with other kinds of fish. If you want a stock that will jell, increase cooking time to 40 minutes. *Makes about 1 litre/1¾ pints*

1 kg/2 lb whole fish heads and bones,
  broken into 5–7.5 cm/2–3 inch
  pieces

1 litre/1¾ pints water

1 Remove gills, Wash heads and bones thoroughly to rinse away all traces of blood. Use a small knife to open any sealed pockets of blood, as it will make the stock bitter.

2 Place heads, bones and water in a 2.5 litre/4 pint soufflé dish. Cover tightly with microwave cling film. Cook at 100% for 20 minutes.

3 Pierce film with the tip of a sharp knife, then remove from oven. Leave covered until bubbling stops, about 3 minutes. Uncover carefully and strain through a fine sieve lined with a single layer of muslin. Cool and skim. Store, tightly covered, in the refrigerator or freezer.

VARIATIONS

SEAFOOD FUMET Use 850 g/1¾ lb prawn shells and 1 kg/2 lb fish heads and fish bones, cleaned. Use 600 ml/1 pint water and 600 ml/1 pint white wine instead of all water. Proceed as for Fish Stock, cooking for 12 minutes. *Makes 1.2 litres/2 pints*

FISH FUMET Use 1 kg/2 lb fish heads and bones, 1 celery stick cut into 5 cm/2 inch lengths, 1 small peeled carrot cut into 2.5 cm/1 inch lengths, 3 parsley springs, ½ bay leaf, 1 whole leek or medium-size onion, peeled and cut into chunks, 600 ml/1 pint *each* water and white wine, and a pinch *each* of dried thyme and savory. Proceed as for Fish Stock. *Makes 1.2 litres/2 pints*

VEGETABLE STOCK

—◆•◆—

This basic vegetarian stock is good to have on hand for everyday cooking if you are a vegetarian, or for when you are having vegetarians as guests. It is cloudy when finished and is best used for bean soups, vegetable soups, and pulse soups (lentils, for instance). This stock has no salt or pepper; if you want, add to taste. You can also use the cooking liquid reserved from making Tomatoes Stuffed with Tabbouleh (page 75) or strained Tomato and Cabbage Soup (page 93) for a vegetarian stock with a strong tomato flavour. *Makes 750 ml/1¼ pints*

4 cloves garlic, smashed and peeled
1 small onion, peeled and halved
Stalks from 1 bunch parsley
1 medium carrot, trimmed, peeled and
  cut into 2.5 cm/1 inch lengths
2 celery sticks, trimmed, stringed and
  cut into 2.5 cm/1 inch lenghts
1 baking potato (500 g/1 lb), scrubbed
  and cut into 2.5 cm/1 inch chunks

1 litre/1¾ pints water, part replaced
  with strained liquid from soaking
  dried mushrooms, if available
1 bay leaf
Pinch dried thyme
Pinch dried oregano

1 Put vegetables into the container of a food processor and process until coarsely chopped.

2 Scrape into a 2.5 litre/4 pint soufflé dish. Add water, bay leaf, thyme and oregano. Cover tightly with microwave cling film. Cook at 100% for 25 minutes.

3 Pierce film with the tip of a sharp knife, then remove from oven. Uncover and strain through a fine sieve, pressing on vegetables to extract all the liquid.

Additional vegetables. To change the flavour and colour of this stock, add 1 large cored tomato, or 60 g/2 oz washed spinach leaves, or 30 g/1 oz mushroom peelings and stalks.

ORIENTAL VEGETABLE STOCK

This is a clear stock with a zing of flavour. It is only mildly salty so increase the amount of soya sauce if you wish. *Makes 1 litre/1¾ pints*

1 litre/1¾ pints water
6 5p piece-size slices fresh root ginger, peeled
60 g/2 oz fresh coriander stalks and leaves

6 cloves garlic, smashed and peeled
30 g/1 oz onion or spring onion greens, thinly sliced
1 teaspoon dried chilli flakes
2 tablespoons tamari soya sauce

1 Put all ingredients in a 2 litre/3½ pint glass jug or bowl. Cover tightly with microwave cling film. Cook at 100% for 15 minutes.

2 Pierce film with the tip of a sharp knife, then remove from oven. Uncover and strain through a fine sieve, pressing on vegetables to extract all the liquid.

Nearly endless additions. Add 1 sheet of nori (shredded), or 1 tablespoon dashi, or 45 g/1½ oz thinly sliced cabbage, or 1 tablespoon lemongrass powder (sereh) or two 15 cm/6 inch pieces lemon grass, bruised with the handle of a knife. If you don't need a clear stock, add 1 teaspoon sesame oil.

MEAT OR FISH GLAZES

Classic French cooking makes use of highly reduced, concentrated essences of various kinds of meat and fish stocks to enrich sauces or to use as the basis of sauces. Glace de viande, for example is made from a stock based on gelatine-rich veal bones and intensely flavoured with beef. Sometimes vegetables are included in the making of glaze, bringing the mixture close to a demi-glace or a reduced Sauce Espagnole (page 321).

Once you discover how easy it is to make a concentrate in the microwave oven, without the bother of filthy pans or ruinous scorching, you will, as I do, make a quantity and freeze it. It keeps virtually forever. Salt is never added to a stock for concentrate, as the reduction would make it overly intense.

Place your unsalted stock in a glass measuring jug at least half again as large as the amount of stock. Cook, uncovered, at 100% until the liquid visible in the jug is reduced to the quantity you want. You usually want a 4-to-1 reduction. That is, 250 ml/8 fl oz stock will give you 60 ml/2 fl oz glaze.

ROUX

— ◆ ◆ ◆ —

Although flour generally cooks oddly in the microwave oven, a good amount of roux—fat and flour cooked together—does well. Keep it on hand to make basic Béchamel (page 316). Roux can also be stirred into cooked food in the same way that beurre manié is in classic French cooking. Do not try to use beurre manié, however; it won't work.

The Creoles of New Orleans have a rich-tasting, special Brown Roux that ordinarily cooks slowly on top of the stove, requires constant stirring, and risks burning. None of this happens when Brown Roux is prepared in the microwave oven. Make a quantity and then whip up your Gumbos and Shrimp Creole quickly and easily.

Roux keeps, refrigerated, virtually indefinitely. *Makes 5½ tablespoons*

60 g/2 oz unsalted butter   6 tablespoons plain flour

1 Heat butter in a 1 litre/2 pint soufflé dish, uncovered, at 100% for 3 minutes.

2 Remove from oven. Thoroughly whisk in flour. Cook, uncovered, at 100% for 2 minutes.

To make 3 tablespoons. Reduce butter to 30 g/1 oz and flour to 4 tablespoons. Heat butter in a 1 litre/2 pint glass measuring jug for 2 minutes and cook with flour for 2 minutes.

To make 200 ml/7 fl oz. Increase butter to 125 g/4 oz and flour to 105 g/3¾ oz. Heat butter for 4 minutes and cook with flour for 3 minutes.

VARIATION

BROWN ROUX Prepare Roux; cook after addition of flour for 6 minutes, stirring twice. To make 350 ml/12 fl oz, increase cold butter to 250 g/8 oz and flour to 210 g/7½ oz. Heat butter for 4 minutes. Whisk in flour and cook for 9 minutes, whisking 3 times. Always remove Brown Roux immediately after cooking from container and whisk vigorously to prevent scorching.

GAMMON HOCKS

— ◆ ◆ ◆ —

There are numerous recipes from America's South that call for gammon hocks and use their cooking liquid. I find it easier and better to precook the gammon hock so as not to overcook the other elements in the recipe.

Check frequently, every 10 minutes or so, to make sure the film keeps a tight seal; if it does not, replace with fresh microwave cling film. *Makes 1 gammon hock and 175 ml/6 fl oz cooking liquid*

1 meaty, smoked gammon hock (knuckle), about 250 g/8 oz, washed and split in half	500 ml/16 fl oz water

1 Put gammon hock and water in a 1 litre/2 pint glass measuring jug. Cover tightly with 2 sheets of microwave cling film. Cook at 100% for 35 minutes.

2 Pierce film, with the tip of a sharp knife then remove from oven and uncover carefully.

To make 2 gammon hocks. Arrange 3 split hocks (about 750 g/1½ lb), cut sides down, in a 2.5 litre/4 pint soufflé dish. Add 600 ml/1 pint water. Cover and cook at 100% for 35 minutes.

LIGHTLY COOKED CRUSHED TOMATOES

M ake the best of off-season tomatoes with this cooked-down concentrate, or profit from an abundance of fresh tomatoes in season. There is virtually no limit to its uses. Freeze in 150 or 300 ml/¼ or ½ pint portions for making sauces or soups, or freeze in smaller, ice cube-size portions to add intense tomato flavour to a dish. See DEFROSTING in the Dictionary. *Makes about 1 litre/1¾ pints*

12 medium tomatoes (about 2 kg/4 lb)

1 Core an cut a deep X across the bottom of each tomato. Place in a 2.5 litre/4 pint soufflé dish. Cook, uncovered, at 100% for 20 minutes, stirring once.

2 Remove from oven. Pass through a food mill fitted with a medium disc. There should be about 2 litres/3½ pints cooked tomatoes.

3 Return tomatoes to soufflé dish. Cook, uncovered, at 100% until almost all liquid has evaporated; this will take about 45 minutes.

4 Remove from oven. Let cool completely. Store, tightly covered, in the refrigerator or freezer (freeze in small quantities).

To make 500 ml/16 fl oz. Use 6 tomatoes (about 1.25 kg/2½ lb). Cook for 12 minutes and pass through food mill; there will be about 1 litre/1¾ pints tomatoes. Return to oven and cook until almost all liquid has evaporated, about 20 minutes.

BASIC TOMATO PASTE

——— • ◆ • ———

I still buy commercial tomato paste, preferably the kind in tubes, but if I want to indulge myself and my food, I make my own. I never did it pre-microwave because it took 6 hours. Now I do it once or twice a year because it is so much better and takes only 1½ hours. Freeze in very small quantities, 1 to 2 tablespoons—just what will be needed for a recipe.

Caution: Just because this is cooked in a microwave oven does not mean the tomatoes will not burn. Stirring is important to guard against overcooking in 'hot spots'. *Makes 350 ml / 12 fl oz*

2 kg/4 lb plum tomatoes, washed and
   cored

1 Place tomatoes in a 2.5 litre/4 pint soufflé dish. Cook, uncovered, at 100% for 20 minutes.

2 Remove from oven. Pass through a food mill fitted with a fine disc.

3 Return tomatoes to soufflé dish. Cook, uncovered, at 100% until paste is of desired thickness, stirring occasionally; this will take from 1 hour to 1 hour 15 minutes.

4 Remove from oven. Cool. Store, tightly covered, in the refrigerator or freezer.

DUXELLES

——— • ◆ • ———

Duxelles, cooked chopped mushrooms and shallots, is one of the best secrets of French cooking. A little bit enriches a sauce, more makes a soup, more still a stuffing for fish. Use 2 tablespoons or so to fill an omelet. Substitute Duxelles for meat in Lasagne (page 136) for a vegetarian dish of singular complexity of taste. If you have Duxelles around, it makes a handy hors d'oeuvre, as in Grilled Stuffed Mushroon Caps: Fill clean, medium mushroom caps with 1 tablespoon Duxelles each. Sprinkle each with ½ teaspoon freshly grated Parmesan cheese. Place on a baking sheet under a preheated grill and cook about 30 seconds, or until the cheese melts.

When cooking Duxelles, you may see a little butter in the mixture at the end of the cooking time, but there should be no mushroom liquid left. If there is, continue to cook, uncovered, in 1- to 2-minute increments until it has evaporated. The cooking time varies, depending on the size of the chopped mushrooms; the larger the mushroom pieces, the shorter the cooking time.

Freeze some Duxelles in ice cube trays, then store in freezer bags, for days when you want to toss just one or two cubes into a Béchamel or pasta sauce. Freeze in larger quantities for use as stuffing. *Makes 350–500 ml/12–16 fl oz, depending on the wateriness of the mushrooms*

125 g/4 oz unsalted butter
500 g/1 lb mushrooms or mushroom stalks, wiped clean and finely chopped
125 g/4 oz shallots, peeled (about 5 shallots)

30 g/1 oz (tightly packed) parsley leaves
2 teaspoons sea salt
½ teaspoon freshly ground black pepper

1 Heat butter in a 1 litre/2 pint soufflé dish, uncovered, at 100% for 2 minutes, until melted. Add mushrooms and stir to coat. Cook, uncovered, at 100% for 5 minutes.

2 Put shallots and parsley in the container of a food processor and process until finely chopped.

3 Remove mushrooms from oven. Stir in shallots, parsley, salt and pepper. Cook, uncovered, at 100% for 8 minutes.

4 Remove from oven.

To make 175 ml/6 fl oz. Halve all ingredients. Proceed as for Duxelles, cooking mushrooms for 4 minutes. Add shallots, parsley, salt and pepper and cook for 5 minutes.

PEPPER PURÉES

Columbus may have been dismayed that his new route did not take him to the haunts of the spice trade. Nevertheless, it is hard to see how the cooks of the world got on before he found the land from which hot chillies came. They quickly turned up in food from Africa, Asia, Arabia, Egypt and Europe. I don't think Australians of British descent use chillies, but Malaysia is virtually pickled in them. Chillies are available green and red, fresh, dried and smoked. They are related to sweet peppers or capsicums.

All peppers and chillies are good for cooking, and make wonderful sauces when puréed. Some purées are suitable for use on their own. Others are sauces in the sense that the Tabasco sauce you buy in bottles is. You use them in small quantities to season foods. Hotness and thickness will vary depending on the proportion of chillies to sweet peppers, whether you remove the seeds from the chillies, and how you purée them. A food mill will remove most of the skin and seeds. A blender or food processor will pulverize them.

In addition to hotness and texture, it is nice to keep colour in mind. If possible, use all green, all red, yellow and green, or yellow and red peppers together. The result will be beautiful clear colours, not muddy ones.

When working with chillies, fresh or dried, you may want to wear rubber kitchen gloves; the oil in the flesh of the chillies and their seeds can be extremely irritating to the skin. Never touch your face with your hands while working with chillies.

These chillies and peppers are cooked in microwave-safe roasting bags. (If you don't have any, all of these recipes, except that using 1.25 kg/2½ lb of peppers, can be cooked in a 2.5 litre/4 pint soufflé dish tightly covered with microwave cling film. The bag does a slightly better job, however.) If you are using an oven with a turntable, the bag must be closed in such a way that, when it fills with steam, it won't interfere with the turning of the turntable. When opening the bag (or the film), be very careful if chillies are enclosed because the steam carries some of the hot oils. Use a long knife to puncture the film and release the steam, and avert your face.

RED PEPPER PURÉE

◆◆◆

This elegant, mild sauce has a fresh taste and a glorious colour. It could be made equally well with yellow peppers. Either version could be the base of a cold soup if mixed with cornflour-thickened chicken stock and a little yogurt. Warm, it is a terrific sauce for ravioli or tortellini. Try it under one of the vegetable timbales (page 262). I also use it when steaming fish (page 173). In the hot variations, use equal weights of the hot fresh chillies of your choice. *Makes 750 ml/1¼ pints*

1.25 kg/2½ lb red peppers, cored and
   seeded (about 5 very large peppers)

1 Put peppers in a microwave-safe roasting bag and close tight. Cook at 100% for 15 minutes.

2 Remove from oven and carefully open the bag. Put peppers through a food mill fitted with a medium disc.

To make 250 ml/8 fl oz. Use 350 g/12 oz red peppers, cooking for 6 minutes.

VARIATIONS

HOT AND SWEET RED PEPPER SAUCE Use 350 g/12 oz red peppers and 60 g/2 oz fresh red chillies, cored, quartered, and seeded. Proceed as for Red Pepper Purée, cooking for 6 minutes. Add 1 teaspoon sea salt to puréed sauce. *Makes 250 ml/8 fl oz. For 500 ml/16 fl oz,* double ingredients and cook for 15 minutes.

HOT PEPPER SAUCE Use this sauce in place of Caribbean green chilli sauces that are usually shaken from bottles. Use 350 g/12 oz green peppers (about 2 peppers) and 600 g/1¼ lb fresh green chillies, stemmed and seeded. Proceed as for Red Pepper Purée, cooking for 18 minutes. Pass through a food mill fitted with a fine disc. Stir in 1 teaspoon sea salt and 2 tablespoons fresh lime juice. Store in a tightly covered glass jar. *Makes 300 ml/½ pint*

FIERY PEPPER SAUCE Use in place of the hottest red pepper sauces from Louisiana (Tabasco) or Thailand. You may make this with variously coloured chillies, but the resulting sauce will be muddy. For a sauce as brilliant as it is strong, use chillies of the same colour, all red or all green.
   Use 500 g/1 lb fresh chillies, stemmed, seeded and deribbed. Proceed as for Red Pepper Purée, cooking for 12 minutes. Pass through a food mill fitted with a fine disc. Store in the refrigerator in a tightly covered glass jar or bottle. *Makes 125 ml/4 fl oz*

SEARING PEPPER SAUCE Make Fiery Pepper Sauce, but do not remove seeds or ribs from chillies. This sauce is slightly thicker than the other hot sauces—spoon, don't shake—and so strong that you can substitute it for the hottest pepper sauce you can buy and use only half the amount called for.

CHINESE CHILLI SAUCE Make Hot Pepper Sauce, using red peppers and fresh red chillies and adding 15 g/½ oz dried, hot, red chillies. Five minutes before the end of the cooking time, carefully open the bag—away from your face, as chilli steam can burn—and add 8 smashed and peeled garlic cloves; reclose the bag and complete cooking and puréeing. Use rice wine vinegar instead of lime juice. Add salt. Keep in a tightly closed jar in the refrigerator. *Makes about 300 ml/½ pint*

SUPER HOT CHILLI PASTE Stir 60 g/2 oz dried chillies into 250 ml/8 fl oz water in a 1 litre/2 pint glass measuring jug. Cover tightly with microwave cling film. Cook at 100% for 8 minutes. Purée in blender. *Makes 125 ml/4 fl oz*

CHILLI OIL

Muskier tasting than the purées, Chilli Oil is frequently used in small amounts in Chinese cooking to jazz things up. It can be quickly make in the microwave oven. Make it at least 2 days before you plan to use it. *Makes 125 ml/4 fl oz*

5 dried, small red chillies, or 2
   tablespoons dried chilli flakes
125 ml/4 fl oz vegetable oil

1 Put peppers and oil in a blender or food processor and process until well combined. Scrape into a 500 ml/1 pint glass measuring jug and cover tightly with microwave cling film. Cook at 100% for 3 minutes.

2 Pierce film with the tip of a sharp knife, then remove from oven and let cool.

3 Uncover and pour into a clean jar or bottle. Store, tightly covered, away from heat or light.

SPICE POWDERS

One of my favourite cookery books was published some time ago in India. It advises the housewife to send her spices to the spice mill only in the care of a family member or trusted servant, so that the valuable spices won't be stolen. She is also enjoined to mix her spices when they come back warm from the spice mill, or to put them in the raging sun to toast.

I do not frequent a spice mill whose crushing stones warm the spices as they grind them, nor do I live in a land of scorching sun. So the microwave oven has become my mundane sun, an electric coffee mill my mill stones—not exotic, but very effective. An endless group of spice powders and curries can be made. Here are a few that I have found useful. Don't make too much at a time.

SPICE POWDER I

———— ♦ ————

A mild, warm blend. *Makes 4 tablespoons*

2 tablespoons coriander seed
2 tablespoons mustard seed
2 teaspoons cumin seed

2 teaspoons fennel seed
½ teaspoon crushed dried chilli

1 Spread all ingredients in an even layer in a flat dish. Cook, uncovered, at 100% for 6 minutes, shaking pan once.

2 Remove from oven. Let cool completely. Grind to a fine powder in a spice grinder or clean electric coffee mill. Store in an airtight container at room temperature.

To make 1½ tablespoons. Halve all ingredients, cooking for 6 minutes.

VARIATIONS

SPICE POWDER II Add 1 teaspoon celery seed and 4 pinches ground cloves to ingredients for Spice Powder I, cooking for 6 minutes. This is good in vegetable dishes.

SPICE POWDER III Add 1 teaspoon ground mace and 1 teaspoon ground turmeric to ingredients for Spice Powder I cooking for 6 minutes. Use in place of commercially prepared curry powders.

CRAB BOIL

◆ • ◆

In the United States, spicy mixtures are made for seasoning crabs and other seafoods as they cook. While they can be bought in packages, I prefer this homemade blend. Try it with prawns. *Makes 4 tablespoons, enough for 24 crabs*

1 tablespoon chilli powder
1 tablespoon sea salt
½ bay leaf
1 tablespoon mustard seed
1 tablespoon dry mustard powder

1 teaspoon celery seed
1 teaspoon cumin seed
1 teaspoon oregano
1 teaspoon cayenne pepper
1 teaspoon paprika

Combine all ingredients. Sprinkle over crabs or other shellfish such as prawns and cook as directed.

BASIC VEGETABLE BRAISE

French recipes for a braise or a stew often call for the inclusion of a mirepoix, a mixture of herbs and chopped vegetables that has been briefly cooked ('sweated'). This can be quickly done in the microwave oven. The Italians have a similar preparation, called Soffrito, with which the main ingredient of a recipe is cooked to imbue it with flavour before final cooking. Spanish and Spanish-derived cuisines use a mixture called, almost identically, Sofrito, for the same purpose. It is nice to be able to reclaim these important culinary elements without too much work. Feel free to chop all the vegetables and herbs together in a food processor.

MIREPOIX

—————◆◆————

Makes about 250 ml/8 fl oz

45 g/1½ oz unsalted butter
2 carrots, trimmed, peeled and coarsely
  chopped
2 celery sticks, trimmed, stringed and
  coarsely chopped
½ small onion, peeled and coarsely
  chopped, or the well-washed white of
  1 leek, coarsely chopped

1 tablespoon finely chopped parsley
  (optional)
Pinch dried thyme (optional)
1 clove garlic, smashed, peeled and
  chopped (optional)

1 Heat butter in a 2.5 litre/4 pint soufflé dish, uncovered, at 100% for 3 minutes.

2 Remove from oven. Add vegetables and parsley, thyme and garlic. Stir to coat. Cook, uncovered, at 100% for 3 minutes.

VARIATIONS

SOFFRITO The Italian version uses the same vegetables as the French, without the thyme. The major difference is that olive oil, pancetta or lard is substituted for the butter, though even in Italian cooking butter is sometimes used. A Soffrito is a very personal thing, with each cook changing the proportion of the vegetables and adding herbs and even, from time to time, some peeled, seeded and chopped tomato or Parma ham. Proceed as for Mirepoix.

SOFRITO This is as prominent in Spanish cooking as the previous two are in their cuisines. It varies enormously from region to region in Spain. Olive oil is always the fat. It may be as simple as 60 g/2 oz peeled, seeded and coarsely chopped tomato, which you should cook for 5 minutes. A fancy Sofrito might contain olive oil, onions (finely chopped), garlic and tomatoes, plus 1 small green or red pepper—cored, seeded and finally chopped, 45 g/1½ oz finely diced ham, a bay leaf, 2 tablespoons finely chopped parsley, and even some chopped chorizo (60 g/2 oz). Cook for 6 minutes. This is good with eggs or with prawns.

GARLIC CREAM

For those who like garlic, this makes a terrific sauce for fish, grilled chicken, or roast leg of lamb. It is gentle and mellow, thickened by the thoroughly cooked garlic. Cook chicken and rabbit in it. Mash potatoes with it. Use it in Brandade de Morue (page 50). *Makes 300 ml/½ pint*

2 heads garlic
250 ml/8 fl oz double cream
125 ml/4 fl oz Chicken Stock (page
  286) or stock from a cube

½ teaspoon sea salt
¼ teaspoon freshly ground black pepper

1 Place garlic on a flat, hard surface and cover with a cloth. Whack once or twice with a heavy saucepan. Remove the cloth; separate the cloves, discarding any loose, papery skin. (There is no need to peel each garlic clove.)

2 Combine all ingredients in a 2 litre/3½ pint glass jug or bowl. Cook, uncovered, at 100% for 10 minutes.

3 Remove from oven. Pass through a food mill, fitted with a fine disc, into a 1 litre/2 pint soufflé dish. Cook, uncovered, at 100% for 8 minutes. The cream should be thick enough to lightly coat a spoon.

To make 600 ml/1 pint. Double all ingredients, cooking for 15 minutes.

To make 4 tablespoons. Divide all ingredient quantities by 4, cooking for 7 minutes. You may substitute 1½ teaspoons Chicken Glaze (page 291) for stock.

VARIATIONS

GARLIC-CREAM MASHED POTATOES Mix 4 tablespoons Garlic Cream with each mashed, microwave-cooked baking potato.

COLD CREAM OF GARLIC SOUP Mash 1 cooked baking potato and blend with 4 tablespoons Garlic Cream and 175 ml/6 fl oz Chicken Stock (page 286) or stock from a cube until perfectly smooth. Season with sea salt and freshly ground black pepper. Serve well chilled.

SOYA SAUCE GLAZE

◆ ▸ ◆

There are times when a flavourful glaze adds a little extra something to a simple piece of fish and seals the surface. This is an easy one for salmon or swordfish steaks (2 cm/¾ inch thick), or 2.5 cm/1 inch fillets of halibut, cod, monkfish, etc., or shelled prawns. Be sure to cook glaze in a 1 litre/2 pint glass measuring jug, though it may seem large—the ingredients boil up furiously and could otherwise make a huge, sticky mess. Oriental Barbecue Sauce (page 223) makes a good glaze too. *Makes 125 ml/4 fl oz, enough for 4 fish steaks or fillets, or 2.5 kg/ 5 lb shelled prawns*

250 ml/8 fl oz tamari soya sauce

4 tablespoons '2 to 1' Simple Syrup (page 488) syrup

1 Combine soya sauce and syrup in a 1 litre/2 pint glass measuring jug. Cook, uncovered, at 100% for 10 to 12 minutes, until reduced to 125 ml/4 fl oz.

2 Remove from oven.

For fish steaks or 2.5 cm/1 inch thick fillets. Brush both sides with glaze. Let marinate for 5 minutes. Brush each side again. Cook, uncovered, at 100% for appropriate times listed in the Dictionary; halfway through cooking time, turn fish over and brush with glaze. When done, remove from oven and let stand, lightly covered with a sheet of paper towel, for 2 minutes.

For 500 g/1 lb shelled raw prawns. Toss with 1½ tablespoons glaze. Place in a 2.5 litre/4 pint soufflé dish with 2 thin slices peeled, fresh root ginger and 1 lemon, quartered. Cover tightly with microwave cling film. Cook at 100% for 2 to 3 minutes, until prawns are pink; halfway through cooking time, shake dish to redistribute prawns for even cooking. See Dictionary for cooking times for other quantities of prawns, and adjust amounts of glaze, ginger and lemon accordingly.

VARIATION

SPICY SOYA GLAZE Add 3 5p piece-size pieces peeled, fresh root ginger, 1 tablespoon sesame oil, 1 large pinch dried chilli flakes, and 3 garlic cloves, smashed and peeled, to glaze before cooking. Cook; strain and use.

ORIENTAL GLAZE

· · ·

This glaze is delicious on Crispiest Duck (page 200). Glaze duck with it before grilling. Then remove duck to a warm platter and combine remaining glaze with liquid in pan. Serve on the side as gravy. This glaze can be used on pork—chops or roasts—veal and chicken. *Makes enough for 1 duck*

5½ tablespoons tamari soya sauce
6 cloves garlic, smashed and peeled
2 tablespoons grated fresh root ginger

250 ml/8 fl oz Chicken Stock (page 286, with 4 cloves garlic, smashed and peeled, and ½ teaspoon ground cumin added to the bones), or stock from a cube
1 tablespoon sugar

Combine soya sauce, garlic and ginger in a 1 litre/2 pint glass measuring jug. Cover tightly with microwave cling film. Cook at 100% for 5 minutes. Pierce film with the tip of a sharp knife, then remove from oven. Stir in stock and sugar.

PRAWN BUTTER

· · ·

Prawn shells are full of flavour, so instead of throwing them out, make this butter. It can be used as part of the butter in a Beurre Blanc (page 314), in the Roux for Basic Béchamel (page 316), to cook prawns or vegetables that are to be served with prawns, or stirred at the last minute into a sauce for prawns. Like all butters, it freezes well. *Makes 350 g/12 oz*

500 g/1 lb unsalted butter

Shells from 2 kg/4 lb prawns

1 Put butter and shells into the container of a food processor. Process until shells are coarsely chopped.

2 Scrape mixture into a 2.5 litre/4 pint soufflé dish. Cook, uncovered, at 100% for 15 minutes, stirring twice.

3 Remove from oven. Strain through a fine sieve, pressing on shells to extract as much butter as possible. Prawn butter, tightly covered, keeps for 2 weeks in the refrigerator or for 2 months in the freezer.

To make 125 g/4 oz. Use 175 g/6 oz unsalted butter and shells from 500 g/1 lb prawns, cooking for 10 minutes.

PRAWN CREAM

Here is another use for prawn shells, one that is slightly less rich than Prawn Butter. Seasoned, it makes a sauce all on its own for fish, possibly fish steamed with a few prawns. It can be used as the liquid in Basic Béchamel (page 316). Add a few chopped prawns during the last 30 seconds of cooking time along with some finely cut chives and, if desired, a few spoonfuls of Duxelles (page 294) for an elegant sauce. *Makes 250 ml/8 fl oz*

250 ml/8 fl oz double cream   Shells from 500 g/1 lb prawns

1 Combine cream and prawn shells in a 1 litre/2 pint soufflé dish. Cover tightly with microwave cling film. Cook at 100% for 5 minutes.

2 Pierce film with the tip of a sharp knife, then remove from oven. Let stand, covered, for 5 minutes.

3 Uncover and strain through a fine sieve, pressing on shells to extract as much liquid as possible. Store tightly covered. Prawn Cream will keep for 4 days in the refrigerator or for a few months in the freezer.

COCONUT MILK

This may not be a standard ingredient of American and European cooking, but it certainly is used all over India, Southeast Asia, and the islands of the Pacific. It smooths curries—I use it in Chicken Curry (page 183) and Curried Prawns (page 151). It keeps well and freezes. I'm sure you will find many more uses for it.

This is better coconut milk, or cream, than I can make in conventional ways. It is also better than the canned kinds. To tell the truth, I never used to make it because it was just too much work. Now that opening coconuts is easy, I keep Coconut Milk on hand. It can also be made with packaged, desiccated coconut from the supermarket, but be sure not to get the sweetened kind.

The leftover coconut can be dried or toasted. If you want rich coconut cream, make the coconut milk a day ahead to give the cream time to form. *Makes 300 ml/½ pint*

To open a coconut. Using a hammer and nail, drive holes through each of the three eyes of a 1 kg/2 lb coconut. Make sure these holes pierce to the centre of the coconut; they allow steam to escape. Drain the liquid from the coconut into a bowl and set aside. Place the whole coconut in a microwave-safe roasting bag and close tight. Cook at 100% for 6 minutes 30 seconds. Remove from oven and open bag, being careful of steam. Add the liquid collected in the bag to the reserved coconut liquid. The coconut will be cracked in several places; simply remove the hairy shell.

With a vegetable peeler, remove the papery brown skin from the coconut and cut the flesh into several pieces. Grate in a food processor.

Freshly grated flesh from a 1 kg/2 lb coconut

5½ tablespoons reservered coconut liquid
250 ml/8 fl oz milk

1 Combine all ingredients in a 2 litre/3½ pint glass jug or bowl. Cover tightly with microwave cling film. Cook, uncovered, at 100% for 7 minutes.

2 Remove from oven. Uncover and strain through a sieve lined with muslin, pressing on the coconut to extract as much liquid as possible.

VARIATION

COCONUT CREAM Cook and strain Coconut Milk. Cover tightly with polythene and refrigerate overnight. Coconut cream will rise to the top and may be skimmed; you will have about 5–6 tablespoons. Remaining milk is excellent.

DRIED OR TOASTED COCONUT

◆ ◆ ◆

Use coconut on everything from sandwich cakes to curry. Toasting crisps the coconut and emphasizes the nutty flavour. Open and prepare the coconut as for Coconut Milk (page 306).

Spread the grated flesh of a 1 kg/2 lb coconut in a 30 cm/12 inch round dish. For dried coconut, cook, uncovered, at 100% for 5 minutes, stirring twice; for toasted coconut, cook for 10 minutes, stirring three or four times.

BREADCRUMBS

◆ ◆ ◆

It annoys me to pay for dry breadcrumbs when I always have leftover bread around. Dried and lightly toasted in the microwave oven, breadcrumbs are thrifty and perfect. If making crumbs from French bread, allow for a little more weight of bread since the crusts are thicker. Crumbs can be made successfully from darker-grained breads like pumpernickel and rye bread. They add a little variety to life. *Makes about 150 g/5 oz*

500 g/1 lb loaf white bread

1 Trim crust from bread. Crumble bread in food processor.

2 Spread crumbs in a thin layer in a 35 × 22.5 cm/13 × 9 inch oval or rectangular dish. Cook, uncovered, at 100% for 8 minutes, stirring twice during cooking.

3 Remove from oven. Cool. For very fine crumbs, crumble again in food processor. Store tightly covered.

VARIATION

PUMPERNICKEL CRUMBS Use 500 g/1 lb trimmed pumpernickel bread, cooking crumbs in four batches for 4 minutes each.

BUTTERED AND SEASONED BREADCRUMBS

When you have made a fair amount of breadcrumbs, it is often pleasant to make all or some of them into Buttered and Seasoned Crumbs. These crumbs keep well either at room temperature or refrigerated. Then they will be on hand if you want to make Bread Stuffing or to use them as a coating for fish, pork or chicken either in microwave cooking or for a topping before a brief browning under a conventional grill. Sicilians sometimes use seasoned crumbs like these as a topping for pasta, particularly pasta with sardines. *Makes 1.4 litres/44 fl oz*

125 g/4 oz unsalted butter
2 teaspoons dried sage
1 teaspoon dried thyme

1 teaspoon savory
Pinch freshly ground black pepper
500 g/1 lb Breadcrumbs

1 Place butter in a 35 × 27.5 × 5 cm/14 × 11 × 2 inch rectangular dish. Cook, uncovered, at 100% for 2 minutes. Stir in herbs and pepper. Cook, uncovered, for 1 minute 30 seconds.

2 Remove from oven. Stir in breadcrumbs, stirring well to distribute the butter and herbs evenly. Cook, uncovered, for 3 minutes, stirring once.

BREAD STUFFING

Bread stuffing is delicious and traditional in roasted birds. It is a delight inside a pocket made in a thick pork chop, and it can be cooked on its own to use as a starch either in a conventional oven at 200°C/400°F/Gas 6 just until browned. *Makes 750 ml/1¼ pints*

1 green pepper, cored, seeded and cut into 7.5 cm/3 inch pieces
1 medium onion, peeled and quartered
1 celery stick, trimmed, stringed and cut into 7.5 cm/3 inch pieces
60 g/2 oz unsalted butter

600 ml/1 pint Buttered and Seasoned Breadcrumbs (page 307)
175 ml/6 fl oz Chicken Stock (page 286) or stock from a cube
1 teaspoon sea salt
¼ teaspoon freshly ground black pepper

1 Place green pepper, onions and celery in the container of a food processor. Process until finely chopped.

2 Heat butter in a 2.5 litre/4 pint soufflé dish, uncovered, at 100% for 4 minutes. Stir in green pepper, onions and celery. Cook, uncovered, at 100% for 8 minutes, stirring once.

3 Remove from oven. Scrape mixture into a large mixing bowl. Stir in remaining ingredients. Let stand for 5 minutes; taste for sesoning before using.

CROÛTONS

◆ ◆ ◆

You really need a turntable for this—hot spots in your oven will cause uneven browning. *Makes 125 g/4 oz*

125 g/4 oz unsalted butter

125 g/4 oz cubes white bread, 1 cm/½ inch square (crusts trimmed)

1 Heat butter in a 35 × 22.5 × 5 cm/14 × 11 × 2 inch dish, uncovered, at 100% for 4 minutes. Add bread and stir to coat. Cook, uncovered, at 100% for 5 minutes.

2 Remove from oven and stir thoroughly. Cook, uncovered, at 100% for 5 minutes longer.

3 Remove from oven and let cool. Store tightly covered.

VARIATION

TRIANGULAR CROÛTES Trim crusts from 6 slices white bread. Cut each slice diagonally to form 4 triangles. Heat 5 tablespoons olive oil in a 35 × 22.5 × 5 cm/14 × 11 × 2 inch dish, uncovered, at 100% for 2 minutes. Arrange bread in a single layer in dish. Cook, uncovered, at 100% for 3 minutes, turning once. Drain on a double thickness of paper towel.

GOAT CHEESE CROÛTONS

◆ ◆ ◆

These are wonderful with a salad. You can use any kind of goat cheese (chèvre) as long as it isn't too dry. You can cook the bread before dinner and top with the cheese. Pop into the oven while you are tossing your salad. The croûtons will be ready when you are. Put one on each salad plate or pass a plate of them. They also make a good hors d'oeuvre. *Serves 10*

10 slices (5 mm/¼ inch thick) French
    bread cut on the diagonal
3 tablespoons olive oil

150 g/5 oz goat cheese, preferably 5
    cm/2 inch diameter small log,
    without cinders
Finely chopped chives, or freshly
    ground black pepper (optional)

1 Arrange bread slices in a ring around inside edge of a 25 cm/10 inch platter. Brush lightly with olive oil.

2 Cook, uncovered, at 100% for 4 minutes.

3 Slice cheese into 10 pieces, each 5 mm/¼ inch thick.

4 Turn croûtons over. Top each with a slice of cheese. Sprinkle with chives or pepper, if desired. Brush with remaining olive oil.

5 Cook, uncovered, at 100% for 1 minutes.

CHOUX PASTRY

This basic dough makes impressive little puffs that are astoundingly useful. It is also just about mindlessly easy to make in the microwave oven. The dough can be baked in a conventional oven, for uses both sweet and savoury: split and filled as hors d'oeuvres—with a spoonful of Duxelles (page 294) or Fresh Mango Chutney (page 407) or a snail in Snail Butter (page 310)—as part of the classic French dessert croquembouche, and as miniature profiteroles filled with Confectioner's Custard (page 381) and topped with Chocolate Sauce (page 378). *Makes 12 to 15 small puffs*

125 ml/4 fl oz water
60 g/2 oz unsalted butter
75 g/2½ oz plain flour

½ teaspoon sea salt
2 whole eggs

1 Place water and butter in a 1 litre/2 pint glass measuring jug and heat, uncovered, at 100% for 4 minutes, until mixture boils.

2 Remove from oven and pour into the container of a food processor. Add flour and salt and process for 1 minute 30 seconds.

3 Add eggs, one at a time, processing 30 seconds after each addition. Pastry should just hold a soft shape. (Recipe may be prepared in advance to this point; pastry will keep, tightly covered and refrigerated, for 2 days.)

4 Bake conventionally, as per traditional recipes.

SNAIL BUTTER

Quick to make, easy to store and very useful. Form this butter into a roll; refrigerate or freeze; then slice off pieces to use as needed. It is a good topping for steamed fish or chicken, freshly cooked vegetables, rice and mashed potatoes. Obviously, it gets used with snails (page 64), and is a standard part of Clams Casino (page 62). *Makes 250 g/8 oz*

4 cloves garlic, smashed and peeled
1 bunch parsley, washed and stalks removed (reserve stalks for soup)

2 tablespoons white wine
1 teaspoon sea salt
250 g/8 oz unsalted butter

1 Put garlic and parsley in the container of a food processor. Process until finely chopped. Add remaining ingredients and process until well blended and pale green in colour.

2 Scrape mixture on to a sheet of greaseproof paper and shape into a log. Wrap tightly in cling film and refrigerate. Snail Butter will keep for 2 to 3 weeks refrigerated, for 2 months frozen.

SAVOURY SAUCES

N o matter what the nouvelle cuisines and 'plain' cooks tell you, a good sauce has been the making of many a meal. The trouble with most sauces, however, was that they took so long to make. That's no longer true. Even the great stock based classics of French cooking are simplified with stocks that cook in half an hour in the microwave oven. Equally, the tomato-based sauces of Italian cooking can be zipped through.

I give recipes for sauces from scratch, but I am not above a little cheating. I identify those sauces that will not be damaged by stock from a cube, canned tomatoes, or even bottled tomato sauces.

One thing about sauces is that they pretty much need to hang together. That means they are usually bound in some way, with what the French call a liaison. All this means is that you don't want puddles of fat in your sauce or to be able to see too clearly the ingredients from which it is made.

The deglazing sauces are nothing more than pan juices dissolved in water, stock and/or wine. After your meat has cooked, usually roasted, simply pour off the fat. If you have roasted in a pan that can go into the microwave oven, add your stock or wine to the pan. Stir. Cook, uncovered, at 100% for 2 minutes. Sitr, scraping the bottom of the pan. Correct the seasonings and serve as is, or swirl in 15–30 g/½–1 oz butter, or thicken the sauce. To thicken, dissolve 1 tablespoon cornflour in 2 tablespoons cold water for each 250 ml/8 fl oz of sauce to be thickened. Whisk into sauce and cook, uncovered, for 3 minutes at 100%. You could also thicken the sauce with Roux (page 292).

Other sauces are thickened with egg yolks, or they are emulsions held together by forcing oil or butter to marry with egg yolks or an acid reduction or lots of gelatine, as provided by the bones in very rich stocks.

By the way, there are sauces that I do not suggest that you make in the microwave oven—Béarnaise, for example. You can make the reduction for a Béarnaise in the microwave oven and melt the butter for it; but don't try to whisk it in the oven.

CLARIFIED BUTTER SAUCE

◆ ◆ ◆

This is what you are supposed to get with boiled lobster and hot artichokes. It is nothing other than sharpened with Clarified Butter (page 424), some strained lemon juice, if liked. You can also cook fresh herbs (1 tablespoon finely chopped for each 125 g/4 oz butter) or spices like cumin or chilli powder (1 teaspoon for each 125 g/4 oz) along with the butter.

BROWNED BUTTER SAUCE

◆ ◆ ◆

Browned Butter Sauce, or beurre noisette, is exquisite for brains, skate and all manner of other fish. Cooked Brain (page 235) or fish are warmed briefly in the sauce. (Consult the Dictionary for cooking times for fish fillets.) Small quantities of the thinner fillets may be entirely cooked in the sauce below. The only difficulty in making this sauce has been getting the butter brown without burning it. This microwave technique makes it easy. *Makes 125 ml/4 fl oz, enough for 4 generous servings*

125 g/4 oz unsalted butter
2 tablespoons drained and rinsed capers
1 tablespoon fresh lemon juice

Sea salt
Freshly ground black pepper

1 Place butter in a 1 litre/2 pint glass measuring jug. Cover lightly with a sheet of paper towel. Cook at 100% for 8 minutes.

2 Remove from oven. Strain through a sieve lined with a sheet of paper towel. Pour into a 27.5 × 21 × 5 cm/11 × 8½ × 2 inch dish and add remaining sauce ingredients. Cook, uncovered, at 100% for 1 minute.

ALMOND BUTTER SAUCE

◆ ◆ ◆

This is simple, quick, classic sauce for fish or chicken. Cook the sauce first, then cook the main ingredient and reheat the sauce for 30 seconds if it seems cold. *Makes 150 ml/¼ pint*

125 g/4 oz unsalted butter
75 g/2½ oz blanched almonds
4 tablespoons chopped parsley
2 tablespoons white wine

6 tablespoons Chicken Stock (page 286), Fish Stock (page 289), or stock from a cube

1 Heat butter in a 27.5 × 20 × 7.5 cm/11 × 8 × 3 inch oval dish, uncovered, at 100% for 4 mintues.

2 Remove from oven. Stir in remaining ingredients. Cook, uncovered, at 100% for 5 minutes 30 seconds, until almonds are golden brown.

BEURRE BLANC REDUCTION

Keep this sauce base in the freezer. Simply defrost and whisk up with butter as needed. Use 2 tablespoons strained reduction for every 250 g/8 oz unsalted butter. This is also the base for Béarnaise sauce. Use in any good standard recipe. Melt your butter in a large measuring jug lightly covered with paper towel in the microwave oven. *Makes 350 ml/12 fl oz*

750 ml/1¼ pints dry white wine
750 ml/1¼ pints white wine vinegar
125 g/4 oz shallots, peeled and chopped

45 g/1½ oz fresh parsley, chopped
3 tablespoons dried tarragon or 5½ tablespoons fresh tarragon

1 Put all ingredients in a 35 × 22.5 × 5 cm/14 × 11 × 2 inch dish. Cook, uncovered, at 100% for 40 minutes.

2 Remove from oven. Let cool before freezing or straining through a fine sieve, pushing firmly and freezing strained liquid.

To make 250 ml/8 fl oz. Halve ingredients, cooking in a 32.5 × 22.5 cm/13 × 9 inch rectangular or oval dish for 25 minutes.

BEURRE BLANC

If you don't have Beurre Blanc Reduction handy (page 314), you can make this complete sauce quickly, to be used for steamed or poached fish and for chicken. If you have fresh tarragon, use double the quantity of dried. Some people strain their reduction. It makes a lighter, more elegant, but slightly less savoury sauce. If you add 2 tablespoons of double cream to the reduction after it is cooked, your sauce will be more stable. It does not, however, reheat well. You can put it in a warmed thermos flask and then use when you are ready.

Beurre Blanc can be varied; but it won't be *blanc* (white) anymore. In whatever version, it holds together because of the high amount of acid in the reduction.

If you have made a quantity of Beurre Blanc Reduction, make sauce with 1½ tablespoons unstrained reduction or 1 tablespoon strained reduction and 125 g/4 oz of butter. *Makes 125 ml/4 fl oz*

4 tablespoons dry white wine
2 tablespoons tarragon vinegar
2 tablespoons very finely chopped
  shallots
½ teaspoon dried tarragon or 1
teaspoon chopped fresh tarragon

125 g/4 oz unsalted butter, cut into 8
  pieces, at room temperature
Sea salt
Freshly ground black pepper

1 Combine wine, vinegar, shallots and tarragon in a 250 ml/8 fl oz glass jug or bowl. Cook, uncovered, at 100% for 8 minutes.

2 Remove from oven. The liquid should have evaporated, leaving only moistened shallots; if mixture is still quite liquid, return to oven and cook at 100% for 1 to 2 minutes longer.

3 Uncover. Whisk in butter, 2 pieces at a time. Season with salt and pepper. Serve at once.

VARIATIONS

BEURRE ROUGE Substitute red wine and red wine vinegar for the wine and vinegar. Proceed as for Beurre Blanc.

SAFFRON BEURRE BLANC This is a nice colour. It is good with steamed scallops or steamed fish fillets. Make Beurre Blanc, omitting dried tarragon. You may substitute white wine vinegar for the tarragon vinegar. After your reduction has been made, put through a fine sieve. Place in a clean pan—not aluminium—and add 8 threads saffron or a knife-point of saffron powder and 2 tablespoons double cream. Over lowest heat on top of the stove, whisk in butter. Taste for salt and pepper and perhaps a dash of lemon juice and Tabasco sauce.

MUSTARD CREAM SAUCE

— ♦ — ♦ —

Mustard holds this cream sauce together and thickens it. Since it is so important, use a good kind. It won't work with coarsely gound—grainy—mustard. The sauce is good on veal, rabbit, and chicken. *Makes 500 ml/16 fl oz*

250 ml/8 fl oz milk
125 ml/4 fl oz double cream
125 g/4 oz Dijon mustard

1 tablespoon lemon juice
¼ teaspoon sea salt
¼ teaspoon freshly ground black pepper

1 Combine all ingredients in a 2 litre/3½ pint glass jug or bowl. Cook, uncovered, at 100% for 12 minutes.

2 Remove from oven.

BASIC BÉCHAMEL

— ♦ — ♦ —

This standard white sauce of French and Italian cooking can taste like glue if not cooked long enough, and have lumps if not made properly. The method here is close to infallible. The gluten content of flour and its ability to thicken liquids vary enormously depending on the hardness of the wheat. Summer wheat will yield a soft (low-gluten) flour, such as British plain flour, and winter wheat a hard (high-gluten) flour. You will need less flour if using one milled from hard winter wheat. *Makes 500 ml/16 fl oz*

60 g/2 oz unsalted butter, cold in one
    piece
6 tablespoons plain flour

500 ml/16 fl oz milk
1½ teaspoons sea salt
Freshly ground black pepper

1 Heat butter in a 1 litre/2 pint glass measuring jug, lightly covered with a sheet of paper towel, at 100% for 3 minutes.

2 Remove from oven. Uncover and thoroughly whisk in flour. Cook, uncovered, at 100% for 2 minutes.

3 Remove from oven and whisk in milk. Cook, uncovered, for 3 minutes at 100%. Whisk to remove lumps, and cook for 3 minutes longer.

4 Remove from oven. Whisk thoroughly and season with salt and pepper.

To make 250 ml/8 fl oz. Halve all ingredients. Heat butter for 1 minute; cook butter and flour for 1 minute 30 seconds. Whisk in milk and cook for 2 minutes. Whisk and cook for 2 minutes longer. Season.

To make 1 litre/1¾ pints. Increase butter to 125 g/4 oz, flour to 105 g/3¾ oz and milk to 1 litre/1¾ pints; increase salt to 2 teaspoons. Heat butter in a 2 litre/3½ pint glass jug or bowl for 2 minutes 30 seconds; cook butter and flour for 5 minutes. Whisk in milk and cook for 5 minutes. Whisk to remove any lumps and cook for 5 minutes; whisk again and cook for 3 minutes longer. Season.

VARIATIONS

THICK BÉCHAMEL Increase butter to 125 g/4 oz and flour to 70 g/2½ oz and cook as for Basic Béchamel.

THIN BÉCHAMEL Decrease flour to 4 tablespoons and cook as for Basic Béchamel.

MORNAY SAUCE

Mornay is a Béchamel or white sauce with cheese. It is good with vegetables, eggs, and fish. *Makes 300 ml/½ pint*

30 g/1 oz cold unsalted butter, in one piece
30 g/1 oz plain flour
300 ml/½ pint milk

½ teaspoon sea salt
Pinch freshly ground black pepper
30 g/1 oz Parmesan cheese, freshly grated

1 Heat butter in a 1 litre/2 pint glass measuring jug, uncovered, at 100% for 2 minutes.

2 Remove from oven. Thoroughly whisk in flour. Cook, uncovered, at 100% for 2 minutes (1 minute in a combination, convection-microwave oven).

3 Remove from oven. Add milk and whisk until mixture is smooth. Cook, uncovered, at 100% for 3 minutes 30 seconds.

4 Remove from oven. Add salt, pepper and cheese and whisk until smooth. Cook, uncovered, at 100% for 3 minutes.

To make 450 ml/¾ pint. Increase butter and flour to 45 g/1½ oz *each* and milk to 450 ml/¾ pint. Heat butter for 3 minutes; cook butter and flour for 3 minutes. Whisk in milk and cook for 6 minutes; add cheese, whisk, and cook for 4 minutes.

VELOUTÉ

· • ·

Velouté is a somewhat more elegant version of Béchamel. There are people who claim that this was the real Béchamel, and only later did milk substitute for stock. The sauce can be lightened by using all stock instead of a stock and cream mixture. It can be made with prepared Roux (page 292). It can also have herbs stirred in; but don't get too jazzy—this is an elegant sauce that should let the stock flavour sing through.

Velouté makes a good base for soup. Stir in 250 ml/8 fl oz vegetable purée and thin with 250 ml/8 fl oz stock, if necessary. Season. Makes about 4 servings of soup. *Makes 500 ml/16 fl oz*

30 g/1 oz unsalted butter
2 tablespoons plain flour
250 ml/8 fl oz double cream

250 ml/8 fl oz Chicken Stock (page 286) or stock from a cube
Sea salt
Freshly ground black pepper

1 Heat butter in a 2 litre/3½ pint glass jug or bowl, uncovered, at 100% for 2 minutes.

2 Remove from oven. Thoroughly whisk in flour. Cook, uncovered, at 100% for 2 minutes.

3 Remove from oven. Whisk in cream and stock. Cook, uncovered, at 100% for 2 minutes; stir and cook for 3 minutes more.

4 Remove from oven. Add salt and pepper and whisk until smooth.

VARIATIONS

FISH VELOUTÉ Halve butter and flour. Omit cream and substitute 125 ml/4 fl oz Fish Stock (page 289) for stock. Heat butter in a 1 litre/2 pint glass measuring jug, uncovered, at 100% for 1 minute. Stir in flour, 1 tablespoon *each* very finely chopped carrot, celery and onion, and 1 parsley sprig, very finely chopped. Cook, uncovered, at 100% for 3 minutes. Remove from oven and whisk in stock, salt and pepper. Cook, uncovered, at 100% for 2 minutes. *Makes 125 ml/4 fl oz*

CURRY VELOUTÉ Add 1 tablespoon Spice Powder III or curry powder when adding flour. Proceed as for Velouté.

MUSHROOM SAUCE Increase butter to 60 g/2 oz. Add flour and cook as for Velouté. Add 125 g/4 oz cleaned and sliced mushrooms (you may substitute dried mushrooms for part of the fresh mushrooms) and a squeeze of fresh lemon juice, a knife-point of cayenne pepper, and 2 tablespoons finely chopped fresh dill (optional). Cook, uncovered, at 100% for 3 minutes. Finish as for Velouté.

SAUCE POULETTE A versatile sauce to accompany mussels, veal or vegetables. Substitute 250 ml/8 fl oz appropriate cooking liquid for stock and milk for cream. Proceed as for Velouté, cooking for 3 minutes after addition of liquid. Whisk 4 tablespoons of hot mixture into 3 egg yolks; whisk back into mixture. Cook, uncovered, at 100% for 1 minute. Remove from oven and whisk in 1 tablespoon fresh lemon juice and salt and pepper to taste. *Makes 500 ml/16 fl oz*

SAUCE SUPRÊME

This luscious sauce is so good I like to eat it by the spoonful. It's not as heavy as the amount of flour would seem to indicate. The flour gets absorbed by the vegetables and the prolonged cooking. *Makes 500 ml/16 fl oz*

100 g/3½ oz unsalted butter
3 tablespoons plain flour
2 tablespoons finely chopped carrot
2 tablespoons finely chopped onion
2 tablespoons finely chopped celery

250 ml/8 fl oz Chicken Stock or Veal Stock (page 286)
250 ml/8 fl oz double cream
1 teaspoon sea salt
Freshly ground black pepper

1 Heat 45 g/1½ oz of the butter in a 2 litre/3½ pint glass jug or bowl, uncovered, at 100% for 2 minutes.

2 Stir in flour and vegetables. Cook, uncovered, at 100% for 3 minutes.

3 Remove from oven. Whisk in stock and cream. Cook, uncovered, at 100% for 7 minutes, until reduced by one third.

4 Remove from oven and season with salt and pepper. Add remaining butter, stirring until melted. Strain sauce through a fine sieve.

VARIATION

SAUCE IVOIRE Prepare Sauce Suprême and whisk 2 teaspoons Chicken or Veal Glaze (page 291) into the finished sauce.

PARSLEY SAUCE

• • •

This is basically a cornflour-thickened Béchamel flavoured with herbs. If you prefer this method, you can make all your white sauces this way, rather than thickening them with a flour and butter roux.

Parsley Sauce is traditional with fish. *Makes 250 ml/8 fl oz*

30 g/1 oz parsley leaves, finely chopped
2 tablespoons thinly sliced chives
1 tablespoon plus 1 teaspoon cornflour

150 ml/¼ pint milk or Fish Stock (page 289)
6 tablespoons double cream
1 teaspoon sea salt

Combine all ingredients in a 1 litre/2 pint glass measuring jug. Cover tightly with microwave cling film. Cook at 100% for 5 minutes.

WATERCRESS SAUCE

• • •

This is another cornflour-bound sauce; but it is the most incredible brilliant green. Once you have made this, I think you will find a dozen ways to use it. Try it under vegetable custards (pages 262–266), with salmon or other fish fillets, with chicken breasts, and with Loin of Veal, hot or cold (page 225). *Makes 400 ml/14 fl oz*

90 g/3 oz watercress sprigs
300 ml/½ pint Chicken Stock (page 286) or stock from a cube
2 tablespoons cornflour

125 ml/4 fl oz double cream
Sea salt
Freshly ground black pepper

1 Put watercress and 250 ml/8 fl oz of the stock into the container of a food processor. Process for 1 minute. Pour into a 1 litre/2 pint measuring jug.

2 Stir cornflour into remaining stock until smooth. Stir thoroughly into watercress mixture. Cover tightly with microwave cling film. Cook at 100% for 4 minutes.

3 Pierce film with the tip of a sharp knife, then remove from oven. Uncover and stir in cream, salt and pepper.

MARCHAND DU VIN SAUCE

───── • • • ─────

This is a quick and easy red wine sauce to accompany grilled and roasted meat.
Makes 350 ml/12 fl oz

5 medium shallots, peeled and chopped
1 clove garlic, smashed, peeled and very
   finely chopped
500 ml/16 fl oz red wine
250 ml/8 fl oz Chicken, Duck or Veal
   Stock (page 286)

1 tablespoon Chicken, Duck or Veal
   Glaze (page 291)
2 teaspoons cornflour dissolved in 1
   tablespoon cold water (optional)
Freshly ground black pepper

1 Put shallots, garlic, wine and 125 ml/4 fl oz of the stock in a 2 litre/3½ pint glass jug or bowl. Cook, uncovered, at 100% for 20 minutes, until reduced by one half.

2 Remove from oven. Stir in glaze and remining stock. If using Marchand du Vin with a roast or sauté, deglaze cooking pan with this mixture; cook on top of the stove until slightly thickened, and season to taste. If using to sauce grilled meats, briskly stir in cornflour. Cook, uncovered, at 100% for 2 minutes. Season to taste.

VARIATION

SAUCE BORDELAISE Prepare Marchand du Vin Sauce. Prepare marrow (page 463) and slice into 5 mm/¼ inch rounds. Spoon sauce over beef fillet or other meat, and arrange 2 or 3 slices of marrow on top of each serving.

SAUCE ESPAGNOLE

───── • • • ─────

This is the ultimate, classic French brown sauce. It is hardly instantaneous in the microwave oven, but it can be made in one afternoon instead of three days the old-fashioned way. I make it and freeze it. To defrost, see page 440. *Makes 750 ml/1¼ pints*

1 small onion, peeled and halved
2 carrots, trimmed, peeled and cut into
   7.5 cm/3 inch lengths
250 g/8 oz cooked ham, trimmed if
   necessary and cut into 5 cm/2 inch
   chunks
1 teaspoon dried thyme

1 bay leaf
125 ml/4 fl oz white wine
2.5 litres/4 pints Veal Stock (page 287)
60 g/2 oz unsalted butter
45 g/1½ oz plain flour
250 ml/8 fl oz Lightly Cooked Crushed
   Tomatoes (page 293)

1 Place onions, carrots, ham, thyme and bay leaf in the container of a food processor. Process until well chopped.

2 Scrape mixture into a 1 litre/2 pint glass measuring jug and add wine. Cook, uncovered, at 100% for 15 minutes. Add 1 litre/1¾ pints of the stock and cook, uncovered, for 20 minutes.

3 Remove from oven and set aside. Heat butter in a 2 litre/3½ pint glass jug or bowl, uncovered, at 100% for 3 minutes. Remove from oven and whisk in flour until smooth. Cook, uncovered, at 100% for 3 minutes.

4 Remove from oven and whisk in vegetable mixture. Cook, uncovered, at 100% for 40 minutes, stirring 3 or 4 times, until reduced to 500 ml/16 fl oz.

5 Add remaining stock and stir well. Cook, uncovered, at 100% for 20 minutes. Stir, and cook for 20 minutes more.

6 Remove from oven and stir in crushed tomatoes. Cook, uncovered, at 100% for 20 minutes.

7 Wet a 60 cm/2 foot square of muslin with cold water and wring out. Place a double thickness of muslin in a sieve. Strain sauce into a clean bowl.

SAUCE AMÉRICAINE

This is a perfect sauce. It is served with lobster, scallops or prawns or even on filleted fish or skinned and boned chicken breasts; but I am happy putting it on rice or Mashed Potatoes (page 252). The truly spiffy can put it under a warm Prawn Pâté (page 56).

Scallops or shelled prawns can be cooked directly in the sauce. Precook the other foods and serve topped with sauce. *Makes 400–500 ml/14–16 fl oz*

250 g/8 oz tomatoes, cored and coarsely chopped
125 g/4 oz Prawn Butter (page 304)
2 tablespoons olive oil
250 ml/8 fl oz Cognac
250 ml/8 fl oz white wine (somewhat sweet, if possible)
250 ml/8 fl oz Fish Stock or Clam liquor (page 289)

2 tablespoons Veal Glaze (page 291)
2 tablespoon very finely chopped shallots
¼ teaspoon Quatre-Épices (page 478)
Pinch cayenne pepper
Pinch dried tarragon
4 drops Tabasco sauce
1 tablespoon fresh lemon juice
Sea salt
Freshly ground black pepper

1 Combine all ingredients except Tabasco sauce, lemon juice, salt and pepper in a 27.5 × 20 × 7.5 cm/11 × 8 × 3 inch dish. Cook, uncovered, at 100% for 30 minutes, until mixture is reduced by two thirds.

2 Remove from oven. Pass through a food mill fitted with a fine disc. Return mixture to dish. Cook, uncovered, at 100% for 4 minutes.

3 Remove from oven. Stir in Tabasco sauce and lemon juice, and season to taste. Sauce may be put through a fine sieve if you are a perfectionist. I prefer the tiny lumps.

VARIATION

SCALLOPS OR PRAWNS À L'AMÉRICAINE Use 1 kg/2 lb medium scallops or prawns. Stir into finished sauce. Cook, uncovered, at 100% for 5 minutes, stirring once. If using queen scallops, cook for only 3 minutes. Taste and add lemon juice, cayenne and 15 g/½ oz extra Prawn Butter, if desired.

TOMATO SAUCE FROM A JAR, MADE DELICIOUS

You can substitute the same quantity of Lightly Cooked Crushed Tomatoes (page 293) for bottled sauce. Add 1 teaspoon dried thyme and ½ teaspoon dried oregano to the tomatoes. *Makes 1 litre/1¾ pints*

4 tablespoons olive oil
100 g/3½ oz onion, peeled and sliced
5 cloves garlic, smashed and peeled
1 medium red pepper and cored, seeded and sliced
1 medium yellow pepper, cored, seeded and sliced
30 g/1 oz parsley finely chopped

1½ young courgettes, thinly sliced
400 g/14 oz jar or can tomato spaghetti sauce (not containing meat or chunks of vegetable)
¼ teaspoon dried thyme
Sea salt
Freshly ground black pepper

1 Heat oil in a 27.5 × 21 × 5 cm/11 × 8½ × 2 inch dish, uncovered, for 2 minutes. Stir in onions and garlic and cook for 4 minutes.

2 Remove from oven. Add remaining ingredients and cover tightly with microwave cling film. Cook at 100% for 5 minutes.

CHUNKY TOMATO SAUCE

⋅ ◆ ⋅

This is the perfect Italian tomato sauce with a good fresh taste. It is a basic sauce capable of many variations. Allow about 250 ml/8 fl oz of sauce for each 250 g/ 8 oz cooked pasta. I generally make the larger quantity and freeze it in convenient small portions. See Dictionary for DEFROSTING. *Makes 1 litre/1¾ pints*

1 medium onion, peeled and quartered
15 g/½ oz parsley leaves
3 cloves garlic, smashed and peeled
5½ tablespoons vegetable oil (a good olive oil is best)

1 litre/1¾ pints Lightly Cooked Crushed Tomatoes (page 293)
2 teaspoons sea salt
¼ teaspoon freshly ground black pepper

1 Put onions, parsley and garlic in the container of a food processor and process until finely chopped.

2 Heat oil in a 2.5 litre/4 pint soufflé dish, uncovered, at 100% for 2 minutes. Stir in onion mixture. Cook, uncovered, at 100% for 8 minutes, stirring once.

3 Remove from oven. Stir in crushed tomatoes, salt and pepper. Cook at 100% for 6 minutes.

4 Remove from oven. Taste and adjust seasoning.

To make 500 ml/16 fl oz. Use a small onion and 2 small garlic cloves; halve all other ingredients. Proceed as for Chunky Tomato Sauce, cooking onion mixture for 6 minutes. Add crushed tomatoes and cook for 4 minutes.

VARIATIONS

TOMATO CREAM SAUCE Prepare 500 ml/16 fl oz Chunky Tomato Sauce. Add 250 ml/8 fl oz double cream, 2 teaspoons fresh lemon juice, and a large dash of Tabasco sauce. Cook, uncovered, at 100% for 4 minutes. Adjust seasonings to taste. *Makes about 750 ml/1¼ pints*

FRESH TOMATO SAUCE WITH BASIL This sauce uses Lightly Cooked Crushed Tomatoes straight from the refrigerator; if using freshly cooked tomatoes that are still warm, shorten cooking time to 8 minutes. Omit parsley. Add 15 g/½ oz whole basil leaves. Increase garlic to 8 cloves; omit salt. Combine in a 1 litre/2 pint soufflé dish. Cook, uncovered, at 100% for 10 minutes.

SALSA PUTTANESCA Heat 2 tablespoons olive oil in a 1 litre/2 pint glass measuring jug, uncovered, for 2 minutes. Stir in 1 small onion, peeled and very finely chopped; cook, uncovered, for 3 minutes. Add 350 ml/12 fl oz Chunky Tomato Sauce, 45 g/1½ oz tuna packed in olive oil (drained), 1 tablespoon anchovy paste, 2 tablespoons *each* red wine, chopped oil-cured olives and chopped capers, and freshly ground black pepper to taste. Cook, uncovered, at 100% for 4 minutes. *Makes 500 ml/16 fl oz*

MEXICAN CHILLI SAUCE Heat 1 tablespoon vegetable oil in a 1 litre/2 pint glass measuring jug, uncovered, for 2 minutes. Stir in 1 finely chopped spring onion, 2 tablespoons coriander leaves and 1 seeded, finely chopped fresh green chilli. Cook, uncovered, at 100% for 4 minutes. Stir in 500 ml/16 fl oz Chunky Tomato Sauce. Cook, uncovered, at 100% for 5 minutes. Remove from oven and let stand until room temperature. Stir in 2 teaspoons fresh lime juice and sea salt to taste. *Makes 500 ml/16 fl oz*

TOMATO SAUCE WITH BASIL

$\bullet\ \bullet$

This is a quick sauce based on canned tomatoes. It's perfectly respectable and delicious. *Makes 750 ml/1¼ pints*

2 cans (400 g/14 oz each) chopped
  tomatoes, Italian plum preferred
3 tablespoons olive oil
5 cloves garlic, smashed, peeled and
  very finely chopped

2 teaspoons sea salt
Freshly ground black pepper
2 tablespoons shredded fresh basil
  leaves
1 tablespoon tomato paste

1 Place tomatoes, oil, garlic, salt and pepper in a 2.5 litre/4 pint soufflé dish. Cook, uncovered, at 100% for 6 minutes.

2 Remove from oven. Stir in basil and tomato paste. Cook, uncovered, at 100% for 3 minutes.

SALSA BOLOGNESE

• • •

This is a terrific version of Italian meat sauce for pasta. Just tumble it on to cooked spaghetti or ziti, use in Lasagne (page 136), and over Fried Polenta (page 124). *Makes 1 litre/1¾ pints*

15 g/½ oz dried funghi porcini
1 small carrot, trimmed, peeled and cut into 7.5 cm/3 inch lengths
1 small onion, peeled and quartered
1 stick celery, trimmed, stringed and cut into 7.5 cm/3 inch lengths
60 g/2 oz pancetta, cut into 2.5 cm × 3 mm × 3 mm/1 × ⅛ × ⅛ juliennes

250 g/8 oz minced pork
250 g/8 oz minced beef
125 g/4 oz minced veal
1 kg/35 oz canned Italian plum tomatoes, coarsely chopped, with liquid
2 teaspoons sea salt
¼ teaspoon freshly ground black pepper

1 Place mushrooms in a small bowl and pour water over to cover. Heat, uncovered, at 100% for 1 minute.

2 Remove from oven. Let stand at room temperature for 10 minutes. Drain mushrooms, rinse thoroughly under cool running water, and squeeze dry. Chop very finely.

3 Place carrots, onions and celery in the container of a food processor and process until finely chopped. Set aside.

4 Place pancetta in a 2.5 litre/4 pint soufflé dish. Cook, uncovered, at 100% until pancetta is lightly browned and has begun to render its fat, about 4 minutes. Set aside.

5 Combine minced meats with reserved vegetables and mushrooms. Add to pancetta. Cook, uncovered, at 100% until lightly browned and cooked through, about 20 minutes, stirring 4 times.

6 Remove from oven. Drain liquid from pan. Stir in tomatoes, salt and pepper. Cook, uncovered, at 100% for 35 minutes, stirring 4 times. TThe sauce will be very thick.

MUSTARD BARBECUE SAUCE

— • ◆ • —

Use 4 tablespoons of this sauce to baste 6 split chicken wings. To use the rest as a dipping sauce, put in a 500 ml/1 pint glass measuring jug and cover tightly with microwave cling film; cook at 100% for 5 minutes. *Makes 175 ml/6 fl oz*

150 g/5 oz spicy brown mustard
100 g/3½ oz cane molasses

4 cloves garlic, smashed and peeled
¼ teaspoon Searing Pepper Sauce (page 297) or ½ teaspoon Tabasco sauce

Thoroughly combine all ingredients.

RED BARBECUE SAUCE

— • ◆ • —

Use half this uncooked sauce to coat chicken wings before cooking them (see Dictionary for cooking times). To use the remaining sauce for dipping cooked wings, put in a 500 ml/1 pint glass measuring jug and cover tightly with microwave cling film; cook at 100% for 5 minutes. This recipe makes enough sauce to cook and accompany 12 split wings, or a rack of spareribs (see Dictionary). *Makes 330 ml/11 fl oz*

250 ml/8 fl oz tomato ketchup
60 g/2 oz dark brown sugar
4 cloves garlic, smashed and peeled
2 tablespoons cider vinegar

½ teaspoon sea salt
Freshly ground black pepper
½ teaspoon Tabasco sauce

Thoroughly combine all ingredients

SATAY SAUCE

— • ◆ • —

Use this piquant dipping sauce for the marinated chicken below. Serve coriander and spring onions in separate bowls. *Makes 400 ml/14 fl oz.*

4 tablespoons Chicken Stock (page 286) or stock from a cube
125 ml/4 fl oz tamari soya sauce
70 g/2½ oz sugar
½ star-anise pod or ½ teaspoon five spice powder
6 cloves garlic, smashed and peeled

2 teaspoons dried red chilli flakes or, preferably, crushed dried chillies
90 g/3 oz smooth peanut butter
2 tablespoons fresh lime juice
Fresh coriander leaves, for serving
Thinly sliced spring onions, for serving

1 Combine stock, soya sauce, sugar, anise, garlic and chilli flakes in a 1 litre/2 pint glass measuring jug. Cover tightly with microwave cling film. Cook at 100% for 3 minutes.

2 Pierce film with the tip of a sharp knife, then remove from oven. Let cool for 5 minutes.

3 Uncover. Whisk in peanut butter and lime juice. Serve with cooked, marinated chicken.

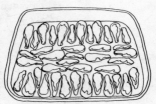

SATAY MARINADE

Makes enough to marinate 2 kg/4 lb chicken joints

3 tablespoons tamari soya sauce
2 tablespoons fresh lime juice
12 cloves garlic, smashed and peeled

½ teaspoon ground cumin
8 slices 5p piece-size fresh root ginger, peeled

Combine all ingredients in a dish large enough to hold chicken. Add chicken and marinate, tightly covered, for at least several hours, or overnight if desired. Cook for times in Dictionary.

CRANBERRY SAUCE FOR DUCK OR GOOSE

Frankly, at Christmas, I often use cranberry sauce right out of a can, or I chunk up an uncooked relish in the food processor. This another kind of sauce altogether, a superbly elegant one for the most festive of dinner parties. *Makes 250 ml/8 fl oz*

60 g/2 oz unsalted butter (15 g/½ oz cut into bits)
4 tablespoons sugar
2 tablespoons fresh orange juice
100 g/3½ oz fresh cranberries or frozen, defrosted, cranberries
1 teaspoon dark rum

Freshly ground black pepper
1 teaspoon Veal Glaze (page 291)
4 teaspoons skimmed pan juices (from the roasted bird) or Chicken Stock (page 286)
4 drops Tabasco sauce
1 teaspoon sea salt

1 Heat 45 g/1½ oz of the butter in a 20 cm/8 inch square dish, uncovered, at 100% for 2 minutes.

2 Remove from oven. Add sugar, orange juice and cranberries. Cover tightly with microwave cling film. Cook at 100% for 3 to 4 minutes, until most of the cranberries have popped.

3 Pierce film with the tip of a sharp knife, then remove from oven. Uncover and whisk in remaining ingredients.

To make 500 ml/16 fl oz. Double all ingredients, cooking sauce for 5 to 6 minutes.

CHERRY SAUCE FOR ROAST BIRDS

I have the prettiest little cherry tree. If I'm lucky, I get to the cherries before the birds. In season, you can buy pie cherries. This is the kind of sauce, called Montmorency, that was always meant to go with duck, not that heavy, thickly sweet stuff with dessert cherries.

If you roast your chicken or grill your crispiest Duck in a pan that can go in the microwave oven, the pan can be deglazed in the oven instead of on top of the stove. See the introduction to this chapter for instructions. *Makes 600 ml/1 pint*

1 roast chicken, 1.25–1.5 kg/2½–3 lb,
  or Crispiest Duck (page 200)

THE SAUCE

250 g/8 oz sour cherries, stalks
  removed and stoned
18 shallots, peeled
125 ml/4 fl oz Chicken or Duck Stock
  (page 286) or stock from a cube
3 tablespoons red wine

1 teaspoon brandy or kirsch
3 tablespoons sugar
1 teaspoon sea salt
½ teaspoon freshly ground black pepper
2 tablespoons cornflour dissolved in 4
  tablespoons cold water

1 Roast chicken in conventional oven, or cook Crispiest Duck. Keep warm.

2 Combine sauce ingredients except cornflour in a 1 litre/2 pint glass measuring jug. Cover tightly with microwave cling film. Cook at 100% for 5 minutes.

3 Pierce film with the tip of a sharp knife to allow steam to escape, then remove from oven. Uncover and strain through a fine sieve. Reserve strained sauce and cherries.

4 Remove chicken or duck to a serving platter. Warm meat juices in the roasting pan over high heat on top of the stove. When juices are bubbling, add strained cherry sauce. Continue to cook, stirring to incorporate any browned bits from the pan into the sauce.

5 Briskly stir in cornflour. If sauce is in a microwavable dish, cook, uncovered, at 100% for 3 minutes 30 seconds. Otherwise, cook over the stove just until thickened. Taste and correct seasoning with salt and pepper.

6 Stir in cherries and serve in a sauceboat.

BLACKBERRY SAUCE

This is fabulous with Crispiest Duck (page 200). Make the berry purée ahead. Prepare duck, skim cooking juices, and finish sauce while duck is grilling. Garnish with a few whole blackberries and a blackberry leaf, if possible. Serve with mountains of Mashed Potatoes (page 252) topped with butter. This makes a highly unusual sauce for venison, too. *Makes 500 ml/16 fl oz*

300 g/10 oz blackberries or black
    raspberries
150 g/5 oz sugar
4 cloves garlic, smashed and peeled

4 tablespoons Duck Stock (page 286)
    or pan juices from duck
4 tablespoons raspberry vinegar
1 teaspoon freshly ground black pepper
1 teaspoon fresh lemon juice

1 Combine berries, sugar and garlic in a 1 litre/2 pint glass measuring jug. Cover tightly with microwave cling film. Cook at 100% for 4 minutes.

2 Pierce film with the tip of a sharp knife, then remove from oven and uncover carefully. Remove garlic from berry mixture and set aside. Place mixture in a blender or food processor and purée. Strain mixture through a fine sieve. There should be about 350 ml/12 fl oz.

3 Return mixture to measuring jug. Add stock, vinegar and reserved garlic. Cover tightly with microwave cling film. Cook at 100% for 5 minutes.

4 Pierce film, then remove from oven. Add pepper and lemon juice. Taste and correct seasoning, if necessary.

PAPAYA CUMIN SAUCE

A cooling, tart, and mildly spiced sauce that is as good with Scallop Mousse (page 56) as it is with Crispiest Duck (page 200). The papaya seeds are edible, with an astringent flavour, and can be used to garnish the food you are saucing. Place the seeds in a sieve and rinse to remove pulp. Drain on paper towel. *Makes 300 ml/½ pint*

1 ripe papaya (about 500 g/1 lb),
    halved lengthways and seeded
125 ml/4 fl oz Chicken Stock (page 286)
1 tablespoon plus 2 teaspoons fresh
    lemon juice

¾ teaspoon ground cumin
½ teaspoon sea salt
⅛ teaspoon freshly ground black pepper
Pinch cayenne pepper

1 Spoon papaya flesh into a 1 litre/2 pint glass measuring jug. Add remaining ingredients except for 1 tablespoon of the lemon juice. Cover tightly with microwave cling film. Cook at 100% for 10 minutes.

2 Pierce film with the tip of a sharp knife, then remove from oven. Let stand for 3 minutes.

3 Purée mixture in a blender or food processor. Beat in remaining 1 tablespoon lemon juice.

MAYONNAISE

No, I don't make it in the microwave oven; but every cookery book needs one. *Makes 250 ml/8 fl oz*

3 egg yolks
2 teaspoons fresh lemon juice
125 ml/4 fl oz olive oil

125 ml/4 fl oz vegetable oil
Sea salt
Freshly ground black pepper

1 Place yolks and lemon juice in the container of a food processor and process until well blended.

2 With the machine running, add oils in a thin stream and process until thoroughly incorporated and mixture is smooth. Season to taste with salt and pepper.

AÏOLI

This is a garlicky mayonnaise often used in fish soups and stews. *Makes 150 ml/ ¼ pint*

2 eggs
4 teaspoons fresh lemon juice
12 drops Tabasco sauce
2 teaspoons sea salt

¼ teaspoon freshly ground black pepper
125 ml/4 fl oz light olive oil
6 to 8 cloves garlic, smashed and peeled

1 Place eggs, lemon juice, Tabasco sauce, salt and pepper in the container of a food processor. Process until well blended.

2 With the machine running, add oil in a thin stream until thoroughly incorporated and the mixture is smooth.

3 Add garlic and process until smooth.

PESTO

◆ ◆ ◆

No, this doesn't get made in the microwave oven, either, but it is a useful basic sauce. If you wish to freeze Pesto, do not add the cheese. Beat in the cheese after defrosting, and serve at room temperature. *Makes 250 ml/8 fl oz*

Leaves from 1 large bunch basil (about 60 g/2 oz) or parsley
2 cloves garlic, smashed and peeled
175 ml/6 fl oz olive oil
25 g/¾ oz pine nuts or walnuts

30 g/1 oz Parmesan cheese, freshly grated or Gorgonzola, crumbled
¾ teaspoon sea salt
¼ teaspoon freshly ground black pepper

1 Put basil and garlic in the container of a food processor and process until coarsely chopped. With the motor running, add oil in a thin stream.

2 Add nuts, cheese, salt and pepper. Process until nuts are finely chopped.

TONNATO SAUCE

◆ ◆ ◆

This is so good with the Loin of Veal (page 225) that I had to include it. It is also good with vegetable custards (pages 262–266)—not white ones. *Makes 350 ml/12 fl oz*

1 can (200 g/7 oz) tuna, drained
2 anchovy fillets
1½ tablespoons drained capers
150 ml/¼ pint Mayonnaise (page 332)
1½ tablespoons olive oil

1½ tablespoons Veal Stock (page 287) or stock used to poach the loin
1½ tablespoons fresh lemon juice
2 tablespoons chopped parsley
Sea salt

1 Put tuna, anchovies and capers in the container of a food processor. Process until mixture is smooth. Add Mayonnaise and process until smooth. With the machine running, add oil, then stock, in a thin stream.

2 Add lemon juice, parsley and salt to taste. Process briefly to mix. Taste and add more lemon juice to salt if desired. Refrigerate, tightly covered.

DESSERTS

◆ ◆

I am an odd duck. Even in great restaurants, I have frequently been known to order a green salad while everybody else is having dessert. At home, I am ordinarily more than satisfied with a piece of fruit and some cheese. There are times, though, when even I want something sweet, something self-indulgent.

FRUIT DESSERTS

Cooking fruits, fresh and dried, is one of the microwave oven's triumphs. To poach fresh fruits, see individual fruits in the Dictionary. Use in all sorts of combinations or with poached dried fruits. See Dictionary also for small-oven timings.

Herewith a few desserts that take fruit a few marvellous, fresh-tasting steps further. They start out taking almost no time at all to prepare, and go on to take just a little more. Simple as they are, they are good enough to end any meal, and each one is as pretty as the fruit from which it is made.

LIGHT POACHED PEARS

· · ·

This delicious, easily prepared desert can be eaten cold or warm. It is a slimmer's delight because no sugar is added. The pears cook absolutely evenly and have more flavour than conventionally poached pears since they lose none of it to the poaching liquid. Serve plain, with double cream, Crème Anglaise (page 380), or with Blueberry Sauce (page 336). A very nice accompaniment to the pears are crisp Florentines (page 368) or Ginger Lace Biscuits filled with ginger cream (page 369). *Serves 6*

6 Conference or Bosc pears, peeled and cored
2 tablespoons fresh lemon juice
6 pieces lemon zest, each 5 cm/2 inches long
6 pieces orange zest, each 5 cm/2 inches long
6 whole cloves

1 Rub pears with juice to prevent discolouring. Place 1 piece lemon zest and 1 piece orange zest inside each core cavity. Stick a clove in side of each pear.

2 Place pears in a ring inside rim of a 25 cm/10 inch soufflé dish that is 7.5–10 cm/3–4 inches deep. Cover tightly with microwave cling film. Cook at 100% for 8 minutes.

3 Pierce film with the tip of a sharp knife, then remove from oven. Carefully pour off juices. Add to Blueberry Sauce, if desired.

4 Serve warm or cold, either plain or centred on a dessert plate in a pool of Blueberry Sauce or double cream.

To poach other quantities. Divide ingredient quantities accordingly, cooking 1 pear in a microwave-safe roasting bag for 3 minutes. Place 2 or 4 pears in containers just large enough to fit, cover and cook 2 pears for 4 minutes 30 seconds, 4 pears for 7 minutes.

VARIATION

PEARS IN PARCHMENT Wrap a single pear, prepared as for Light Poached Pears, in a 20 cm/8 inch square of parchment paper. Cook at 100% for 4 minutes. Serve in untwisted paper as in a pastry shell.

BLUEBERRY SAUCE
◆ ◆ ◆

This delicious sauce goes particularly well with Light Poached Pears. Try it also under Puff Pastry (page 383) feuilletés split and layered with fresh blueberries and Confectioner's Custard (page 381). *Makes 350 ml/12 fl oz*

300 g/10 oz blueberries
3 tablespoons caster sugar

6 tablespoons pear juice, from Light Poached Pears (page 335)
⅛ teaspoon ground cinnamon

1 Pick over berries, discarding any that are overripe, green or discoloured. Put into a 1 litre/2 pint glass measuring jug.

2 Sprinkle with sugar. Cover tightly with microwave cling film. Cook at 100% for 3 minutes.

3 Pierce film with the tip of a sharp knife, then remove from oven. Uncover, pour into the container of a food processor and purée. Pass through a fine sieve.

4 Add pear juice and cinnamon. If serving with Light Poached Pears, allow 4 tablespoons sauce for each portion.

PEARS IN RED WINE
◆ ◆ ◆

If you want the traditional pears poached in French fashion in red wine, the microwave oven cooks the red wine syrup in short order and the pears even more quickly. I don't like the pears too sweet, but you can increase the sugar to 400 g/14 oz. (This poaching syrup can be used for other fruits, such as peaches.)

The pears will darken in colour the longer they are allowed to sit in the syrup. I have allowed ½ pear per person, thinking you might want to serve each portion with some cinnamon ice cream, or with some Crème Anglaise (page 380). *Serves 4*

POACHING SYRUP

200 g/7 oz caster sugar	1 cardamom pod, crushed
500 ml/16 fl oz red wine	2 whole cloves
1 piece cinnamon stick, 4 cm/1½ inches long	2 Conference or Bosc pears (200–250 g/ 7–8 oz each), peeled, cored and halved
4 whole allspice berries	
Pinch freshly grated nutmeg	

1 Combine all ingredients except pears in a 2 litre/3½ pint glass jug or bowl. Cook, uncovered, at 100% for 3 minutes. Stir well. Cover tightly with microwave cling film. Cook at 100% for 5 minutes longer.

2 Pierce film with the tip of a sharp knife and then remove from oven. Arrange pears in a 21 × 17.5 × 6 cm/8½ × 7 × 2½ inch dish, cored side up, alternating wide and narrow ends. Pour liquid over pears. Cover tightly with microwave cling film. Cook at 100% for 12 minutes.

3 Pierce film, then remove from oven. Cool pears in syrup. Serve pears with a little of the syrup.

To poach 1 pear. Halve all ingredients, cooking syrup for 2 minutes 30 seconds; cook pears in syrup for 3 minutes.

To poach 4 pears. Double all ingredients, cooking syrup for 4 minutes; cook pears in syrup for 17 minutes.

POACHED RED PLUMS

◆ ◆ ◆

These plums are a good compôte on their own, or are good in a mixed compôte contributing a little of their syrup. I make this at the end of summer when pears are too hard. Greengages can be poached the same way. Add 2 minutes to each poaching time. Leftover syrup can be refrigerated and reused. The nicely coloured syrup from the red plums can be refrigerated and added, 2 tablespoons at a time, to inexpensive sparkling wine to make a beautiful and festive drink. *Makes 6 plums*

POACHING SYRUP
500 ml/16 fl oz water
400 g/14 oz caster sugar
1 piece cinnamon stick, 2.5 cm/1 inch
  long
1 tablespoon vanilla essence

3 pieces lemon zest, 7.5 × 2.5 cm/3 × 1
inch

6 firm red plums (about 500 g/1 lb)

1 Combine water, sugar and cinnamon in a 2.5 litre/4 pint soufflé dish. Cook, uncovered, at 100% for 3 minutes. Remove from oven and stir well. Cover tightly with microwave cling film. Cook at 100% for 6 minutes.

2 Pierce film with the tip of a sharp knife, then remove from oven. Uncover and stir in vanilla and zest. Add plums. Cover tightly with microwave cling film. Cook at 100% for 8 minutes.

3 Pierce film, then remove from oven. Uncover and store, tightly covered, in the refrigerator.

To poach 10 plums. Cook in the same quantity of syrup for 10 minutes.

To poach 16 plums. Cook in two batches in the same quantity of syrup; six plums for 8 minutes, ten plums for 10 minutes.

BOURBON PEACHES

◆ ◆ ◆

These peaches are more than a dessert, they are the song of the American South. I make them when peaches are in season and use them all winter. While one can be served to each guest as a dessert with some plain whipped cream and a crisp biscuit, or with vanilla ice cream, a half peach would be delicious with baked ham or a roast loin of pork. The peaches will keep, covered with syrup and refrigerated, for a good year. *Makes 15 peaches*

250 ml/8 fl oz water
400 g/14 oz caster sugar
1.25 kg/2¼ lb very small hard peaches
  (about 15), each pricked once
½ orange, squeezed and shell reserved
½ lemon, squeezed and shell reserved

4 whole cloves
3 whole allspice berries
½ teaspoon ground ginger
250 ml/8 fl oz Kentucky sour mash
  bourbon whiskey

1 Combine water and sugar in a 2 litre/3½ pint glass jug or bowl. Cover tightly with microwave cling film. Cook at 100% for 15 minutes. Stir twice during cooking, making sure to reseal film tightly after opening.

2 Pierce film with the tip of a sharp knife, then remove from oven. Uncover and add peaches. Stir in remaining ingredients except bourbon. Cover tightly with microwave cling film. Cook at 100% for 5 minutes.

3 Pierce film, the remove from oven. Uncover and let cool slightly. When peaches are cool enough to handle, slip off their skins. Pack peaches into a tall, narrow container.

4 Strain poaching syrup through muslin. Stir in bourbon and pour over peaches to cover. Cover tightly and refrigerate until ready to use.

RUMMY BANANAS

If it weren't for the rum, this would make a cosy children's dessert. On the other hand, I have served it as a party dessert, to a chorus of contented sighs. Sometimes I make a small version for myself—an ideal self-indulgence and comfort food. You can serve this with Florentines (page 368) and ice cream, but it's good enough all on its own. *Serves 6*

175 ml/6 fl oz dark rum
75 g/2½ oz dark brown sugar
30 g/1 oz unsalted butter
1 piece (5 cm/2 inches) vanilla pod or
  ½ teaspoon vanilla essence

2 tablespoons fresh lemon juice
Zest of ½ lemon, cut into julienne strips
2 thin slices fresh root ginger
6 bananas (1.25–1.5 kg/2½–3 lb)

1 Combine rum, sugar, butter, vanilla pod, lemon juice, zest and ginger in a 1 litre/2 pint glass measuring jug. (If using vanilla essence, do not add it until step 2.) Cover tightly with microwave cling film. Cook at 100% for 3 minutes.

2 Pierce film with the tip of a sharp knife, then remove from oven. Uncover and stir. (Add vanilla essence if you are using it.) Set aside.

3 Peel bananas and remove 1 cm/½ inch from each end. Arrange pinwheel-fashion in a 25 cm/10 inch round dish. Pour rum mixture over bananas. Cover tightly with microwave cling film. Cook at 100% for 5 minutes 30 seconds. Pierce film before removing from oven.

To serve 2. Use 5½ tablespoons rum, 2 bananas, and halve remaining ingredients. Fit bananas into a dish just large enough to hold them, cooking for 3 minutes.

Arrange bananas pinwheel-fashion in a 25 cm/ 10 inch round dish. Other longish foods such as quartered artichokes can be arranged in the same way with the thicker end towards the outside of the dish.

MAPLE SYRUP-BAKED APPLES

B aking apples in the microwave oven is so quick that I even am willing to make one for my own dinner. The apple skins are edible and the apples are evenly cooked all the way through. Also, the apples don't explode into a disorderly mess. You can certainly use other apple varieties in this recipe, but check the Dictionary for cooking times. Check it also if you're using a very small (400 to 450 watts) oven. *Serves 6*

6 Granny Smith or Bramley apples
   (250–275 g/8–9 oz each), cored, with
   a 4 cm/1½ inch collar peeled from
   top of apple
1 tablespoon currants

3 tablespoons chopped walnuts
Grated zest of 1 orange
2 tablespoons fresh orange juice
3 tablespoons fresh lemon juice
175 ml/6 fl oz maple syrup

1 Arrange apples in a 30 × 23.5 × 6 cm/12 × 9½ × 2½ inch oval dish so that they don't touch each other or the sides of the dish. Divide currants, walnuts and zest evenly among apple cavities.

2 Combine juices and syrup and pour around apples. Cover with microwave cling film, airtight but loose enough so that film isn't stretched over tops of apples if they stand higher than sides of dish. Cook at 100% for 9 minutes.

3 Pierce with the tip of a sharp knife, then remove from oven. Let stand for 5 minutes (apples will continue to steam).

4 Uncover and serve warm with some of the syrup.

To bake other quantities. Divide ingredient quantities accordingly. See Dictionary for cooking times.

PEACH CRISP

$\bullet\!\!\!-\!\!\!\bullet$

This is an easy dessert for summer days when peaches are plentiful and ripe. The brown streusel topping made with dark pumpernickel breadcrumbs is good enough to make in extra quantity and have on hand for another time, hence this recipe gives you about twice the quantity you need for the peaches. The chocolate richness is a perfect contrast to the fresh fruit taste. This could also be made with nectarines, apricots, or peeled apple slices that have been tossed in a little lemon juice. *Serves 4*

STREUSEL
40 g/1¼ oz blanched almonds
15 g/½ oz good quality plain chocolate
4 tablespoons caster sugar
75 g/2½ oz breadcrumbs from stale,
   dark Russian pumpernickel, trimmed

60 g/2 oz unsalted butter
500 g/1 lb peaches, peeled and sliced
   into 8 wedges each (about 4 peaches)

1 Place almonds, chocolate and sugar in the container of a food processor. Process until finely ground. Stir in breadcrumbs.

2 Heat butter in a 1 litre/2 pint glass measuring jug, uncovered, at 100% for 2 minutes. Remove from oven and add crumb mixture. Stir to moisten crumbs with butter. (This streusel mixture may be made in advance and kept, tightly covered and frozen, until needed.)

3 Layer peach slices in a 1 litre/2 pint soufflé dish. Sprinkle with half of the streusel mixture. (Freeze remaining streusel mixture.) Cook, uncovered, at 100% for 6 minutes.

4 Serve hot, with cream or ice cream.

To serve 1. Peel and slice a peach. Put in a 125 ml/4 fl oz ramekin and sprinkle with 2 tablespoons streusel mixture. Cook for 2 minutes.

To serve 2. Peel and slice 2 peaches. Put in a 500 ml/16 fl oz soufflé dish and sprinkle with 3 tablespoons streusel mixture. Cook for 4 minutes.

FIGS IN RED WINE

A ripe, sun-warmed fig is sweet and voluptuous whether eaten alone or paired with lightly salty prosciutto. Sometimes figs aren't perfectly ripe, or you just want another kind of dessert. That's when this poached fig dessert comes into its own. The ring mould helps to hold the figs upright in an arrangement that permits them to cook evenly. Serve cold or warm. This is good with double cream or Crème Anglaise (page 380). *Serves 6*

8 teaspoons caster sugar
125 ml/4 fl oz Marsala or port
¼ teaspoon ground allspice
⅛ teaspoon ground cloves

⅛ teaspoon freshly ground black pepper
1 piece (5 cm/2 inches) vanilla pod,
  split lengthways
12 ripe figs, preferably black

1 Combine sugar, wine, allspice, cloves, pepper and vanilla pod in a 25 cm/10 inch glass ring mould. Arrange figs evenly around mould.

2 Cover tightly with microwave cling film. Cook at 100% for 5 minutes.

3 Pierce film with the tip of a sharp knife, then remove from oven. Serve figs warm with their poaching liquid.

To serve 1. Substitute ¼ teaspoon vanilla essence for vanilla pod, and divide all other ingredient quantities by 4; combine all ingredients in a 500 ml/16 fl oz soufflé dish, cover and cook for 1 minute 30 seconds to 2 minutes.

To serve 3. Halve all ingredients except vanilla pod; arrange figs in a 20 cm/8 inch glass ring mould, cover and cook for 3 minutes.

APPLE CHARLOTTE

— • • —

Charlottes are old-fashioned desserts, made either with a contrast of buttery crisped bread and meltingly fruity acid apple filling topped with whipped cream or as a chilled dessert set with gelatine. This elegant version is part of the classic French repertoire. Don't try to make a smaller version, as the apples will burn before the charlotte cooks. *Serves 4 to 6*

60 g/2 oz unsalted butter
10 slices firm white bread, crusts
  removed
125 g/4 oz caster sugar

1 kg/2 lb Granny Smith apples, peeled,
  cored and thinly sliced
2 tablespoons fresh lemon juice
250 ml/8 fl oz double cream, whipped,
  for serving

1 Heat butter in a 500 ml/1 pint glass measuring jug, uncovered, at 100% for 1 minute 30 seconds. Set aside.

2 Preheat conventional oven to 180° C/350° F/Gas 4.

3 Trim bread to line a 1.5 litre/2½ pint soufflé dish: using a 5 cm/2 inch round biscuit cutter, cut out enough bread rounds to cover bottom of dish, overlapping slightly; cut enough 2.5 × 5 cm/1 × 2 inch pieces to fit, overlapping, around sides of dish.

4 Place bread shapes on a baking sheet. Brush on one side with melted butter. Toast in conventional oven until lightly brown.

5 Generously butter dish and dust with 2 tablespoons of the sugar.

6 Remove toast from oven. Arrange overlapping rounds, golden side down, over bottom of soufflé dish. Arrange overlapping rectangles around sides. Reserve any extra pieces.

7 Toss apple slices with remaining sugar and lemon juice. Layer slices in lined dish. Arrange any remaining toast on top of apples.

8 Cover tightly with microwave cling film. Cook at 100% 5 minutes.

9 Pierce film with the tip of a sharp knife, then uncover and cook for 8 to 10 minutes longer, until set.

10 Remove charlotte from oven. If apple mixture has reduced dramatically during cooking, you may want to trim toast edges even with top of filling. Set a plate over top of dish (charlotte will continue to steam) and let stand until cool enough to handle.

11 Unmould charlotte on to a serving plate. Serve warm or cold. Slice with a serrated knife, and serve with whipped cream.

KEY LIME PIE

◆•◆

Once upon a time, the Florida Keys had a large crop of small, dark green limes that yielded small quantities of a wonderfully aromatic, flowery tasting juice that was often made into diaphanous pies topped with a cloud of whipped cream— no longer. Today when Key limes are available, they come from Mexico during a short winter season. This is not a thick, heavy meringue pie. It is a chiffon pie, light as foam, that needs to be made a morning or day ahead. Substitute fresh lemon juice for the lime juice for lemon chiffon pie. *Makes one 22.5 cm/9 inch pie*

350 ml/12 fl oz milk
3 eggs, separated
100 g/3½ oz caster sugar
125 ml/4 fl oz Key lime juice, squeezed
    from 12 Key limes or 3 to 4 regular
    limes

1 tablespoon powdered gelatine
4 tablespoons water
175 ml/6 fl oz double cream
Sweet Tart Pastry (page 383), baked
    and left in its tin
2 tablespoons icing sugar

1 Heat milk in a 1 litre/2 pint glass measuring jug, uncovered, at 100% for 2 minutes.

2 Whisk together egg yolks and caster sugar. Whisk in hot milk. Return mixture to jug. Cook, uncovered, at 100% for 2 minutes. Remove from oven and stir in lime juice.

3 Combine gelatine and water in a 250 ml/8 fl oz glass jug or bowl. Heat, uncovered, at 100% for 45 seconds. Remove from oven and stir into lime mixture. Place mixture in the refrigerator and chill, stirring occasionally, until it begins to set.

4 Whip cream to soft peaks and fold into lime mixture. Pour into tart shell and refrigerate for 2 hours.

5 When pie is set, whisk egg whites to soft peaks. Continue whisking, adding icing sugar by teaspoonful, until whites are stiff.

6 Heat conventional grill. Spread meringue over pie, making sure to cover lime filling completely. Place pie under grill and brown lightly. Refrigerate if not eating immediately.

PUDDINGS AND CUSTARDS

There is some part of my soul that remains forever a child. No dessert pleases that side of me as much as puddings and custards. I even cool my puddings uncovered in the refrigerator so that my spoon breaks a skin, making a hole into which to pour double cream. Grown-ups will want to cover the desserts loosely before cooling so that no skin develops. Such desserts are closely related to custard sauces. Indeed, a flavoured Crème Anglaise (page 380) can be served with almost any of these desserts as an added decadence.

CHOCOLATE PUDDING

This lovely dessert is adapted from a recipe of Larry Forgione's. He is the chef-owner of An American Place in New York. In the microwave oven it is as easy and as rapid as any mix, but how different! I will put it up against a French pot de crème or mousse any time. Use very good chocolate; it's worth it. Don't worry about making eight portions when there are only four people eating. These delights will keep up to a week, loosely covered, in the refrigerator. I promise they will disappear. *Serves 8*

500 ml/16 fl oz milk
100 g/3½ caster sugar
150 g/5 oz good-quality plain
  chocolate, grated
2 tablespoons cornflour
2 tablespoons unsweetened cocoa
  powder

2 tablespoons water
2 eggs
4 egg yolks
30 g/1 oz unsalted butter
1 tablespoon dark rum
2 tablespoons vanilla essence

1 Place milk, sugar and chocolate in a 2 litre/3½ pint glass jug or bowl. Cook, uncovered, at 100% for 4 minutes, stirring twice during cooking. Remove from oven and set aside.

2 Sift together cornflour and cocoa powder. Add water to make a smooth mixture.

3 Stir cornflour into chocolate mixture. Whisk in whole eggs and yolks. Cook, uncovered, at 100% for 2 minutes. Remove from oven, stir thoroughly and cook for 2 minutes more.

4 Remove from oven and pour mixture into the container of a food processor. Add butter, rum and vanilla and process until smooth. Pour into individual cups or a 2 litre/3½ pint serving bowl and chill.

BUTTERSCOTCH PUDDING

◆ ◆

A nice discovery of working with the microwave oven has been to find out how easy it is to make caramel, the base for butterscotch—no scorched pans, scorched sugar, or disastrous crystals. See Dictionary for notes on CARAMEL.
Serves 8

200 g/7 oz caster sugar	175 g/6 oz unsalted butter
4 tablespoons water	2 eggs
250 ml/8 fl oz double cream	4 egg yolks
2 tablespoons cornflour	2 teaspoons vanilla essence
250 ml/8 fl oz milk	

1 Combine sugar and water in a 2 litre/3½ pint glass jug or bowl. Cover tightly with microwave cling film. Cook at 100% for 8 minutes, until light and gold.

2 Pierce film with the tip of a sharp knife, then uncover carefully and stir in cream. Cook, uncovered, at 100% for 3 minutes.

3 Remove from oven. Dissolve cornflour in 4 tablespoons of the milk. Add to caramel mixture.

4 Stir in remaining milk, butter, eggs and yolks. Cook, uncovered, at 100% for 2 minutes.

5 Remove from oven and stir until smooth. Cook, uncovered, at 100% for 2 minutes longer.

6 Remove from oven and pour into the container of a food processor. Add vanilla and process until smooth. Pour into individual cups and chill for at least 1 hour before serving.

POLENTA PUDDING WITH RASPBERRIES

◆ ◆

Most of us think of polenta as that lush Italian cornmeal dish that is eaten instead of potatoes or rice, or that is fried to make a wonderful base for sauces as a first course. The very clever northern Italians, however, came up with another, less expected polenta dish, a creamy yellow dessert with fresh fruit, served with a sauce of the same fruit. If you want it to be yet more magnificent, serve with Crème Anglaise (page 380). This would be luscious after a light main course such as fish with vegetables.

If this is more desert than you need for your dinner, don't worry; you will finish it happily the next day. *Serves 8*

250 g/8 oz fresh raspberries	Grated zest of 1 lemon
185 g/6½ oz caster sugar	1 teaspoon vanilla esence
1 litre/1¾ pints water	¼ teaspoon sea salt
90 g/3 oz cornmeal (maize meal)	Unsalted butter, for the mould

1 Toss together raspberries and 4 tablespoons of the sugar in a small, shallow dish. Cook, uncovered, at 100% for 4 minutes. Remove from oven and reserve.

2 Combine water, cornmeal, zest and remaining sugar in a 2 litre/3½ pint glass jug or bowl. Cook, uncovered, at 100% for 12 minutes, stirring twice.

3 Remove from oven and let stand for 10 minutes, stirring once or twice. Stir in vanilla and salt.

4 Set aside half of the raspberry mixture. Place remaining mixture in the container of a food processor and process until smooth, adding water if necessary to make a thin sauce. Reserve.

5 Stir raspberry mixture that was set aside (not sauce) into the polenta just until marbled—don't completely incorporate it. Pour into a buttered 22.5 × 10 cm/ 9 × 4 inch bowl or 1 litre/2 pint pudding basin. Chill for 4 hours, until firm.

6 Unmould on to a serving dish and serve with the reserved sauce.

CRÈME BRÛLÉE

There is a territorial dispute as to whether this great classic dessert originated at an English university—the most common notion—or was a Spanish recipe, brought to England by a chef. Whatever, it has become wildly popular everywhere. It is a shallow pool of thin custard alluringly topped with a thin, hard, translucent golden brown sugar glaze that must be rapped sharply with the back of a spoon in order to fracture it before the dessert is eaten. The glazing must be done under a conventional grill, but making the custard is simplified by the microwave oven.

You should make the custards at least 6 hours before you intend to glaze them. The custards may be variously flavoured although it is not traditional. *Serves 4*

350 ml/12 fl oz milk
2 eggs
2 tablespoons caster sugar

1 teaspoon vanilla essence
125 g/4 oz light brown sugar, to
  caramelize tops of custards

1 Heat milk in a 1 litre/2 pint glass measuring jug, uncovered, at 100% for 4 minutes.

2 Remove from oven. Whisk together eggs, sugar and vanilla until well combined. Whisking constantly, add hot milk in a thin stream. Divide mixture evenly among four 12.5 cm/5 inch individual tart or quiche dishes.

3 Place dishes, evenly spaced, around turntable in oven. Cook, uncovered, at 50% for 6 minutes. If not using an oven with a turntable change position of custards halfway through cooking and add 15 seconds cooking time.

4 Remove from oven. Cover custards with buttered greaseproof paper, placing directly on custards, to prevent a skin from forming. Let cool to room temperature and refrigerate for at least 6 hours.

5 Preheat conventional grill.

6 Sift 3 tablespoons brown sugar over each custard, completely covering the top, particularly the edges. Fit dishes into a metal pan. Fill gaps between dishes with ice and add water to a depth of 3 mm/¼ inch.

7 Grill just until sugar melts, about 4 minutes. Watch carefully to avoid burning. Remove from oven and rub each caramel crust with ice for 30 seconds to harden it.

8 Refrigerate until ready to serve, which should be fairly soon or the glaze may dissolve.

To serve 6. Use 500 ml/16 fl oz milk, 4 eggs, 4½ tablespoons caster sugar, 2 teaspoons vanilla, and 90 g/3 oz brown sugar. Heat milk in a 1 litre/2 pint glass measuring jug for 5 minutes; cook custards for 6 minutes.

To serve 8. Double quantities of milk, eggs and caster sugar; use 1 tablespoon vanilla and 125 g/4 oz brown sugar. Heat milk in a 2 litre/3½ pint glass jug or bowl for 7 minutes; cook custards for 8 minutes.

BREAD PUDDING

◆ ◆ ◆

There is nothing homelier or better than a bread pudding. If you have stale bread—which is how this dessert originated, as did pain perdu—use it. Do not toast as in step 2; instead melt butter for 3 minutes at 100%, then toss in bread and proceed. This is another recipe with many possible variations. Stir in 45 g/ 1½ oz chocolate morsels, or add 30 g/1 oz peeled apple cut into 5 mm/¼ inch cubes and stirred with ¼ teaspoon ground cinnamon. Substitute fresh raspberries turned in 2 tablespoons Poire William (pear brandy) for the raisins. As long as you respect the proportions, the dish size and the cooking time, you can give your imagination free rein. *Serves 4*

30 g/1 oz raisins
125 ml/4 fl oz warm water or bourbon
  whiskey
100 g/3½ oz white bread, crusts
  removed and cut into 1 cm/½ inch
  cubes

60 g/2 oz unsalted butter
2 tablespoons caster sugar
3 egg yolks
250 ml/8 fl oz double cream
2 teaspoons vanilla essence

1 Soak raisins in water for 10 minutes.

2 Place bread in a 23.5 × 17.5 × 5 cm/9½ × 7 × 2 inch dish and cook, uncovered, at 100% for 4 minutes, stirring once. Remove from oven and set aside.

3 Drain raisins and set aside.

4 Heat butter in a 500 ml/1 pint glass measuring jug, uncovered, at 100% for 2 minutes. Remove from oven. Drizzle half the melted butter over bread and stir to coat.

5 Whisk together sugar, egg yolks, cream and vanilla. Whisk in remaining melted butter and stir in raisins. Pour mixture over bread and cook, uncovered, at 100% for 3 minutes.

6 Remove from oven. Cover dish with a plate and let stand for 5 minutes. Serve warm.

RICE PUDDING

• • •

What is the matter with Mary Jane?
... It's lovely rice pudding for dinner again!
A.A. MILNE

I would be delighted with rice pudding again; but then I am not a Victorian child subjected to it with startling frequency.

For those who like their rice pudding with a baked topping, pour finished pudding into four individual gratin dishes. Heat grill. Combine 100 g/3 ½ oz sugar with 1 tablespoon ground cinnamon. Sift over puddings to coat. Place dishes on a baking sheet. Put under grill about 2 minutes, or until the puddings glaze. Allow to cool; refrigerate or serve warm. *Serves 4*

75 g/2½ oz raisins
175 g/6 oz long-grain rice, parboiled, not instant (see Note below)
500 ml/16 fl oz milk
4 tablespoons caster sugar
1 vanilla pod, split lengthways
500 ml/16 fl oz double cream
2 egg yolks

1 Combine raisins, rice, milk, sugar and vanilla pod in a 2.5 litre/4 pint soufflé dish. Cook, uncovered, at 100% for 10 minutes. Stir, and cook for 10 minutes longer.

2 Remove from oven. Whisk together cream and egg yolks, and stir into rice mixture.

3 Cook, uncovered, for 1 minute. Stir, and cook for 1 minute longer.

4 Remove from oven and stir. Let sit for 5 minutes before serving. Serve with additional double cream, Tart Apricot Purée (page 385) or Fresh Strawberry Sauce (page 379).

Note. To substitute short-grain (pudding) rice, use 200 g/7 oz. Put the rice in a 2.5 litre/4 pint soufflé dish and cover tightly with microwave cling film. Cook at 100% for 10 minutes or until just boiling. Pierce film with the tip of a sharp knife to release steam, then remove from oven and uncover. Drain rice and rinse with cold water.

TAPIOCA PUDDING

• • •

As a child, I hated what we called 'fish eyes and glue'. As a grown-up cook, I couldn't understand the French haute cuisine penchant for thickening with tapioca. Tapioca really gets magnificently cooked in the microwave oven; I am a convert to these creamy and delicious desserts that are even good warm. *Serves 5 to 6*

500 ml/16 fl oz milk	1 egg
3 tablespoons tapioca (instant type)	1 teaspoon vanilla essence or 1 teaspoon
3 tablespoons caster sugar	almond essence
Pinch sea salt	

1 Stir together milk, tapioca, sugar and salt in a 2 litre/3½ pint glass jug or bowl. Cover tightly with microwave cling film. Cook at 100% for 5 minutes. Pierce film with the tip of a sharp knife to release steam, then uncover and stir well. Cook, uncovered, for 4 minutes more.

2 Remove from oven. Stir well. Beat together egg and vanilla. Stirring constantly, pour 125 ml/4 fl oz tapioca into egg and then pour mixture back into tapioca. Cook, uncovered, at 100% for 1 minute.

3 Remove from oven. Stir well and cover with polythene, placing it directly on pudding to prevent a skin from forming. Serve warm or chilled.

To Serve 10 to 12. Double all ingredients. Cook as for Tapioca Pudding in a 2.5–3 litre/4–5 pint soufflé dish for 8 minutes. Stir and cook, uncovered, for 5 minutes more. Add eggs and vanilla as for Tapioca Pudding and cook for 1 minute more. Serve in soufflé dish or pour into 125 ml/4 fl oz ramekins and chill.

VARIATION

CHOCOLATE TAPIOCA for 5 or 10 Proceed as for Tapioca Pudding. After final cooking and while pudding is still hot, whisk in 60 g/2 oz grated plain chocolate (for smaller portion) or 125 g/4 oz chocolate (for larger portion). Finish and serve as for Tapioca Pudding.

STEAMED PUDDINGS

It occurred to me forcibly as I was labouring to make decent cakes in the microwave oven that exactly the things that were causing me problems with the cakes would help make perfect steamed puddings. This didn't make me any happier about the cakes, but when I did get around to trying steamed puddings, I was happy to find my suspicions were right.

I love steamed puddings and their moist texture somewhere between cake and pudding. Until the microwave oven, I made them infrequently, as they required long steaming in a pan of simmering water that needed to be constantly checked and topped up. Now they are no more difficult or time-consuming than any other dessert.

Most of them would welcome a topping of unsweetened whipped cream, or Ginger Cream (page 369).

THANKSGIVING PUDDING

——————— ◆·◆ ———————

I'm afraid I've got rather satiated with the rich, traditional pies associated with Thanksgiving—pumpkin, pecan and mincemeat. Wanting something equally good but a little less heavy, I devised this steamed pudding. Pumpkin can replace the acorn squash, if you like. Place 350 g/12 oz of 2.5 cm/1 inch cubes of pumpkin flesh in a large glass measuring jug and cook, tightly covered with microwave cling film, for 8 minutes. *Serves 8*

150 g/5 oz unsalted butter
1 acorn squash (about 500 g/1 lb), halved and seeded
220 g/7½ oz dark brown sugar
5 eggs
125 ml/4 fl oz double cream
40 g/1⅓ oz plain flour, sifted
1 teaspoon vanilla essence

¾ teaspoon ground cinnamon
¼ teaspoon ground allspice
Candied orange peel, for garnish (optional)
2 tablespoons pomegranate seeds, for garnish (optional)
Double cream, for serving (optional)

1 Butter a 22.5 × 10 cm/9 × 4 inch ceramic bowl or a 1 litre/2 pint pudding basin with 30 g/1 oz of the butter.

2 Place squash halves, side by side, in a rectangular dish just large enough to hold them. Cover tightly with microwave cling film. Cook at 100% for 8 minutes.

3 Pierce film with the tip of a sharp knife, then remove from oven. Uncover and let cool to room temperature.

4 Put sugar and remaining butter, cut into 8 pieces, in the container of a food processor and blend.

5 Scrape the cooked squash from its shell into the processor. Add remaining ingredients except garnishes and cream and blend to a smooth mixture.

6 Pour into prepared bowl. Cover tightly with microwave cling film. Cook at 100% for 9 minutes, until set; if pudding looks moist in the centre, that is fine.

7 Pierce film with the tip of a sharp knife, remove from oven and cover top of bowl with a heavy plate; this will keep the pudding hot. Let stand for 15 minutes.

8 Unmould pudding on to a serving plate. Garnish with candied orange peel and pomegranate seeds. Serve warm with whipped cream, if desired.

To make individual puddings. Cook in 2 batches of four 125 ml/4 fl oz ramekins each for 2 minutes.

To make a single, smaller pudding. Halve the ingredients and halve the cooking time; cook in a smaller bowl (17.5 × 10 cm/7 × 4 inches) or 750 ml/1¼ pint pudding basin. From this quantity you can, of course, prepare 1 batch of individual puddings.

STEAMED CHOCOLATE PUDDING

This rich and moist pudding is a dessert to dream about. *Serves* 8

150 g/5 oz unsalted butter
250 g/8 oz plain chocolate
100 g/3½ oz light brown sugar
1 teaspoon vanilla essence
125 ml/4 fl oz double cream

40 g/1⅓ oz plain flour, sifted
½ teaspoon baking powder
3 eggs
Double cream, for serving (optional)

1 Butter a 22.5 × 10 cm/9 × 4 inch ceramic bowl or a 1 litre/2 pint pudding basin with 30 g/1 oz of the butter.

2 Grate chocolate in a food processor. Add remaining butter, cut into 8 pieces, and sugar. Process until thoroughly combined.

3 Add remaining ingredients, except cream for serving, and process to a smooth mixture.

4 Pour into prepared bowl. Cover tightly with microwave cling film. Cook at 100% for 5 minutes, until set.

5 Pierce film with the tip of a sharp knife, then remove and cover top of bowl with a heavy plate; this will keep the pudding hot. Let stand for 10 minutes.

6 Unmould pudding on to a serving plate. Serve warm or cold, with whipped cream if desired.

To make individual puddings. Cook in 2 batches of four 125 ml/4 fl oz ramekins each for 1 minute 30 seconds.

To make a single, smaller pudding. Halve all ingredients and halve cooking time; cook in a smaller bowl (17.5 × 10 cm/7 × 4 inches) or 750 ml/1¼ pint pudding basin. From this quantity you can, of course, prepare 1 batch of individual puddings.

STEAMED PEAR PUDDING

Unlike the other steamed puddings, this is pale in colour. The strong, but somehow mysterious flavour and perfume of pears comes as a pleasant surprise.
Serves 8

150 g/5 oz unsalted butter
750 g/1½ lb ripe Conference or Bosc
   pears (about 3 pears)
4 tablespoons fresh lemon juice
200 g/7 oz caster sugar
5 eggs

125 ml/4 fl oz double cream
40 g/1⅓ oz plain flour, sifted
1 teaspoon vanilla essence
½ teaspoon ground cinnamon
½ teaspoon ground ginger
¼ teaspoon ground cloves

1 Butter a 22.5 × 10 cm/8 × 4 inch ceramic bowl or a 1 litre/2 pint pudding basin with 30 g/1 oz of the butter.

2 Peel, halve and core pears. Rub with lemon juice to prevent discolouration. Set in a 1 litre/2 pint glass measuring jug or soufflé dish and cover tightly with microwave cling film. Cook at 100% for 3 minutes.

3 Put remaining ingredients, including remaining butter cut into pieces, in the container of a food processor. Pierce film, covering pears with the tip of a sharp knife, then remove from oven and add them to processor. Blend to a smooth mixture.

4 Pour into prepared bowl. Cover tightly with microwave cling film. Cook at 100% for 9 minutes, until set.

5 Pierce film, with the tip of a sharp knife, remove from oven and cover top of bowl with a heavy plate; this will keep the pudding hot. Let stand for 15 minutes.

6 Unmould pudding on to a serving plate. Serve warm.

To make individual puddings. Cook in 2 batches of four 125 ml/4 fl oz ramekins each for 2 minutes.

To make a single, smaller pudding. Halve the ingredients and halve the cooking time; cook in a smaller bowl (17.5 × 10 cm/7 × 4 inches) or 750 ml/1¼ pint pudding basin. From this quantity you can, of course, prepare 1 batch of individual puddings.

STEAMED PAPAYA PUDDING
• • •

As steamed puddings go, this is rather exotic; but my, it is good, especially when other fruit desserts are in seasonally short supply. *Serves 8*

500 g/1 lb papaya, peeled, seeded and cut into 5 cm/2 inch pieces	125 ml/4 fl oz soured cream
150 g/5 oz unsalted butter	40 g/1⅓ oz plain flour, sifted
200 g/7 oz caster sugar	1 teaspoon vanilla essence
6 eggs	1 teaspoon ground cardamom

1 Place papaya in a 1 litre/2 pint glass measuring jug. Cover tightly with microwave cling film. Cook at 100% for 4 minutes.

2 Butter a 22.5 × 10 cm/9 × 4 inch bowl or a 1 litre/2 pint pudding basin with 30 g/1 oz of the butter.

3 Pierce film covering papaya, then remove from oven. Place in the container of a food processor with remaining ingredients, including remaining butter cut into small pieces, and blend to a smooth mixture.

4 Pour into prepared bowl. Cover tightly with microwave cling film. Cook at 100% for 9 minutes, until pudding is set.

5 Pierce film with the tip of a sharp knife, remove from oven and cover top of bowl with a heavy plate; this will keep the pudding hot. Let stand for 15 minutes.

6 Unmould pudding on to a serving plate. Serve warm, with additional soured cream if desired.

To make individual puddings. Cook in 2 batches of four 125 ml/4 fl oz ramekins each for 2 minutes.

To make a single, smaller pudding. Halve the ingredients and halve the cooking time; cook in a smaller bowl (17.5 × 10 cm/7 × 4 inches) or 750 ml/1¼ pint pudding basin. From this quantity you can, of course, prepare 1 batch of individual puddings.

CAKES AND BISCUITS

I am about to tell you with hideous honesty the severe limitations of baking in the microwave oven. Before I do, I want to boast and tell you that the recipes I have included are terrific. You can make any of them with a perfect assurance of success, a success and a rapidity far beyond that possible in a conventional oven.

In addition, the confirmed baker will find that many elements of baking—component parts of recipes—are quickly and well accomplished in the microwave oven: Confectioner's Custard, Melting Chocolate, Blanching Nuts, Toasting Nuts, Praline Powder and Paste, Apricot Glaze, Ganache, Chocolate Glaze, White Mountain Icing, Melting Butter, and many more.

Now we must go on to the unfortunate limitation of excellence. This is a touchy subject because so many baking recipes have been written for the microwave oven. If you like them, by all means use them. I find that most are unsuccessful (including most that I tried to develop myself). I will not give you recipes that I do not consider as good as any to be made.

One of the troubles with baking arises from the odd way that the starches in wheat flour—particularly gluten, which is in fact a protein—absorb liquid in the microwave oven; they tend to turn gluey. Rather than creating a pleasant crumb, you get a wet and soggy layer. Where I have lined cake tins with paper towel, it is to encourage a dry surface. Additionally, flour does not brown in baking, so flour-based cakes stay a ghastly colour. The baking problem is compounded by the tendency of eggs to become rubbery quickly in the microwave oven. As if all of this were not enough, the very size and shape of cakes mean that they cook unevenly in the microwave oven. Where I have shielded the outside of the pan with aluminium foil, it is to prevent the outside of the cake from cooking before the centre.

The more 'gluten-dependent' doughs for bread are a disaster. You will either get wet cardboard (tasting as if one of those clever people who puts sawdust into commercial products to lower the calories and up the fibre had sabotaged your kitchen in the night) or a heavy sodden mass that looks and weighs the same as one's child's first attempt at bread baking. You can, however, raise yeasts and doughs splendidly.

Similar, if less intense, problems arise for pastry. High sugar content doughs such as Sweet Tart Pastry (page 383) will brown only slightly. Puff Pastry (page 383) cooked in small batches is sufficiently spectacular—rising higher than any I have baked conventionally—to make it worth putting up with its pale colour (you can always glaze it briefly under the grill). Almost all other pastries toughen before they cook through.

Cakes such as tortes and biscuits that are almost or totally flour-free, using nuts or chocolate to hold them together, can be extraordinarily good. There are several of them in this chapter. Substituting fine oatmeal or rice flour for wheat flour where appropriate works well; but these flours have no gluten and cannot be used in risen cakes. Substituting wholemeal flour or wheat germ for part of the plain flour helps, but results are far from perfect. Note that in the Sponge Cake, the American Chocolate Layer Cake, and the Apricot Tea Cake, cornflour has been substituted for all or part of the flour. Potato flour can be substituted in equal quantities in all recipes where cornflour is used. If you love to bake and want to experiment, this is a direction that might well be worth following. Please, let me know what happens.

I have tried hundreds of recipes, most of them discarded as total disasters or less than marvellous. Here are the very worthy survivors.

CAKES

All of these recipes were developed and tested in full-power ovens: 650 to 700 watts. In a medium-power oven (around 500 watts) they take about half again as long. Some recipes have been tested for lower wattages. For the others, I am sorry, but you are on your own. In some cases you cannot make a full-size cake in a small oven.

If you have never baked cakes in the microwave oven before, there are things I should warn you about so you are not surprised. As they cook, egg-risen cakes will look like soufflés that are about to spill over, but actually they will deflate instead. When taken from the oven or the pan, they will not look entirely familiar. Many cakes will shrink more from the sides of the tins than conventional cakes. There is no surface browning, and they may seem slightly moist. This extra moisture will generally be absorbed as the cake sits. When you turn the cake out, if it seems gelatinous on the bottom, put it back in the oven, as is, for 1 minute at 100%. If cake are not iced immediately, they should be tightly wrapped in polythene, since they have formed no protective crust to keep in the moisture. This open texture is perfect for icing.

Soufflé dishes or moulds vary in thickness and in the structure of their upper edge. If possible, use glass soufflé dishes. They heat more quickly and cool off more quickly than ceramic. Since the glass soufflé dishes often come in nests, you will have all the sizes you may need.

Tins are prepared in a number of ways to permit the cakes to rise and/or cook properly. Tins should be prepared as indicated for best results. Sometimes the outside—not the bottom—of the pan is wrapped in aluminium foil. This helps certain cakes to cook through before the edges get overcooked. Some tins are prepared by being buttered and then coated with sugar to keep the cakes moist and to help them rise. This may leave a moist layer on the bottom of the cake. We find that as the cake sits unmoulded, the moisture absorbs. If you dislike the moisture, try lining the mould with paper towels as for Sponge Cake (page 358).

APRICOT TEA CAKE

This is a light and lovely moist cake to serve plain with tea or, at the end of a meal, with espresso. Its appearance will be like that of the Sponge Cake, but it will have orange-coloured flakes. Use leftovers to make a trifle. *Serves 8*

15 g/½ oz unsalted butter
100 g/3½ oz plus 2 tablespoons caster sugar
6 eggs, separated
4 tablespoons Sweet Apricot Purée (page 386)

Pinch sea salt
60 g/2 oz cornflour, sifted
1 tablespoon vanilla essence
Apricot Glaze (page 384) (optional)

1 Heat butter in a 2 litre/3½ pint soufflé dish, uncovered, at 100% for 1 minute. Remove from oven and spread melted butter around dish to coat. Coat bottom and sides of dish with 2 tablespoons sugar.

2 Beat egg yolks and remaining sugar until light and lemon-coloured, about 2 minutes. Fold in apricot purée, salt, cornflour and vanilla.

3 In a clean bowl, whisk egg whites to soft peaks. Fold one third of whites into yolk mixture and combine well. Fold in remaining whites. Pour into prepared soufflé dish. Cook, uncovered, at 100% for 7 minutes.

4 Remove from oven. Let cool for 5 minutes. Turn out carefully on to a serving plate. Glaze with Apricot Glaze, if desired. If not serving immediately, store tightly wrapped in two layers of polythene.

To make a half-size cake in a small oven. Halve all ingredients. Cook in a 1.5 litre/2½ pint soufflé dish for 9 minutes 30 seconds, using a turntable.

SPONGE CAKE

This is a tremendously useful cake. Served as a whole cake, icing sugar can be sifted over it using a paper doily as a pattern—charming for tea. As layers, it can be made into a Big City Strawberry Shortcake (page 360) or the all-time favourites for which variations follow. *Makes 1 cake, or 2 layers*

7 eggs, separated
200 g/7 oz plus 1 tablespoon caster sugar
1 tablespoon boiling water

1 teaspoon vanilla essence
60 g/2 oz plain flour
60 g/2 oz cornflour

1 Line bottom and sides of a 2 litre/3½ pint soufflé dish with paper towels cut to fit. Cut a 10 cm/4 inch wide strip of parchment paper long enough to encircle the dish; secure to outside of dish with string to form a 2.5 cm/1 inch collar above rim.

2 Beat egg yolks for 30 seconds, until eggs begin to thicken. Gradually beat in 100 g/3½ oz of the sugar and continue beating until very thick, about 2 minutes. If not using an electric beater, this will have to be carried out in a bowl placed over a saucepan of hot water.

3 Stir in water and vanilla essence. Sift together flour and cornflour and gently fold into mixture, about a third at a time.

4 In a clean bowl, whisk egg whites until frothy. Add remaining 1 tablespoon sugar and whisk until soft peaks form. Stir about one quarter of the whites into mixture, then fold in remaining whites.

5 Pour mixture into prepared dish. Cook, uncovered, at 100% for 5 minutes 30 seconds or just until set. Do not overcook or the cake will toughen.

6 Remove from oven and let cool on a wire rack for 10 minutes. Turn cake out on to rack; gently peel off paper towel; let cool completely.

7 If desired, cut horizontally into 2 equal layers, using a bread knife or serrated metal spatula.

To make a half-size cake in a small oven. Use 4 eggs and halve remaining ingredients. Cook in a 1.5 litre/2½ pint soufflé dish for 8 minutes, using a turntable.

VARIATIONS

CHOCOLATE-HAZELNUT SANDWICH CAKE Split cake into 2 layers. Spread bottom layer with Hazelnut Cream (page 367). Replace top layer. Coat with Ganache (page 387).

LEMON SANDWICH CAKE Add 1 teaspoon grated lemon zest to the cake mixture before baking. Split into layers. Spread bottom layer with Lemon Curd (page 386). Replace top layer. Glaze with Apricot-Lemon Glaze (page 385).

CHOCOLATE TRUFFLE SANDWICH CAKE Split cake into 2 layers. Make a double quantity of Ganache (page 387). Into one half of the warm Ganache, beat until smooth 60 g/2 oz unsalted butter and 1 tablespoon brandy. Spread Ganache with added butter on bottom layer. Replace top layer. Pour on remaining, plain Ganache. When Ganache is set, top cake with shaved bittersweet chocolate.

BIG CITY STRAWBERRY SHORTCAKE

— • • —

When I was growing up in New York City, the original Lindy's restaurant, domain of Leo Lindy himself, was going strong. There they served the most glorious of strawberry shortcakes. I was driven to re-create my Big City Strawberry Shortcake. Variations with other berries are given, but nothing quite matches the grandeur of the layers separated and topped with oversize whole strawberries. *Serves 6 to 8*

1 tablespoon plus 1 teaspoon powdered gelatine	4 tablespoons caster sugar
4 tablespoons cold water	1 Sponge Cake (page 358)
750 ml/1¼ pints double cream	600 g/1¼ lb strawberries, washed and hulled

1 In a 250 ml/8 fl oz glass jug or bowl, sprinkle gelatine over water. Heat, uncovered, at 100% for 1 minute.

2 Remove from oven and let cool (do not allow to harden).

3 Whip cream until nearly doubled in bulk. Beat in sugar. Gradually beat in gelatine and continue beating until stiff. Refrigerate for 15 minutes before using.

4 Split cake into 2 layers. Place bottom layer, cut side up, on a serving plate. Spread with 1 cm/½ inch layer of cream. Arrange a layer of berries, bottoms down, over the cream. Cover with more cream to make an even layer. Top with second cake layer, and spread top and sides with more cream. Cover top densely with a layer of beautiful strawberries.

VARIATIONS

BLUEBERRY BASH Replace each strawberry layer with a solid layer of blueberries. This will take about 600 g/1¼ lb. Drizzle some Blueberry Sauce (page 336) over all and pass additional sauce in a pitcher.

PERFECT PEAR SHORTCAKE Make 2 Sponge Cakes, split each into 2 layers, and brush top of each layer with a glaze of 100 g/3½ oz quince or other pale green jelly warmed with 1 tablespoon water. Replace strawberries with 6 poached pears (see Dictionary), cut lengthways into thin slices. Add 2 to 3 tablespoons Poire William (pear brandy) to cream mixture when adding sugar. Drizzle Raspberry Sauce (page 379) over top and on dish around base of cake.

AMERICAN CHOCOLATE LAYER CAKE

• • •

Nothing caused as much dispute in the kitchen as whether this cake or the two basic variations was best. The American Chocolate Layer Cake was defended by an American purist who felt that the open texture and medium chocolate intensity produced the most authentic version. The Truffled Chocolate Gâteau has more chocolate and rises higher. And the European Dark Chocolate Cake is broader and flatter, and has a moister, more intense chocolate flavour than either of the other two. It was the crowd pleaser, even though it seemed to me more like torte than the American idea of a layer, or sandwich, cake.

What is shown by comparing the recipes is how relatively minor changes in the proportions of ingredients totally alter the way cakes bake in the microwave oven. It is not just a change in taste, but a change in texture and even dimension.

Makes one 17.5 × 11 cm/7 × 4½ inch cake that can be cut into two 17.5 × 5.5 cm/ 7 × 2¼ inch layers; fill to serve 6 to 8

15 g/½ oz unsalted butter
100 g/3½ oz plus 2 tablespoons caster sugar
125 g/4 oz good-quality plain chocolate

6 eggs, separated
Pinch sea salt
60 g/2 oz cornflour, sifted
1 tablespoon vanilla essence

1 Heat butter in a a 2 litre/3½ pint soufflé dish, uncovered, at 100% for 1 minute. Remove from oven and spread melted butter around inside of dish to coat. Coat bottom and sides of dish with 2 tablespoons of the sugar. Set aside.

2 Place chocolate in a 1 litre/2 pint glass measuring jug. Cover tightly with microwave cling film. Cook at 100% for 2 minutes (1 minute 30 seconds in a combination convection-microwave oven).

3 Pierce film with the tip of a sharp knife, then remove from oven. Beat together egg yolks, salt and remaining sugar until light, about 2 minutes. Stir in melted chocolate, cornflour and vanilla.

4 In a clean bowl, whisk egg whites to soft peaks. Fold one third of the whites into chocolate mixture and stir gently to combine. Fold in remaining whites. Pour mixture into prepared dish. Cook, uncovered, at 100% for 6 minutes.

5 Remove from oven and let stand for 5 minutes. Turn out on to a serving platter. When cool, slice cake horizontally into 2 layers. Fill and ice with Chocolate Fudge Icing (page 362). If not icing cake immediately, wrap tightly in polythene.

To make a half-size cake in a small oven. Halve all ingredients. Cook in a 1 litre/ 2 pint soufflé dish for 7 minutes, using turntable.

VARIATIONS

TRUFFLED CHOCOLATE GÂTEAU Double the quantity of chocolate and heat for 3 minutes 30 seconds (2 minutes to 2 minutes 30 seconds in a combination convection-microwave oven). Proceed as for American Chocolate Layer Cake, cooking cake for 8 minutes. Cake will be 17.5 × 12.5 cm/7 × 5 inches. Split into 3 layers, each 2 cm/¾ inch thick. Fill between layers with Chocolate Truffle mixture (page 376) and glaze with Ganache (page 387). (To make a half-size cake in a small oven, halve all ingredients and cook in a 1 litre/2 pint soufflé dish for 8 minutes, using a turntable.)

EUROPEAN DARK CHOCOLATE CAKE Double the quantity of chocolate and heat for 3 minutes 30 seconds (2 minutes to 2 minutes 30 seconds in a combination convection-microwave oven). Use 5 eggs and reduce cornflour to 40 g/1⅓ oz. Proceed as for American Chocolate Layer Cake, cooking cake for 6 minutes. Cake will be 17.5 × 6 cm/7 × 2½ inches. Leave whole or split into 2 layers. Fill with Chocolate Truffle mixture (page 376) and glaze with Ganache (page 387). (To make a half-size cake in a small oven, halve all ingredients and cook in a 1 litre/2 pint soufflé dish for 8 minutes 30 seconds, using a turntable.)

ORANGE CHOCOLATE CAKE To European Dark Chocolate Cake add grated zest of 1 orange to mixture and 1 tablespoon orange liqueur to icing.

MOCHA CAKE To any of the three basic cakes, add 1 tablespoon instant espresso powder to mixture and 1 tablespoon coffee liqueur to icing.

SACHERTORTE Spread bottom layer of European Dark Chocolate Cake with raspberry jam and add 1 tablespoon raspberry liqueur to icing.

CHOCOLATE FUDGE ICING

I have never felt that I had to invent the wheel. One of my favourite chocolate icings is in *Joy of Cooking*. I have adapted it for microwave cooking. *Makes enough to fill and ice one 17.5 cm/7 inch sandwich cake*

200 g/7 oz caster sugar
125 ml/4 fl oz double cream
60 g/2 oz plain chocolate, cut into 2.5 cm/1 inch pieces

½ teaspoon vanilla essence
30 g/1 oz unsalted butter

1 Stir together sugar and cream in a 1 litre/2 pint glass measuring jug. Cover tightly with microwave cling film. Cook at 100% for 4 minutes.

2 Pierce film with the tip of a sharp knife, then remove from oven. Uncover and add chocolate and vanilla, stirring well until chocolate is melted. Let cool to room temperature.

3 When chocolate mixture has cooled, beat in butter. Continue beating until mixture is of spreading consistency, about 5 minutes. If icing is slightly warm, refrigerate for 15 minutes until slightly thickened.

REINE DE SABA

A classic French cake adapted for the microwave oven—flour is changed to cornflour—this is about as rich and elegant as a simple chocolate sandwich cake can get. It will last for several days if you want to make it ahead and if you can keep people from nibbling at it. *Serves 6*

125 g/4 oz plus 10 g/⅓ oz unsalted butter
45 g/1½ oz currants
2 tablespoons bourbon whiskey
125 g/4 oz plain chocolate
135 g/4½ oz caster sugar

3 eggs, separated
40 g/1⅓ oz cornflour, sifted
30 g/1 oz blanched almonds, finely ground
Ganache (page 387), for glazing

1 Butter the bottom of a round 20 × 5 cm/8 × 2 inch dish using 10 g/⅓ oz of the butter, and cover bottom with greaseproof or parchment paper cut to fit. Shield sides of dish: Cut a strip of aluminium foil 7.5 cm/3 inches wide and long enough to encircle dish; wrap foil around outside of dish and secure by folding excess 2.5 cm/1 inch over rim.

2 Put currants in a 500 ml/1 pint glass measuring jug and pour bourbon whiskey over. Heat, loosely covered with paper towels, at 100% for 2 minutes. Remove from oven and reserve.

3 Place chocolate in a clean 500 ml/1 pint glass measuring jug and heat, uncovered, at 100% for 2 minutes (1 minute 30 seconds in a combination convection-microwave oven).

4 With an electric beater, cream remaining butter and sugar for 2 minutes, until light.

5 Add egg yolks one at a time, incorporating each thoroughly before adding the next. Stir in chocolate, cornflour, almonds and currants.

6 In a clean bowl, whisk egg whites until stiff. Fold into yolk mixture until just incorporated.

7 Pour into prepared dish. Cook, uncovered, at 100% for 2 minutes longer. (If using a small oven, cook, uncovered, for 5 minutes using a turntable. Remove foil shield; cook 4 minutes longer.)

8 Remove cake from oven, cover with a plate and let sit for 10 minutes.

9 Turn out on to a cooling rack. When completely cool, glaze with Ganache.

ITALIAN CHOCOLATE CAKE

As I looked for a virtually flourless cake, I remembered Edda Servi Machlin's Egg-White Chocolate Cake from her book, *Classic Cuisine of the Italian Jews*. With her kind permission, I have adapted it to the microwave oven. *Makes one 17.5 cm/7 inch cake*

8 egg whites
45 g/1½ oz unsweetened cocoa powder, sifted
200 g/7 oz caster sugar
3 tablespoons vegetable oil
45 g/1½ oz shelled hazelnuts, toasted, skins removed and coarsely chopped

45 g/1½ oz blanched almonds, toasted and coarsely chopped
30 g/1 oz shelled walnuts, toasted and coarsely chopped
½ teaspoon sea salt
Icing sugar, for dusting cake

1 Shield the sides of a 20 × 7.5 cm/8 × 3 inch round glass or ceramic dish: Cut a strip of aluminium foil 10 cm/4 inches wide and long enough to encircle dish; wrap outside of dish and secure by folding excess 2.5 cm/1 inch over rim.

2 Stir together 2 of the egg whites, the cocoa powder, sugar and oil until combined. Stir in nuts and set aside.

3 Whisk remaining 6 egg whites and salt to stiff peaks.

4 Fold one third of whites into nut mixture until well incorporated. Gently fold in remaining whites and pour mixture into prepared dish.

5 Cover dish loosely with paper towels and cook at 100% for 2 minutes. (If using a small oven, cook for 4 minutes, using a turntable.)

6 Remove from oven and cover dish with a plate. Allow cake to stand, covered, for 5 minutes (cake will continue to cook).

7 Turn cake on to a serving plate and dust with icing sugar. Serve when cool.

PUMPERNICKEL TORTE

This torte is made in two layers, cooked successively in the same dish. It will be easiest, therefore, to keep microwave cling film and cooling racks handy when making it. *Serves 10 to 12*

30 g/1 oz soft butter, or 1 tablespoon
   light oil
75 g/2½ oz blanched almonds
30 g/1 oz good-quality plain or
   bittersweet chocolate
175 g/6 oz fine, dry Pumpernickel
   Crumbs (page 307)

150 g/5 oz caster sugar
6 whole eggs, separated
325 g/11 oz raspberry jam
Ganache (page 387), to glaze cake
   (optional)

1 Thoroughly coat the interior of a 25 cm/10 inch flan dish with half of the butter, or brush on half of the oil.

2 Place almonds and chocolate in the container of a food processor. Process until finely ground (do not overprocess). Add to crumbs and stir to combine.

3 Beat together 100 g/3½ oz of sugar and the egg yolks until light and lemon-coloured, about 2 minutes.

4 Whisk egg whites to soft peaks. Whisking constantly, add remaining sugar by the tablespoon until incorporated and whites hold stiff peaks. Fold one third of whites into yolk mixture. Fold in half of crumb mixture, then fold in remaining whites and crumb mixture.

5 Pour one half of mixture into prepared dish. Cook, uncovered, at 100% for 4 minutes.

6 Remove from oven. Gently turn out cake on to a wire rack and let cool. Grease dish again with remaining butter or oil. Pour remaining mixture into prepared dish. Cook as above.

7 Remove from oven. Remove cake to a rack to cool as in step 6. Let cakes stand for 5 minutes. Wrap each tightly in 2 sheets of polythene until ready to use. (Cake may be prepared to this point up to 1 day in advance.)

8 Assemble the cake: Sandwich layers together with jam and brush sides of cake with jam. Glaze with Ganache, if desired.

NUT CAKE WITH HAZELNUT CREAM

— • • • —

The Austrians love their nut cakes almost as much as they do their strudel. This recipe was developed from a turn-of-the-century Viennese cookery book; it needed almost no modification. The luxury-loving Viennese never were very keen on flour in their tortes.

The Hazelnut Cream and the Coffee Glaze are splendid recipes for other uses. The cream could go between Sponge Cake layers, the glaze on simple biscuits. *Serves 8 to 10 (it is very rich)*

Unsalted butter, for the dish
150 g/5 oz caster sugar
6 eggs, separated
125 g/4 oz shelled walnuts, finely ground

45 g/1½ oz fine, dry Breadcrumbs (page 306) or store-bought, unseasoned breadcrumbs
Hazelnut Cream (see following recipe)
Coffee Glaze (see following recipe)

1 Butter a 30 × 5 cm/12 × 2 inch round dish and coat with 2 teaspoons of sugar.

2 Beat together egg yolks and remaining sugar until lemon-coloured.

3 In a clean bowl, whisk egg whites until stiff. Fold one third of the whites into yolk mixture. Fold in walnuts and Breadcrumbs. Fold in remaining whites.

4 Pour into prepared dish and cover loosely with paper towels. Cook at 100% for 6 minutes (top will look moist).

5 Remove from oven. Allow to cool in dish for 8 to 10 minutes. Turn out on to cooling rack.

7 Using a serrated knife, slice cake in half horizontally to make 2 layers. Spread Hazelnut Cream on bottom layer and place second layer over the first. Cover tightly and refrigerate while preparing Coffee Glaze. (You may prepare the cake to this point up to 1 day in advance.)

8 Prepare Coffee Glaze. As soon as it is ready, pour it over top of cake. Do not spread glaze; simply tilt cake to distribute glaze over top. Let cool to room temperature.

HAZELNUT CREAM

◆ ◆ ◆

250 /8 oz unsalted butter
4 tablespoons caster sugar

125 g/4 oz hazelnut Praline Powder
 (page 388)
2 tablespoons strong coffee

1 Cream butter and sugar until light. Beat in Praline Powder. Add coffee and beat until creamy.

2 If not using immediately, store in a cool, not refrigerated, place.

COFFEE GLAZE

◆ ◆ ◆

125 g/4 oz icing sugar

2 tablespoons strong coffee

1 Combine sugar and coffee in a 500 ml/1 pint glass measuring jug. Cover tightly with microwave cling film. Cook at 100% for 3 to 4 minutes.

2 Pierce film with the tip of a sharp knife, then remove from oven and use hot glaze immediately.

BISCUITS

Most biscuits should be made in a conventional oven. But, strangely, the more elegant and difficult biscuits—thin lacy Florentines, Ginger Lace Biscuits, and Tuiles—are easy and rapid in the microwave oven, which caramelizes them just enough without risk of scorching. These are typically the finishing touches served with homemade sorbets, ice creams and poached fruits. For the 'more is never enough' crowd, they can even be served with Bavarian creams and custards. If only a few biscuits are needed to go with a dessert, extra mixture can be refrigerated or even frozen. The mixture is so rich that it will defrost rapidly at room temperature.

Do not substitute plastic jugs for glass in these recipes. The mixtures will cook too rapidly.

FLORENTINES

These may be the most elegant of the thin, crisp accompaniment biscuits. They are studded with the fresh zests of lemons and tangerines and redolent of sliced almonds.

I like these biscuits left plain, but it is always possible to gild the lily. They can be spread on the bottom with melted chocolate. Unglazed, these biscuits will last for several days in a tightly closed tin. *Makes 2½ to 3 dozen*

125 g/4 oz cold unsalted butter
4 tablespoons soured cream
100 g/3½ oz caster sugar
90 g/3 oz honey
1 tablespoon finely grated tangerine or satsuma zest

1 tablespoon finely grated lemon zest
45 g/1½ oz blanched flaked almonds
40 g/1⅓ oz plain flour, sifted
Vegetable oil, for the cooking platter
Bittersweet chocolate (optional)

1 Heat butter in a 500 ml/1 pint glass measuring jug, loosely covered with paper towels, at 100% for 2 minutes.

2 Stir together butter, soured cream, sugar, honey, zests and almonds until well blended. Stir in flour just enough to mix.

3 Lightly coat a 30 cm/12 inch round flat platter with oil. Drop teaspoonfuls of mixture in a ring inside rim of platter, with 5 cm/2 inches between each biscuit (cook 6 to 8 at a time). Cook, uncovered, at 100% for 3 minutes.

4 As oven heats with successive batches, cooking time will shorten to 2 minutes 30 seconds. Allow each batch to cool for 2 minutes after baking, then remove with a metal palette knife to cooling rack.

5 When completely cool, spread flat side of each biscuit with melted chocolate, if desired.

GINGER LACE BISCUITS

Also called Brandy Snaps, these are a classic teatime treat from before Mrs. Beeton right up to the present. *Makes 2½ dozen*

60 g/2 oz cold unsalted butter
55 g/scant 2 oz dark brown sugar
80 g/2⅔ oz golden syrup or cane
  molasses syrup
½ teaspoon ground ginger
60 g/2 oz plain flour, sifted

1 teaspoon fresh lemon juice
Vegetable oil, for the cooking platter
500 ml/15 fl oz double cream
  (optional)
45 g/1½ oz crystallized ginger, diced
  (optional)

1 Combine butter, sugar, golden syrup and ground ginger in a 1 litre/2 pint glass measuring jug and cook, uncovered, at 100% for 4 minutes.

2 Remove from oven an briskly stir in flour and lemon juice.

3 Lightly coat a 30 cm/12 inch round platter with vegetable oil. Drop teaspoonfuls of mixture in a ring inside rim of platter, with 5 cm/2 inches between each biscuit (cook about 6 biscuits per patch). Cook, uncovered, at 100% for 2 minutes 30 seconds.

4 As oven heats with successive batches, cooking times will shorten to 2 minutes. Allow each batch to cool for 1 minute after baking.

5 Oil the handle of a wooden spoon. With a metal palette knife, carefully lift each biscuit off platter and gently wrap it around handle. As each biscuit is shaped, transfer it to cooling rack.

6 If desired, just before serving, make Ginger Cream: whip cream to soft peaks. Fold in diced ginger. Using a piping bag fitted with a large star nozzle, pipe cream into both ends of each biscuit.

Note. Biscuits may be left flat and served without cream, as for Florentines (page 368).

TUILES

• ◆ •

These are the most common of the thin and crisp French petit fours biscuits. They get their name from their supposed resemblance to the classic terracotta tiles on the roofs (*tuiles*) of certain French houses.

As with Ginger Lace Cookies, the oven will heat up with successive batches. The same precautions apply. *Makes 2 to 3 dozen*

60 g/2 oz cold unsalted butter
60 g/2 oz blanched almonds or shelled walnuts, finely ground
100 g/3½ oz caster sugar

2 egg whites
1 egg yolk
1 teaspoon vanilla essence
Vegetable oil, for the cooking platter

1 Heat butter in a 500 ml/1 pint glass measuring jug, uncovered, at 100% for 2 minutes.

2 Place remaining ingredients except oil in the container of a food processor and process until well combined. With the motor running, pour in melted butter in a thin stream.

3 Generously grease a 30 cm/12 inch round platter. Drop mixture by teaspoonfuls 5 cm/2 inches apart (make about 4 biscuits per batch). Cook, uncovered, at 100% for 2 minutes 30 seconds to 3 minutes. (As the oven heats with successive batches, cooking time will be shorter.)

4 Remove from oven. Lift biscuits off platter with a metal palette knife and drape over the handle of a wooden spoon to cool.

OAT CRISPS

• ◆ •

With her kind permision, I have adapted this recipe of Maida Heatter's from *Great American Cookies* for the microwave oven. These delicious wafers give a sensation of instant health. They would be good with coffee or caramel ice cream or Bourbon Peaches (page 338). *Makes 6 dozen*

30 g/1 oz unsalted butter
3 eggs
¾ teaspoon ground cinnamon
1 teaspoon vanilla essence
½ teaspoon sea salt

300 g/10 oz caster sugar
4 teaspoons baking powder
275 g/9 oz quick-cooking porridge oats
45 g/1½ oz plain flour, sifted
Vegetable oil, for the cooking platter

1 Heat butter in a 250 ml/8 fl oz glass jug or bowl, uncovered, at 100% for 1 minute 30 seconds. Reserve.

2 Beat eggs until foamy. Add cinnamon, vanilla, salt and sugar and beat until well mixed, about 2 minutes.

3 Add melted butter and remaining ingredients except vegetable oil and blend well.

4 Lightly coat a 30 cm/12 inch round, flat platter with vegetable oil. Drop the mixture by ½ teaspoonfuls on to the platter in a ring around the inside rim. (Make about 6 biscuits per batch.) Cook, uncovered, at 100% for 3 minutes, until biscuits are just golden at centres.

5 As oven heats with successive batches, cooking time will shorten to 2 minutes 30 seconds. With a metal palette knife, remove biscuits to a rack to cool. Store in an airtight container for up to a week.

Note. Mixture can be make a day in advance and kept, tightly covered, in the refrigerator.

FUDGY BROWNIES

Everybody has his or her own notion of what makes the perfect brownie. I like the fudgy ones thick with nuts and raisins. Make these in small batches. They cook so quickly you can have them fresh whenever you want. It takes about 5 minutes to whip them up and 8 minutes to cook them. You don't have to shield them; the tight covering helps them to cook evenly. *Makes* 16

125 g/4 oz unsalted butter	1 teaspoon vanilla essence
90 g/3 oz plain chocolate	Pinch sea salt
4 tablespoons caster sugar	¼ teaspoon baking powder
220 g/7½ oz light brown sugar	90 g/3 oz plain flour, sifted
2 eggs	

1 Place butter and chocolate in a 2 litre/3½ pint glass jug or bowl. Cover tightly with microwave cling film. Cook at 100% for 2 minutes.

2 Pierce film with the tip of a sharp knife, then remove from oven. Uncover and whisk until combined. Whisk in all sugar and then eggs, one at a time. Stir in vanilla.

3 Sift together salt, baking powder and flour. Fold into chocolate mixture. Pour into a 20 cm/8 inch square or oval dish. Cover tightly with microwave cling film. Cook at 100% for 4 minutes. Pierce film, then uncover and cook for 2 minutes longer.

4 Remove from oven. Cut into squares and let stand until cool.

VARIATIONS

CHUNKY FUDGY BROWNIES When folding in dry ingredients, stir in 45 g/1½ oz raisins and 45 g/1½ oz coarsely chopped walnuts. Cook as for Fudgy Brownies.

REBECCA'S RASPBERRY BROWNIES Substitute 80 g/2⅔ oz Raspberry Jam (page 393) for the caster sugar and omit raisins and walnuts. Proceed as for Fudgy Brownies.

CAKEY BROWNIES Reduce chocolate to 60 g/2 oz and omit caster sugar, vanilla, raisins and walnuts. Decrease flour to 80 g/2⅔ oz and increase baking powder to ½ teaspoon. For the sugar, you can use either light brown or caster. Proceed as for Fudgy Brownies, cooking, covered, for 3 minutes. Uncover and cook for 2 minutes longer.

THE ORIGINAL CHOCOLATE SANDWICH BISCUIT

◆ ◆ ◆

One day for pure escapism, I was reading *A Thousand Ways to Please a Husband, with Bettina's Best Recipes*, by Louise Bennett Weaver and Helen Cowles Le Cron, published in 1917, a morally edifying text based on the notion that good cooking and prudent housekeeping would render a marriage not only happy, but endlessly romantic in a vine-covered cottage. It was filled with marvellous cautionary tales about good wives and bad wives who were rescued by Bettina's smarmy example. Oh, for simpler times. Among the recipes, I found one for dry chocolate biscuits to be sandwiched together with White Mountain Frosting.

They keep for a long time and would be nice with a cup of coffee or a glass of milk. (I don't know if Bettina would approve of the caffeine.) *Makes 12*

45 g/1½ oz plain chocolate
30 g/1 oz unsalted butter
4 tablespoons caster sugar
1 egg

45 g/1½ oz fine, dry Breadcrumbs (page 306) or unseasoned, store-bought breadcrumbs
½ teaspoon vanilla essence
White Mountain Frosting (see following recipe)

1 Place chocolate in a 500 ml/1 pint glass measuring jug. Heat, uncovered, at 100% for 1 minute 30 seconds to 2 minutes, until melted.

2 Remove from oven and set aside. Cream butter and sugar until light. Beat in egg. Stir in Breadcrumbs, vanilla and melted chocolate.

3 Line a 30 cm/12 inch round platter with parchment or greaseproof paper, cut to fit. Spread batter in a thin layer over entire platter. Cook, uncovered, at 100% for 3 to 4 minutes, just until firm.

4 Remove from oven and allow to cool. Gently turn biscuit circle out on to a clean surface. Peel parchment from bottom. Cut out 24 biscuits using a 4 cm/ 1½ inch round biscuit cutter.

5 Sandwich two biscuits together with White Mountain Frosting (page 373) or buttercream as filling.

WHITE MOUNTAIN FROSTING

* • •

This frosting is normally made for cakes, not just for sandwiching biscuits. It's a sort of marshmallow event. If you want to fill as well as ice the cake, you will need double quantity. *Makes enough to ice but not to also fill a cake*

200 g/7 oz caster sugar
⅛ teaspoon cream of tartar
4 tablespoons water

1 egg white
½ teaspoon vanilla essence

1 Combine sugar, cream of tartar and water in a 1 litre/2 pint glass measuring jug. Cover tightly with microwave cling film. Cook at 100% for 5 to 6 minutes, until syrup registers 116° C/238° F on a sugar thermometer (soft ball stage).

2 Beat egg white until foamy.

3 Pierce film covering syrup to release steam, then remove from oven. Beating constantly, add sugar syrup to white in a thin stream until incorporated. Continue to beat until cool (mixture will thicken as it cools). Beat in vanilla.

4 If not using immediately, cover bowl with a damp towel for up to 30 minutes.

To make enough to ice and fill a cake. Double ingredients, cooking sugar mixture for 7 minutes 30 seconds.

VARIATION

COCONUT FROSTING Dry 125 g/4 oz unsweetened grated coconut (page 306). Fold into double quantity White Mountain Frosting. Fill and ice a sandwich cake. Sprinkle 45 g/1 ½ oz more grated coconut on top and sides.

ALMOND SHORTBREAD

This dry cake, from the usually abstemious Scots, is so rich in butter that it is a concealed sin. This almond version may just go it one better. Make ahead to keep on hand for unexpected guests. *Makes two 22.5 cm/9 inch round shortbreads*

175 g/6 oz plain flour
125 g/4 oz cornflour
165 g/5½ oz blanched almonds, toasted and ground (see Note below)
200 g/7 oz caster sugar

125 g/4 oz cold unsalted butter, cut into 1 cm/½ inch pieces
2 to 3 tablespoons water
10 g/⅓ oz softened unsalted butter

1 Combine flour, cornflour, almonds and sugar in the container of a food processor. Process briefly to combine. Add butter, pulsing on and off, just until mixture is crumbly. Add water and pulse twice, or just until mixture pulls together into a mass.

2 Divide dough in half. Shape each half into a 20 cm/8 inch round on a sheet of polythene.

3 Thoroughly coat a 30 cm/12 inch flat platter with the softened butter. Turn one round on to the platter and peel off the polythene. Cook, uncovered, at 100% for 2 minutes 30 seconds to 3 minutes, just until set.

4 Remove from oven. Carefully transfer the shortbread to a flat surface to cool. Score the shortbread lightly into 8 wedges. Cook and score the second round.

5 Let shortbreads cool completely. Store in a tightly covered tin.

Note. To toast 165 g/5½ oz blanched flaked almonds, place in a 35 × 27.5 × 5 cm/14 × 11 × 2 inch dish and cook, uncovered, at 100% for 10 minutes, stirring twice.

PEANUT BRITTLE

◆—◆—◆

This is a childhood delight that cooks quickly and without risk in the microwave oven. Don't eat it with weak teeth. Don't expect to keep it for long, either; it just seems to vanish. *Makes 750 g/1½ lb*

200 g/7 oz caster sugar
165 g/5½ golden syrup
125 ml/4 fl oz water

250 g/8 oz shelled raw peanuts,
    blanched or unblanched
Vegetable oil, for the baking sheet

1 Combine sugar, syrup and water in a 2 litre/3½ pint glass jug or bowl. Cook, uncovered, at 100% for 3 minutes.

2 Remove from oven and stir thoroughly. Add peanuts; stir again. Cover tightly with microwave cling film. Cook at 100% for 15 minutes.

3 Lightly coat a palette knife and a large baking sheet or 40 × 30 cm/16 × 12 inch marble slab with vegetable oil. Pierce film to release steam, then remove from oven. Uncover carefully. Pour mixture on to oiled surface. With the oiled palette knife, spread peanuts to distribute them evenly through cooling syrup. Let harden.

4 When brittle is cool, break into chunks with a wooden mallet or rolling pin. Store in an airtight container.

CHOCOLATE PECAN TURTLES

◆—◆—◆

These rich sweets are an American childhood dream with chewy caramel and the richest of chocolate coatings. They may be unfamiliar; but not once eaten. *Makes about 2 dozen turtles*

135 g/4½ shelled pecan halves
100 g/3½ oz light brown sugar
100 g/3½ oz golden syrup
175 ml/6 fl oz double cream
Pinch sea salt

1 teaspoon vegetable oil, for work
    surface
1 teaspoon vanilla essence
175 g/6 oz plain chocolate, broken into
    small pieces

1 Spread pecan halves in a single layer in a 27.5 22.5 × 5 cm/11 × 9 × 2 inch rectangular dish. Cook, uncovered, at 100% for 4 minutes 30 seconds. Remove from oven and reserve.

2 Stir together sugar, syrup, cream and salt in a 2 litre/3½ pint glass jug or bowl. Cover tightly with microwave cling film. Cook at 100% for 5 minutes. Prick film to release steam. Leaving jug or bowl in oven, uncover and stir mixture. Re-cover and cook at 100% for 4 minutes. Prick cling film to release steam.

3 Remove from oven and uncover carefully. Stir in reserved pecans and vanilla.

4 Lightly oil a marble slab or baking sheet and a fork. Using the oiled fork, drop mixture by teaspoonful amounts on to oiled surface. Let stand to harden.

5 When caramel is hard enough to handle, place chocolate in a 500 ml/1 pint glass measuring jug. Cover with a double layer of paper towels. Cook at 100% for 2 minutes 30 seconds.

6 Remove from oven and uncover. Dip each caramel into chocolate, covering top half of the sweet. Place on greaseproof paper and let stand at room temperature until chocolated has hardened. Do not refrigerate.

CHOCOLATE TRUFFLES

Everybody seems to love truffles. There are truffles made without the butter, but I prefer these richer ones. I also prefer truffles that are rolled in unsweetened cocoa; but there are those who think they are eating a truffle only if it has been dipped in chocolate. To dip in chocolate, melt 90 g/3 oz bittersweet chocolate (page 433). Allow to cool to room temperature. Dip cold formed truffles (using a toothpick if you want), one by one, into melted chocolate. Set on a cake rack over a baking sheet. When all truffles have been dipped, place in refrigerator. *Makes about 30 truffles*

1 recipe quantity Ganache (page 387), at room temperature
60 g/2 oz unsalted butter

1 tablespoon Cognac
90 g/3 oz unsweetened cocoa powder, sifted, for coating truffles

1 Beat together all ingredients, except cocoa, until well combined. Pour into a 1 litre/2 pint soufflé dish. Chill for 2 hours.

2 When thoroughly chilled, scoop up balls of truffle mixture with a melon baller, dipped in warm water between scoops. Roll each truffle in cocoa powder. Store, tightly covered, refrigerated, in additional cocoa powder.

SWEET SAUCES

There are times when the difference between a ho-hum dessert and a gala one is a good sauce. This little group is quickly made in the microwave oven and can bless everything from ice cream to simple cake to custards and pastry.

CHUNKY BLUEBERRY SAUCE

This luscious sauce is simply perfect over pancakes or ice cream or with shortcake. For a more elegant version to serve with desserts, add 2 tablespoons Poire William (pear brandy) or triple sec to cooked berries and purée through a sieve. See also the Blueberry Sauce that accompanies Light Poached Pears (page 335). *Makes 350 ml/12 fl oz*

300 g/10 oz blueberries   3 tablespoons caster sugar

1 Pick over berries, discarding any that are overripe, green or discoloured. Put into a 1 litre/2 pint glass measuring jug.

2 Sprinkle with sugar. Cover tightly with microwave cling film. Cook at 100% for 3 minutes. Pierce film with the tip of a sharp knife before removing from oven.

CARAMEL SAUCE

Serve this quick and easy sauce warm with Apple Charlotte (page 343), under a square of Puff Pastry (page 383) that has been split in half and filled with Confectioner's Custard (page 381), or poured over ice cream. *Makes 250 ml/ 8 fl oz*

100 g/3½ oz caster sugar   125 ml/4 fl oz double cream
2 tablespoons cold water   15 g/½ oz unsalted butter

1 Combine sugar and water in a 1 litre/2 pint glass measuring jug. Cover tightly with microwave cling film. Cook at 100% for 4 to 5 minutes, until syrup just begins to turn light gold.

2 Pierce film with the tip of a sharp knife, then remove from oven, uncover carefully, and slowly pour in cream. Stir in butter. Cook, uncovered, at 100% for 1 minute to 1 minute 30 seconds, until dark gold.

BUTTERSCOTCH SAUCE

• • •

The major difference between this and Caramel Sauce is that this is much richer. It is the classic sauce for ice cream sundaes. I don't know anybody sophisticated enough to resist its wiles. *makes 500 ml/16 fl oz*

125 g/4 oz unsalted butter
175 g/6 oz light brown sugar
90 g/3 oz golden syrup

2 tablespoons double cream
½ teaspoon sea salt
½ teaspoon vanilla essence

1 Put 60 g/2 oz of the butter and the sugar, syrup, cream and salt in a 2 litre/3½ pint glass jug or bowl. Cover tightly with microwave cling film. Cook at 100% for 5 minutes.

2 Pierce film with the tip of a sharp knife, then remove from oven. Uncover and whisk in vanilla essence and remaining butter. Serve warm or at room temperature.

3 To store, let cool to room temperature and cover tightly; it will keep in the refrigerator for up to 4 months. Reheat for 1 minute, uncovered, at 100%; stir and serve.

CHOCOLATE SAUCE

• • •

Imagine a warm dark pool of this around a steamed pudding dusted with icing sugar. It is also surprisingly good with Light Poached Pears (page 335). *Makes 350 ml/12 fl oz*

125 g/4 oz good-quality plain
  chocolate, broken into 4 cm/1½ inch
  pieces
4 tablespoons strong coffee

30 g/1 oz unsalted butter
2 tablespoons double cream
2 tablespoons dark rum

1 Place all ingredients in a 2 litre/3½ pint glass jug or bowl. Cover tightly with microwave cling film. Cook at 100% for 5 minutes.

2 Pierce with the tip of a sharp knife, then remove from oven. Uncover and whisk sauce until smooth. Serve warm or at room temperature.

Note. This sauce will keep very well refrigerated, in a tightly covered glass jar, for a week or more. Reheat for 1 minute, uncovered, at 100%; stir and serve.

NESSELRODE SAUCE

◆ ◆

There was a time when eating ice cream meant a trip to an ice cream parlour. Eating was done on little marble-topped tables or at a grand Victorian soda fountain. Those were the days of Nesselrode Sauce, too good to be forgotten. *Makes 750 ml/1¼ pints*

1 jar (175 g/6 oz) maraschino cherries, drained and coarsely chopped (juice reserved)
100 g/3½ oz candied mixed fruits
325 g/11 oz orange marmalade

45 g/1½ oz candied ginger, coarsely chopped
150 g/5 oz roasted, unsalted mixed nuts, coarsely chopped
125 ml/4 fl oz dark rum

1 Put all ingredients in a 2 litre/3½ pint jug or bowl. Stir in one half of the reserved maraschino juice.

2 Cook, uncovered, at 100% for 5 minutes.

3 Remove from oven and stir well. Let sauce ripen stored in a tightly covered jar in the refrigerator for at least 2 days. Serve over vanilla ice cream.

Note. The sauce will keep, tightly covered, for months.

FRESH STRAWBERRY SAUCE

◆ ◆

This sauce owes nothing to microwave cooking; but it will be good with many of your microwave-prepared desserts, particularly Big City Strawberry Short-cake (page 360). Serve on the side in a jug. Raspberry Sauce can be made by substituting raspberries for the strawberries and whirring in a food processor or blender. Strain, if desired. *Makes 250 ml/8 fl oz*

350 g/12 oz strawberries, hulled and mashed with a silver fork

½ teaspoon fresh lemon juice
2 tablespoon caster sugar

Combine all ingredients well and allow to macerate for at least 5 minutes before serving.

CRÈME ANGLAISE

I could call this Custard, but it seems so French to me that it would be in disguise in English. A little Crème Anglaise seems to go with every dessert that isn't frozen. Poached fruit—pears, plums and peaches—chocolate mousse and un-iced cakes all enjoy this pairing. The flavour can be varied by substituting rum, triple sec or another alcohol for the vanilla essence. *Makes 600 ml/1 pint*

500 ml/16 fl oz milk
6 egg yolks

4 tablespoons caster sugar
1 teaspoon vanilla essence

1 Heat milk in a 1 litre/2 pint glass measuring jug, uncovered, at 100% for 3 minutes. Remove from oven.

2 Whisk together egg yolks and sugar. Gradually whisk hot milk into egg mixture. Return mixture to jug. Cook, uncovered, at 100% for 2 minutes.

3 Remove from oven and whisk vigorously for 30 seconds. Return to oven and cook for 1 minute longer.

4 Remove from oven. Whisk in vanilla essence. Strain sauce through a fine sieve into a clean bowl. Refrigerate, tightly covered, until ready to use.

To make 250 ml/8 fl oz. Halve all ingredients, cooking milk and egg mixture for only 1 minute 30 seconds. Remove from oven, whisk in vanilla essence, strain, and cover.

SWEET BASICS

There are some sweet things that are not desserts on their own, or accompaniments to desserts. They are parts of desserts. Quick and easy to make in the microwave oven, they permit you to invent your own combinations. See the Index for additional icings, fillings, glazes, toppings and syrups.

CONFECTIONER'S CUSTARD

Filling profiteroles, or forming a thin layer under fruit in large or individual tarts, Confectioner's Custard is widely used. See Sweet Tart Pastry (page 383) and Apricot Glaze (page 384), which is used to brush the raw fruit. If can be flavoured by flavouring the milk as it heats, as in the variations that follow.

Do not try to freeze and defrost. It takes longer to defrost than to make from scratch. Also, Confectioner's Custard made with cornflour loses some thickening when frozen and defrosted. *Makes 600 ml/1 pint*

500 ml/16 fl oz milk
75 g/2½ oz caster sugar
2 tablespoons cornflour

6 egg yolks
2 teaspoons vanilla essence

1 Heat milk in a 1 litre/2 pint glass measuring jug, uncovered, at 100% for 4 minutes. Remove from oven and set aside.

2 Sift together sugar and cornflour. Whisk into egg yolks. Gradually whisk in hot milk. Return mixture to jug and cook, uncovered, at 100% for 2 minutes.

3 Remove from oven and whisk vigorously. Return to oven and cook for 1 minute longer.

4 Remove from oven and whisk in vanilla essence. Strain through a fine sieve into a clean bowl. Refrigerate, tightly covered, until ready to use.

VARIATIONS

CHOCOLATE CONFECTIONER'S CUSTARD When whisking in vanilla, also whisk in 90 g/3 oz of chopped bittersweet chocolate.

COFFEE CONFECTIONER'S CUSTARD When heating milk, add 1½ tablespoons instant coffee or espresso.

RASPBERRY CONFECTIONER'S CUSTARD Instead of whisking in vanilla, stir in 3 tablespoons good raspberry jam and 2 tablespoons Framboise (raspberry liqueur).

ORANGE CONFECTIONER'S CUSTARD Use only 350 ml/12 fl oz milk. When whisking milk into egg-yolk mixture, add 125 ml/4 fl oz orange juice. For vanilla, substitute 2 tablespoons triple sec and the grated zest of 1 large orange.

ALMOND CONFECTIONER'S CUSTARD Substitute an equal quantity of Amaretto or almond essence for the vanilla. At the same time, stir in 4 tablespoons Praline Powder (page 388).

CRUMB CRUSTS

Most crusts do not cook well in the microwave oven—they do not colour and are heavy—but crumb crust, which implies precooked flour, does just fine. Fill with your favourite mixture, or the Lemon Curd (page 386). If filling with a precooked mixture, first cook Crumb Crust, uncovered, at 100% for 2 minutes; let it cool completely before filling. *Makes enough for one 20–22.5 cm/8–9 inch crust*

PUMPERNICKEL CRUST
90 g/3 oz fine, dry dark Pumpernickel Crumbs (page 307)
30 g/1 oz blanched almonds, coarsely ground
15 g/½ oz bittersweet chocolate, grated
4 tablespoons caster sugar
60 g/2 oz unsalted butter, melted

MELBA TOAST CRUST
90 g/3 oz melba roast crumbs
4 tablespoons caster sugar
Grated zest of ½ orange
Grated zest of ½ lemon
60 g/2 oz unsalted butter, melted

BISCUIT CRUST
90 g/3 oz digestive biscuits, crushed
4 tablespoons caster sugar
Grated zest of 1 orange
¼ teaspoon ground ginger
60 g/2 oz unsalted butter, melted

Combine ingredients and mix well. Press firmly over bottom and up sides of a 20–22.5 cm/8–9 inch glass pie tin or flan dish.

SWEET TART PASTRY

·•·

Because of the high proportion of sugar, this pastry cooks well and will tan, if not brown. It is a classic tart shell to fill with a Confectioner's Custard (page 381), a layer of fruit, and a light topping of Apricot Glaze (page 384).

If you want to roll out several pastry cases at one time, do. Then freeze in disposable pie or flan tins. Stack when frozen. When needed, remove frozen pastry to microwave-safe pie tin or flan dish. Bake frozen exactly as for fresh pastry. *Makes enough for one 22.5 cm/9 inch tart shell or four 11 cm/4½ inch tartlets*

300 g/10 oz plain flour	Grated zest of 1 lemon
150 g/5 oz caster sugar	2 eggs, lightly beaten
Pinch sea salt	1 tablespoon iced water
150 g/5 oz unsalted butter, cut into	2 tablespoons milk (optional)
1 cm/½ inch pieces	

1 Sift together flour, sugar and salt. Rub in butter until mixture is mealy, or process briefly in a food processor with on/off pulses until mixture is like crumbs.

2 Add zest, eggs and water and stir just until dough can be gathered into a ball. Do not overmix. Wrap in polythene and chill 30 minutes before using.

3 Lightly flour work surface. Roll out pastry 3 mm/⅛ inch thick. Fit into pie tin or flan dish—try to avoid stretching dough as you work with it. Chill dough in mould for 15 minutes. If desired, brush with milk. The finished pastry will have more shine, but may be a little tougher.

4 Cook, uncovered, at 100% until pastry looks quite dry, about 4 minutes for a 22.5 cm/9 inch tart, or 2 minutes to 2 minutes 30 seconds for 4 tartlets.

5 Remove from oven. Let cool 2 minutes. Remove from mould(s) and let cool completely on a wire rack.

PUFF PASTRY

·•·

Microwave-baked puff pastry will not brown and therefore should be served in conjunction with brightly coloured fruits and vegetables. It does rise impressively high whether you make it yourself or, in haste, use store-bought. Don't overcook or it will crumble on you. There are so many books with wonderful, if long, recipes for puff pastry that one is not included here. What follows are instruction for baking squares and vol-au-vents made from defrosted frozen puff pastry. *Serves 4*

4 squares (7.5 cm × 3 mm/3 × ⅛ inch)
   defrosted frozen puff pastry, each
   square pricked 5 times with a fork.

1 Place pastry squares evenly spaced around the inside rim of a 30 cm/12 inch round platter. Cook, uncovered, at 100% for 6 minutes. If you are using a small oven, cook for 9 minutes.

2 Remove from oven. Split horizontally and serve warm or at room temperature with Confectioner's Custard (page 381) and fresh raspberries.

To make 8 squares. Prick 8 squares and place around the inside rim of a 30 × 25 × 1 cm/12 × 10 × ½ inch platter. Cook for 8 minutes.

To make 2 squares. Prick 2 squares and place on a 25 cm/10 inch flan dish. Cook for 2 minutes 30 seconds. (If you are using a small oven, cook for 4 minutes 30 seconds.)

VARIATION

VOL-AU-VENTS Place 4 frozen vol-au-vents around the inside rim of a 30 cm/ 12 inch platter. Cook, uncovered, at 100% for 8 minutes. (If you are using a small oven, place vol-au-vents on a 25 cm/10 inch flan dish and cook for 14 minutes.) To make 2 vol-au-vents, place on a 25 cm/10 inch flan dish and cook at 100% for 3 minutes 30 seconds. (If you are using a small oven, cook for 5 minutes 30 seconds.)

APRICOT GLAZE

◆ ◆

While apricot jam can be briefly heated in the microwave oven and then put through a sieve, homemade glaze is better. The kitchen smalls wonderful while it is cooking. *Makes 350 ml/12 fl oz*

500 g/1 lb ripe apricots (about 7),   200 g/7 oz caster sugar
   halved and stoned   4 tablespoons water
2 tablespoons fresh lemon juice

1 Place apricots in a 2 litre/3½ pint glass jug or bowl. Stir in lemon juice, sugar and water. Cover tightly with microwave cling film. Cook at 100% for 10 minutes.

2 Pierce film with the tip of a sharp knife, then remove from oven. Uncover and pass through medium disc of food mill. Place a fine sieve over a clean 2 litre/3½ pint glass jug or bowl and pass purée through sieve. Cook, uncovered, at 100% for 12 minutes more.

3 Remove from oven. Let stand until cool. Pour into a jar with a lid and refrigerate tightly covered. To use, heat, uncovered, at 100% for 2 minutes.

VARIATION

APRICOT-LEMON GLAZE Increase lemon juice to 6 tablespoons, increase sugar by 2 tablespoons, and omit water.

See also Coffee Glaze (page 367).

TART APRICOT PURÉE

⎯⎯ • ♦ • ⎯⎯

Use this tart purée to make Danish and other sweet pastries, or stir 250 ml/8 fl oz into the base mixture for 1 litre/2 pint of vanilla ice cream and freeze. *Makes 350 ml/12 fl oz purée*

250 g/8 oz dried apricots 2 tablespoons caster sugar
350 ml/12 fl oz water 2 tablespoons fresh lemon juice
1 piece (5 cm/2 inches) vanilla pod

1 Combine apricots, water, vanilla pod and sugar in a 1 litre/2 pint glass measuring jug. Cover tightly with microwave cling film. Cook at 100% for 7 minutes.

2 Pierce film with the tip of a sharp knife, then remove from oven. Uncover, drain apricots, and discard vanilla pod.

3 Pour into the container of a food processor, add lemon juice, and pufee until smooth, about 1 minute.

SWEET APRICOT PURÉE

◆•◆

This easy-to-make purée can be kept on hand for use as a soufflé base, Bavarian cream flavouring, or filling for a sandwich cake. Try 125 ml/4 fl oz stirred into Confectioner's Custard (page 381). See Apricot Tea Cake (page 358). This purée is even good as jam. *Makes 175 ml/6 fl oz*

90 g/3 oz dried apricots
125 ml/4 fl oz water
4 tablespoons caster sugar

1 piece (5 cm/2 inches) vanilla pod
2 tablespoons fresh lemon juice
2 teaspoons grated lemon zest

1 Combine all ingredients in a 500 ml/1 pint glass measuring jug. Cover tightly with microwave cling film. Cook at 100% for 6 minutes.

2 Pierce film with the tip of a sharp knife, then remove from oven. Uncover and discard vanilla pod.

3 Pour into the container of a food processor and purée.

VARIATION

SPICY AND CHUNKY APRICOT JAM Add 3 5p piece-size pieces of peeled fresh root ginger to apricots as they cook. Remove along with vanilla pod. After removing from food processor, stir in 30 g/1 oz chopped blanched almonds or macadamia nuts.

LEMON CURD

◆•◆

Serve with berries, plain cake, toast, or in a Crumb Crust (page 382), where it can be topped with meringue and briefly grilled to make a superior lemon meringue pie. Use as filling in Lemon Sandwich Cake (page 359). Put into tartlets made with Sweet Tart Pastry (page 383) and top with sliced berries. *Makes 250 ml/8 fl oz*

125 g/4 oz unsalted butter
100 g/3½ oz caster sugar
4 tablespoons fresh lemon juice

Grated zest of 1 lemon
3 eggs, beaten

1 Place butter, sugar, juice and zest together in a 1 litre/2 pint glass measuring jug. Cover tightly with microwave cling film. Cook at 100% for 4 minutes.

2 Pierce film with the tip of a sharp knife, then remove from oven, uncover and stir well.

3 Whisk 4 tablespoons of lemon mixture into the eggs to warm them. Whisking constantly, pour egg mixture back into remaining lemon mixture.

4 Cook, uncovered, at 100% for 2 minutes. Remove from oven and whisk until smooth. Cook for 2 minutes longer.

5 Remove from oven and immediately pour into the container of a food processor. Process for 30 seconds until smooth. Cool before serving.

GANACHE

This is the classic, smooth chocolate that glazes cakes in the best French tradition. The cake is placed on a cooling rack over a large plate and the glaze is poured over it and allowed to flow down the sides. It is important to remember not to touch it once it is poured on the cake, or it will not stay shiny. Many of the chocolate truffles in the world are simply leftover Ganache, chilled and formed with a melon baller before being rolled in cocoa. See Chocolate Truffles (page 376) for another version. *Makes 500 ml/16 fl oz*

250 ml/8 fl oz double cream

250 g/8 oz good-quality plain chocolate, grated

1 Heat cream in a 1 litre/2 pint glass measuring jug, uncovered, at 100% for 2 minutes 30 seconds.

2 Remove from oven. Add chocolate, stirring until melted and mixture is smooth.

CARAMEL

This is the hard-crack caramel that is often allowed to harden in a thin transparent disc on an oiled baking sheet. This thin disc is scored into wedges before it cools and the wedges arranged on top of cakes like dobosh torte. *Makes 125 ml/4 fl oz*

100 g/3½ oz caster sugar

4 tablespoons water

1 Combine sugar and water in a 1 litre/2 pint glass measuring jug. Cover tightly with microwave cling film. Cook at 100% for 5 minutes 30 seconds.

2 Pierce film with the tip of a sharp knife, then remove from oven. Uncover carefully and use.

To make 250 ml/8 fl oz. Use twice the amount of sugar and water, cooking caramel for 8 minutes.

PRALINE POWDER

Makes 250 g/8 oz

150 g/8 oz blanched almonds or
  hazelnuts
200 g/7 oz caster sugar

4 tablespoons water
Vegetable or safflower oil, for the
  baking sheet

1 Place almonds in a single layer on a plate. Cook, uncovered, at 100% for 5 minutes, until golden. Set aside.

2 Combine sugar and water in a 2 litre/3½ pint glass jug or bowl. Stir thoroughly to dissolve completely. Cover tightly with microwave cling film. Cook at 100% for 4 minutes.

3 Without taking measure from oven, pierce film with the tip of a sharp knife and uncover very carefully. Continue cooking, uncovered, 4 to 5 minutes longer, until golden brown. Do not stir.

4 Remove from oven. Lightly oil a baking sheet. Add almonds to hot syrup and stir to coat. Pour on to oiled sheet all at once.

5 Allow to cool. When cool to the touch and hard, break praline into 2.5–5 cm/1–2 inch pieces.

6 Put praline pieces in the container of a food processor. Process only to a fine powder; do not overprocess, or powder will become a dense paste.

Note. To clean glass jug or bowl, fill with cold water and heat, uncovered, at 100% for 12 to 15 minutes. Remove from oven, pour off water. Repeat if there is still undissolved caramel stuck on.

VARIATION

PRALINE PASTE Continue to process Praline Powder until it becomes a dense paste. For a smoother paste, add 15 g/½ oz cocoa butter and process until thoroughly incorporated.

JAMS & ...

These are the grace notes, the added flourishes that I sometimes remember after the song has faded. They are jams, jellies, preserves, salsas, relishes, fruit butters, chutneys, apple sauce, pickles, mustards and the like, friends to have in the cupboard or refrigerator and to pull out as needed. They are the makings of breakfast, brunch and afternoon tea. If I were Pennsylvania Dutch, there would be more of them; no meal would be deemed adequate without the traditional seven sweets and seven sours.

While preserves can be made out of season, it seems to me to miss the whole point—and they cost more. If you are smitten by the preserving urge in autumn or winter, work with cranberries or dried fruit. Try the Fresh Mango Chutney (page 407). Make mustards and Kimchi (page 404). Wait until spring for rhubarb and strawberries, until summer for raspberries, blackberries, sour cherries and sweetcorn.

These are not foods you need, except perhaps at Christmas, Passover, Easter. On the other hand, they are a nice afternoon's project. They make welcome presents; they don't demand immediate eating. Before you start, make sure you have enough jars on hand. They might as well be attractive; that way they can go right on the table, or be lovely when the gift wrapping is torn away.

I go one step further and wrap each kind in a different bright colour of tissue— Strawberry Jam in clear red, Cranberry Jelly in maroon, Peach Chutney in apricot, for example—so that when it comes time to give a gift, they are colour-coded. I can pick an assortment, put them in a colourful bag or into a basket, tie with a ribbon, and I am ready to go. Since I also make flavoured vinegars, like raspberry, I usually include a bottle of that as well. Jars of Spiced Mixed Nuts (page 466) are nice in the assortment, along with some of your own Chunky Tomato Sauce (page 324) or Mexican Chilli Sauce (page 325).

Sterilizing jars in the microwave is unsatisfactory, I am told by the health experts. This is one time when I listen. I sterilize the jars on top of the stove while I am cooking. I proceed to bottle in classic fashion following the instructions of the jar manufacturers.

JAMS, JELLIES AND PRESERVES

I may have fantasies about being an old-fashioned cook making everything from scratch; but, sadly, they just are not true. My breads are more often bought than baked, and I resort to cans and jars more than I might like. I grow herbs and vegetables, but I cannot bear to raise chickens. I am redeemed from my own obloquy by rows of translucent jars lined up in a shallow, nineteenth-century jam cupboard. They contain summer's fruits, some from my own trees, some bought: I make jams, jellies, preserves, fruit syrups to pour over pancakes and waffles, and dense, spicy apple, peach and apricot butters.

Technically, preserves are everything you put up for keeping. I use the word in its other sense, as a preparation that retains the shape of the whole fruit. In a jam, the fruit is squashed. In a jelly, you really don't sense the fruit except as a flavour. Fruit butters are thick and savoury, but they don't jell. Syrups pour.

I find I don't need to make huge quantities. This way I can preserve the fruit as it ripens or gets picked. Making preserves becomes a little bit of cooking rather than a major chore. By the time the last bits of autumn fruit have been added—a few jars made here, a few jars made there—it adds up to a handsome collection and gives more variety. I use small jars, 125–175 g/4–6 oz. That way I don't have to eat the same preserve every day or risk having them go bad once opened. Small jars also make more charming presents in an assortment.

If opened or unopened preserves crystallize, open the jar and put it in the microwave oven for 1 minute at 100% and it will smooth out.

Chunky Blueberry Sauce (page 377) is somewhere between a perserve and syrup (sauce). It is worth preserving. Your own favourite recipes can also be adapted for the microwave oven by following the recipes with respect to cooking times and proportions of fruit to sugar.

Jams, jellies and preserves are made quickly and cleanly in the microwave oven. I don't use any pectin because I don't like preserves to be too hard, and all the ones I tried jelled satisfactorily when cooked according to these recipes. I find that using a thermometer does not tell much. Instead, I have a simple test. To check jam for the proper consistency, place a small amount on a plate and put in the freezer until well chilled. If a spoon pulled through the jam leaves a wide track, it is ready. If it is not yet jelled, put it back, uncovered, in the microwave oven for 5 minutes at a time, testing after each 5 minutes. Place in sterilized jars and seal according to jar manufacturer's instructions, or refrigerate. If you want to seal your jam with paraffin, it must be melted in the conventional oven or on top of the stove in a double boiler; microwaves pass right through it.

Many people don't like or cannot digest the tiny seeds in berries. They will be happier making the jams that have been put through a food mill. Some may want to go so far as to put the jam through a fine sieve after it comes out of the food mill.

The amounts of sugar and lemon juice in the recipes are not absolute. They will depend on the sweetness of the fruit and your palate. Don't play around too much, or you may upset the jelling. I don't like my jams and preserves too sweet. If you like them very sweet, add an extra 4 tablespoons sugar for each 200 g/7 oz used below.

Because of the heat and steam in cooking jam, be sure to use large enough pieces of cling film to cover. On 35 × 27.5 × 5 cm/14 × 11 × 2 inches dishes, use 2 pieces of overlapping film, lengthways. To stir, use the technique of cutting a slit with the tip of a sharp knife through the film; stir with a wooden spoon, making sure to scrape the bottom of the dish to get any undissolved sugar. Patch with a piece of film that amply overlaps the slit. If you remove film, be careful, because the sugar-steam is hot. Re-cover as above.

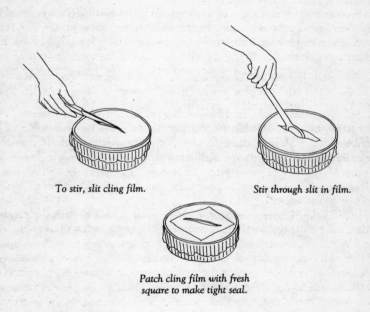

To stir, slit cling film.   Stir through slit in film.

Patch cling film with fresh
square to make tight seal.

STRAWBERRY PRESERVES

❖ ❖ ❖

Wait until you smell these preserves some cold winter's morning. You will become a preserving convert. Strawberry Preserves should be made in season from fully ripe fruit that is not huge. Berries that are 2.5 cm/1 inch or smaller are best; don't use bad or mushy berries. You get less preserves from the same volume of strawberries as raspberries because strawberries contain more water.
Makes 350 ml/12 fl oz

600 g/1¼ lb strawberries, wiped clean and hulled

200–250 g/7–8 oz caster sugar
2 teaspoons fresh lemon juice

1 Toss together berries and sugar in a 2.5 litre/4 pint soufflé dish. Let stand for 5 minutes. Cover tightly with microwave cling film. Cook at 100% for 10 minutes. Slit film and stir well. Re-cover and cook at 100% for 10 to 15 minutes longer, until very thick.

2 Pierce film with the tip of a sharp knife to release steam, then remove from oven. Uncover and stir in lemon juice. Divide preserves among sterilized jars. Seal with 3 mm/⅛ inch of melted paraffin, if desired.

To make 750 ml/1¼ pints. Double quantities of ingredients. Cook in a 35 × 27.5 × 5 cm/14 × 11 × 2 inch dish. Cook 15 minutes; stir; cook 15 minutes; uncover; stir; cook 20 minutes, or until very thick.

VARIATION

STRAWBERRY JAM Make preserves. After final cooking, pass the mixture through a food mill fitted with the medium disc. Finish as for preserves.

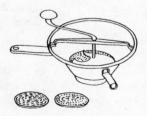

Use a food mill when making jams to remove seeds, skin and pips from the fruit.

RHUBARB-STRAWBERRY JAM

———— ◆ ◆ ————

I like this tarter version of Strawberry Jam. The strawberry flavour still dominates, and the jam is a little lighter in colour. Don't worry about stringing the rhubarb. Just remove any strings that really get in your way while slicing. If the jam seems stringy once it's cooked, pass through a food mill fitted with a medium disc. This can be made into a very good pie filling (see variation). *Makes 1 litre/1¾ pints*

500 g/1 lb rhubarb, washed, trimmed and cut into 5 mm/¼ inch diagonal slices	300 g/10 oz strawberries, wiped clean and hulled
	500 g/1 lb caster sugar

1 Combine all ingredients in a 2.5 litre/4 pint soufflé dish. Cover tightly with microwave cling film. If your oven does not have a turntable, place soufflé dish on a large plate. Cook at 100% for 10 minutes. Pierce film with the tip of a sharp knife to release steam, then uncover and cook for 10 minutes longer. If any liquid bubbles out of the dish during cooking, simply scrape off turntable or plate back into dish at end of cooking.

2 Remove from oven. Divide jam among sterilized jars. Seal with 3 mm/⅛ inch of melted paraffin, if desired.

VARIATION

RHUBARB-STRAWBERRY PIE FILLING Make jam, reducing final cooking time to 6 minutes uncovered. Add 2½ tablespoons tapioca, cover tightly, and cook for 4 minutes longer. Pour into baked Sweet Tart Pastry (page 383) or a Crumb Crust (page 382). Cover with meringue or whipped cream, if desired.

RED RASPBERRY JAM

———— ◆ ◆ ————

Raspberries are too fragile to really hold their shape when cooked, and so can't be made into preserves. I don't put the jam through a food mill, but most people like at least some of the seeds removed, so I tell you to put it through a food mill. If you really want to get all the seeds out, you will then have to put it through a fine sieve.

The smaller amount of sugar produces a fairly tart jam. If you like yours sweeter, use the larger amount.

Raspberry jam is useful for baking as well as for breakfast. It is a wonderful clear red. To melt for baking, open a 175 g/6 oz jar of raspberry jam that has been sieved. Stir in 2 teaspoons Framboise or triple sec or water. Place open jar in centre of microwave oven. Heat at 100% for 30 seconds. Stir and use.

Black raspberries hold their shape better than red raspberries and so can be made into preserves. Follow the variation for Black Raspberry Jam, but do not put it through the food mill. This will be less tart than Red Raspberry Jam. *Makes 1 litre/1¾ pints*

1 kg/2 lb red raspberries   400–500 g/14–16 oz caster sugar

1 Combine berries and sugar in a 35 × 27.5 × 5 cm/14 × 11 × 2 inch dish. Cover tightly with microwave cling film. Cook at 100% for 15 minutes. Slit film and stir well. Re-cover and cook for 15 minutes longer. Pierce film with the tip of a sharp knife to release steam, then uncover and stir once more. Cook, uncovered, for 15 minutes longer.

2 Remove from oven. Pass through the fine disc of a food mill. Divide among sterilized jars. Seal with 3 mm/⅛ inch of melted parafin, if desired.

To make 500 ml/16 fl oz. Halve all ingredients. Combine berries and sugar in a 2.5 litre/4 pint soufflé dish and let stand for 5 minutes. Cook for 10 minutes. Uncover and cook for 8 to 10 minutes longer, until thick.

VARIATION

BLACK RASPBERRY JAM Substitute an equal amount black raspberries for red raspberries and proceed as for Red Raspberry Jam. Stir in 4 teaspoons fresh lemon juice after final cooking. To make 350 ml/12 fl oz, proceed as for Red Raspberry Jam, using black raspberries instead of red raspberries. Add 2 teaspoons fresh lemon juice after final cooking.

SOUR CHERRY PRESERVES

I have two dwarf cherry trees with perfectly round crowns. Studded with pink-white blooms in the spring and round, light red fruits in early summer, they look like a child's drawing. My only problem is that the birds usually decide that the fruit is ripe just before I do. I have had to resort to shrouding at least one tree in bird netting and crawling up under the net to pick. Fortunately, there is lots of fruit and it is easy to pick.

This is the kind of preserve you can't buy. It is made with whole Montmorency cherries. I often bottle it with the stones in. Then, it is a pink-red jelly with glints of orange, with the fruit trapped in it. It is very beautiful. I don't mind spitting the stones out as I eat; but this is not for everyone. If you put it through a food mill, you will get a smaller amount of a cross between jam and jelly. It won't be clear, but is still beautiful.

The tart-sweet flavour is good with cheese. Try a mild, soft goat cheese instead of cream cheese. *Makes 500–600 ml/16–20 fl oz*

450 g/15 oz sour cherries
200 g/7 oz caster sugar

2 tablespoon fresh lemon juice

1 Combine cherries and sugar in a 2 litre/3½ pint glass jug or bowl. Cover tightly with microwave cling film. Cook at 100% for 10 minutes. Slit film and stir well. Re-cover and cook for 10 minutes longer.

2 Pierce film with the tip of a sharp knife to release steam, then remove from oven. Uncover and skim. Test consistency (page 390). When jelled, stir in lemon juice.

3 Divide preserves among sterilized jars. Seal with 3 mm/⅛ inch of melted parafin, if desired.

VARIATION

SOUR CHERRY JELLY Make Sour Cherry Preserves. After final cooking, pass throuh the medium disc of a food mill. If the jelly is still not as clear as you like it, pass through a sieve. You will have about 400 ml/14 fl oz after passing through the food mill, and 300 ml/½ pint after passing through the sieve.

RED CURRANT JELLY

— • ◆ • —

The red stuff you buy in jars never seems to taste like red currants, but rather like sugar and pectin tinted red, which is how I suspect it is made. It's a shame. Red currants have a delicious, fresh, acid flavour. If you buy them in season, or have a few bushes, you can keep that flavour in a brilliant jelly that is tradtionally served with meat, particularly game, as well as being used in pastries and sweets.

The most tedious part of cooking or serving red currants is stripping the tiny berries from their tiny stalks. With this method you don't need to. You cook the berries in bunches. All you have to do is rinse them first. Red currants are hard to pick, but even I can manage a good amount. *Makes 600 g/1¼ lb*

500 g/1 lb fresh red currants, with stalks	250 g/8 oz sugar

1 Combine red currants and sugar in a 2 litre/3½ pint glass jug or bowl. Cover tightly with microwave cling film. Cook at 100% for 5 minutes. Pierce film with the tip of a sharp knife. Without taking dish from oven, uncover and stir, wiping down insides with a damp cloth to prevent sugar from crystallizing. Cook, uncovered, at 100% for 10 minutes longer. Test consistency (page 434).

2 Pass jelly through the fine disc of a food mill to remove stalks and pips. If you like a clearer jelly, pass through a double thickness of dampened muslin or a jelly bag.

3 Divide among sterilized jars. Seal with 3mm/⅛ inch of melted paraffin wax, if desired.

APPLE JELLY

This is a beautiful, clear, naturally red jelly. It makes the perfect base for Hot Pepper Jelly or Apple Mint Jelly. For the latter, you will use green-skinned apples instead of red for a more appropriate colour. Mint jelly is traditional with roast lamb. Hot Pepper Jelly has become popular because of the Mexican and Tex-Mex food craze. I like it with toast and cream cheese, but I think most people use it with meat.

At the end, you will have a nice dividend of 750 ml/1¼ pints of apple sauce. *Makes 600 g/1¼ lb*

1.5 kg/3 lb tart red apples, quartered 600 g/1¼ lb sugar	1 lemon, quartered and seeds removed

1 Combine all ingredients in a 23.5 × 13.5 cm/9½ × 5½ inch round dish. Cover tightly with microwave cling film. Cook at 100% for 20 minutes.

2 Remove from oven. Uncover and pass through the fine disc of a food mill.

Strain jelly through a double thickness of dampened muslin or a jelly bag. Reserve pulp and use as apple sauce. Place jelly in a clean 3 litre/5 pint dish. Cook, uncovered, at 100% for 25 minutes, or until setting point is reached.

3 Remove from oven. Divide among sterilized jars and seal with 3 mm/⅛ inch of melted paraffin wax, if desired.

VARIATIONS

HOT PEPPER JELLY Make Apple Jelly, adding 15 dried hot chillies for the final 5 minutes of cooking time. Strain through a sieve.

APPLE MINT JELLY Substitute equal amount Granny Smith apples for red apples. Add 45 g/1½ oz coarsely chopped mint leaves for final 3 minutes of cooking time. Strain through a sieve.

PLUM JAM

I am surprised people don't make more Plum Jam because it is so delicious. To quarter the plums, cut all the way around the circumference to the stone, then twist apart. Cook with stones, which add natural pectin and flavour. They will separate out in the food mill.

The colour and flavour of the jam will depend on the plums used. Dark-skinned plums will give you a bright red, prune plums a softer rose colour. Greengage jam will be green. If you find those little gold-yellow plum called mirabelles, cook them for 12 minutes. The jam will be a wonderful golden colour and smell like honey. *Makes 500 ml/16 fl oz*

750 g/1½ lb red plum, washed and quartered

150 g/5 oz caster sugar

1 Combine plums and sugar in a 2 litre/3½ pint glass jug or bowl. Cover tightly with microwave cling film. Cook at 100% for 10 minutes.

2 Pierce film with the tip of a sharp knife, then remove from oven. Uncover and stir, scraping the bottom of the jug or bowl to get any undissolved sugar.

3 Pass plums through a food mill fitted with a medium disc. Return to glass jug or bowl. Cook, uncovered, at 100% for 3 minutes.

4 Remove from oven. Divide among sterilized jars. Seal with 3 mm/⅛ inch of melted paraffin, if desired.

APPLE SAUCE

⬩◆⬩

Apple sauce can be a dessert. It can also go on potato pancakes or make a side dish with roast loin of pork. Fresh is so much better than canned or bottled. Make it as you need it. Made with red-skinned apples, it will have a lovely rosy colour. There is another easy way to come by Apple Sauce: as a variation of Apple Butter (see following recipe).

One reason to use this recipe is that you don't add the sugar until step 4. That lets you taste and use less sugar if you want. You could even use a sugar substitute. To make Apple Sauce with other apple varieties, see timings in Dictionary. *Makes 750 ml/1¼ pints*

6 Granny Smith apples	Pinch grated nutmeg
Fresh lemon juice, for rubbing apples	Pinch ground allspice
200 g/7 oz caster sugar	30 g/1 oz unsalted butter

1 Core the apples and peel a 4 cm/1½ inch strip around the top. Rub cut surfaces with lemon juice. In the largest container you have, with or without a tightly fitting lid, arrange the apples in a ring so that they do not touch. If using a container with a lid, add 2 tablespoons water. If using a container without a lid, cover tightly with microwave cling film. Cook at 100% for 9 minutes 30 seconds. If using cling film, pierce it with the tip of a sharp knife.

2 Remove from oven. Uncover and drape apples with a clean towel. Let stand for 5 minutes.

3 Scrape apples and any juices into the container of a food processor. Process until smooth.

4 Scrape into a 1 litre/2 pint glass measuring jug and add remaining ingredients. Cook, uncovered, at 100% for 2 minutes.

5 Remove from oven. Let stand until cool. Store, tightly covered and refrigerated, for up to a week.

To make 350 ml/12 fl oz. Halve ingredients. Cook apples for 4 minutes. Cook apple sauce for 1 minute.

VARIATION

HORSERADISH APPLE SAUCE Make 350 ml/12 fl oz Apple Sauce. Do not add seasonings or butter. When sweetened apple sauce is cold, stir in bottled horseradish sauce. Serve chilled with boiled beef or roast pork.

APPLE BUTTER

— • ◆ • —

I remember making apple butter on American Indian day at summer camp. It was a long process and there was always the risk of scorching the apple butter as it reduced itself to a dark brown pulp. To be authentic, we used maple syrup because the Indians didn't have refined sugar. I didn't like it much and I was discouraged by the amount of stirring required.

The microwave oven changes all that—almost no stirring and it is quickly done. I substitute sugar, part white and part brown, for the maple syrup. It gives it more apple flavour. If you want to be authentic, use 350 g/12 oz maple syrup instead of the sugars, but it will be sweeter.

Apple Butter has a pleasant spiciness, and it can be used as a relish with pork or venison. *Makes 500 ml/16 fl oz*

750 g/1½ lb Bramley apples, quartered
90 g/3 oz dark brown sugar
100 g/3½ oz caster sugar
½ cinnamon stick or ½ teaspoon ground
  cinnamon

3 whole allspice berries
3 whole cloves
Pinch freshly grated nutmeg

1 Combine all ingredients in a 27.5 × 21 × 10 cm/11 × 8½ × 4 inch dish. Cover tightly with microwave cling film. Cook at 100% for 15 minutes.

2 Pierce film with the tip of a sharp knife, then remove from oven. Uncover and pass through the medium disc of a food mill. Return to dish. Cook, uncovered, at 100% for 10 minutes longer.

3 Remove from oven. If you want a smoother butter, pass through the fine disc of a food mill.

4 Pack in sterilized jars, or let stand until cool and store, tightly covered and refrigerated, for up to 2 months.

To make 1 litre/1¾ pints. Double amount of apples and sugar. Use 1 stick cinnamon or ¾ teaspoon ground cinnamon, 6 allspice berries, 5 cloves and ¼ teaspoon nutmeg. Cook in a 35 × 27.5 × 5 cm/14 × 11 × 2 inch dish for 20 minutes. Pass through food mill and cook for 10 minutes longer.

VARIATION

APPLE SAUCE Use all caster sugar instead of half dark brown sugar. Do not cook for the final time after passing through the food mill. You will have a little more Apple Sauce than you would have Apple Butter.

PEACH BUTTER

◆ ◆ ◆

Lighter in colour and more sophisticated than the Apple Butter, this can be served as a jam, or used as a relish with grilled fish or chicken. *Makes 500 ml/16 fl oz*

750 g/1½ lb peaches, washed, stored
   and quartered
125 ml/4 fl oz water
1 tablespoon cider vinegar
200 g/7 oz caster sugar

½ teaspoon ground cinnamon
4 whole cloves
¼ teaspoon ground mace
1 piece (5 cm/2 inches) vanilla pod

1 Combine all ingredients in a 2.5 litre/4 pint soufflé dish. Cover tightly with microwave cling film. Cook at 100% for 10 minutes.

2 Pierce film with the tip of a sharp knife, then remove from oven. Uncover and pass through the fine disc of a food mill. Return to soufflé dish. Cook, uncovered, at 100% for 5 minutes.

3 Remove from oven. Let stand until cool. Store, tightly covered and refrigerated, for up to 2 months.

To make 1 litre/1¾ pints. Double all ingredients, cooking in a 35 × 27.5 × 5 cm/ 14 × 11 × 2 inch dish for 15 minutes. Pass through food mill and cook, uncovered, for 7 minutes 30 seconds longer.

QUINCE PASTE

◆ ◆ ◆

A Viennese speciality called Quittenkase, this is a translucent sweet that jells hard enough to mould and then slice. It is usually served as dessert, like the South American guava paste that is made the same way. Small slices can accompany cream cheese or a mild goat cheese, and it's a nice addition to brunch. Almost all ordinary preserves made with quinces turn a light reddish-pink. This cooks so quickly in the microwave oven that it stays gold. If you store it, tightly wrapped in two layers of polythene and refrigerated, it will change colour with time. *Makes 1 litre/1¾ pints*

1.25 kg/2½ lb qunices, washed and
   quartered

½ lemon, cut into wedges
400 g/14 oz caster sugar

1 Combine quinces and lemon in a 2 litre/3½ pint glass jug or bowl. Cover tightly with microwave cling film. Cook at 100% for 10 minutes.

2 Pierce film with the tip of a sharp knife, then remove from oven. Uncover and remove all pieces of quince that can be easily pierced with the tip of a sharp knife. Re-cover dish and cook for 5 minutes longer.

3 Pierce film, then remove from oven. Uncover and stir in sugar. Pass through the fine disc of a food mill.

4 Scrape mixture into a 27.5 × 21 × 5 cm/11 × 8½ × 2 inch dish. Cook, uncovered, at 100% for 15 minutes, stirring once or twice.

5 Remove from oven. Pour into one or more glass or ceramic moulds or bowls. Let stand until cool. Store, tightly covered and refrigerated, for up to 2 months.

VARIATION

GUAVA PASTE Substitute an equal quantity of guavas for quinces and proceed as for Quince Paste.

RELISHES & ...

Relishes, pickles, savoury jellies and chutneys are meant to introduce a meal or go with the main course. They are not breakfast food. Often they are quite chunky or contain whole fruits or vegetables. Almost every cuisine seems to have characteristic dishes like this. Think of ketchup. Today, it is smooth tomato stuff out of a bottle, but there are also mushroom ketchups, walnut, and the like.

Pickled black walnuts, cornichons and many other kinds of standard pickles can be made if you have access to the ingredients. I didn't. Onions à la Monégasque (page 48), Onions in Barbecue Sauce (page 267), and Saffron Onions (page 48) can all be preserved and eaten as relishes.

BEETROOT AND APPLE RELISH

• •

This quickly made relish has crunch from the apples and colour and sweetness from the beetroots. It is good with fish or pork. *Makes 1 litre/1¾ pints*

350 g/12 oz beetroots, rinsed and stalks removed
½ Granny Smith or Bramley apple, peeled, cored and cut into 5–10 mm/ ¼–½ inch dice

60 g/2 oz onion, peeled and chopped
2 tablespoons cider vinegar
½ teaspoon pickling salt
1 tablespoon caster sugar
Pinch freshly ground black pepper

1 Arrange beetroots in a circle towards the edge of 2.5 litre/4 pint soufflé dish or a casserole with a tightly fitting lid. If using soufflé dish, cover tightly with microwave cling film. If using casserole, add 2 tablespoons water. Cook at 100% for 10 to 11 minutes, or until the beetroot can easily be pierced with the tip of a knife. If using cling film, prick it with the tip of a sharp knife.

2 Remove from oven. Uncover. Slip off beetroot skins and cut into 5–10 mm/ ¼–½ inch cubes.

3 Combine beetroots with remaining ingredients in a 1 litre/2 pint glass measuring jug glass. Cover tightly with microwave cling film. Cook at 100% for 4 minutes.

4 Pierce film, then remove from oven. Uncover and divide among sterilized jars, or let stand until cool and store, tightly covered. Refrigerate for up to 2 months.

CRANBERRY SAUCE

• • •

Come Christmas, I need a surefire recipe for a glistening cranberry mould. They don't get better, quicker or easier than this one. *Makes 500 ml/16 fl oz*

350 g/12 oz fresh or frozen cranberries
200 g/7 oz caster sugar

125 ml/4 fl oz cranberry juice
Pinch pickling salt

1 Combine all ingredient in a 2 litre/3½ pint glass jug or bowl. Cook, uncovered, at 100% for 10 minutes.

2 Remove from oven. Rinse a 2.5 litre/4 pint soufflé dish with cold water. Pour Cranberry Sauce into dish. Refrigerate, loosely covered, for 4 to 6 hours, until firm. Run a knife around edge of dish and unmould on to a serving platter.

VARIATION

CHUNKY CRANBERRY NUT SAUCE Add 60 g/2 oz coarsely chopped pecans and segments from 1 orange, zest and pith removed, cooking for 12 minutes.

MAPLE SWEETCORN RELISH

• • •

I can eat this by the spoonful; but it really is made to go with hamburgers, grilled steak, meat loaf, ribs, grilled fish or fried chicken, the picnic and barbecue foods. While it is by far best with fresh sweetcorn, if you run out in winter and crave a batch, it can be made with vacuum-packed canned sweetcorn kernels. In spite of the chillies, this is only mildly spiced. *Makes 1 litre/1¾ pints*

250 g/8 oz fresh sweetcorn kernels
(from 3 ears) or canned kernels in
water, drained
½ small green cabage, cut into 5 mm/¼
inch cubes
1 small onion, peeled and finely
chopped
75 g/2½ oz red pepper, cored, seeded
and diced
75 g/2½ oz green pepper, cored, seeded
and diced

1 tablespoon Dijon mustard
250 ml/8 fl oz cider vinegar
125 ml/4 fl oz maple syrup
1½ teaspoons dry mustard
1 tablespoon pickling salt
2 teaspoons crushed dried red chillies or
10 small dried red chillies
1 tablespoon finely chopped fresh root
ginger
4 large cloves garlic, smashed, peeled
and very finely chopped

1 Combine all ingredients in a 2.5 litre/4 pint soufflé dish (if you are using canned sweetcorn, do not add it now). Cover tightly with microwave cling film. Cook at 100% for 5 minutes. Pierce film with the tip of a sharp knife, then uncover; add canned sweetcorn if you are using it. Cook, uncovered, at 100% for 3 minutes longer.

2 Remove from oven. Divide among sterilized jars. Seal.

BREAD AND BUTTER PICKLES

I usually like my pickles sour, but these crunchy, sweet and sour slices are a pretty and worthwhile exception. Unlike many pickles, these can be eaten as soon as they are made. I refrigerate them because they taste better cold and crisp.
Makes 1 litre/1¾ pints

1.5 kg/3 lb small, unwaxed pickling cucumbers, washed, trimmed and cut into 5 mm/¼ inch slices (in food processor if you want)
1 medium onion, peeled and sliced
1 large clove garlic, smashed and peeled

3 tablespoons pickling salt
450 g/15 oz caster sugar
¾ teaspoon turmeric
¾ teaspoon celery seed
1 tablespoon mustard seed
350 ml/12 fl oz white vinegar

1 Combine cucumbers, onions, garlic and salt in a large bowl. Cover with 2 trays of ice cubes or crushed ice and stir well. Let stand for 3 hours.

2 Drain cucumbers and discard liquid. Set aside.

3 Combine remaining ingredients in a 23.5 × 13 cm/9½ × 5½ inch round dish. Cook, uncovered, at 100% for 6 minutes. Add reserved cucumber mixture. Cover tightly with microwave cling film. Cook at 100% for 12 minutes.

4 Pierce film with the tip of a sharp knife, then remove from oven. Uncover and divide among sterilized jars. Seal.

KIMCHI

I've never had a Korean meal that didn't include these pickled winter vegetables. Sometimes the Kimchi is red in colour. I prefer this pale, not overly spicy version. In Korea, they used to bury the crocks of Kimchi in the ground to keep it cold while it fermented. This recipe is not that authentic, but it smells a lot better. I like it with French foods like pâté, with cold sliced meat, or as part of a mixed hors d'oeuvre. You have to start this the day before you preserve it to let the cabbage soak and wilt. *Makes 1 litre/1¾ pints*

750 g/1½ lb mooli (white radish), peeled
4 tablespoons pickling salt
250 ml/8 fl oz water
750 g/1½ lb Chinese leaves, washed and cut across the vein into 4 cm/1½ inch slices

4 large spring onions, cut into 5 cm/2 inch lengths
4 large cloves garlic, smashed and peeled
3 slices peeled fresh root ginger, julienned
10 whole small dried chillies

1 Cut mooli across into 3 mm/⅛ inch slices, using the slicing disc on the food processor.

2 Combine salt and water in a deep, non-metal dish; a medium-size crock would be perfect. Add mooli and cabbage and cover tightly with polythene. Let stand overnight, stirring occasionally.

3 Drain vegetables and reserve salted water.

4 Place spring onions, garlic and ginger in the container of a food processor. Process until finely chopped. Add to drained vegetables and mix well.

5 Pour reserved water back into a 1 litre/2 pint glass measuring jug and cook, uncovered, at 100% for 5 minutes.

6 Remove from oven. Divide vegetables among sterilized jars. Add chillies and pour liquid over vegetables to within 1 cm/½ inch of top of jar. Store, tightly covered and refrigerated, for at least 2 days before serving.

DILLY CARROTS

I'm not so fond of dilled green beans; I don't like the colour they turn. Carrots, on the other hand, stay a beautiful orange and remain crisp. This is an ideal low-calorie cocktail snack. You can reuse the brine. *Makes 2 litre/3½ pints*

1.5 kg/3 lb small fresh carrots, trimmed, peeled and cut into sticks 5 mm/¼ inch across and 2.5 cm/1 inch shorter than height of jar
1 bunch fresh dill
8 cloves garlic, smashed and peeled

1½ teaspoons dried chilli flakes
1½ teaspoons dried dill seed
500 ml/16 fl oz cider vinegar
500 ml/16 fl oz water
4 tablespoons pickling salt

1 Fit carrots, standing up, around the inside rim of sterilized jars, leaving a space in the centre. Place 2 large dill sprigs and 1 clove garlic into the centre of each jar. Set aside.

2 Combine remaining ingredients in a 2 litre/3½ pint glass jug or bowl. Cook, uncovered, at 100% for 6 minutes.

3 Remove from oven. Pour liquid over carrots to within 1 cm/½ inch of top of jar. Set aside any extra liquid. Arrange filled jars in an evenly spaced circle—not touching—around inside rim of turntable or around inside edge of oven. Cook, uncovered, at 100% for 10 minutes.

4 Remove from oven. Pour reserved liquid into jars to cover carrots, if necessary. Store, tightly covered and refrigerated, for up to 2 months.

PICKLED PEACH RELISH

This relish has the prettiest colours, and is good and spicy, a surprise with cold meats, chicken or fish. *Makes 750 ml/1¼ pints*

4 tablespoons cider vinegar
4 tablespoons caster sugar
5–6 large, firm to medium ripe peaches, peeled, stoned and chopped

150 g/5 oz red pepper, cored, seeded and chopped
1 fresh chilli, seeded and chopped
1 teaspoon grated peeled fresh root ginger

1 Stir together vinegar and sugar in a 2 litre/3½ pint glass jug or bowl. Cover tightly with microwave cling film. Cook at 100% for 3 minutes.

2 Pierce film with the tip of sharp knife, then remove from oven. Uncover and stir in peaches, chilli and ginger. Cook, uncovered, at 100% for 4 to 6 minutes, until peaches are tender.

3 Remove from oven. Pack in sterilized jars, or let stand until cool and store, tightly covered and refrigerated, for up to 2 weeks.

PEACH CHUTNEY

◆ ◆ ◆

This is a wonderful and unusual summer chutney that is best if allowed to mature for at least one day before eating. Serve it with baked ham or roast chicken as well as curry. I also like it on a plate with tuna fish salad or egg salad and sliced tomato. *Makes 1 litre/1¾ pints*

1 lemon, cut into 5 mm/¼ inch slices, each slice quartered and seeds discarded
3 cloves garlic, smashed, peeled and quartered
300 g/10 oz caster sugar
75 g/2½ oz raisins
150 g/5 oz blanched almonds
4 slices peeled fresh root ginger, cut into matchsticks
6 cardamom pods, crushed and hulls discarded

½ teaspoon dried chilli flakes
150 g/5 oz shallots, peeled
175 ml/6 fl oz cider vinegar
1 teaspoon black mustard seed
1 teaspoon cumin seed
1 teaspoon pickling salt
750 g/1½ lb peaches—firm to medium ripe—trimmed, stoned and cut into 5 cm/2 inch chunks
250 g/8 oz celery, trimmed, stringed and sliced on the diagonal

1 Combine all ingredients except peaches and celery in a 2.5 litre/4 pint soufflé dish. Cook, uncovered, at 100% for 5 minutes.

2 Add peaches and stir well. Cover tightly with microwave cling film. Cook at 100% for 5 minutes.

3 Pierce film with the tip of a sharp knife, then remove from oven. Uncover and stir in celery. Place in sterilized bottles and seal, or let stand until cool and store, tightly covered and refrigerated, for up to 2 months.

FRESH MANGO CHUTNEY

◆ ◆ ◆

This chutney can be made in midwinter. It is a classic, and good to keep on hand to go with curries, ham sandwiches, simply cooked fish and scrambled eggs. A slightly underripe papaya can be substituted for the mango. Mango chutney that you can buy has so little fruit these days that it's worth making your own. *Makes 500 ml/16 fl oz*

1 large ripe mango, peeled and cut into
   1 cm/½ inch thick slices
1 tablespoon Spice Powder III (page
   299) or curry powder
¼ teaspoon celery seed
Pinch ground cloves
1 fresh green chilli, roasted, peeled and
   sliced
1 teaspoon pickling salt
1 tablespoon vegetable oil

6 thin slices peeled fresh root ginger
75 g/2½ oz brown sugar
125 ml/4 fl oz tomato juice
125 ml/4 fl oz water
2 teaspoons cornflour dissolved in
   4 tablespoons water
2 teaspoons fresh lemon juice
1 tablespoon chopped fresh coriander
1 tablespoon chopped fresh mint

1 Stir together all ingredients except lemon juice, coriander and mint in a 2.5 litre/4 pint soufflé dish. Cook, uncovered, at 100% for 5 minutes. Stir well. Cook for 5 minutes longer.

2 Remove from oven. Stir in remaining ingredients. Store, tightly covered and refrigerated, for up to 2 months.

VARIATION

FRESH SPICY MANGO CHUTNEY Add 1 small onion, diced; 1 small tomato, seeded and diced; 3 cloves garlic, smashed, peeled and sliced; 30 g/1 oz slivered almonds; 30 g/1 oz raisins, and an additional ½ tablespoon mint. Increase lemon juice to 1 tablespoon. Decrease sugar to 2 tablespoons and cornflour to 1 teaspoon. Omit celery seed, cloves, chilli, tomato juice and coriander.

DICTIONARY OF FOODS AND TECHNIQUES

Cooking in the microwave oven is different from other kinds of cooking. If you read the first chapters of this book, you will see exactly how. It is not just that cooking times are different, but also that they are dependent on the weight and dimensions of the foods. Buying a small scale and learning to use it makes a valuable ally. The way the food cooks also depends on the way you wrap it, the size of the dish (the kind you eat from or the kind you use in the microwave oven) and the amount of liquid (see pages 31–32), assorted vegetables or other ingredients cooked with the food. How it cooks even depends on the amount of fat protein, sugar, fat and water in the food.

All this will seem unfamiliar at first. If you think of it in baking terms, it may be easier to understand and accept. When you read a cake recipe, you don't begin by changing the size of the tin, the cooking time or the cooking temperature. You know that would change the results and might create disaster.

In researching the basic information for this book, I have tested as many possible basic variations for the cooking of a certain kind of food as possible. I am sharing the results with you in this Dictionary, food by food and technique by technique. These are not recipes. They are results of tests that tell you how things work.

My hope is that this Dictionary will make it possible for you to really cook in the microwave oven, not just follow recipes. I wish I had had it when I started this book. Now I have it, and I use it almost every time I cook in the microwave oven. If I want to change recipe or make it for fewer or more people I look in the Dictionary.

For instance, if a recipe calls for 4 cooked, split and boned chicken breasts, and you want to cook 8 split and boned breasts, look up CHICKEN; you will find out the cooking time and what kind of container to use. Go on from there. As you can see, you can't cook the breast as you would on top of the stove for the same amount of time but in a larger container, nor can you just multiply the cooking time by two. You need the information in the Dictionary.

If you want to cook more than 8 breasts, you will find there is no cooking time given. That means a larger quantity was tried but didn't cook well. *When a technique or quantity does not work, it has been omitted.* Since the cooking time for the 8 breasts is only 8 minutes, do it twice for 16 breasts. If you have a small oven and know that most of the recipes were tested in a large oven, look to page 18 to see how to modify the recipe, or look in the Dictionary. Alternate cooking times are given for small quantities of chicken in the small ovens, but no times for large quantities. This means that larger quantities are not realistic in a small oven. You can always try if you want.

When you want to make chicken stew, but none of the recipes in the book is exactly what you want, look at CHICKEN again. You will see that for a 2 kg/4 lb bird you can include 500 g/1 lb of vegetables and 500 ml/16 fl oz of liquid, that you cook in a 2.5 litre/4 pint soufflé dish, cover tightly with microwave cling film and cook at 100% for 22 minutes. You might decide to use onions, carrots and mushrooms and 350 ml/12 fl oz chicken stock and 125 ml/4 fl oz cream.

Season as you want. If you have a question about how those seasonings will act in the microwave oven, look them up as well. If the stew is too thin when it has finished cooking, look up THICKENING or CORNFLOUR and find out what to do.

Now, I don't really have to do all that anymore. Some of it I remember; some of it I can figure out. But I probably will look up CHICKEN all the same.

More simply, let's say I want to cook artichokes for a crowd. That's not a recipe; that's a simple Dictionary cooking time and technique. I just look up ARTICHOKE and I'm in business. If there are any questions about what some of the words like 'tightly cover' mean, look in the Index for a reference, or check the general information chapters in the front of the book, complete with clear illustrations.

Cooking in the microwave oven is different, but it is well worth learning. The more you do, the less you will have to look up. If you're at all like me, this Dictionary will stay useful.

Cross-references to other entries in this Dictionary appear in SMALL CAPITAL LETTERS. Recipe titles are capitalized. All cooking times are for large ovens unless specifically stated.

·A·

ACORN SQUASH This delicious winter squash is better cooked in the microwave oven than any other way. The resulting squash is smooth, not fibrous. Because it cooks so rapidly in the microwave oven, you will be able to prepare it more often.

Cooked acorn squash can be a wonderful component of soups, purées and even desserts. See Acorn Squash Soup, Acorn Squash Purée and Thanksgiving Pudding. For cooking times, see SQUASH.

ALCOHOL Many flavours used in cooking are carried in alcohol, ranging from red wine to vanilla and the other estracts, from brandy or Cognac to pastis. Alcohol, and hence the flavours it carries, volatilizes much more quickly in microwave cooking than by other means. It is therefore unnecessary to flame such high-proof alcohols as brandy when adding them to food to be cooked in the microwave oven; if this eliminates a measure of drama from cooking, it certainly adds safety. The percentage of spirits in any given recipe should be increased by one half if cooked for a short time, and doubled if cooked for more than 7 or 8 minutes.

ALLSPICE See SPICES

ALMOND These nuts can be bought in the shell, shelled (with the skin left on) or blanched (with skin removed). They are often blanched and ground into a fine powder or paste for use in baking, curries and old recipes for soup. To grind, use a nut grater (which looks much like a rotary cheese grater) or grind in a food processor. Use a blender to make paste.

Almonds often require some preparation, such as toasting, before they can be used in a recipe, and in this the microwave oven is an invaluable helper. Seasoned, toasted almonds make a good snack with drinks. For blanching, salting, spicing and toasting, see NUTS. See also Pralines, Praline Paste and Praline Powder.

ANISEED These small seeds taste like a subtle version of liquorice and are often used to flavour liquors. They are sadly underused in seasoning food. Try toasting them whole and sprinkling on chicken or veal stew or powdering them in an electric coffee mill (30 g/1 oz of whole aniseeds will yield 4 tablespoons ground seed). See GRINDING and TOASTING.

APPLE The microwave oven bakes apples beautifully, keeping the skin a good colour. It also quickly prepares apple purée, with or without butter or sugar for applesauce. See Maple-Syrup-Baked Apples.

Remember that apples will not caramelize when they are baked, but stay pale in colour. They will darken with the longer cooking of Apple Butter.

COOKING TIMES FOR APPLES

Times are the same for large and medium ovens. For small oven, add 1 minute per apple to cooking time. Core apples; peel top 4 cm/1½ inches; rub cut sides with lemon; arrange the apples in a container just large enough to hold them in a ring so that they do not touch. If using a container with a lid, add 2 tablespoons water. If using a container without a lid, cover tightly with microwave cling film. If using cling film, prick with the tip of a sharp knife after cooking.

Granny Smith apples 250–275 g/8–9 oz each. See illustration page 34.

1 apple	3 min. (rest, covered, 5 min.)
2 apples	3 min. 30 sec. (rest 5 min.)
4 apples	5 min. 15 sec. (rest 5 min.)
6 apples	9 min. (rest 5 min., puncture wrap and drape apples with a towel)

Dessert apples About 200 g/7 oz each

1 apple	1 min.45 sec.
4 apples	4 min.

Cooking apples About 300 g/10 oz each.

1 apple	2 min. 30 sec.
4 apples	4 min. 45 sec.

Yield

750 g/1½ apples	about 600 ml/1 pint applesauce

APRICOT The brief season for these glorious, sweet little fruits is one of early summer's delights. The rest of the year we can enjoy them dried. The dried fruit makes good jam, is much used as a glaze in baking, and is the base for wonderful purées to be used in desserts like soufflés and in sauces, sweet or savoury. To plump dried apricots, see SOAKING, dried fruit. See also Sweet Apricot Purée, Tart Apricot Purée and Apricot Sauce.

ARROWROOT This starch is expensive and doesn't work well for last-minute thickening in the microwave oven; replace with CORNFLOUR, BEURRE MANIÉ or ROUX.

ARTICHOKE Artichokes are the flowers of one of the desirable thistles; on the stalk, allowed to go to seed and dried, they make spectacular dried arrangements. Globe artichokes are big, roundish, green and mature in the summer season of the area in which they are planted—July in California, December in Chile. There is another kind of artichoke, small, pointed and slightly purplish in colour, that is meant to be eaten whole. See Baby Artichokes à la Grecque.

The microwave oven is a blessing for cooking artichokes. It eliminates the need for water, time (as much as half an hour), the tricky business of balancing a plate on the artichokes to keep them submerged, and the dangers and mess of dealing with a large pan of boiling water when you are done with it. It turns out artichokes that are rich in vitamins, never soggy and so green that some guests may have trouble believing they are cooked. It even means that fancy recipes calling for artichoke bottoms become feasible once again. Simply let the cooked artichokes cool; pull off the leaves;

scrape out the chokes with a silver spoon and rub the cleaned bottom with a cut lemon.

The procedure for cooking globe artichokes is simple. Trim the artichokes (most easily done with a serrated knife): Cut each stalk flush with the bottom of the artichoke; cut 2.5 cm/1 inch off the top of the artichoke. Neatly trim off other prickly leaf tips. Pull off any browned bottom leaves. As you work, rub all cut surfaces with lemon to keep them from discolouring. See illustration page 46.

Place artichokes in a container just large enough to hold them, in a ring so that they do not touch. If using a container with a lid, add 2 tablespoons water. If using a container without a lid, cover tightly with microwave cling film. If using cling film, prick with the tip of a sharp knife after cooking. Cook at 100%. With a fingernail, press the bottom of an artichoke; it should give. Remove from the oven. Let stand 5 minutes.

COOKING TIMES FOR ARTICHOKES

Baby artichokes 25 g/¾ oz each, about 18 per 500 g/1 lb. Remove round bottom leaves; trim leaf tips; cover tightly.

500 g/1 lb artichokes with 500 ml/16 fl oz stock and 175 ml/6 fl oz olive oil, turned once (1.5 litre/2½ pint soufflé)	12 min

Small artichokes 60 g/2 oz each. Trim as baby artichokes; cover tightly.

4 artichokes	10 min.
8 artichokes	11 min.
16 artichokes	14 min.
8 artichokes with 300 ml/½ pint liquid, turned once (2.5 litre/ 4 pint soufflé)	13 min.

Large artichokes 250–350 g/8–12 oz each. Place in containers and arrange as in general introduction.

1 artichoke	7 min.
1 artichoke	12 min. (small oven)
2 artichokes	10 min.

2 artichokes	20 min. (small oven with turntable)
4 artichokes	15 min.
6 artichokes	19 min.

Yields

250 g/8 oz artichoke	30 g/1 oz heart
6 average hearts	185 g/6½ oz
185 g/6½ oz hearts	185 g/6½ oz purée

ASPARAGUS Another vegetable that cooks quickly and well in the microwave oven without any water—no tying in little bunches—and that keeps its colour.

Trim the asparagus by snapping off the woody ends. Peel, if desired, from just below the tip to the end with a vegetable peeler. When cooking whole spears, lay them two to three deep (pointing in the same direction) in a rectangular baking dish. Cover tightly with microwave cling film and cook at 100%.

Tips or short pieces to be cooked before incorporation in another dish should be placed, by the 250 g/8 oz batch, in a container or containers just large enough to hold them. Cover tightly with microwave cling film. If using one container, place in centre of oven. Several containers should be placed in a circle so they do not touch. Prick cling film after cooking.

However you cook asparagus, carefully uncover it as soon as it comes out of the oven; wrapped, the asparagus will continue to steam and can overcook very quickly. If you are using the asparagus tips or pieces in a dish where they will be reheated, place them in a sieve immediately after cooking and run plenty of cold water over them to keep them firm.

COOKING TIMES FOR ASPARAGUS

Whole spears Trim. Arrange 2 or 3 deep in a dish just large enough to hold them; cover tightly.

125 g/4 oz	4 min. (small oven)
250 g/8 oz	2 min. 30 sec.
250 g/8 oz	5 min. (small oven)
500 g/1 lb	4 min. 15 sec.
1 kg/2 lb	7 min.

Tips and/or stalks 2.5–5 cm/1–2 inch lengths. Place in containers and arrange as in general instructions.

250 g/8 oz	3 min.
500 g/1 lb	4 min. 30 sec.

Yield

500 g/1 lb asparagus	500 ml/16 fl oz purée

AUBERGINE This vegetable comes into its own in the microwave oven. Now it is true that you will not get a charred taste cooking it this way, nor can you fry it in the microwave oven, but you will get a lightness of taste and lack of bitterness. Skins on whole aubergines—pricked a few times so the vegetables don't explode while cooking—have a nicer colour than those of aubergines cooked any other way. The flesh stays a lovely pale green that is attractive for dips. See Classic Aubergine Appetizer and Aubergine Appetizer with Oriental Seasonings.

LARGE PURPLE AUBERGINE

COOKING TIMES FOR LARGE WHOLE PURPLE AUBERGINE

Prick several times with a fork; set on 2 layers of paper towel, uncovered.

250 g/8 oz	8 min.
500 g/1 lb	12 min.
500 g/1 lb	16 min. (small oven)
1 kg/2 lb	18 to 20 min.

SMALL PURPLE AUBERGINE

These are miniature versions of the large aubergine. The best are 7.5–10 cm/3–4 inches long. They are attractive halved and stuffed (see page 72). They are also excellent as part of a mixed vegetable dish.

COOKING TIMES FOR SMALL PURPLE AUBERGINE

Halved and stuffed 10 cm/4 inches long; cover tightly.

6 aubergines; stuff after 3 min. (22.5 cm/9 inch flan dish)	7 min.

CHINESE AUBERGINE

These are the long thin aubergines in various colours that are so often pictured in Chinese paintings.

COOKING TIMES FOR WHOLE CHINESE AUBERGINE

Prick several times with a fork; cook in a dish just large enouth to hold them; cover tightly.

250 g/8 oz	10 to 12 min.
500 g/1 lb	15 min.

AVOCADO I really don't like cooked avocados. I buy them ripe and use them raw in salads and dips. If fate has brought you a hard avocado and you absolutely must use it, cut it in half lengthways and remove the stone. Place avocado halves, side by side, thin end next to fat end, in a container just large enough to hold them. Cover tightly with microwave cling film. Cook for 1 minute at 100%. Prick film; remove from oven; uncover and run halves under cold water. The avocado will be softer, edible— but not my choice

⎯⎯⎯ B ⎯⎯⎯

BACON Cooking bacon in the microwave oven is a trick most people seem to have learned, and it certainly beats cooking it in hot fat in a frying pan. The timing depends on the thickness and number of rashers and how crisp you want them. Bacon rashers cooked in the microwave oven stay flat—great for sandwiches—and the cleaning is minimal. Be careful; remember that you are dealing with hot fat. The fat in the meat permits browning.

Do not let the rashers overlap or they will not cook properly. If cooking 2 rashers, place 2 sheets of paper towel under them on a plate. Cover loosely with another sheet. To cook 4 to 8 slices, arrange on 4 sheets of paper towel. Cover loosely with 1 sheet. Cooking bacon is an instance where oven size and power make a big difference.

Sometimes you may need, as for Clams Casino, to blanch bacon, meaning to partially cook it in water (which also eliminates salt). To blanch bacon rashers, whole strips or pieces of any size, place in a shallow container and add water to cover. Cook, uncovered, at 100%. It is a simple matter to cut raw bacon into pieces if the rashers are cold and you use a sharp knife or scissors. Defrosting softens bacon, making it easy to separate frozen rashers.

BLANCHING TIMES FOR BACON

Rashers Arrange in a single layer in a shallow container, uncovered.

8 bacon rashers with 250 ml/8 fl oz water	2 min. 30 sec.

COOKING TIMES FOR BACON

Thin-sliced streaky bacon In large microwave oven, arrange as above.

2 rashers	2 min. for moist bacon
	3 min. for crisp bacon
4 rashers	2 min. 30 sec., moist
	3 min. 30 sec., crisp
6 rashers	4 min., moist
	4 min. 45 sec., crisp
8 rashers	6 min., moist
	6 min. 45 sec., crisp

Thin-sliced streaky bacon In medium or small microwave oven, arrange as above.

2 rashers	2 min. 30 sec. for moist bacon
	4 min. for crisp bacon
4 rashers	3 min., moist
	5 min. 30 sec., crisp
6 rashers	4 min. 45 sec., moist
	6 min. 30 sec., crisp
8 rashers	Ovens too small

Streaky bacon rashers Cut 5 mm/¼ inch thick. In any oven, arrange as above.

2 rashers	4 min.
4 rashers	5 min. 30 sec.
6 rashers	6 min. 30 sec.
8 rashers	7 min. (large oven only)

Back bacon In any oven, arrange on a single sheet of paper towel—uncovered.

2 rashers	1 min.
4 rashers	1 min. 45 sec.
6 rashers	2 min. 15 sec.

DEFROSTING TIMES FOR BACON

Rashers In unopened package, heat at 100%.

500 g/1 lb	1 min.

LARDONS

These thick match-shaped strips of bacon are cooked or 'rendered' and used as a classic garnish for Chicken in Red Wine and other kinds of stews. Buy bacon in a piece of the thickness your recipe requires. When cooked, remove lardons from fat with a slotted spoon. Save the fat for the recipe if needed. The lardons can be reheated briefly by placing them on a piece of paper towel in the microwave oven and heating at 100% for 30 seconds.

COOKING TIMES FOR LARDONS

Bacon lardons Cut 5–10 mm/¼–½ inch bacon rashers into strips 5 cm/2 inches long and 5–10 mm/¼–½ inch thick. Place in a single layer; cover loosely with a sheet of paper towel.

125 g/4 oz bacon	7 min.

BAKING Technically, baking is anything done in an oven, usually without added liquid, or even in an enclosed pan on top of the stove without liquid.

Cakes, pies, biscuits and breads, even soufflés, are what most of us consider to be baking. To tell you the truth, this is not where the microwave oven shines. You can't use your usual baking recipes and expect them to work. Soufflés won't work no matter what you do.

I have developed some fabulous baking recipes (see Cakes and Biscuits, pages 356–376). If you read the introduction to that section and the introduction to Cakes, you will see what the problems are and how you can avoid them.

Baking problems involve the protein gluten (the stretchy part of starch in wheat flour and to a lesser extent in other starches) and the way it absorbs water. Avoiding wheat flour is the best solution; otherwise you will have an overly wet, unpleasant food. However, yeast, baking powder and bicarbonate of soda need gluten to accomplish the magic of rising.

Egg-risen mixtures have problems of their own. They tend to rise too fast and then collapse, tough and unpleasant, which is what happens to soufflés. However, if the eggs are carefully balanced against a nongluten starch like cornflour, the whole thing can be made to work. Try my recipes before plunging in to adapt your own. They may give you some guidelines.

Nonsweet, nonbread-baking works very well in the microwave oven, the kind of baking that used to be done in the breadbaker's oven after the bread came out: stuffed vegetables, baked (not roasted) meats such as pot roasts and casseroles (excluding cassoulet, which needs to form a crust). The difference between my results and those of the bread oven is that my method doesn't take overnight, only minutes.

Proving or rising dough works well in the microwave oven. See RAISING.

BAKING POWDER The microwave oven has very little effect on the way this works; but because most flour baking is unsatisfactory in the microwave oven, you will not be using much of it. When you do use it, remember that it only has about a 4-month shelf life once opened. It's too bad no one packages it in more reasonable sizes; but, as it's cheap it's worth the trouble of replacing.

BALSAMIC VINEGAR See VINEGAR.

BANANA We tend to eat one kind of banana, the large, yellow, sweet ones, mostly raw. The future will probably bring the broader knowledge of various plantains, many of them intended mainly for cooking. Even the ubiquitous banana makes a wonderful dessert when cooked. See Rummy Bananas.

We have become accustomed to bananas that are picked so very green that not only are they still green by the time we buy them, but they remain green in our fruit baskets. The microwave oven can—and here it is tempting to say 'magically'—ripen this fruit for you. This is better for feeding babies than hard, underripe fruit.

Shield a banana in its skin for 2.5 cm/1 inch at either end with doubled aluminium foil (see illustration page 21). Cook 1 minute at 100% in a large or medium microwave oven, for 1 minute 30 seconds in a small oven.

Yields

scant 250 g/8 oz	1 large banana
1 large banana	125 ml/4 fl oz purée
1.25 kg/2½ lb	6 large bananas
6 large bananas	675 ml/22 fl oz purée

BARLEY One of the first grains man cultivated. At one time it was the principle grain used in peasant bread-making. Today, sadly, it has declined in culinary popularity, although vast quantities of it are used in the production of spirits. It is a nice change from rice and potatoes both as a side dish (see Creamy Barley) and as a soup ingredient (see Mushroom Barley Soup).

In cooking, we generally use pearl barley, which is husked, cooks rapidly and has a pleasant texture. If you have had the barley on the shelf for along time, it is liable to be very hard and dry. Add 5 minutes to the cooking times below and add more liquid if needed.

COOKING TIMES FOR MEDIUM PEARL BARLEY

Risotto technique Uncovered.

50 g/1⅔ oz barley with 250 ml/8 fl oz stock (20 × 15 cm/8 × 6 inch flat oval dish)	16 min.
200 g/7 oz barley with 750 ml/1¼ pints stock (30 × 22.5 × 5 cm/12 × 9 × 2 inch flat oval dish)	27 min.
200 g/7 oz barley as above	43 min.(small oven)

Boiled Cook in a 2.5 litre/4 pint soufflé; cover tightly with 2 sheets microwave cling film; omit resting time.

200 g/7 oz barley with 1 litre/1¾ pints water	30 min.
400 g/14 oz barley with 1.5 litres/2½ pints water	30 min.

BASIL I use this loveliest of herbs frequently, and I am delighted that it is now available fresh, year-round, in many supermarkets. There are two basic varieties, the large-leaf French basil and the smaller-leaf bush basil, which is generally used to make pesto in the Genoan style. Bush basil is more peppery and aromatic. Look for crisp leaves without any black spots. Wash thoroughly and, if cutting, cut across the veins in the leaves. Often, basil leaves are nicest when used whole. They make a wonderful addition to summer salads. See DRYING, herbs.

BATTER Batter-based breads, cakes and pancakes are almost useless in microwave cooking.

BAY LEAF Even more than with the other dried herbs, be careful with this one or you will get a bitter flavour. If in doubt, use less. Most recipes call for too much bay leaf in any case. Consider adding it only for the last 4 to 5 minutes of the cooking time.

Remember to remove any leaves before serving or reheating a dish; people can choke on them.

BEAN CURD See SOYA

BEANS When I first started using the microwave oven, I was so infatuated with its speed that I dismissed any usage that wasn't super-quick. After I calmed down a little, I realized that the reduced time involved in soaking dried beans and cooking them the microwave way was the difference between almost never cooking them from scratch and feeling free to use them as an ingredient.

Some pulses cook as beans do. See PULSES or specific kind of pulse.

Canned beans are obviously no problem; you are just reheating.

FRESH BEANS

GREEN, WAX, HARICOT VERT or FRENCH YARD-LONG BEANS and other fresh pole and bush beans are quick, not watery, and retain their colour in the microwave oven. Top, tail and string as necessary. If the beans are very large, or if the recipe calls for it, either cut into lengths or halve lengthways. Cooking times are based on beans in 250 g/8 oz amounts, sprinkled with water, in a container or containers just large enough to hold them. Cover tightly with microwave cling film. If using one container, place in centre of oven. More containers should be placed in a circle so that they do not touch. Prick cling film after cooking.

BROAD BEANS

Dried BROAD BEANS do not cook to best advantage in the microwave oven. You blanch them to make shelling easier. Cook them on top of the stove.

DRIED BEANS

Dried-bean cooking times are determined by the size of the beans. It seems odd, but smaller beans take slightly longer to cook because there are more of them to the 500 g/1 lb. The cooking times for these beans follow.

Never salt the beans before cooking, as it

toughens the skin. All dried beans must be soaked before cooking.

Large dried beans: black beans, blackeyed beans, cannellini, kidney beans, red beans, pink beans, pinto beans.

Small dried beans: flageolets, haricot beans.

Legumes: Broad beans, chick-peas, lentils, split peas.

SOAKING DRIED BEANS AND PEAS

To soak 150–300 g/5–10 oz dried beans of any size or pulses, place in a 2.5 litre/4 pint soufflé dish with 500 ml/16 fl oz water. Cover tightly with microwave cling film. Cook at 100% for 15 minutes. Remove from oven and let stand, covered, for 5 minutes. Uncover and add 500 ml/16 fl oz very hot water. Re-cover and let stand for 1 hour. Drain.

COOKING TIMES FOR LARGE DRIED BEANS

Put *presoaked* beans in 2.5 litre/4 pint soufflé; cover tightly with 2 sheets microwave cling film.

185 g/6½ oz beans with 1 litre/1¾ pints warm water	35 min. (rest 20 min.)
375 g/13 oz beans with 1.5 litres/2½ pints warm water	45 min. (rest 20 min.)

COOKING TIMES FOR SMALL DRIED BEANS

Put *presoaked* beans in a 2.5 litre/4 pint soufflé; cover tightly with 2 sheets microwave cling film.

150–300 g/5–10 oz beans with 1 litre/1¾ pints warm water	40 min. (rest 30 min.)

COOKING TIMES FOR FRESH BEANS

Whole green and wax beans, trimmed Place in containers and arrange as in general instructions.

125 g/4 oz beans	3 min. 30 sec. to 4 min.
125 g/4 oz beans	5 min. (small oven)
250 g/8 oz beans	4 min. to 4 mins. 30 sec.
250 g/8 oz	6 min. (small oven)
500 g/1 lb	6 to 8 min.

Whole haricots verts and yard-long beans, trimmed Arrange in a single layer; cover tightly.

125 g/4 oz beans with 250 ml/8 fl oz water (1 litre/2 pint measuring jug)	6 min.
500 g/1 lb beans with 750 ml/1¼ pints water (35 × 27.5 × 5 cm/14 × 11 × 2 inch dish)	15 min.

BEEF This may still be one of our favourite foods, no matter what we have learned about limiting its ingestion for our health's sake. When it comes to cooking those most favourite cuts of all, the steaks and roasts, the microwave oven is of no earthly use at all; no amount of browning mixture or glaze will conceal the fact that these cuts would have cooked better in a conventional oven, on a barbecue, in a sauté pan or under a grill. Use the microwave oven for DEFROSTING.

It also has limitations in cooking pot roast and stew. If you wish to brown the meat before cooking, do so on top of the stove; browning pans are inadequate. Prolonged microwave cooking has a tendency to toughen meat; do not exceed recipe times. Do not use too much liquid: it is inefficient, boils the meat and makes a less good sauce. Follow the timings and proportions below or in recipes selected from the Index.

Such foods can be eaten when ready or reheated, which mellows the flavours (see MELLOWING).

The recipes I have worked out are very good, and they certainly save time. They are not fancy. They are the kind of homely food I relish at parties as well as on my own.

Dishes made with minced meat such as meat loaf, chilli and pasta sauces can be very successful. See Leonard Schwartz's Meat

Loaf, Chunky Beef Chilli, and Salsa Bolognese.

COOKING TIMES FOR BEEF

Brisket Cover tightly.

1.1 kg/2¼ lb with 350 ml/ 12 fl oz liquid and 500 g/1 lb vegetables, turned once (2.5 litre/4 pint soufflé)	60 mins.

Chuck Cover tightly.

1 kg/2 lb, 5 mm/¼ inch cubes, with about 1 litre/ 1¾ pints liquid and 350 g/12 oz vegetables (35 × 27.5 × 5 cm/14 × 11 × 2 inch dish)	15 min.
1 kg/2 lb, 2.5 cm/1 inch cubes, with 250 ml/8 fl oz liquid and 500 g/1 lb vegetables (2.5 litre/4 pint soufflé)	18 min.
1.5 kg/3 lb, 1 cm/½ inch thick slices, with 350 ml/ 12 fl oz liquid and 500 g/1 lb, vegetables (2.5 litre/4 pint soufflé)	15 min.

Minced beef Cover tightly.

1 kg/2 lb with about 1 litre/1¾ pints liquid and 350 g/12 oz vegetables (35 × 27.5 × 5 cm/14 × 11 × 2 inch dish)	5 min.

Meat Loaf

1 kg/2 lb minced beef with 500 ml/15 fl oz thick liquid, uncovered (22.5 × 12.5 × 7.5 cm/9 × 5 × 3 inch loaf dish)	12 min., stand 10 min.
1.5 kg/3 lb minced meat with 3 eggs and 350 g/12 oz vegetables, shaped as below and covered tightly for half of cooking time:	4 min
250 g/8 oz loaf (in 25 cm/10 inch round dish)	
500 g/1 lb loaf (or a 25 cm/10 inch round dish)	7 min.
8 250 g/8 oz loaves (30 cm/12 inch round dish)	8 min.
1 kg/2 lb loaf (22.5 cm/9 inch ring mould)	9 min.

BEEF STOCK See Meat Stocks

BEEF GLAZE See Meat Glazes.

BEEF LIVER Beef liver is particularly good in pâtés, where its strong taste has a contribution to make. If you can buy it, it should be considerably cheaper than other livers. Substitute it happily in Country Pâté and Pâté with Chinese Black Beans, but not in Scandinavian Liver Pâté, where its taste would be overwhelming. It is really not worth cooking on its own.

BEETROOT Often sold precooked to be sliced into salads, combined with potatoes in purées or included in soups and stews. When baked, beetroot retain a maximum of colour and flavour. Microwave cooking achieves the same effect rapidly and with almost no mess.

Trim the leaves down to within 2.5 cm/ 1 inch of the beetroot. (If they are small, save them for POT GREENS.) Scrub beetroots well. Arrange beetroot in a circle towards the edge of 2.5 litre/4 pint soufflé dish, or a casserole with a tightly fitting lid. If using soufflé dish, cover tightly with microwave cling film. If using casserole, add 2 tablespoons water. Cook at 100% for timings below, or until the beetroot can easily be pierced with the tip of a knife. If using cling film, prick with the tip of a sharp knife. If using immediately, cool slightly, trim the tops and slip off the skins. (You can then clean your hands with some lemon if you don't wish to be mistaken for Lady Macbeth.)

Precooked beetroots will last, well wrapped and refrigerated, for over a week and are worth keeping on hand. See Cold Beetroot Borscht and Beetroot and Potato Purée.

COOKING TIMES FOR BEETROOT

Small beetroot 60 g/2 oz each. Put in a

dish at least 1 cm/½ inch deep and large enough to hold them in a single layer; cover tightly.

250 g/8 oz	8 min.
250 g/8 oz	12 min. (small oven)
500 g/1 lb	12 min.
750 g/1½ lb	16 min.

Large beetroots As above.

325 g/11 oz	20 min.
1.25 kg/2½ lb	25 to 30 min.

Yields

4 small beetroots	250 g/8 oz
250 g/8 oz	150 ml/¼ pint purée

BEURRE MAINÉ This standard of the French repertoire is simply made of equal quantities of flour and butter worked together to form a smooth paste. It is easily done in the food processor. You can make a quantity ahead and roll it up in polythene to use as needed. About 1 tablespoon of beurre mainé thickens 250 ml/8 fl oz of sauce. It must be stirred into your stew or other saucy item about 5 minutes before the end of cooking time. Generally, I have found FLOUR or Roux to be better last minute thickeners.

BICARBONATE OF SODA We use this not so much as a raising agent, but to counteract the acidity of buttermilk or other ingredients in some recipes.

BLACK BEAN For cooking times, see BEANS. Chinese black beans require no presoaking if the recipe requires 3 minutes or more cooking time. If not, barely cover with water in a glass jug or bowl. Cover tightly with microwave cling film. Heat at 100% for 1 minute 30 seconds.

BLACKBERRY Both the fat, cultivated varieties and the firmer, seedier wild ones are some of the most aromatic and delicious of berries. Substitute equal weights in Black Raspberry Jam and Big City Strawberry Shortcake.

BLACK-EYED BEAN For cooking times, see BEANS, dried

BLACK RASPBERRY These blackberry look-alikes have a more mysterious flavour. Substitute equal weights of black raspberries in Big City Strawberry Shortcake.

BLANCHING *VEGETABLES* are blanched—usually in copious, salted water—to precook them briefly so they hold their colour and flavour for more prolonged cooking. This is usually unnecessary in microwave cooking since vegetables cook so quickly and retain their colour so well. (Cook spinach and watercress, for example, directly in butter or liquid such as stock for terrific results.)

Most vegetables are blanched before freezing. Cook in water for half the normal times given for individual vegetables in this Dictionary. (Since water takes time to come to the boil, the vegetables will be less than halfway cooked.) Run cold water over blanched vegetables to stop the cooking process. Freeze.

Certain *NUTS* and *PULSES*, fresh and dried, are blanched to remove their skins. I find that the skins are much more easily removed after microwave cooking than any other method. See BEANS, NUTS and PULSES.

You will sometimes need to blanch *BACON* before using in certain recipes. See BACON

BLUEBERRY This is one berry that cooks not only more quickly but also infinitely better in the microwave oven, making richly flavoured sauces for ice creams and other desserts. Blueberry sauces are worth making in quantity when the berries are in season; store them in sterile jars or freeze the sauce in small (60 g/2 oz) quantities. Defrost in a plastic-topped glass or a microwave-safe plastic bag at 100% for 2 minutes. See Blueberry Sauce.

BOILING Most of the time you don't want to boil foods in a great deal of liquid. It slows things down. There are times when you do want to bring some liquid to boil—a soup, perhaps, or some liquid to add to a stew or to a purée to make a soup. 250 ml/8 fl oz of liquid in a 500 ml/1 pint glass measuring jug, tightly covered, takes between 2 minutes 30 seconds and 3 minutes 30 seconds at 100%. The lowest time is for water, wine and tomato juice. Three minutes covers stock, cold cream, sugar water and heavily salted water. The longest time is needed for refrigerated milk.

BOLETUS EDULIS See CEP.

BOURBON WHISKEY This strongly flavoured liquor is hard to use subtly in cooking. It is a little easier with the microwave oven because of the rapid volatilization. Bourbon is also the name of the best Mexican vanilla. See ALCOHOL

BRAISING Normally means slow, moist cooking in a tightly closed environment. Tight covering with microwave cling film mimics perfectly the pots closed with a dough seal of earlier times. Braising gradually breaks down the fibres of meats and vegetables, making them tender, and it produces marvelous gravies by extracting the flavours and gelatinous qualities of the foods and integrating them. It is like stewing, but with less liquid; and because of the rapidity of microwave cooking, it is a more successful method. Care must be taken when braising meats not to overcook them and toughen them. See Braised Leeks, Ossobuco and Chicken Fricassée.

BRAINS These ae something we are all delighted to have, but few of us eat, which is a shame. Brains are highly esteemed as food in other parts of the world. They cook wonderfully in the microwave oven, either as an ingredient for a first-course cold dish (see Brain Salad) or with a nutty brown butter enlivened by capers, lemon or vinegar. Try heating them (1 set, tightly covered with microwave cling film) with 15 g/½ oz butter, a little ham (125 g/4 oz, slivered), 2 sliced mushrooms and 75 g/2½ oz cooked or defrosted peas, enriched with

175 ml/6 fl oz Sauce Espagnole or 2 tablespoons Meat Glaze if you have it on hand. This will serve four as a first course, two as a main course.

COOKING TIMES FOR BRAINS

Trimmed With 125 ml/4 fl oz liquid; cover tightly.

1 set brains (1 litre/2 pint soufflé)	8 min.
1 set brains with 600 ml/1 pint chopped vegetables (2 litre/3½ pint soufflé)	12 min.

BRAN The husk of wheat or other grain. Comes under the heading of what's good for you. A small amount can be sprinkled into muffins and breads without changing the cooking times. Try a tablespoon sprinkled over cooked carrots.

BRANDY The generic name for fruit alcohols, grape included. Only those made from grapes in the Cognac region of Franch are called Cognac. See ALCOHOL.

BREAD Shares the difficulties of all things made with wheat flour (see BAKING, problems). Although many authors give bread recipes for the microwave oven, I find that classic breads raised with yeast are always better made in a conventional oven, especially considering the time and energy spent kneading. In the microwave oven, raised breads become a wet, spongy mess. Steamed breads, however, work well, cooking in less than one quarter of the normal, messy time spent in a bain-marie.

Most breads raised with bicarbonate of soda or baking powder (banana and nut, for example) also work well. Tea breads and muffins respond very erratically, and since they take so little time in a conventional oven, I see no benefit to making them in the microwave oven. Use the microwave oven to speed the proving and raising of yeast doughs if you like. See RAISING and REHEATING.

BREADCRUMBS Frequently used dried or buttered. See Breadcrumbs recipe.

BROAD BEAN This bean does not cook well in the microwave oven. See BEANS.

BROCCOLI One of those foods that seems to cook miraculously in the mcirowave oven. No longer do we risk soggy tops when the stalks are cooked through or nasty fibrous stalks when the florets are perfect. Our broccoli stays radiantly green and healthy. Salt is better added just after cooking, but it can be dissolved in the tiny amount of water sprinkled on before cooking. It can be served cold by placing it under cold running water immediately after removing from the oven; do not sauce until just prior to eating or it will discolour. Hot, cooked broccoli makes a lovely purée to serve with any roast or grilled meat or fish. It also is a perfect base for a hot or cold soup.

Do not try to cook whole heads—too uneven. If cooking a large quantity, arrange flower tops towards the centre of the dish with stalks pointing outward. Just a few stalks can be lined up. Florets and/or peeled and sliced stalks—good, cold, in chicken salad—can be cooked in 75 g/2½ oz batches in 500 ml/1 pint measuring jug(s) or in a dish just large enough to hold them in a single layer, tightly covered with microwave cling film. When cooking more than one batch, arrange jugs in a circle. Prick cling film with the tip of a sharp knife after cooking. One medium head will generously serve two people.

COOKING TIMES FOR BROCCOLI

Longer times are for old broccoli, or for medium or small ovens.

Stalks separated In a single layer in a dish just large enough to hold them; cover tightly.

250 g/8 oz with 1 tbsp water	4 to 6 min.
500 /1 lb with 1½ tbsp water	6 to 8 min. 30 sec.
1 kg/2 lb with 3 tbsp water	8 to 10 min.
1.25 kg/2½ lb with 4 tbsp water	12 min.

Yields

1 medium head broccoli	600 g/1¼ lb, untrimmed 425 g/15 oz, trimmed

BROCCOLI DI RAPE More stalk than floret, it has a pleasant bitter taste and is frequently used in Italian cooking. Serve as a first course, as a vegetable or over pasta. See Spaghetti with Bitter Broccoli Sauce.

COOKING TIMES FOR BROCCOLI DI RAPE

Cut into 5 cm/2 inch pieces Cover tightly.

350 g/12 oz broccoli di rape with 6 tbsp olive oil heated for 3 min. (27.5 × 21 × 5 cm/11 × 8½ × 2 inch dish)	7 min.
750 g/1½ lb broccoli di rape with 175 ml/6 fl oz olive oil heated for 4 min. (35 × 27.5 × 5 cm/14 × 11 × 2 inch dish)	10 min.

Yields

2 bunches	750 g/1½ lb, untrimmed
750 g/1½ lb	600 g/1¼ lb, trimmed

BROWNING In traditional cooking, meats are often sautéed before stewing or braising in order to sear them, sealing in their juices. In microwave cooking, that process is not necessary, since cooking proceeds so quickly that there is no excessive loss of juice. You will need much less fat than in conventional cooking; fats are used only for their flavours. I don't think you'll miss the browning in the finished flavour.

Meat browns when it roasts in the conventional way. This does not happen in the microwave oven, and all the coloured glazes in the world cannot disguise this fact. This lack of sealing, or searing, is one reason meat does not truly roast in the microwave oven. See ROASTING. If you wish a browned outer surface, sauté the food briefly on top of the stove; then complete cooking in the microwave oven, as in Ossobuco. When there are darkly coloured sauces, as in Chicken in Red Wine, you will not miss the dark colour of the pieces of meat that you would have if they had first been browned.

Browning of FATS does take place in the microwave oven. See BACON and BUTTER.

Browning of SUGARS—caramelization—is an important aspect of working with sweets. It is brilliantly easy and fabulously good in the microwave oven. See CARAMEL and Pralines. Many vegetables and fruits have high sugar contents that will caramelize. See Classic French Onion Soup and Apple Butter.

Surface browning of CHEESES, GRATINS and CASSEROLES cannot be done in the microwave oven. The surface of the food cooks no differently than the inside does. Where a browned CRUST or SKIN is desired, the best solution is to virtually complete the cooking in the microwave oven, and then brown briefly under a grill. See Macaroni Cheese and Crispiest Duck.

Of course, you can also glaze foods as long as you realize you are not roasting them. See Barbecued Chicken Legs.

BRUSSELS SPROUTS These miniature cabbages grow decoratively up the plant's stalks, hiding under leaves. Traditional at Christmas, combine with one third their weight in blanched chestnuts and toss with butter. Don't overcook them, as they easily become mushy. Oven size does make a difference in cooking times.

COOKING TIMES FOR BRUSSELS SPROUTS

Large and medium ovens Trim bottoms; rinse; in a single layer in a dish just large enough to hold them; cover tightly.

175 g/6 oz	2 min.
350 g/12 oz	3 min.
550 g/18 oz	4 min. 45 sec.
750 g/1½ lb	6 min. 45 sec.

Small oven Prepare as above.

175 g/6 oz	4 min.
350 g/12 oz	6 min.
550 g/18 oz	Oven too small

BURGHUL Cracked wheat. It is a wonderful grain to serve with dishes prepared in the microwave oven since it requires little attention and tastes good hot or cold. You must remember to allow time for the water or stock to come to the boil and for the burghul to steep, or your main dish will be ready before the burghul. To serve burghul piping hot, after steeping and just before serving, cover tightly with microwave cling film and heat in the microwave oven for 4 minutes.

For basic burghul to serve 6 to 8 people, combine 275 g/9 oz burghul with 1.75 litres/3 pints boiling water; let stand 25 minutes. Drain if necessary.

Sliced mushroom, onions or garlic, and herbs and/or spices may be cooked in the microwave oven in a little melted butter and added to the burghul: Heat 90 g/3 oz butter at 100% for 3 minutes; stir in 250 g/8 oz sliced mushrooms, 2 teaspoons ground cumin, 2 tablespoons finely chopped parsley and 3 cloves finely chopped garlic. Cook, uncovered, at 100% for 5 minutes. Stir into steeped burghul with salt and pepper to taste just before reheating in the microwave oven.

BUTCHER'S SALT See SALT.

BUTTER In this book I always use unsalted so that it will contain less water and be fresher. In a day when we all have freezers, there is no reason for salted butter. See Index for butter sauce recipes and compound butters like Snail Butter (no snails in it) that can be used for various recipes. See also FATS and SOFTENING.

Unless specified, all butter in this book is cooked from cold, straight from the refrigerator.

Butter contains varying amounts of water. If it contains a great deal of water, you may hear the butter pop when it is being melted. This can also happen in metal-lined multiuse ovens if condensing moisture drops back into the butter; the butter may spit and mess up the oven. Always melt butter in a fairly large container. If spitting continues to haunt you, loosely cover the container with paper towels

CLARIFIED BUTTER

This removes the water and remaining milk solids that tend to burn during high-heat cooking. Sometimes it is aged to make GHEE for Indian cooking. I tend to be lazy about clarifying butter, but here is how it is done: Cut the butter into 15 g/½ oz pieces. Heat, loosely covered with paper towel, at 100% to melt. Skim solids from surface of liquid and discard. Pour off clear liquid carefully leaving the milky solids behind.

MELTING TIMES FOR BUTTER

Cut into 15 g/½ oz pieces. Cover loosely with paper towel; cook at 100%.

125 g/4 oz or less butter (500 ml/1 pint measuring jug)	*2 min.*
250 g/8 oz butter (1 litre/2 pint measuring jug)	*2 min. 30 sec.*
500 g/1 lb butter (2 litre/ 3½ pint glass jug or bowl)	*4 min.*

Yields

125 g/4 oz butter	*5½ tbsp clarified butter*
250 g/8 oz butter	*175 ml/6 fl oz clarified butter*
500 g/1 lb butter	*275 ml/13 fl oz clarified butter*

BROWNED BUTTER

Browned butter (beurre noisette) has a rather different flavour. Strain through a sieve lined with paper towel.

BROWNING TIMES FOR BUTTER

Cut into 15 g/½ oz pieces. Cover loosely with paper towel; cook at 100%.

125 g/4 oz butter (1 litre/ 2 pint measuring jug)	*8 min.*
250 g/8 oz butter (1 litre/ 2 pint measuring jug)	*10 min.*

Yields

125 g/4 oz butter	*125 ml/4 fl oz browned butter*
250 g/8 oz butter	*250 ml/8 fl oz browned butter*

BUTTERMILK Today's buttermilk—the liquid left after the butter is churned—tastes little like the thick clabbered stuff I remember from my childhood. It is thin and innocuous, drunk by some and used by others to give a tart edge to the taste of scones and other baked goods, where its acid is generally offset with a little bicarbonate of soda.

BUTTERNUT SQUASH Cut this squash in half and scoop out fibres and seeds. For cooking times, see SQUASH.

BUTTON ONION These small, generally white onions no bigger than 1 cm/½ inch in diameter used to be a highlight of midsummer. Now they are being specially grown and are available almost year-round.

Rather than peeling them raw, it is easier to cut off the stalk end, blanch them and then pop the skins right off. See ONIONS. While they can be butter-glazed or mixed with Béchamel, they are most spectacular à la Grecque or Monégasque.

•C•

CABBAGE Great green cabbage got a terrible reputation during the many years that it was virtually the only green, nonroot vegetable to last through the winter. It was generally old, overcooked and smelly. Let us not give up on this wonderful family of vegetables that has taken such a bad rap. Young cabbage shredded and wilted (melted) in butter with seasonings is good as a vegetable dish, or as part of a recipe.

To cook in wedges: Remove any shabby outer leaves, core cabbage and cut into wedges. To blanch whole leaves as containers for stuffings: Remove unattractive outer leaves; core deeply; cook the cabbage head whole. If leaves are still difficult to pull away intact, cook 1 minute more.

See also BRUSSELS SPROUTS, CHINESE LEAVES, PAK CHOI, RED CABBAGE and SAVOY CABBAGE.

COOKING TIMES FOR GREEN OR WHITE CABBAGE

Shredded cabbage Cover tightly; season fat or liquid if desired.

250 g/8 oz (1 litre/2 pint measuring jug)	4 min.
250 g/8 oz (1 litre/2 pint measuring jug)	6 min. (small oven)
350 g/12 oz with 1 tbsp liquid or 30 g/1 oz fat (2 litre/3½ pint soufflé dish)	12 min.
1 kg/2 lb with 1 tbsp water or 45 g/1½ oz fat (2.5 litre/4 pint soufflé dish)	12 to 14 min.

Whole leaves Use cabbage whole, deeply cored, set uncovered on turntable or plate

1.25 kg/2½ lb cabbage	5 min.

Wedges Cut each wedge 125–150 g/4–5 oz, about 6–8.5 cm/2½–3½ inches at the widest part. Arrange in a shallow dish in a ring, petal-fashion, with core edge toward outside of dish; cover tightly.

2 wedges (20 cm/8 inch dish)	8 min.
2 wedges (20 cm/8 inch dish)	12 min. (small oven)
4 wedges (25 cm/10 inch dish)	12 min.
6 wedges (30 cm/12 inch round dish)	16 min.

COOKING TIMES FOR RED CABBAGE

Shredded Cover tightly.

1.1 kg/2¼ lb with 35 g/ 1¼ oz butter and 175 g/6 oz onion; 175 ml/6 fl oz liquid added after 8 min. (30 × 25 × 7.5 cm/12 × 10 × 3 inch dish)	18 min.

CALAMARI See SQUID.

CALF'S LIVER The liver of very young veal is delicate in taste and texture. It should not be overcooked. I think it is best sautéed or grilled. In this book it is used to make Scandinavian Liver Pâté. Try to get for kosher calf's liver; because of the way the animals are killed, the liver is more delicate. Make sure the butcher has removed the external membrane and the big veins.

CANNELLINI See BEANS for cooking times.

CAPER Salted, preserved flower buds that make a nice addition to Browned Butter Sauce and give an edge to the flavour of some of the blander meats such as veal escalopes and brains. Oddly, the smaller buds are considered choicer than the larger ones. Taste capers for saltiness before using them. If unpleasantly salty, run them under cold water in a small sieve. Be stingy when adding salt or acid to a dish or sauce containing them.

CAPON A bird that is born male but grows up neutered. Do not attempt to roast in a microwave oven (see ROASTING). Capon may be steamed for use in salads or sauced dishes. For timing and method, see CHICKEN, whole bird.

CARAMEL Thanks to the way sugar cooks in the microwave oven, making caramel of different colours and hardness is easy, rapid and reliable. Tight wrapping causes condensation from steam to continually wash the insides of the cooking container, eliminating problems of crystallization; and cooking in a glass jug or bowl permits you to see exactly the colour the caramel is turning and to stop it if it is becoming too dark. Pans used for making caramel on top of the stove are frequently ruined or hard to clean. This is no problem in the microwave oven.

Caramel is nothing but cooked sugar that has browned from the heat. As a sweet, the sugar has been sufficiently cooked, usually with a small amount of water, so that it liquifies. This sweet caramel may vary in colour from pale gold to very dark brown, and from reasonably soft—employable in chewy sweets—to the hard-crack stage used in nut brittles and as a rich stained-glass covering for cakes and other desserts.

I must emphasize how important a tight seal is here. If you don't get one, the sugar will cook unevenly and will crystallize. Use a large enough piece of microwave cling film to extend 7.5 cm/3 inches down the sides of the jug or bowl (and wrap the handle), and to have enough give so that it attaches firmly to the glass above and below the handle as well as below the spout.

Avoid stirring, as this may cloud the caramel. If stirring is absolutely necessary, use a metal spoon lightly coated with a vegetable oil. The less hard stages of caramel will be very lightly coloured. The caramel—hard in particular—continues to darken after it comes out of the oven. Be very careful when removing the film from hot sugar mixtures as the steam is very hot. Prick the film to release the steam; pull an edge of the film away from the container and lift.

Other kinds of foods caramelize as well, so that when we roast a bird or piece of meat to a rich brown exterior in a conventional oven, we would also call this caramelization. Onions, with their high sugar content, caramelize as they cook and their liquid is driven off. See French Onion Soup.

See also SUGAR, SIMPLE SYRUP, Pralines, Caramel Sauce and Peanut Brittle.

COOKING TIMES FOR SUGAR AND CARAMEL

To make 250 ml/8 fl oz, stir together 200 g/7 oz sugar with 5½ tbsp warm water to remove any lumps. Place in a 1 litre/2 pint glass measuring jug. Cook tightly covered at 100% in a large oven. Prick film before moving from oven.

Soft ball	5 min.
Hard ball	6 min.
Hard crack	7 min. 30 sec.
Caramel, coloured and hard	9 min.
Caramel, coloured and hard	16 to 17 min. (small oven)

CARAWAY If these tasty seeds have been sitting around your kitchen for some time getting musty just waiting for you to sprinkle them on buttered noodles, they may benefit from a brief but rejuvenating toast. See TOASTING, small seeds and GRINDING.

Yield

1 tbsp, whole   ¾ tbsp, ground

CARDAMOM Often a component of curry powder, this otherwise underused spice can be bought ground or in its seed pod, which is a papery husk containing many small seeds. While whole pods can be cooked in stocks that are to be strained, I generally crumble the pods between my fingers to remove the husks and separate the seeds before using them. See GRINDING and TOASTING, whole spices. See also Steamed Papaya Pudding.

CARP Long-lived freshwater fish that grow to great size and are related to the decorative goldfish in the bowl, carp can be either light, clean, medium-soft-fleshed, or it can be nasty if coming from muddy waters. It can be cooked as any white-fleshed, milk-tasting fish (see FISH for cooking times) and is a traditional component of Gefilte Fish.

CARROT These basic vegetables cook rapidly in the microwave oven without getting mushy. This means that they can be added to a stew or soup right at the beginning of the cooking time and emerge as recognizable pieces of carrot.

Try to avoid buying those huge roots known as chefs' specials because some chefs buy them to minimize peeling time. These monsters have thick cores and tend to be bitter. When buying small carrots, check to see if they are real babies, or midgets or dwarves. The two latter kinds are genetically small but full-grown; peel and cook as other carrots. True baby carrots, about 2 cm/¾ inch wide at the top and 7.5–12.5 cm/3–5 inches long, may not even need peeling, especially if they have just been pulled from the garden.

Scrub carrots with a hard brush, and peel if the skin has any gritty texture or bitter taste. Cooking in butter and a little bit of sugar and salt is particularly nice. Arrange with the thin tips towards the centre of a dish or place in a microwave-safe plastic bag. Season and add butter. Seal. Cook at 100%. Oven size does affect cooking times.

COOKING TIMES FOR CARROTS

Times are the same in large and medium ovens. For standard carrots, peel and cut in juliennes or crossways into 3–5 mm/⅛–¼ inch green tops; arrange in 2 or 3 layers in a dish just large enough to hold them; cover tightly.

Plain carrots Peel and cut in juliennes or into rounds; cover tightly.

125 g/4 oz	4 min. 30 sec.
250 g/8 oz	6 min. 30 sec.
350 g/12 oz	7 min.
500 g/1 lb	8 min.
1 kg/2 lb	11 min.

Glazed whole, small carrots About 12 per 500 g/1 lb. Peel; arrange in a dish just large enough to hold them; cover tightly.
250 g/8 oz with 15 g/½ oz 8 min.
 butter and 1 tbsp sugar

Yields

250 g/8 oz	150 ml/¼ pint purée

CASHEW I know people ruthless enough to pick these marvellously rich and expensive nuts out of nut mixtures, leaving the shattered peanuts for me. In addition to being gobbled solo, they are sometimes added to curries and curried salads. You may want to toast them lightly before using. See NUTS, toasting.

CAULIFLOWER If you need a large whole head, bring a pan of water to the boil and proceed in traditional fashion; it will be too big to cook evenly in a microwave oven. Small heads, under 750 g/1½ lb with the leaves, and florets, those small rounded tips about 5 cm/2 inches long and 5 cm/2 inches across at their widest, cook quickly and well in a microwave oven, either alone (to toss with a little butter or top with Mornay) or in soups and puréed (see Cream of Cauliflower Soup).

COOKING TIMES FOR CAULIFLOWER

Florets Cook in a single layer in a dish just large enough to hold them; cover tightly.

250 g/8 oz florets	4 min.
250 g/8 oz florets	6 min. (small oven)
500 g/1 lb florets	7 min.
500 g/1 lb florets	10 min. (small oven)
750 g/1½ lb florets	9 min.

Whole head Core and trim; cook in a dish just large enough to hold it; cover tightly.
1 small head, 750 g/1½ lb 7 min.
 with leaves, or 550 g/18
 oz cored and trimmed

Yield

1 small head   500 ml/16 fl oz
                                     purée

CAVIAR At their very best, these salted
fish eggs should be left alone except for the
spoon (bone, shell or tortoise shell if
possible) that conveys them to your mouth.
In any case, don't cook caviar. Stir into a
cooked dish like scrambled eggs after the
food is cooked.

CAYENNE A spicy red pepper pod
usually bought dried and ground. See
CHILLI.

CELERIAC This knobby root, once
peeled, is delicious raw; it is also excellent
cooked in soup or puréed with potatoes—1
part celeriac to 3 parts potato.

COOKING TIMES FOR CELERIAC

Trim, peel and cut into 1 cm/½ inch dice.
Cook in tightly sealed microwave-safe
cooking bags in 175 g/6 oz amounts. Add 1
minute 30 seconds to cooking times for
quantities of less than 750 g/1½ lb in small
ovens.

350 g/12 oz celeriac	6 min.
600 g/1¼ lb celeriac	9 min.
1.25 kg/2½ lb celeriac	15 min.

Yields

1 celeriac, 325 g/11 oz	125 ml/4 fl oz purée
600 g/1¼ lb celeriac	250 ml/8 fl oz purée

CELERY This lovely vegetable, traditionally a herb, is massively ignored except
for inclusion in chicken soup or chicken or
tuna fish salad, or for display in a cut-glass
bowl with olives. Even there it tends to be
misused. Celery needs to be well washed
and then stringed thoroughly by peeling
with a vegetable peeler.

Try cooked celery, leaves included,
mixed with Basic Béchamel, Mornay or
Sauce Suprême. Brown under the grill. Try
adding 1 part cooked celery to 2 parts
cooked potatoes before mashing them. For
a spectacular soup, puréed or not, combine

150 g/5 oz cooked celery, 350 ml/12 fl oz
Chicken Stock and either 150 g/5 oz cubed,
cooked potatoes or 250 ml/8 fl oz Sauce
Suprême. A touch of cream would not go
amiss. Salt and pepper to taste.

COOKING TIMES FOR CELERY

Trim, string and slice 5 mm/¼ inch thick.

To steam celery Cook in tightly sealed
microwave-safe cooking bags in 75 g/2½ oz
quantities.

150 g/5 oz celery with ½ tbsp water	2 to 3 min.
300 g/10 oz celery with 1 tbsp water	5 to 6 min.

To sweat celery Cook in a 1 litre/2 pint
glass measuring jug with butter melted at
100% for 2 min.; cover tightly.

75 g/2½ oz celery with 10 g/⅓ oz butter	4 min.
150 g/5 oz celery with 15 g/½ oz butter	6 min. 15 sec

Yield

2 sticks celery   125 g/4 oz

CELERY SEED The seeds of this spice
are so small that they sometimes get caught
in the teeth. They do a lot for a chicken or
tuna fish salad. They cook in the microwave
oven much as they do any other way. See
TOASTING, small seeds.

CEP The generic name for this wonderful, fleshy wild mushroom is Boletus edulis.
Cèpes is the French name. The Italians call
them funghi porcini, the Germans steinpilz
('stone mushroom') or herenpilz ('master
mushroom') and the Russian belyi grib. The
cep has a large fleshy cap whose underside
looks like a sponge, with allover pores that
have no discernible arrangement. The
somewhat more fibrous stem is shaped like
a baluster and is almost as thick in the
middle as the cap itself is wide.

Ceps are picked in late summer and
autumn. When fresh, they are usually
grilled whole or vigorously cooked in olive
oil (done better on top of the stove). Sliced,

both fresh and dried, they are a wonderful component of sauces, soups, stews and grain dishes, darkening and intensifying the taste. They will do wonders added to dishes made with common, fresh store-bought mushrooms. 30 g/1 oz dried ceps added to risotto during the final cooking time makes a lovely dish. See SOAKING, ceps, and DRYING, mushrooms.

CEREAL See GRAINS.

CHANTERELLE This heavenly golden-yellow, trumpet-shaped wild mushroom, also called girolle, is sometimes found fresh in the shops but is more often sold dried. If you pick chanterelles, as I do, you can begin to look for them in late spring and on into early summer. Store-bought ones may come from differnent climates and be available into fall and early winter. They are best cooked in hot butter or olive oil, and they like garlic and fresh herbs. A few added to your Duxelles or Mushroom Soup can make a vast improvement. They are German favourites called *Schwarzwalder* ('Black Forest') *pfifferlinge*.

CHEESE It will not make a nice brown crust in the microwave oven. It will do other things very well: melt without separating, recover from the refrigerator or even from that dread malady, unripeness. See Index for recipes.

CHERRY Fresh and raw are the best ways to enjoy sweet dessert cherries. Sour cherries and pie cherries, such as Montmorency, do well in sauces and pie fillings. They also make a terrific tart preserve (see Sour Cherry Jelly). See Cherry Sauce for Roast Birds.

CHESTNUT The microwave oven can blanch and cook chestnuts very well, but it doesn't give them a roasted flavour. It does make peeling them wonderfully simple. Cut an X with a sharp knife into the flat side of each one. Cook for the appropriate time, then peel as soon as they are cool enough to handle; return any difficult ones to the oven

for 1 additional minute. Cook peeled chestnuts for the additional time indicated before using them in a recipe. Add to Brussels sprouts, desserts, stuffings and purées.

COOKING TIMES FOR CHESTNUTS

Raw, unshelled chestnuts Cut as above; arrange in a single layer in a shallow dish just large enough to hold them, uncovered.

250 g/8 oz	6 min.
500 g/1 lb	8 min.
750 g/1½ lb	11 min.

Shelled chestnuts Cook and peel as above. Arrange in a single layer in a shallow dish just large enough to hold them, uncovered.

250 g/8 oz	4 min.
500 g/1 lb	6 min.
750 g/1½ lb	8 min.

CHICKEN Chicken can be poached, stewed, steamed and braised perfectly in the microwave oven. It cooks rapidly, staying moist and cooking evenly. You cannot roast in a microwave oven. The birds cook best in joints, whether skinned and boned or not. See also POUSSIN.

CHICKEN JOINTS

Chickens, depending on their size and your recipe, may be quartered, or jointed. One jointed chicken yields 2 brests, 2 thighs and 2 drumsticks, as well as backbone, wings and neck. Use the last three in the dish or use for stock. When cooking breasts from very large birds, you may cut them crossways into 2 pieces. Use pieces whole, skinned or skinned and boned. Skinning reduces calories; boning shortens cooking time and reduces the flavour but makes for more elegant eating when it comes to a saucy dish or stew.

Many traditional chicken recipes call for browning the pieces as a first step. Microwave cooking does not require this, nor does it do it well. You can lightly brown small quantities in a browning dish (see page 26). I have found, as in the Chicken in Red Wine, that highly flavoured preparations do not require browning. If the unbrowned skin will offend you, remove it before cooking. If you insist on the classic browning of a number of chicken pieces before putting them in to stew, do it on top of the stove.

A flavoured butter or stuffing under the skin will flavour and baste the meat and colour the cooked skin.

Chicken with the bone in is best cooked in liquid in the microwave oven. Look at the Index for recipes for tomato sauces, stocks, barbecue sauces and marinades.

Skinned and boned chicken pieces can be cooked individually by placing them in a deep soup dish or small flan dish and covering with a tight-fitting lid or microwave cling film. Following timing in charts that follow. Flavour by cooking in stock, marinate, or sprinkle with herbs and spices.

While skin-on and bone-in pieces can overlap slightly, they will cook more evenly in one layer. Follow dish indications in recipes. See also illustration of arrangement of chicken pieces, page 191.

Microwave cooking of boneless parts is a quick way to cook chicken for salad or any of the many recipes that use precooked chicken.

Cooking times are given for chicken in various pieces, with the skin and bone, without the skin and bone and in different quantities of liquid and/or vegetables. Since the time will vary depending on what is cooked with the chicken, this permits you to develop your own recipes.

Know the appetites of the eaters and the size of the meal you are planning before deciding how many pieces of chicken to allow per person. If cooking 2 servings in 2 separate dishes, see page 25 for timing information. If you want to serve seconds and feel that you need more than the maximum number of chicken pieces given below, do not attempt to multiply the number of pieces. Make 2 batches; that way the chicken will be hot and ready when your guests are ready for a second serving.

See also browning dishes (page 26), adjusting cooking times for oven size (page 18), arranging foods in microwave (page 33) and microwave oven racks (page 25).

COOKING TIMES FOR CHICKEN BREASTS

Breasts, skinned and boned (In the UK, what is called a breast is actually a half breast, weighing about 125 g/4 oz.) Cover tightly.

1 breast (15 cm/6 inch dish)	2 min. 30 sec.
1 breast as above	3 min. (small oven)
2 breasts (small flan dish)	3 min. 30 sec. 4 min. (small oven)
4 breasts (25 cm. 10 inch round dish)	5 min.
4 breasts with 275 g/9 oz vegetables (2.5 litre/4 pint soufflé dish)	9 min.
4 breasts as above	6 min. (small oven)
6 breasts (35 × 27.5 × 5 cm/14 × 11 × 2 inch dish)	6 min. (small oven)
8 breasts, about 1.5 kg/3 lb, with 4 tbsp stock (35 × 27.5 × 5 cm/14 × 11 × 2 inch dish or 30 cm/ 12 inch round dish	8 min.

Breasts, skin and bone left on Cover tightly.

1 breast stuffed under the skin, accompanied by 1 portion cooked vegetable (small flan dish)	2 min. 45 sec. 4 min. 30 sec. (small oven)
1 breast as stew, with 175 ml/6 fl oz liquid and 125 g/4 oz raw vegetables (large deep soup dish or flan dish)	12 min.
2 breasts steamed in 4 tbsp stock (20 cm/8 inch round dish)	5 min. 30 sec.
4 breasts steamed in 4 tbsp stock (10 × 25 cm/8 × 10 inch oval dish)	7 min. 30 sec.

COOKING TIMES FOR CHICKEN LEGS AND LEG PIECES

Each leg is composed of a drumstick and a thigh piece. A complete leg, 2 thighs or 2 drumsticks cook in the same amount of time. On average, each piece will weigh just under 125 g/4 oz. A whole leg, therefore, will weigh just under 250 g/8 oz.

Before cooking drumsticks you must make a cut, to the bone, all the way around the base of the thin end of the drumstick; this will allow the meat to shrink as it cooks, and the skin won't become so distended with steam that the drumstick explodes. To cook drumsticks only, arrange them spoke-fashion in a circular dish with the thick ends towards the outside of the dish, or alternate thin and thick ends if cooking them in a rectangular dish.

Times are for bone-in pieces. It is easier to bone chicken legs after they are cooked. Pieces may be skinned or not; it will make no difference to the timing. Legs seem to cook better with some liquid.

Whole legs, all thigh or all drumstick Cover tightly.

1 whole leg or 2 pieces with 4 tbsp stock (15 cm/6 inch round dish)	5 min. 7 min. 30 sec. (small oven)
1 whole leg with 175 ml/6 fl oz liquid and 125 g/4 oz vegetables (1 litre/2 pint soufflé dish)	12 min.
2 whole legs or 4 pieces with 4 tbsp stock (27.5 × 15 cm/11 × 6 inch rectangular dish)	7 min. 30 sec. 9 min. (small oven)
4 whole legs or 8 pieces with 4 tbsp stock or coated with sauce (27.5 cm/11 inch round dish)	11 min.
2 whole legs or 4 pieces with 10 g/⅓ oz butter, uncovered, turned once (22.5 cm/9 inch square browning dish)	6 min.
4 whole legs or 8 pieces with 15 g/½ oz butter, uncovered, turned once (25 cm/10 inch square or round browning dish)	10 min. 30 sec.

COOKING TIMES FOR CHICKEN WINGS

Before cooking wings, cut off the wing tips and save them in your freezer until the next time you make stock. Divide wings at joint into 2 pieces. Six wings (12 pieces) make about 500 g/1 lb. The tips from these will give you 125 g/4 oz to save. I can see no reason for ever cooking chicken wings without a sauce. All times below are with sauce, tightly covered.

Wings Remove tips; split in two; cover tightly.

6 wings, 12 pieces, with 5½ tbsp sauce (22.5 cm/ 9 inch square dish)	6 min.
6 wings as above	12 min. (small oven)
12 wings, 24 pieces, with 125 ml/4 fl oz sauce (25 × 20 cm/10 × 8 inch dish)	10 min.
24 wings, 48 pieces, with 150 ml/¼ pint sauce (35 × 27.5 cm/14 × 11 inch dish)	14 min.

WHOLE BIRDS

Whole birds should be jointed. They cook better in the presence of liquid; this can be water, stock or ingredients for a sauce. Whole chickens are less expensive than the same weight of joints.

When cooking a whole chicken in joints, arrange with thick part of drumsticks and thigh pieces towards the outside, and breast pieces and any other parts being cooked in the centre, skin side down.

COOKING TIMES FOR WHOLE BIRDS

Cover tightly (2.5 litre/4 pint soufflé or casserole).

1.25 kg/2½ lb bird with 175 ml/6 fl oz stock	15 min.

1.25 kg/2½ lb bird with 1 litre/1¾ pints liquid and 350 g/12 oz vegetables	17 min.
1.3 kg/3 lb bird with 60–175 ml/2–6 fl oz liquid	17 min.
1.8 kg/4 lb bird with 500 ml/16 fl oz liquid, and 500 g/1 lb vegetables, if liked	22 min.

CHICKEN GLAZE A concentrate made from chicken stock, used to lend a strong chicken flavour to recipes where no extra liquid is needed. It may, for instance, be stirred into Beurre Blanc and served with chicken brests. About 1 tablespoon glaze to each 250 ml/8 fl oz of sauce or stew is a good rule of thumb. See Meat Glazes.

CHICKEN LIVER Chicken livers are little dividends inside some whole chickens. Don't throw them out. If you don't have immediate use for them, put them in a freezer container, cover with milk and freeze. As you acquire more livers, add them to the container and cover with more milk. Defrost them when you want to make a pâté.

This is one of the few ingredients that can genuinely be sautéed and browned in a browning dish. They will also cook gently in the microwave oven in hot fat without toughening as long as they are not overcooked. Always heat the fat—chicken or butter—for 3 to 5 minutes (depending on the quantity) before adding the livers. If browning, heat the browning dish for 4 minutes at 100% before adding butter.

All livers should be cleaned of connective membranes, veins and fat before cooking.

DEFROSTING TIMES FOR CHICKEN LIVERS

Frozen in 250 ml/8 fl oz milk Cook, uncovered, at 100%. Drain after cooking.

250 g/8 oz	7 min. (stir after 5 min.)
500 g/1 lb	9 min. (stir after 5 min.)

COOKING TIMES FOR CHICKEN LIVERS

Halved Cook in a single layer, uncovered.

250 g/8 oz with 15 g/½ oz butter, turned once (22.5 cm/9 inch square browning dish)	2 min.
500 g/1 lb with 30 g/1 oz butter, turned once (25 cm/10 inch square or round browning dish)	3 min.

CHICKEN STOCK This is one of the most useful basic preparations in the kitchen. In today's rushed world, I would guess that it is provided by re-constituted stock cubes in most home kitchens—even mine. There is now a good and rapid alternative. The basic stock that I make is unseasoned by vegetables or seasonings since those can always be added to adapt to the dish in about 7 minutes of microwave cooking time. Since it is unsalted, it is perfect for reduction in CHICKEN GLAZE. I seldom make less than 1 litre/2 pints (bones may be accumulated in a container in the refrigerator). I freeze what I don't use in 250 ml/8 fl oz quantities for the future. See Meat Stocks. See also DEFROSTING, homemade staples, and STOCK CUBES.

CHICK-PEA Widely used in all the countries bordering the Mediterranean, they are available canned but hove a slightly mushy texture. Like dried broad beans and unlike most beans, chick-peas have a skin that must be removed before final cooking or eating. For some reason microwave soaking makes the skins easier to slip off. Soak as for dried beans and pulses (see BEANS). Let the cooked chick-peas cool, covered, in their cooking liquid.

COOKING TIMES FOR CHICK-PEAS

Presoaked chick-peas Remove the skins; drain, rinse and return to 2.5 litre/4 pint soufflé; cover tightly.

200 g/7 oz chick-peas with 1 litre/1¾ pints water	35 min.

400 g/14 oz chick-peas with   45 min.
  1.5 litres/2½ pints water

CHICORY Pale greenish-white vegetable with a slightly bitter flavour, best known in this country as a salad leaf, it can also be braised. You can vary the ingredients in the braising liquid (keep quantities and times the same).

COOKING TIMES FOR CHICORY

Whole chicory Braised in a dish just large enough to hold them; cover tightly.

2 chicons with 5½ tbsp liquid	8 min.
2 chicons as above	12 min. (small oven)
8 chicons with 250 ml/8 fl oz liquid	16 min.

CHIFFONADE A technique of thinly slicing leafy greens across the veins. (The heavy veins of spinach, sorrel, basil and other green leaves often make the cooked vegetable stringy.) Neatly line up the leaves in stacks for easy slicing.

CHILLI Spicy pod peppers or capsicums, both fresh and dry, red and green. The name also refers to the dishes made from them, in their native Mexico, the southwestern United States and Thailand, China and Hungary (with paprika), which have avidly adopted them as their own. See SOAKING, dried chillies.

Scads of sauces, differing in intensity, to shake and spoon, can be made following the method in Red Pepper Purée. They are much better than the bottled sauces. Make them when the chillies are in season; jar and refrigerate or bottle.

I dearly love Southwestern American chilli dishes, which can be varied practically ad infinitum. You can substitute venison, chicken, turkey, rabbit or pork for the beef, and vary the mix of seasonings, the amount of tomato, the presence or absence of chocolate. To invent your own, use Chunky Beef Chilli and respect the proportion of liquid to solid. I have not found any advantage when cooking in the

microwave oven to first cooking the chillies in fat, as is usual in most top-of-the-stove recipes. Again, if you really feel the need to brown the meat, do it first on top of the stove.

CHINESE BLACK BEAN See BLACK BEAN.

CHINESE LEAVES This is a type of oriental cabbage that has elongated oval heads of pale green, tightly packed, crinkly leaves.

COOKING TIMES FOR CHINESE LEAVES

Cut across into 5 cm/2 inch lengths Cover tightly.

250 g/8 oz with 30 g/1 oz butter (27.5 × 21 × 5 cm/11 × 8½ × 2 inch dish)	4 min. 30 sec. (large oven) 8 min. 30 sec. (small oven)
500 g/1 lb with 60 g/2 oz butter (27.5 × 20 × 7.5 cm/11 × 8 × 3 inch oval dish)	7 min.

CHIVES Although these thin, tubular herbs—each a separate tiny plant even though they grow in clumps—are available dried and freeze-dried, I think they are only worth using fresh. When cutting, don't take the tips off of an entire clump or you will kill all the plants in it. Instead, cut off entire individual leaves. Either snip with scissors or slice with a sharp knife; do not attempt to chop—too messy. If chopping with other herbs or ingredients in a food processor, cut into 2.5 cm/1 inch lengths first, or the long leaves will wrap themselves around the spindle. When fresh chives are not available, substitute thinly sliced spring onion greens.

CHOCOLATE Chocolate is at once an everyday delight and an arcane subject for specialists, who navigate their way amid warnings about the difficulties of tempering, scorching and seizing up. As an instinctive rather than a scientific cook, I was always rather intimidated by this. Imagine my delight when I found out how liberating it is to work with chocolate in the microwave oven: Properly handled, it becomes hassle-free. See Chocolate Glaze.

Remember that as chocolate cools, it acts as a thickening agent. Add, as in chilli, for the last 3 minutes of cooking time, or it gets too hot and separates. Bitter chocolate is good as a background to spicy flavours.

When melting chocolate alone, do so in a shallow dish. Uncoated metal interior of convection-microwave ovens will melt chocolate more quickly. When adding to a hot mixture, chop or grate first. Chocolate melted at 100%, covered, will not lose its temper. Usually, when chocolate is melted for sweets or other coating, it is put through a complex series of controlled heatings and coolings called tempering so it stays shiny and smooth. Temper in the microwave oven by melting half the chocolate, sitr in remainder, grated.

MELTING TIMES FOR CHOCOLATE

Break into 15–30 g/½–1 oz pieces. Heat at 100%; cover tightly.

30 g/1 oz	45 sec.
30 g/1 oz	2 min. (small oven)
45 g/1½ oz	1 min.
45 g/1½ oz	2 min. 30 sec. (small oven)
60 g/2 oz	2 min.
60 g/2 oz	1 min. 15 sec. (convection-microwave oven)
125 g/4 oz	2 min.
125 g/4 oz	1 min 30 sec (convection-microwave oven)
125 g/4 oz	3 min. (small oven)
250 g/8 oz	3 min. 30 sec.
250 g/8 oz	2 min. to 2 min. 30 sec. (convection-microwave oven)

CHOP To cut up into even but not regular (that would be diced) pieces that are faily small but not really tiny. Chop with a knife, or in the food processor with short pulses.

CHRISTOPHENE This tropical vegetable, imported from the Caribbean, Southeast Asia and East and West Africa, is also called chow-chow, chayote and vegetable pear. Now becoming widely available, the Christophene is shaped like an avocado, has a waxy yellowish skin, a large stone and subtle, aromatic flavour. I strongly prefer cooking it in the microwave oven, where it doesn't get waterlogged and keeps its delicate pale green colour

COOKING TIMES FOR CHRISTOPHENE

Prick whole vegetable 4 times; set on paper towel, uncovered.

1 christophene	6 min.
2 christophene	9 min. 30 sec.
4 christophene	15 min.

Yields

1 christophene	250 g/8 oz
250 g/8 oz	60 g/2 oz cooked pulp and 2 shells

CHUNKS These are irregular pieces of food that are not even on all sides. They are larger than cubes and thicker than slices.

CHUTNEY I love this kind of chunky, spicy fruit preserve. Almost any kind of fruit or non-leafy vegetable may be used; the mango version is often served as an accompaniment to curries. It is also a wonderful (if less classic) friend to simple grilled or roasted fish, birds and meat. Unfortunately, the bottled chutneys that I used to chop up and spread on bread with cream cheese or use with thinly sliced tomatoes as a sandwich have gotten more liquid (less fruit) over the years. Now that I have the handy, rapid microwave oven, I make my own. Try putting chutney in a toasted cheese sandwich. See Fresh Mango Chutney and Peach Chutney. You can easily substitute firm pears or apples for mangoes and add nuts.

CINNAMON The inner bark of a tree, it comes in tight, dry rolls called sticks or quills. The best comes from Ceylon; ask for it. It is available ground, too. Use the quills when infusing liquids; the dry powder will separate out.

CLAMS American varieties are available in a wide range of sizes, with hard as well as soft shells (those with soft shells are commonly called steamers). In Britain, clams are becoming more widely available, and they are very popular in France. Littlenecks, the smallest hard-shell clams, are young and ideally should be no more than 4 cm/1½ inches across, but you will find them up to 5 cm/2 inches. Save the very smallest to eat raw—they are too good to cook. The medium-size, middle-aged cherrystones are about 7.5 cm/3 inches across. The granddaddy quahogs are over 8.5 cm/3½ inches across and are often called chowder clams. Hard-shell clams need only vigorous scrubbing and a check to make sure that all shells are tightly closed before cooking; discard any that seem the least bit open. Soft-shell clams have a protruding neck and, once the clams are cooked, clam-eaters will have to pull the black skin off the necks as they go along.

Littlenecks are usually served raw, on the half-shell; but they and their larger relatives are terrific contributions to seafood dishes and are good cooked on their own. Soft-shell clams are almost always eaten simply steamed, with the steaming liquid, lemon and melted butter on the side. Quahogs are usually cooked, chopped and added to soup or chowder. When cooking clams, if not using the liquor they yield, save it, frozen, for use later in chowders and substitute for FISH STOCK. See New England Clam Chowder and Clams Casino.

COOKING TIMES FOR CLAMS

Cook clams in a single layer, set on hinge ends and fit into a dish 5 cm/2 inches deep; cover tightly. Clams are cooked as soon as they open; they don't have to gape.

Steamers 12 per 500 g/1 lb.

14 clams with 30 g/1 oz butter in a small soufflé dish	6 min. (small oven)
18 clams with 30 g/1 oz butter in a small soufflé dish	4 min.
36 clams	6 min.
36 clams divided among 2 dishes	8 min.

Littlenecks 8 to 10 per 500/1 lb.

6 clams	2 min. 30 sec. to 3 min. 30 sec. (depending on size of clams)
6 clams	4 min. (small oven)
12 clams (750 g/1½ lb)	4 min.
24 clams (1.5 kg/3 lb)	7 min.
48 clams	11 min.

Cherrystones 3 per 500 g/1 lb.

15 clams	9 min.

Quahogs 2 per 500 g/1 lb

16 (3.6 kg/8 lb) clams (35 × 27.5 × 5 cm/ 14 × 11 × 2 inch dish)	20 min.

CLAM LIQUOR This is the liquid from cooked clams (as well as from other molluscs such as mussels and oysters). As clams vary in juiciness, yields may be different. Save any clam liquor that you are not going to use in the dish under preparation; it can be used instead of FISH STOCK to make Fish Velouté or as a base for soups, and can be frozen for later use. See DEFROSTING, homemade staples.

Yields

750 g/1½ lb steamers	5½–8 tbsp
1.5 kg/3 lb littlenecks	175 ml/6 fl oz
2.5 kg/5 lb cherrystones	400 ml/14 fl oz
4 kg/8 lb quahogs	900–1.2 litres/ 1½–2 pints
36 mussels (about 1 kg/2 lb)	250 ml/8 fl oz
12 oysters (about 1 kg/2 lb)	125 ml/4 fl oz

CLARIFYING CLARIFYING BUTTER is very simple and safe in the microwave oven—you won't get burned when the water in the butter spits as it is driven away. See BUTTER, clarified.

CLARIFYING STOCKS AND SAUCES to make them absolutely transparent— important for aspics and consommés—is a tedious chore on top of the stove and always a little suspenseful: Will it work?

The microwave oven lets you breathe easy. Its strange effect of rubberizing egg whites is consummately useful and good here.

To clarify 1 litre/1¾ pints of stock: Place stock in a 2 litre/3½ pint glass jug or bowl. Beat 5 egg whites until stiff, and stir them, with their shells, into stock with 250 g/8 oz very lean beef or other appropriate, coarsely minced meat. Let these solids collect on surface of liquid. Cook, uncovered, at 100% for 6 minutes. Wet a clean tea towel with warm water, wring it out and line a sieve with it. Place over large bowl. With a slotted spoon scoop egg whites and shells and meat into sieve. Slowly pour over hot stock. It should come through crystal clear; if not, repeat clarifying with 5 freshly beaten egg whites.

Stock can also be clarified by omitting meat; proceed exactly as above, omitting the minced meat. The stock will be more subtle and not quite as intense.

CLEMENTINE Small, almost seedless tangerines, the best of which come from Morocco, they are a delicious addition to our winter fruits. The peel can be dried and makes an excellent seasoning. See DRYING.

CLOVE Usually means the nail-shaped spice, really the dried, unopened flower bud of the clove tree. Always use carefully; the flavour is strong. It is available whole and ground. If you don't use it often, buy whole cloves and grind them as needed; they will be more pungent. Ground cloves are always used in baking. Whole cloves are stuck into a ham before glazing.

One of the nicest ways of using this spice in microwave cooking is the old-fashioned trick of sticking a clove into a fruit or vegetable so that it can be readily located and, if necessary, extracted so that no one bites down on a still-hard stick. In microwave cooking, there is the added benefit that the clove flavour gently permeates the food into which it is stuck. See Light Poached Pears and Braised Onions. See also GRINDING.

Cloves have historically been a very dear spice. Do not confuse them with their inexpensive imitator, oil of clove, which is made from the bark of an American tree and used as a flavouring, anesthetic and breath freshener.

COCOA BUTTER Cocoa beans are fatty little devils, almost one half fat. In the chocolate-making process the cocoa butter is pressed out of the beans. At a later point some of the cocoa butter is put back. The surplus cocoa butter is a valuable commodity for cooking, a rich fat that stays solid at higher temperatures than butter or oil. It used to be much more called for in the kitchen than it is today. Consequently, the only way I have been able to buy it recently is at old-fashioned chemists where it is sold in sticks for use on the skin. If you want to buy some for the kitchen, make sure nothing in the way of scent or preservatives has been added. See Praline Paste.

COCONUT Most of us will cheat and buy this desiccated and canned or sealed in airtight bags. The important thing is to check when it is sweetened; sweetened may be all right for some baking, but you don't want to find it in your curry. The microwave oven can be of great help in opening your coconut. See the following recipes: Coconut Milk, Coconut Cream, Shredded Coconut and Toasted Coconut.

COCONUT MILK OR CREAM This is not the natural juice of the coconut, but a liquid made by cooking shredded coconut in milk and then straining. It is a basic ingredient of spicy dishes from India, Thailand, Indonesia, the Philippines and the Caribbean, all areas where the coconut grows lavishly; see, for example, Chicken Curry. Coconut milk also is essential to a piña colada. Fresh is better than canned, although canned may be used. Be careful not to buy sweetened coconut milk or cream if it is to be used in curry. See Coconut Milk.

COD Europe's most popular fish for centuries, either fresh or dried (even in countries such as Portugal, where fresh fish is plentiful). Cod is white-fleshed, tends to flake when cooked and is medium-firm. It falls apart if overcooked. Fresh cod can be cooked in steaks, fillets and medallions; for cooking times, see FISH. Salt (dried) cod must be soaked before use. The simple microwave way of soaking salt cod is a delight—it takes only 20 minutes—while the conventional way takes a couple of days and endless streams of cold running water.

SOAKING AND DESALTING SALT COD

Skinned salt cod fillet, 250 g/8 oz. Rinse 2 min. under cold running water. Place in 25 × 7.5 cm/10 × 3 inch round dish with 750 ml/1¼ pints cold water. Cover tightly. Cook at 100% for 5 min. Uncover; drain. Rinse under cold water. Repeat twice.

COGNAC By most people's standards, this is the best of grape brandies coming from the Cognac region in France's Charente. See ALCOHOL.

CONCASSÉ A French term for a simple tomato preparation often used in the making of sauces, or lightly seasoned and used as a sauce on its own. There is a dispute as to whether it consists of tomatoes that have been peeled (see PEELING, tomatoes), cut in half across the fat part, gently squeezed to remove juice and seeds, and cleaned of remaining seeds with the flick of a finger or spoon before being chopped up, or whether it is also lightly cooked to dry it slightly and concentrate the flavours. (It is not cooked long enough to make a true sauce.) I favour the second, slightly cooked version; see Lightly Cooked Crushed Tomatoes. One advantage of this kind is that it can be frozen and used as needed.

CONCH This large, baroque shell provides something wonderful to eat only when it is exquisitely fresh. Then, the long fibrous muscle is best sliced thinly and eaten raw in a serviche. If you want to make conch chowder, prepare the chowder

mixture (see New England Clam Chowder) and substitute thinly sliced raw conch for the clams; stir in while the mixture is still hot; cover tightly and cook at 100% for 1 minute 30 seconds. Substitute any FISH STOCK for the clam liquor.

CORIANDER This plant yields both an aromatic, tender, green-leaved herb (cilantro in Spanish-speaking countries, Chinese parsley in Oriental recipes) and a dry spice that is the light, small, brown seed of the same plant. It has an earthy, pungent fragrance that people either love or loathe. See DRYING, herbs and GRINDING.

CORNFLOUR The most satisfactory last-minute thickening to use in the microwave oven. Generally, it is added in a slurry of 2 parts water to 1 part cornflour; 2 tablespoons water with 1 tablespoon cornflour thickens 250 ml/8 fl oz of thin sauce. Use less if the sauce is already thick. When adding cornflour, leave the cooking dish in the oven. Uncover carefully and quickly stir in the cornflour slurry; cover tightly with fresh microwave cling film. (See illustration page 27.) At 100%, the sauce will take about 2 minutes to thicken if you have moved like lightning and up to 4 minutes if you have been poking around. It will have a nice silky texture.

Cornflour also stars in microwave baking, where its abilities to hold things together without problem-causing gluten is invaluable, see Cakes and Biscuits.

CORNMEAL This grain makes wonderful polenta in the microwave oven. The Italian dish is usually made with a coarsely ground meal, although finer ground cornmeal works perfectly well. See POLENTA and Soft Polenta, Firm Polenta and 'Fried' Polenta. If hot cereal for breakfast makes a comeback, the microwave oven combined with cornmeal could star.

COURGETTE See SQUASH

COUSCOUS A form of miniature pasta and the dish made with it, prevalent in the countries bordering the southern Mediterranean, particularly Morocco, and in Sicily and Spain. The authentic dish is made by steaming the couscous over a spicy stew. However, a nonauthentic version that I find a delicious adjunct to roast lamb or chicken is Couscous made in the style of risotto.

COVERING Lids, paper, cling film and so forth—this is a large and important subject in microwave cooking since it truly is a major determinant of the speed and manner in which foods cook. See pages 26–28 for a full discussion.

CRAB Crabmeat, easier by far to use than whole crab, is available fresh, frozen and canned. Remember that it is already cooked. When preparing it in the microwave oven, make your sauce separately (mornay, for instance), combine it with the crabmeat that you have picked over (to remove any cartilage) and reheat briefly in the microwave oven or brown under a grill.

CRANBERRY These bog berries are now available, frozen, year-round. Many relishes are best made with raw cranberries. However cooked, they also make wonderful sauces and jellies.

CRAWFISH See LOBSTER.

CREAM Is there anything more voluptuous than the really rich double cream and whipping cream? I doubt it. If you are using a large amount of cream in the microwave oven, be sure to use a large, deep container—it has a nasty tendency to boil over.

CREAM CHEESE See SOFTENING, cream cheese.

CREAM OF TARTAR Baking powder or a component of anonymous baking powders. You do little baking with wheat flour in the microwave oven; it is farily irrelevant here.

CUBE Meats, peeled and vegetables and peeled fruits are frequently cut into even, 6-sided cubes before cooking. Unless a size is given in a recipe, this normally means that each side of the cube is around 1 cm/½ inch square. A dice is smaller than a cube.

CUMIN This warm-tasting spice is one of my favourites. It often crops up in prepared chilli powders (though you can get chilli powder made just with chilli and add as much cumin as you want). Cumin is wonderful in a host of other dishes and is best ground fresh from the seeds. See GRINDING

CURRANT These tiny jewel-like berries come in red, black and white. With them you can make some of the world's best Redcurrant Jelly, tart and sweet. Dried currants are often used in fruit cakes, buns and mincemeat. See SOAKING, dried fruit.

CURRY A blend of several spices, usually including dried chillies, turmeric, cardamom, cumin, ginger and coriander. (There is a rarely used Indian leaf herb whose name sounds, to Occidental ears at any rate, like 'curry' and thus that name has been given to both the spice powder and the dishes made with that leaf.) 'Curry' powders are commercially available in various qualities. Some Indian recipes call for particular blends, for which the spices are often toasted first. See TOASTING, whole spices, Chicken Curry and Green Vegetable Curry.

CUTTLEFISH See SQUID.

·D·

DAB See SOLE. For cooking times, see FISH.

DANDELION GREENS In early spring, these greens can be picked out of any garden. Never pick from a garden or field that has recently been sprayed with weed killer. Always pick the smallest leaves.

The French use dandelion leaves in a salad typically sprinkled with bacon lardons and dressed with their rendered fat. In the American South, dandelion greens are often popped into Spring Pot Greens. For purposes of cooking time, consider them soft greens.

Yields

1 bunch dandelion	250 g/8 oz, with stems
250 g/8 oz with stems	150 g/5 oz, cleaned and stemmed

DAUBE There are many different explanations for the derivation of the word *daube*, the French name for a dish made by the long, moist cooking of meat that has not been previously browned. The explanation I favour takes into account the numerous countries that have similar dishes with seemingly related names and techniques: the various *adobos* of the Spanish-speaking countries, the Italian *addobbo* and even the English nonculinary 'daub.' The similar words all relate to a root word meaning 'to whiten' (used also to describe the whitewashing of walls and thence to the covering materials of the walls, *adobe*—the same kind of earthenware from which pots are made).

In different regions of France there developed, over the centuries, earthenware pots of particular shapes specifically suited to the preparation of specific sorts of dishes. A *daubière* is taller than it is wide, with a bulbous bottom and a narrower neck. In later evolution, but before the universal appearance of ovens, the *daubière* lid was hallowed to hold hot coals, providing for top as well as bottom heat. This pot gave its name to a group of dishes in which meat is tightly covered and slowly cooked to a rich flavour, tasting slightly of the earthenware pot. The lack of browning and the tight sealing are perfect for the microwave oven. See Sliced Beef Casserole.

DEFROSTING One of my greatest pleasures in writing about microwave cooking is the feeling that I will be helping people to once again eat delicious fresh food. It really takes no more time to make food fresh in the microwave oven than to defrost it. Fresh tastes much better.

How you wrap and prepare foods for FREEZING determines how well and quickly you can defrost them.

Preprogramming. If you have an oven with a preprogrammed defrost cycle that you trust, use it. I tried seven different programmes from different manufacturers. No two were the same. I also did not find their programmes gave a better result than defrosting at 100% for a shorter time. Large blocks of food such as roasts and family-size quantities of soup got hot, slightly cooked or recooked, no matter what method was used.

Pack food for freezing in smallish quantities so as not to risk ruining it in the defrosting. Small quantities can either be defrosted or cooked, no matter what methods are used. In most cases, small quantities of frozen, raw foods (such as a single fish fillet or skinned and boned breast of chicken) are best cooked from frozen, often in stock or sauce. See FREEZING.

Large quantities, such as roasts, sometimes defrost better at 30%. This may be difficult to locate on your oven due to manufacturer paranoia. (It is as if stove manufacturers refused to tell you what temperature the settings on their ovens mean.) The most usual euphemisms are 'low defrost', 'medium low', 'simmer', '3' and 'low' or 'defrost' where there are fewer settings.

HOMEMADE STAPLES

Stocks, tomato purées and the like, glazes, reductions, for Beurre Blanc, Duxelles,

Sauce Espagnole, fruit sauces, and purées are the exceptions to the basic rule of fresh. These should be frozen in small quantities. Since you use modest quantities at a time, this will prevent you from having to defrost too much at once, which takes too long and wastes food. Defrosting these foods in the microwave oven does not leave them cold, as they would be if defrosted in the refrigerator, but the degree of recooking is not critical here.

Some generalizations can be made. Very small quantities, the kinds that are used to enrich a sauce or accompany a single portion of fish or chicken, will take the same time no matter what food is involved. Large and medium oven times should be roughly equal; in a small oven, allow 30 seconds more.

DEFROSTING TIMES FOR LIQUIDS, SMALL AMOUNTS

Frozen cube Put in a ramekin or small soufflé dish; cover tightly; defrost at 100%.

1 tbsp	45 sec. to 1 min.
2 tbsp (30 g/1 oz)	1 min. to 1 min. 30 sec.
4 tbsp (60 g/2 oz)	1 min. 30 sec. to 2 min.

In larger quantities, a judgement has to be made as to the density of the liquid, or the solidity and butteriness of the purée. Take the lid off the freezer container. If the container is microwave-safe, cover it with microwave cling film; if not, empty the contents into a suitable bowl or measure.

DEFROSTING TIMES FOR THIN LIQUIDS

Stocks, juices and light sauces such as tomato Cover tightly; defrost at 100%

125 ml/4 fl oz	2 min. to 2 min. 30 sec.
250 ml/8 fl oz	4 to 5 min.
350 ml/12 fl oz	6 min. to 6 min. 30 sec.
500 ml/16 fl oz	8 min.
780 ml/26 fl oz	15 min.

DEFROSTING TIMES FOR MEDIUM-WEIGHT LIQUIDS

Purées and sauces with some fat (such as Espagnole, Béchamel, Duxelles and Sorrel) Cover tightly; defrost at 100%.

125 ml/4 fl oz	4 min. 30 sec.
150 ml/¼ pint	5 min.
250 ml/8 fl oz	9 min.
300 ml/½ pint	10 min.

DEFROSTING TIMES FOR THICK LIQUIDS

Thick sauces and heavy purées (such as potato and broccoli) Cover tightly; defrost at 100%.

125 ml/4 fl oz	2 min.
250 ml/8 fl oz	3 min. 30 sec.
500 ml/16 fl oz	500 ml/16 fl oz

For defrosting prepared PASTA DISHES, see Macaroni and Cheese.

RAW INGREDIENTS

Raw ingredients are occasionally acceptable when frozen and defrosted. Sometimes they are a necessity. What is bought frozen should be kept frozen until it is time to defrost and cook it. Food should be cooked as soon after defrosting as possible. Single-portion quantities of raw ingredients—vegetables, skinned and boned chicken breasts and filleted fish or fish steaks—should be cooked from the frozen, not thawed first. Roasts over 3–3.6 kg/7–8 lb should not be defrosted in the microwave oven; flat legs of lamb and loins of pork defrost most successfully.

MEAT

Beef joints (braising cuts) 1.6 kg/3½ lb. When buying, ask the butcher to cover the joint with pork back fat. This helps protect the surface. Unwrap meat; place in casserole with tightly fitting lid or container just large enough to hold meat. If using container without lid, cover with microwave cling film. Heat at 30% for 25 min. Turn over; heat 20 min. at 30%. If using cling film, pierce with the tip of a sharp knife each time container is to be uncovered. Season and roast or cook as desired.

Beef, steak Don't do it.

Lamb, leg (spring lamb) About 2 kg/4 lb, in a 35 × 22.5 × 5 cm/14 × 9 × 2 inch dish. Shield shank with aluminium foil. Cook, uncovered, at 100% for 15 min. Remove foil and continue cooking for 6 min. Then season and cook for 20 min. in a very hot oven for medium rare. Serves 6. See Roast Leg of Lamb.

Lamb, leg About 3.2 kg/7 lb, in a 35 × 22.5 × 5 cm/14 × 11 × 2 inch dish. Shield shank with aluminium foil. Cover tightly with microwave cling film. Cook at 100% for 14 min. Uncover, remove foil. Re-cover and cook at 100% for 14 min. more. Then season and cook for 20 min. in very hot oven for medium rare. Serves 10.

Lamb chops Don't do it.

Pork loin Boned and rolled, 1.5–1.8 kg/ 3–4 lb, unwrapped in casserole with tightly fitting lid or container just large enough to hold meat for 20 to 30 min. at 30%. If using container without lid, cover with microwave cling film and prick at end of defrosting. Let sit 5 min. after taking from oven. Roast normally.

Pork chops To defrost chops to be cooked in sauce in the microwave oven, lengthen the cooking time in the sauce.

4 thin chops in sauce	*add 2 min.*
4 thick chops with 250 ml/8 fl oz tomato sauce	*Covered at 100% for 20 min.*

Spareribs Do not defrost. Cook frozen in sauce. Cook 30 min. for each frozen rack.

Bacon To soften and separate, see BACON.

Chicken joints are best defrosted in their cooking liquid. To arrange, see page 34. For skinned and boned breasts:

2 chicken breasts In 125 ml/4 fl oz liquid (and 60–125 g/2–4 oz vegetables, if desired) in a 21 × 16 × 5 cm/8½ × 6½ × 2 inch dish, tightly covered. Cook at 100% for 5 min., turn over, re-cover tightly, and cook 3 min. longer.

4 chicken breasts In 500 ml/16 fl oz stock or light sauce (and 125–250 g/4–8 oz vegetables, if desired) in a 27.5 × 20 × 5 cm/11 × 8 × 2 inch dish, tightly covered. Cook at 100% for 5 min., turn over, re-cover tightly, and cook 4 min. longer.

Duck is often bought frozen. Remove from plastic package. In container, tightly covered with microwave cling film, or in casserole just large enough to hold, defrost 20 mins. at 30%. Turn over and defrost another 20 mins. at 30%. If using film, pierce with tip of sharp knife. Uncover and put in roasting pan. Carefully pry open tail end (it will still be slightly frozen). Remove pockets of fat. With your hand, wiggle the packet of neck and innards stored inside the bird until you can free and remove it (it may take a minute or two). Roast as is, or joint for microwave cooking. See DUCK.

Quail is available frozen, in packages of two or four. Unwrap and defrost at 30% for 5 minutes, turning over once.

Fillets Individual fish fillets are better wrapped and frozen in individual serving portions, 150–250 g/5–8 oz. Defrost in the cooking sauce where feasible. Unwrap fillets; place without sauce in small flan dish; cover tightly with microwave cling film. Prick film after defrosting. Cook afterwards. This technique is good for slimmers who want to keep portion-controlled pieces of fish on hand.

500 g/1 lb fillet (10 cm/4 inches wide), tightly covered	*7 min. at 30%*
Small fillets (175–250 g/6–8 oz), 1 in a small dish	*1 min. at 100%, turn over, 30 sec. at 100%, rest covered 1 min.*
	1 min.30 sec. at 100%, turn over, 1 min. at 100%, rest covered 1 min. (small oven)

2 in a flan dish	1 min. 30 sec. at 100%, turn over, 1 min. 30 sec. at 100%, rest covered 1 min. 2 min. at 100%, turn over, 2 min. at 100%, rest covered 2 min. (small oven)
4 in a large flan dish	1 min. 30 sec. at 100% turn over, 2 min. at 100%, rest covered 2 min. Do not do in small oven

Boned or unboned steaks Defrost at 100% in a dish just large enough to hold, covered with microwave cling film. Prick film after defrosting.

250 g/8 oz steak (2.5 cm/1 inch thick)	1 min. 30 sec., turn over, 30 sec.; cook.

Whole fish Remove the head and tail if the fish is too long to fit in the oven. Place diagonally in container just large enough to hold; cover tightly with microwave cling film. Shield (see page 19) 5–7.5 cm/2–3 inches of tail end and around cut where head was removed in doubled aluminium foil. For fish over 1.3 kg/3 lb, or without head and tail, start with a defrosting time of 25 minutes at 30%. Add 5 minutes for each pound over 1.3 kg/3 lb. Turn over once during cooking time. Remove foil for final one third of cooking time. Prick film each time container is to be uncovered.

Small fish Place fish in a container just large enough to hold; cover tightly with microwave cling film. Prick film each time container is to be covered. Defrost at 100%; turn over once.

1 fish, 400–500 g/14–16 oz	2 min.
2 fish, 400–500 g/14–16 oz each	3 min. 30 sec.

Large, thick fish Defrost at 30%; turn over twice. See illustration page 19 to shield fish.

3.7 kg/8 lb fish, 2.9 kg/6¼ lb without head and tail	45 min.; remove foil after 30 min.
3.4 kg/7½ lb fish, 2.6 kg/5¾ lb without head and tail	35 min.; remove foil after 30 min.
1.8 kg/4 lb fish, 1.6 kg/3½ lb without head and tail	30 min.; remove foil after 20 min.
1.5 kg/3¼ lb fish with head and tail	25 min.; remove foil after 15 min.

Tiny prawns To cook, 1½ min. longer

250 g/8 oz packet	2 min. at 100%

Crawfish tail Cover each tightly.

90–125 g/3–4 oz tail	30 sec.
150–175 g/5–6 oz tail	50 sec.
200–250 g/7–8 oz tail	1 min. 45 sec.
275–350 g/9–12 oz tail	2 min. 30 sec.

VEGETABLES

Even though I prefer fresh vegetables, I often cook frozen ones because I have a garden and I know no way of growing exactly the right amount. There is only one commercially prepared frozen vegetable that I use with any frequency—honest. It is often better than fresh petit pois. These vegetables should be considered blanched, not raw. Sometimes I use peeled and frozen button onions to save myself work.

HOME-FROZEN VEGETABLES Asparagus and other whole vegetables frozen without prior blanching should be cooked directly from the frozen. Add 30 seconds to the cooking time for every 250 g/8 oz of frozen asparagus.

Small vegetables such as peas, all kinds of fresh beans and sliced vegetables should be taken out of their wrapping and placed in a sieve. Run warm, not hot, tap water over them so that the pieces can be separated. Drain and cook immediately as if fresh. If vegetables defrost fully before cooking, reduce cooking time by one quarter.

Treat vegetables that have been cooked in butter or sauce or have been made into purée before freezing like homemade staples (heavy purées).

COMMERCIALLY PREPARED FROZEN FOOD Such foods come with packet instructions. If, even with this book in hand, you want to defrost commercially prepared frozen food, you don't need my help except for two warnings: (1) Even if the instructions don't tell you to, put the packet on a plate or in a bowl. Some of the contents will invariably spill over and mess up the oven. Also, the polythene pouches are hard to handle when hot. It's easier to take a plate out of the oven. (2) Wait a minute or two after taking a polythene pounch of food out of the oven before opening it. Even if you have pricked the pouch as instructed, there will still be enough steam in the bag to give you a nasty burn. Unless you let it cool slightly, it is hard to avoid the steam because the bag flops as you open it.

HOMEMADE FROZEN PREPARED FOOD In my house these are the result of miscalculation: too much prepared for the number of people or the appetites. I do not cook and freeze ahead now that I have a microwave oven except for homemade staples and vegetables. If I have leftovers and cannot bear to throw them out now rather than later, I pack them up in quantities that are reasonable for one or two people, in order to freeze. Larger quanties, especially if there are chunks of meat in them, will take too long to defrost. This is not just defrosting, but defrosting and REHEATING in one operation. Increase the defrosting times for homemade staples (heavy purées) by one third.

DICE Fruits, vegetables and meats are sometimes cut into even 6-sided shapes before cooking. Unless a specific size is given in the recipe, they are to be 5 mm/¼ inch square on each side.

DILL The feathery leaves and small, flat, oval seeds of this plant are one of Russia's gifts (along with rhubarb, soured cream and yogurt) to the culinary world. The seeds and dried flowers are normally used in pickling. The seeds are also good in salads. Fresh dill is wonderful in cucumber salad and chicken soup. Many preparations that call for mint are equally successful with dill.

I never used dried dill in the past because it was such an ugly colour. With microwave-oven DRYING dill stays green, wonderful for those with plentiful fresh dill in the summer and none in the winter. Use a teaspoon of dried dill to substitute for each tablespoon of fresh.

DRYING Before freezers and refrigerators, food that wasn't bottled (preserved) was often dried. Even today, some foods such as herbs, apricots, prunes, raisins and seeds are routinely dried. Still other foods that used to be dried for preserving have become expensive and sought-after specialities because of their particularly good flavour, different from that of their fresh progenitors. Examples would be sun-dried tomatoes from Italy, dried mushrooms from many parts of the world, and salted and dried cod.

Some foods can be dried satisfactorily in the microwave oven. Others cannot, particularly those that have a high ratio of water to solid matter. I tried for weeks to create the equivalent of sun-dried tomatoes, to no effect. True *Boletus edulis*, or CEP, dries very successfully. Its slimier, wetter cousins don't.

Most dried foods need to be soaked in olive oil, water or stock before they are used in a dish. There are some exceptions to this when cooking in the microwave oven. When included in soups and stews, dried mushrooms, other than MORELS, do not need to be presoaked; see Mushroom Barley Soup. Morels need to be presoaked to remove grit and sand. There may be dishes, such as sautées, for which you want to presoak other dried mushrooms. See SOAKING.

To dry coconut, see page 306.

DRYING HERBS

Microwave drying is standard practice for

me. The colour and fragrance are the next best thing to fresh. Scatter 45 g/1½ oz of washed and dried herb leaves or sprigs in an even layer on a double layer of paper towel. Do not cover. Cook for 4 minutes at 100%. Keep tightly covered.

DRYING MUSHROOMS

Fairy rings, chanterelles, lactarii and ceps all dry successfully. After wiping clean or washing only with a damp paper towel, dry mushrooms thoroughly. Slice ceps 3 mm/ ⅛ inch thick through the stalk. Leave fairy rings whole. Cut chanterelles into quarters from top to bottom, or sixths if very large. Halve lactarii. Cover a doubled layer of paper towel, 1 sheet large, with a single layer of mushrooms. Cook, uncovered, at 100% for 3 minutes. Turn mushroom slices over on to fresh towel and cook 2 minutes at 100%. If the mushrooms are not light and perfectly dry, leave on a dry sheet of paper overnight. When perfectly dry, store in a tightly closed glass bottle.

DRYING ZEST

Oranges, lemons and tangerines are not usually dried at home, but the zests are a nice ingredient to have available to season stews or add, pulverized, to baked foods. Peel oranges and lemons very thinly with a potato peeler, taking none of the bitter white pith. Cut zest into strips about 5 mm/ ¼ inch wide. Peel tangerines; turn peel orange side down and scrape off the white pith (using the edge of a silver spoon, if possible). Cut zest as above.

The zest of 1 orange or 2 lemons spread out on a double sheet of paper towel and covered with a single sheet will dry in 2 minutes 30 seconds at 100%, to make 3 tablespoons.

The zest of 1 tangerine, 1 large clementine or 2 small clementines will take 2 minutes at 100% and make 2 tablespoons.

DUCK Properly cooked, duck takes advantage of the microwave oven's differential cooking properties (fat cooks more quickly than meat) more than almost any other food. Duck's plentiful extra fat also renders magnificently in the microwave oven. I am as pleased by the recipes for duck as anything I have done in the oven, and it is gratifying that this technique makes it reasonable to cook duck for only one or two people. See Crispiest Duck for timings on duck; see Duck Confit for this very special dish, so fashionable today in salads but traditionally used in cassoulet or simple grilled to serve with potatoes cooked in the duck fat. See also RENDERING.

Ducks make wonderful stock and glaze. Duck livers are large and may be substituted by weight for other livers in recipes for pâtes. They also make very special creamy mousses on their own. The other innards can be made into a confit. If you are cooking one of today's numerous recipes for skinned and boned duck breast (magret), save the bones for stock and render the skin in flat pieces and use on a salad.

DUCK STOCK See Meat Stocks. See also CLARIFYING, stocks and sauces.

DUCK GLAZE See Meat Glazes.

E

EGGS All recipes in this books use British size 3 eggs, or Australian 55's. These kitchen staples have idiosyncracies in microwave cooking: To wit, never try to cook an egg in its shell, as it will explode. In fact, even a whole egg yolk will explode unless pricked once or twice with the tip of a sharp knife before cooking. Strangely enough, this doesn't result in a gooey mess, and the yolk keeps its shape very well. In Aubergine, Tomato and Fennel with Eggs or Baked Eggs, simply break the eggs where you want them; quickly prick each yolk a couple of times, and continue to cook according to the recipe. I hope this will bring back all the delicious baked egg dishes of the classic repertoire.

BINDING WITH EGG YOLKS This presents few problems. A sauce will curdle if the yolks get too hot or aren't sitrred thoroughly or frequently enough. Follow recipes exactly. Allow 1 yolk for each 125 ml/4 fl oz of sauce. See Chicken Fricassèe for technique. *CUSTARDS* work on the same principle; see Crème Brûlée. The classic French dessert sauce Crème Anglaise and the indispensable tart ingredient, Confectioner's Custard, are thinner versions of the custard.

QUICHE is made with a custard. I do not find crusts satisfactory in the microwave oven. If you are willing to settle for a quiche without a crust, see page 138 for a very successful recipe. You can bake the crust in a traditional oven, then fill and bake in the microwave oven.

EGG WHITE-RAISED DISHES Soufflés are a disaster. When I first tried a soufflé in the oven and peeked through the glass door, I was ecstatic; I thought we were all going to be making the highest, best soufflés the world has ever seen. As this soufflé finished its rising act and continued to cook in order to set, my beautiful dome collapsed into a sad pancake. No fiddling with soufflé recipes worked. I have tried every recipe in every book that claim to be for soufflés in the microwave oven. Not one of them is worth making.

Prepare your soufflé bases in the microwave oven, then bake the soufflé conventionally; Basic Béchamel and virtually any vegetable, fruit or fish purée will make a good soufflé base. However, the fallen-soufflé technique is the basis of many of the cakes in this book.

Now, as for my own idiosyncracies as opposed to those of eggs themselves: There are those who prepare *SCRAMBLED EGGS* and *OMELETS* (which they don't seem to differentiate sharply) in the microwave oven. I don't like the texture (too fluffy), and I don't like constantly opening the door during a short cooking period. Make your omelets and scrambled eggs on top of the stove.

EGG AND CRUMBING This never works in the microwave oven: You get a gluey mess.

EMULSIFICATION The binding together of a fat (oil or butter) and an acid (such as vinegar) or a protein (such as egg yolks). An emulsion is a uniform suspension of minuscule fat droplets throughout a liquid, achieved either by rapid beating and/or warming to form a stable mixture. Mayonnaise and the infamous Hollandaise are emulsions.

Emulsions such as egg-bound sauces and custards that involve stirring and the heat of actual boiling do splendidly in the microwave oven. (See EGGS.) It seems foolish to me to open the microwave oven every 15 seconds, as readers are often directed, to stir something like a Hollandaise. Be content to use the microwave oven to melt the butter for Hollandaise: make the sauce itself on top of the stove.

Other sauces are thickened in other ways. See Savoury Sauces and Sweet Sauces, and CORNFLOUR.

EVAPORATION The liquid in foods or added to them partially evaporates in microwave cooking unless tightly covered. Sometimes evaporation is desirable, as in Risotto and in REDUCTIONS.

F

FATS One of the nice things about cooking in a microwave oven, particularly for those of us on a perpetual diet, is that very little fat is needed since foods do not stick to the cooking pan (and we cannot really sauté). Except for recipes where the food is cooked entirely in fat, a sort of melting procedure (see treatment of onions in risotto recipes, pages 107–115), think of fats primarily as flavourings when cooking in the microwave oven.

Many different kinds are used in cooking: animal fats such as bacon, butter, chicken, duck, pork back fat, lard and suet; vegetable oils such as corn and soya; fruit oil such as olive; and the seeming infinity of seed and nut oils such as coconut, hazelnut, sesame, walnut, sunflower, cottonseed (used mainly in margarine), safflower, almond and even mustard. Each has its own taste.

The flavour of a fat changes with heating. Some of the expensive oils, such as almond, walnut and hazelnut, taste much better cold and should rarely be heated (and then only slightly, as for a warm salad dressing). The flavour of other fats changes very noticeably when they are heated enough to brown, like butter and bacon, but the browned taste is often desirable. Some fats, like sesame oil, have an entirely different flavour when the seed or nut is toasted before the oil is extracted. (Oriental sesame oil is made from seeds toasted first and so is brown in colour, rather than pale gold-to-clear.)

Fats can go rancid if kept too long in too warm an environment. Groundnut oil, a neutral oil to start with, quickly develops an 'off' taste, especially if kept in a clear bottle in a well-lighted place. While animal fats freeze well, the oils don't. Even refrigerating an oil such as olive (containing some fruit pulp and acid) may be enough to make it cloud and separate. Other oils, such as nut oils, that contain tiny solid particles separate when refrigerated.

Fats have different melting and burning temperatures. For melting techniques for animal fats, see BUTTER and RENDERING. If you respect the cooking times and quantities in the recipes, you will have no problem with fat burning.

DEEP-FAT FRYING

Since manufacturers of microwave ovens often counsel against deep-fat frying and will invalidate the warranties of any oven used for it, it has been thought better to omit recipes for this procedure in this book.

For deep-fat frying, neutral-flavour oils such as corn, safflower and ground nut tend to be most satisfactory. However, the Italians deep-fry in olive oil.

When it comes to deep-fat frying at a high temperature, you can use a saturated or unsaturated fat, because the heat will convert unsaturated fat molecules into saturated ones. The same is true for margarines. For use in salad dressings, on bread or when the fat isn't subjected to heat, saturated fats probably are not as good for you as either polyunsaturated or mono-unsaturated fats, particularly if you have a tendency to coronary artery disese or high cholesterol. Mono-unsaturated fats used to be thought less good for you than polyunsaturated; but in the fast-moving world of nutritional information, it has now been found that there are actually some health advantages to mono-unsaturated fats like olive oil. They certainly have more taste.

FAT, PORK BACK Solid, unmelted pork fat without meat streaks. This also comes salted. The fat used in pâtés and to line pâté moulds must always be the unsalted kind. (Have the butcher slice the fat for lining; it will save much time and effort.) See SALT PORK.

FENNEL There are two different, but related, plants called fennel. One is a weed that can be cultivated as a herb; it grows along the shores of the Mediterranean and in California. Its feathery tops, which look a lot like dill, are used in fish dishes, and its dried stalks are used as fuel for fires over which fish is grilled.

The other is Florence fennel, a root vegetable that looks sort of like a bulbous celery. It is terrific raw, thinly sliced, in salads with a lemony dressing. It also makes a good and unusual cooked vegetable, and this is where the microwave oven comes in. It cooks the vegetable quickly without leaving it fibrous or turning it mushy. I have added fennel to vegetable dishes (see Aubergine, Tomato and Fennel) and have served it on its own (see Fresh Fennel). If you can't find fennel, try substituting celery hearts or celeriac.

COOKING TIMES FOR FENNEL

Large bulb fennel 7.5 cm/3 inches diameter, about 250 g/8 oz each. Trim and cut into 6 wedges each; cover tightly.

1 bulb fennel	*3 min. 30 sec., rest 2 min.*
2 bulbs fennel	*5 min., rest 2 min.*

FENNEL SEED The seed of the fennel is used as a spice, whole or ground. See GRINDING. The flavour is something halfway between dill seed and anise, slightly liquorice.

FIGS Fresh, fully ripe figs are one of the world's great pleasures, and they require no cooking. However, there are times when they are less than radiant but would be a welcome change as a dessert. They can be poached. See SOAKING, dried fruit.

COOKING TIMES FOR WHOLE FRESH FIGS

With 125 ml/4 fl oz liquid per dozen figs; cover tightly.

3 figs (500 ml/16 fl oz dish)	*1 min. 30 sec. to 2 min.*
6 figs (20 cm/8 inch ring mould)	*3 min.*
12 figs (25 cm/10 inch ring mould)	*5 min.*

FISH All fish cook magnificently in the microwave oven except for those that are simply too large; double-check size, especially if you have a turntable. Also,

pieces more than 10 cm/4 inches thick will not cook terribly evenly (but they don't in a fish kettle or the oven either). Fish stays moist without any hardening of its surface. When in doubt, undercook. You can always put it back for a few more minutes.

Fish cook with relative uniformity from type to type. Cooking time depends on the shape, thickness and quantity of bone. There are a couple of exceptions: monkfish and paupiettes (fillets rolled around a stuffing). Fish timings are based on the use of an oven with a turntable or the use of a separate turntable. *If you are not using a turntable*, all cooking times over 5 minutes should be interrupted at the halfway point and the cooking dish rotated 45 degrees. If the total cooking time is more than 15 minutes, rotate 45 degrees after each third of cooking time. All fish cooking times are based on tight covering with microwave cling film. For additional information about arranging fish in a cooking dish, see page 34. All cooking times given here are for large or medium-size ovens, unless otherwise indicated.

To cook more than 1 dish of fish at a time, see page 143. To cook fish with seafood, see Cod with Clams Livornese.

See also individual varieties, especially MONKFISH, TROUT and TUNA; DEFROSTING, fish and seafood; and SEAFOOD COMBINATIONS.

FILLETS

I am defining these as halves or quarters of fish removed lengthways from the bones. Cooking times are the same whether they are skinned or not. If the skin is on, slash it across the width so the fillet does not curl. Line up fillets, in a single layer if possible, in a rectangular dish (it need not be greased). Season and cover tightly with microwave cling film. Added liquid is not necessary; it will lengthen the cooking time and should be kept to a minimum (in any case, it need not cover the fillet). If adding liquid, about 4 tbsp per 150 g/5 oz fillet is adequate. Each 125 ml/4 fl oz will extend the cooking time 30 seconds.

COOKING TIMES FOR FILLETS

1 cm/½ inch thick fillets, 125 g/4 oz each Steamed; cover tightly on a plate just large enough to hold them.

1 piece	1 min.
1 piece	1 min. 30 sec. (small oven)

1 cm/½ inch thick fillets, 175–250 g/ 6–8 oz each Steamed; cover tightly.

1 piece	2 min.
1 piece	3 min. 30 sec. (small oven)
2 piece	2 min. 30 sec.
4 pieces	5 min.
6 pieces	7 min.

2.5 cm/1 inch thick fillets, 175–250 g/ 6–8 oz each Steamed; cover tightly.

1 piece	3 min.
1 piece	4 min. 30 sec. (small oven)
2 pieces	4 min. 30 sec. 6 min. (small oven)
4 pieces	6 min.
6 pieces, about 1.3 kg/3 lb	8 min. to 8 min. 30 sec.

PAPILLOTES

Portions of fish, seasoned or plain, often conventionally cooked in folded parchment paper and tightly sealed. The same may be done in a microwave oven; but cooking in a tightly covered dish will do the same thing. (Aluminium foil cannot be used in this way and greaseproof paper becomes soggy and unattractive.) Place individual fillet flat on half of a heart-shaped piece of parchment paper. Roll over edges of paper to securely enclose fish.

COOKING TIME FOR PAPILLOTES

1 cm/½ inch thick fillets Steamed; cover tightly.

1 piece	45 sec. to 1 min.
2 pieces	1 min. 30 sec.
More than 2 pieces	Oven usually too small

PAUPIETTES

These are individual fillets split lengthways down the centre. Any bones and membrane are removed, and the pieces are rolled individually, starting with the head end. Sometimes a stuffing is placed inside the roll. Add 15 seconds to the cooking time for each stuffed paupiette. Cover tightly with microwave cling film.

COOKING TIMES FOR PAUPIETTES

Unstuffed Steamed; cover tightly.

1 piece	45 sec.
2 pieces	1 min. 30 sec.
4 pieces	2 min.
8 pieces	3 min.

STEAKS

These are defined as cuts across the fish with or without bone and are usually cut from larger fish. They will cook for the same amount of time either way. Time variations for added liquid are as for fillets. Steaks, if on the bone, should be arranged in a circle with the thin belly-flap pieces towards the middle. Cover tightly with microwave cling film. If you wish to add flavour to these thicker cuts, marinating works very well. Serve immediately.

COOKING TIMES FOR STEAKS

2 cm/¾ inch thick boneless steaks 250–275 g/8–9 oz each Steamed; cover tightly.

1 piece	3 min.
1 piece	4 min. 30 sec. to 5 min. (small oven)
2 pieces	4 to 5 min.
2 pieces	6 to 7 min. (small oven)
4 pieces	8 min.

2.5 cm/1 inch thick boneless steaks 175 g/6 oz each Steamed; cover tightly.

1 piece	3 min.
1 piece	4 min. (small oven)
2 pieces	4 min. 30 sec.
4 pieces	6 min.
6 pieces	8 min. to 8 min. 30 sec.

MEDALLIONS

These are really variants of steaks. I cut them from 4 cm/1½ inch thich steaks or fillets using a stainless-steel biscuit cutter 5 cm/2 inches in diameter. They are best arranged in a ring, allowing 1 cm/½ inch between medallions, 1 cm/½ inch from the edge of the cooking dish. Vegetables may be placed in the centre of the ring. Cover tightly with microwave cling film. Serve immediately. Medallions cook particularly well because of their dimensions and look attractive on the plate. Save any trimmings for fish burgers, Paupiettes with Provençal Fish Sauce, Swordfish Quenelles and pâtés.

COOKING TIMES FOR MEDALLIONS

4 cm/1½ inch thick medallions Steamed; cover tightly.

2 pieces	1 min. 30 sec.
2 pieces	4 min. (small oven)
4 pieces	2 min. 30 sec. to 3 min.
6 pieces	4 min.
12 pieces	6 min.

WHOLE FISH

Gutted, with or without head and tail. The skin does not have to be slashed since the bones will hold the fish straight. More liquid may be used so as to slow the surface cooking time. Tightly cover with microwave cling film in a dish just large enough to hold. Prick and remove film after cooking and let fish rest covered with a towel.

To cook more than 1 fish: If fish are very small (sardines, for example), arrange spoke-fashion with tails towards the centre; arrange 2 larger fish head to tail; continue this arrangement for more fish.

COOKING TIMES FOR WHOLE FISH

250 g/8 oz fish Poached; cover tightly.

1 fish with 90 g/3 oz onions and 175 ml/6 fl oz liquid	4 min.
4 fish with 175 g/6 oz onions and 350 ml/12 fl oz liquid	10 min., rest 2 min.

250–350 g/8–12 oz fish Poached; cover tightly.

1 fish with 250 ml/8 fl oz liquid	4 to 5 min.
2 fish with 350 ml/12 fl oz liquid	5 min.
4 fish with 550 ml/18 fl oz liquid	6 min.

350 g/12 oz fish Steamed with 30 g/1 oz liquid; cover tightly.

1 fish	2 min.
2 fish	3 min. to 3 min. 30 sec.
4 fish	5 to 6 min.

500 g/1 lb fish Poached; cover tightly.

1 fish with 250 ml/8 fl oz liquid	4 to 5 min., turn over once
2 fish with 350 ml/12 fl oz liquid	6 min., turn over once
4 fish with 550 ml/18 fl oz liquid	10 to 11 min., turn over once

1–1.3 kg/2–3 lb fish Poached; cover tightly.

1 fish	10 to 11 min.

Larger, defrosted whole fish Steamed; cover tightly. See DEFROSTING.

750 g/1½ lb fish, with head and tail	8 min. (large oven), 12 min. (small oven)
1 kg/2 lb fish, with head and tail	11 min. (large oven), 14 min. (small oven)
1.25 kg/2½ lb fish, with head and tail	14 min.
2.7 kg/6 lb fish, head removed: weight 2 kg/4½ lb	18 in.
3.7 kg/8 lb fish, head removed: weight 2.7 kg/6 lb	22 min.

FISH STOCK This wonderful gelatinous stock can be made from the head and/or bones of any white-fleshed fish (except the flat fish) that have been thoroughly washed to remove any blood—remove gills also—and cut into smallish pieces. Stock made with flat fish—sole, plaice and the like—turns bitter on top of the stove in about 10 minutes; in the microwave oven the same thing happens in 5 minutes. Use cod, haddock, halibut and so on and you will have better, richer stocks with more gelatine. Do not use the bones of oily fish, such as salmon, mackerel, sturgeon and herring unless the stock is to be used with those fish; the taste will be too particular.

Fish stocks are wonderful bases for any number of fish soups or sauces for fish. CLAM LIQUOR can be substituted for fish stock or used as a portion of the liquid in making fish stock; it will give a more intense flavour.

When buying fillets, ask for the bones and freeze them if you don't have time to make stock. See DEFROSTING, thin liquids, for defrosting times. See also CLARIFYING, stocks and sauces; clarified fish stock is used primarily for Aspic or for cold jellied summer soups.

FISH GLAZE Like the other glazes, this is a luxury to have on hand when fitting classic sauces to fish or seafood dishes. See Beurre Blanc. It can also be added to the sauce of a quick-cooking fish recipe if the flavour seems a little faded.

FIVE-SPICE POWDER This Chinese seasoning has a strong liquorice taste thanks to star anise. It is available, in jars, in the spice section of supermarkets. A smaller amount of star anise may be substituted.

FLAGEOLET For cooking times, see BEANS.

FLOUR Flour has been made not only from almost every grain known to man (wheat, rice, oats) but from nuts (acorn and chestnut), starchy fruits (cassava) and roots (arrowroot) as well. Those flours with a substantial amount of gluten, such as hard-wheat flours, behave disastrously in the microwave oven and should be avoided wherever possible except for very special cases (see Roux). This is why there are few conventional baking recipes in the microwave repertoire.

Every recipe in this book works. The ones you won't find here (French bread, for example) are absent not on a whim, but because there was no way I could get a result that I considered good. The rising of yeast doughs can be aided substantially by the microwave oven. See RAISING.

FRENCH BEANS See HARICOT VERT.

FREEZING Just a few general notes: Mark your container with a waxy marker or a label; later you will know what you have. Make sure frozen foods exclude air or are covered with a layer of liquid to avoid freezer burn. See DEFROSTING.

WRAPPING For whole foods or fillets such as fish, pork joints, and skinned and boned chicken breasts, first wrap separately and in greaseproof paper or cling film before wrapping in freezer foil or freezer paper. Wrap singly for even defrosting.

For jointed birds, wrap joints separately so that you can make as many servings as you wish.

For meat cut up for stew, drape a large piece of freezer wrap on a flat plate. Place the pieces of meat on it in a single layer. Fold wrap over meat. Freeze on plate. Remove plate when frozen. This will help the meat to defrost evenly in the cooking liquid.

LIQUID OR SEMILIQUID FOODS Divide into reasonably small quantities among microwave-safe plastic containers. A 500 ml/15 fl oz quantity defrosts much more rapidly than a litre; 2 separate 500 ml/15 fl oz quantities will go more quickly and evenly than 1 litre. Use containers that can be put directly in the microwave oven—containers larger than needed for the amount to be frozen, since liquids expand in freezing and tend to boil over when being defrosted. Remember that the lids of such containers are almost never meant for the microwave oven; remove them and cover the container with microwave cling film. Flimsy plastic containers will get dangerously soft when heated. Do not freeze in paper containers, as they may disintegrate by the time defrosting is accomplished.

Very small quantities of sauces and reductions, from 1 to 4 tablespoons, can be frozen in plastic ice cube trays. When thoroughly frozen, store cubes of an equal size in a freezer bag.

FOODS TO BE REHEATED IN A SPECIAL CONTAINER Foods that are cooked in special containers and that hold their shape once cooked, such as Meat Loaf and Macaroni Cheese, should be allowed to cool in the cooking container. Then invert on to cling film, aluminium foil or freezer wrap and wrap tightly. Freeze. To defrost, remove from wrapper; return to original container and defrost, covered if the amount is large. Place container on a dish to avoid spills.

Vegetables are best frozen lightly blanched in the size pieces you wish to finally cook them in. Freeze in freezer bags. Turn out into blanching containers, and defrost and heat.

FRUIT All the fruits and berries cook brilliantly in the microwave oven. Refer to specific entries in this Dictionary.

GAME It used to be that any animal that appeared naturaly in a habitat and raised itself in the wild was considered game, from fish to venison. A hare was game, some rabbits were game. These days, the lines of definition are blurring. Most of the venison and pheasant served in this country are farm-raised. Today, game seems to mean animals that used to be caught wild, whether they actually are now or not.

Generally, game cannot be roasted in the microwave oven (but see POUSSIN). Cook game birds and rabbit as you would CHICKEN, adjusting the seasonings. Cook red-meat game as you would lean BEEF as it has almost no fat.

GARLIC Yes, I love it. Yes, many people do not. Most of us know that garlic cooked for a serious amount of time changes character. It becomes soft and sweet and tends to thicken the liquid in which it cooks. This sometimes desirable effect occurs (except to elephant garlic) with miraculous rapidity in the microwave oven. Almost any quantity of cloves, smashed, peeled and covered with 250–350 ml/8–12 fl oz of stock and tightly covered, will cook to that wonderful stage in about 8 minutes. This means that in long-cooking dishes you will need a much larger quantity of garlic than you might imagine. It also means that if you want a sharp garlic taste, add the garlic 3 minutes before the end of cooking, or after removing the food from the oven.

Recipes in the book call for garlic cloves to be 'smashed and peeled'. Garlic is a living thing, like a flower bulb. When you cut it, it gives off a bitter odour and flavour. Smashing the bulb first will prevent this from happening, and will also make it easier to peel. If you discover that the clove has a green centre (or 'germ'), fish out and discard the green part, as it tends to be bitter and tough.

Whole heads of cooked garlic make a wonderful garnish for people who love garlic and don't mind eating with fingers. Serve a whole head to each person; encourage eaters to remove 1 clove at a time and pull the pulp out between their teeth. (Give them a place to discard the garlic skins.) See Roasted Garlic.

GELATINE A natural component of animal bones and certain plants (some seaweeds, mosses and fruits). Tapioca, for example, is made from the root of the cassava. Those neat little sachet of commercial gelatine are made from gelatine extracted from bones, purified and powdered. You can generally figure that 1 packet (11 g/0.4 oz), which is equivalent to 4 teaspoons, will set 600 ml/1 pint of liquid if it's not very acid (grapefruit juice, lemon juice and white wine all require half again as much gelatine) and does not contain pineapple, papaya, kiwi or fig (all of which contain an enzyme that will dissolve the gelatine).

One sachet of gelatine sprinkled on 5–6 tablespoons cold water in a 250 ml/8 fl oz glass jug or bowl (or 2 sachets sprinkled on 150 ml/¼ pint water in a 500 ml/1 pint measuring jug), allowed to 'soak' or absorb water for 2 minutes, can then be dissolved, tightly covered, at 100% in 30 seconds. Remove from oven and stir. Continue with recipe.

Agar-agar is a seaweed gelatine used in vegetarian recipes. Unlike bone-derived gelatine, agar-agar sets at room temperature. When it is being used to coat and layer a mould for an aspic, it may get too hard to work with. To remedy this, simply cover the aspic and stick it back in the microwave oven for 30 seconds.

GHEE A form of clarified butter, allowed to cool before it is used. In some parts of India it is aged until it acquires what is to a Western palate a distinctly high taste. Julie Sahni in her brilliant book *Classic Indian Vegetarian and Grain Cooking*, says of ghee that it is '... made by heating butter long enough to allow the moisture present in the milk solids, which causes spoilage, to evaporate. The slow heating and cooking process gives the clarified butter a gentle nutty aroma, a pale yellow colour when cool, and a distinctly grainy texture. The unmistakable taste of authentic usli ghee is due to the lactic flavour present in the butter.' See BUTTER, clarified.

GINGER This is a rhizome (such as irises grow from). Fresh ginger should be thin-skinned, light in colour and juicy. It is also available dried and ground for use in baking. If fresh root ginger is to be used as a flavouring only—in stir-frying, for example—and will not be eaten, it need not be peeled. Never add it before prolonged cooking; it will only give the dish a hot flavour without any fruity, acid freshness. Five minutes or so in the microwave oven is plenty. A few slices tucked under a fish fillet while cooking perfumes the entire fish.

A trick when fresh root ginger is to be eaten is to grate it. A Japanese bamboo wasabi grater is ideal for eliminating strings.

GIROLLE See CEP.

GLAZE (GLACE DE VIANDE) In cooking, there are basically three types of glazes: thick glazes, such as a barbecue sauce, which give colour and flavour to meats as they cook or after they cook (they do not substitute for true roasting); sweet glazes of chocolate, sugar or fruit purée to seal or ice cake layers and pastry; and savoury glazes, made by reducing a stock (see Meat Stocks). Commercially, savoury glazes are sometimes called concentrates. See Index for glaze recipes.

GOAT CHEESE Goat cheese is made in abundance, and only partially for its distinctive flavour. Mainly, it is made because goats can feed on much poorer and higher land than cows can. The cheese comes from many countries and may have very different textures and flavours; most are rather crumbly. Fresh, young, chalk-white cheeses are an interesting ingredient. See Goat Cheese Croûtons.

GOOSE These wonderful, fat birds are always Christmas, Scrooge and Tiny Tim to me. For this purpose, roast in a conventional oven and enjoy with sage stuffing. Goose, like duck, can be made into a confit; joint the goose so that the pieces and weights match those of the duck in Duck Confit and proceed as for duck.

GOOSEBERRY These fat members of the currant family come in several different varieties, including the romantically names cloudberries. Most gooseberries are a pale acid green or a soft pinky mauve. Gooseberry jelly can be made as is Redcurrant Jelly.

GORGONZOLA Creamy blue cheese from Italy. I often prefer Gorgonzola to Roquefort, which often has an enormous quantity of salt. My favourite kind, Dolcelatte, is made from cream-rich summer milk.

GRAINS The seeds of grasses, used ground as flour. Some, such as wild rice, are cooked whole for a side dish, in desserts or as a cereal. See specific grains in this Dictionary.

GRATING Cheese and chocolate can be grated in a food processor fitted with a grating disc, in a small, rotary hand-held cheese grater or on a four-sided grater. Grate firm vegetables such as carrots, potatoes and even cabbage on a four-sided grater or in a food processor.

GREEN BEAN Fresh green beans and their pale look-alikes, wax beans, are a pleasure to cook in the microwave oven. No pots of water, no salt unless you choose, and bright colours, lots of vitamins and a perfect crisp but cooked texture.

See BEANS for cooking times. A portion of green beans placed in the dish around a piece of fish or a chicken breast will up the combined cooking time by only 20 seconds (1 minute for HARICOTS VERTS). If you really must salt the beans (they have enough flavour and cook better without it), add it to the water with which you sprinkle the beans. If you wish to cook the beans in tomato sauce or other liquid, add 1 minute for each 125 ml/4 fl oz.

GRINDING Grinding of nuts and seeds, including spices, can be done with a mortar and pestle, but that is work.

Small quantities of nuts and all spices are best ground in a simple electric coffee mill reserved for that purpose; use it to grind allspice, anise, caraway, cardamom, cloves, coriander, cumin, fennel, etc. The quantity of seed that you can grind at home depends to an extent on the size of your machine, but a good rule of thumb is 2 to 3 tablespoons.

Large quantities of nuts can be ground in the food processor. (Seeds and coffee beans cannot; they are too light and fly around so madly that many of them entirely escape the blades.) Here again, the quantity you can grind at one time depends on the capacity of your machine. Don't fill the container more than halfway full; in order to bring all the unchopped nuts down from the top, you'd have to overprocess the nuts closest to the blades. Grind nuts with pulses rather than a continuous, butter-producing whir. If the recipe contains sugar, it is safer to grind the nuts with the sugar.

GUAVA These semitropical fruits come in a wide variety of colours, from yellow to red purple. They are fairly hard (even when ripe), difficult to peel, full of seeds and are almost never eaten raw. Sounds unappealing; but cooked guavas are a delicacy. The most succulent preparation is a firm, if slightly gritty, jelly paste eaten as a dessert in South American countries along with cream cheese. Prepare in the same way as Qunice Paste.

·H·

HADDOCK A white-fleshed fish often used interchangeably with cod. There is a vigorous debate as to which is better. Haddock is often smoked, and the cure was originally developed in the fishing village of Findon, south of Aberdeen. Arbroath Smokies are smaller smoked haddock. See FISH for cooking times. See also COD for soaking.

HAKE This white-fleshed fish is cooked in ways similar to haddock and cod. In Spain, where it is vastly popular, it is called by the more melodious name of *merluza*. In Portugal, where it is the most widely used fresh fish, it is called *pescada*. Whiting is a rather soft member of the hake family; a favourite preparation is Whiting with Parsley Sauce. See FISH for cooking times.

HALIBUT The largest member of the flat fish family, a cousin to sole and plaice. Some halibut grow to be 6 feet long, which explains why they are usually cooked as filleted steaks rather than whole or a single whole fillets. For this reason halibut tends to get cooked more like hake, haddock and plaice than like the other flat fishes, although it may be steamed and served with Almond Butter Sauce or Browned Butter Sauce with Capers. See FISH for cooking times.

HAM It is many things to many different people. To a pig, it is its hind leg. Things are confused because the Corsicans, among others, make hams that are neither meant to be cooked nor are they smoked. Such hams are called 'raw' in the various languages of their countries; they are salted either in brine or by having salt rubbed into the meat, after which they are hung in a cool, dry, airy place to age and loose excess water. Then they are scrubbed with fresh water. The most famous of these raw hams is probably *prosciutto crudo* from Parma, also called Parma ham. *Jambon de Toulouse* is a sort of unsmoked Bayonne ham (an elegant, mildly smoked French ham meant to be eaten without further cooking). France has many other country hams meant to be eaten raw (*cru*). The Spanish version is *jamón serrano* ('mountain ham').

A whole English ham should not be cooked in the microwave oven, but lovingly tended at length in traditional ways. Be satisfied with preparing the accompanying vegetables in the microwave oven.

HARE See RABBIT.

HARICOT VERT These French green beans are usually under cooked in this country, but must be cooked sufficiently to develop their flavour. For cooking times, see BEANS.

HAZELNUT These lovely shiny, brown-shelled nuts are eaten plain, as well as being used in cakes, pastries and ice creams. *Nocciole*, the Italian ice cream, is one of my favourites. In Spain and in France the nut is ground to thicken savoury sauces. For blanching and toasting, see NUTS. Like almonds, they make excellent Praline.

HERBS This is one of the largest groups of food seasonings. See specific herbs in this Dictionary. A great pleasure of the microwave oven is its ability to dry fresh herbs better than any other method I know. See DRYING, herbs.

HERRING A large and, to me, confusing family of fish. Along with sardines and anchovies, which are relatives, it accounts for most of the fish eaten worldwide. Since such fish swarm in large schools, they are easy to net. Over the centuries their plenitude has been preserved by smoking, salting—both dry and in brine—and pickling. Salted herrings need to be desalted before they can be prepared; follow the directions for soaking and desalting COD. For cooking times, see FISH.

HONEY Long before man knew how to extract sugar from beetroot or cane, his sweet tooth led him to discover the extremely efficient factories of the bees. Today honeys from all over the world are sold here, each with its own distinctive taste, often based on the particular nectar of the flowers that have fed the bees. Honey is usually slathered on breakfast toast; don't forget that you can cook with it. When substituting honey for sugar in a recipe, remember that it is significantly sweeter than the equivalent weight of sugar.

To reconstitute honey or jam. Cook 350 g/ 12 oz in jar, top removed, covered tightly with microwave cling film for 1 minute 30 seconds.

HORSERADISH A herb grown for its pungent, eye-watering, sharp root. Peel; grate in a food processor to avoid skinned knuckles and tears; prepare raw. Horseradish quickly loses its authority when cooked. A little stirred at the last minute into a sauce for kidneys, along with some mellowing cream, is very nice.

I

ICE CREAM Most homemade ice cream is made with a custard base such as Crème Anglaise. It may be flavoured either by adding crushed fruit or by flavouring the cream with which the custard is made; for example, steep coffee beans in the cream, tightly covered, for 4 minutes at 100%. After custard is made, cool; make ice cream.

J

JALAPEÑO These dark green, ovoid hot chillies, about 7.5 cm/3 inches long, are frequently used in the Mexican and Tex-Mex cookery. They are most often sold here in cans. See CHILLI.

JAM See PRESERVING.

JICAMA A large brown root with crisp, white, slightly starchy flesh. It can be cooked, but I see no reason for it; it is at its best raw, thinly sliced or cut in juliennes. To cook jicama, at the most cut it up to inexpensively replace water chestnuts in stir-fried dishes.

JULIENNE Meats and vegetables, raw and cooked, are often cut into even strips to be used raw or before cooking. Unless the specific size is given in the Dictionary, julienne size is 3 mm × 3 mm × 5 cm/$\frac{1}{8}$ × $\frac{1}{8}$ × 2 inches. Lardons, before cooking, are normally fatter and shorter, 5 mm × 5 mm × 2.5 cm/$\frac{1}{4}$ × $\frac{1}{4}$ × 1 inch.

JUNIPER BERRY The taste of gin, predominantly flavoured by these round, dried black berries, can be added to any dish. Simply crush a few into it while it cooks. This flavour adds a nice note to cabbage, fish and poached pineapple or Light Poached Pears. Use 3 berries per person; crush with fingertips before adding.

·K·

KALE If the leaves have very pronounced ribs, separate the ribs from the leafy parts. Kale may also be cooked as PAK CHOI.

COOKING TIMES FOR KALE

Braised Cook in a 35 × 27.5 × 5 cm/14 × 11 × 2 inch dish; cover tightly.

1 kg/2 lb kale with 750 ml/1¼ pints water and 125 g/4 oz pork fat	*30 min.; uncover for last 5 min of cooking time*

Yields

1 bunch with stalks	*600 g/1¼ lb, raw*
600 g/1¼ lb, raw stalks removed	*500 g/1 lb, raw*

KEY LIME Almost no Key limes grow any longer in the Florida Keys. Certainly, none are grown commercially, but they are grown commercially in Mexico. They are worth searching for with their strong perfume, slightly bitter taste and dark green and (when ripe) plentiful juice (which freezes well). When you find them, buy lots.

KIDNEY BEAN Dark red, dried beans that often pop up in chilli. They are also used to make delicious Refried Beans. For cooking times, see BEANS.

KIWI This public relations success fruit originally comes from New Zealand and is now being grown in California. Much of its popularity is due to the brilliant green of the flesh, in which small black seeds make decorative patterns. The taste is similar to bananas. It is not a fruit to cook, but good sorbet can be made with its purée. See SIMPLE SYRUP.

KOHLRABI A cool, pale green relative of broccoli, it is round like a root vegetable, but the knob is a swelling in the stem from which its leaves grow. When you buy it, the leaves will have been, or should be, snapped off, leaving rather Turkish-looking arched points on the outside. When precooking kohlrabi to slice or mash and stir with butter, it is easier to peel it after it is cooked. Of course, Stuffed Kohlrabi must be peeled before cooking. This neglected vegetable should return to popularity with the benefits of microwave cooking: It cooks quickly, stays green and does not get watery.

COOKING TIMES FOR KOHLRABI

Small kohlrabi 8 to 10 per 500 g/1 lb. Cook 250 g/8 oz quantities in tightly sealed microwave safe cooking bags.

250 g/8 oz	*4 to 5 min.*
500 g/1 lb	*6 min.*

Large Kohlrabi 4 per 500 g/1 lb; cook in a tightly sealed microwave-safe cooking bag.

2 kohlrabi	*4 to 5 min.*

Small, stuffed kohlrabi Each kohlrabi with 2 tbsp stuffing; cover tightly.

2 kohlrabi with 1 tsp water (small soufflé dish)	*3 to 4 min.*
8 kohlrabi with 1 tbsp. water (22.5 cm/9 inch soufflé dish)	*7 min.*

· L ·

LAMB As with beef, leave the chops and joints to the frying pan, conventional oven and grill. The one time when roasting comes into the picture at all is when you have a frozen leg stashed in the freezer for last-minute guests or when you buy a frozen leg. It can be rapidly defrosted and cooked immediately. See DEFROSTING, lamb, or Roast Leg of Lamb. Other than that, use the microwave oven to make Lamb Steaks, Irish Stew and Moroccan Stuffing.

COOKING TIMES FOR LAMB

Stewing lamb, bone in Cook in a 2.5 litre/4 pint soufflé dish; cover tightly.

1 kg/2 lb lamb with 750 ml/1¼ pints liquid and 500 g/1 lb vegetables	18 min.
1 kg/2 lb lamb with 350 ml/12 fl oz liquid and 1 kg/2 lb vegetables	25 min.

LAMB STOCK A lot of flavour for very little work comes from lamb stock. Try substituting this stock and cubed lamb in Mushroom-Barley Soup. See Meat Stocks and CLARIFYING, stocks and sauces.

LARDON See BACON, lardons.

LEEK I love leeks, tiny whole ones for grilling and big fat ones for braising, leeks in soups and sauces, and to make meltingly good nests for fish, seafood and chicken. Before cooking leeks, it is important to clean them very well. They are kept white and tender at the bottom by being planted in a trough. As they grow, dirt is shoveled into the trough to hide the root end from chlorophyll-producing light. To clean them, first cut off the roots, being careful not to cut them off so high that the leaves fall apart. Slit the green leaves on either side down to the white part. If the leeks are very wide, take the tip of a sharp knife and cut a cross into the root end. Soak them in cold water, rinse and dry.

If you've never tried leeks on their own as a vegetable, try Braised Leeks. I like these so much I eat them as a first course, hot or cool. Leeks are also a lovely ingredient in other dishes (see Leek and Potato Soup). Melt them in butter or oil; place a spoonful of melted leeks in the shell under an opened oyster; top with Sauce Suprême or Mornay made with the oyster liquor and dry white wine or vermouth; slip under the grill for an elegant first course. Two tablespoons under a fish fillet adds splendid flavour. Stir some into a Sauce Suprême made with chicken stock to serve with quickly cooked chicken breasts.

COOKING TIMES FOR LEEKS

Whole medium leeks Braise in a dish just large enough to hold them in a single layer; half-cover with stock; cover tightly.

250 g/8 oz	20 min.
500 g/1 lb	30 min.
1 kg/2 lb	40 min.

Sliced 3 mm/⅛ inch thick or into juliennes Melted, with 30 g/1 oz butter per 500 g/1 lb, uncovered.

250 g/8 oz leeks (20 cm/8 inch round dish)	4 min.
500 g/1 lb leeks (1 litre/2 pint soufflé dish)	6 min. 15 sec.

Yield

2 medium leeks	250 g/8 oz untrimmed

LEMON Another of my favourite tastes is that of lemon juice. I always mean freshly squeezed juice, never bottled or frozen. Except where it is used in a marinade, as in some of the fish dishes, lemon should be added at the end of cooking or after the dish comes from the oven. Lemon quickly loses its aromatic freshness when cooked.

I find its quantity one of the most difficult to specify in a recipe. The juice of 1 lemon makes no sense. We have all had the experience of straining at a stony lemon that after much effort gives us only a teaspoon or so of juice. There are also gushers, lemons that prodouce 4 tablespoons or more of impeccable juice. Why not then just given quantities? I do; but I always feel guilty. Lemon juice varies so much in acidity that one time you may need very little and at others much more.

Recipes that read 'salt to taste'—an instruction I like since we all have different salt tolerances and palates—add more problems. The tastes of salt and acid make each other stronger. When adding them both to a recipe, alternate them and taste as you go along, so you don't have any nasty surprises. Many such dishes, when cooked in the microwave oven, should be seasoned at the end.

Lemon zest, the yellow part of the skin, is a nice addition to fish and fruit cooked in the microwave oven. It doesn't need to be blanched first. It may also be dried to add to fruit desserts, but it is not quite as good as orange or tangerine zest. See DRYING, zest.

LEMON BALM This lovely perennial herb is only good fresh. Do not bother to dry it.

LEMON GRASS An inedible seasoning (too tough), much used in Thai and Vietnamese cooking, it is available fresh, dried and dried and powdered (usually as sereh powder). It is a delightful addition to chicken soup. The fresh herb should be bruised by smacking with a heavy knife or pan before being added to the soup. The dried herb is better off with a little microwave oven-intensified soaking. See SOAKING, herbs.

LEMON SOLE See SOLE. For cooking times, see FISH.

LENTIL One of the staples of cooking from India through Europe, this pulse is available in many colours: red, yellow, orange, brown and greenish. Sadly, the brilliant little discs all turn muddy when cooked. Lentils are available in normal and quick-cooking varieties; I find it really makes little difference which you use when cooking in the microwave oven. Lentils make terrific winter soups and mushes, usually served with sausage in Italy,

Hungary and Germany. See Green Lentil Soup. They have an intense enough flavour to be a worthy mainstay of vegetarian cooking. In India, where they are cooked as dhal, they are a component of almost every meal. Their protein combines with that of rice to make a rich nutritional complex.

As with other dried pulses, lentils are sometimes very old and dry when you buy them. If they are not sufficiently cooked at the end of the resting time, re-cover and cook at 100% for another 5 minutes. When you cook them, cover them with a double layer of microwave cling film; cook at 100%.

COOKING TIMES FOR LENTILS

Green or brown lentils Cook in a 2.5 litre/4 pint soufflé dish; cover tightly; rest, covered, for 20 min.

200 g/7 oz lentils with	35 min.
1 litre/1¾ pints water	
400 g/14 oz lentils with	35 min.
1.5 litres/2½ pints water	

Red, yellow or orange lentils Cook in a 2.5 litre/4 pint soufflé dish; cover tightly; rest, covered, for 20 min.

200 g/7 oz lentils with	10 min.
1 litre/1¾ pints water	
400 g/14 oz lentils with	10 min.
1.5 litres/2½ pints water	

LETTUCE A large family of leafy greens usually used in salads, lettuce cooks well—try whole as a light vegetable to serve with fish (see Braised Lettuce) or cooked shredded with peas. It is not an old wives' tale: Lettuce is a natural calmative.

LIAISON See EMULSIFICATION and THICKENING, sauces.

LIME Aside from their pairing with tonic and appearance in Bloody Marys in the last ten years, these smallish, green citrus fruits are used mainly for their juice. Seviche relies on it. See also KEY LIME.

LIQUEURS These alcoholic drinks, often sweet, are made with fruit (orange or pear, for example), nut (almond, hazelnut), herb (angelica) and spice (anise, caraway) flavourings. Many of the most famous originated in monasteries as restoratives or cordials. See ALCOHOL for advice on cooking with liqueurs in the microwave oven.

LIVER See BEEF LIVER, CALF'S LIVER, CHICKEN LIVER and DUCK LIVER; see Pâté in Index.

LOBSTER This crustacean is blue-black when alive and red when cooked. A similar creature is the crawfish, which is a dull brownish-red. Unlike the lobster, the crawfish has no claws. (See DEFROSTING, crawfish tail, for timing.) Fresh (live) lobsters should be boiled or steamed on top of the stove.

—————◆M◆—————

MACADAMIA These expensive Hawaiian nuts can be used in cooking, but it seems a shame, as they are so delicious on their own. You can use them, toasted and ground, for an especially rich dusting on baked goods and other sweets. See NUTS, toasting and GRINDING.

MACE Available dried and ground, this spice tastes a lot like nutmeg, which is hardly surprising since it is made from the nutmeg husk. It is less expensive, and also less aromatic. If substituting for nutmeg, increase the quantity to taste. While you do not need both spices in the kitchen, their slightly different flavours make for an interesting comparison.

MACERATING See SOAKING.

MACKEREL Of all the fish that swim in the sea, many are mackerel. All mackerel are oily. They make good soups and stews with pungent greens such as kale. Otherwise, they are usually cooked in acid liquids, such as white wine or tomato sauce, to balance the oil. Depending on the variety and size, they can be cooked whole, filleted or as steaks. See FISH for cooking times.

MANDOLINE An excellent French tool that predates the food processor. It is much like an old-fashioned cabbage slicer except that it is metal and can be adjusted for different thicknesses of slicing and julienning. Use it when perfectly even cutting is important. It is the ideal substitute for a good sharp knife or a food processor with assorted slicing discs.

MANGE-TOUT The thin, edible pod peas so much seen in Chinese restaurants. If you are adding them to a stew or Chinese-style dish, lay on food, tightly covered, for the final 1 minute 30 seconds cooking time.

Mange-touts really should not be cooked in much water. 90 g/3 oz will feed at least two people. To cook as a separate vegetable in the microwave oven, string; heat 10 g/⅓

oz butter or 2 teaspoons water for each 90 g/3 oz of mange-touts for 2 minutes, uncovered, at 100%; stir in mange-touts; cook as below. SUGAR SNAP PEAS cook as for mange-touts.

COOKING TIMES FOR MANGE-TOUTS

Mange-touts Cover tightly.

125 g/4 oz (1 litre/2 pint measuring jug)	2 min.
125 g/4 oz as above	3 min. (small oven)
250 g/8 oz with 350 ml/ 12 fl oz water (1 litre/2 pint measuring jug)	3 min.

MANGO There are many different varieties of this fruit. The most delicious are flattened ovals with skin that is green when picked, yellow when the mango is ripe. The flesh is golden apricot in colour. The only trouble with the mango is freeing the delectable flesh from skin and stone. It is easier to extract the flesh of underripe mangoes than ripe ones; this is no help when you wish to enjoy one raw, but it is nice to know for those times you want to make chutney or curry. See Fresh Mango Chutney.

MAPLE SYRUP Sweeter than cane sugar, maple syrup and honey were the staple sweeteners in American Colonial days until molasses, rum and sugar were traded with the Caribbean countries. Syrup made from the first run of sap is the best, though mildest in flavour and palest in colour. Different states and Canada have different designations for the various grades of syrup. It is a shame to squander Fancy, Grade AA, Pale or whatever the first-run designation might be on cooking, where its elegant flavour will be lost. Use a medium-grade syrup if it is going to be cooked at all; it will have a distinct maple flavour, though not as overpowering as that of a dark maple syrup.

MARJORAM This annual version of oregano is somewhat milder in flavour. It is used extensively in Italian cooking. See DRYING, herbs.

MARROW Both a vegetable and the soft centre of bones. The best animal marrow for cooking is that found in the leg bones of veal; it is one of the things that makes Ossobuco so succulent. Many classic French recipes call for marrow that has been removed from the bone and sliced on top of steaks or into sauce (see Marchand du Vin).

Cooking bone marrow is one of the chores that the microwave oven performs superbly, better and more reliably than other ways. Be sure you really have veal bones. If the veal is superannuated, really an overgrown, milk-fed calf, it will have bloody, stringy marrow. Make sure the marrow you buy is white to pale pink and uniform in colour. Have the bones cut into 5–7.5 cm/2–3 inch lengths with marrow showing at both ends; soak in heavily salted water—4 tablespoons salt to each 250 ml/8 fl oz cold water— for an hour. Rinse in clear water and dry. Stand the pieces up, not touching, in a soufflé dish deep enough to hold them. Cover tightly with microwave cling film. After cooking at 100% for the recommended time, pierce the film, then remove from the oven and let the bones cool just until you can handle them. Free the marrow with a thin sharp knife by running the blade all around between the marrow and the bone at each end of the bone. Gently shake out the marrow.

COOKING TIMES FOR MARROW BONES

Cut into 5–7.5 cm/2–3 inch lengths and soak as above Stand in a dish just large enough to hold them without touching; add 2 tbsp water per bone; cover tightly.

2 pieces bone, about 125 g/4 oz	1 min.
4 pieces bone, about 250 g/8 oz	2 min.
8 pieces bone, about 500 g/1 lb	4 min.

MAYONNAISE A cold emulsion of oil and egg yolk flavoured with vinegar or lemon juice, it is a very useful uncooked sauce (see page 332). It may be coloured and flavoured with green herbs or Lightly Cooked Crushed Tomatoes. Serve with cooked fish, seafood or poultry to make a salad.

MELLOWING A way of reheating to improve meat stew flavours. See page 206.

MILK When heating or cooking milk in a microwave oven as for New England Clam Chowder or Basic Béchamel, be sure to use a large container. Milk boils up easily, making a mess. One nice thing about cooking it in a microwave oven rather than on top of the stove is that you are much less likely to scorch the milk (and will not have a nasty pan to clean).

SCALDING TIMES FOR MILK

Cook in a 1 litre/2 pint glass measuring jug; cover tightly.

250 ml/8 fl oz milk	1 min. 30 sec.
500 ml/16 fl oz milk	3 min.

MILLET One of the world's oldest grains. It is still used in Russian cooking, and before sweetcorn hit Italy, Italians made their polenta with it. To cook millet, substitute it for couscous in Risotto of Couscous. You can vary the liquid and the seasonings as you wish. Millet makes a nice change from potatoes.

COOKING TIMES FOR MILLET

400 g/14 oz millet with 1 litre/1¾ pints liquid (35 × 27.5 × 5 cm/14 × 11 × 2 inch dish)	10 min., uncovered

MINT A herb of which there are many different kinds. They freeze terribly but dry well, retaining green colour and much of their flavour. Dried mint makes an agreeable tea. It is an ingredient essential to many Moroccan dishes. See DRYING, herbs.

MIRIN This Japanese sweetened wine is a component of many sauces, giving them what Westerners may think of as their characteristic Japanese flavour. Mirin can be a nice addition to the repertoire of Western seasonings; see Pâté with Chinese Black Beans. Mirin is available in Japanese food shops.

MOLASSES A by-product of sugar refining. The best grade has some sugar left in it; the darker the molasses, the less sweet it is. Recipes using molasses usually call for bicarbonate of soda to neutralize its acid.

MONKFISH Newly popular (although long esteemed in France as lotte), this firm, white-fleshed fish is generally sold as a skinned, boneless tail. It requires longer cooking than most fish. Braising is ideal. See Monkfish in Green Sauce.

COOKING TIMES FOR MONKFISH

150 g/5 oz fillets Cover tightly.

2 fillets with 125 ml/4 fl oz liquid, 3 tbsp oil and 175/6 oz vegetables (22.5 cm/9 inch flan dish)	5 min.
6 fillets with 125 ml/4 fl oz liquid, 4 tbsp oil and 400 g/14 oz vegetables (27.5 × 20 cm/11 × 8 inch oval dish)	8 min.

MOREL One of the most expensive mushrooms, it is usually available dried since it is hard to locate—you don't even tell your best friend where your patch is—and has a short season. The dried reconstitute beautifully and quickly in the microwave oven. See SOAKING, dried mushrooms.

MULLET The king of this fish family is the famed French Mediterranean rouget. For cooking times, see FISH.

MUSHROOM In this book, 'mushrooms' without a modifying adjective means commercially grown agaricus mushrooms, with white caps and pinkish-brown gills. Scores of other mushrooms are great delicacies. A few are cultivated; many more are picked wild. They are available fresh and dried. See individual varieties: CEP, CHANTERELLE, MOREL and SHIITAKE. See DRYING, mushrooms, and SOAKING, dried mushrooms. See also Duxelles.

COOKING TIMES FOR MUSHROOMS

Sliced With 1 tsp fresh lemon juice per 250 g/8 oz; cover tightly.

250 g/8 oz (27.5 × 20 cm/11 × 8 inch oval dish)	3 min.
250 g/8 oz as above	4 min. 30 sec. (small oven)
500 g/1 lb (27.5 × 20 cm/11 × 8 inch oval dish)	3 min.
1 kg/2 lb (35 × 27.5 × 5 cm/14 × 11 × 2 inch dish)	6 min.

Whole caps With 1 tsp oil per 250 g/8 oz; cover tightly.

250 g/8 oz (27.5 × 20 cm/11 × 8 inch oval dish)	8 min.
500 g/1 lb (27.5 × 20 cm/11 × 8 inch oval dish)	12 min.
1 kg/2 lb (35 × 27.5 × 5 cm/14 × 11 × 2 inch dish)	15 min.

MUSSELS The shells of most varieties are blue-black, but there is also a brown-shelled Venetian kind and a startlingly green-shelled New Zealand variety. Size tells you nothing about quality. Often the smallest shells have particularly nutty and delicious meat inside while the large shells have flabby meat; and sometimes the biggest are succulent. The most important thing is to get mussels that have been growing in clear, cold seawater on rocks or on special 'mussel farm' constructions.

The only tricky part about cooking mussels is cleaning them. Some farmed mussels have no beards and require virtually no cleaning. For other mussels, scrape off the beard with a sharp knife, then scrub under cold water with a plastic scrubbing pad. If you want to store cleaned mussels before cooking, refrigerate in a clean polythene bag; do not keep in water or they will become watery. In the microwave oven, they may be cooked, tightly covered with microwave cling film, with or without added liquid. They are done when they begin to open.

Save the liquor given off as you cook mussels for adding to soups. (See CLAM LIQUOR.) Mussels make a nice addition to fish and barely affect cooking time. See Cod with Mussels Livornese.

COOKING TIMES FOR MUSSELS

16 to 18 per 500 g/1 lb Cook in a 2.5 litre/4 pint soufflé dish standing up, hinge end down; cover tightly.

500 g/1 lb	3 min.
500 g/1 lb	6 min. (small oven)
1 kg/2 lb	7 min.
1 kg/2 lb with about 175 ml/6 fl oz liquid	8 min.
2 kg/4 lb; cook 2 dishes of 36 mussels each simultaneously, using microwave trivet. Reverse positions after 8 min.	15 min.

MUSTARD The tiny seeds that are ground to make prepared mustard grow almost all over the world. Toasted mustard seed is used in many Indian dishes. Mustard powder usually has some flour added to it. Mustard powder and prepared mustard both act as thickening agents when cooked with milk or cream as in Dijon Snails. See TOASTING, small seeds.

N

NUOC NAM This salty liquid sauce made by fermenting fish is a staple of Indonesian, Cambodian, Vietnamese, Laotian, Thai and other Malaysian cuisines. Adjust quantities as for SALT

NUTMEG A large hard seed, dried and ground as a spice. A little bit goes a long way, whether sprinkled on punches or into spinach or cake and biscuit dough. Nutmeg has a tendency to be overpowering, and the microwave oven will bring out every bit of nutmeg flavour you put in.

NUTS See varieties in Dictionary. See also GRINDING.

To *blanch nuts*, put them in a flat container in a single layer. Add water and cook at 100%. Rub off the skins with your hands or between layers of towelling.

BLANCHING TIMES FOR NUTS

Arrange in a single layer in a shallow dish. Add 125 ml/4 fl oz water per 500 g/1 lb nuts; cover tightly.

125 g/4 oz	1 min. 30 sec.
250 g/8 oz	3 min.
500 g/1 lb	6 min.

Toasting times for nuts vary with their different amounts of oil.

TOASTING TIMES FOR NUTS

Arrange in a single layer in a shallow dish; cook at 100%, uncovered.

Almonds

175 g/6 oz	5 min.

Macadamia nuts

150 g/5 oz	4 min.

Peanuts

250 g/8 oz	3 min.
500 g/1 lb	4 min.

Pine nuts

250 g/8 oz	8 to 10 min. (stir twice during cooking)

Walnuts or pecans

150 g/5 oz	4 min. 30 sec.

SPICING NUTS

Generally speaking, you can spice just about any nut there is. And you can make sweet spiced nuts or piquant spiced nuts.

Spiced mixed nuts: Heat 1 teaspoon vegetable oil, uncovered, in a 25 cm/10 inch flan dish at 100% for 2 minutes. Add 1 tablespoon chilli powder, 4 drops Tabasco sauce and 1 teaspoon sea salt. Cook, uncovered, at 100% for 1 minute. Add 350 g/12 oz unsalted nuts and stir to coat. Cook, uncovered, at 100% for 5 minutes, stirring once. Vary seasonings.

To *salt nuts*, proceed as for Spiced Mixed Nuts, substituting sea salt for the chilli powder and omitting the Tabasco sauce.

─────────●─────────

OATMEAL Oatmeal is used mainly in baking and as breakfast cereal; except perhaps in Scotland, it is much less used than it once was. Cereal companies have responded by making quicker-cooking porridge oats. Use large cooking dishes or measuring jugs; porridge tends to boil over.

COOKING TIMES FOR PORRIDGE

Traditional porridge made from coarse oatmeal Cover tightly.

4 tbsp with 250 ml/8 fl oz water; uncover after 4 min. 30 sec. (2 litre/3½ pint jug or bowl)	*9 min. 30 sec. to 10 min. 30 sec.*
90 g/3 oz with 500 ml/16 fl oz water; uncover after 5 min. (2 litre/3½ pint jug or bowl)	*13 to 14 min.*

Porridge oats (not quick-cooking) Cover tightly.

scant 30 g/1 oz with 175 ml/6 fl oz water (1 litre/ 2 pint measuring jug)	*2 min. 30 sec., stand 1 min.*
scant 30 g/1 oz as above	*4 min. (small oven), stand 30 sec.*
40 g/1⅓ oz with 350 ml/ 12 fl oz water (2 litre/3½ pint jug or bowl)	*3 min. 30 sec., stand 1 min.*

OATS Grain from which oatmeal is made. Oats au naturel are horse feed.

OCTOPUS See SQUID.

OFFAL Animal innards are selectively eaten in our country. I remember when sweetbreads were cheap; they have become a costly speciality. Tongue gets made into sandwiches with relatively little fuss. Brains, kidney, heart, lung and intestine are commonly avoided I think, in part, because offal requires cooking procedures different from those we perform all the time, and that makes us nervous. The microwave oven vastly simplifies and improves this kind of cooking. See BRAINS, SWEETBREADS and TONGUE.

OIL See FATS.

OKRA When trimming this vegetable for stewing, it is important not to remove the entire stalk end or cut into the okra pod itself; it you do, you'll find that every slimy tale you've heard about it is true. If you trim carefully, though, your efforts will be rewarded with succulent, well-behaved okra. On the other hand, if you are using it in a gumbo to act as a thickener, you will have to slice it acros to let the viscous thickener out.

COOKING TIMES FOR OKRA

Stewed whole okra Trim stalks; cook in a 22.5 cm/9 inch square dish, uncovered.

250 g/8 oz okra (add 500 ml/16 fl oz thick liquid and cover tightly)	*3 min. in 4 tbsp oil*

OLIVE OIL Now that it's been discovered that mono-unsaturated fats are actually good for you or, in the most pessimistic rendering, no worse for you than polyunsaturated, we can all enjoy the wonderful olive oils with glee. Italy, France, Spain, Portugal, Greece and California all produce a wide variety of qualities and tastes. I generally buy small quantities of unfamiliar oils until I determine what I think each will be best for.

Apart from deep-fat frying, olive oil is used mainly as a flavouring in microwave cooking. It seldom gets so hot that it loses its essential flavour, which is why I use good, fruity oils but not ones so heavy that their flavour will overwhelm everything cooked in them. Your own palate is the only reliable guide for you. See FATS and FRYING.

ONION This large vegetable family, with its relatives the LEEK, SHALLOT, GARLIC and CHIVE, is a cooking staple, as much a flavouring as a major ingredient. Flavour depends on the onion variety and the soil it grows in and, sometimes on their age as well. When cooking, taste a little bit of the onion you have; if it is very sharp, reduce the quantity in the recipe. (If slicing an onion makes you cry more than usual, it probably is quite sharp.)

The sweeter the onion, the more likely it is to brown well with microwave cooking, except for red onions, which never brown well, no matter how they are cooked. Unfortunately, browning onions takes a long time even in the microwave oven. The advantage is you don't have to stand and stir and worry about scorching.

Since onions vary so wildly in size and weight, I have tried in these recipes to give you the size of the onion being used, or the weight.

Button onions seem delightful, until you realize you have to peel them. The microwave oven makes this easy: Trim the root ends; blanch onions. If they are very young, reduce the cooking time by about 15 seconds. When cool enough to handle, simply pop them out of thie skins.

BLANCHING TIMES FOR BUTTON ONIONS

Arrange in a single layer. Cook in a 27.5 × 21 × 5 cm/11 × 8½ × 2 inch oval dish, uncovered.

250 g/8 oz onions with 1 tbsp water	1 min.
500 g/1 lb onions with 2 tbsp water	2 min.

COOKING TIMES FOR ONIONS

Button onions, blanched Peel; cook in a 1 litre/2 pint soufflé dish; cover tightly.

250 g/8 oz onions with 6–8 tbsp liquid	8 min.
250 g/8 oz onions with 125–250 ml/4–8 fl oz liquid	10 min.
500 g/1 lb onions with 250–500 ml/8–16 fl oz liquid; stir once	15 min.

Whole small white onions 12 per 500 g/1 lb; peel; cook in a 25 cm/10 inch dish; cover tightly.

1 kg/2lb onions with 500 ml/16 fl oz sauce	10 min.

Whole Italian-flat onions 6 × 8 × 1 cm/ 2½ × 3¼ × ¼ inch; peel and trim; cook in a 35 × 27.5 × 5 cm/14 × 11 × 2 inch dish; cover tightly.

750 g/1½ lb with 400 ml/ 14 fl oz sauce; uncover last 10 min. cooking time	25 min.

Sliced onions To caramelize, cook, sliced, uncovered.

250 g/8 oz with 60 g/2 oz butter (1 litre/2 pint soufflé dish)	30 min.
500 g/1 lb with 125 g/ 4 oz butter 35 × 27.5 × 5 cm/14 × 11 × 2 inch dish)	40 to 50 min.

Finely chopped onions Cook in a shallow dish with fat previously heated for 2 min., uncovered.

60 g/2 oz onions with 30 g/1 oz fat (20 cm/ 8 inch square dish)	2 min.
60 g/2 oz as above	3 min. (small oven)
75 g/2½ oz onions with 60 g/2 oz fat (25 cm/ 10 inch flan dish)	2 min.
125 g/4 oz onions with 60 g/2 oz fat (25 cm/ 10 inch flan dish)	4 min.
125 g/4 oz as above	5 min. (small oven)
150 g/5 oz onions with 125 g/4 oz fat (35 × 27.5 × 5 cm/14 × 11 × 2 inch dish)	3 min.
250 g/8 oz onions with 125 g/4 oz fat (35 × 27.5 × 5 cm/14 × 11 × 2 inch dish)	3 min.

ORANGE As with all citrus fruits, oranges should be fresh wherever possible. When juice or zest is included in a recipe, it should be cooked for a minimum of time. The microwave oven does a good job of drying zests. See DRYING, zest.

OREGANO Often confused with marjoram, this perennial herb and its edible flowers have a strong, robust taste. Too often it dominates pasta sauces and pizza. Use with discretion. When using fresh in the microwave oven, slightly increase the quantity over the usual amounts, and decrease the quantity when using dry. See DRYING, herbs.

OSSOBUCO Thick cuts through the veal knuckle in a rich and unctuous Italian sauce cook wonderfully in the microwave oven. The centre round of bone and marrow acts like a magnet for the microwaves. Suddenly, it is feasible to cook veal knuckle for one or two people—consider that 4 pieces cook in 16 minutes at 100%! See recipe for Ossobuco or devise your own using the same times and proportions of liquid.

COOKING TIMES FOR SLICED VEAL KNUCKLE (OSSOBUCO)

Veal knuckle Thick slices, about 6 cm/ 2½ inches each. Brown on top of the stove for 10 min.; cover tightly.

2 knuckles with 4 tbsp liquid and 125 g/4 oz vegetables (20 × 15 cm/8 × 6 inch oval dish)	*12 min.*
4 knuckles with 125 ml/4 fl oz liquid and 250 g/8 oz vegetables (27.5 × 20 × 5 cm/11 × 8 × 2 inch dish)	*16 min.*
6 knuckles with 150 ml/¼ pint liquid and 325 g/11 oz vegetables (35 × 27.5 × 5 cm/14 × 11 × 2 inch dish)	*22 min.*

OYSTERS I eat oysters raw. No reasonable amount of cooking is going to make a bad oyster safe, so I might as well eat them raw. There are times when it is nice to slip a few faintly cooked oysters into a sauce, or even to turn them into a dish like Oysters Rockefeller or Oysters Florentine.

You can open the scrubbed oysters for cooking in the microwave oven. Remove them from their shells; twist off the top shell and discard. Save the liquor in the shells to use in the sauce, or in other fish dishes (see CLAM LIQUOR).

OPENING TIMES FOR OYSTERS

Cook in a single layer in a shallow dish, hinges down. 6 per 500 g/1 lb. Cover tightly.

6 oysters	*2 min.*
12 oysters	*4 min.*
24 oysters	*9 min.*

––––––• **P** •––––––

PAPAYA A delightful fruit—almost as good as a mango, but a lot easier to peel and seed—that has a slightly orange-yellow skin when ripe. All too often it is available only green, and I seldom have the wit to think enough ahead to buy it and ripen it for a special meal. Fortunately, there are dishes that use underripe papaya to advantage: Chicken Curry, Papaya and Cumin Sauce and Steamed Papaya Pudding. The easiest way to deal with papaya is to cut it in half lengthways, scoop out the seeds, then scoop out the flesh.

PAPRIKA I have an aunt, a rather difficult lady, who used to admonish her daughter to be very careful: 'Once a girl gets a bad name ...' The sentence would trail off with dire implications. Well, paprika did some awful things, almost as bad as parsley. It ended up flaunting itself all over fish and chicken and even boiled potatoes until nobody wanted it anymore. If paprika promises to be good and show up only where it has something to offer, like in Chicken Paprikàs, I think we can consider being seen in its company again.

Paprika is the name the Hungarians gave to Ameriacn pod peppers when they turned them into a seasoning. It is available both as a powder and as a paste in different degrees of pungency (see Pepper Purées to make your own). Paprika adds no flavour to food if simply sprinkled over it dry; it needs to be cooked, which it already is in paste form.

PARMESAN More bad cheese—indeed, I am tempted to say sawdust—has been sold masquerading as the real Italian cheese from Parma. Buy Parmesan in bulk. Look for aged cheese. Grate it yourself as you need it (see GRATING) since it rapidly fades in taste once grated. It keeps well, tightly wrapped, in a chunk. Then when you add it to foods such as Risotto, you will really enjoy it. Also consider eating it on its own with a pear instead of dessert, or scatter slivers of it on mushroom-rocket salad.

PARSLEY A Victorian tale: 'The Green Menace, or Virtue Reclaimed', edifyingly told in three parts, being parsley, its dangers; parsley addiction; and parsley, redemption through restraint. When I first began my green temperance league, the signs of parsley abuse were already widely spread. Sprigs showed up in the strangest places. I feared the day a cooking student would proudly show me a chocolate cake luridly wreathed in parsley, 'for a little colour'. As cooks have become more aware of the possibilities inherent in contrasts and arrangements of food on the plate, this danger has faded. Abstinence is not the solution. Remember that parsley is a wonderful herb with very good flavour, an important seasoning in its own right.

There are two principal kinds of parsley, common curly parsley and Italian flat-leaf parsley. Both are delicious. Contrary to popular supposition, curly parsley is stronger-tasting than flat-leaf. Young parsley of either kind will be better and more delicate than the older, tougher sprigs and may need to be increased in quantity. For maximum flavour, parsley needs to be cooked; this is particularly nice in the microwave oven, since it will keep its colour. See Parsley Sauce. The stalks can be saved for soup whenever you find only the leaves are called for. I dislike the quantity 'a bunch of parsley' (though I'm guilty of the mistake myself); no two bunches are ever the same. See DRYING, herbs and advice on quantities, page 444.

PARSNIP A delightful vegetable, the parsnip has a sweet, nutty flavour. Add some cooked, puréed parsnips to mashed potatoes, or stir them into a winter vegetable soup or, cooked and cubed, into a winter version of Chicken Fricassée. Parsnips are unexpectedly elegant in Parsnip Creams.

COOKING TIMES FOR PARSNIPS

Cut into 4 cm/1½ inch chunks; cover tightly.

250 g/8 oz parsnips with 125 ml/4 fl oz liquid (1 litre/2 pint measuring jug)	5 min.
250 g/8 oz parsnips with 125 ml/4 fl oz liquid (1 litre/2 pint measuring jug)	9 min. (small oven)
500 g/1 lb parsnips with 250 ml/8 fl oz liquid (2 litre/3½ pint jug or bowl)	8 min.
1 kg/2 lb parsnips with 350 ml/12 fl oz liquid (1 litre/2 pint soufflé dish)	11 min.

Yield

500 g/1 lb cooked, trimmed parsnips with 250 ml/8 fl oz liquid	500 ml/16 fl oz purée

PARTRIDGE Perfect, plump partridges should be roasted or grilled; should an older one come your way, it could be happily substituted in the Mini-Chartreuse. Serve roasted, pleasant with Braised Red Cabbage, Parsnip Creams or one of the vegetable purées, pages 251–260.

PASTA I love pasta, but almost never cook it in the microwave oven. It's too slow, due to the relatively huge quantity of water. It is better cooked on top of the stove and then combined with a soup or sauce that has been prepared separately in the microwave oven. Do remember to allow enough time for boiling your water, as well as for cooking your pasta, so that the microwave part of the recipe is not far ahead of the pasta.

PEA Unfortunately, the season for fresh peas is very short, so this is one case where I often counsel frozen. I use the tiny petit pois. Unwrap frozen peas; place in sieve; run warm tap water over the peas until they separate. One small packet will then heat, tightly covered, with or without 15 g/½ oz of butter, at 100% in 2 minutes. (To heat in a small oven, prepare as for a large oven and cook for 4 min. 30 sec.) When adding to recipes, remember that frozen peas are basically cooked; you are adding them just for the length of time it takes them to heat.

When tender, fresh peas are available, cook, with or without butter, salt, and a few fresh mint leaves, tightly covered.

COOKING TIMES FOR FRESH PEAS

Large peas Cover tightly.

150 g/5 oz with 5 g/⅙ oz butter (500 ml/1 pint measuring jug)	4 min.

Tiny new peas Cover tightly.

300 g/10 oz (1 litre/2 pint measure)	3 to 4 min.

Yield

750 g/1½ lb peas, unshelled	250 g/8 oz peas, shelled

PEACH One of the many fruits that poach perfectly in the microwave oven. You can also make delicious Peach Butter.

COOKING TIMES FOR PEACHES

Whole, small peaches About 75 g/2½ oz each. Prick each with a fork; cover tightly.

1 kg/2 lb peaches in 500 ml/16 fl oz syrup (2 litre/3½ pint jug or bowl)	5 min.

Quartered and stoned for Peach Butter Cover tightly.

750 g/1½ lb peaches with 125 ml/4 fl oz liquid and 100 g/3½ oz caster sugar (2.5 litre/4 pint soufflé dish)	15 min.
1.3 kg/3 lb peaches with 250 ml/8 fl oz liquid and 100 g/3½ oz caster sugar (35 × 27.5 × 5 cm/14 × 11 × 2 inch dish)	22 min. 30 sec.

PEANUT See Peanut Brittle. See also NUTS toasting.

PEAR Today, pears are often better for a longer season than apples, since they must always be picked underripe and allowed to ripen off the tree, or they will be mushy. Storing the underripe fruit in the refrigerator keeps them in good shape for a pretty long time. This underripeness is actually an asset when cooking pears for a desert; use firm varieties such as Conference or Bosc. Pears cooked in a microwave oven do not need any additional sugar, and they will cook evently.

COOKING TIMES FOR FIRM PEARS

Whole Peel and core; arrange in dish in which they will just fit and cover tightly.

1 pear	3 min.
1 pear	4 min. 30 sec. (small oven)
2 pears	4 min. 30 sec.
2 pears	8 min. (small oven, with carousel)
4 pears	7 min.
6 pears	8 min.

Halved Peel and core; arrange (see page 337) in a single layer; cover tightly.

1 pear in 250 ml/8 fl oz syrup (small dish at least 6 cm/2½ inches deep)	7 min.
2 pears in 500 ml/16 fl oz syrup (21 × 17.5 × 6 cm/8½ × 7 × 2½ inch dish)	12 min.
4 pears in 1 litre/1¾ pints syrup (30 × 27.5 × 6 cm/12 × 11 × 2½ inch oval dish)	17 min.

PECAN see NUTS, toasting.

PECTIN This is the other element, besides sugar, that makes jams and jellies set. Fruits that are rich in pectin, such as quince, are often added to low-pectin fruits like apples to make a jam set. (Pectin is also available in bottles.) I don't like preserves that are too firm; none of the recipes in this book calls for added pectin, and I think you will find them satisfactory.

PEELING The peeling of hard fruits and vegetables is best done with a potato peeler.

Tomatoes, when really ripe, need no special treament. Run the back of a knife blade firmly along the tomato to losen the skin, then peel. Tomatoes that are not ripe can be cooked for 30 seconds in boiling water, then peeled and cored. Results in the microwave oven are too uneven.

Peaches can be treated as tomatoes. To peel the brown skin from nuts, see NUTS, blanching. For help with peeling chestnuts, see CHESTNUT.

PEPPERS Large sweet pod peppers, now available in a dizzying variety of colours. They make wonderful sauces (see Red Pepper Purée), contribute colour and flavour to vegetable dishes, and are terrific stuffed either hot or cold as a first course or as a main course.

COOKING TIMES FOR PEPPERS

Whole Core and seed; cook in a tightly closed microwave-safe cooking bag.

250 g/8 oz	4 to 5 min.
250 g/8 oz	6 to 7 min. (small oven)
500 g/1 lb	6 min.

Whole, as a stuffed vegetable Stuff; stand in a deep 25 × 20 cm/10 × 8 inch dish; cover tightly.

4 large peppers, about 1 kg/2 lb, with 125 ml/ 4 fl oz liquid	20 min., stand 5 min.

PEPPER, BLACK There is no sense in using black peppercorns whole; you're just wasting pepper. Pepper is one of the trickiest ingredients to use in microwave cooking; following quantities in standard recipes will give wildly over-peppered results. It isn't so much that the pepper gets acrid, as it will with prolonged conventional cooking; but the briefer, more intense microwave cooking seems to elicit every last bit of pepper flavour from the spice. Begin by cutting your usual pepper quantities to one quarter, until you get a feel for it, or add pepper when foods come out of the microwave oven and are still warm.

PEPPER, WHITE This ground pepper is stronger in taste than black and, like it, should be used sparingly in microwave cooking. It is used primarily in elegant white sauces where black flecks would be a distraction. See PEPPER, BLACK.

PEPPERMINT See MINT.

PERCH Many fish are disguised under the name of perch. There are several different kinds of true perch; they live in fresh water and are generally small. Freshly caught, they are at their best pan-fried. They can be poached whole, like TROUT. For cooking times, see FISH.

PHEASANT See GAME.

COOKING TIMES FOR PHEASANT

Whole bird Cook in a shallow 30 cm/12 inch oval dish, uncovered.

1–1.25 kg/2¼–2½ lb bird   15 min.
with 250 g/8 oz fruit or
vegetables

PIGEON See POUSSIN.

PIKE These long, thin, freshwater fish are often hard to come by. If you can order one, or if you know a friendly fisherman, try the classic Quenelle with pike; while other fish and seafood, such as scallops, can be cooked this way, the firm, fine, somewhat neutral flesh of pike is ideal. If you have filleted pike left over, see FISH for cooking times.

PINEAPPLE The symbol of hospitality, most pineapples used to come exclusively from Hawaii. Today, they come from Puerto Rico and other Caribbean islands, and some far-flung areas as well. There are different varieties coming on to the market. Some of the most sweetly ripe and aromatic are the small, reddish-skinned fuits from the Caribbean. The old test for ripeness—tugging on a leaf to see if it comes out easily—is not as reliable as it used to be. To examine for ripeness, gently press the bottom; it should give slightly, without feeling soft or mushy—signs that it may be overripe, have brown spots and be fermented. When you have one that feels right, smell it. It should give off the aroma of fresh, sweet pineapple.

Most fresh pineapple is eaten raw. There is one very nice way of preparing it that works well in the microwave oven: Cut the top from the pineapple; quarter. Trim and discard the strip of core; cut the flesh from the skin. Replace the flesh on the skin and slice it, crossways, into bit-size pieces. Arrange quarters spoke-fashion on a plate, leaf ends towards the centre. Cover tightly with microwave cling film. Cook as for 'boats' and serve warm with vanilla ice cream.

COOKING TIMES FOR FRESH
PINEAPPLE

1.8 kg/4 lb pineapple for compote Trim, peel, quarter and core cook in a 25×20×5 cm/10×8×2 inch dish; cover tightly.

4 quarters pineapple   8 min.

1.8 kg/4 lb pinapple to serve as 'boats' Trim, quarter and core; skin, slice across and arrange on skin; cover tightly.

4 quarters pineapple (2   10 min.
dishes 30 × 25 × 5 cm/
12 × 10 × 2 inch); cook
simultaneously on a
microwave trivet

PINE NUT The seeds that are shaken out of certain pine cones when they are ripe. Pine nuts are often used in Italian food. In pesto, no prior cooking is needed. To top ice cream or some stews, they are nice toasted. See NUTS, toasting.

PINTO BEAN For cooking times, see BEANS.

PISTACHIO A bowlful of these little nuts in their natural beige or dyed red shells can cause an addiction and a room littered with shells. As you open them, you will notice that they have a thin, papery skin over their softish green flesh: remove before making into ice cream or adding (about 30 g/1 oz) to Veal Pâté. Blanch as peanuts; see NUTS, blanching.

PITA Heats and puffs in the microwave oven at 100% for 1 minute.

PLAICE A flat fish that is best when small. See SOLE. For cooking times, see FISH..

PLUM 'A plum ripe for the picking' tells us the high esteem in which plums have been held. There are countless variaties, from the tiny mirabelles to huge greengages. There are pointy purple prune plums, and red plums with golden flesh that can be as small as mirabelles and almost as large as greengages.

Because of their high sugar content, plums have long been used throughout Europe to prepare brandies, which are frequently named after the type of plum from which they are made.

All plum varieties poach well, and most make good jam. Watch out for mirabelles, though; they will turn to alcohol practically while you look at them.

Prunes are dried plums. They can be cooked with almost no liquid, their skins pricked once or twice with a fork, and tightly covered with microwave cling film, to put in a compote or eat alone. They can also be poached in a syrup with or without wine. Small prunes can be stoned; little prunes should be left whole.

COOKING TIMES FOR PLUMS

Whole plums About 6 per 500 g/1 lb. Poach in a 2.5 litre/4 pint soufflé dish in 500 ml/16 fl oz syrup (see SIMPLE SYRUP); cover tightly.

6 plums	8 min.
10 plums	10 min.
16 plums	Cook in 2 batches as above, reusing syrup

POACHING Cooking food in a large quantity of liquid, often liquid to cover, at a temperature below boiling. Unless you want to poach in a sugar syrup (see Figs in Red Wine) or other flavoured liquid, poaching is inefficient in the microwave oven. It is preferable to steam the food with a minimal amount of added liquid.

POIRE WILLIAM The French name for a variety of pear, unusually used to describe a delicious, nonsweet, white brandy (alcool blanc) or eau-de-vie made from pears. Most Poire William is made in Switzerland. My favourites are made in the Haute Savoie of France and come in slim, long-necked bottles like Alsatian wine bottles. True Poire William is expensive. Drink very cold in small quantities at the end of a meal. Splash a little on a fruit salad or add to a fruit dessert. When using in a cooked dish, add as close to the end of the cooking time as possible to preserve flavour. Watch out for pear liqueurs that are sweetened, as they are never as freshly fruity. See ALCOHOL.

POLENTA The Italian name for cornmeal and cornmeal mush. Before the arrival of sweetcorn in Italy, various grains and pulses were cooked in similar fashion to make those diet staples, porridges. See CORNMEAL.

POUSSIN This small chicken (weighing about 500 g/1 lb), with quail and small pigeons (often called squabs), are the only bird that cook well whole in the microwave oven: The interior cavities are not so large that timing becomes odd and cooking uneven. While the birds do not roast, a flavoured butter stuffing under the skin not only improves the flavour, it also causes the skin to turn an attractive colour. Allow 1 bird per person. See Pigeon Seasoned with Butter Under the Skin.

COOKING TIMES FOR POUSSIN

Whole poussin Stuff butter under skin, uncovered.

1 poussin with 30 g/ 1 oz butter (dinner plate)	4 min.
1 poussin as above	5 min. 30 sec. (small oven)
2 poussins with 60 g/2 oz butter (serving plate)	6 min.

PORK Here again, I do not believe that the microwave oven roasts. However, a good compromise is achieved in Smothered Pork Roast. I see no reason for us all to waste money attempting to pan fry, or grill pork in the microwave oven, particularly today's leaner pork. It can be stewed in chunks, or minced, or enjoyed in chops as an entire dish or in pieces as part of a robust pasta sauce.

New guidelines for cooking pork indicate that it is safe to eat once it reaches a uniform internal temperature of 60° C/140° F. I realize that pork can be cooked as concerns taste and texture in the microwave oven without reaching the requisite internal temperature, and I have developed recipes that are unquestionably safe. If you have any doubts when following or adapting recipes, use a little instant-reading thermometer. See also DEFROSTING, meat.

COOKING TIMES FOR PORK

Thin pork chops Cut 1–2 cm/½–¾ inch thick. Cover tightly.

1 chop about 150 g/ 5 oz, with 4 tbsp sauce (15 cm/6 inch round dish)	4 min.
6 chops about 1 kg/ 2 lb, with 250 ml/ 8 fl oz sauce (30 cm/12 inch square dish)	8 min.

Thick pork chops Cut 2.5–4 cm/1–1½ inches thick. Cover tightly.

4 chops, about 1 kg/ 2 lb, with 1.6 kg/ 3½ lb vegetables (35 × 27.5 × 5 cm/14 × 11 × 2 inch dish)	16 min.

Spareribs Cover tightly.

1.6 kg/3½ lb ribs brushed with sauce (35 × 27.5 × 5 cm/14 × 11 × 2 inch dish)	20 min., then grill 4 min.

Pork loin joint Cover tightly.

1.6 kg/3½ lb joint with 750 g/1½ lb vegetables; uncover for last 15 min. of cooking time (27.5 × 20 × 5 cm/11 × 8 × 2 inch dish)	cook 35 min. at 100%, then grill as desired.

Sausage Cut into 5 cm/2 inch lengths, uncovered.

1 kg/1 lb sausage, last 7 min. of cooking time with 125 ml/4 fl oz sauce and 750 g/ 1½ lb vegetables; cover tightly (27.5 × 20 × 5 cm/11 × 8 × 2 inch dish)	17 min.

POTATO I am going to get myself in real trouble discussing potatoes, since one of the first things that everybody tried and marvels at is 'baking' potatoes in the microwave oven. I have given the cooking times for baked potatoes here because I think that potatoes so cooked are useful in myriad preparations, such as mashed potatoes and pruées. I do not think that a baking potato cooked in the microwave oven is a baked potato as I understand it: with a crisp skin and light, mealy flesh. Of course, if you've been baking potatoes wrapped in foil in a regular oven, you won't see the difference. Baking potoates cooked for a good hour in a very hot oven are real baked potatoes.

Potatoes in general do something funny in the microwave oven. When they are fully cooked, they will still have a somewhat firm, waxy texture. This is an asset when making soups or stews, where you want them to retain their shape rather than fall apart, but is less wonderful if you want to make potatoes Lyonnaise or baked potatoes. When the potatoes have cooked in the microwave oven, take them out immediately and, holding them in a doubled cloth, squeeze each potato gently, making a lighter potato but not entirely solving the problem. Oddly, letting them cool and then reheating for about 2 minutes helps. On the other hand, it's hard to beat the rapidity of the microwave timings, especially when you remember you don't need to wait for the oven to heat or for water to come to the boil. Potatoes cooked in fat do better (probably because nobody expects them to be mealy). Under the proper circumstances (see Potato Galette), they will even brown. If you are cooking larger quantities than those given below, you are better off cooking them on top of the stove or in a conventional oven.

COOKING TIMES FOR POTATOES

Times are the same for large and medium ovens. For 275–300 g/9–10 oz baking potatoes, add 1 minute to cooking times in large and medium ovens.

Whole baking potatoes 200–250 g/7–8 oz each. Prick twice with a fork; place 1 potato in centre; arrange more potatoes spoke-fashion; do not cover.

1 potato	7 min.
1 potato	10 min. (small oven)
2 potatoes	11 min.
2 potatoes	18 min. (small oven)
3 potatoes	16 min.
4 potatoes	20 min.

Whole new potatoes Cover tightly.

250 g/8 oz potatoes with 7 g/¼ oz butter; stir once (1 litre/2 pint soufflé dish)	8 min.
500 g/1 lb potatoes with 3 tbsp oil; stir once (1.5 litre/2½ pint soufflé dish)	10 to 15 min.
500 g/1 lb potatoes in circle shallow round dish with 2 tbsp water	10 min.
2 kg/4 lb potatoes with 175 ml/6 fl oz oil; stir once (35 × 27.5 × 5 cm/14 × 11 × 2 inch dish)	20 min.

Sliced Cover tightly.

250 g/8 oz with 7 g/¼ oz butter (1 litre/2 pint soufflé dish)	4 to 5 min.
500 g/1 lb with 15 g/½ oz butter (2 litre/3½ pint soufflé dish)	4 to 5 min.

Peeled and cubed 1 cm/½ inch potatoes, boiled Cover tightly.

250 g/8 oz with 250 ml/8 fl oz water (1 litre/2 pint measuring jug)	8 min.
500 g/1 lb with 500 ml/16 fl oz water (2 litre/3½ pint jug or bowl)	15 min. 30 sec.

PRALINE See ALMOND.

PRAWNS Despite all the brouhaha about fish and seafood, this is still a universal favourite. There was a time when all prawns were born equal. Today, increasing sophistication and the demands of a growing market have introduced us to many unfamiliar kinds of prawn. Some of them we can even find unfrozen. (Usually the prawns you find reposing on ice in the fishmonger's have been frozen on the boat and defrosted in the shop.)

See Prawn Pâté, Prawn Butter and Prawn Cream.

COOKING TIMES FOR PRAWNS

Times are the same for large and medium ovens. These are 'medium' prawns, about 24 per 500 g/1 lb. When cooking prawns en masse, not arranged in in a single layer, shake the cooking dish about halfway through the cooking time to redistribute them for even cooking.

Raw prawns in the shell Cover tightly.

125 g/4 oz (small flan dish)	45 to 55 sec.
250 g/8 oz (22.5 cm/9 inch flan dish)	2 to 3 min.

350 g/12 oz (1.5 litre/ 2½ pint soufflé)	3 min. to 3 min. 30 sec.
500 g/1 lb (2 litre/3½ pint soufflé)	3 to 4 min.

Peeled raw prawns Cover tightly.

125 g/4 oz (small flan dish)	1 to 2 min. 1 min. 30 sec. (small oven)
250 g/8 oz (22.5 cm/9 inch flan dish)	2 to 3 min.
350 g/12 oz (1.5 litre/ 2½ pint soufflé)	2 to 3 min.
1 kg/2 lb (35 × 27.5 × 5 cm/14 × 11 × 2 inch dish)	7 to 8 min. (stir once)

Butterflied raw prawns Cover tightly.

125 g/4 oz (small flan dish)	25 to 30 sec. 45 sec. (small oven)
250 g/8 oz (22.5 cm/9 inch flan dish)	1 min. to 1 min. 30 sec.
350 g/12 oz (1.5 litre/ 2½ pint soufflé)	2 to 3 min.

PREHEATING They say microwave ovens don't heat up. Well, they do. The air and moisture in the oven warms, and that shortens already short cooking times. See, for example, the biscuits on pages 368–371. This heating effect can be useful in creating a warm, protected environment for something like RISING.

PRESERVING Usually means making jams and jellies. In a larger sense, it means storing things so that they will not spoil and includes DRYING, FREEZING, salting and smoking.

Jams, jellies and fruit butters can be made in the microwave oven; see pages 389–401. Since I am not a frontier farm wife putting things by for a long, hard winter, I find making them in small batches in the microwave oven ideal. I usually don't want to pick more than that quantity of fruit anyhow. The process is so controllable that I always get a set.

Jars and lids for preserves are best sterilized on top of the stove. If the jam or jelly is boiling hot, it can be placed immediately in the sterile jars and sealed with paraffin (which must be melted on top of the stove—it is impervious to microwaves).

PRUNES see PLUMS.

PULSES The dried seeds of leguminous plants are what the rest of the world had instead of dried beans before America was discovered. In season, many of them, such as broad beans, peas and chick-peas, are cooked fresh; many more are usually dried and later soaked and boiled. Many also have skins on the individual pulses that must be removed for palatability whether cooked fresh or dried. See individual pulses BROAD BEAN, CHICK-PEA, LENTIL, and BEANS for soaking times.

·Q·

QUAIL Good as these small birds are (60 g/2 oz each), I have some hesitation about serving them at dinner parties, especially when I don't know the guests very well. It is very hard to eat quail without using your fingers. They are good quartered and deep-fried as finger food for a cocktail party, and they are delicious split and grilled or sautéed. One especially succulent recipe for quail cooked in the microwave oven is Mini-Chartreuse. Quail are now widely available frozen. See DEFROSTING.

QUATRE-ÉPICES This classic French seasoning is made up of 1 part each ground ginger, nutmeg and clove, and 3 parts freshly ground black pepper. See Smooth Country Pâté.

QUINCE There exist both quince bushes and quince trees. The trees have pink an white blooms on dark bare branches in the spring; they are beautiful and fragrant. The bushes have red blooms and thorns, and attract humming birds. The fruits are fuzzy, knobby, yellow-green and hard to peel. I know of no one who eats them raw, but they are good in compotes and a boon beyond belief to the world of jam and jelly-making. Qunices are rich in natural pectin, and for that reason are often combines with fruits like apples, whose jelly is more difficult to set; in cases such as these, usually one quarter of the total fruit weight is quince. (See PECTIN.) There is one oddity about cooking quince in the microwave oven. Ordinarily, cooked quince turns a pale pinkish-orange; in the microwave oven it stays yellow-gold.

The Austrians make a Quince Paste (*Quittenkäse*) that is a delicious dessert or sweetmeat when thinly sliced.

R

RABBIT Increasingly, rabbit is available frozen in supermarkets. It can be cooked in the same ways and for the same times as comparable weights of chicken. Hare is somewhat larger and stronger-tasting. Defrost as in Rabbit in Mustard Cream. See also DEFROSTING.

RADICCHIO There is much to be said about the large family of red chicories. Some are second growths, forced in a cold (slightly above freezing), dark environment to intensify the red colouration. Other species of radicchio are field-grown. All are early-spring or late-autumn-to-winter vegetables due to their need for cold weather. The kind most commonly available in this country, Red Verona, looks like an undernourished red cabbage except that it is softer and costs more.

Other kinds of radicchio are more oval in form. Some are quite loose; some are splotched and speckled or red on green; some have pointed leaves. All radicchio are natives of the Veneto around Venice; there they are so varied and important (grown for cooking as vegetables more than for use in salad) that whole cookery books have been written about them. The most desirable radicchio for cooking is Treviso.

When radicchio is cooked, it generally loses its beautiful red colour. It retains more of it when cooked in the microwave oven. I have developed two classic Italian recipes into microwave oven recipes, with some improvement: See Risotto with Radicchio and Red Vermouth, and Radicchio Gratin.

COOKING TIMES FOR WHOLE RADICCHIO

Cook in a tightly sealed microwave-safe cooking bag.

500 g/1 lb radicchio	5 min.
1 kg/2 lb radicchio	8 min.

RAISIN To plump or macerate, see SOAKING, dried fruit.

RISING I don't usually use the microwave oven to raise my doughs. Firstly, it is frequently in use for something else. Secondly, I prefer doughs to be cold for a longer length of time; I think they develop more flavour. Nevertheless, there are times when I am in a hurry.

Prepare dough and place in a bowl to rise as usual. Cover with a damp sheet of paper towel. Set bowl in a dish 7.5 cm/3 inches deep and add water to almost fill the dish. Heat at 100% for 1 minute, and leave oven door closed for 15 minutes. Now rotate the bowl one-quarter turn, and heat again for 1 minute. Let stand again for 15 minutes more. Dough should be doubled in bulk.

RASPBERRY See Raspberry Jam. See also PRESERVING.

RECIPES Expanding or reducing them in quantity is one of the trickiest problems when working or playing with the microwave oven.

To adjust microwave recipes: Look up the major ingredient in your recipe in this Dictionary. See if you can find a formula that resembles the proportions in your recipe and is for the quantity you want, and follow that. Do not change the proportions of liquid to solid. If, for instance, you have a recipe for beef stew that calls for 500 g/1 lb of meat and you want to cook 1 kg/2 lb, look up BEEF. Locate beef, 1 kg/2 lb. Multiply your liquid ingredients and your vegetables by 2. Adjust those quantities so that they conform to the formula, and cook as indicated.

RED BEANS These large dried beans are widely used in Mexican cooking. See BEANS for cooking times. They are delicious in Refried Beans.

RED CABBAGE This dark, almost purple cabbage with a winy taste is not good in salads, where it often shows up 'for colour'. It is very special in sweet and sour soups like Winter Borscht, and as a vegetable, Sweet and Sour Red Cabbage. These wonderful traditional dishes had left my repertoire because red cabbage normally takes a long time to cook. The microwave oven has returned them to frequent use.

Shredded Cover tightly.

1.25 kg/2½ lb cabbage   18 min.
with 30 g/1 oz fat and
175 ml/6 fl oz liquid
added after 8 min. (30
× 25 × 7.5 cm/12 ×
10 × 3 inch dish)

RED SNAPPER This is probably the most highly esteemed of America's southern Atlantic coastal fish. Red snapper is a member of a big family. While they may be very large, the most common sizes in fishmongers here are smallish fish to feed two to four. The rose-red scalloped skin stays red during cooking, which has put the fillets in demand in restaurants with nouvelle cuisine and new American cooking.

   Generally, the fish is cooked whole or in fillets, rarely in steaks. When buying or cooking a whole fish, remember that because the snapper has a big head and heavy bones, more than one third of its weight will not be edible. It has very white flesh, a medium flake and is medium firm. See FISH for cooking times.

REDUCTION When cooked uncovered, liquids evaporate quickly in the microwave oven. Do not reduce salted liquids or vegetable mixtures. If you have cooked something and are left with too much water that you cannot drain—a purée, for instance—place it for a short time, uncovered, in the microwave oven at 100%. The microwave is also efficient for other kinds of reduction, where you are intentionally intensifying the taste or texture of a liquid. See Beurre Blanc or Béarnaise to make a reduction of aromatic vegetables and liquid. This may take too long in low-powered (small and medium) ovens to make it worthwhile. Where

feasible, reduce in a glass measuring jug so that you know precisely what your result is.

REDUCTION TIMES FOR STOCK TO GLAZE

Cook uncovered at 100%.

6 tbsp liquid (250 ml/8 fl oz jug or bowl) Yields 1½ tbsp	*8 min.*
250 ml/8 fl oz liquid (500 ml/1 pint jug) Yields 4 tbsp	*12 to 15 min.*

REDUCTION TIMES FOR STOCK TO DOUBLE STRENGTH

Cook uncovered at 100%.

1 litre/1¾ pints liquid (35 × 27.5 × 5 cm/14 × 11 × 2 inch dish)	*30 min.*
1.5 litres/2½ pints liquid (35 × 27.5 × 5 cm/14 × 11 × 2 inch dish)	*40 min.*

REHEATING It takes so little time to make things fresh in the microwave oven that, by and large, it is better not to reheat. When planning to reheat, shorten cooking time slightly. If you want to work ahead, make your sauces, purées, caramels and other components. Arrange your vegetables for cooking. Set up your seafood and fish dishes ready for cooking. Cover them both tightly with microwave cling film. When the time comes, cook them.

   Meat stews may actually profit from reheating. I call that mellowing; see page 206 for times. To make risotto and other rice dishes ahead, or to reheat, see page 109. I'm not mad for bread reheating in the microwave oven. The choice seems to be between dry bread and soggy crusts. Wrap bread in a triple layer of microwave-safe paper towel and reheat at 100% for 2 minutes. See also DEFROSTING.

TO REHEAT SAUCES, STOCKS, PURÉES

To bring from refrigerated to boiling, cover tightly; cook at 100%.

125 ml/4 fl oz	*4 min.*
250 ml/8 fl oz	*5 min.*

500 ml/16 fl oz	4 min., stir, 2 min.
1 litre/1¾ pints	4 min., stir, 4 min.

RENDERING When a solid fat or almost pure fat (bacon, chicken fat, duck fat, pork fat) is cooked, the fat liquefies, and the solid matter can be skimmed out as cracklings or lardons—particularly rapid and painless in the microwave oven. See BACON for rendering lardons. Lardons are good tossed with a salad of frisée or batavia and a dressing made with 2 parts of the warm bacon fat, 1 part vinegar, salt and pepper. The rendered fat keeps indefinitely refrigerated and is used for cooking.

POULTRY FAT

To render *duck fat*, remove the solid fat from the inside of ducks and trim it from skin flaps as well. Using scissors, cut fat into 1 cm/½ inch square pieces. Cook in batches of 600 ml/1 pint each: Place in a 2.5 litre/4 pint soufflé dish and cover with a sheet of paper towel; cook at 100% for 25 minutes. Remove cracklings to drain fat. You can include duck skin cut into strips as part of the measured fat.

To render *chicken fat (schmaltz)*, proceed as for duck, above, using both skin and fat. Some people add a peeled, quartered onion or 5 whole garlic cloves as fat renders.

Yield of fat from:

2.3–2.5 kg/5–5½ lb duck	500–800 ml/16–28 fl oz rendered fat
1.8 kg/4 lb chicken	250 ml/8 fl oz rendered fat

SUET

Cut it into chunks and process until coarsely shredded. Cook as duck fat.

CRACKLINGS

Solids left when fat is rendered. Store, tightly covered, in the refrigerator for up to 2 weeks. Heat in a single layer on a sheet of paper towel at 100% for 30 seconds. Serve instead of nuts; sprinkle with sea salt or on salads or mashed potatoes.

RHUBARB Early in chilly northern springs, one of the most decorative of perennial food plants pushes up year after year. Its pink-to-red stalks and dark-green leaves are inviting indeed. Originally a Russian plant, it has been used all over Europe and North America to make spring tonics—a wise move in earlier times, since it is rich in vitamins that would have been lacking all through the dark winter. Be careful, though, of the leaves; they contain too much oxalic acid to be human fodder. Incidentally, if someone in the family is prone to the insult of kidney stones, you might omit rhubarb from the menu.

Vitamin C in pill form and the winter arrival of warm-climate citrus fruits have vitiated the need for rhubarb, but it still merits a place in garden and kitchen for its taste. Fibrous, like celery, it is best cooked by first being cut across the stalk into 5 mm/¼ inch diagonal slices. Then it can be cooked rapidly, retaining more colour and flavour than when cooked traditionally for a longer time. Added to early strawberries it is delicious in jams and pies. See Rhubarb-Strawberry Jam.

Rhubarb freezes beautifully if it is first blanched: Cook each 125 g/4 oz of cut stems for 1 minute in 350 ml/12 fl oz of '1 to 1' SIMPLE SYRUP. Freeze in 300 ml/½ pint microwave-safe plastic containers. To defrost, uncover container; cover tightly with microwave cling film. Cook at 100% for 4 minutes. Allow to sit until completely defrosted. Use as fresh rhubarb.

COOKING TIMES FOR RHUBARB

Fresh rhubarb as a side dish Scrub, trim and slice 3 mm/⅛ inch thick; cover tightly.

250 g/8 oz rhubarb with 4 tbsp sugar (1 litre/2 pint measuring jug)	3 min. 30 sec.

RICE One of the most adaptable grains, or starches, it is the staple food of over half of the population of the world. Different regions and culinary cultures have developed countless rice varieties. The major descriptive categories have to do with the shape (round or oval), width (in India, superfine, fine or coarse) and length (long, medium or short), whether its brown (bran) layer under the husk has been removed, and whether it is raw or processed (precooked, converted and so forth). Some varieties of rice are even described by their scent as well as their colour. Often the most useful way to describe a rice is by the dish in which it is most commonly used. No matter what the kind of rice, the best grade has unbroken grains.

It is difficult to give an exact amount of liquid for cooking rice as it will vary with the age of the grain. Old rice, like all old grains, takes considerably more cooking liquid than does 'new' rice. In India, the home of the pilaf method, rice is often specially aged to be cooked in this way.

In many instances you are better off cooking rice as a side dish on top of the stove; while the rice is cooking, the main business of meal preparation can go on in the microwave oven. As in timing all starches, just be sure your calculations include time for the water to come to a boil, or your microwave-cooked main course may be ready before your rice.

Some special rice preparations become joyously easy in the microwave oven. Imagine a risotto that can be cooked in the microwave oven while you busy yourself with other things—no standing over the stove dribbling in stock and stirring.

Rice pilaf (also known as pilaff, pilaw, pilau) has many pseudonyms because it is a basic preparation common to an enormous part of the rice-eating world, from Bulgaria and Greece through most of the Middle East, and throughout India. It is normally differentiated from risotto in two ways: first, by the long grain used (see RICE, basmati, and RICE, patna); second, by the fact that after the rice is initially cooked in oil, the liquid is added all at once rather than a little at a time. (In the Near East, the procedure is a little different and entails endless soakings of the rice. I don't find it works any better.) The rice is then cooked covered. In microwave cooking, the liquid is added all at once to both preparations, and it is the variety of rice type and the covering that make the difference.

RICE, AMBRA This other northern Italian rice is slightly longer and more pointed than its cousin, arborio, and makes a somewhat less glutinous risotto. Italians often prefer seafood risottos with ambra, in part for its pale-gold colour.

RICE, ARBORIO (Sometimes called avorio.) A short (though not as short as the Oriental rices) oval grain with an opaque white spot near the midpoint, grown in the Po Valley north of Venice. It suits risotto as it stays firm, yet releases a fair amount of starch, giving the dish its creamy texture. See also RICE, AMBRA, and Risotto.

RICE, BASMATI Julie Sahni, in *Classic Indian Vegetarian and Grain Cooking*, translates basmati as 'queen of fragrance'. It is a highly esteemed Indian and Pakistani rice: long, thin, white and expensive. It has a delicate warm smell, somewhere between nuts and tea. It is usually cooked pilaf-fashion.

RICE, BROWN Rice that has not had its external germ removed. Because it is more nutritious than rice that has (e.g., white rice), it has become extremely popular in recent years. Any kind of rice can be prepared in this way; but the most commonly available are Carolina-type rices, sometimes converted, and Oriental rices, notably in macrobiotic diets. All brown rice takes longer to cook than the comparable white grain. Cook it on top of the stove; it doesn't do as well in the microwave oven.

RICE, CAROLINA Unless I specify a special rice in a recipe, I am talking about Carolina rice. Up until the Civil War, the States of North and South Carolina were a prolific rice-growing area. Exporting to the world at large. A long-grain rice, rounded in profile, was developed there, and it became the American standard. Even though little rice is grown in the Carolinas today, that type is called Carolina rice. It is of a medium hardness and can be used in most recipes, though it will not make a true risotto (it is not starchy enough and gets soft too quickly) or a true pilaf (the grains do not stay separate enough as it cooks). However, you can cook it in either of those fashions (see pages 107–115, 117–121) for very good flavour.

RICE, 'CONVERTED' See RICE, PAR-BOILED.

RICE, GLUTINOUS See RICE, PARBOILED.

RICE, LONG-GRAIN This should only be a physical description of rice that tends to cook up with individual fluffy grains rather than in a 'sticky' or risotto-like fashion. There are many different kinds of long-grain rice from various regions, with different degrees of fluffiness when cooked.

RICE, ORIENTAL (SHORT-GRAIN) Where chopsticks or hands are the eating tools and rice the staple food (eaten in conjunction with almost every meal), it is desirable that the rice cook in such a way that it more or less sticks together, so that it can be easily picked up. This is the rice of sushi; the Japanese-grown version has a smallish oval grain and, instead of arborio's central white mark, it has a central dark mark.

RICE, PARBOILED There are two kinds, quick-cooking rice (which I have nothing to do with) and a rice that is really power-steamed rather than boiled. It takes a little longer to cook than other long-grain rices, and it holds its shape well. It can be substituted for patna and basmati rices in pilafs and for arborio rice in risotto.

RICE, PATNA Originally referring to a very fine-quality, long-grain Indian rice, the name now indicates only rice grown from a patna-type seed and suitable for cooking pilaf. You can substitute basmati rice or converted rice.

RICE, STICKY A short-grain, almost round rice that is sticky when cooked. Also called glutinous rice and Oriental round short-grain rice.

RICE, SWEET This is usually used in sweet Oriental dishes. It is sometimes also called glutinous or sticky—very confusing.

RICE, WILD The microwave oven cook wild rice better than any other method I have tried. One has to fuss very little, and the results are remarkably consistent. This dark-brown native North American grain is not rice at all, but rather a grain shaped like rice. These days it is often not wild. The best-quality wild rice is longish, fat and glossy, with no loose husks and an herby, tea-like fragrance. The object of its preparation is to swell it and expose the more tender inner meat.

COOKING TIMES FOR WILD RICE

Cover tightly. Let stand 15 minutes after cooking with microwave cling film lightly pierced by a knife tip.

80 g/2⅔ oz rice with 250 ml/8 fl oz water (1 litre/2 pint measuring jug)	7 min.; stand; drain
80 g/2¾ oz rice as above	12 min.; stand; uncover, cook 12 min. (small oven)
160 g/5⅓ oz rice with 500 ml/16 fl oz water (2 litre/ 3½ pint jug or bowl)	12 min.; stand; drain (large oven)
160 g/5⅓ oz rice as above	20 min.; stand; uncover, cook 10 min. (small oven)
200 g/7 oz rice with 750 ml/1¼ pints water (27.5 × 21 × 7.5 cm/11 × 8½ × 3 inch dish)	18 min.; stand; uncover, cook 10 min.

RICE WINE A light, clear, marginally sweet wine used by the Japanese for cooking. It is available in Japanese food shops. One kind is MIRIN.

RIPENING See BANANA or AVOCADO.

ROASTING No, never, not in the microwave oven. Painting food with coloured glazes doesn't mean that they have browned on their own. By the time such browning takes place, the food is cooked to death. You have a regular oven. Use it. The results will be much better.

ROCK SALT See SALT.

ROSEMARY This richly aromatic herb often associated with lamb can be found in several varieties. Some look like small pine trees, and in the south of France are trimmed into hedges. Others are hanging and crawling plants grown on stone walls and used as ground cover. In northern climes, plants need to be transferred to pots and brought indoors in the winter.

This is one herb where the fresh and dried are fairly close in flavour and quantity used. Of course, fresh is still preferable. See DRYING, herbs. See also page 37 for amounts to use in the microwave oven.

ROTATING Moving food in a flat circular motion. I think much less of this needs to be done than is called for in most books. If your oven has a turntable, or if you have purchased a separate one (see page 18), you don't need to worry about rotating. Additionally, the tight wrapping you do with microwave cling film creates a mini-environment that helps even out the cooking. If you will be unhappy unless you rotate the food, see page 18.

RYE A widely used grain for bread in cold climates, for whisky in warm ones. Sadly, due to the problems with bread and gluten-based baking, rye is not of much use in the microwave oven.

—— • S • ——

SAFFRON These tiny pistils from a special fall-blooming crocus are available whole or ground. The same weight of saffron will be much smaller when ground. It is always very expensive, which is why I don't use it very much, and it has the most beautiful colour, the colour of Tibetan monks' robes. The flavour is slightly musky, a background taste. It is much used in Indian cooking, usually with rice. In Milan, it is used in the risotto that accompanies veal knuckle (Ossobuco). See Saffron Risotto.

SAGE A perennial herb with many varieties such as pineapple, variegated and red. Fresh sage is frequently used in Italian and other Mediterranean cooking with green beans and in stews. Dried, it is used in stuffings and in meat loaf. Sage flowers are edible. See DRYING, herbs. See also page 37 for adjusting herb quantities when cooking in the microwave oven.

SALMON One of the great fish families. Its rich fat even turns out to be good for us. The Atlantic, Pacific, farmed, ocean and spring-run river varieties all have different colours and tastes, but they cook the same way. See FISH for cooking times.

SALMON TROUT See SEA TROUT.

SALT It may be hard to remember that salt is not a uniform staple, but can vary in texture and flavour. I prefer salt with a neutral flavour and a coarse texture. In most of the recipes in this book, I have called for coarse sea salt as the most readily available salt without added chemicals. In pickling recipes, this is unacceptale since the minerals in sea salt may distort the colour, keeping ability and flavour of the finished product. For pickles, you will have to locate pickling or pure rock salt.

In the U.S., I use kosher salt. The Australian equivalent seems to be butcher's salt. If possible, avoid table salt (common salt) with its added chemicals. If substituting table salt in the recipes in this book, divide salt quantity by 3.

SARDINE Many of us have never seen these excellent little fish except in cans. When they are avialable fresh in this country, they are almost always imported. It should be noted that baby herrings of species other than pilchards are often substituted.

Fresh sardines are at their absolute best sprinkled with salt and grilled out-of-doors. Second best is still good enough for me. Sardines that are cooked and then marinated are highly esteemed in Venice; see Marinated Sardines. Arrange many in a single layer, spoke-fashion, heads out, tails to the middle. See FISH for cooking times.

SAUCE Different from a gravy in that it is made apart from the food on which it is to be served. Some sauces use the pan juices or a stock made with a similar principal ingredient. See Savoury Sauces for meats, vegetables, fish and the like. See also Dessert Sauces.

SAUTÉEING You can cook in fat in the microwave oven, but you cannot truly stir-fry or sauté, as it is impossible to keep the food moving. The positive side of this is that you can cook without the fat called for in sautéeing.

SAVORY, SUMMER An annual herb that grows in a somewhat disorderly fashion, it is good with HARICOTS VERTS, in egg dishes and as part of a herb mixture to season eggs. When using it fresh in the microwave oven, increase standard quantities by one third. I often grow more than I need; then I dry it in the microwave oven; see DRYING, herbs.

SAVORY, WINTER This perennial herb grows as a small round bush. Most varieties have delicate, edible, attractive white flowers. A strong-tasting herb, it is best used in stews and wild mushroom dishes; it accompanies pork with brio. Try adding ¼ teaspoon dried to each 175 g/6 oz of cannellini beans before cooking them (see BEANS). Use slightly less dried winter savory than usual when cooking in the microwave oven. This is another herb that, like rosemary, is almost the same dried and fresh. See DRYING, herbs.

SAVOY CABBAGE The most tender of the cabbages, it has a largish firm head and pale-green, crinkly leaves.

COOKING TIMES FOR SAVOY CABBAGE

Shredded Cook in a 1 litre/2 pint glass measuring jug; cover tightly.

250 g/8 oz cabbage	*4 min.*

SCALLOP Gourmets the world over are all scallop-lovers. Aphrodite, goddess of love, beauty and fertility, rose from the sea and rode it on a scallop shell, which was not inappropriate as the scallop is one of the most beautiful of shells. Scallop shells were worn as pendants by her worshipers at Knidos. St James the Apostle wore the scallop as his emblem, and it became the emblem of the many thousands of pilgrims in the Middle Ages who flocked across Europe to Campostela, Spain, where his principal shrine was located. The French name for scallops and the many dishes made with them is *coquille* ('shell') *Saint-Jacques* ('St. James'). *Concha* ('shell') *de peregrino* ('pilgrim') is its Spanish name.

The most edible parts of the scallop are its large, white, central muscle and its *roe* a delightful reddish-orange quarter moon found in many varieties.

Scallops come in many sizes. Generally, different sizes indicate different species. A *queen scallop* is not an immature *common* or *ordinary scallop*, but rather one that is small at maturity.

Scallops vary in quality. The best have a white, semi-translucent flesh that is medium firm. Less fortunate scallops growing in less flavoured waters have flesh that is more ivory in colour, more opaque and considerably firmer. All scallops must be carefully cooked so that their considerable liquid content is not lost and they become dry. The darker-coloured ones will be direr and less tender in any case.

Judging freshness is a little problematic. They do not begin to smell fishy with age. Instead, their natural sweetness becomes more intense, and they begin to spew liquid. Sometimes they get mushy.

Queen scallops are best wiped dry and sautéed very briefly in butter with fresh herbs and perhaps a shallot or two. Do not salt until removing from pan. They are almost as good briefly cooked in the microwave oven. See Sauté of Queen Scallops.

Ordinary scallops cook perfectly and without fat in the microwave. Simply arrange in a cooking dish in a single layer; use a dish with a lip or some depth to it, to hold the liquid the scallops give off. If a small number is being cooked, arrange in a circle towards the outer edge of the dish. Cover tightly with microwave cling film. They are fully cooked when they just turn white and opaque. Any extra cooked juices may be saved to add to fish sauces or stocks.

COOKING TIMES FOR SCALLOPS

Queen scallops In butter.

250 g/8 oz with 15 g/½ oz butter (22.5 cm/9 inch browning dish, uncovered)	*2 min. (small oven)*
250 g/8 oz (flan dish, cover tightly)	*4 min. (small oven)*
350 g/12 oz with 15 g/½ oz butter (22.5 cm/9 inch browning dish, uncovered)	*1 min. 30 sec.*
750 g/1½ lb with 30 g/1 oz butter (25 cm/10 inch browning dish, uncovered)	*2 min.*

Ordinary scallops Steamed; cover tightly.

250 g/8 oz (flan dish)	*2 min. 4 min. (small oven)*
250 g/8 oz with 175 g/6 oz vegetables (flan dish)	*3 min*

500 g/1 lb (2.5 litre/4 pint soufflé)	3 min.
500 g/1 lb with 250 g/8 oz vegetables (2.5 litre/4 pint soufflé)	7 min.
750 g/1½ lb (27.5 × 21 × 5 cm/11 × 8½ × 2 inch dish)	5 to 7 min.
1 kg/2 lb (35 × 27.5 × 5 cm/14 × 11 × 2 inch dish)	9 to 10 min.
1 kg/2 lb with 500 g/1 lb vegetables (35 × 27.5 × 5 cm/14 × 11 × 2 inch dish)	11 min.

SCHMALTZ The Yiddish word for rendered chicken fat. It is more important in kosher cooking than in other kinds, since butter may not be used with meat. Seasoning varies from cook to cook. For some, an onion must be cut into the fat as it renders; for others some garlic, to achieve the flavour they desire. See RENDERING, chicken fat.

Schmaltz is also descriptive of a kind of particularly fat herring.

SEA BASS An ocean-dwelling bass species. Cook it as you would cook salmon. See FISH for cooking times.

SEA BREAM These are very good fish, not great fish. Depending on the size—you don't want to cook a piece more than 4 cm/1½ inches thick—you may be dealing with a whole fish or a fillet; steaks don't work too well. Whole fish should be slashed through the skin and rubbed with olive oil, lemon juice, salt and pepper. A few garlic cloves can be tucked inside. Then it should be grilled, preferably outdoors. Fillets cook rapidly in their own juices or prepared as for the grilled, whole bream. See FISH for cooking times.

SEA SALT See SALT.

SEAFOOD COMBINATIONS Putting clams, oysters, mussels together or with fish raises the problem that it may take longer for some shells to open than others, or longer than the fish to cook. Arrangement helps (see pages 33–34) by keeping the clams, for example, to the faster-cooking dish edge and putting the fish in the centre. For model recipes, see Cod with Clams Livornese or Simple Fish Stew.

SEA TROUT These are brown trout (see TROUT) that have taken to the sea. They are also called salmon trout because they eat the same food as the salmon, and their flesh turns a paler version of the same colour. The flesh itself is firm, but with a smaller flake and les fat than salmon. Sea trout are usually cooked whole or in fillets. Cook as salmon; use the less seasoned sauces. See FISH for cooking times.

SESAME OIL The oil pressed from these seeds is available in two ways, colourless and tasteless, or brownish in colour because the seeds have been toasted before pressing. This brownish oil, also called Oriental sesame oil, is the one used in this book.

SESAME SEED See TOASTING, small seeds.

SHALLOT Another member of the onion (allium) family. Shallots with red-brown skins are milder than those with bluish-grey ones. They seem to have grown larger and easier to peel than they used to be; but they are still small and persnickety, and you can't bang them first as you do garlic. They are essential for Beurre Blanc, and are excellent pickled like onions.

SHERRY A fortified wine (alcohol is added) from Spain, it comes in many different varieties, from bone dry to rich, sweetish and creamy. When sherry is called for in a recipe, it is usually a medium sherry of modest quality, but never 'cooking' sherry, which is a disaster. A bottle of sherry, recorked, keeps practically indefinitely. As with all alcohols, if adding it to a recipe to be cooked in the microwave oven longer than 7 or 8 minutes, double the quantity.

SHIITAKE Mushrooms with dark-brown tops an pale-beige gills used in Oriental cooking are mainly available in this country dried, listed in cookery books as dried Chinese mushrooms. They are increasingly available fresh. If dried mushrooms are called for, do not substitute fresh; it changes the flavour of the dish. Break into pieces dry without stalks into stews, sauces and other dishes with at least 4 tablespoons liquid and at least 3 minutes or more cooking time. For use in stir-fry, see SOAKING, dried mushrooms.

SIEVE To force a soft, generally cooked food through a sieve in order to purée it and remove any hard particles. Sieving to purée can be done in a food mill (page 31). It cannot be done in a food processor or blender because it will not remove pips, seeds, skin, etc. When this kind of puréeing is done through a sieve, you will have to push on the sieve firmly with a wooden spoon to push as much through as possible. It is easier if the sieve fits firmly on the bowl into which your purée or sauce will pass.

SIMPLE SYRUP This is a preparation with unlimited usefulness. It is what you use to sweeten anything in which undissolved sugar granules would be unwelcome. Anyone who has drained a glass of lemonade to find a wad of wet sugar at the bottom knows what I'm talking about.

Simple syrup is just that: simple. It is made by boiling sugar and water together. There are two syrups: '1 to 1' and '2 to 1', referring to the proportions of sugar to water. The sweetness will be determined by the percentage of sugar. The density, viscosity and thickness will be determined by the percentage of sugar and the length and heat of cooking time. See also CARAMEL.

Simple syrups can be flavoured by replacing the water, or part of it, with wine or juices and by adding spices. See Index for Fruit, poached.

Simple syrup can be kept refrigerated for a long time, which is nice during the hot days when you will want lemonade and iced tea or coffee. It is very important to cover the cooking dish tightly with microwave cling film. This causes the steam to wash down the sides of the container and avoids the formation of crystals. Use a large cooking dish to that the hot sugar mixture doesn't get near the cling film. When opening the film to stir, do so by pulling it away from the side of the dish to let the steam escape without your getting burned. See page 28 for illustration.

'1 to 1' simple syrup Combine 400 g/14 oz caster sugar and 500 ml/16 fl oz water in a 2.5 litre/4 pint soufflé dish. Cook, uncovered, at 100% for 3 minutes. Stir. Cover tightly with microwave cling film. Cook at 100% for 6 minutes more. (Use it for fruits that will not be cooked, such as lemons for sorbet.)

'2 to 1' simple syrup Combine 400 g/14 oz caster sugar and 250 ml/8 fl oz water in a 2 litre/3½ pint glass jug or bowl. Cover tightly with microwave cling film. Cook at 100% for 15 minutes, stirring twice during cooking time; be sure to reseal tightly after stirring. (Use it to cook fruit. The liquid from the fruit will dilute the syrup.)

SLICE To cut a piece of food lengthways, or across, into even strips that are broader than they are thick and the same length or longer than they are broad. Meats should generally be sliced with a long, thin slicing knife and cut across the grain. Breads, very juicy fruits and vegetables such as tomatoes and oranges are usually better cut across with a serrated knife between the stalk and blossom end. Slice sizes are generally given in the recipes.

SNAILS For all intents and purposes, these denizens of vineyards come in cans and have been cooked. All we do when we cook them is to reheat them in a flavouring. See Snail Butter and Dijon Snails.

SOAKING To soak dried beans and pulses, see BEANS

DRIED FRUIT

To soften, a minimum of liquid is needed. (The soaking of fruit is called macerating, whether for the purpose of reconstituting of flavouring.) Place fruit in a single layer in a dish; sprinkle with water; cover tightly with microwave cling film; cook at 100% for the times below. Sometimes you may want to use more water to soften the fruit for purée. Today, many dried fruits are vacuum-packed, which keeps them from drying out until you open the package. If they dry out once the package is opened and you want to eat them, soak as below. Flavour can be added at the same time the fruits soak by using wine or fortified wine (see SHERRY) as the soaking liquid and adding seasonings.

SOAKING TIMES FOR DRIED FRUIT

Apricots Arrange 'belly' side up; cover tightly.

6 to 10 apricots (small flan dish)	30 sec.
24 apricots with 1 tbsp water	1 min.
250 g/8 oz with 350 ml/ 12 fl oz water (1 litre/ 2 pint measuring jug)	2 min.

Currants Cover tightly.

90 g/3 oz currants with 1 tbsp water (500 ml/ 1 pint measuring jug)	1 min.

Raisins Cover tightly.

175 g/6 oz raisins with 2 tbsp water (500 ml/1 pint measuring jug)	1 min. 30 sec.

DRIED CHILLIES

Do not presoak for use in sauces. Cook in sauce—at least 4 minutes. Reconstitute dried chillies to make them into the freshest-tasting of chilli pastes. Put 60 g/2 oz dried chillies in a 1 litre/2 pint glass measuring jug with 250 ml/8 fl oz water. Cover tightly with microwave cling film. Cook at 100% for 8 minutes.

DRIED HERBS

Dried herbs to be used in non-microwave cooking benefit from being briefly soaked in a small container with cooking liquid or water to cover. Cover tightly. Cook at 100% for 2 minutes.

DRIED MUSHROOMS

Dried mushrooms, particularly slices, do not need to be presoaked if they are being cooked for more than 3 minutes in a dish that contains liquid, such as soup, sauce or stew. When using dried shiitake in such a dish, break into pieces and discard the stalk and the hard place where the stalk attaches to the cap. Morels must always be presoaked because they tend to contain lots of sand. Save the soaking liquid; put it through a dampened cloth in a sieve and use the liquid either in your dish or in other soups and stews.

SOAKING TIMES FOR MORELS

Place in measuring jug with water; cover tightly with microwave cling film and heat at 100%.

30 g/1 oz mushrooms with 4 tbsp water	3 min.
30 g/1 oz as above	4 min. 30 sec. (small oven)
60 g/2 oz mushrooms with 125 ml/4 fl oz water	5 min.
125 g/4 oz mushrooms with 175 ml/6 fl oz water	7 min.

SOAKING TIMES FOR CAPS

Discard stalks of ceps (funghi porcini) or whole shiitake. Swish briskly in cold water to rinse off grit. Arrange bottoms up in a single layer in a 20 cm/8 inch flan dish with 1 tbsp water; cover tightly; cook at 100%; let stand, covered, 4 min.

4 large caps	4 min. (small oven)
20 small caps	2 min.
8 large caps	4 min.

SOFTENING *To soften brown sugar:* Set the opened bag on the microwave turntable. Place a mug of water next to it. Heat at 100% for 2 minutes, and check to see if the sugar is soft enough to use. If not, heat for 1 minute more.

To soften cold butter: Cut 125 g/4 oz of butter into 4 pieces. Put in a glass measuring jug and heat, uncovered, at 100% for 30 seconds. Remove from oven and whisk; the butter will have the consistency of whipped butter.

To soften or eliminate cyrstals from jam, preserves, jelly or honey, see HONEY.

SOFTENING TIMES FOR CREAM CHEESE

Set on a plate; cover tightly.

90 g/3 oz	30 sec.
250 g/8 oz	1 min.

SOLE Part of the large world of bottom-dwelling flat fish, along with flounder, plaice, dab and turbot. It is distinguished in the culinary world by having hundreds of classic preparations assigned to it. Pride of place is usually given to Dover sole, caught in the English Channel (though there are Venetians who would make a strong argument for their *sfoglia*, the same species but tending to be smaller and more delicate).

Both Dover and lemon sole have 2 fillets. They divide easily down a prominent central line into 2 half-fillets. Larger fish should always be divided into the 4 pieces. For microwave cooking, arrange the thicker, centre edge of the half-fillets towards the edge of the dish. Half-fillets are used for making paupiettes (see FISH). Some eaters may want a whole fish—2 fillets, 4 half-fillets—for themselves as a main dish, or 1 fillet—2 half-fillets—as a first course. Others may be satisfied with half the quantity.

Dover sole is firm-fleshed and is never meant to flake in cooking. I prefer it cooked whole, grilled or sautéed briefly so that the flesh doesn't harden. Melted butter and a little lemon are all it needs. Forget the fancy sauces that just mask the flavour.

Lemon sole has a medium-firm flesh and is better cooked in fillets, as the tough skins will make it hard to cook the subtle flesh evenly. Lemon sole can be cooked in butter or poached. They like the protection of a goodish amount of liquid and should not be vigorously sautéed. This makes them perfect candidates for microwave cooking. They may be substituted in any recipe

calling for fish fillets. Cook individual frozen fillets directly from frozen, adding 1 minute of cooking time for each whole fillet (30 seconds for a half). See FISH for times.

Sole are responsible for one important culinary confusion. In many French cookery books (and in the books that use them as a source, without too much reflection), we are told never to cook fish stock for more than 20 to 30 minutes. This was a warning that used to puzzle me, an avid maker of fish soups that used long-cooked fish stocks, until I began to work in restaurant kitchens. There I discovered that the bones most commonly used for stocks were sole and other flat fish frames. So much 'sole' is sold filleted and used in restaurant dishes that the bones are in plentiful supply. These bones do indeed turn bitter when cooked longer than 20 minutes. So, yes, if using sole bones for stock, keep the cooking brief, 5 minutes in a microwave oven.

SORREL The thought of sorrel soup has sustained me through many hot weeding sessions. I prefer the small wild sorrel to the larger leaves of French sorrel, a garden perennial. Both have what are called shield or lance-shaped leaves. They look rather like arrowheads to me. All sorrels need to be thoroughly washed, dried and the leaves piled up going in the same direction so that they can be thinly slices, into strips 3 mm/$\frac{1}{8}$ inch wide, across the central vein (so they won't be stringy). This is called *chiffonade*. Never cook sorrel in an aluminium or coated aluminium pan. The sorrel will look and taste nasty due to the interaction of its considerable acids with the aluminium.

Sorrel makes a classic French classic sauce for shad. The sauce can be easily thinned to make a cold soup that is one of the delights of spring and summer.

COOKING TIMES FOR SORREL

Cut into *chiffonade*; cover tightly.

60 g/2 oz sorrel with 15 g/½ oz butter (1 litre/2 pint measuring jug)	2 min.

250 g/8 oz sorrel with 60 g/ *2 oz butter (2.5 litre/4 pint soufflé)*	*3 min.*

SOURED CREAM When called for in this book, commercially soured cream is intended. Soured cream is much used in Hungarian and Russian recipes. Unfortunately, it is just as fattening as single cream. It also tends to separate when cooked at too high a heat. The best method is to add it towards the very end of the cooking time. See Pork Chops with Sauerkraut.

SOYA These beans are among the most nutritious and widely grown of foods and are rich in an oil that has extensive commercial use. I like them neither as a vegetable nor as an oil. Processed, turned into soya sauce and bean curd, they are one of the Orient's greatest gifts to cooking, appreciated particularly by vegetarians whose diet might otherwise be poor in protein.

The *soya sauce* called for in the recipes in this book is the commercial brand most commonly available. I prefer tamari soya sauce which is authentically fermented and has a richer taste. It may be substituted in all recipes in this book, to their benefit.

True Chinese and Japanese soya sauces, usually marketed as shoyu, have a variety of distinct tastes; you may want to try them and substitute according to your results. One caution: Chinese soya sauce is often very salty.

Bean curd (tofu) is sold in many shops in two main forms: pillows 7.5 × 5 × 5 cm/3 × 2 × 2 inches, and cubes. The pillows are firmer and drier. Both are usually sold packed in water. When you get them home, rinse them off and re-cover with cold water to store. 125 g/4 oz of tofu per person, cut into 2.5 cm/1 inch squares, may be stirred into any of the vegetable stews or casseroles before cooking. Add 30 seconds of cooking time to the recipe for each portion of tofu added. This will make nutritious vegetarian dishes.

SPAGHETTI SQUASH Also called spaghetti marrow and vegetable spaghetti. Cooking spaghetti squash takes approximately the same amount of time in the microwave oven as in regular cooking. I would cook the squash conventionally and make the sauce in the microwave oven.

COOKING TIMES FOR SPAGHETTI SQUASH

Halve lengthways; cover each half tightly.
1 squash, 2.2 kg/4¼ lb	*20 min.*

SPICE Buy spices in small quantities and unground if possible; ground spices quickly lose the valuable flavour you have paid for. Most of these seeds and nuts need grinding before cooking. Exceptions are mustard seed, anise, caraway and other spices that are either used as is or toasted before use. See GRINDING; see also TOASTING, whole spices.

If spices are in glass bottles, they should be stored in a dark place away from the heat of the stove. Both light and heat affect them adversely. Read about spices and learn what makes for good ones. Pay a little more for the best; it makes a big difference in the food.

Microwave cooking tends to accentuate spices' effect, extracting all the volatile flavours. In most recipes, you can decrease spice quantities by one third. In long-cooking recipes, more than 15 minutes in the oven, you may want to return to something nearer standard quantities. For more specific information about quantities see page 37.

For specific information, see ANISEED, CARAWAY, CARDAMOM, CAYENNE, CELERY SEED, CHILLI, CLOVE, CUMIN, CURRY, DILL, GINGER, JUNIPER BERRY, MACE, NUTMEG AND PAPRIKA. See also Spice Powders.

SPINACH Cooking spinach, either plain (no water needed) or in malted butter, takes the same brief time in the microwave oven. It is not only quick and clean, but also produces unusually bright green spinach, a joy in Creamed Spinach. The flavour is so intense you may very well not need any salt. If you find it is too strong for you, try cooking it uncovered.

COOKING TIMES FOR SPINACH

Stalks removed.

125 g/4 oz spinach (27.5 × 21 × 5 cm/11 × 8½ × 2 inch dish, uncovered)	4 min. (small oven)
250 g/8 oz spinach (35 × 27.5 × 5 cm/14 × 11 × 2 inch dish, uncovered)	4 min.
1 kg/2 lb spinach (tightly sealed microwave-safe cooking bag or in a 5 litre/8 pint casserole with a tightly fitting lid)	5 min. 30 sec.

SPLIT PEA I went to a progressive school where all the children learned how to cook—a fairly radical notion at the time. I made pea soup and was proud of myself. I went home and insisted on cooking it for my parents. What I prepared for them with so much fanfare was a thick, green, unappetizing sludge; that ended my split pea soup efforts. As I was creating recipes for this book, I realized that split peas must be tested. To my surprise, this rapid, controllable cooking method made my peace with both the peas and the soup.

It is inefficient to cook split peas in the microwave oven with all the liquid you will want for soup. Presoak and cook as you would large dried beans (see BEANS). Purée, then make one of the soups on page 96. The joy of this method is that, having no evaporation, you don't risk scorching, making library paste or leaving uncooked peas in the pot.

Consider using the purée as a vegetable with roast pork or Oriental Glazed Duck. If desired, stir some room-temperature butter and salt into the split peas after cooking. Yellow and green split peas cook exactly the same way. The taste isn't wildly different, either. The choice depends on the history of a dish and the colours on your plate.

Yield

200 g/7 oz dry peas	500 ml/16 fl oz purée

SPRING ONION Both the green part and the white part, sliced, are frequent inclusions in Oriental recipes. Young spring onion greens can be substituted, very thinly sliced, for the less available fresh chives, even though they have a slightly different flavour. Spring onions also make an attractive vegetable when braised; see Spring Onions à la Grecque. See also LEEK.

SQUASH The many varieties of squash, which are becoming increasingly popular in this country, fall into either of two categories: winter squash or summer squash, thick-skinned and thin-skinned, respectively. For cooking times of winter varieties (acorn and butternut), see SQUASH, winter. For cooking times of summer varieties (courgette, custard marrow or pattypan), see SQUASH, summer. See SPAGHETTI SQUASH for that vegetable's own particular cooking times. Occasionally you may find, at high prices, tiny baby vegetables in the shops. They are more beautiful than good-tasting. Remember that of the normally sized squash, particularly the summer varieties, smaller—say 7.5–10 cm/3–4 inches long—is better. If you must cook the baby squash, steam whole at times below.

SUMMER SQUASH

COOKING TIMES FOR SUMMER SQUASH

Trim ends and wash well. Times are the same for large and medium ovens. For small oven, add 1 minute to cooking times.

Quartered lengthways Arrange in a dish just large enough to hold squash in no more than 2 layers; cover tightly.

125 g/4 oz	8 min.
250 g/8 oz	8 to 9 min.
500 g/1 lb	10 min.
1 kg/2 lb	12 to 14 min.

5 mm/¼ inch crossways slices or 5

mm/¼ inch juliennes Arrange as above; cover tightly.

125 g/4 oz	2 min. 30 sec.
250 g/8 oz	3 min. 30 sec.
500 g/1 lb	5 min.
1 kg/2 lb	8 min. 30 sec.

Yield

1 small courgette	125–150 g/4–5 oz

WINTER SQUASH

Varieties include acorn and butternut. Acorn squash is a marvellous vegetable on its own, unseasoned. *To make Seasoned Squash:* Sprinkle flesh of each cleaned squash half with salt and pepper and a little ground ginger or nutmeg, and place a 15 g/½ oz knob of butter in the cavity before wrapping. *To make Glazed Squash:* For each half combine 1 tablespoon maple syrup with 1 teaspoon lemon juice, a pinch each of salt, pepper and cumin; swirl over flesh, letting any excess glaze pool in the cavity, or top after cooking with maple syrup or brown sugar and glaze under the grill. Each half makes a single serving, either as is or scooped out and puréed with butter. See Acorn Squash Purée.

Cooked acorn squash can be a wonderful component of soups, purées and even desserts. See Acorn Squash Soup and Thanksgiving Pudding.

Cooking times for acorn squash apply to butternut squash as well.

COOKING TIMES FOR WINTER SQUASH

Halve winter squash. Remove seeds and fibres. (Wash seeds and toast in conventional oven.) For acorn and butternut, place seeded halves side by side (for butternut, place a large end next to a narrow end) in a dish just large enough to hold them. Cover tightly with microwave cling film.

250 g/8 oz	5 min.
500 g/1 lb	7 min.
500 g/1 lb	10 min. (small oven)
1 kg/2 lb	15 min.
1.5 kg/3 lb	20 min.

Yield

500 g/1 lb squash	250 ml/8 fl oz purée

SQUID A member of a many-legged family of ink-bearing undersea animals whose large heads are also their bodies. Familiar as *calamari fritti* (fried rings and curly legs) in Italian restaurants. They are available fresh and frozen and can be cooked in other ways, notably stuffed. Their longish funnel-shaped body seems made for stuffing once the legs and innards, including the quill that contains the ink, have been removed. The legs can be chopped to add to the stuffing. While the ink can be a pleasant addition to a sauce, it is not copious enough to make really dark black risottos and pastas; for that you need cuttlefish. Most books say you should peel the thin speckled membrane from the body of the squid. I find it unnecessary. See Stuffed Squid. Briefly cooked, squid are a fine salad component; see Calamari Salad. They main thing is never to overcook them, or they will toughen.

Cuttlefish (*seppie* in Italian) is more round-oval than the elongated-oval squid and generally much larger. Its most prominent virtue is the generous quantities of ink in its sac; it also contains a second sac with a yellow fluid that is used in stews. Instead of a quill it has a large bone inside, the kind that canaries have in their cages for pecking. They are available frozen. See defrosting times on page 494.

To clean a cuttlefish, hold it over a bowl and tug gently on the legs. All the innards may come out at the same time. If not, reach into the head-body and pull out any remaining structures. Try not to break the ink sac. If the sac has broken, pour the ink through a course sieve. If the sac is intact, hold the tip of one end with your fingers, gently squeeze the sac with the thumb and forefinger of your other hand and slide them away from the first hand. It is much like squeezing the last toothpaste out of the tube. Wash your hands. In similar fashion, remove the liquid from the yellowish sac into another bowl. Cut the legs and tentacles free, in one piece. Discard remnants and bone. Wash the now-empty head. Do not bother to peel. Cut into strips as required by the recipe.

Cuttlefish are generally stewed to take advantage of their ink and other fluids. The ink is added to the cooking liquid for the last few minutes to warm and thicken. If cooked too long at too high a heat, it will coagulate, giving an unpleasantly grainy texture. When the ink is added to Risotto to make Black Risotto, it must be measured. The stock quantity is then reduced by the amount of ink, and the ink is stirred in 3 minutes before the risotto is done. The squid body is sliced into rings and gently, briefly cooked in olive oil or butter with garlic and parsley, salt and pepper, if desired. The white squid is then arrayed dramatically on top of the dark risotto. Allow 1 small cuttlefish for each 200 g/7 oz of cooked risotto.

The last member of the family to get much culinary attention is the *octopus*—not the giant creature from the deep seen in late-night movies, but a smaller relative. There are no octopus recipes in this book; I just don't have the patience or energy for octopus, which must be repeatedly clubbed or slammed on rocks to tenderize it before cooking. I have seen fishermen in Greece work on an octopus for half an hour at a time. Then the pieces are charcoal-grilled and are delicious.

COOKING TIMES FOR SQUID

Rings Tentacles separated, body cut into rings; cover tightly.

350 g/12 oz squid with	2 min. 30 sec.
175 g/6 oz vegetables	
(1 litre/2 pint soufflé)	

Stuffed Cook with 2 tbsp stuffing per squid, uncovered.

750 g/1½ lb squid with	5 min.
125 ml/4 fl oz sauce	
(30 cm/12 inch round	
dish)	

DEFROSTING TIMES FOR CUTTLEFISH

750 g/1½ lb cuttlefish,	40 min. at 30%
covered tightly (2.5	
litre/4 pint soufflé)	

STEAMING Many foods are best steamed in the microwave oven, rather than poached or boiled. Fish, chicken and vegetables require little or no added liquid as they are very liquid themselves. To get the foods to steam, it is very important to cover them tightly with microwave cling film (see page 26). Some of the advantages of steaming are the lack of a need for fat, the evenness and rapidity of cooking, the bright colour and retained vitamins of vegetables.

STEWING The leisurely cooking of meats, vegetables and seafoods, and fruit, alone or in combination, in seasoned liquids. It works very well in the microwave oven. Due to the tight sealing, which eliminates evaporation and assures evenness of cooking, you must use less liquid than called for in standard recipes.

STOCK See CHICKEN STOCK, STOCK CUBES and Meat Stocks. See also CLARIFYING, and sauces, and DEFROSTING, homemade staples.

STOCK CUBES If it is necessary to use these instead of homeade stock, be sure to add the appropriate amount of liquid. Remember, stock made from cubes is very salty and you may want to eliminate or reduce the amount of salt called for in the recipe. Stock cubes may also contain MSG (monosodium glutamate) and should be avoided when cooking for people sensitive to it. See CHICKEN STOCK and meat stocks.

STRAIN This is to place something that has been cooked in a liquid in a sieve to remove the liquid.

STRAWBERRY These wonderful red fruits—both the small, pointy Alpine or wild variety from everbearing plants and the large, roundish, originally American variety propagated by runners from their plants—are at their best fresh and in season. I really don't like what happens to strawberries when they are cooked or frozen: They get fuzzy. The one great exception is Strawberry Jam. If you do want to freeze a bumper crop in syrup rather than berry by berry (to save room), make SIMPLE SYRUP ('2 to 2'): 1 litre/1¾ pints syrup to any equal amount berries. Allow syrup to cool 4 minutes, uncovered, after it comes out of the microwave oven. Stir in washed, hulled and dried (sliced if you wish) berries. Place in freezer containers and freeze immediately.

STURGEON I find it confusing that a fish that brings a premium price when smoked, and whose eggs sold as caviar bring very high prices, itself sells at comparatively modest prices. This is no doubt because people don't know how to cook it. In Russia, it is a highly desired prime ingredient for fish soup, *solianka*.

Sturgeon has exceedingly firm flesh with a colour like that of veal, to which it is often compared. Although it is an oily fish, it is not self-basting due to its firmness, so it is not a candidate for grilling. It also toughens if boiled or poached whole. The best results are obtained by filleting the fish, then cutting it into crossways slices and cooking it like veal or tuna. See Index for tuna recipes. See FISH for cooking times.

Incidentally, in the realm of little-known facts, the cartilaginous spinal marrow of sturgeon is in great demand in Russian recipes as a thickening, in Coulibiac and other delicacies. It is sold dried and called *vesiga*. When you cook the stock for *solianka*, you can easily remove it from the spine. Use as is, or dry—cut in 5 cm/1 inch lengths—on a sheet of paper towel; uncovered, for 3 minutes at 100%. Store tightly covered and refrigerated.

SUET Hard, white animal fat, the best of which cushions beef, veal and mutton kidneys (leaf lard). It can be used raw and flaked or finely shredded for pastry, or melted to make a superior (in terms of taste if not nutrition) frying fat. See RENDERING.

SUGAR Sugar is one of those surprises in microwave cooking. While it dissolves fairly slowly in water and needs to be stirred, on its own it cooks very quickly, acting almost as a magnet for the microwaves. Heavily sugared mixtures will cook more quickly. It is impossible to create a true caramelized glaze on top of a cooked mixture in the microwave oven; sugar mixtures, however, will increase in density and caramelize rapidly in the microwave oven. Caramelizing in this way is a delight: no untoward crystals, no burned and hard-to-clean pans, perfect control. Always uncover sugar mixtures carefully to avoid the hot steam. See CARAMEL and SIMPLE SYRUP; see also Pralines.

BROWN SUGAR

Brown sugar, dark or light, is sugar with some of the molasses left in or added. Due to its high moisture content, it tends to coalesce into a solid block once the packet is opened. It can be easily softened in the microwave oven; see SOFTENING.

SUGAR SNAP PEA An edible pod pea with fully formed peas inside, this has been touted as a recent innovation, but nineteenth-century strains existed. Sugar snap peas must be strung, from both ends. They are at their best flung on top of stew to steam for the last 2 minutes of cooking time in the microwave oven. Do not overcook, or the pods become mushy. Cook as for MANGE-TOUT.

SUNFLOWER SEED A few large sunflowers will cheer up a vegetable garden. Their heads will provide enough seeds for a long winter by the fire. When the petals begin to go, cut off the flowers and bring indoors. Turn flowers upside down on a clean piece of paper. The seeds will drop out by themselves; after a few days you can shake the flower to hasten the dropping of the seeds. Toast in a conventional oven.

SWEATING In French cooking, vegetables are sometimes diced, then slowly cooked in a little fat to evaporate some of their water and intensify their taste. This can be done rapidly in the microwave oven by tossing the vegetables with melted butter and cooking, uncovered, at 100% for 2 to 3 minutes.

SWEDE This large, waxy yellow turnip has a sharper taste than a regular turnip. If it is to be puréed or steamed, it requires longer cooking than a regular turnip. On the other hand, julienned and quickly blanched, it can be used instead of celeriac in a mustard vinaigrette or mayonnaise for a first-course salad.

COOKING TIME FOR SWEDE

Cut into 1 cm/½ inch cubes; cover tightly.

750 g/1½ lb swede	*15 min.*
with 125 ml/4 fl oz water (2 litre/ 3½ pint jug or bowl)	

Yield

750 g/1½ lb raw	*400 ml/14 fl oz purée*

SWEETBREADS Cooked almost exclusively—and often incorrectly—in restaurants, sweetbreads become easy to cook with the microwave oven. The result is better than any other method: less cleaning, blanching, firming and so forth, and better texture at the end. Suddenly, sweetbreads are easy, and there is no longer a reason to have to omit them in sneaky guilt from classic preparations such as *financière*. See Summer Pâté with Veal, Sweetbreads and Spinach.

COOKING TIMES FOR SWEETBREADS

Trimmed; cover tightly.

600 g/1¼ lb sweetbreads with 90 g/3 oz vegetables and 250 ml/8 fl oz liquid (2.5 litre/4 pint soufflé dish)	*5 min.*

SWEETCORN The silk is easier to remove once the ear of sweetcorn is cooked. If you wish to serve sweetcorn in the husk without silk, tear the husk down far enough to strip away the silk, then pull husks back up.

COOKING TIMES FOR CORN-ON-THE-COB

Cobs with silk and husk intact 2 to 3 per 500 g/1 lb. Place in a single layer on turntable or a platter, uncovered.

1 cob	*2 min.*
1 cob	*7 min. (small oven)*
2 cobs	*5 min.*
2 cobs	*12 min. (small oven)*
4 cobs	*9 min.*
6 cobs	*14 min.*

SWEET POTATO Both yellow and white, these starchy tubers are often confused with yams. White sweet potatoes are sweeter than the yellow and take about 3 minutes longer to cook. Both do well in purée, a use to which they are frequently put in the Caribbean, but will take much more butter and cream to come smooth than white potatoes. Cook for following times for purée or pie.

COOKING TIMES FOR SWEET POTATOES

Whole Prick and set on paper towel, uncovered.

1 kg/2 lb yellow potatoes (about 2 large)	*13 to 15 min.*

SWORDFISH This large game fish produces marvellous boneless steaks for grilling. They are also very good cooked in the microwave oven. Medallions and cubes for specific recipes are easily cut from thick steaks. A healthy fat content keeps the tightly grained and firm flesh moist. Do not overcook. See FISH for cooking times.

T

TAMARI See SOYA.

TAPIOCA I hated this when I was a child; but it cooks so thoroughly in the microwave oven that it is a treat. Use for dessert or, as in older French recipes, to thicken soups. Cooked in the microwave oven, there is no stirring during the cooking, no first bringing the liquid to the boil. The quick-cooking tapioca available in shops today is preferable.

COOKING TIMES FOR QUICK-COOKING TAPIOCA

For dessert Makes 600 ml/1 pint. Cover tightly.

3 tbsp tapioca with 500 ml/16 fl oz milk, 1 egg and 3 tbsp caster sugar (2 litre/3½ pint glass jug or bowl)	10 min.

To thicken soup Cover tightly.

1 tbsp tapioca with 500 ml/16 fl oz stock (1 litre/2 pint measuring jug)	10 min.

TARRAGON Russian tarragon is not worth growing. French tarragon with its leaves tasting slightly of liquorice is a delight. Tarragon should never be cooked for a long time. Its leaves, whole or chopped, may be added to stews like Chicken Fricassée and Veal Fricassée or to sauces like Sauce Suprême and Sauce Espagnole a few minutes before serving. Use about 1 tablespoon fresh leaves to each 250 ml/8 fl oz of sauce or every 500 ml/16 fl oz of stew. Normally, I don't like dried tarragon. It tastes like bad tea. Microwave-oven-dried tarragon is far superior in colour and flavour. If you don't have the space to freeze tarragon (in whole branches, then stored loosely wrapped in a freezer bag), try drying it. See DRYING, herbs.

TEMPERING Usually done to chocolate that is melted for glazing or dipping to keep it shiny and stable. It does not need to be done when chocolate is melted in the microwave oven; it will not lose its temper if melted exactly as described. See CHOCOLATE, melting.

THICKENING Many soups, sauces and purées need to be thickened at the end of their cooking times. See CORNFLOUR and EMULSIFICATION. See also Roux.

THYME There are two major forms of this herb, bush and creeping. There are many varieties of each of these forms: different colours of leaves and flowers and different nuances to the taste (lemon, for one). It is the bush kind that is generally used as part of a bouquet garni and in meat and mushroom preparations. It has a strong flavour. It dries magnificently. Reduce quantities for use in microwave cooking by about half for both fresh and dried. See DRYING herbs.

TIMING It is not only that almost everything cooks more quickly in the microwave oven. Remember, too, that you do not have to allow time for water to come to the boil; that time is included in the recipe. To time a meal, or the proper preparation of courses in a meal, see Microwave Basics (pages 29–38).

TOASTING The browning of the sugary part of a usually dry food in the presence of heat. Do not attempt to make breakfast toast in the microwave oven. The toast dries out before it browns, it will brown unevenly. Many other foods are often toasted before using in a recipe. Many of them will do well in the microwave oven.

To toast *croûtons*, see page 308.

To toast *nuts*, see NUTS, toasting.

To toast *coconut*, see page 306. You can toast coconut that has already been used in the making of coconut milk or cream.

To toast *whole spices and small seeds* (such as mustard, caraway or sesame), spread a quantity, up to 4 tablespoons, in a shallow layer in a flat dish. Cook, uncovered, at

100% for 6 minutes. This is particularly desirable before making curry powder. See Spice Powders, page 299. It also can rescue herb seeds that are a little old. Large raw seeds such as sunflower toast better in the conventional oven.

TOMALLEY The greenish liver of lobsters, crayfish and large prawns should never be thrown away. Tomalley is a flavourful addition to Mayonnaise to be served with cold lobster or to other fish sauces. Try whisking it into a fish stock-based Sauce Suprême or a Sauce Américaine. It adds creamy texture and a mysterious richness of background flavour.

TOMATILLO The tomatillo is not a tomato, even if its name means small tomato and it is sometimes called husk tomato or green tomato. Related to the ground cherry and cape gooseberry, it originally comes from South America, and is most used in Mexican and southwestern American cooking. It grows in a papery husk that has to be removed before cooking; after removing it, you'll find the tomatillo is sticky and should be washed.

TOMATO I love tomatoes. To my mind, one of the best reasons to put in the work of planting a vegetable garden and maintaining it all season long is to have sun-warm, vine-ripened tomatoes of a broad range of colours, sizes, textures and flavours available in one sense-startling glut, and the joy of preserving them in so many guises for winter-long pleasure! There is a deadening uniformity in the very low standard of commercial tomatoes. Do not despair. I enjoy them within their limits: I use commercially canned tomatoes, packed whole, in juice, Italian plum preferably; tomatoes canned as juice, paste (better in tubes), chopped, commercial pasta sauce and even ketchup.

Microwave cooking can help us with many of the pedestrian tastes involved in cooking tomatoes. It helps us make sauces and pastes quickly enough so that some of the acid freshness of the tomato remains. In addition, it is a joy to cook stuffed tomatoes in the microwave oven; they retain their shape and colour and don't collapse.

While tomatoes are used frequently in this book, I have restrained myself. Wanting this book to be as usable as possible with commonly available ingredients, I do not call for glorious reddish-gold tomatoes or firm, green tomatoes, nor for those wonderful little Italian tomatoes that dry and sweeten as they hang from drying racks. I use all of these and recommend that you try them when you can get them. In early autumn, when the acrid smell of late tomatoes is in the air and they can be bought by the inexpensive bushel, do at least consider preserving some for winter use; with the microwave oven, it is easy.

Most of the basic tomato recipes are better made in the microwave oven. See Lightly Cooked Crushed Tomatoes and Chunky Tomato Sauce.

TONGUE Fresh tongue does not cook as well in the microwave oven as on top of the stove; but smoked or pickled tongue does very well, and in 20 minutes (plus soaking, if necessary) becomes a valid quick dinner for a crowd.

TROUT Almost all the trout we get to eat is farm-raised. Some varieties go to sea and acquire different names there; they also appear in larger forms in lakes, where they acquire yet a third set of names. If I were you, I would let your fisherman be responsible for the name of the fish. What you buy in the fishmonger will probably be a rainbow weighing about 400 g/14 oz.

If I could make one reform in trout cookery it would be to get anglers and fishmongers alike to gut the trout through the gills rather than slitting the stomach. Trout have very thin flesh on the stomach flaps, and it dries out when the fish are gutted by slitting. This becomes particularly important when cooking Blue Trout (au Bleu), my favourite way.

Normally, trout can only be cooked au bleu when freshly caught with their natural, protective slime intact. With the aid of the microwave oven, I can get a creditable result with bought trout, even with trout that have been frozen. See Blue Trout. For defrosting times see DEFROSTING, fish and seafood.

TRUFFLE This precious underground growth, black or white, is highly esteemed by eaters and cooks. The white Italian truffle should not be washed or cooked. It should be brushed with a soft toothbrush to remove sand and grit, then thinly shaved over hot risotto or egg pasta in a cream sauce. If you have the truffles or the money, try it. Black truffles really need to be cooked to bring out all their potential. Again, if you have some, stud the French Pâté with them and watch it all come together.

These expensive delights are echoed in name, shape and colour by Chocolate Truffles, made, basically, of cream and chocolate.

TUNA Different varieties are found in salt waters in most parts of the world where the water is not gelid. The American white meat (for canning purposes), albacore tuna, is light-fleshed throughout. Most tuna are whiter where they are fatter, in the belly; this belly meat is called *ventresca* in Italy and *toro* in Japan, where it is the most highly esteemed cut for sashimi.

There are many different sizes and kinds of tuna, each with its own name in different parts of the world. Mahi-mahi and ahi, which have turned up recently on American menus, are not new fish, merely different tunas called by their Hawaiian names.

I am a great defender of canned tuna and the tuna fish sandwich. When it comes to fresh tuna, my favourite way of eating it is raw. That does not mean that I don't also adore it grilled, steamed and stewed. Cooked tuna seems to be a different fish altogether. It develops its characteristic smell, darkens in colour and becomes firmer. Although liberally supplied with fat, it will dry out if overcooked.

Tuna is generally sold in filleted steaks. At this point it can be cut into medallions, cubes or other portions for cooking. See

FISH for cooking times.

TURBOT The most highly esteemed of the European flat fish, with firm, gelatinous white flesh and a nice fat layer under the skin. Turbot is almost always poached or steamed plain and served with a little melted butter or Hollandaise to let its delicate flavour and texture shine. This makes it a perfect candidate for microwave cooking. You cannot cook a whole turbot larger than will fit in the largest dish that your oven will accommodate. You can, however, use a larger fish by cutting off with a heavy shears the fins on the two sides—dorsal and ventral. Turbot cooks well in steaks from larger fish and fillets from smaller specimens. See FISH for cooking times.

TURKEY Once more, the microwave oven does not roast. When you want a glorious, festive, crisply browned bird, light up the regular oven.

If you want to cook individual joints of turkey, or enough for salad, cook as CHICKEN by weight without bone.

TURKEY STOCK While your turkey is roasting, place giblets and neck (no liver!), 1 small peeled and quartered onion and 1 stick of celery in a 2 litre/3½ pint glass jug or bowl with 750 ml/1¼ pints of water or Chicken Stock. Cover tightly. Cook for 20 to 40 minutes at 100%. Slice gizzard and heart; remove meat from neck. Use meat and stock to make gravy. After your guests have demolished the turkey, reclaim the bones. Rinse them off and cut them up; proceed as for Chicken Stock with Vegetables.

TURNIP Here, I mean all-white or white and purple turnips. They are peeled before cooking. See SWEDE for yellow turnips.

COOKING TIMES FOR TURNIPS

Diced Cover tightly.

4 turnips, 500 g/1 lb (2 litre/3½ pint glass jug or bowl)	6 min.
4 turnips as above	10 min. (small oven)

V

VANILLA This is one of the only ugly orchids, but it has the advantage of being the only one with a usable seed. The whole pod is long and thin and dark brown. For the purposes of cooking, vanilla is available as an essence in an alcohol base, as a powder and as whole pods. Watch out for artificial vanilla essences and flavourings, they have a disagreeable aftertaste. Vanilla is often thought of either in ice cream or in combination with chocolate. It is good both ways; it is also a taste that goes well with seafood sauces.

I have only recently learned that the French trick of storing valilla pods in caster sugar is not the ideal way. They are supposed to be stored in the refrigerator in a tightly closed glass jar or tube. I may go on storing an odd pod in sugar; I like the way the sugar tastes and smells, particularly in a cup of tea. I have found, however, that for this purpose I can rinse off and use again a piece of pod that has given the first blush of its youth to a custard or a fruit-poaching syrup.

Where feasible (not in biscuits), pods are always preferable to essence. This is particularly true in microwave cooking. You will get unexpectedly vivid flavours from the pod, while the essence will tend to dissipate and more will be required (see ALCOHOL). A 5 cm/2 inch piece of vanilla pod split lengthways equals 1 teaspoon vanilla essence.

VEAL This is expensive meat, and will be very pale pink if milk-fed, with a delicate texture and flavour.

While it is true that the microwave oven will not roast, it is less important in the case of veal than beef. Veal is easily dried out and toughened by dry-heat cooking. The moist method available in the microwave oven will produce superior results. Think of the texture of the best Vitello Tonnato and you will get the idea.

One of my favourite tricks of the microwave oven is its ability to cook Ossobuco in short order, even Ossobuco for one or two—unthinkably silly by any other method. Two other star turns are the cooking of bone MARROW and the extraction of gelatine from bone to make stock. See Meat Stocks.

Carefully time when braised and stewed veal will be ready. It should be served instantaneously, or it will toughen. Do not overcook.

COOKING TIMES FOR VEAL

Pie veal Cut into 5 cm/2 inch cubes; cover tightly.

1 kg/2 lb veal with 675 ml/22 fl oz liquid and 500 g/1 lb vegetables (2.5 litre/4 pint soufflé dish)	15 min., stand 10 min., then 4 min.
1 kg/2 lb veal with 350 ml/12 fl oz liquid (2.5 litre/4 pint soufflé dish)	10 min., stand 10 min.

Veal knuckle Cut across the bone, 6 cm/2½ inches thick; cover tightly.

750 g/1½ lb (2 pieces) with 6 tbsp liquid and 45 g/1½ oz vegetables (20 × 15 cm/8 × 6 inch dish)	12 min, stand 15 min.
1.5 kg/3 lb (4 pieces) with 175 ml/6 fl oz liquid and 90 g/3 oz vegetables (27.5 × 20 × 5 cm/11 × 8 × 2 inch oval dish)	16 min., stand 15 min.
2 kg/4½ lb (6 pieces) with 250 ml/8 fl oz liquid and 275 g/9 oz vegetables (35 × 27.5 × 5 cm/14 × 11 × 2 inch dish)	22 min., stand 15 min.

Loin Boned; cover tightly.

750 g/1½ lb with 125 ml/4 fl oz liquid (22.5 × 12.5 × 7.5 cm/9 × 5 × 3 inch dish)	6 min.

VEAL STOCK See Meat Stocks. See also DEFROSTING, homemade staples, and CLARIFYING, stocks and sauces.

VEAL GLAZE See Meat Glazes.

VEGETABLE OIL By this I do not mean olive oil, sesame oil, walnut or hazelnut oil. I mean the neutral-tasting oils made from various seeds and grains. They are cold- or hot-pressed. Aside from that, the vegetable oils can be used interchangeably.

VEGETABLE PEAR See CHAYOTE.

VEGETABLES Vegetables cook brilliantly in the microwave oven. When cooking a variety of them at once, make sure that they cook evenly by arranging slow-cooking vegetables towards the outside of the dish and quick-cooking vegetables in the centre. See Pasta Primavera (page 133).

SLOW-COOKING VEGETABLES: broccoli, carrots, cauliflower, cherry tomatoes, green beans, peas, red cabbage, sugar snap peas.

QUICK-COOKING VEGETABLES: asparagus, peppers, mushrooms, red onion slices, spring onions, courgettes.

VERMOUTH A fortified red or white wine (alcohol is added) made with various herbs and spices. It may be aged or not, dry or not. While some may be sweet, I generally call for the stronger, more bitter-tasting ones in my recipes. A little dry white vermouth can be used in sauces for fish instead of white wine. If you have these wines in the house, experiment with them. A deep-red aged vermouth would be very good included in Pears in Red Wine.

VINEGAR After one set of yeasts has produced wine from fruits or grains, another set comes along and turns the wine into vinegar—not something you want to have happen to your best bottles, but a lovely fate for apple juice and lesser wines. Vinegar retains some flavour from its starting liquid and can acquire more from the way it is aged or from having things steeped in it.

For instance, the best raspberry vinegar is made from raspberries that are fermented; however, most, even the fancy imports, are made by adding a raspberry syrup to a plain wine vinegar. There is still another way of making raspberry vinegar that I prefer to the syrup method. Fresh raspberries are macerated in white vinegar. If enough raspberries are used, this gives a fresh fruity taste and nose. The syrup kind smells and tastes like boiled sweets.

Special vinegars are aged over a long period of time in a succession of casks of decreasing size in different woods. Balsamic, for example, acquires a rich, sweetish, complex taste that is very attractive. Even though it is quite high in acid, due to its flavour balance, it tastes less acidic than plain white vinegar. Balsamic vinegar is a good substitute for soya sauce for those who must diminish their salt intake. If a recipe calls for both vinegar and soya sauce, substitute two thirds as much balsamic vinegar.

Other special vinegars include Japanese rice vinegar—clear, with a hint of yellow and a light, pleasant flavour. Sherry vinegar has a nutty flavour and does well in salads made with nut oils and even actual nuts in the dressing. Malt vinegar has a medium depth of flavour and is favoured for sprinkling on fish and chips.

·W·

WALNUT Available in the shell and shelled, whole, in pieces and halves, they are lovely seasoned and toasted (see NUTS, toasting). Walnuts are less oily and firmer than pecans, and hence easier to grind (see GRINDING). Walnut oil is very full-tasting, but it goes rancid quickly and can even get a rancid taste when cooked. I prefer to use it cold in salad dressings.

WARMING See REHEATING.

WATER The presence of water is very important in the microwave oven, since much of the cooking is done by generated steam. Since the oven will generate steam from the liquid already in most foods, quantities of additional water are not generally needed. However, water takes a relatively long time to heat, so it is important to minimize water and liquids containing water in recipes for the microwave oven.

When cooking recipes in this book, it is important not to increase the proportion of liquid. When making your own recipes, look first for a similar one already adapted for the microwave oven and be guided by it. An advantage of little water usage is that you don't throw the vitamins out with the cooking water.

WATERCRESS Watercress risks falling into parsley's trap: over-use as decoration (see PARSLEY). Remember that watercress is a green with a sharp, peppery taste and should be used to take advantage of this, not used just for decoration. It needs cooking to set its colour; in the microwave oven, the colour will be radiant. Consider substituting watercress for part of the spinach in soups and purées, and don't season with pepper until the cooking is done. See Watercress Sauce.

WATERLESS COOKING Most foods have a high water or fat content, they really don't need added liquid to cook well in the microwave oven as long as they are tightly wrapped. See STEAMING.

WAX BEAN See BEANS.

WHEAT See FLOUR.

WHISK A handle with thin wires attached to it, used to beat sauces and other mixtures in order to smooth out lumps. It is sometimes used to beat in air, as for egg whites and cream. Some mixers have whisk attachments.

WHITE BEAN See BEANS, dried.

WHITEBAIT Tiny fish, a gaggle of which are usually fried whole and eaten like chips. They should be cooked in a deep-fat-fryer, since they need to be lightly dusted with flour before frying.

WHITING A white-fleshed fish of the hake family, with rather soft flesh. Its fillets can be substituted for hake, but will not be quite as good. See Whiting with Parsley Sauce. See FISH for cooking times. See illustration, page 179.

WINE See ALCOHOL.

WORCESTERSHIRE SAUCE A quick way to get colour and flavour into sauces such as Red Barbecue Sauce, page 327.

Y

YAM Cooking times (except for white yams, which take forever) are the same as for SWEET POTATO.

YARD-LONG BEAN Known also as Philippine bean and long bean. See BEANS, fresh, for cooking times.

YEAST Yeast doughs can be given a boost in rising with the microwave oven. See RISING.

YOGURT This is not the fountain of youth. It is a delightful, acid-tasting ingredient for cooking. All yogurt called for in this book is unsweetened and unflavoured. Low-fat yogurt will cut down on calories. Yogurt, like soured cream, tends to separate with heat; it should be stirred in a the end of the cooking time. See Cold Curried Tomato Soup with Yogurt.

Z

ZEST The thin outer rind of citrus fruits, widely used in cooking and baking. It should have no pith—the white, bitter, inner rind—clinging to it. The easiest way to remove zest is to peel it off in strips from whole fruits using a potato peeler. Some recipes may call for these strips to be cut lengthways into thin sliver-like strips.

When zest is being used as decoration rather than cooked as an ingredient, it is often blanched. Place strips of zest in a single layer in a soup plate; sprinkle with 2 tablespoons water. Cover tightly; cook at 100% for 1 minute. See DRYING.

INDEX

acorn squash: purée, 257
  soup, 102–3
  Thanksgiving pudding,
    352–3
aïoli, 332–3
alcohol, 37
almonds: almond butter
    sauce, 313–14
  fillet of sole with, 164–5
  praline powder, 388
  shortbread, 374
  tuiles, 370
aluminium foil, shielding
    with, 20, 26
American chocolate layer
    cake, 361–2
anchovies: tonnato sauce,
    333
anise seafood stew, 87
apples: apple butter, 399
  apple charlotte, 343
  beetroot and apple relish,
    402
  chicken breasts Normande,
    184–5
  jelly, 396–7
  maple syrup-baked, 340–1
  sauce, 398, 399
apricots: glaze, 384–5
  sweet purée, 386
  tart purée, 385
  tea cake, 358
arcing, 19
aromatics, 37
arranging food, 33, 34
arrowroot, 36
artichokes, globe: baby
    artichokes à la Grecque,
    47
  miniature artichokes à la
    Grecque, 46–7
  and onions à la Grecque,
    45
  stuffed, 73–4
asparagus: asparagus creams,
    263–4
  soup, 103
aubergines: aubergine,
    tomato and fennel, 281
  classic appetizer, 41–2
  stuffed, 72–3
avgolemono chicken, 190

bananas, rummy, 339–40
barbecue sauce: chicken with,
    188–9
  mustard, 327
  onions in, 267
  red, 327
barbecued spareribs, 222–3
barley: beef-barley soup, 102
  creamy barley, 120–1
basil: pesto, 333
  summer vegetables with,
    276
  swordfish with tomato
    and, 157–8
  tomato sauce with, 325
batavia soup, 79
beans: chillied, 127–8
  *see also individual types of
    bean*
béchamel sauce, 316–17
beef: beef-barley soup, 102
  beef in red wine, 211
  chunky beef chilli, 208–9
  fillet of beef with morels,
    216
  fillet of beef Provençale,
    215
  heart of the home beef
    stew, 208
  Leonard Schwartz's meat
    loaf, 212–14
  light beef stock, 287
  old-fashioned meat loaf,
    214–15
  salsa Bolognese, 326
  sliced beef casserole,
    211–12
  Stroganoff meatballs, 69
  stuffed cabbage leaves,
    278–9
  topside steaks with tomato
    sauce, 217
  traditional pot roast, 210
beetroot: beetroot and apple
    relish, 402
  beetroot and potato purée,
    259–60
  cold beetroot borscht, 105
  hot beetroot and red
    cabbage borscht, 92
  traditional hot borscht,
    91–2
beurre blanc, 314–15
beurre noisette, 313
big city strawberry shortcake,
    360

Billi bi, 83
biscuits, 368
  almond shortbread, 374
  biscuit crusts, 382
  Florentines, 368–9
  fudgy brownies, 371–2
  ginger lace biscuits, 369
  oat crisps, 370–1
  original chocolate
    sandwich biscuit,
    372–3
  tuiles, 370
bitter broccoli *see* broccoli
black beans: pâté with
    Chinese black beans,
    59–60
  soup, 97
black-eye beans, 128–9
blackberry sauce, 330–1
blueberries: blueberry bash,
    360
  chunky sauce, 377
  sauce, 336
borscht: cold beetroot
    borscht, 105
  hot beetroot and red
    cabbage borscht, 92
  traditional hot borscht,
    91–2
Bourbon peaches, 338–9
brains, 235–6
  braised brains with turnip
    sauce, 236–7
brandade de morue, 50–1
brandy snaps, 369
bread: bread pudding, 349
  breadcrumbs, 306–7
  buttered and seasoned
    breadcrumbs, 307–8
  croûtons, 309
    goat cheese croûtons,
    309
  stuffing, 308
bread and butter pickles, 404
broccoli, 240–1
  pasta with bitter broccoli
    sauce, 135
  purée, 254–5
  sliced fresh tuna with
    broccoli florets, 162–3
  timbale, 262
browned butter sauce, 313
brownies, fudgy, 371–2
browning dishes, 20, 26
Brussels sprouts, turbot with,
    166–7